THE BLUE ANNALS

In the staggering immensity of Tibetan historiography, the present English translation of *The Blue Annals* of Ḥgos lotsa.ba Gzhon.nu.dpal by George N. Roerich has made it a classic like the history of Herodotus.

— PROF. LOKESH CHANDRA

GEORGE NICHOLAS DE ROERICH

(August 16,1902 — May 21, 1960)

GEORGE NICHOLAS DE ROERICH was a prominent 20th century Tibetologist. He is known for his contribution to Tibetan dialectology, his monumental translation of *The Blue Annals,* and his *11-volume Tibetan-Russian-English Dictionary* (published posthumously).

THE BLUE ANNALS

(In Two parts)

GEORGE N. ROERICH

A New Revised Edition which include
"A Place Name Index"
and
Foreword by

PROF. LOKESH CHANDRA

(PART -II)

MOTILAL BANARSIDASS PUBLISHERS
PRIVATE LIMITED • DELHI (INDIA)

3rd Revised Edition : Delhi, 2016
Second Edition : Delhi, 1976
First Edition: Kolkata, 1949

ISBN: 978-81-208-0471-5

MOTILAL BANARSIDASS
41 U.A. Bungalow Road, Jawahar Nagar, Delhi 110 007
8 Mahalaxmi Chamber, 22 Bhulabhai Desai Road, Mumbai 400 026
203 Royapettah High Road, Mylapore, Chennai 600 004
236, 9th Main III Block, Jayanagar, Bangaluru 560 011
8 Camac Street, Kolkata 700 017
Ashok Rajpath, Patna 800 004
Chowk, Varanasi 221 001

By arrangement with the Asiatic Society of Bengal.

MLBD Cataloging-in-Publication Data

I. The Blue Annals (In Two Parts) by GEORGE N. ROERICH
Includes bibliography and several indexes
ISBN : 978-81-208-0471-5
I. Tibetan Literature II. Tibetan Philosophy
III. Roerich, George N. IV. Buddhism

Printed in India
by RP Jain at NAB Printing Unit,
A-44, Naraina Industrial Area, Phase I, New Delhi–110028
and published by JP Jain for Motilal Banarsidass Publishers (P) Ltd,
41 U.A. Bungalow Road, Jawahar Nagar, Delhi-110007

FOREWORD

A sacred past, the authority of roots, the profundity of the moral and political order, the confluence of idealized and realistic time, and the mandate of Heaven in the descent of their royal order, has endowed Tibet with a unique historical consciousness. A large body of ancient Tibetan historical works exists from genealogies of kings, epic history, biographies of outstanding monks, family chronicles, Chos-hbuṅ or histories of Buddhism, annals of monasteries, transmission lineages (thob.yig) of great masters, down to composite annals that present a continuing sequence of the Tibetan state in the eternity of Dharma. The incarnation of eminent *kalyāṇamitras* and the advent of Indian masters and their collaboration with Tibetan *lotsavas* have been meticulously documented by Tibetan historical texts to show the living wholeness of their cultural transformation after the advent of Buddhism. *Sba.bśed* by the Minister from Sba is the great record of the Samye monastery and pertains to the earliest period of Tibetan history. He was a Minister to King Khri.sroṅ.ldeḥu.btsan (r. 755-780). His authority has been unequalled and he has been cited by all Tibetan historians for the last thousand years. The *Ocean Annals of Amdo*[1] (written in 1865) list more than five hundred titles on folios 4-9, and Akhu Rinpoche (1803-1875) has a list of hundreds of rare historical texts.[2]

In the staggering immensity of Tibetan historiography, the present English translation of *The Blue Annals* of Ḥgos lo-tsa.ba Gzhon.nu.dpal by George N. Roerich has made it a classic like the history of Herodotus. It is a comprehensive narrative of the royal period, the early and later spread of

---

1 Lokesh Chandra, *Ocean Annals of Amdo,* Parts 1-3, New Delhi, 1975.

2 Lokesh Chandra, *Materials for a History of Tibetan Literature,* New Delhi 1963, part 3 pages 503 f.

Buddhism, the translations of mantrayāna tantras and new tantras, the renderings of the basic Prajñāpāramitā and Tantra texts by Rin.chen.bzaṅ.po the great translator puruṣottama, and many others. The renaissance of Buddhism by Atiśa and his lineage, the story of the 'Path and Fruit' doctrine of the Sa.skya.pas, and the spiritual lineages of Rṅog lotsava, Mar.pa, Ko.brag.pa, Ni.gu and Kha.rug.pa are a glorious heritage of doctrines. The tenth book of *The Blue Annals* relates the origin and development of the Kālacakra-tantra and its precepts. The Kālacakra has assumed special importance as His Holiness the Dalai Lama XIV has been giving its empowerments over the years. The Kulika king Durjaya introduced a new era in 806 A.C. The Kulika kings gave rise to *Kalkī,* the concept of the tenth *avatāra* of Viṣṇu, who will vanquish the *mlecchas.*

The Blue Annals is a fundamental work for the history of Tibet, for the development of sects in Tibet, and the transmission of maṇḍalas of the Vajrāvalī and of Avalokiteśvara (the term 'cycle' stands for maṇḍala). *The Blue Annals* clearly contraposits China and Tibet when it says: "Just as the Bodhisattva Mañjuśrī took over China, in the same manner the Bodhisattva Mahāsattva Ārya Avalokiteśvara protected this country of Tibet" (p. 1006). Avalokiteśvara and his mantra *Oṁ Maṇipadme Hūṁ* reached Tibet during the reign of Lha.tho.tho.ri whom Pandita Buddharakṣita and Lotsava Li.the.se brought books from India. Because of them the kingdom prospered. This became known as "Beginning of the Dharma." Another tradition says that during his reign, a casket containing Buddhist sūtras and a golden stūpa appeared at the royal palace, in 373 A.C. The king and court preserved them as objects of veneration and the realm received great blessings (Crystal Mirror 6.139). This falls in the reign of the Gupta Emperor Samudragupta (ruled 330-380 A.C.), whose domains extended from the Himalayas to the South. It seems that contacts of India and Tibet began with the sacred offering of sūtras and stūpa to the Tibetan king, leading to the establishment of commercial relations. The very name Samudragupta refers to his role in trans-oceanic (*samudra*) trade and this leads us to the surmise that Tibet must have exchanged goods of daily use (like fabrics, salt, etc.) with their gold which could be mined easily with simple tools.

The Blue Annals is the only Tibetan historical work that begins with a Sanskrit hymn, the *Trikāya-stava*, cited from the Sekoddeśa.ṭīkā of Naropa. Ḥgos lotsava was conversant with Sanskrit. He laments that he could not write the history of the reign of Aśoka, "as I did not hear of any one possessing an Indian royal chronicle" (p. 35). He names the places where Lord Buddha spent forty five summer retreats (pp. 21-22). *The Blue Annals* deserve a new and simplified narration, with few transmission lineages and other details, to bring out its rich exposition of Buddhism both in India and Tibet. The several Indian teachers who went to Tibet and introduced more and more disciplines reflect the Buddhist ambience in India in their respective centuries.

This reprinting of *The Blue Annals* is a splendid contribution to Tibetology in particular, and to Buddhology in general as it provides glimpses of Buddhism in the years of its decline, for example, the declining years of Odantapuri with fifty-three monks and Vikramaśīlā with about a hundred monks. These Annals are an exposition of a sophisticated mind about the renaissance of *Dharma* in the gigantic creative ferment of the Land of Snows.

—LOKESH CHANDRA
September 12, 2014

CONTENTS

Foreword by LOKESH CHANDRA V
Introduction xi

PART I

Book I The Beginning of the Story of the Doctrine. The Royal Chronicle. The Period of the Early Spread of the Doctrine 1
II Later Spread of the Doctrine. The Story of the Beginning of the Period of the Later Spread of the Docrine 63
III The Early Translations of the Mantrayāna Tantras 102
IV The New Tantras (gsan-snags gsar-ma) and the Followers of the "Path and Fruit" (Lam' Bras) Doctrine 204
V The Venerable Lord (Jo-bo-rje, Atiśa) and his Spiritual Lineage 241
VI rNog lo-tsā-ba, Pa-tshab lo-tsā-ba and their Lineage. The Origin (of the teaching) of the Mādhyamika, the Nyāya and the "Five Treatises" of Maitreya-Asaṅga 328
VII The Preaching of the Tantras 351
VIII The Spiritual Lineage of the Lord Translator Mar-pa which was known as Dwags-po bKa-brgyud 399
IX The Book on Ko-brag-pa and Ni-gu 726

PART II

X	The Kālacakra	753
XI	The Mahāmudrā	839
XII	The Early, Later and Intermediate Lineages of zi-byed	867
XIII	The (system) of gCod-yul and Kha-rag-pa	980
XIV	The Cycle of the Mahākaruṇika and that of the Vajrāvalī	1006
XV	The Origin of Religious Schools such as the Four Tshogssde, and Others, Queries and Replies (concerning the "Blue Annals", zu-lan). The Story of the Printing of this Edition	1062

*

INDEXES

Sūtra & Śāstras (Sanskrit)	1095
Personal Names (Sanskrit)	1104
Book Titles (Tibetan)	1123
Personal Names (Tibetan)	1138
Chinese Names	1265
Mangol Names	1267
A Place Name Index	1269
List of Errata	1305

BOOK X.

The Kālacakra.

I shall (now) relate the story of the origin of the Śrī Kālacakra-Tantra (dPal Dus-kyi 'khor-lo'i rgyud) and its precepts. Now the general account of the propagation of the Mahāyāna Guhyamantra (Theg-pa čhen-po gSaṅ-sṅags) in Jambudvīpa: In the beginning, in the East, king Pradyotacandra (Rab-gsal zla-ba) and others obtained the Yoga-Tantras, such as the Sarvatathāgatatattvasaṃgraha (De-kho-na-ñid bsdus-pa, Kg. rGyud-'bum, No.479) and others, and preached them. Then the ācārya Nāgārjuna and his disciples obtained the Yoga-Tantras, including the Guhyasamāja and others (the Anuttara-yoga-Tantras were also called Mahāyoga-Tantras, or rNal-'byor čhen-po'i rgyud), and preached them. They spread from the South. After that from the West Śrī Kambala (dPal La-ba-pa) and others discovered the Yoginī-Tantras (rNal-'byor-ma'i rgyud) in the country of Oḍḍīyāna (O-ḍi-yan). They also spread towards Madhyadeśa. After that, there appeared from the realm of Śambhala commentaries (on the Kālacakra-Tantra) composed by Bodhisattvas (here Bodhisattvas mean the kings of Śambhala), such as the Śrī Kālacakra and others. They spread towards Madhyadeśa. In the Vimalaprabhā (Vimalaprabhā-nāma-mūla-tantrānusārinīdvādaśasāhasrikālaghukālacakratantrarājaṭīkā, Tg. rGyud, 1347; also Kg. rGyud-'bum, No. 845) it is said: "Here the fixing of chronological calculations (byed-pa-la ṅes-pa): In 600 years from the time of the Tathāgata—the period of Mañjuśrī ('Jam-dpal); in 800 years from that time—the era of the Mlecchas (the starting year of the Kālacakra chronology is the first year of the Hijra, calculated from the year 624 A. D., instead of 622 A. D.); by lowering the era of the Mlecchas by 182 years, (one obtains) the time of Rigs-ldan rgyal-dka' (Kulika Durjaya), during which Kulika Durjaya introduced the "lesser" chronology (mentioned in the Kālacakra. Kulika Durjaya is said to have introduced the system of calculations known as byed-pa'i rtsis in 806 A. D.)." This date should be regarded as a correct calculation based on the era of the Mlecchas. "The past Prabhāva year, etc." mean the cycles of sixty years of which the first was the Prabhāva (Rab-byuṅ) year (Me-yos, Fire-Hare year, 1027 A. D.) and which (are designated) as "Prabhāva and others."[1]

Each period of sixty years, which preceded the present years (were called) the "past Prabhāva" (the past Vibhava, past Śukla, etc). Basing themselves on the above quotation, most of the later scholars maintained that the time of the appearance of the Kālacakra in Madhyadeśa corresponded to the beginning of the first cycle (rab-byuṅ) of the "past" years ('das-lo). But it seems to me that the Kālacakra had appeared in Āryadeśa long before that time, for in the Sahajasaṃvara-sādhana (Tg. rGyud, No. 1436) composed by the mahāsiddha (Vajra)ghaṇṭapāda is found the second śloka of the introduc- (14)
tory verse of the Vimalaprabhā: "(He) was impressed by the Bhagavatī Prajñā (Viśvamatā), which though formless, yet has a form" (rnam-par-bčas kyaṅ rnam-med bčom-ldan 'das Śes-rab-ma ste de-yis 'khyud). Also because after Ghaṇṭapāda (came) Rus-sbal-žabs (Kūrmapāda). He (transmitted it) to Dza-landha-ri-pa (Jālandharapāda); the latter to Kṛṣṇapāda (Nag-po-pa); the latter to Bhadrapāda (bZaṅ-po-žabs); the latter to Vijayapāda (rNam-rgyal-žabs); the latter to Tilli-pa (Tailipāda); the latter to Nā-ro-pa. Thus from Ghaṇṭa(pāda) till Nā-ro-pa there have been eight teachers in the Line. Also

1 According to some authorities the Kālacakra-Tantra was preached by the Buddha in his 80th year at Śri Dhānya-kaṭaka (Amarāvati in the Sattenapalle Tāluka of Guṇṭūr District, Madras) upon the request of Sucandra (Zla-bzaṅ). According to Bu-ston Rin-po-čhe the Buddha preached the Kālacakra system in the year of his Enlightenment (see Dus-'khor Čhos-'byuṅ, fol. 13a, volume IV /ṅa/of the "Collection of Works," or gSuṅ-'bum). According to him the "statement made by some that the Buddha had preached it (the Kālacakra) in the year of his passing into Nirvāṇa at Śrī Dhānya-kaṭaka should be rejected."

because Nā-ro-pa and Kālacakrapāda, father and son, were contemporaries. Further, because it is said in the gŚin-rJe gśed-kyi 'khor-lo'i gsal-byed (this is the Yamāriyantrāvali, Tg. rGyud, No. 2022), composed by Śrī Virūpa, that he had written the text basing himself on the Kālacakra. Also because, when relating the story of Tsi-lu-pa's (Celuka) search for the Kālacakra, it was said that the ācārya had read (it) in the vihāra of Ratnagiri (Rin-čhen ri-bo) which had been left undamaged by the Turuṣkas, and was of the opinion that, in general, for the (attainment) of Enlightenment the Mahāyāna Guhyamantra (gsaṅ-sṅags) was necessary, and that the text had to be studied with the help of the commentary by the Bodhisattvas. Accordingly he proceeded in search of the Kālacakra (so the Kālacakra must have been in existence at that time). Thus it has to be admitted that the system of Kālacakra seems to have reached Āryadeśa at an early date, and that (the system) became known to many people in the time of Kālacakrapāda, father and son. The statement by gLan-baṅ-so-ba and others that the first translation (of the Kālacakra) into Tibetan was that of Gyi-Jo, seems to be correct, because the coming of the paṇḍita Somanātha (Zla-ba mgon-po) took place in the later life of Gra-pa mṄon-śes, who said that in his youth he had heard the Kālacakra from (his) uncle. Bu(ston) and Dol-(pa-pa) were the two great expounders of the Kālacakra in the Land of Snows (Gaṅs-čan-gyi khrod, i. e. Tibet). These two first obtained it from the spiritual descendants of Rwalo-(tsā-ba), but later they studied it according to the tradition of 'Bro lo-tsā-ba. Thus Rwa and 'Bro have been the chief (expounders of the Kālacakra in (2a)
Tibet). In connection with this, the followers of the tradition of 'Bro used to say that: Kālacakrapāda, the Eldest (Dus-žabs čhen-po) obtained it from Kulika (Rigs-ldan). Then Kālacakrapāda, the Junior (Dus-žabs-pa čhuṅ-ṅu), Somanātha (Zla-ba mgon-po), sGom-pa dKon-mčhog-bsruṅs (the ascetic Ratnagupta), sGro-ston gNam-la-brtsegs, Yu-mo, his son Dharmeśvara, the scholar Nam-mkha'-'od, Se-čhen Nam-mkha'

rgyal-mtshan, the Dharmasvāmin 'Jam-dbyaṅs gsar-ma, Kun-mkhyen Čhos-sku 'od-zer, Kun-spaṅs Thugs-rJe brtson-'grus, Byaṅ-sems rGyal-ba ye-śes, Kun-mkhyen Yon-tan rgya-mtsho, and the Dharmasvāmin Kun-mkhyen čhen-po. The followers of the Raw-lo tradition state as follows: Kulika (Rigs-ldan), Tsi-lu-pa (Celuka), Piṇḍopa, Kālacakrapāda, the Eldest (Dus-žabs čhe-ba), Kālacakrapāda, the Junior (čhuṅ-ba), Mañjukīrti, the Nepālese Samantaśrī, Rwa Čhos-rab, Rwa Ye-śes seṅ-ge, Rwa 'Bum-seṅ, the Venerable (rJe-btsun) rGwa-lo, Roṅ-pa Śes-rab seṅ-ge, and the bla-ma rDo-rJe rgyal-mtshan. The latter taught (the system) to Bu-ston Rin-po-čhe. Further, sKyi-ston 'Jam-dbyaṅs obtained it from Roṅ-pa Śes-rab seṅ-ge, Kun-mkhyen čhen-po obtained it from him. Bu-(ston) and Dol-pa-pa, the two, obtained the system according to the tradition of Rwalo-tsā-ba. Later they obtained many precepts according to the tradition of 'Bro lo-tsā-ba and others. The accounts about the teacher in whose time the Kālacakra had been obtained from Kulika (Rigs-ldan) in Āryadeśa, and the (first) disciples on whom it was bestowed, are at variance. According to the rGyud-la-'Jug-pa'i man-ṅag rin-po-čhe Za-ma-tog kha-'byed-pa (The opening of the Casket containing the precious precepts to serve as an introduction to the Tantra) by gLan-baṅ-so-ba Čhos-kyi dbaṅ-phyug, a disciple of Tre-po mgon-po: By the words "handed-down from the siddha and his followers" it is meant that it had continued in a regular succession. Now the Lineage: king Pad-ma-dkar-po (Puṇḍarīka), a manifestation of the Bodhisattva Avalokiteśvara, who was indicated in the last śloka of the prophecy (given by Buddha about the kings of Śambhala), taught (the system) to the ācārya Kālacakrapāda. This ācārya belonged to the kṣatriya caste of Madhyadeśa in (2b) India, and was born after his royal parents had performed the rite ensuring the birth of a noble son (kulaputra). He was learned in the five branches of knowledge, and was known to be a manifestation of Ārya Mañjuśrī. He was blessed by the Venerable Tārā, whose face he saw clearly. After he had acquired all the "lower perfections" (eight in all), the Vene-

rable One once told him: "In the Northern Śambhala there exist many Tantras and commentaries taught and prophesied by the Buddha. Go in search of them and listen to them!" He then thought of going there. In the opinion of some scholars he had joined a caravan of merchants, and proceeded there. Some said that he was guided there by a phantom monk. Again some said that the Venerable Tārā herself helped him (i. e. preached to him). Again some said that when he decided to proceed to Śambhala, and was preparing (for the journey), he visited Śambhala in his vision, and obtained the doctrines from Ārya Avalokiteśvara himself (Rigs-ldan Pad-ma dkar-po). This last statement should be accepted. When he was residing in Madhyadeśa, Tsi-lu-pa preached the system to five paṇḍitas: Piṇḍo ācārya, 'Dul-ba 'byuṅ-gnas blo-gros (Vinayākaramati), Thar-pa 'byuṅ-gnas-sbas-pa (Mokṣākaragupta), Seṅ-ge rgyal-mtshan (Siṃhadhvaja), and mTha'-yas rnam-par rgyal-ba (Anantajaya). When they had mastered it, he journeyed to Puṣpahari (written in later works Pu-la-ha-ri, a hill near Nālandā, according to Čhag lo-tsā-ba), and stayed there preaching the system to Nā-ro paṇ-čhen and others. Though all of his disciples were endowed with excellent qualities, one named Piṇḍo ācārya especially distinguished himself. This was due to the fact that in a former existence he had been a shortwitted monk, and had performed a sādhana in order to improve his intellect. After receiving a prophecy by a deva in his dream, he made out of coral an image of Kurukullā and inserted it into the mouth (3a)
of a dead woman. He sat cross-legged on the corpse and meditated for seven days. Then (the dead woman) looked up at him and uttered: "What do you want?" At that time if he would have said that he wished to get by heart whatever had been seen by him, he would have obtained it. But being disappointed with his intelligence, he asked: "I wish to be able to commit to memory all that which has been written by me". And so it happened, and he became known as paṇḍita Piṇḍo ācārya. He became known in Madhyadeśa

as Vāgīśvarakīrti, and was attended by twelve junior paṇḍitas. He heard the Doctrine from the ācārya Kālacakrapāda (Dus-žabs-pa), and was able to memorize the whole text after listening to it once. The holder of his Spiritul Lineage (was) one named dGe-bsñen Byaṅ-čhub (Upāsakabodhi). His son was a very great paṇḍita who studied under his father's brother dGon-pa-ba (Āraṇyaka). He obtained (the system) together with Nā-ro-pa from Kālacakrapāda, the Senior, and became known as Kālacakrapāda, the Junior. Moreover differences in the views impressed by the "father" and "son". These "father" and "son" having once said while residing in Madhyadeśa that "One who does not know the Kālacakra, would not know the Vajrayāna", caused displeasure among paṇḍitas, who having gathered in Madhyadeśa, prepared seats at Vikramaśīla and held a debate. J̌o-bo čhen-po (Kālacakrapāda) could not be defeated. Then all rose from their seats, and he placed his foot on their heads. Except Dā-bodhisattva (Dānaśīla), all obtained instruction in the Kālacakra from him. He became also known as Dus-'khor-ba (Kālacakrapāda, the Junior) and propagated widely the system. At that time there was in the country of Kāśmīra an excellent brāhmaṇa scholar named bZaṅ-po (Bhadra) or Sūryaketu, when he was teaching the Doctrine to Paṇḍita Sonasati, Lakṣmīkara, Dānaśrī, Candrarāhula, Somanātha, and others, the Paṇḍita Vinayākaramati ('Dul-ba 'byuṅ-gnas blo-gros) sent the Sekoddeśa (Kg. rGyud-'bum, No. 361) and the Sekaprakriyā (dBaṅ-rab-byed, Kg. rGyud, (3b)
No. 365), and he having given them to read to the paṇḍitas, all were filled with wonder. In particular, the Teacher Somanātha of Kāśmīra was filled with great faith, and having discontinued his studies there, proceeded in search of that system. In Madhyadeśa he met Dus-'khor-ba and asked him for instruction in the Kālacakra. The latter having given him instruction, he became an accomplished scholar in the complete commentary of the Tantra, in the Tantra itself, the precepts, and in the initiation rite. This Teacher be-

longed to a Brahmin family and till the age of ten he studied his father's doctrine, and was able to memorize sixteen ślokas after reading them once. After that his mother introduced him to Buddhism. He having mastered the science of the Kāśmīrī Ñi-ma rgyal-mtshan (Śūryaketu) and Kālacakrapāda, the Junior, became a paṇḍita. He, intending to spread the system in Tibet, proceeded there, and asked gÑos-'byuṅ-po: "Are you able to translate this book?" The latter replied: "I am unable to translate it, but there is a way out of it. I shall send a message to the son of the kalyāṇa-mitra lČe-pa of bZaṅ-yul in gYor-po who will be able to assist you with money." He sent a messenger, after which lČe, father and son, invited him. They requested him, and a proper translation (of the text) was made by him. The great achievement of these 'father' and 'son' was that, in general, they were endowed with a proper reverence, and attended on all translators and paṇḍitas, and, in particular, they possessed a great knowledge of the Mahāyāna Guhyamantra. They used to spend all their wealth for the sake of religion. When they first met the great Kāśmīrī teacher (Somanātha), they presented him with three golden sraṅs, a complete set of garments, including a mantle, and begged him to stay. After that they saw him off as far as Čhu-śul and furnished him with thirty loads of wine. A-ža rGya-gar-rtsegs also acted as translator, and for a whole year he (4a)
fed thirty men and horses. (When they had finished the translation of the text), he presented him as remuneration thirty golden sraṅs, as well as another thirty sraṅs on various occasions. In all he presented him sixty golden sraṅs, and pleased him. After that the lo-tsā-ba and the paṇḍita were invited by 'Gar-ston of the Northern Upland, the kalyāṇa-mitra Gra-pa, and the scholar rDo-rje-rgyan of sKar-čhuṅ to their residences. While they were receiving instruction in the Tantra itself and its commentary, the kalyāṇa-mitra lČe, father and son, also listened to it. After that the Kāśmīrī Somanātha proceeded to India to present offerings to (his)

Teacher and the Vajrāsana. When he had offered a great quantity of gold, he removed his doubts concerning (the Kālacakra) assisted by his former brother in initiation (sṅa-ma'i mčhed-po) 'Dul-da'i 'byuṅ-gnas blo-gros (Vinayākaramati) and Siṃhadhvaja (Seṅ-ge rgyal-mtshan). When he (Somanātha) again returned to Tibet, lČe, father and son, obtained once more the Kālacakra from him. There appears to have existed a later translation (of the text) by 'Bro lo-tsā-ba. lČe, father and son, taught it to the bla-ma 'Go-čhen-po (Head guru) of Dol, named Ñi-ma. The latter preached it to the great scholar kLubs Saṅghakīrti. The latter to his son. The latter to gLan, the Great (gLan čhen-po). Again, according to the second Lineage: When the Great Kāśmīrī Teacher (Somanātha) arrived in Tibet for the second time, he was pleased by the reverence and service paid to him by the kalyāṇa-mitra dKon-mčhog-bsruṅ of 'Phan-yul and his disciple, who attended on him for a considerable time. He therefore bestowed on them the explanation of the Tantra itself, its commentary (Vimalaprabhā), together with the precepts, which he had not given to other Tibetan scholars. They (dKon-mčhog-bsruṅ dpon-slob-gñis) bestowed them on the Venerable (rJe-btsun) Yu-mo, the Great. From him the great scholar Tre-bo mGon-po, the Great, and the Master of the Doctrine Se received them. The great scholar (mkhas-pa'i skye-bo Tre-bo mgon-po) taught (the system) to gLan. He taught it also to kLubs Jo-sras. The latter to gLan Čhos-kyi dbaṅ-phyug.

Again, according to the third Lineage: Dus-kyi 'khor-lo-ba, the Last, and Śrī Ñā-ro-pa (transmitted it) to Mañju- (4b)
kīrti and Abhayākara. These two taught the Tantra and commentary (Vimalaprabhā) to the bla-ma gÑan lo-tsa-ba and rGwa lo-tsā-ba, who expressed the desire to study the Tantra only. The Venerable 'Gos also studied under these two teachers, and thus till the Master (mṅa'-bdag, Se Čhos-kyi mṅa'-bdag).

Again, according to the fourth Lineage: Abhaya and his

brother taught it to the paṇḍita Samantaśrī, the lo-tsā-ba and paṇḍita. The latter to kLubs. Further, Anupamarakṣita, Sādhuputra, Dharmākaraśānti, and Vikṣāntadeva. The latter to the great Kaśmīrī paṇḍita Śākyaśrībhadra, matchless on the surface of the Earth. He to gLan, 'father' and 'son'—so it is said. According to the Dus-kyi 'khor-lo'i bsdus-don, composed by the bla-ma bSod-nams 'od-zer-ba: "Thus in the Realm of Śambhala exists the Kālacakra-Tantra together with its commentary and precepts, but in the Āryadeśa of India, (the Kālacakra) was first obtained in Śambhala from a manifestation of a Bodhisattva by an Indian named the monk bSod-sñoms-pa, the Great (Piṇḍo-pa). It is not known what Bodhisattva manifested himself in him. The latter (taught it) to the Southern brāhmaṇa Dārikapā(da). The latter to Tsi-lu-pa (Celuka). The latter to Kālacakrapāda. The latter to Dus-'khor-ba, the Great. The latter to two of his disciples—Bodhibhadra and Sādhuputra. Bodhibhadra had three disciples: the guru Abhaya, Tsa-mi-ba, the Great (Tsa-mi Saṅs-rgyas grags-pa), and Abhiyukta (Abhi-dzu-kta). Sādhuputra had two disciples: Dharmākara and Bhāskara. The ācārya Se lo-tsā-ba said that he had listened (to the exposition of the Kālacakra) once by the guru Abhaya, twice by Tsa-mi, then (to the exposition of) the first part (of the text) by Abhiyukta, and once by Bhāskara. From him gÑos 'Od-ma obtained it, who said that he had studied it for three years. Then the teacher Se lo-tsā-ba proceeded to dbUs. In his absence he (gÑos 'Od-ma) marked with white the passages in the text that were not understood by him. On his (Se-lo's) way from dbUs to India, gÑos 'Od-ma asked about these passages, and when Se-lo was coming to India all his doubts (5a)
were removed. He then obtained the exposition of all the texts, together with their initiation rites and precepts, and all his doubts were removed. bKra-śis rin-čhen and gÑos-sgom obtained it from 'Od-ma. The latter meditated on the precepts and obtained the signs of spiritual realization. He also obtained the permission (luṅ) to preach the text, but

he did not know it well. bKra-śis rin-čhen listened to it for 12 years, and knew it, as well as 'Od-ma himself, and thus became like a well-filled vase. He also obtained the teachings of Rwa, 'Bro, Gyi-J̌o, and others, and used to say that 'there was no one better than himself'. The ācārya Dus-'khor-ba obtained it from him on thirty-two occasions, and mastered it in the manner of a vase filled to the brim. The scholar (mkhas-grub) famous by the name of Bhikṣu Ratnaśrī and U-rgyan-pa obtained it from him. I obtained the system from the latter."

Again, according (to another) Lineage: the ācārya Kālacakrapāda, the Senior, was the son of a yoginī who took him with her to Śambhala. (There) a monk of an extremely beautiful appearance, blessed him, and he developed the ability of committing to memory a thousand ślokas every day. After that the boy heard the Mūla-Tantra (not included in the Canon), the Sañcaya-Tantra (bsDus-pa'i rgyud, Paramādibuddhoddhṛta-Śri-Kālacakra-nāma-Tantrarāja, Kg. rGyud-'bum, No. 362) and the commentary (Vimalaprabhā) recited by the monk who was a manifestation of Avalokiteśvara. He committed these texts to memory and then proceeded to Madhyadeśa. This boy on being ordained, became known as Tsi-lu-pa (Celuka); he was also known by the name of Tshim-bu-ba. When the ācārya Tsi-lu-pa was residing (at the court) of the king of Ka-ṭa-ka (Orissa), he had three disciples, who made the request that the Tantra and the commentary might be written down in the form of a book. So he wrote it down, and the books were entrusted to the three disciples. One (of them) became a paṇḍita, another became an adept (sādhaka), but the third was unable to progress beyond the stage of an ordinary human being. Then the troops of a foreign king invaded the country. They (5b)
(the disciples) hid the Tantra and its commentaries (the Vimalaprabhā, the rDo-rJe sñiṅ-'grel, and the Phyag-rdor don-'grel) in a pit, and fled away. After the war was over, they returned, and searched for the (hidden books). (They discovered) that the last paragraphs of the two lesser commen-

taries (the rDo-rJe sñiṅ-'grel and the Phyag-rdor don-'grel) were missing. The disciples again requested him to write down (the missing portions), but he declined, saying: "the ḍākinīs have hidden them, and therefore it is improper to write them now." After Tsi-lu-pa proceeded towards the East to Kusumpura (Me-tog khyim). Upāsakabodhi obtained the system from him. This disciple Bodhi used to say that "if he does not understand the Kālacakra, the Doctrine, and especially the Guhyamantra (gSaṅ-sṅags) cannot be understood by him." All the paṇḍitas having assembled, said: "This is incorrect! Let us debate it!" They conducted a debate at Vikramaśīla. The Master (Bodhi) asked them about the contradictions in the upper and lower sections of the different Tantras from the stand-point of the Kālacakra, but they did not dare (to debate on the subject). They all begged his forbearance, and asked the Master to instruct them in the Kālacakra, and in this manner the doctrine spread. The Master's name became Dus-kyi 'khor-lo-ba. Khams-pa Žu-lo obtained the system from his disciples Mañjukīrti and Abhayākara. gÑan-lo also obtained it. The bla-ma 'Gos obtained it from these two

There exists a slight disagreement as to the origins of the Lineages of Rwa and 'Bro between the accounts given by Bu Rin-po-čhe in his gČes-pa'i lde-mig (Vol. IV/ṅa/of the gSuṅ-'bum), by gLan Čhos-dbaṅ, by the scholar bSod-nams 'od-zer-ba, and in the account of the Lineage of gÑan lo-tsā-ba. In particular, the one who was called Piṇḍo-ācārya was stated by some to have been the Teacher of Kālacakrapāda, the Senior, and again by others to have been the disciple of Kālacakrapāda. Some maintain that he (Piṇḍo) was identical with Ṅag-gi dbaṅ-phyug grags-pa. They seem to imply that he was Ṅag-gi dbaṅ-phyug, one of the four gate-keepers (of Vikramaśīla), but this does not seem to be possible. Because in the treatise Yan-lag bdun-ldan (Saptāṅga, Tg. rGyud, No. 1888), composed by him (i.e. by the gate-keeper Ṅag-gi dbaṅ-phyug), he expressed many different views on the fourth initiation, but never mentioned the system of Kālacakra.

On the other hand it can be said about the Kālacakra-sādhanagarbhālaṃkāra (Dus-kyi 'khor-lo'i sgrub-thabs sñiṅ-po-rgyan, Tg. rGyud, No. 1365), composed by the ācārya bSod-sñoms-pa (Piṇḍo) that the very name of the śāstra shows that it (6a) deals with the Kālacakra. Even if one were to accept as true the statement of the Rwa-pas (followers of Rwa) that prior to Kālacakrapāda, the Great, there had existed two teachers of the Kālacakra, it would not be a contradiction to say that Kālacakrapāda had received a blessing from Kulika himself, who taught him the Tantra. Because, as stated by Ñi-ma-dpal, Vajradhara himself, assuming the form of Avadhūti-pa, had bestowed the precepts of the Sadaṅga-yoga (yan-lag drug) on the ācārya Anupamarakṣita (dPe-med-'tsho), and because others also maintained that Tilli-pa, a disciple of Vijayapāda (rNam-rgyal-žabs), who was the last of a numerous Lineage of teachers of the Cakrasaṃvara Cycle, was a direct disciple of Vajradhara. The ācārya Anupamarakṣita could not be later than the ācārya Nā-ro-pa, since Nā-ro-pa in his Sekoddeśa-ṭīkā (Tg. rGyud, No. 1351) quoted his teaching. In general, even some of the accounts by Indian teachers, can be unreliable, for instance in the commentary on Śūnyaśrī's Sadaṅga-yoga (Guṇapūrṇī-nāma-Sadaṅgayoga ṭippanī, Tg. rGyud, No.1388) translated by dPaṅ (dLo-gros brtan-pa), Sūryaśrī (Ñi-ma-dpal) is stated to have been a disciple of Čhos-'byuṅ ži-ba (Dharmākaraśānti), but, according to a statement of the Precious mahā-paṇḍita (Śākyaśrībhadra), Sūryaśrī (Ñi-ma dpal) had been the teacher of Dharmākaraśānti (Čhos-'byuṅ ži-ba. The Commentary on the Sadaṅga-yoga, though stated to have been the work of Sūryaśrī, seems to have contained, as indicated by the title, notes written down by one of his disciples. In two Indian books, consulted by me, the very same statement is made. The statement that the concluding paragraphs of the Hevajra-Tantra (brTag-gñis) and of the Saṃvara-ṭīkā had been hidden away by ḍākinīs, is unreliable, because it is certain that the sizes of these books translated into Tibetan were the same as those of the original books composed

by the Bodhisattva, for in the Vajragarbhaṭīkā (rDo-rJe sñiṅ-'grel, Hevajrapiṇḍārtha-ṭīkā, Tg. rGyud, No. 1180) the above commentary on the Saṃvara-Tantra is described as a commentary on the twelve and half ślokas (of the Mūla-Tantra), and the entire commentary on these ślokas is extant in Tibetan, and because in the Saṃvara commentary (Tg. rGyud, No. 1402) itself it is stated that the Mūla-Tantra and the "topics of the Six Extremities" (six ways of explaining the Tantra), as expounded in the ṭippaṇī, composed by the Bodhisattva, should be studied by one proceeding to a country, situated South and North (since they have been lost in Madhyadeśa), and further, because in the Vajragarbhaṭīkā it is stated; "by (6b)
this the last chapters, such as the chapter on conduct (caryā), are meant" (This means that the author himself had omitted the last chapters, and not that they had been hidden by ḍākinīs). Though there exist various accounts which agree and disagree, they all agree (in stating) that Abhaya, who belonged to the line of gÑan and Se lo-tsā-ba, Mañjukīrti, who belonged to the line of Rwa-lo, and Somanātha, who belonged to the line of 'Bro-pa, have been direct disciples of Kālacakrapāda, the Junior. They also agree in that Kālacakrapāda, the Junior, was a direct disciple of Kālacakrapāda, the Senior, and therefore one is not to be troubled by it. It is somewhat difficult to accept the statement that the first (first year of the first cycle of sixty years, i. e. 1027 A. D.) of the "past" years ('das-lo) of the period of 403 years (Me-kha rgya-mtsho) corresponds to the year of the introduction of the Kālacakra in Madhyadeśa, for Abhaya had composed the "Introduction to the Kālacakra" (Kālacakrāvatāra, Tg. rGyud, No. 1383) which says that about 60 years must have elapsed since the appearance of the Kālacakra (when he was composing the book). In the account of Čhag lo-tsā-ba it is stated that Ratnarakṣita had said that not sixty years had passed, but 45 years. If we were to synchronize this date with the dates given by Tibetan teachers, (we would see) that it corresponds to the sixteenth year of Mar-pa and Gra-pa mṄon-śes, and

that at that time the Kālacakra had already appeared in Tibet. It seems to me that Śrī Bhadrabodhi, the father of Kālacakrapāda, the Junior, was the person who had translated the Kālacakra with Gyi-Jo. It is also stated that one Nālandā-pa, a disciple of Kālacakrapāda, the Junior (Dus-žabs-pa chuṅ-ba), had on one occasion visited Tibet, etc. The Kāśmīrī Somanātha was able to commit to memory 16 ślokas after reading them once, and was endowed with a pure perfection of controlling the acyuta-bodhicitta (byaṅ-sems 'dzag-med). Besides the Kālacakra, he preached in Tibet the secret meaning of the sGron-gsal (Pradīpodyatana), as well as taught the rTsa-ba śes-rab (Prajñā-nāma-mūlamādhyamakakārikā, Tg. dbU-ma, No. 3824). I had seen the text which was transmitted in his Lineage. Having mastered the Tibetan language, he made an excellent translation of the Don-dam bsñen-pa (Srī Paramārthaseva, Tg. rGyud, No 1348). Later he journeyed to mṄa'-ris, and it was said that he had also translated the Great Commentary on the Kālacakra (Vimalaprabhā, Tg. rGyud, No. 1347). lČe, father and son, obtained the Kālacakra from Somanātha. From them 'Gro Ñi-ma obtained the system. Again it is known that they (lČe, father and son) had also (7a)
obtained it from gÑan lo-tsā-ba and other teachers. Yu-mo was also a disciple of his, but the stream of his teaching (of the Kālacakra) seems to have been interrupted. sGom-pa dKon-mčhog-bsruṅs having disposed of his entire property, realized six golden sraṅs for it, and having tied a silk scarf to his neck placed it in the hand of the paṇḍita, and thus offered him his own body, speech and mind (in Tibet a horse which is presented has always a scarf tied to its neck). The Teacher bestowed on him the exposition of the commentary on the Tantra (i. e. the Vimalaprabhā) together with its complete precepts. Having heard it (recited) in the translation of 'Bro, he had to accept 'Bro as his Teacher. Thus when enumerating the Lineage, he used to say: Somanātha, 'Bro lo-tsā-ba, and sGom-pa dKon-mčhog-bsruṅs.

sGro-ston gNam-la-brtsegs was a scholar who in his early

life had studied the Piṭakas, and when he grew older came to Somanātha, who said to him: "If you take my belongings to Mañ-yul (Ladak), on my return to Tibet I shall bestow on you the system". Some of his other friends told him: "one cannot buy the system from the paṇḍita, you had better ask our sGom-pa for it". Following this advice, he requested sGom-pa dKon-mčhog-bsruṅs (Ratnagupta) to bestow on him the commentary on the Tantra together with the precepts. The Teacher bestowed the complete system on him, and he practised it, and achieved excellent results. Later, when the paṇḍita (Somanātha) came again to Tibet, he went to meet the paṇḍita, who said to him: "I shall now give you the system". sNam-la-brtsegs replied: "When I was young, you did not wish to bestow it on me. But now, when I am old, I shall not ask for it". The paṇḍita said: "you are satisfied with the precepts of dKon-mčhog-bsruṅs. If not from me, from whom else did they originate?" and saying so, he thrashed him. sNam-la-brtsegs replied: "Yes, yes, it is due to the grace of the great Teacher!" Then the paṇḍita asked him: "What did he give you?" He replied: This and that". The paṇḍita said: "I do not possess more than this! Now take an oath that you will not preach it to others", saying so, the paṇḍita placed his rosary on his neck. gNam-la-brtsegs replied: "This was not preached by you, Teacher! (why then should I take an oath?)"—"O wicked one!" exclaimed the paṇḍita, and threw a handful of sand at his head. After that the paṇḍita said: "Well, now you may preach it to others, but you should preach the complete text, from end to end (mgo-lus)". In this manner he obtained (7b)
the permission. In the same manner, when Yu-mo made a similar request to the paṇḍita, the latter said, pointing at his luggage: "Carry this to Nepāl! I shall give it later". After asking the advice of his friends, he asked sGro-ston for it. The latter bestowed on him the commentary on the Tantra (Vimalaprabhā) together with the precepts, as well as the Pradīpodyotana (sGron-gsal) with its precepts. After that he

went to 'U-yug, and practised meditation, and obtained realization (siddhi). He had excellent disciples, and passed away at the age of 82. His disciples known as Wa-brag dkar-ba and one known as gÑal-pa Gro spent a considerable time immured ('dag-'byar) practising the bKa'-gdams doctrine. Later they came to Yu-mo and practised the precepts, and on the very first day they obtained all the (ten) signs (of meditation). They realized that the Kālacakra was the best path and meditated (according to the system). They were endowed with a great faculty of prescience.

gÑos sGyi-khuṅ-pa: when he had reached the age of 70, he met bLa-ma čhen-pa (Yu-mo). He preached to Ṅor-rJe. The latter taught (the Kālacakra) to Dol-pa 'Gas-ston dBaṅ-phyug-grub. The siddha Dharmabodhi has been a disciple of Yu-mo Tre-po mGon-po having obtained all the precepts and the basic text, taught them extensively. His Lineage had many branches. The scholar Dharmeśvara was the son of the Great Teacher (Yu-mo), and was born in the latter's 56th year. He taught the Sekoddeśa (Kg. rGyud, No. 361) when he was twelve. At the age of 16, he taught the Great Commentary on the Tantra (rGyud-'grel čhen-mo, Vimalaprabhā, Tg. rGyud, No. 1347). He debated (on the Doctrine) with numerous scholars, such as rGya-gliṅ-pa and others, and defeated them. His disciple Khaṅ-gsar-pa Nam-mkha'-'od was learned in the Piṭakas, such as the Rigs-tshogs-drug (the six Treatises by Ārya Nāgārjuna), and other. texts. He taught the "Great Commentary on the Tantra" (the Vimalaprabhā) and was endowed with an excellent mystic trance.

Dharmeśvara's daughter Jo-'bum: in her childhood she was influenced by her mother, practised magic, and caused the death of many enemies. After that she practised meditation (according to the method) of the Saḍaṅga-yoga (Yan-lag drug-gi rnal-'byor) and in this actual life she became an āryā, (8a)
equal to a natural yoginī (ārya or 'phags-pa are called those who had attained the stage of darśana-mārga).

Her brother Se-mo-čhe-ba Nam-mkha' rgyal-mtshan: in

his childhood he suffered from a deficient hearing and speech, and therefore there was not much hope (for him). Later he attended on Khaṅ-gsar-pa Nam-mkha'-'od and mastered the Commentary on the Tantra (Vimalaprabhā). He practised the Sadaṅga and the "Six doctrines" of Nā-ro, and obtained a perfect mystic trance. He was able to recollect clearly (his) numberless former existences. Because he resided at Se-mo-čhe, he became known as the siddha Se-mo-čhe-ba.

His disciple 'J̌am-sar Śes-rab 'od-zer: his native place was Upper Myaṅ. He attended on gÑal-žig and others, and became very learned in numerous Piṭakas. For many years he purified his body performing austerities. For a considerable time he propitiated Vajrapāṇi and felt confident, thinking "none among gods and demons are able to transgress my command." When he was going to preach at rKyaṅ-'dur, and was fording the gTsaṅ-po river, on the road leading towards the residence of Se-mo-čhe-ba, at the hermitage of Groṅ-čhuṅ, some asuras caused a shower of stones to fall, but he burst into a song saying that he having become indifferent towards the eight mundane dharmas, did not know fear. At the feet of Se-mo-čhe-ba he mastered the Commentary on the Tantra (Vimalaprabhā) together with its branches, and the initiation rite (of the Kālacakra). He practised meditation of the sampannakrama degree and within one day obtained the (ten) signs (of meditation), and thus became a Master of Yoga (yogeśvara, rnal-'byor-gyi dbaṅ-phyug). He had great faith in precepts, and used to say: "If these precepts would have been accompanied by diligence towards meditation possessed by the great ascetics of the Dwags-po bKa'-brgyud sect, then this country (Tibet) would have been filled with siddhas." Later he had a vision of the face of Munīndra and his retinue, and offered the Sapta-aṅga (1. Phyag-'tshal-ba, salutation; 2. mčhod-pa, offering; 3. bśags-pa, confession; 4. rJes-su yi-raṅ-ba, extolling virtue; 5. bskul-ba, request to Buddha to set in motion the Wheel of Law; 6. gsol-ba 'debs-pa, request to the Buddha to live long; 7. psṅo-pa, the offering of one's own meritorious acts for the welfare of others). The rite was first described in the Āryabhadracaryāpraṇidhānarāja (Kg. gZuṅs-'dus, No. 1095). "Having removed all his doubts in regard to the Cause, Path and Effect of Enlightenment before the Buddha, I did not request him to expound the Doctrine", said he. When preaching the Piṭakas, he used to teach it abiding in a state of perpetual trance (samāhita, mñam-par bžag-bžin). In his dreams he visited numerous paradises, such as Sukhāvatī and others. He established meditative schools in hermitages and maintained them with (8b) the help of his precepts. He thus obtained the power of preaching and meditating. His disciple the bla-ma Čhos-sku 'od-zer: he was a natural son of gSer-sdiṅs-pa gŽon-nu-'od and was born in the year Wood-Male-Dog (śiṅ-pho-kyi—1214 A.D.), which follows on the year Water-Female-Hen (čhu-mo-bya—1213 A.D.), during which the Kha-čhe paṇčhen returned to Kāśmīra. Čhos-sku 'od-zer's story (rnam-thar) was briefly told in the Chapter on the school of the Guhyasamāja-Tantra (See Book VIII /na/, fol. 10a and b.). (Here I shall tell) in detail about his meeting with the Dharmasvāmin 'Jam-gsar. He was told by gSer-sdiṅs-pa to go there, because he had a karmic connection (las-'brel) with 'Jam-gsar-ba. So he visited him, and while he was listening to the initiation rite of Yamāntaka, he was the Teacher as Yamāntaka. He also listened to the exposition of all the scriptures, philosophy and precepts. When he was listening to the initiation rite of the Kālacakra, he saw the Teacher as rDo-rJe-śugs, and reported the matter to the Teacher, who replied: "I also feel proud (when practising meditation of the utpanna-krama degree, the adept develops in himself the sensation of pride /ahaṃkāra/ of being the deity on which he was meditating), thinking "Am I not rDo-rJe-śugs? We, Teacher and disciple, should not be handicapped by hindrances." When he entered the maṇḍala (during his initiation), he saw a clear vision of the jñāna-maṇḍala (/of the Kālacakra/jñāna-maṇḍala, or ye-śe dkyil-'khor, the true maṇḍala of a deity; samaya-maṇḍala, or dam-tshig dkyil-'khor, the maṇḍala created by the adept in his Mind). At the time of obtaining the fourth (initiation), as soon as the Teacher had said: "Now you should assume a posture like me, and keep your Mind free from thoughts (mi-rtog-pa)", the fluctuations ('gyu-ba) of his Mind, big or small, came to an end, and he was able to transform them into the mystic trance of the Great Bliss (bde-stoṅ čhen-po). Later while practising meditations in his meditative cell (sgom-khaṅ), he suddenly achieved success, and the Dharmasvāmin told him that "he had reached the final stage of 'clearness' (gsal-ba, the two qualities of meditation are 1. gsal-ba or clearness, and 2. brtan-pa /sthira/ or steadiness)." He taught at this monastic college the Doctrine, such as the Pramāṇaviniścaya and other subjects. The Dharmasvāmin praised him highly. When he came to Se-mo-čhe-ba to get from him an Introduction to the Doctrine (čhos-'brel), the latter said: "You two ('J̌am-gsar-ba and Čhos-sku 'od-zer) through many existences have been Teacher and disciple". From him Čhos-sku 'od-zer heard the complete Commentary on the Tantra (Vimalaprabhā) with its branches. He benefitted others by bestowing initiations, preaching the Tantra and precepts.

His disciple Kun-spaṅs (the ascetic) Thugs-rJe brTson-'grus: he was born at Dab-phyar sPaṅ-sgaṅ in Northern La-stod, in the year Water-Female-Hare (čhu-mo-yos—1243 A.D.; according to the Re'u-mig in 1242 A.D. /čhu—stag/). (9a)
In his youth he mastered the Piṭakas. He also looked after numerous monks at the monastic college of rKyaṅ-'dur, and was famous as a proficient debater. On one occasion during his studies, he listened to the complete exposition of the Kālacakra by the All-Knowing (Kun-mkhyen) Čhos-sku 'od-zer. He obtained precepts, and while he practised meditations, he opened many samādhi-dvāras (gates of trance). Once, when an accident endangered his life (a handicap which arose during

his practice of the prāṇāyāma), Kun-mkhyen-pa (Čhos-sku 'od-zer) perceived it, and came by himself (without being called). Kun-mkhyen-pa said: "If you would have died this time, you would have obtained the four "bodies" (the four kāyas or bodies are: 1. svabhāva-kāya, ṅo-bo-ñid sku, Body of Absolute Existence; 2. Jñāna-dharmakāya, Ye-śes čhos-sku, Body of Absolute Wisdom; 3. Saṃbhoga-kāya, loṅs-spyod rdzogs-pa'i sku, Body of Glory; 4. Nirmāṇa-kāya, sprul-sku, Apparitional Body), and saying so, he removed the dangers threatening his life. After that he left his work as a student and preacher, and concentrated exclusively on meditation, and became known as Kun-spaṅs-pa. He heard the different exposition of the Sadaṅga-yoga (of the Kālacakra), whatever were found in Tibet. He transferred his residence to the mountains of the North, and while meditating, he subdued by the power of his concentrated Mind many demons. He was invited to J̌o-naṅ by J̌o-mo Nags-rgyal (the local deity of J̌o-naṅ), and he promised the goddess to come there after three years. When the time came, he journeyed there, founded a monastery, and looked after numerous disciples to whom he imparted both teachings and hidden precepts. Among them: Byaṅ-sems rGyal-ba ye-śes, La-stod-pa dBaṅ-rgyal, Mun-me Brag-kha-ba, and Son-pa Kun-rgyal are known as the "Four Sons of Kun-spaṅs-pa".

Byaṅ-sems rGyal-ba ye-śes: he was born in the year Fire-Female-Serpent (me-mo-sbrul – 1257 A.D.). In his childhood, Kar-ma-pa Pa-śi-pa (baγśi) accepted him (as disciple) against his father's will, taught him the Kar-ma-pa doctrines, and looked after him (by supplying him) with (his) worldly needs. Later he proceeded to J̌o-mo-naṅ and listened to (the exposition) of all the basic texts of Kun-spaṅs-pa, the latter's hidden precepts, and practised (meditation) according to them.

La-stod-pa dBaṅ-rgyal: he practised meditation and attained remarkable results. During the same time he also composed a guide-book on the teachings of (his) Teacher, beginning with the "Bar-du dge-ba", or second section (lit.

"useful in the middle". Most of the Tibetan Guide-books are divided into three sections: 1. Thog-mar dge-ba, "useful in the beginning", 2. Bar-du dge-ba, "useful in the middle" and 3. mTha'-mar dge-ba, "useful in the end". The Guide-book on the Sadaṅga-yoga was divided into six branches. The first two branches/yan-lag/ corresponded to the Thog-mar dge-ba, the next two to the Bar-du dge-ba, and the last two to the mTha'-mar dge-ba. La-stod-pa dBaṅ-rgyal wrote a Commentary on the last four branches of the Sadaṅga-yoga). He improved the meditations of many (disciples) and removed their handicaps. (9b)

Mun-me Brag-kha-ba Grags-pa seṅ-ge: he was born in the year Wood-Female-Hare (śiṅ-mo-yos—1255 A. D.) at rGyal-te Thaṅ-kar in Northern gYas-ru. He belonged to the gLan clan. In his youth he was ordained by the Phro-phu Rin-po-čhe bSod-nams seṅ-ge, and received the name of Grags-pa seṅ-ge. Later he received the final monastic ordination in the presence of the same upādhyāya dbU-ma-pa Ser-'bum acting as ācārya, and Bu-ston seṅ-ge-'od acting as Secret Preceptor. From Phya-ru-ba Seṅ-ge-dpal of Sa-skya he heard the rNam-'grel (Pramāṇavārtika), the Treatises of Maitreya, the "Six Treatises of Nāgārjuna," and the Tantra class were perfectly mastered by him. However he was of the opinion that meditation represented the Essence of the Doctrine, and therefore he asked Kun-spaṅs-pa and Byaṅ-seems rGyal-ye at J̌o-mo-naṅ for guidance in the Sadaṅga-yoga (sByor-ba yan-lag drug), and asked them to expound the Tantra. They said to him: "Go to Roṅ!" He then heard the "Commentary on the Tantra" (Vimalaprabhā) together with its precepts from Akara-siddhi, the youngest son of rGwa lo-tsā-ba. He held in high esteem meditation at the hermitage of Gya'-luṅ. Subsequently he helped many disciples by preaching (to them) the Commentary on the Tantra (Vimalaprabhā) and by giving them guidance. Later in the year of the Tiger (stag-lo—1338 A. D.), when a great snow-fall happened in the kingdom, Lo-be-ba Kun-bzaṅ acted as (his) supporter, and settled him at

Brag-kha. He stayed there in seclusion and recited the mantra of the Kālacakra 10,000,000 times, made 1,000,000 ablutions, and many wonderful signs took place, as for example flames assuming the form of precious stones, etc. Every day he practised meditation on the utpannakrama and sampannakrama degrees, besides the six āsanas (lus-sbyoṅ drug) of the body. He named as his four chief guide-books: the sByor-drug (Ṣaḍaṅga), the dMar-khrid, the gČod, and the gZer-lṅa, and mainly followed their prescriptions. During the summer seclusion, he spent most of his time in the continuous practice of gČod (rGyun-gČod). He used to send all the property which came into his hands to the monastery of his Teacher. He was endowed with the faculty of prescience, and all his prophecies concerning the future events at Sa-skya came true. He passed away at the age of 89 in the year Water-Female-Sheep (čhu-mo-lug—1343 A.D.) amidst wonderful (10*a*)
signs. After the cremation (of his remains), his body was transformed into a heap of relics. His disciples were the Dharmasvāmin bLa-mo Dam-pa and the dKa'-bču-pa gŽon-nu seṅ ge blo-gros, Waṅ-mo Žu-ba gŽon-nu-dpal, and many others. From Sroṅ-pa Čhos-dpal, a disciple of Sron-pa Kun-rgyal, Brag-nag-pa Čhos-skyoṅ-dpal obtained the system of Sron. The bKa'-bču-pa gŽon-nu seṅ-ge obtained it from him. Sron-pa Kun-dga'-rgyal has been the zu-gur-čhe (<mong. Ĵarɣuči) of the Mongol Emperor, and was ordained by bLa-ma 'Phags-pa, who introduced him to the study of the Piṭaka. Later he obtained guidance from Kun-spaṅs-pa, and obtained perfect results (in his meditation). He met Avalokiteśvara and Śa-ba-ri dBaṅ-phyug (one of the great mahāsiddhas). His precepts which were known as the "Method of Sron" (Sron-lugs), slightly differed from others, and through them he benefitted others. dPal-ldan bLa-ma obtained the "Method of Sron" (Sron-lugs) from the following three: Sron-pa Kun-dga' rgyal, his disciple Čhos-dpal, and the mahā-upādhyāya bSod-nams grags-pa. In this manner Kun-spaṅs-pa laboured for a long time for the welfare of others,

and then entrusted the abbotship to Byaṅ-sems rGyal-ye. He passed away at the age of 71, in the year Water-Female Ox (čhu-mo-glaṅ—1313 A.D.). Byaṅ-sems rGyal-ba ye-śes, aged 57, occupied the abbot's chair of J̌o-naṅ in the year Water-Female-Ox (čhu-mo-glaṅ—1313A.D.). Many kalyāṇa-mitras, such as the bla-ma Kun-bsod-pa and others, and many great men, such as the great official Byaṅ-rdor and the great official Yon-btsun, and others, became his disciples. He used to say: "Most of those who had received my guidance, have obtained perfect results. At least there had been none who did not complete the (ten) signs (of meditation)". He occupied the chair for eight years, and then passed away at the age of 64 in the year Iron-Male-Ape (lčags-pho-spre'u—1320 A.D.). He being an extraordinary man, the story of his life was written by the Dharmasvāmin Raṅ-byuṅ rdo-rǰe.

mKhas-btsun Yon-tan rgya-mtsho, a disciple of Byaṅ-sems-pa: he was born in the year Iron-Ape (lčags-spre— (10b) 1260 A.D.). At the age of 61, he occupied the abbot's chair. He handed over the chair in the year Fire-Male-Tiger (me-pho-stag—1326 A.D.), and died at the age of 68 in the year Fire-Female-Hare (me-mo-yos—1327 A.D.). His native place was sPeṅ-pa of mDog. In his childhood he followed on numerous scholars at Sa-skya, such as 'J̌am-dbyaṅs-pa and others, and studied well the Piṭaka. He journeyed to the Imperial Palace in the retinue of 'J̌am-dbyaṅs-pa (mČhims 'J̌am-dpal-dbyaṅs or 'J̌am-dbyaṅs gsar-ma). With 'J̌am-dbyaṅs-pa's permission, he soon returned to dbUs and gTsaṅ. Having come to J̌o-mo-naṅ, he thoroughly absorbed the initiation rite (of the Kālacakra system), and the Tantra from both Kun-spaṅs-pa and Byaṅ-sems-pa, and received their guidance. His Mind concentration acquired a lofty character, and he became the object of worship of all living beings

Kun-mkhyen Śes-rab rgyal-mtshan (a famous scholar of the J̌o-naṅ-pa sect, known generally under the name of Dol-

po-pa. His image is found in the J̌o-khaṅ of Lha-sa among those of the most famous Teachers of Tibet), who had become his disciple: he was born in the family known as Ban-tshaṅ of Dol-pa. In his youth he became a disciple of sKyi-ston 'J̌am-dbyaṅs-pa, uncle and nephew. He studied the Piṭakas, such as the bKa'-čhen bži ('Dul-ba, mDzod, Phar-phyin, dbU-ma) and others, also the Tantras, such as the initiation of Vajramālā (rDo-rJ̌e phreṅ-ba) and others. He especially studied the exposition of the Kālacakra after the method of Rwa by both the uncle and nephew ('J̌am-dbyaṅs-pa). He preached the bKa'-bži ('Dul-ba, Phar-phyin, mDzod, dbU-ma) at Sa-skya from his youth. Inspite of the fact that others did not like him doing so, he also added the Bodhicaryāvatāra, and preached it. He visited the monastic colleges of dbUs and gTsaṅ, took part in debates and became known as a good scholar. He studied extensively with many teachers. At J̌o-mo-naṅ he obtained the Commentary on the Tantra (Vimalaprabhā) together with its hidden precepts from mKhas-btsun Yon-tan rgya-mtsho. After having practised the precepts, he experienced an incomparable result. At the age of 35 he occupied the chair. Till his death he used to preach and meditate (bśad-sgrub). He erected the sKu-'bum mthoṅ-grol-čhen-mo. Following his orders, two of his disciples Ma-ti paṇ-čhen and the lo-tsā-ba bLo gros-dpal re- (11a)
vised in the year Wood-Male-Dog (śiṅ-pho-khyi—1334 A.D.) the translation of the Kālacakra. The Great All-Knowing (Kun-mkhyen čhen-po, Śes-rab rgyal-mtshan) having taken as basis this translation, composed an abridgement (bsdus-don—piṇḍārtha) on the Great Commentary on the Tantra (rGyud-'grel čhen-mo, i.e. the Vimalaprabhā) and notes. Further, he composed numerous short treatises (śāstras) on initiations and meditation, on astrology, etc. After the erection of the sKu-'bum čhen-mo, a new kind of meditation was produced in him. He said: "It seems to me, that having created Mount Meru (i.e. the Great caitya), the Ocean gushed forth" (this was a reference to his famous treatise Ṅes-don rgya-mtsho,

"The Ocean of Direct Meaning (nīta-artha)". He composed learned treatises on the doctrine of gžan-stoṅ (refutation of the raṅ-stoṅ doctrine of Candrakīrti), such as the Ṅes-don rgya-mtsho, the bsDus-don (its Summary), and Sa-bčad (its analysis), a commentary on the Uttaratantra (rGyud bLa-ma), the Abhisamayālaṃkāra, a Commentary on the General Doctrine (bsTan-pa spyi-'grel), the bKa'-bsdu-bži-pa (the "Fourth Council". In the bKa'-bsdu-bži-pa he outlined the theory of the existence of a Natural Buddha/raṅ-bžin saṅs-rgyas/ in all living beings), and others, which filled dbUs and gTsaṅ (the Ṅes-don rgya-mtsho and the bKa'-bsdu-bži-pa are two famous texts of the J̌o-naṅ-pa sect. Monks of the dGe-lugs-pa school are forbidden to keep these books within the precincts of the monastery). When many scholars, disagreeing, with his theory (grub-mtha'), came to discuss the matter with him, their refutations were melted similar to snow when reaching the ocean. Having installed the lo-tsā-ba on the abbot's chair, he proceeded to dbUs, took up residence in Lha-sa and taught the guide-book on the Saḍaṅga-yoga. The territory of Lha-sa became filled with (monks) practising ritualistic dances (ñams-skyoṅ-ba'i gar). Later he proceeded to dPal J̌o-mo-naṅ, and at the age of 70 in the year Iron-Female-Ox (lčags-mo-glaṅ—1361 A.D.) proceeded to Sukhāvatī (born in 1292 A.D.). His disciples Kun-spaṅs Čhos-grags dpal-bzaṅ-po, Phyogs-las rNam-rgyal, Ña-dbon Kun-dga'-dpal, and many others were learned men, who practised the Saḍaṅga-yoga. They filled all the mountain valleys and lands of dbUs and gTsaṅ with adepts (sādhaka) practising the Saḍaṅga-yoga. This Meditative Lineage spread greatly in Khams also. Even nowadays there appear to exist numerous adepts (sādhakas) observing the rule of the periods of three half-months and three years on the banks of the rMa-čhu (Huang-ho. Followers of J̌o-naṅ-pa are still found round lṄa-ba in South Amdo/ on the borders of Ssŭ-ch'uan/).

Now the Dharmasvāmin Phyogs-las rnam-rgyal (Bo-doṅ Phyogs-las rnam-rgyal): He was a native of mṄa'-ris and was born in the year Fire-Male-Horse (me-pho-rta—1306 A.D.). In his youth he proceeded to dbUs and studied at Čhos-'khor-gliṅ the Sūtra-piṭaka, such as the Prajñāpāramitā, the Nyāya, and other branches of knowledge. He became a great scholar. He also took part in debates in both dbUs and gTsaṅ. Once when he was taking part in a debate, he met the Dharmasvāmin Kun-mkhyen čhen-po Śes-rab rgyal-mtshan, and was filled with faith. He took up residence at Jo-naṅ proper, and obtained from Kun-mkhyen čhen-po the exposition of the Tantra and the initiation rite of the Kālacakra, together with the hidden precepts, as well as many other doctrines. He practised the precepts, and an excellent mystic trance was (11*b*) produced in him. He regarded Kun-mkhyen čhen-po as the chief among his teachers. Kun-mkhyen čhen-po's disciple Byaṅ-pa Ta'i-dban-pa after consulting Kun-mkhyen čhen-po, and his disciple, founded the monastery (čhos-sde) of Ṅam-riṅs (Lha-rtse ; at present the monastery belongs to the dGe-lugs-pa sect). Kun-mkhyen čhen-po spent some time there. Then he entrusted (the monastery) to Phyogs-las rnam-rgyal, and himself proceeded to Jo-mo-naṅ proper. Phyogs-las rnam-rgyal taught the Piṭakas for a considerable time, in particular the Prajñāpā-ramitā class and Logic. He gathered round himself many clever disciples. Later he handed over the chair to bsTan-pa'i rgyal-mtshan, and at the age of 49 became abbot of Jo-mo-naṅ. (fol. 12a: The words "že-dgu-pa-la..." refer to this passage). After five years he handed over this monastery also, and proceeded to dbUs. At 'Tshal-dbus-gliṅ he preached to a large congregation of disciples the initiation rite of the Kālaca-kra-Tantra and the hidden precepts. After that he journeyed towards Yar-kluṅs. When he was residing at rṄor, the lo-tsā-ba Byaṅ-čhub rtse-mo heard from him the higher initiation (mčhog-dbaṅ) of the Kālacakra. Having come to Yar-kluṅs, he stayed at Khra-'brug and other places, and established numerous disciples on the virtuous path. After that he pro-ceeded to gTsaṅ and took up residence at Se-mkhar-čhuṅ. His life: he was born in the year Fire-Male-Horse (me-pho-

rta—1306 A. D.) and lived to the age of 81, in the year Fire-Male-Tiger (me-pho-stag—1386 A. D.). My Teacher Saṅs-rgyas rin-čhen-pa obtained (the Doctrine) from him. He was born in the year Earth-Female-Hare (sa-mo-yos—1336 A. D.) at sNe'u-mkhar as son of mKhas-grub Čhos-dpal-pa, holder of the Lineage of scholars and meditation. Possessed of the spiritual heritage (gotra) of the Mahāyāna, in his childhood he never quarrelled with his playmates. From his youth, he listened to the exposition of numerous secret doctrines (gter-čhos) of his ancestors, such as the exposition of the Hevajra-Tantra (brTag-gñis) according to the method of rṄog, the (Vajra)kīla (Phur-bu), and Hayagrīva Cycles of the "Old" believers (rÑiṅ-ma), the bLa-ma gSaṅ-'dus (a rÑiṅ-ma book), and other texts. After that he journeyed to rTses-thaṅ and (12a)
attended on Čhos-seṅ-pa, the Great, and the ācārya 'Od-zer-dpal-pa, studied the Prajñāpāramitā, and took part in philosophical debates. After that he took up the study of the Pramāṇavārtika. While he was memorizing the Commentary, he felt a desire to hear the (exposition) of the Kālacakra. He then obtained from the Lo-čhen Byaṅ-čhub rtse-mo on one occasion the complete text of the Great Commentary on the Tantra (Vimalaprabhā), and on another occasion half of the text. He obtained the complete text on two occasions from the lo-tsā-ba Nam-mkha' bzaṅ-po. From the Dharmasvāmin Phyogs-pa the complete initiation of the Kālacakra, and twice the exposition of the Great Commentary of the Tantra, as hidden precepts the Sadaṅga-yoga, and the Sevasādhana (U-rgyan bsñen-sgrub). From the Dharmasvāmin Phyogs-pa's disciple rTogs-ldan sṅo-ñal-ma Ye-śes rgyal-mtshan he obtained the Commentary on the Tantra (Vimalaprabhā) together with notes by Phyogs-las rnam-rgyal. From the ācārya 'Jam-sgeg he obtained the Śrī Paramārthasevā (Tg. rGyud, No. 1348) and the lTa-'dod mdor-bstan (Tg. rGyud, No. 2304). From Yar-'brog-kha-ba-luṅ-pa Žaṅ-ston bSod-nams grags-pa he obtained the Commentary on the Tantra (Vimalaprabhā) together with notes by Kun-mkhyen čhen-po. From Ri-ston bLo-čhen-'od

he obtained the translation of the Commentary on the Tantra by Lo-grags-pa, which was handed down from Man-luṅs-pa and the lo-tsā-ba Grags-pa rgyal-mtshan, and the Sekoddeśa-ṭīkā of Nā-ro-pa. When Kun-mkhyen čhen-po came to Lhasa, he took up the final monastic ordination in his presence, and obtained from him several of the lesser doctrines. Among these he held in high esteem the method of Phyogs-las rnam-rgyal. After that he consecrated himself to meditation. During his practice of the Sadaṅga-yoga, he suffered during nine years from a disease. and felt the upper and lower parts of his body burning as if scorched by glowing charcoal. However he did not interrupt his meditation. Having been relieved of his affliction, his meditation greatly improved. He preached the exposition of the Commentary on the Tantra (Vimalaprabhā). He constantly gave guidance to numerous disciples in the practice of the Sadaṅga-yoga, who included priests and laymen, males and females. During a considerable time he laboured for the welfare of others. He passed away at the age of 86 in the year Wood-Male-Dragon (śiṅ-pho-'brug—1424 A. D.). He attended on the Blessed Maitreya in the Abode of Tuṣita, which had been the abode of his former incarnations. I obtained from him the complete initiation rite of the Kālacakra, as given in the book on the maṇḍala (12b)
rites composed by Kun-mkhyen čhen-po (Śes-rab rgyal-mtshan). I also obtained the text of the Great Commentary on the Tantra (Vimalaprabhā), the guide-book on the Sadaṅga-yoga, the Sekoddeśa with the commentary by Nā-ro-pa, as well as other commentaries (on the Kālacakra) by Bodhisattvas (i.e. by the kings of Śambhala). The Rin-po-čhe bSod-bzaṅ-ba also studied thoroughly the Kālacakra with its branches and secret precepts under the Dharmasvāmin Phyogs-las rnam-rgyal and the scholar Ña-dbon. During a considerable time he looked after disciples by bestowing on them guidance, expositions and initiations. He also composed a text-book on initiation rites (dBaṅ-sgrub. dBaṅ-sgrub means the first part of the initiation rite, which precedes the introduction

of the disciple into the maṇḍala), and became the Teacher of all great men. The Dharmasvāmin De-bžin gśegs-pa and mThon-ba Don-ldan also became his disciples. This yogeś-vara who had attained the stage of a scholar and a siddha, passed away at the age of 93 in the year Water-Female-Ox (čhu-mo-glaṅ—1433 A.D.). His disciple the dKa'-bču-pa Pad-ma-bzaṅ-po-ba expounded on many occasions the commentary on the Tantra (Vimalaprabhā), as well as composed a large commentary on the Vimalaprabhā. Further, the Dharmasvāmin Čhos-bzaṅ Ñi-ma, a disciple of Rin-po-čhe bSod-nams bzaṅ-po, founded the hermitage of gYa'-snaṅ, and upheld the Doctrine by preaching the Kālacakra, as well as by meditation. There appeared many adepts (sādhakas) who concentrated solely on the practice of the Sadaṅga-yoga. Again, 'Jam-dbyaṅs Čhos-kyi mgon-po-ba, a disciple of Kun-mkhyen čhen-po, took over the chair of gYag-sde paṇ-čhen, and for a long time preached the Kālacakra. He had many learned disciples, including 'Jam-dbyaṅs Rin-rgyal-ba and others. Having come to the monastic college of rTses-thaṅ, he preached the Commentary on the Tantra (Vimalaprabhā) to many piṭakadharas, of whom the best student (gsan-pa-po, lit. "a hearer") was the mahā-upādhyāya Rin-po-čhe rGyal-mtshan bzaṅ-po. He was born in the year Iron-Male-Tiger (lčags-pho-stag—1350 A.D.), when Bu-ston Rin-po-čhe was 61. He studied all the Piṭakas, and especially the "Four Books" (13a) (bKa'-bži), at gSaṅ-phu and rTses-thaṅ. He was greatly attached to the practice of the Pratimokṣa, and possessed an excellent bodhicitta. He studied under 'Jam-dbyaṅs Čhos-mgon-po, and having become learned in the Kālacakra, he used to say (jokingly) that all the passages (in the Vimalaprabhā) uttered by Avalokiteśvara, which said (that the rest of the text) was easily understood, represented a prophecy indicating him (for he had understood them without difficulty). He benefitted a multitude of people by preaching to them. He composed in verses a ritual book on the utpannakrama degree of the Kālacakra, and made the Kālacakra the object of his constant meditation. He heard the hidden precepts of the Sadaṅga-yoga from Saṅs-rgyas bLo-gros-pa, the mahā-upādhyāya of the Tshogs-čhen-mo-bas. He was of benefit to others by preaching to them, and passed away at the age of 76 in the year Wood-Female-Serpent (śiṅ-mo-sbrul—1425 A.D.). My Teacher Śākyaśrī was a disciple of 'J̌am-dbyaṅs Čhos-mgon-po, and had studied extensively the Kālacakra. He also listened to its exposition by the mahā-upādhyāya Rin-po-čhe rGyal-bzaṅ-ba and the Rin-po-čhe bSod-bzaṅ-ba. He also listened to the exposition of most of the Kālacakra works of Bu-ston by a bla-ma known as dBaṅ-rin-pa, who resided at rGyal-lha-khaṅ ('Phan-po), a direct disciple of Bu-ston Pin-po-čhe. The mahā-upādhyāya Las-kyi rdo-rǰe (Teacher of rǰe Tsoṅ-kha-pa) revealed to him that he had been in a previous life a kalyāṇa-mitra of sNar-thaṅ learned in the Kālacakra. In a dream he saw himself climbing a long stairway, and when he had reached the bum-pa (the spherical part) of a caitya, he saw in the corner of a shining maṇḍala of Kālacakra the Dharmasvāmin Kun-mkhyen čhen-po (Dol-po-pa Śes-rab rgyal-mtshan). Since he saw himself being blessed by Dol-po-pa, he used to say that he had understood many doctrines. He proceeded to Sukhāvatī at the age of 80 in the year Earth-Male-Dragon (sa-pho-'brug—1448 A.D.).

Further, the upādhyāya of J̌e-rdziṅ-tshogs-pa, named Rin-čhen tshul-khrims, obtained the Kālacakra system together (13b)
with its hidden precepts from the Dharmasvāmin Kun-mkhyen čhen-po. He practised meditation and attained great wisdom (mahā-jñāna, ye-śes čhen-po). His disciple Žo-luṅ mTsho-kha-ba benefitted numerous living beings with the help of precepts of the Sadaṅga-yoga. The disciple of Rin-čhen tshul-khrims-pa, the Dharmasvāmin bSod-nams rgyal-mtshan possessed a perfect knowledge of the Sadaṅga-yoga and guided numerous disciples. Again, the disciple of Kun-mkhyen čhen-po, 'J̌am-dbyaṅs bLo-gros rgyal-mtshan, known as sMan-čhu-kha-pa, looked after many disciples with the help of

initiations, by preaching to them the Tantra, by expositions, and hidden precepts. His disciple the Dharmasvāmin sMi-ri-ba founded the monastery of sMi-ri. He introduced many disciples to meditation. There were about eighty of those who observed a yearly seclusion (lo-mtshams-pa). Even nowadays this rule has not been infringed. Further, the disciple of Byaṅ-sems rgyal-ye, the kalyāṇa-mitra who was born at Dar-yul Bye-ma, and who was a disciple of sTag-luṅ Rin-po-čhe Saṅs-rgyas-dpal and of Ṅo-pa Dar-śe, obtained the hidden precepts of the Ṣaḍaṅga-yoga from Byaṅ-čhub sems-dpa' rGyal-ba ye-śes. He visited Wu-t'ai-shan (Ri-bo rtse-lṅa) and other places, practised meditation and was known to have been a siddha. He spread the Doctrine of the Ṣaḍaṅga-yoga in the Northern Quarters. A disciple of Yon-tan rgya-mtsho-ba and Rin-po-čhe Śes-rab 'bum-pa, named Seṅ-ge-dpal, propagated the Doctrine of the Ṣaḍaṅga-yoga in the Northern Quarter.

Bo-doṅ Rin-po-čhe Rin-čhen rtse-mo, who had become one of the nine "sons" of gÑal-žig, obtained the exposition of the Kālacakra and all its hidden precepts from the bLa-ma Se-mo-čhe-ba. He also erected a large image which became known by the name of Dus-'khor Lha-mo-čhe of Bo-doṅ Rin-rtse. (14a) He recited diligently 10,000,000 mantras without leaving his mat. While he was making oblations (homa), the flames assumed the shape of auspicious signs, such as the lucky diagram (śrīvatsa, dpal-be'u), the svāstika (gyuṅ-druṅ 'khyil-ba) etc. He used to preach the Kālacakra, and had numerous disciples. In particular, there appeared 18 'parasol holders' (gdugs-theg-pa). He bestowed guidance, and had disciples possessing miraculous powers. At the age of 51 he proceeded to Śambhala.

Bo-doṅ Rin-po-čhe's disciple sTag-sde-ba Seṅ-ge rgyal-mtshan: he was born in the year Water-Male-Ape (čhu-pho-spre'u—1212 A.D.) at Pha-li-luṅ. He obtained from the Bo-doṅ Rin-po-čhe the Prajñāpāramitā, the Pramāṇa (Logic), and the Abhidharma, and especially the exposition of the initiation of the Kālacakra together with its hidden precepts. After the death of the Dharmasvāmin, he took over numerous monasteries, such as Log-groṅ and others, and preached there. He had many learned disciples, such as the brothers Śoṅ, dKon-gžon, the Senior and Junior (čhe-čhuṅ), Thur-śe, the Senior and Junior, and others. Among his early disciples there were 13 'holders of the Parasol' (gdugs-theg-pa). Later sNa-tsha-roṅ-pa Śer-gžon, sTag-sde-ba brTson-rgyal, the bLa-ma dGe-'dun-brtan, the upādhyāya Yon-mgon, and others obtained initiations (from him). These disciples surpassed in learning the Teacher himself. He passed away at the age of 83 on the 8th day of the Tiṣya month (rGyal) of the year Wood-Male-Horse (śiṅ-pho-rta—1294 A.D.). Śoṅ-ston rDo-rJe rgyal-mtshan, born at Boṅ-ra of sPyad-luṅs Śar-kha, studied under sTag-sde-ba numerous śāstras, such as Logic (Pramāṇa), etc. Having copied about forty pages of the Kālacakra, he presented them as remuneration, and thus obtained the complete initiation into the Kālacakra. He also listened to the exposition of the Tantra and its Commentary (Vimalaprabhā), based on the translation of 'Bro (lo-tsā-ba). He studied under Gro-luṅ-pa mDo-sde rgyal-mtshan many Tantric treatises (śāstras) and astrology. When the bLa-ma 'Phags-pa returned to Tibet, he presented him with a well- (14b) composed śloka of praise. Having said that he intended going to study the work of a translator, he begged 'Phags-pa to send him on (to India), and the latter said: "It is a good idea! But it is difficult to acquire the ability of translating new texts. Study well and interrogate paṇḍitas. Because of the shortness of my study with the Dharmasvāmin, I do not know properly the sDebs-sbyor me-tog-gi čhuṅ-po (a treatise on prosody) composed by the Lord himself (Sa-skya paṇ-čhen), the Tshig-gi gter (name of a grammatical work by Sa-skya paṇ-čhen), and other texts. Therefore you should at any rate master them!" saying so, he gave him the above mentioned books, five golden sraṅs, and ten pieces of silk. Having reached Nepāl, he attended for five years on the paṇḍita

Mahendrabhadra and mastered the five lesser sciences (mṅon-brJod, sñan-ṅag, sdebs-sbyor, zlos-gar, and rtsis). He especially studied the science of grammar. Then he proceeded to Sa-skya, and p epared a good translation of the Śrī-Kālacakra-Tantra together with its commentary (Vimalaprabhā). This (translation) was seen by the Precious 'Phags-pa who sent him a letter praising him because "he possessed better faculties than the lo-tsā-bas who had previously translated the Kālacakra-Tantra". Śoṅ (-ston) translated for the first time the dPag-bsam 'khri-śiṅ (Bodhisattvāvadāna-kalpalatā, Tg. sKyes-rabs, No. 4155), as well as corrected some other translations. He also introduced the study of Sanskrit grammar, prosody, and lexicology (in Tibet). He taught the work of a translator to his own younger brother Śoṅ bLo-gros brtan-pa, and preached the Kālacakra-Tantra and its Commentary. bLo-brtan preached it to sGra-tshad-pa Rin-čhen rgyal-mtshan and to the lo-tsā-ba mČhog-ldan. 'J̌am-dbyaṅs sKyi-ston obtained it from the latter, and Kun-mkhyen čhen-po (Śes-rab rgyal-mtshan) obtained it from him.

Further, the bLa-ma dPal-ldan Seṅ-ge-ba, known to have been learned in the "Seven Treatises on Logic" (Tshad-ma-sde-bdun) which he had studied under the lo-tsā-ba mČhog-ldan, obtained them (the Kālacakra-Tantra and the Vimalaprabhā) in the translation of Śoṅ. He also (15a)
obtained the translation by Rwa from Roṅ-pa Śes-rab seṅ-ge. Kun-spaṅs Čhos-grags dpal-bzaṅ-po obtained from him the complete exposition (of the system) according to the initiation rite and translation by Śoṅ. Again, Kun-mkhyen 'Dzims-pa obtained (the Kālacakra) from mṄon-gra-ba Rin-čhen rtse-mo. From him and from the bla-ma rGwa-lo the complete methods of 'Bro and Rwa were obtained by the monk Tshul-khrims-'bar, a native of dbUs. Dus-'khor-ba Ye-śes rin-čhen obtained it from the latter. Kun-mkhyen Yon-tan rgya-mtsho obtained it from him. Again, the Lord of Scholars (mKhas-pa'i dbaṅ-po) dPaṅ bLo-gros brtan-

pa obtained it from sTag-sde-ba (dPaṅ bLo-gros brtan-pa, and his brother Śoṅ-ston rDo-rJe rgyal-mtshan are considered to have been the founders of philological studies in Tibet /rig-gnas includes grammar, prosody, etc./). He was born in the year Fire-Male-Mouse (me-pho-byi-ba—1276 A.D.) at south Khyam of La-stod. His mother having died early, he was brought up on sheep's milk. In his childhood, the Dharmasvāmin Byaṅ-gliṅ-pa and the mahāsiddha U-rgyan-pa looked after him, saying: "he will become a great kalyāṇa-mitra!" At the age of 7, he was ordained by the mahā-upādhyāya gSer-khaṅ-pa and Me-ston 'Dul-'dzin, and studied the Vinaya (Pratimokṣa-sūtra). At the age of 13, he made a new exposition of it. Then having heard of the fame of sTag-sde-ba, he proceeded to Tsha-sna, and obtained many Pitakas of the Tantra and Sūtra classes from sTag-sde-ba. He especially mastered the Kālacakra. When he reached the age of 19, sTag-sde-ba died. He studied with the lo-tsā-ba mČhog-ldan the Ka-lā-pa (Tg. sGra, No. 4282) and the Candra-pa (Tg.sGra, No. 4269). He also studied the Kāvyā-darśa (sÑan-sṅags me-loṅ, Tg. Sgra, No. 4301). He learned the Prākṛta language from the A-tsa-ras (ācārya) whom he chanced to meet. From a time he became a great translator. On seven occasions he visited Nepāl. He translated and revised the translations of numerous texts of the Tantra and Sūtra classes. He also composed numerous commentaries on Logic (Pramāṇa), Abhidharma, and (other) branches of knowledge. In short, during his life-time there was no better scholar than he. Later he proceeded to dbUs and opened the mental eyes of numerous Piṭakadharas at Ne'u-thog, Guṅ-thaṅ, sTag-luṅ, and other monasteries. The great descendants of dPal Sa-skya-pa, such as 'Jam-pa'i dbyaṅs Don-yod rgyal-mtshan, his brother and others showed him respect on other occasions, also when he was not preaching the Doctrine. He also acted for a short while as abbot of the monastery of Bo-doṅ-ye. While the Dharmasvāmin bSod-nams rgyal-mtshan was listening to the recitation of the text of the (15b)

permission (luṅ) of the Commentary on the Kālacakra Tantra, he insisted that he should practise it in real earnest. He spent a long time at gNas-po-čhe and preached his method of meditation, and his fame spread upwards as far as Ya-tse (mṄa'-ris), and downwards as far as China. Having completed his labours for the welfare of others, he passed away at the age of 67 in the year of Water-Male-Horse (čhu-pho-rta—1342 A.D.). dPal-ldan Byaṅ-čhub rtse-mo obtained, (the system) from the scholar dPaṅ, whose nephew he was. He was born in the year Water-Female-Hare (čhu-mo-yos—1243 A.D.) in Southern La-stod. In his childhood he became the disciple of the Venerable dPaṅ and mastered the three Piṭakas, the precious class of the Tantras, and the Sanskrit language. He also studied the lesser sciences, and mastered them all. By order of dPal-ldan bLa-ma Dam-pa he became abbot of Bo-doṅ. When dPal-ldan bLa-ma Dam-pa proceeded to the Imperial Court, he attended on him as far as sTag-luṅ. The sTag-luṅ Rin-po-čhe Ratnākara made the following request to dPal-ldan bLa-ma Dam-pa: "Let this lo-tsā-ba rTse-mo act as preceptor of my nephew". bLa-ma Dam-pa agreed, saying he was at liberty to do so. The one known as Nephew Nam-mkha' dpal-bzaṅ-po was an incarnation of Dharmeśvara, son of Yu-mo. He recollected clearly all former events. rTse- (16a)
mo bestowed on him the Commentary on the Kālacakra-Tantra (Vimalaprabhā) together with the hidden precepts, and other doctrines. Nam-mkha' dpal-bzaṅ po became an unrivalled great scholar and wrote many treatises. Later, when residing at the monastery of sTag-luṅ, he entrusted the monastery to bKra-śis dpal-brtsegs, and himself concentrated on meditation only in the mansion called Thaṅ-lha-mdzod. Later the great lo-tsā-ba (lo-čhen) stayed at Yar-kluṅs, gDan-sa Thel, and Guṅ-thaṅ, and satisfied numerous scholars by a shower of religion, which included the Śrī-Kālacakra and other systems. In particular, sPyan-sṅa Grags-pa Byaṅ-čhub-pa obtained many doctrines (from him). He saw the great lo-tsā-ba meditating by day and by night, without leaving it, and

imitating his example, he stayed alone in darkness in a small hut, and devoted himself solely to mind concentration. After that he journeyed towards gTsaṅ and stayed at Čhu-mig Riṅ-mo. He established many disciples in initiation, and gave them his guidance, and passed away at the age of 78 in the year Iron-Male-Ape (lčags-pho-spre'u—1320 A.D.).

The lo-tsā-ba Nam-mkha' bzaṅ-po, a disciple of the great lo-tsā-ba, who was learned in Grammar, Logic, and the Kālacakra, also attended on the great lo-tsā-ba (Byaṅ-čhub rtse-mo), and preached extensively the Kālacakra in other localities. The nephew of the great lo-tsā-ba, the lo-tsā-ba Grags-pa rgyal-mtshan and his nephew dPal 'J̌igs-med grags-pa accepted the doctrines of former teachers, and with the help of their learned labours, worked for the welfare of numerous disciples, and became Masters of the Doctrine. This 'J̌igs-med grags-pa was born in the year Wood-Female-Hare (śiṅ-mo-yos—1315 A. D.) and passed away at the age 77 in the year Iron-Female-Sheep (lčags-mo-lug—1391 A.D.). It also stated that he was born in the year Water-Female-Ox (čhu-mo-glaṅ—1313 A.D.). The disciples of dPal 'J̌igs-med grags-pa, who were devoted to their teacher, and who were continuously praising him, were the (16b) Lord of Men (Mi 'i bdag-po) rNam-rgyal grags-pa, who was very learned, and the great scholar bSod-nams rnam-par rgyal-ba.

bSod-rnam-par rgyal-ba: he at first studied many Piṭakas, and having become a learned man, he proceeded to Yar-'brog to visit 'J̌igs-med grags-pa, and heard many doctrines from him.

He had great faith in his interpretation of the essence of the Tantras. He composed numerous treatises, headed by a Commentary on the Kālacakra in seven volumes and a detailed exposition of Tantric vows (gSaṅ-sṅags-kyi dam-tshig) of more than ten pages. Further, he listened to the exposition of the Kālacakra proper by Don-grub kun-dga', a scholar who had studied for a long time the system of Kālacakra.

Now (here is an account) of (the school) which is known as the tradition of Rwa of Śrī-Kālacakra: The ācārya Tsi-lu-pa having first obtained the Kālacakra, his disciple was bSod-sñoms-pa (Piṇḍo); the latter's disciple was Kālacakrapāda, the Senior (Dus-žabs-pa čhe-ba); the latter's disciple—Kālacakrapāda, the Junior (Dus-žabs-pa chuṅ-ba); the latter's disciple—Mañju-kīrti; the latter's disciple—the paṇḍita Samantaśrī of Ye-raṅ in Nepāl. Rwa lo-tsā-ba rDo-rJe grags-pa's nephew, named Rwa Čhos-rab was very learned in the Tantra class. He especially mastered the doctrines possessed by Rwa rDo-rJe grags-pa, invited to Tibet the paṇḍita Samantaśrī, and (assisted by him) made a good translation of the Kālacakra-Tantra together with its Commentary—the Vimalaprabhā, and listened to its exposition. He also translated many branches of the Kālacakra, pleased the paṇḍita with his offerings, and escorted him as far as Nepāl. The paṇḍita was pleased and presented him the hat of 'Bum-phrag gsum-pa (Sthirapāla. 'Bum-phrag gsum-pa, seems to be a title given to him, because he had memorized 300,000 ślokas). Having gone to dbUs, he laboured extensively for the welfare of numerous inhabitants of Khams and dbUs. He preached the doctrines, especially the Kālacakra, to Rwa Ye-śes seṅ-ge. The latter taught it to Rwa 'Bum-seṅ, who (taught it) to the Venerable rGwa-lo (-tsā-ba). (17a)

rGwa-lo: When during the reign of Khri-sroṅ lde-btsan, king of Tibet, sBa gSal-snaṅ and Saṅ-śi were sent as envoys to invite Buddhist monks (hwa-śaṅ) from China, they invited one Mi-ñag (a native of Mi-ñag) who had been a hwa-śaṅ, and the king made him his chaplain (mčhod-gnas).

Among the Lineage of numerous mantradharas who had practised the teachings of the basic texts of the Mahāyāna, were: at Yar-'brog-sgaṅ-Mi-ñag gŽon-nu sñiṅ-po, his son gŽon-nu Seṅ-ge, and the latter's son Rig-'dzin sñiṅ-po, who settled in the country of rGya-ma of Roṅ. His son rDo-rJe seṅ-ge took over mKhar-phug of Roṅ. The eldest of his four sons, named Ye-śes rdo-rJe, was a learned man,

and attained spiritual realization. He took over the monastery of dBen-dmar, the seat of one called dBaṅ-phyug rgyal-pa, who had obtained the siddhi with the help of precepts known as the dbYug-čhos of the Mahāmudrā (dbYug-čhos means a secret doctrine written on a roll of paper, and hidden inside a bamboo stick, used as a walking staff by yogins). rGwa-lo was born to him in the year Water-Female-Hog (čhu-mo-phag —1203 A.D.). On being recognized as an incarnation of rGwa-lo, he was called rGwa-lo. His real name was rNam-rgyal rdo-rje. In his childhood he met the Kha-čhe paṇ-čhen (Śākyaśrī) at Ṅur-smrig, who perceived that he was to become a remarkable man. He (Śākyaśrī) took the boy with his hand and pronounced an auspicious śloka. During his studies, the boy became afflicted by the "king" (rGyal-po, a demon of the gNas-byuṅ čhos-skyoṅ class). He proceeded to Thar-pa to (interview) dPyal, and the affliction left him. There for three years he studied the Sanskrit alphabet. He listened to the exposition of the Hevajra and (Vajra) vārahī Cycles, and afterwards preached them. All were filled with amazement. From Rwa 'Bum-seṅ he obtained the doctrines of the tradition of Rwa, and especially the Kālacakra. He practised meditation, and obtained the perfection of speech, and gained the faculty of composing new mantras. He taught the Kālacakra and had many disciples. He died at the age of 80 in the year Wood-Horse (čhu-rta—1282 A.D.). His chief disciple (was) the Venerable Man-luṅs-pa, the Great (a famous Tibetan pilgrim who wrote a lengthy account of the holy places of India /Man-luṅs-pa'i lam-yig/, on which the Byaṅ Śamba-la'i lam-yig by dPal-ldan Ye-śes, the Third Paṇ-čhen bLa-ma of bKra-śis lhun-po, was based). He was born in the year Earth Female-Hog (sa-mo-phag—1239 A.D.). In the year Iron-Male-Mouse (lčags-pho-byi-ba – 1300 A.D.) he took the vow in front of the Mahābodhi at Vajrāsana not to partake of more than a single grain of rice and a drop of water per day, while expecting a prophecy by the Mahābodhi image. (17*b*)
On the 12th day (after his vow) the host poured some

water over his head but he scarcely felt it. On the 18th day the Mahābodhi (image) spoke to him, saying: "O son of noble family! Proceed to Mount Potala, and practise the virtuous conduct in the manner of Bodhisattvas in the presence of the Bodhisattva Avalokiteśvara". Having received this prophecy, he rose and proceeded southwards. While staying at the caitya of Śrī Dhānya kaṭaka (Guntur District, Madras), a splinter of seṅ-ldaṅ wood (Khadira, Acacia catechu) injured his foot, and he bled profusely. After healing his wound, he obtained the Paramākṣarasukha (mčhog-tu mi-'gyur-ba'i bde). Then attired as an Indian yogin he crossed over the surface of the Ocean, as if walking on hard ground, and proceeded towards Potala. rGwa-lo had many disciples: the bLa-ma 'Phags-pa, Rin-po-čhe Khro-phu-ba, Lho-pa Grub-seṅ, Thaṅ-ston lo-tsā-ba, and others. His eldest son rGya-gar grags-pa whose ordination name was bLo gros nam-mkha' dpal became learned in all the doctrines of his father, including that of Kālacakra, and took over the manastery of dbEn-dmar. He built a vihāra, performed (there) extensive religious works, and passed away. His second son Śes-rab seṅ-ge was born in the year Iron-Female-Hog (lčags-mo-phag—1251 A.D.). In his youth he studied grammar (i.e. Sanskrit Grammar) and the Kālacakra. At the age of 16, he taught the Kālacakra. At the age of 20, he proceeded to Thar-pa (situated near Gyangtse) and obtained the doctrine from dPyal. At the age of 22, he came to sTag-sde seṅ-rgyal and for five years studied the Prajñāpāramitā and Logic. He became especially learned in Logic. He took part in philosophical debates in dbUs and gTsaṅ. At the age of 30, he was ordained and received the final monastic ordination in the presence of the bla-ma Čhos-rgyal 'Phags-pa and the upādhyāya mČhims. He listened the expositions of many (18a) doctrines. He invited the lo-tsā-ba Grags-pa rgyal-mtshan, and listened to the exposition of the Vajramālā initiation, Tantric texts, including the Mañjuśrīmūlatantra (Kg. rGyud-'bum, No. 543), etc., as well as the sMan-dpyad

yan-lag brgyad (The "Eight branches of Medical Science," Tg. gSo-rig-pa, No. 4306). He took over the monastery of dbEn-dmar, and preached there for a long time. He also preached many doctrines at various other monasteries, such as Thar-pa Khro-phu, bSam-yas, sTag-lun, gŽu Kun-dga' ra-ba, Śans-rTse-gdon, Čhu-mig, sTon-mo-lun, gYus-dGa'-ldan, and others. At the age of 41, he entrusted dbEn-dmar to the bla-ma rDo-rje rgyal-mtshan and himself settled at dMu. He founded Śambhar (gTsan) and built there a vihāra. He copied the Tantra section of (the bKa'-'gyur) and the Vinaya, and laboured for the welfare of living beings. At last, he bestowed an initiation on the newly born Dharmasvāmin bSod-nams rgyal-mtshan, and died at the age of 65 in the Wood-Female-Hare (śin-mo-yos—1315 A.D.). He had many disciples among the descendants of Sa-skya-pa, including the Ti-śrī (Ti-shih) Kun-blo and others; numerous disciples among great men, and many disciples who were learned men, virtuous and benevolent, such as the lo-tsā-bas Yar (Yar-kluns Grags-pa rgyal-mtshan), Thar (Thar-pa lo-tsā-ba Ñi-ma rgyal-mtshan), dPan (dPan bLo-gros brtan-pa). He had in particular many disciples learned in the Kālacakra. The third son (of rGwa lo) the ācārya rNal-'byor looked after the country. The fourth son—the bLa-ma Ākarasiddhi mastered the Kālacakra according to the traditions of Rwa and 'Bro, as well as the complete systems of dPyal-ba and Sa-skya-pa. His son the bla-ma rDo-rje rgyal-mtshan was born in the year Water-Female-Sheep (čhu-mo-lug—1283 A.D.). In his youth he studied grammar and was ordained by 'Jam-dbyans Rin-rgyal acting as upādhyāya, and the ācārya Śes-gyal acting as ācārya. At the age of 16, he took over the monastery of dbEn-dmar. He maintained a school (bśad-grwa) of Kālacakra, and received the final monastic ordination in the presence of the upādhyāya bKa'-bži-pa and (18b)
the upādhyāya Žal-sna-ba. He studied the grammar of Candragomin (Tsandra-pa/Candra-vyākaraṇa-sūtra, Tg. sGra, No. 4269/) and different kinds of alphabets with the Thar-

pa lo-tsā-ba, and studied the Abhidharma and many hidden precepts (upadeśa) and propitiation rites (sādhana). He obtained from the bla-ma Śes-rab seṅ-ge-ba all the instructions pertaining to initiation rites, especially those of the Kālacakra, and mastered them in the manner of a vase filled to the brim. Further, he obtained from the upādhyāya Žal-sṅa-ba the Vinaya and the Abhidharmakośa. From mDzo-po Lhas-pa Saṅs-rgyas sgom-pa (he obtained) the Vajramālā, transmitted through the Lineage of sGaṅ lo-tsā-ba, the Guhyasamāja, the Saṃvara Cycle according to the method of Atīśa, hidden precepts of the "Path and Fruit" doctrine (Lam-'bras), etc. Further, he studied many Tantras. He also obtained from Sri'u čhuṅ-pa bLo-ldan seṅ-ge the Guhyasamāja, the Yoga (Tantra), the gSaṅ-ldan (Tg. rGyud, No. 2584), the gDan-bži (Kg. rGyud-'bum, No. 430), and other texts. bLa-ma Śes-rab seṅ-ge having died, he took over Śambhar and dbEn-dmar. For a long time he carried on the preaching of the Kālacakra. After that he was invited by the Great Emperor, because his fame had encompassed all quarters. He proceeded to the Imperial Court in the Dog year (khyi-lo—1310 A.D. This must be the Iron-Dog year /lčags-khyi/), and installed faith in the Great Emperor and all his ministers. He died at the age of 43 in the year Wood-Female-Ox (śiṅ-mo-glaṅ—1325 A.D.).

Bu-ston Rin-po-čhe obtained from him the Kālacakra. At first he studied with Thar-pa lo-tsā-ba the Grammar by Candragomin and mastered the work of a translator. He fostered the incomparable hidden precepts of the Sadaṅga-yoga which were transmitted in the Lineage of Anupamarakṣita (dPe-med-'tsho), meditated, and a wonderful experience was produced in him. He inquired into numerous difficult points of the Kālacakra, and committed them to memory. Later he visited the bla-ma rDo-rje rgyal-mtshan at Śambhar. During the nine months of his residence there, he attended the daily recitations of the Commentary on the Tantra (Vimalaprabhā), and they conducted detailed investigations (into the system). He also made a thorough study of astrology, and studied the "lesser" branches of the Kālacakra. Following the advice of rDo-rje rgyal-mtshan, he translated the Commentary on the Sekoddeśa in 360 ślokas (Tg.rGyud, No.1354). Having come to Ža-lu (gTsaṅ), he chose the Kālacakra as the subject of his seasonal (19a) preaching, and preached it. He also composed many treatises (śāstras) on the Kālacakra. Later he obtained numerous hidden precepts of the Saḍaṅga-yoga by Kun-spaṅs-pa, which were in the possession of the bla-ma 'Phags-'od-pa. While he was writing down notes on the Vimalaprabhā (Commentary on the Tantra), he revised the translation made by Śoṅ. He wrote it out properly, after it had been translated by two translators at Jo-naṅ. In general, (one can say) that although there were many men learned in the system of the Kālacakra, as well as many siddhas, in the domain of the detailed exposition of the system, Bu himself was preeminent, the chief and the best. Through his continuous teaching of the Kālacakra, he obtained numerous disciples, the chief among whom was dPal-ldan bla-ma Dam-pa, who never left behind the book containing the Kālacakra, and studied it with great diligence even while touring the country. Having examined all the Commentaries and many different works translated previously, he wrote on many branches of the Kālacakra, such as the "Maṇḍala rite" (mÑon-dkyil). He also composed a Mahā-ṭīkā. While he was preaching it at sÑe-thaṅ, more than 500 scholars possessing this text gathered there. Later he made a revision of the Mahā-ṭīkā. Even at the end of his life, he used to bestow complete initiations on numerous great kalyāṇa-mitras, though himself suffering from an ailment. The Dharmasvāmin Bu's successor, the lo-tsā-ba Rin-čhen rnam-rgyal-ba also made the Kālacakra the subject of his seasonal preaching, and taught it. His Spiritual Lineage exists until now. The Dharmasvāmin Rin-po-čhe Śaṅs-pa Kun-mkhyen-pa obtained the complete Cycle of the Kālacakra from Čhos-kyi dpal-ba of Goṅ-gsum bde-čhen, a disciple of the All-knowing Bu (-ston), and benefitted numerous living beings. The Venerable Tsoṅ-kha-pa, the Great, also heard the initiation rites, the exposition (of the system), and the hidden precepts of the Kālacakra from Goṅ-gsum bde-čhen-pa. He (Tsoṅ-kha-pa) taught the complete exposition of the Commentary on the Tantra (Vimalaprabhā) in the year Earth-Male-Dog (sa-pho-kyi—1418 A.D.). Being a Master of the Doctrine, the Lord All-knowing (Tsoṅ-kha-pa's) preaching of the system on a single occasion only became like a banner which was never lowered, not like the others who had preached (the system) on a hundred occasions. Such was the statement by my Teacher. Again, from bSod-nams lhun-grub, who was a clansman of the bla-ma rDo-rJe rgyal mtshan, the bla-ma Ṅag-gi dbaṅ-phyug grags-pa obtained the Kālacakra Cycle with its branches. He looked after many disciples, and was learned in both the direct and indirect meanings of the Kālacakra (in the Kālacakra draṅ-don or neya-artha means "meaning made easy", and corresponds to the utpannakrama degree; ṅes-don or nīta-artha means "sublime meaning", and corresponds to the sampannakrama degree). He had the faculty of attracting the minds of others with the help of rites, such as dance and song recitals, etc. He was also learned in astrology and composed a treatise (śāstra) on it. His maṇḍala rite received a great spread. The Dharmasvāmin rGod-phrug ras-pa used to say that once when he was listening to his exposition of the guide to the Saḍaṅga-yoga, he saw the Teacher as Śa-ba-ri dBaṅ-phyug. Again, the Se lo-tsā-ba gŽon-nu tshul-khrims studied the Commentary on the Kālacakra-Tantra (Vimalaprabhā) on two occasions with Tsa-mi, on one occasion with Abhaya, on one occasion with Bhāskara, and the first part of the Commentary with Abhiyukta. (19b)

While both Abhaya and Mañjukīrti had been disciples of Nā-ro-pa, Abhaya had been also a disciple of Tsa-mi. Bhāskara was also called Bhāskaradeva, meaning "Sun god" ('Od-byed-lha), the disciple of Śrīdhara (dPal-'dzin). When Se lo-tsā-ba came to Tibet, he taught the system to

gÑos Dar-ma-'od. The latter taught it to Dus-'khor-ba bKra-śis rin-čhen. The latter to Dus-'khor-ba Saṅs-rgyas rdo-rǰe. The latter to Śrī U-rgyan-pa. The latter taught it extensively basing himself on the translation by Tsa-mi, at La-stod, Yar-kluṅs and other localities. sÑe-mDo-ba obtained it from Grub-čhen-pa (U-rgyan-pa), and latter taught it to the Dharmasvāmin Raṅ-byuṅ-ba (Raṅ-byuṅ rdo-rǰe) according to the translation by Tsa-mi. rGwa lo-tsā-ba obtained the hidden (20*a*)
precepts of the Sadaṅga-yoga from Tsa-mi, as well as studied it under Abhaya. He practised meditation and attained spiritual realization (siddhi). His fame spread as far as Zaṅs-gliṅ (according to some authors—Ceylon, according to others—Tāmralipti). Having come to Tibet, he bestowed these precepts on Žaṅ-'tshal-pa and others. He laboured for the welfare of others by bestowing initiations and precepts throughout dbUs, gTsaṅ and Lower Khams. He lived to the age of 89.

Again, when the paṇḍita Vibhūticandra was preaching Grammar to about five disciples in Nepāl, there came a yogin wearing a black lion-cloth. At first the disciples wondered at him, and informed the paṇḍita. The latter understood that this was Śa-ba-ri dBaṅ-phyug. He then requested the yogin to bestow on him the Sadaṅga-yoga, the essence of all the Tantras, and the latter bestowed it on him. The yogin stayed for 21 days, and said that he was going to Kāśmīra. When he had left, the paṇḍita (Vibhūticandra) asked all the Tibetans, who had come to Nepāl: "Who was the most famous kalyāṇa-mitra in Tibet at the present time?" They replied that "the greatest was Ko-brag-pa". The paṇḍita then sent a letter to Ko-brag-pa saying that he possessed the profound precepts of Śa-ba-ri dBaṅ-phyug (in Tibetan also called Ri-khrod-pa dBaṅ-phyug. See. A. Gruenwedel: Die Geschichten d. Vierundachtzig Zauberer/Mahāsiddhas/, p. 148), and that he should come to receive them. Ko-brag-pa despatched suitable presents to the paṇḍita and his retinue, and requested the paṇḍita to visit Tibet. When the paṇḍita reached Diṅ-ri, he bestowed the hidden precepts on Ko-brag-pa, dPyal A-mo-gha, gYuṅ-phug-pa, Ñeg-po Čhos-ldan, and Mar-ston gYaṅ-'bar. The paṇḍita himself also listened to the hidden precepts preached by Ko-brag-pa. These precepts spread greatly. The ascetic Žaṅ when preaching the pratyāhāra (restraining organs) stage of the Saḍaṅga-yoga (so-sor sdud-pa), used to base himself on this system only. The Kha-čhe paṇ-čhen (Śākyaśrī) bestowed on the lo-tsā-ba dPyal Čhos-kyi bzaṅ-po the Commentary on the Hevajra-Tantra (brTag-gñis), composed by Nā-ro-pa, and the latter's secret precepts on the Saḍaṅga-yoga (sByor-ba yan-lag drug). These secret precepts the lo-tsā-ba expounded in a book entitled the "Key to the Casket of Precious Stones" (Rin-po-čhe sgom-gyi lde-mig). gÑal-pa Hrul-po, a disciple of the lo-tsā-ba (Khro-phu lo-tsā-ba), composed a commentary on it. The book exists nowadays. But the best of the initiations and precepts of Śrī-Kālacakra (originated) from the Venerable Great scholar (mKhas-pa čhen-po) Śrī Vanaratna (dPal Nags-kyi rin-čhen). This Precious Great paṇḍita was born[1] as the son of a king in the town of Dam-pa (Sadnagara) in Eastern India (Chittagong District, E. Bengal). At the age of 8, he received the noviciate from one named Buddhaghoṣa (Saṅs-rgyas-dbyaṅs), who led many hundreds of thousands of monks, was learned in all sciences and endowed with a great faculty of prescience, and who acted as upādhyāya, and one named Sujataratna, who led many tens of thousands of monks, and who acted as ācārya, at the vihāra called Mahācaitya. He studied many sciences under these upādhyāya and ācārya, as well as with other scholars. The upādhyāya produced in him a Mental Creative Effort towards Enlightenment. He listened to the exposition of numerous profound initiations and hidden precepts. At the age of 20, he received the final monastic ordination from his former upādhyāya and ācārya. Then having become an ascetic, he journeyed to Seṅga'i gliṅ (Ceylon). He spent six years

(20b)

1 In 1384 A.D. (Śiṅ-byi-lo, Wood-Mouse year).

there. He visited many sacred places and miraculous images, many wonderful miracles taking place. From the ācārya Dharmakīrti he obtained the Vinaya-āgama, the 'Od-ldan (Tg. 'Dul-ba, No. 4125), and other texts. He practised chiefly the mind concentration. Then when he was about to return to Jambudvīpa, he had a vision of Saṅs-rgyas Gaṅs-čhen-mtsho (Hemasāgara). Unharmed by heretics, he journeyd to the kingdom of Kaliṅga in Southern India. There a great paṇḍita named Mi'i ñi-ma (Narāditya), famed as a scholar in (21a)
Jambudvīpa, praised him in the following verse:

"Great sthavira Vanaratna,
Who has realized the freedom from Worldly attachment (Virāga)
Having cleansed the turbid defilement produced in the World,
O beings! Follow on him with devotion, in order to pacify the Saṃsāra."

He worshipped him for a considerable time. Again he proceeded towards the Śrī Dhānya-kaṭaka mahā-caitya, and stayed for some time in the hermitage of Nāgabodhi (kLu'i byaṅ čhub). At first he met Śa-ba-ri dBaṅ-phyug. Then while en route to Magadha, he studied with the heretical paṇḍita Harihara the book Kalāpa (Kalāpasūtra, Tg. sGra, No. 4282), a version which was seven times larger than the one known in Tibet. Most of his time he spent in meditation practising the Sadaṅga-yoga. He especially practised meditation (according to Sadaṅga-yoga), observing periods of three years, three half-months and three days (according to the Yoga method advocated in the Kālacakra, a yogin should observe the following periods in meditation: three years, three half-months and three days; during these periods the physical organism is believed to undergo a complete change) in a forest situated beyond the river called Ka-na-kra-śo-tam. He attained an excellent mind concentration and met Virūpakṣa, the Lord of Yoga, in a vihāra called Uruvāsa, and his disciple the siddha Pāghala. (In this vihāra) a miraculous stone image of Ārya

Avalokiteśvara spoke to him: "Go to Tibet! After attending on a king, you will be of benefit to many!" In accordance with this prophecy, he first proceeded to Nepāl, and there obtained from the great paṇḍita Śīlasāgara the Bodhicittotpāda according to the method of the Bodhisattvacaryāvatāra. He reached Tibet in the year Fire-Male-Horse (me-pho-rta—1426 A.D., Vanaratna is often called "Paṇḍita mtha'-ma" or "The Last Paṇḍita".) On his arrival at Lha-sa and Yar-kluṅ a few people only came to ask him about religion. He therefore returned again to Nepāl. While he was residing at the vihāra of Śāntapurī of 'Phags-pa Śiṅ-kun (Svayambhū-caitya in Nepāl), there came first the bla-ma Saṅs-rgyas-dbyaṅs (Buddhaghoṣa), and after that, Śrī Śa-ba-ri dBaṅ-phyug. They drew the maṇḍala-cakra, and bestowed on him the initiation into the Cycle of Saṃvara, and in particular the uttara-abhiṣeka (of Kālacakra), following which he experienced an immutable Bliss. Again, Si-tu Rab-bstan-pa having des- (21b) patched as messenger one named Bod rgyal-ba, invited him, and he journeyed to rGyal-rtse (Gyangtse). About that time he met sMra-ba'i khyu-mčhog čhen-po Roṅ-ston, the All-Knowing. He bestowed several precepts on him and other kalyāṇa-mitras. Later he proceeded to Lha-sa. There, while residing on the Srin-po-ri with the "Great Lion of Speech" (sMra-ba'i seṅ-ge, Roṅ-ston), he received an invitation from the Dharmasvāmin Grags-pa 'byuṅ-gnas-pa. He spent some time at the great monastic college of rTses-thaṅ, where the Dharmarāja Grags-pa 'byuṅ-gnas and his chief minister obtained from him several initiation rites of the Saṃvara Cycle, according to the method of Lū i-pa. After that, the Teacher and his supporter (Grags-pa 'byuṅ-gnas) proceeded together towards Goṅ-dkar. About that time Grags-pa 'byuṅ-gnas received on the Srin-po-ri the initiation of Acala according to the Anuttara (-Tantra). He (Vanaratna) had a vision of the Saṃvara image (found at that place) to be alive (this image had been erected by Vibhūticandra on advice from Śākyaśrī-bhadra). Then the great paṇḍita and his disciples proceeded to sPa-gro (Bhutan), and spent some time there. There he met Padmasambhava. After that in the year Fire-Male-Dragon (me-pho-'brug—1436 A.D.) he proceeded to sNe-gdoṅ. Shortly afterwards he took up residence at rTses-thaṅ. He bestowed the complete precepts of the Ṣaḍaṅga-yoga according to the system of the great ācārya Anupamarakṣita on us, the 32 Piṭakadharas, headed by the mahā-upādhyāya of sNar-thaṅ-bSod-nams-mčhog-grub-pa, the great Grags-bzaṅ-pa, the Great bLo-gros rgyal-mtshan-pa, the mahā-upādhyāya of Thel-pa-Kun-rgyal-ba, and Čhos-kyi grags-pa, the Lord of Speech. In the past Bu-(ston) Rin-po-čhe had studied the hidden precepts according to the method of Anupamarakṣita (dPe-med-'tsho) with the Thar-pa lo-tsā-ba, however, with the exception of the pratyāhāra and the dhyāna-aṅga, the prāṇā-yāma (srog-rtsol) and the other three aṅgas (of these precepts) belonged to the systems of other paṇḍitas (and not to that of Anupamarakṣita). But here (in these precepts) all the six branches (aṅga) belonged to the system of Anupamarakṣita. Therefore his grace was very great. The Spiritual Lineage (22a) of the above precepts: Avalokiteśvara, the ācārya Anupama-rakṣita, dPal-'dzin dGa'-ba (Śrīdharanandana), 'Od-byed-lha (Bhāskaradeva), 'grub-thob Ñi-ma-dpal-ye-śes (the siddha Sūrya-śrījñāna), Čhos-'byuṅ ži-ba (Dharmākaraśānti), Ratnarakṣita, Mi-dbaṅ-blo (Narendrabodhi), Phyogs-grol (Muktipakṣa), Śākyarakṣita, rJe Legs-skyes (Sujata), and Saṅs-rgyas-dbyaṅs (Buddhaghoṣa). The latter bestowed (them) on the Dharma-svāmin the Precious Great Paṇḍita (Vanaratna). At rTses-thaṅ after completing the exposition of the "Guide to the Ṣaḍaṅga-yoga", he (Vanaratna) bestowed (on us) the initiation of Acala of the Anuttara-Tantra, and the blessing of (Vajra)vārahī, according to the six texts of the Vārahī Cycle (Phag-mo gžuṅ-drug: Tg. rGyud, Nos. 1551, 1552, 1553, 1554, 1555, 1556). Next year he (Vanaratna) bestowed on the Dharmarāja Grags-pa 'byuṅ-gnas the complete initiation of the Vajramālā according to the system of the ācārya Abhaya, having divided it into forty-five maṇḍalas. Its Spiritual

Lineage: Vajradhara, Vajra-yoginī (Vajravārahī), Abhayākara, Nāyakapāda ('Dren-pa'i žabs), sTobs-bču-dpal (Daśabalaśrī), Vikhyātadeva, Śrībhadra, Lalitavajra, Dharmagupta, Ratnākara, Padmavajra, Ratnakīrti, Buddhaghoṣa, the Dharmasvāmin the Precious Mahā-paṇḍita (Vanaratna. dGe-bśes dGe-'dun čhos-'phel tells me that a detailed biography of Vanaratna exists in manuscript form in Tibet. The rNam-thar contains valuable information on Ceylon). After having attended the initiation rite performed by the Dharmarāja, numerous great Piṭakadharas, who had mastered the sacred scriptures, received the full initiation into the same maṇḍala (i.e. the maṇḍala into which was initiated Grags-pa 'byuṅ-gnas).

The Spiritual Lineage of the Great Commentary Śrīsaṃpūtatantrarājaṭīkāmnāyamañjarī-nāma (Man-ṅag sñe-ma, Tg. rGyud, No. 1198) which was bestowed (by Vanaratna) on the Dharmarāja Grags-pa 'byuṅ-gnas-pa and five other Piṭakadharas: Abhaya, Nāyaka, Ratnabuddhi, Dharmagupta (Čhos-sbas), Sahajakīrti (Lhan-skyes-grags), Dharmaśrī, Śākyadhvaja (Śākya rgyal-mtshan), Vāgīśvarakīrti (Ṅag-dbaṅ-grags), Ratnakīrti (Rin-čhen-grags), and the Precious Mahā-paṇḍita (Vanaratna). Again he (Vanaratna) proceeded to Nepāl via sKyi-roṅ escorted by a retinue sent by the king, and decided to go to Vajrāsana in order to erect a large image of the mahā-guru Buddhaghoṣa. Robbers having heard that he had become the spiritual teacher of the Tibetan king, waited for him on the road, and because of this he had to postpone his journey (22b) there. He sent a man with offerings to Vajrāsana. In Nepāl proper, he erected a beautiful golden image of Vajradhara which he considered to represent Buddhaghoṣa, and in the meantime laboured for the welfare of others by preaching various doctrines, etc. He spent his entire time in work which was without equal, and concentrated mainly on meditative practice. Later he again came to Tibet in the year Water-Female-Hen (čhu-mo-bya—1453 A.D.). On his way, he bestowed on Byaṅ-pa, father and son, and their numerous retinue the initiation into the Saṃvara Cycle, etc., as well as preached during the journey many other doctrines. Having reached Yar-kluṅs, he bestowed on the Great Lord Kun-dga' legs-pa and his retinue, as well as on sMra-ba'i dbaṅ-phyug ("The Lord of Speech") bSod-nams rnam-par rgyal-ba and on many other great Piṭakadharas, the complete initiation into the Sadaṅga-yoga. On some he bestowed the exposition of the saṁpannakrama degree of the Vajravārahī Cycle. Further, he preached to the monastic congregations at rTses-thaṅ, gSaṅ-phu, Guṅ-thaṅ (Lha-sa), and other monasteries. By establishing a multitude of people in various localities in the mental Creative Effort towards Enlightenment, etc., he brought to an end their Phenomenal Existences (saṃsāra, i.e. they obtained emancipation). He was invited to gDan-sa Thel and other places. He laboured extensively for the welfare of others, as well as for his own, and observed wonderful signs of mental concentration. He seems to have been the most popular among the paṇḍitas who visited Tibet in later times. Especially in the exposition of the sublime meaning (nīta-artha) of the Vajrayāna, his grace was like the restoration of the life-string (srog-'thud-pa). At our first meeting, he bestowed on me several initiations, such as the initiation into the maṇḍala of Mañjuvajra, the complete initiation into the Kālacakra according to rites described in the Commentary on the Tantra (Vimalaprabhā), which was accompanied by certain other rites (not mentioned in the Vimalaprabhā and belonging especially to the Kālacakra).

Its Lineage: Ādi-Buddha, from Sucandra to Kulika Vijaya (Rigs-ldan rnam-rgyal), Kālacakrapāda, the Senior, Kālacakra- (23a) pāda, the Junior, Śākyasiṃhadhvaja (Śākya-seṅ-ge rgyal-mtshan), Gautamaśrī, Madhaṅgarasvāmin, Ratnamaṅgala, Jinālaṃkāra, Swāmin Matimant, Śākyarakṣita, Sujata, Buddhaghoṣa, the Dharmasvāmin the Precious Mahā-paṇḍita (Vanaratna). In the above manner, this Precious Great paṇḍita, though he hadno opportunity to expound the Great Commentary on the Tantra (Vimalaprabhā), restored the precepts of both the utpannakrama and sampannakrama degrees of the

Kālacakra, and his grace was great. Later the lo-tsā-ba and scholar bSod-nams rgya-mtsho having come to Nepāl, obtained numerous precepts from the Precious Great Paṇḍita and their practical application (lag-tu blaṅ-ba), and the accounts of the mystic experiences of the mahā-paṇḍita, etc. The detailed account can be had from him. Further, he (bSod-nams rgya-mtsho) completed the translation of the commentary Vasanta-tilaka-nāma (dPyid-kyi thig-le žes-bya-ba, Tg. rGyud, No. 1448), composed by the ācārya Kṛṣna (Nag-po-pa), which was left untranslated, wich the exception of the commentary on the ten Detailed Expositions (rGyas-bstan, name of the first chaptets of the Vasantatilaka), and bestowed its "permission" (luṅ, permissson to read the text). During his second (visit to Tibet) the paṇḍita on being requested by the Precious Dharmasvāmin sPyan-sṅa Ṅag-gi dbaṅ-phyug, composed a guide on the Śrī-Cakrasaṃvarapañcakramavṛtti (Dril-bu Rim-lṅa, Tg. rGyud, No. 1435) as well as expounded the text. The practice based on the Pañcakrama, which existed formerly in Tibet, belonged to the 'sạnimitta' class (mtshan-ma-daṅ-bčas-pa), but the one he bestowed belonged to the sampanna-krama degree of the "animitta" class (mtshan-ma-med-pa). Its Spiritual Lineage: Vajradhara, Vajra-yoginī (Vajravārahī), Vajraghaṇṭa (rDo-rJe dril-bu-ba), Kūrmapāda (Rus-sbal-žabs), Jālandharapāda, Kṛṣṇa (Nag-po-pa), Bhadrapāda (bZaṅ-po-žabs), Vinayapāda (rNam-rgyal-žabs), Tillipa, Nā-ro-pa, Yogendratilaka (rNal-'byor-dbaṅ-po'i thig-le), Pad-ma-dkar-po, Ye-śes-'dzin (Jñānadhara), dGe-ba'i blo (Kalyāṇamati), Buddha-jñāna (Saṅs-rgyas ye-śes), the Great Lord Sujata (rJe-čhen-po Legs-skyes), Phyogs-grol (Diṅmuka), Dharmakīrti (Čhos-kyi grags-pa), Ratnakīrti (Rin-čhen grags-pa), the Precious Dhar-masvāmin Mahā-paṇḍita (Vanaratna). Further, he bestowed on dPal bSod-nams rnam-par rgyal-ba and others the rDzogs-rim Saṅs-rgyas 'čhar-pa by Lū-i-pa, the Kye'i rdo-rJe'i rdzogs-rim sÑiṅ-po brgya-pa composed by Āryadeva (Pratipattisāra-śataka, Tg. rGyud, No. 2334), and the commentary on it (23b) composed by Herukadeva (Tg. rGyud, No. 2335). Vana-

ratna performed extensive religious works in Tibet, such as translations of each of the above mentioned texts, etc. He again returned to Nepāl, as prophesied by his Teacher and his tutelary deity. He devoted himself exclusively to meditation at the hermitage of Govicandra, met the mahāsiddha Lū-i-pa and others, and was pleased. He constantly supported the beggars of Nepāl by giving them food and material gifts, as well as satiated the fortunate ones with different kinds of doctrines. At the age of 85, in the eighth month of the year Earth-Male-Mouse (sa-pho-byi-ba—1468 A.D.) he said: "I shall now hold the feast of going to the Tuṣita Heaven", and offered a great feast to all the 'Ju-'Ju of Nepāl, and to a crowd of beggars. After that, till the eleventh month, various supernatural phenomena, such as flower showers, earth tremours, rainbows inside his house, etc. were observed. Especially on the 18th day of the 11th month, (it was observed) that while the paṇḍita was preaching the Doctrine, streams of white water similar to milk filled the air round his body. Till midnight of the 22nd day he held a Tantric feast with his disciples, holders of (Tantric) vows, and gave out detailed prophecies about profound doctrines and future events. Then having retired to his cell, he sat in the "diamond" (vajra) posture on his meditative mat, holding his body erect, and manifested the state of going to Heaven. In the evening of the 23rd, when people were conveying (lit. inviting) his remains for cremation at the Ram-do-li burial ground (situated near the hill of the Svayambhū-caitya), the whole of the country of Nepāl was enveloped by a great light, the points of the flames of the funeral pyre became entwined with rainbows and rose towards the limitless sky, and numberless great miracles were observed. Even (24a)
the dull Nepālese were filled with an undifferentiated faith and seemed to share in the highest form of emancipation. This Great Soul, free from any kind of defiling defects, conformed to the ideal of an ācārya as described in the Precious Tantra class. He also was endowed with all

the virtuous qualities (listed in the Tantras) without exception, and especially was believed to possess all the marks of a Holy Teacher as described in the Kālacakra-Tantra, and those of a bestower of spiritual realization. Therefore he became our highest and only refuge.

Now the Great Translator bSod-nams rgya-mtsho: In the garland of his former existences, he performed the labours of the three boundless accumulations.

For the welfare of living beings, he reached the end of the Path. Though he had attained the Highest Enlightenment (Abhisambodhi), a state characterized by renunciation and knowledge which cannot be improved upon, there is no doubt that he had assumed the form of a mahāsattva, a leader, who strove to convey the travellers-disciples to the firm ground of salvation. Having equipped the boat of action by crowding the sails of wisdom and commiseration for the benefit of the helpless who had sunk into the dreaded ocean of Phenomenal Existence (saṃsāra), stirred up by a hundred waves of imagination (saṃkalpa, kun-rtog), filled with waves of defilement and the sea monsters of Karma, and surrounded by the fire of the Aśvamukha range (rTa-gdoṅ—the iron mountain range surrounding the Ocean) of the (five) groups of elements, constituting an ordinary individual (upadāna-skandha, ñe-bar len-pa'i phuṅ-po), took rebirth as the equal of ordinary living beings in the eyes of his disciples. The manner of his (24b) labours for the sake of the Doctrine can be best told in eight chapters: The first (chapter) relates the manner of his taking rebirth in the Spiritual Lineage of Saints (siddhas). The king of Ṅan-lam known by the name of 'Od-kyi dKyil-'khor-čan belonged to a family without blemishes. He belonged to the Rog clan. In the past the religious king Khri-sroṅ-lde-btsan in order to establish the Doctrine (in Tibet), had invited the upādhyāya Bodhisattva (mKhan-po Bodhisattva-Śāntarakṣita) and the vidyādhara Pad-ma, who ordained the seven "Men on Probation" (Sad-mi mi-bdun). One of them, named, Ṅan-lam rGyal-ba mčhog-dbyaṅs obtained the spell (siddhi)

of Hayagrīva. Among his descendants there was an uninterrupted succession of scholars and siddhas, and the best among them, in both miraculous powers (siddhi) and knowledge, was the great vidyādhara bSod-nams 'od-zer. He and mother dPal-ldan 'dzom-pa, a natural ḍākinī, had five sons and daughters. He (bSod-nams rgya-mtsho) was born as the eldest of them. At the time (of his being in his mother's womb), his mother saw in her dream that she had found in a spring a golden vajra with five points, and that her Mind and body became filled with bliss. They (mother and child) were nourished by sun-rays and surrounded by rainbows. Music pleasant to the ear resounded. Accompanied by the above miraculous signs, the child was born on the 25th day of the 10th month of the Wood-Male-Dragon year (śiṅ-pho-'brug—1424 A.D.), known as khro-mo or "the fierce" (krodhī), at Khyams Khaṅ-gsar in Yar-kluṅs-bstan-thaṅ. He was named dPal-'byor rgya-mtsho, because an increase in all kinds of gains was observed. Later the Precious mGon-rgyal-ba of gSaṅ-phu Brag-nag gave him the name of bSod-nams rgya- (25a)
mtsho'i sde, a name which corresponded to its meaning. He became known by that name to all. He was brought up with special veneration in the midst of the ocean of plenty. Like a lotus in a lake, he became the nectar of the eyes of all peoples.

The second (chapter): The manner of his manifesting extraordinary deeds as a child. Soon after his birth, when he was being fed on the lap of his nurse, all felt attracted towards him. His daily behaviour differed from that of ordinary people. At the age of 4 or 5, he was taken to bSam-yas, and as soon as he saw the sacred images in the "Temple of the Three Styles" (dbU-rtse-rigs-gsum, or San-yang temple), he performed different kinds of salutations and made offerings (to them). He was overpowered by sadness (ṅes-'byuṅ) towards the World, and deep faith. His hair stood erect and he shed tears. On some occasions he used to preach to his playmates on the subject of the different kinds of suffering of this Phenomenal Existence (saṃsāra) and Hell (durgata), and directed their Minds towards emancipation from them. He was able to master without difficulty the alphabet and even excelled his Teacher. He used to recite regularly mantras and sacred texts. He also composed a beautiful poem, perfect in words and meaning, and presented it to his mother, who was fond of poetry. Because of his (former) practice of meditation of the sampannakrama degree, he (constantly) dwelt in a mystic trance, (in which) he contemplated countless visions, and spent a long time gazing at them. Everywhere he used to erect altars in front of the Three Jewels. In this manner he spent all of his time in virtuous labours which were difficult to perform even by great beings, and always remained alert.

The third (chapter): The manner of his ordination and of his continuous search for knowledge. When he had reached the age of seven, Roṅ-ston-pa sMra-ba'i seṅ-ge accompanied by his disciples came to bSam-yas and revolved the Wheel of (25b)
the Doctrine. The (child) attended the religious class and showed great devotion (towards Roṅ-ston-pa). He felt sad pondering over the sufferings of the Phenomenal Existence which was similar to a fiery pit. He thought that he should take up ordination into the Doctrine. He was ordained by the Dharmasvāmin Roṅ-ston who acted as upādhyāya, Dwags-po bKra-śis rnam-par rgyal-ba acting as ācārya, and the bKa'-bži-pa Śes-rab dpal-ldan as "Time recorder" (dus-bsgo-ba). At the time (of the ordination) the upādhyāya said: "He will become a holy man, the owner of boundless doctrines," and encouraged him with these words. He was given the name of Śākya rin-čhen. While he was engaged in the study of the Pramāṇavārtika and the Prajñāpāramitā under his uncle the ācārya Ṅag-dbaṅ-ba, he used to learn by heart every day three pages of the Pramāṇavārtika. He became an expert in the recitation of sacred texts, and was able to practise the recitation of each sentence backwards. At the age of 13, he preached for the first time the Prajñāpāramitā and the

Pramāṇavārtika, at the religious school of rTses-thaṅ, and filled all present with amazement. Through this the religious king Grags-pa 'byuṅ-gnas felt attracted towards him and said: "I shall adopt this novice as my son!" He paid for his studies and entrusted him to the great dPal-'byor rgya-mtsho-ba. He studied diligently the three great texts of the "Ten Books" during many days and nights. He used to spend his time in work and never slept. His Teacher used to preach daily seven different kinds of texts, and (the boy) used to repeat the text aloud (skyar-čhos-pa). To repeat thus about twenty pages of the "arrow-size" (mda'-tshad, the usual length of a Tibetan block-print page) was not difficult for him. During a journey, he committed to memory the text of the bŚes-sprin (Tg. sPrin-yig, No. 4182) while riding horseback, and completed it during a stage. Such were his wonderful deeds of excellent wisdom which he had acquired by birth, by practice, and by diligence. At the age of 21, he chose the following texts and preached them for many months at the religious assemblies of dPal rTses-thaṅ: The Five Treatises of Maitreya (Byams-čhos sde-lṅa), the dbU-ma rigs-tshogs (it is not clear why 'Gos lo-tsā-ba listed the Ratnamālā and the Mādhyamakakārikā separately from the dbU-ma Rigs-tshogs, the treatises by Nāgārjuna), the Ratnamālā (Tg. dbU-ma, No. 3901), the Suhṛllekha (Tg. Čhos-'byuṅ, No. 4496), the Bodhisattvacaryāvatāra, the Mūlamādhyamakakārikā (Tg. dbU-ma, No. 3824), Mādhyamakāvatāra (Tg. dbU-ma, No. 3861), the Catuḥśataka (Tg. dbU-ma, No. 3846), the Abhidharmasamuccaya, the Abhidharmakośa, the Pañcaskandha-prakaraṇa (Tg. dbU-ma, No. 3866), the Vinaya-sūtra (mDo-rtsa, Tg. 'Dul-ba, No. 4117), the Me-tog phreṅ-rgyud (Tg. 'Dul-ba, No. 4123), the Triśatikā (Sum-brgya-pa, Tg. No. 4124), the Prātimokṣa-sūtra (Kg. 'Dul-ba, No. 2), the "Seven Texts on Logic" (Tshad-ma sde-bdun, with the Pramāṇa-samuccaya /Tg. Tshad-ma, No. 4203/; the mDo of the text stands for Tshad-ma'i mdo, i. e. the Tshad-ma Kun-btus of Diṅnāga), and the Rig-gter (a treatise on Logic composed by

(26a)

the Sa-skya paṇḍita Kun-dga' rgyal-mtshan. The book contains his exposition of Logic (Mūla), and an auto-commentary, strongly criticized by the late Logicians of the Yellow school.). All scholars became filled with admiration towards him. And especially so the Dharmarāja Grags-pa 'byuṅ-gnas-pa who became more than satisfied, and said: "He is the only man who has done more than I had hoped for, among all those whom I had assisted. Now he will be able to become my preacher!" He was very pleased. The first initiation obtained by him in this present life, was the initiation into the maṇḍala of 'Khor-lo čhen-po (a form of Vajrapāṇi) bestowed on him by his father, a great vidyādhara, in his childhood. He was then given the secret name of Akṣobhyavajra (Mi-bskyod rdo-rJe). Further, he obtained many "permissions" (rJes-gnaṅ, to read the texts belonging to the Cycles) of Gur (mGon-po Gur, a form of Mahākāla) and Žal (mGon-po Žal-bži, a form of Mahākāla with four heads), and the Kālacakra. He thought after that that he should satisfy his wisdom by searching for the boundless Doctrine, giving up all partiality towards theories, monasteries, etc. 26b

He proceeded to Na-len-dra (a monastery in 'Phan-yul) and listened to many instructions by Roṅ-ston sMra-ba'i seṅ-ge, such as (the exposition) of the Five Treatises of Maitreya (Byams-čhos-lṅa), the Mūlamādhyamakakārikā, the Mādhyamakāvatāra, the Bodhisattvacaryāvatāra (sPyod-'Jug), the Dul-ba Me-tog phreṅ-rgyud (Tg. rGyud, No. 4123), the three Bhāvanākramas (sGom-rim, Tg. dbU-ma, Nos. 3915-3617), as well as numerous short expositions of the Prajñāpāramitā and the theories of the Mādhyamaka. From the Lord bKra-śis rnam-rgyal he heard the Prajñāpāramitā, Logic, texts belonging to the Mādhyamaka system (dbU-ma-skor, the Mādhyamaka Cycle), the initiation of Hevajra and Nairātma (Kye-rdor yab yum). From rṄog Byaṅ-čhub-dpal, the last of the seven descendants of rṄog, (he heard) the initiation into the seven maṇḍalas of rṄog, and obtained many permissions (luṅ). From dMar-ston rGyal-mtshan 'od-

zer (he obtained) many initiations of the Mantrayāna. From the sNar-thaṅ upādhyāya bSod-nams mčhog-grub-pa (he received) the permission (luṅ) of the Pañcabhūmi of Asaṅga Sa-sde, Tg. Sems-tsam, Nos. 4035-37, 4038, 4039, 4040, 4041-2). From the mahā-upādhyāya Kun-rgyal-ba he obtained) many initiations, such as the Vajramālā (rDo-rJe phreṅ-ba) and the Vajracaryākṛyasamuccaya (Tg. rGyud, No. 3305), the doctrine of the "Path and Fruit" (Lam-'bras), the U-rgyan bsñen-grub (Sevasādhana by U-rgyan-pa), the "Six Doctrines" (of Nā ro-pa), the Mahāmudrā, and many others. He also attended numerous recitals of the Tantric section of the bKa'-'gyur (rGyud-'bum), and many expositions, such as the sGron-gsal (Pradipodyotananāma-ṭīkā, Tg. rGyud, No. 1785) and other texts. Having come to 'Tshur-phu he obtained from 'Jam-dbyaṅs Don-grub 'od-zer whatever initiations, precepts and expositions of texts were found in the Ocean of the dPal Kar-ma-pa doctrine. From the ācārya Ye-śes rgya-mtsho-ba and, after going to Brag-nag, from the Lord Rin-čhen rgyal-mtshan, he obtained the initiation rites of many maṇḍalas of the "Outer" and "Inner" Tantras ("Inner" stands for Anuttara-yoga; "Outer" or Phyi stands for the three other Tantra classes), such as the Kālacakra and others. From 'Gos lo-tsā-ba gŽon-nu-dpal (the author of the Deb-ther sŃon-po) he obtained the Prajñāpāramitā and the "Six Basic Texts of the bKa'-gdams-pas" (bKa'-gdams-gžuṅ-drug. kLoṅ-rdol bla-ma'i gSuṅ-'bum, Book XXV (Ra), fol. 2a:, Śikṣāsamuccaya, Bodhisattvacaryāvatāra, Sa'i dṅos-gži, Sūtrālaṃkāra (Sa-rgyan gñis), Jātakamālā and Udānavarga), and numerous initiations and 'permissions' (rJes-gnaṅ) of the "Old" Tantras (sŃa-'gyur). In particular, the Lo-tsa'i skad-dod (a Dictionary for the use) of translators, the sGra'i Sa-ris (Diagrams /Sa-ris—drawing of figures and letters on a wooden board strewn with ashes/), the Śrī Kālacakra, the sGron-gsal (Tg. rGyud, No. 1785), the Hevajra, etc. as well as the expositions of other Tantras. 274
He used to familiarize himself with the subjects preached by

the Teacher all day long, and in this manner he became a great scholar in numerous Sūtras and Tantras. Further, he mastered the various sciences, such as prosody, medicine and the arts, befitting a scholar. He became without effort the greatest scholar on the field of rites and Tantric methods, such as ritual dancing, songs, and the drawing and outlining of maṇḍalas. In particular, he attended on Vanaratna, the great paṇḍita of Sadnagara (groṅ-khyer Dam-pa) in Eastern India, who had come to Tibet, and obtained from him instruction, such as the Sadaṅga-yoga, the highest of all the Paths of Vajrayāna, and the initiation of the Thirteen Deities of the Saṃvara Cycle according to the system of Ghaṇṭapāda (Dril-bu-pa), with the help of which the great paṇḍita himself had obtained the realization, and the initiation and authorization of the Kālacakra, etc. He saw the mahā-paṇḍita off to Nepāl as far as 'Dol-kha, and obtained from him some extensive expositions of texts, such as the Pratipattisāraśataka by Āryadeva (sÑiṅ-po brgya-pa, Tg. rGyud, No.2334). Though the paṇḍita (Vanaratna) could not give him the complete exposition of the Commentary on the Kālacakra-Tantra (Vimalaprabhā), he gave him a detailed explanation of the difficult points (of the system) in the form of replies to his questions. He understood all the conclusions, and thus his grace in the Kālacakra became great in this region. Later rJe Thams-čad mkhyen-pa (the Lord All-knowing) Byams-pa gliṅ-pa, the Great, and dPal Kar-ma-pa, (the fourth) holder of the Red Crown (žwa-dmar čod-pan 'dzin-pa), bestowed on him numerous initiations, expositions, recitals of sacred texts, etc. He attended on nearly thirty teachers who were learned and possessed siddhis, and thus crossed the Ocean of learn- (27b)
ing, his scholarly fame encompassing the entire Earth.

The Fourth (Chapter): The acquisition of the virtues of an ordained monk. At the age of 22, he acquired the virtues of an ordained monk before a congregation of 20 monks, the mahā-upādhyāya Don-grub dpal-ba of the Tshogs-čhen-pas, who belonged to the immaculate lineage of ordination of the

Great Kashmirian paṇḍita, acting as upādhyāya, the Lord 'Gos lo-tsā-ba gŽon-nu-dpal (it seems that this portion was inserted by the editors of the Text) as karma-ācārya, and the great dPal-'byor as Secret Preceptor (gsaṅ-ston). He became possessed of an excellent pure conduct which was pleasing to Saints (Ārya).

The Fifth (chapter): the opening of the gates of knowledge caused by reflection. During his previous extensive studies, he examined and investigated (the books) in respect of words and their meanings, and did not satisfy himself with the mere hearing (of their exposition). He put questions to his Teacher, put in order (the Teacher's replies) and conducted debates with all those who were considered to be scholars. Thus he mastered the innermost meaning of all sacred texts.

Further, he used to spend his time in seclusion at rTses-thaṅ bSam-gliṅ, Pho-braṅ 'Um-bu bla-mkhar, rGyal-bzaṅs, bSam-yas 'čhims-phu, Khrims-khaṅ-gliṅ, Brag-lha-klu-phug, and other places. He studied all the sacred texts contained in the bKa'-'gyur and elsewhere, and acquired a deep understanding of the essence of the meaning of each word in these texts. While residing at dPal rTses-thaṅ and Las-stod-byaṅ, (he read) twice the bsTan-'gyur, the Collection of Works (bKa'-'bum) by Bu-ston, the De-ñid-'dus-pa (Sarvatathāgata-tattvasaṃgraha-nāma-mahāyānasūtra, Kg. rGyud-'bum, No. (28a)
479), and other texts, all that was to be found in the Tibetan language. In short, wherever he went, he used to read all available sacred texts, large or short. Everyday he used to expand the ocean of his Mind, completely filled with the games of knowledge. He became a great scholar similar to the king of precious gems, fulfilling the desires of all living beings, headed by those who possessed a strong wish for emancipation.

The sixth (chapter): the acquisition of beatitude obtained by the power of blessing (of the Buddha)—by this I mean the manifestation of the manner of acquiring an excellent, realization. This holy man having attained the degree of a fully-enlightened Mahāsattva abiding in the higher stage (Mahābhūmi, sa-čhen-po), manifested the miracle of rebirth as desired by him. From his childhood he turned towards the 'direct' meaning (nīta-artha) of the Doctrine, and because of this, he was able to listen to many kinds of expositions (of the Doctrine) by holy men, showed great diligence, and manifested many kinds of perfection. He obtained the "Six Doctrines" (of Nā-ro-pa) from the Lord 'Gos, the mahā-upādhyāya Kun-rgyal-ba and 'Tshur-phu 'Jam-dbyaṅs go-śrī. He practised their (precepts) and an incontrovertible understanding of the Mahāmudrā state was born in him. On being initiated into the maṇḍala of Śrī-Ḍākārṇavamahāyoginītantrarāja (Kg. rGyud-'bum, No. 372), he became possessed by a deity and experienced an intense beatitude. When he obtained at Brag-nag the initiation rite of the Yoga-Tantra from the Lord Rin-čhen rgyal-mtshan-pa, he got a pure vision, which made him understand the World and all living beings (bčud) to represent the great maṇḍala of the three dPal (dPal-mčhog daṅ-po), rTse (rDo-rJe rtse-mo), and dbYiṅs (rDo-rJe-dbyiṅs. "Sbornik izobzazheniy 300 burkhanov" Bibl. Buddh. V, pp. 26, 77). Later when he was performing (28b) the initiation of the seven maṇḍalas of rŇog for the benefit of his Holiness dPal Čhos-kyi grags pa, the holder of the Red Crown of Śrī Kar-ma-pa (dPal Kar-ma-pa žwa-dmar čod-pan 'dzin-pa), he had a vision of all the seven maṇḍalas of rŇog surrounded by a rainbow. When he came to the sacred place of Tsa-ri-tra, the local deity (žiṅ-skyoṅ, kṣetrapāla) appeared in his proper form, and performed work (on his behalf). He perceived the peculiarities of this sacred place as corresponding to the real forms of ḍākinīs and vīras (dpa'-bo) according to the three phyi-naṅ-gžan (phyi—deities presiding over the Sun, Moon and Stars; naṅ—deities presiding over the inner organs of the body, gžan—other deities). When he was performing twice the rite of preparing nectar pills (bdud-ril-bu) in a skull cup endowed with proper marks, the scent of the medicine enveloped his entire dwelling. The nectar was seen to flow endlessly from a jar of wine (śiṅs-bu). He discovered the sign of Vajra-garuḍa (rDo-rJe nam-mkha'-ldiṅ) at Lho-brag mkhar-čhu. At Gro-bo-luṅ he met the saint (puruṣottama) Mar-pa who gave him his blessing. He then sang the following song:

"In the spiritual palace of North Śambhala,
He was dwelling amidst five hundred queens.
Now he has come into my presence!
Do you see him? Is there (another) fortunate one?"

He sang numerous psalms on his attainment of mental concentration at the above places, as well as at Śam-bu, rGyal-po'i khab, Čhu-bar, 'Tshel-min, bSam-gtan-gliṅ, and other localities, and these psalms were received by all with amazement in respect of their words and meaning. He transformed himself into 'Gos lo-tsā-ba gŽon-nu-žabs, 'Gro-mgon Phag-mo-gru-pa, and dPal-čhe-mčhog (the chief divinity of the rÑiṅ-ma-pas), and preached the Doctrine presiding over an assembly of ḍākinīs. However, he pretended that he had performed in a dream. He said that he had seen smoke coming out between the eye-brows of 'Gos-gŽon-nu'i-žabs which then spread in the sky, and when (29a)
he had looked at it attentively, he saw numberless forms of the śūnya-rūpa (one of the ten visionary forms described in the Kālacakra/Sekoddeśaṭīkā, ed. Carelli /Baroda, 1941/, p. 35: dhūma, smoke; marici, mirage; kha-skya, dyota, fire-fly; dīpa, lamp; jvālā, flame; candra, Moon; āditya, Sun; Rāhu, eclipse; bindu, spot). Later, when he was listening to the recitation of the gNas-brtan-gyi smon-lam čhen-mo by dPal Byams-pa-gliṅ-pa, the Great, he saw the Buddha surrounded by arhats as well as the scenery described in the poem (Sthaviropanimantraṇa by Bhavaskandha, Tg. Sprin-yig, No. 4199). The yakṣa (gnod-sbyin) rDo-rJe bdud-'dul (Vajra-Māradama) laboured on his behalf in his real form. The Dharmarāja Li-byin-ha-ra presented him with the seal of the Master of the Doctrine. He had a clear vision

of the inside of the great stūpa of Byams-pa-gliṅ filled with a thousand Buddhas of the Bhadrakalpa similar to a heap of grain. The Venerable Mañjughoṣa stretching out his right golden hand, placed it on his head and blessed him. dPal Byams-pa-gliṅ-pa, the great, having descended from the Tuṣita heaven, preached to him many doctrines in the symbolical language (dgoṅs-skad, sandhābhāṣā).[1] On many occasions he met the great paṇḍita (Vanaratna), who (appeared to him) in the form of a paṇḍita, a yogin, and a god. After the departure of the great paṇḍita to Tuṣita, he instructed him in a vision to proceed to the Lake of Tsa-ri (Tsa-ri-gyu-mtsho), preached the Doctrine to him, appointed him his chief disciple, and gave him the śrīvatsa emblem of (his) heart. In real life also, the skull-cup which he used in making offerings to his Teacher, acquired the colour of pearl, and out of it appeared a clearly visible image of the great paṇḍita (Vanaratna). The inside and outside of the great stūpa of Byams-pa-gliṅ appeared to his vision of wisdom as a pure sphere. Because of all this he sang the following song:

"The Dharmakāya, free of thought construction, the bodhicitta,
this sacred form endowed with the thirty-seven marks of Enlightenment (the 37 bodhi-pakṣas. See Mhvtpt, 38-44), (29b)
appearing as a great stūpa, displaying 84,000 gates of religion.
Even in the smallest particle of which, there (were found) countless paradises!
Do you see them? Is there a fortunate one?
It appears clearly to the eyes of myself, the yogin!"

He perceived the complete ten signs (rtags-bču) of meditation after hearing the recitation of the guide to the "Six Practices" (sByor drug) by the mahā-upādhyāya Kun-rgyal-ba. He experienced a feeling of beatitude in his body and a wonderful sensation of a change came over him. Of the several different visions (seen by him) before the

1 Prabodh Chandra Bagchi: "Studies in the Tantras". Calcutta, 1939, p. 27.

dKar-ru image of Dam-pa at Diṅ-ri, one (was) the vision of a manifestation which appeared to be the real form of the image. The reflection of the image which he saw in the mirror was a form similar to the image of Bal-thul-ma (name of a famous statue of Dam-pa), with a small Mahābodhi stūpa on the crown of its head. He saw emanating from the space between the eyebrows of this form innumerable signs of siddhi, and a tilaka mark inside which appeared innumerable forms of the śūnya-rūpa. In this manner he obtained numberless visions of the śūnya-rūpa. We find in his life-story the frequent statement that he had seen innumerable forms of the śūnya-rūpa. This means that he had seen by his eye of wisdom the Holy Sphere of Wisdom in which all gods of the utpannakrama and sampannakrama degrees, Buddhas and Holy Bodhisattvas, equal to atoms in numbers, appeared within each atom. At Zaṅs-phu of South Gro-bo-luṅ he was encouraged by a prophecy that he was destined to attain spiritual realization in Nepāl, and obtain the mystic trance, such as the svādīṣṭa (raṅ-byin-rlabs), and he proceeded to Nepāl. The Lord of Miraculous Powers (siddheśvara) Vanaratna having manifested the innate wisdom of initiation (30a) into the maṇḍala of Saṃvara, which is the essence of the undifferentiated "Outer", "Inner" and "Secret" aspects, as well as the union of the thirteen deities (of th Saṃvara Cycle), he became a Bodhisattva Mahāsattva, dwelling on the highest stage, and realizing the samādhi-aṅga, which was called the prabhāsvara of the fourth stage (=the eighth bhūmi) of the Pañcakrama of the Guhyasamāja. The events which took place between his installation as Cakravartin of the Siddhas and his attainment of the state of beatitude of the excellent stage (mčhog-gi gnas=Buddhahood) were described in his songs:

"In the year of Bhānutāra (Ñi-sgrol-byed, śiṅ-spre—1464 A.D.).
in the month of Viśākha, in the southern region,
in the house of Tam-mra of Gro-bo'i kluṅs,

when it was filled by feasting ḍākinīs, (I was told that) the prophecy by the nirmāṇa-kāya (Vanaratna) which said that
'at the time of the ripening of wild rice,
your wish will bear fruit',
would be made manifest.
This is the first encouragement (received by him).
Then in the year of Pārthiva (sa-skyoṅ, śiṅ-bya—1465 A.D.),
in the month of Citra (Nag-pa, the 3rd month of the Tibetan year),
in the virāga-pakṣa (i.e. the kṛṣṇa-pakṣa or the last half of the lunar month),
on the day of Kulika (Rigs-ldan),
at Ku-la Śam-bu, when Caṇḍikā had glorified (me)
by her blessing,
a crow's dropping fell on my head and she said:
'O son! You who wish to meet your father,
will meet danger and obstacles'.
While I was terrified (hearing) this prophecy,
there appeared (again) the form of a red Garuḍa,
and gathered clouds (čhu-'dzin) from the Four Quarters,
and caused a shower of rain to fall which inundated the entire countryside.
After that the black form of Garuḍa was manifested,
and transformed itself into a Mahākāla, and said:
This secret omen indicates that your worldly work will be handicapped by ill-fame.
You should cultivate a desire towards Buddhahood only.'
This was the second encouragement (received by him).
In the same year of Pārthiva (sa-skyoṅ—1465 A.D.),
in the month Čhu-stod (the 6th month of the Tibetan year),
in the śukla-pakṣa (the first half of the lunar month),
in the middle rGyal-ba (the 8th day of the sixth month; according to the Kālacakra the days of a half-month/lunar/ were divided into five groups of days, namely: rGyal-ba daṅ-po, rGyal-ba gñis pa, rGyal-ba mtha'-ma; dGa'-ba daṅ-po, dGa'-ba gñis-pa, dGa'-ba mtha'-ma; rDzogs-pa daṅ-po,

rDzogs pa gñis-pa, rDzogs-pa mtha'-ma; bZaṅ-po daṅ-po, bZaṅ-po gñis-pa, bZaṅ-po mtha'-ma; sTon-pa daṅ-po...... 1st day – dGa'-ba daṅ-po. 2nd day—bZaṅ-po daṅ-po. 3rd day—rGyal-ba daṅ-po. 4th day—sTon-pa daṅ-po. 5th day—rDzogs-pa daṅ-po. 6th day—dGa'-ba gñis-pa. 7th day—bZaṅ-po gñis-pa, etc.).

In the southern 'Island of Jewels' (Rin-po-čhe'i gliṅ, probably Rin-čhen gliṅ, or Ratnadvīpa, Nepāl?),
The grandfather, the black-faced Ri-dags-dgra (Śa-ba-ri),
And my father, a monk in appearance (i.e. Vanaratna) together bestowed their blessing. (30b)
In a wooden house, surrounded by wooden boards,
Mother Mig-maṅs ('Many-eyed', i.e. Vajravārahī) looked after me!
This was secretly revealed to me by one of my own disciples.
It had the sign of a strict secret, and it was said,
'It was improper to reveal it in an assembly'.
This was the third encouragement towards Buddhahood.
Then, the son, wishing to return to his native country (i.e. from Nepāl to Tibet),
Arranged to go there disguised as a merchant.
In the year Wood-Hen (śiṅ-bya, Pārthiva, Sa-skyoṅ, 1465 A.D.), in the month of Aśvinī (dbYug-pa 'dzin-pa 'holding a staff'; Tha-skar—the 9th month of the Tibetan year),
In the dark half of the lunar month (kṛṣṇa-pakṣa), in the third Jaya (rGyal-ba, i.e. the 28th day of the month),
In the region of the North, called Nam-rim (in gTsaṅ),
Near the Palace of the Kālacakra (image),
On an auspicious date (indicated) in the prophecy of the gods.
(I had a vision) of twenty-four deer-eyed (ri-dwags mig) damsels
Naked (phyogs-kyi gos-čan, space-attired), moving through the Sky (i.e. ḍākinīs, mkha'-'gro-ma),
Who had come from definite places (i.e. the 24 sacred places of the Tantras).

All of them were enjoyed by Heruka.

This is a great symbol of the hidden which indicates the Innate Wisdom of those who are able to control the nāḍīs i.e. breath-control).

The above was the fourth encouragement, difficult to obtain.
Afterwards I gradually reached the "Abode of Saints" (siddhas), Chu-bar, which has the shape of the sacred letter "e" (i.e. triangular in shape).

In the month of Kulika-kārttika (the 10th month), in the third dGa'-ba (the 26th day of the month) of the dark half of the month (Kṛṣna-pakṣa), the father (Vanaratna),
wearing a religious robe of golden colour,
and the mother, adorned with rich ornaments,
greeted me, and I felt overwhelmed by joy.
I, the son, wearing the upper garment (saṅgha-tsi<saṃghāṭī, one of the three robes of Buddhist monk) of golden colour,
uttered a prophecy to the parents (i.e. Vanaratna and his retinue), and called their names, saying: "O Vairocana-vajra!" and "O Vajra-Tārā!"
This is the wonder of wonders, a secret symbol (which indicates), that I was not to be differentiated from them!
This was the fifth encouragement towards atttaining Enlightenment (mčhog-čhen, Buddhahood).
Then, travelling leizurely, in the 11th month, in the dark half of the month (kṛsṇa-pakṣa), on the 23rd day (rGyal-ba
gñis-pa or dbus-ma), in the abode Calakoṭa, in the mountains (31a)
called Ñi-ma-mkhar,
In the house of Kuṇḍala, aflame with Inner Heat (gtum-mo, this means that he saw the vision in his centre of kanda),
my father (Vanaratna) properly embraced by a nun and indulging in secret enjoyment,
told me and my friend Dīpaṃ,
that we could now practise the śīkṣa-caryā.
We entered it and beheld a boundless pure Sky.

We offered the prayer of Prabhāsvara,
and we attained the realization of the Self (svasaṃvidyā).
Then my Illusory body (māyāsvadeha), consumed by shining flames,
I threw it away as a snake its skin.
Then I heard a natural voice saying:
'There is still a little (left) of the gross body.'
This was a true sign of prophecy, supreme in excellence.
This was the sixth encouragement. A!
Then on the full moon day of the 12th month,
The father (Vanaratna) initiated my body, speech and mind,
as well as wisdom, into the maṇḍala (sdom-pa) of the thirteen deities of
the grandfather (i.e. Saṃvara).
Again, on my return, I satisfied (my) ordinary disciples with
the same initiation.
Before Dawn, as if in a clear mystic trance,
I saw, with my own eyes, the following vision:
In a good house, a high seat was placed before my father Vanaratna),
who said: 'This mat is for you to sit on!'
Then, on my head,
he placed his right hand endowed with marks,
and initiated me into the mantra of Samvara (lit. "the abode with
no letters," name of a mantra of seventeen letters).
The secret of this symbol is most vast, and its meaning great.
It was the encouragement towards the Hidden.
It is the Seven, by which the Mind, consisting of different
moods (čha-śas-čan), is transformed into the state of non-differentiation.
I was wandering amidst the illusory play of the gNas-bdun
like a child (rDo-rje gnas-bdun, i.e. the seven characteristics
of the Bodhisattva-gotra = Tathāgata-garbha: the Buddha /Saṅs-rgyas/, Dharma /čhos/, Saṅgha /dge-'dun/, bDe-gśegs sñiṅ-po /Tathāgata-garbha/, the four are expounded in the

first chapter of the Anuttara-Tantra, Bodhi /byaṅ-čhub/, Guṇa /yon-tan/, Karma /'phrin-las/. The last three are expounded in the last three chapters of the Anuttara-Tantra. See kLoṅ-rdol bLa-ma'i gSuṅ-'bum,
Book X/Tha/, fol. 5a)
But my father (Vanaratna) explained to me its meaning,
and encouraged me in the realization of the Meaning."

Having said so, let those, who were fortunate, who had obtained the power of the virtue of Faith, who possessed the eye of the Doctrine and that of wisdom, which had become a source of knowledge (pramāṇa), examine it in order to grasp its meaning. After that he proceeded to the Svayambhūnātha-caitya ('Phags-pa Śiṅ-kun in Nepāl), and while holding an assembly at the Śāntapurī vihāra, he met the yogeśvara Śa-ba-ri, who gave him his blessing. He sang many wonderful songs: (31b)

"Blessed by the grand-father Śa-ba-ri,
and by the grace of my blessed father (Vanaratna),
the image of the outer enjoyment melted into the vessel (Mind)
(i.e. all the images of the Outer World sank into the Mind).
Thus the essence of the inner skandhas and dhātus developed into nectar.

May you gods, vīras and ḍākinīs be pleased with it!"

There he pleased the great paṇḍita (Vanaratna) with the three kinds of Joys (čhos-kyi mñes-pa, zen-ziṅ-gi mñes-pa, žabs-tog mñes-pa). He obtained the entire secret treasury of the Hidden precepts in the manner of a vase filled to the brim, such as the Ṣaḍaṅga-yoga, which had been personally imparted by Śa-ba-ri to the great paṇḍita (Vanaratna), the precepts of Padma-Amitāyus (Padmasambhava in the form of Amitāyus) imparted by the vidyādhara Padma, and other texts. He experienced the Wisdom peculiar to the essence of initiation (the fourth initiation). When all his wishes were fulfilled and he was about to proceed to Tibet, the Teacher told him that "the Hidden precepts, which you have heard from me, had all their Lineages, but I (myself), was able to hear all the Doctrine from Śa-ba-ri himself. These Hidden precepts which had

originated with me, should be occasionally preached to the fortunate ones who are in search of the Path of the Yuganaddha (zuṅ-'Jug). These disciples were perceived by the eye of my mystical trance". In this manner he received the great encouragement to labour for the welfare of others. Following his Teacher's prophecy, these (disciples) who were trained and given precepts by the Lord, were able to develop without hindrance the understanding of the Path. Through his pre- (32a)
science he was able to perceive the birth of understanding (in his disciples), by his eye of wisdom he was able to perceive the births and physical traits of individuals, and used to guide them accordingly.

The seventh (chapter): Having thus become the Master of the Ocean of the Piṭaka and of the Tantra class, and having attained realization, the story of his labours for the Doctrine (is as follows). This holy man was of the opinion that the Doctrine of the Enlightened One was the foundation of all happiness and bliss. Besides exerting himself in the protection of the propagation and continuation of the impartial Doctrine by means of various actions, he laid the foundation of the Three Jewels (Triratna) as the basis of the continuation of the Doctrine. He first erected for the shrine of his parents an image of the saṃbhoga-kāya of Maitreya adorned with ornaments, one foot (in height), then a golden image of the Teacher one span (in height). He caused to be made frescoes and paintings for the great vihāra of dPal rTses-thaṅ, and an image of Maitreya, and that of Siddhārtha having 22 spans each. He repaired the bSam-yas khrims-khaṅ-gliṅ, and placed in the centre (of the altar) the images of Mahābodhi with its retinue, the image of Śāntarakṣita (Źi-ba-'tsho), and an image of rGyal-ba mČhog-dbyaṅs, together with two golden caityas enshrining the relics of his father. He also contributed the building material for the erection of the great image at Na-len-dra ('Phan-yul), as if the image was being built by his own hands. Later at the monastery of Byams-pa-gliṅ of Gra, the Lord himself took over charge of the work on the shrine (32b) of the Lord All-knowing bSod-nams rnam-par rgyal-ba. After that with the help of the great alms-giver Sa-la sPyod-pa'i dbaṅ-phyug, the great official Rin-čhen bzaṅ-po and his consort, elevated by fortune and property, accustomed to the giving of alms, with a lofty power of heart, dPal rDo-rJe bde-ma and her son, the great official Rịn-čhen rgyal-po with his brother, erected a bKra-śis sgo-maṅ caitya of the Revolving of the Wheel of the Law, having 32½ fathoms in height and 22 fathoms ('dom) in width on each side, excellent in building material and plan, and an image of Maitreya in his nirmāṇa-kāya aspect represented in the bhadra posture (sitting on a throne, with both legs down, bhadrāsana), having 57 spans at the back. He completed the building of the caitya in 18 months, and the large image in 14 months. This Mount Meru (these statues), built by miracles, which were beyond the Mind of ordinary human beings, manifested inexhaustible wonders and were without equal in this World, fit to be worshipped and admired by all men from scholars to fools, who did not mind the difficulties of a long journey (to worship them). It is impossible for me to describe in writing even a small part (of these images).

Further, while assisted by the above alms-givers, he erected a very large golden image of the Buddhas of the Three Periods, a golden image of the Teacher surrounded by the 16 arhats, he repaired the meditative cell and the vihāra of sPyi-bo at mČhims-phu together with their images, (the monastery) of Gra-thaṅ, and other monasteries. He built the great meditative monastery (sgrub-sde čhen-po) of bSam-gtan-gliṅ, and erected images and painted banners (thaṅ-ka) (33a)
of the Teachers, of the Lord himself, to whom he owed most, and painted images of the principal deities of the four classes of Tantras, etc. He also prepared copies written in gold of the Commentaries and the chief Tantras. Further, he prepared copies of the Sūtras and Tantras together with their commentaries. It is impossible to enumerate all of these (books). On his advice, the king of the Southern Provinces, dPal

bKra-śis Dar-rgyas Legs-pa'i rgyal-po erected a golden image of the Mahāmuni, having 25 spans at the back, as well as a vihāra, a great caitya, a monastery, a golden bKa'-'gyur and bsTan-'gyur written on paper. (On his advice) the nan-so of bSam-lde Grags-pa mtha'-yas prepared a copy of the bKa'-'gyur written in gold including the rGyud-'bum (the Tantric section). He advised the nan-so of Yar-rgyab, the great official Rin-čhen bzan-po and his wife to complete the copying of the golden bKa'-'gyur which they were preparing. Because of internal feuds in Tsa-ri'i gnas-čhen, the skull of (Mid-la), endowed with marks (mtshan-ldan thod-pa), was taken to Dwags-po, and the monastery was about to fall in ruins. He pacified the region with the help of meditation and other means, and established the foundation of the Doctrine. Wherever (the Lord) went, he used to repair and worship stūpas, vihāras, sacred texts, etc. He distributed his income among the monastic congregation in numerous ways.

The story of his work as translator: When the great paṇḍita (Vanaratna) came to Tibet, he acted as interpreter at numerous sermons. He made a new translation of the Pratipattisāraśataka (sÑin-po brgya-pa) and its commentary (Tg. rGyud, Nos. 2334, 2335), as well as translations of many short texts, such as the text on the Vajravārahī Cycle called rDo-rJe rnam-par sgeg-ma (Vajravilāsinī-nāma Vajravārahī-sādhana, Tg. rGyud, No. 1602). He also revised the translations of the Hevajra Cycle, the Vajrapañjara (Gur), the Saṃvara-udbhava (sDom-'byun, Tg. rGyud, No. 373), the Śrī Tattvaviśada-nāma-Śrīsaṃvaravṛtti (Tg. rGyud, No. 1410), and the manual on the rite of the maṇḍala of the 13 deities of the Saṃvara Cycle (bDe-mčhog bču-gsum-ma). These (33b) translations were excellent both in words and meaning. The śāstras composed by him: An exposition of the Commentary on the first two chapters of the Śrī Kālacakra, a pañjikā (bKa'-'grel) on the rDo-rJe sñin-'grel (Hevajrapiṇḍārtha-ṭīkā, Tg. rGyud, No. 1180), and the Phyag-rdor stod-'grel (Tg. rGyud, No. 1402). This is the best text existing in

Tibetan on the Cycle of Sems-'grel (commentaries written by Bodhisattvas in Śambhala and other regions). Further, he wrote notes on the Samādhirāja-sūtra (Ārya-Sarvadharmasvabhāva-samatāvipañcitasamādhirāja-nāma-mahāyānasūtra, Kg. mDo-sde, No. 127), the Ratnakūṭa (Kg. dKon-brtsegs, Nos. 45-93), and the Avataṃsaka (Kg. dKon-brtsegs, No. 44). Further, he composed notes on many Tantras, such as the mKha-'gro rgya-mtsho (Śrī Ḍākārṇavamahāyoginītantrarāja-nāma, Kg. rGyud, No. 372), the mṄon-brJod (Abhidhāna-uttaratantra-nāma,Kg. rGyud-'bum, No. 367), the rDo-rJe mkha'-'gro (Vajra-ḍāka-nāma-uttaratantra, Kg. rGyud-'bum, No. 371), also composed sādhanas and maṇḍala rites, the sDom-pa bču-gsum-ma (the 13 deities of Saṃvara), the Mi-gyo bla-med, the Acala system according to the Anuttara-Tantra (such as Kg. rGyud-'bum, No. 431), the Phag-mo (Vārahī), and most of the sādhanas transmitted by the great paṇḍita (Vanaratna). He composed manuals on the maṇḍala rites of gSaṅ-'dus 'Jig-rten dbaṅ-phyug, the rDo-rJe 'Jigs-byed, the 'Jam-dpal sgyu-dra, the Phyag-rdor dbaṅ-bskur, the rṄog dkyil-bdun (7 maṇḍalas of the rṄog system), the Ži-khro (a rÑiṅ-ma deity), the Phur-bu (Vajrakīla), the rTa-mgrin (Hayagrīva), and others. He composed guide books on the Pañcakrama of the Sadaṅga-yoga, etc., also composed the bKa'-gso bsruṅs-spyi (rite of sacrifice to all the Protectors), the Dud-sol phyi-naṅ, the Lha-mo Dud-sol-ma-phyi and the Lha-mo Dud-sol-ma-naṅ, the gNod-sbyin (Beg-tse), and other rites. His complete Collection of Works (bKa'-'bum) contains about 12 volumes.

The story (of his) worship of the Teacher, the images of the Ratna, and of the monastic congregations: while he was listening to the teaching of his Teacher who preached to him the Sūtras and Tantras, he manifested constant reverence and worship of all. At the end of the preaching of the Doctrine by his teachers, he used always to offer tea (čhos-Ja) to the class. When they had finished preaching the great treatises, he held the festival known as the "Festival of completing (the study) of treatises" (gŽuṅ-rdzogs ston-mo), etc.

When he was attending a class on the Tantras and initiations, he offered a gaṇacakra and a ceremony to the Tantra class. While engaged in the study of secret precepts, he held the festival of khrid-ston (festival of guidance). On all these (34a) occasions, he offered excellent food and suitable presents. He used to perform worship accompanied by acts of reverence of body and speech. In particular, he said: "When the great paṇḍita (Vanaratna) came to Tibet, he offered his eighteen altar covers, and there is no need of enumerating the large offering of gold cloth, etc. presented on many occasions. The great paṇḍita (Vanaratna) having left for Nepāl, he used to send him every year one golden srañs, clothes, etc. Later, at the time of (his) annual and monthly memorial ceremonies he used to present every year large presents to the great monastic congregations. To 'Gos lo-tsā-ba gŽon-nu-žabs he offered first every year, later every month, excellent and tasty food, summer and winter clothes, extensive offerings of gold and barley grain. He also made presents to teachers of equal standing and performed the annual and monthly memorial rites for his own parents, and for deceased teachers. The story of his offerings to the large and small monasteries, etc.: he increased the grants (to various monastic establishments); he offered gaṇacakras (Tantric feasts) to revered teachers at the sacred place of Ca-ri-tra; he paid for the offerings of tea at the great monasteries, such as Tshogs-čhen-pa and others; he arranged for the memorial ceremoñy of the precious upādhyāya; he paid the expenses of feeding Khrims-khañ-gliñ; he secured lands for both bLo and Ka-čhu, etc. At the time of the revolving of the Wheel of the Doctrine of the Ocean of Piṭakas and Tantras during the summer recess at the monastery of Byams-pa-gliñ and at the time of the Great Assembly, many thousands of monks belonging to large and small monastic establishments gathered there, headed by the inmates of the three Tshogs-sde (Tshogs-sde gsum). He supported the great festivals which were admired by all, and during which they used to recite the great praṇidhāna of the Sthaviras and that of Bhaiṣajyaguru in the morning, and various other prayers in the evening, as well as (performed religious plays), which led the people present towards virtuous deeds. He also purchased land-plots to defray the cost of the great and small Tantric rites (sgrub-mčhod). He stimulated faith in great alms-givers who supported the meditative monastery (sgrub-sde) of bSam-gtan-gliṅ. Thus he himself performed an ocean of labours which transgressed the sphere of the Mind. Since his youth, while engaged in the study of Philosophy, he used to make daily sacrifices of two balins before the Ratna, of offering lamps (dkar-me), and of whatever flowers he was able to gather in summer and winter, according to season. During the funeral rites for his parents and his deceased spiritual teachers, and later during the bestowal of initiations of dPal-rtse-dbyiṅs-gsum, Khams-gsum rnam-rgyal (Tg. rGyud, No.2519), and' J̌am-dpal sgyu-'phrul-dra-ba, etc. at bTsan-thaṅ, Khrims-khaṅ-gliṅ, and other monasteries, during the Kālacakra and other ceremonies at the new monasteries, during the sGyu-'phrul dra-ba and other rites at the time of the consecration of the great stūpa at Byams-pa-gliṅ and at the time of his preaching of many "Old" and "New" Tantras, and the "Seven maṇḍalas of rṄog" to the Precious Incarnation of Žwa-dmar-pa at Dol Lhun-grub Lha-rtse and rNam-rgyal, and constantly during the performance of consecration rites, homa offerings and maṇḍala rites, he used to worship according to the number of deities in each of the maṇḍalas, and prepare the usual daily offerings properly and in prescribed numbers, in abundance and cleanly prepared. The above shows that he was endowed with the great miracle of the Heavenly Treasury (Gaganagañja, name of a samādhi). Other people at a mere glance at them were filled with faith and this served as a good example for them. (34b) (35a)

The Revolving of the Wheel of the Law: In general he was of the opinion that meditation represented the essence of the Doctrine, and that he had to show diligence in it.

The Precious great paṇḍita (Vanaratna) had also said : "Since now was the time of gathering the essence of the Doctrine, there was no need of going hither and thither. Meditate chiefly. During the intervals you can preach the method by which one could find the beginning of the Path of yuganaddha. There is no better benefit to others than the preaching of the Path of yuganaddha". Such were his instructions. When his followers begged him to revolve the Wheel of the Law, he replied "Those who keep in their Minds their own benefit and honour, and preach the Doctrine for the sake of gathering a retinue only, can be called hypocrites. Enough of such preachers and students! I, myself, considered the acts of the three main gates (acts of Body, Speech and Mind), especially the act of meditation, to be of benefit to others, but knowing the difference between works that were almost useless and those that were of little use, and those that were useful in all respects, I do not care to perform now insignificant works in the interest of others, but afterwards I intend to perform constantly extensive works in the interest of other: with the help of the power by which I shall be able to benefit beings numerous as the Ocean in the Ocean of Paradises of the Buddhas". Though he did not preach extensively the Piṭakas to his attendants, he satiated them with the nectar of the Doctrine expressing the very essence of the meaning of the Sūtras and Tantras during a single class on religion, according to the state of the disciples' minds. While he was staying at a philosophical college, as (35*b*)
assistant teacher, he was able to increase the wisdom of many wise men. At Brag-nag he taught to many, who had come there from Khams, the theory and the ritual dance of the Yoga rite. To more than fifty men he gave many initiations, such as the 'Jam-dpal sGyu-'phrul dra-ba and others. At mČhims-phu he bestowed on many the initiation of the four divinities of the Hayagrīva Cycle. At rTses-thaṅ he taught the exposition of the Hevajra (brTag-gñis) and

other texts, and numerous initiations, such as the Ži-khro, etc. (100 deities of the rÑiṅ-ma-pas) to the bKa'-bču-pa of Ñan-re and to many others, who included Lhun-sde Rab-'byams-pa and many others. At Thar-pa-gliṅ, sMan-rgyal, gYam-bzaṅs, and other monasteries, he taught to many seekers the initiation of gSaṅ-'dus 'J̌ig-rten dbaṅ-phyug (the Guhyasamāja in the form of Lokeśvara), the secret sādhana of Avalokiteśvara, the exposition of the "Six Doctrines" of the Mahāmudrā (Phyag-čhen čhos-drug, the Six Doctrines of Nā-ro-pa), the exposition of the Samādhirāja-sūtra, etc. At rGyal-po'i-khab he taught to the bla-ma 'Braṅ-ri-ba, to the bla-ma Tshul-la and others the exposition of the Saḍaṅga-yoga, to honoured priests (J̌o-bzaṅs) of Tsa-ri the exposition of dGoṅs-gčig (by 'Bri-khuṅ-pa), the exposition of the "Six Doctrines" of the Mahāmudrā, and the initiation of rDo-rǰe rNal-'byor-ma. At the monastery of dBaṅ-po to the bla-ma 'Braṅ-ri-ba and others the initiation of Saṃvara, Hevajra according to the method of Maitrī and others. At Eastern Lho-brag he preached the Hevajra-Tantra (brTag-pa gñis) and numerous initiations, permissions (luṅ), etc. to dPal Amogha and 'Od-bzaṅ-ba, the master of the house (gzims-dpon) of the Dharmasvāmin Po-doṅ-ba. To bKa'-bču-pa bSod-bzaṅs and others he preached the Summary of the Kālacakra (Dus-kyi 'khor-lo'i spyi-don). At Western Lho-brag he preached on two occasions to more than fifty disciples, including the Dharmasvāmin bsTan-rim-pa, Daṅ-spro-mkhan čhen-po, the bla-ma Dza-sna-ba, sLe'u-čhuṅ-pa, and others, the Saḍaṅga-yoga, the dGoṅs-gčig, the Dril-bu lus-dKyil (the Saṃvara Cycle according to the method of Dril-bu-pa which located all the 24 Tantric sacred places inside the human body), and the bLa-ma gSaṅ-'dus (a rÑiṅ-ma-pa rite). At Yar-'brog Kha-ba kluṅs he preached to the Dharmasvāmin Kun-dga' rgyal-po and to many elders of the mṄon-dga' monastery, and to meditative hermits of the meditative monastery of bSam-sdiṅs—the Saḍaṅga-yoga, the initiation of Saṃvara, the Mahāmūdra, and to numerous (36a)

Tantrics (sṅags-pa rñiṅ-ma-pas) he gave the initiation of Ži-khro, Phur-pa (Vajrakīla), Hayagrīva, etc. according to the wish of each of them. At North La-stod he preached the initiation of Ži-khro, etc., and the exposition of the Guhyagarbha to numerous Tantrics and Bon-pos, including the official (master, bdag-po) Čhud-kha-pa. Later at Byams-pa-gliṅ during the great summer recess he bestowed on the three great Zur, including Byaṅ-čhub rnam-rgyal of Čhos'-khor sgaṅ-pa, and to a thousand monks, residents and non-residents, headed by Čhen-po bSod-nams 'od-zer-ba, the ācārya bsTan-gsal-ba, the ācārya Śes-rab dbaṅ-po, and others, the Samādhirāja-sūtra, the Śikṣāsamuccaya, the Munimatālamkāra, the Sa-sde-lṅa (of Asaṅga), the Be-bum sṅon-po (of Po-to-ba), and the great commentary on the Byams-smon (Byams-pa'i smon-lam-gyirgyal-po, Maitrī-praṇidhānarāja, "Les mDo-maṅ", ed. Lalou, No. 107, p. 42). In this manner he helped to bring out the essence of the sublime meaning (nīta-artha). In particular he preached during many years the great Vinaya of the Mantrayāna (which contained the vows of Mantrayāna) to the inmates of Byams-pa-gliṅ. Further, he preached to the Dharmasvāmin Āryadeva and to many others the Commentary on the Hevajra-Tantra (brTag-gñis) by Vajragarbha (rDo-rje sñiṅ-po, Tg. rGyud, No. 1180), the Nā-ro 'grel-čhen (Vajrapādasāra-saṃgrahapañjikā, Tg. rGyud, No. 1186), the dGoṅs-čig, the Zab-mo naṅ-don, and other texts, and the initiation of Acala according to the Anuttara-yoga-Tantra (Mi-gyo bla-med), etc. Again to many (disciples), headed by the Khams-pa the Kalyāṇa-mitra bKa'-bču-pa, Mi-ñag Rab-'byams-pa Čhos-kyi grags-pa, Rab-'byams-pa bDe-bzaṅ-pa, mÑa'-ris Rab-'byams-pa Śer-rgyal-ba, Rab-'byams-pa Legs-bśad-pa, and to many learned kalyāṇa-mitras he preached extensively on about four occasions the Zab-mo naṅ-don and the dGoṅs-čig. To about fifty students, including Čhos-'khor sgaṅ-pa, the 'Phags-pa gDan-sa-ba dPal-bzaṅ-pa, and others, the Dohā in 160 ślokas (Saraha's Dohā), the Tshul-khrims le'u (the chapter on morality, one of the chapters of the

Bodhisattva-bhūmi), the Mañjusrīnāmasaṅgīti, etc. He also bestowed on many occasions the "Guide on the Sadaṅga-yoga", on virtuous ones, including the Rab-'byams-pa Śer-rgyal-ba, Legs-bśad-pa, and others, as well as on the meditative hermits of bSam-gtan-gliṅ. During that time also he taught the "Guide on the Sadaṅga-yoga" for half a year on more than 30 occasions. The king who observed the Worldly Dharmas Hyendu Kun-dga' rgyal-mtshan the khri-dpon of Yar-'brog with his brother, his son Hyendu Lhun-grub bkra-śis, the Yar-rgyab dpon-čhen (great official) Rin-čhen bzaṅ-po, the queen rDo-rJe bde-ma, her son the great official Kun-dga' rin-čhen rgyal-po, his younger brother the Dharmasvāmin bSod-nams ye-śes dpal-bzaṅ-po, his son the Tshal-pa naṅ-so Lha-dbaṅ-pa with his son, the naṅ-so of bSam-bde Grags-pa mTha'-yas with his minister, rGyal-ba-pa, the khri-dpon of Bya-pa, and his son dPal bKra-śis Dar-rgyas Legs-pa'i rgyal-po with his brother, all honoured him. He bestowed on them numerous hidden precepts, instructions, and initiations which purified their minds and protected them from misfortunes. In particular he bestowed on them the initiation into the three auspicious maṇḍalas (Amitābha-Tārā-Vijaya) and mantras. In this manner the whole country-side became blessed and unconquerable by others. They all became adorned by the Ocean of Worldly and Spiritual values which he bestowed on them by leading them towards the foundation of virtue which represented the method of rendering worldly wealth fruitful. The Lord of Byaṅ-pa rNam-rgyal grags-pa and his son, though proud of their descent in public, privately they greatly esteemed him as their Spiritual Teacher, and on many occasions they used to put him questions on the Doctrine, and honoured him greatly. Especially his Holiness Čhos-kyi grags-pa Ye-śes dpal-bzaṅ-po, the fourth hierarch of the Red Crown (Žwa-dmar čod-paṇ 'dzin-pa) of dPal Kar-ma-pa, a manifestation of the Jina-Naṭeśvara (Gar-dbaṅ) Vajradhara, the Great, begged him, who had been his spiritual preceptor

(36b) (37a)

during many previous existences, to come to Khams, and to become his spiritual preceptor in this life also. He sent the invitation by messenger with large presents. The messenger arrived when the bla-ma was residing in Tsa-ri, but he was unable to go there. Later he purposely journeyed towards dbUs, and they became Teacher and disciple, more intimate than close friends. He at first bestowed on him the initiation of the two-faced Vajravārahī, that of the Thirteen gods of Saṃvara according to the system of Dril-bu-pa (Vajraghaṇṭapāda), Acala according to the Anuttara-yoga-Tantra (Mi-gyo bla-med), the "Seven maṇḍalas of rṄog", the 'Khor-lo sgyu-drug, the Saṅs-rgyas thod-pa (Śrī-Buddha-kapāla-nāma-yoginītantrarāja, Kg. rGyud-'bum, No. 424), the Phur-pa spu-gri (a rÑiṅ-ma book), the rDor-dbyiṅs, the Phyag-rdor dbaṅ-bskur (Ārya-Vajrapāṇyabhiṣeka-mahā-tantra, Kg. rGyud, No. 496), the Dam-tshig gsum-bkod (Trisamayavyuharāja-nāma-tantra, Kg. rGyud-'bum' No.502), the Amitābha initiation according to the method of Dze-ṭā-ri (Jetāri), the initiation of bDe-mčhog Nam-mkha'-daṅ-mñam-pa (Śrī-Khasama-tantrarāja-nāma, Kg. rGyud-'bum, No.386), etc., the rJe-btsan (a Tibetan local deity), the Dud-sol (name of a goddess), the Phyag-bži-pa according to the method of Nāgar-juna, the Nā-ro mkha'-spyod (the Vajravārahī system accord-ing to the method of Nā-ro-pa), the Don-grub-ma (Sarvārthasiddhisādhana-nāma, Kg. rGyud, No. 1552), the 'Jam-dbyaṅs lha-lṅa (five aspects of Mañjughoṣa dwelling on the five Peaks of Wu-t-'ai-shan), the bLa-ma gSaṅ-'dus (a rÑiṅ-ma deity), the Tshogs-bdag (Gaṇapati), the Tshe-riṅ mčhed-lṅa (the five sister-goddesses dwelling on a group of snowy peaks in Southern Tibet, of which Mount Everest is one/Jo-mo gLaṅ-bzaṅ-ma or Jo-mo gLaṅ-ma, name of Mount Everest /), etc., the Hevajra, the Gur (Vajrapañjara), the Samputa (Samputa-nāma-mahā-tantra, Kg. rGyud-'bum, No. 381), the gDan-gži, the Mahāmāyā, the Mañjuśrīnāmasaṅgīti with the explanations of the rṄog Lineage, the Ye-śes rdo-rJe kun-las-btus čhe-ba (Śrī-jñānavajrasamuccaya, Kg. rGyud-'bum,

No, 450), the sÑiṅ-mo rgya-pa, the mūla and its commentary (Tg. rGyud, No. 2249), the Grub-sñiṅ (a work belonging to the Dohā class), the A-ma-na-si (Amanasikāroddeśa, Tg. rGyud, No. 2249/A-ma-na-si is the name of a class of works containing 26 titles. Bu-ston, bsTan-'gyur dkar-čhag, gSuṅ-'bum, Vol.XXVI /La/, fol. 47a; Tg. rGyud, Nos.2229-2254), the Zab-mo naṅ-don (Tg. rGyud, Nos. 2217-2223) and the dGoṅs-čig, the permission (luṅ) of the 'Gro-mgon bKa'-'bum, etc., the Ṣaḍaṅga-yoga, the Guide-book on the sampannakrama degree of Vajrayoginī (rDo-rJe rnal-'byor-ma, i.e. Vajravārahī), and the Pañcakrama of Dril-bu-pa according to the method of the great paṇḍita (Vanaratna), and the collection of precepts including the hidden precepts of bSre-'pho (a book of Mar-pa in 9 sections), the Čhos-drug-mkhar-dkar-ma (hidden by the son of Mar-pa and discovered by guru Čhos-dbaṅ), the precepts of Mā-yā'i rdzogs-rim-pa'i nu-ma (i.e. anuma, name of a system of meditation on 4 letters. Here the Anuma of the sampannakrama degree of Māyā is meant). Thus Čhos-grags listened to the heavy shower of religion, profound and extensive, and became the chief of the sons (i.e. disciples). (37*b*)

Further, on many fortunate ones he bestowed initiations and expositions fulfilling the wish of each of them. He stated that "the Śrī Kālacakra clearly explains, without hiding, the doctrine of yuganaddha, the essence of all the scriptures. If one were to grasp its meaning, one would be able to penetrate all the scriptures of the Sūtra and Tantra classes, for all the others are just means of understanding this doctrine. For it is the essence of the Doctrine". He used to interpret all the doctrines of the Sūtra and Tantra classes with the help of the Kālacakra, never separated from the book, and used to expound it. He clearly sounded the fearless roar of the lion, saying: "The ultimate Goal of all (the Doctrines) is the understanding of the vehicle of yuganaddha." Also he used to say: "One who had placed his faith in this vehicle, if he were to die touching with his fore-head the volume on

the Kālacakra, he would draw nearer to the state of Enlightenment, than he who had studied numerous Piṭakas, and had become a scholar". In this manner he held the doctrine of the Kālacakra in high esteem. He preached extensively on many occasions the sPyi-don (of the Kālacakra, i.e. the Summary on the Kālacakra), as well as extensively preached to many of his attendants and Piṭakadharas, headed by Chos-'khor-sgaṅ-pa. The assemblies of fortunate ones whom he had liberated by giving them guidance on such subjects as the Saḍaṅga-yoga, etc., were numberless. I have given a brief account of these events. In reality (yaṅ-dag-par-na) he was endowed with all the qualities of a kalyāṇa-mitra, such as the sign of possessing the nature (38a)
of a Bodhisattva (Bodhisattva-gotra), courage, eagerness (spro-ba), exertion (brtun-pa), never giving up the vows of morality (śikṣāpāda), never breaking his promises, commiseration towards the low and wicked ones, kindness without cause, the returning of kindness shown to him by others, kindness towards those who attempted on his life, and possessed of extensive knowledge. He was bound by the vows of the Pratimokṣa (ṅes-'byuṅ) accompanied by a Mental Creative Effort towards the Mahāyāna (the Bodhisattva vow), he was not defiled by natural sins, and by transgressions of religious vows, he did not transgress the limits of the precious vows of permission and prohibition (dgag-sgrub). In this manner he perfected his pure conduct (tshaṅs-par spyod-la, brahmacaryā), and was endowed with the complete accomplishments set forth in the Vinaya of the Holy Doctrine, fit for a Teacher. His mind was fully awakened towards the entry into the vehicle of Vajrayāna, and he never transgressed, even for a brief moment, the ordinary and extraordinary vows.

He experienced the Innate Wisdom (Sahaja-jñāna) described in the (third) initiation. He also perceived the affirmation of the fourth initiation (the state of yuganaddha), which is the hidden state of all the Tantras. He possessed the four pratisaṃvedyas (so-so-yaṅ-dag-par rig-pa, the four kinds of intense penetration/Mhvtpt, §13/, obtained on the ninth stage), he was kind and free from pride. He was endowed with all the characteristics of a venerable teacher (śrīmat-guru, dpal-ldan bla-ma), and thus became the sole protector of the entire World including that of the gods. One should remember the Ocean of his life-story and repeat his name. One should reverence him in every way, have faith in him and salute him constantly with great and unshakable faith. What use is there in troubling oneself by writing about the minor miracles of his life? (38*b*)

The eighth (Chapter): his passing into Nirvāṇa. Though the great Bodhisattvas abiding on the lofty stage (mahā-bhūmi, sa-čhen) are liberated from the bondages of birth and death, this expression is used here in order to indicate a technical religious term signifying a feeling of sorrow towards impermanence. While every day he used to bestow profound and minute instructions on the mahā-upādhyāya 'Ṭshal-min Čhos-kyi grags-pa, mṄa'-ris Rab-'byams-pa Śer-rgyal-ba, Čhos-'khor sgaṅ-pa, the Dharmasvāmin rTe'u-ra-pa, Rin-čhen čhos-rgyal, and others, he gathered his apparitional body on the 7th day of the 9th month of the year Water-Male-Tiger (čhu-pho-stag—1482 A.D. This biography must have been inserted by the editor after the death of 'Gos lo-tsā-ba in 1481 A.D.), called dGe-byed (śubhakṛt), at the age of 59. On the 10th day he manifested the appearance of proceeding to Tuṣita, and numerous wonderful signs, such as rainbows, flower showers, scent, etc., were observed by all. The fourth Kar-ma-pa hierarch, the "Holder of the Red Crown" (Žwa-dmar čod-paṇ 'dzin-pa) came there and comforted the disciples, telling them that the Lord had truly gone to Tuṣita. The hierarch stayed with them till the end of the 49th day and exhorted them to meditate. The hierarch was present at the cremation, offered blessings on the occasion of the funeral rites (dgoṅs-rdzogs ṅo-bo bsṅo-ba), performed the consecration ceremonies of the precious "outer" images (images placed for worship, as distinguished from those kept inside

stūpas), and wrote a praise of the Teacher and his Biography, and thus fulfilled the Teacher's wishes. They used white sandal wood for the cremation, as well as myrobalan and scented woods (benzoin, Skrt. sihla), etc. Many relics of different colours, a śārira bright as crystal, and numberless images were recovered (from the ashes), and worshipped by (39a)
the disciples. After the Teacher had manifested the appearance of passing into Nirvāṇa, his mercy (grace) continued to exert itself without break. They erected a precious stūpa (gduṅ-khaṅ) several stories high, made of silver. The door of the stūpa (sgo-khaṅ) and ornaments inlaid with jewels were made of pure gold, and were adorned with countless precious stones, such as ma-rgad (marakata, emerald), ruby (padma-rāga), pearls (mu-tig), saphires (nal), and turquoises. The relic holder was placed on the upper storey of the great stūpa of Byams-pa-gliṅ. (They also prepared) a shrine made of silver and gold, adorned with precious stones, the length of an arrow (mda'-gaṅ-pa) in height, a precious life-size image (of the Teacher), and several other smaller images, made of gold and silver, also several large and small painted banners (ras-bris) of the Teacher, and many hundred stamped images, having mixed medicated clay with his ashes. The Collection of his Works was edited. Later, as desired by him, a large and wonderful silk image of the Venerable Maitreya was reverently prepared by dPal rDo-rJe bde-ma and her son the Dharmasvāmin bSod-nams ye-śes-dpal-bzaṅ-po. Further, his personal disciples and alms-givers erected several of his images in gold and silver, and popularized his Collection of Works. All this became the foundation of the Doctrine, and objects for worship by living beings. Among his chief disciples there were many who spread his method of meditation and his teaching in different localities, but his permanent attendants kept at Dol bSam-gtan-gliṅ and Byams-pa-gliṅ his precepts of the "Guide on the Sadaṅga-yoga", his method of rites (sgrub-mčhod), as well as his large image, (39b)
holy objects which belonged to him, his offering utensils.

and his books. The above brief account was given here in conformity with the authorization of the author of the present work, mentioned above. In the absence of written sources, it was impossible to include in the present work the other accounts (about his Life). We have written the above, because the All-knowing 'Gos, author of the present work, intended to include in this History stories about the Doctrine and various individuals which could be of benefit to the Doctrine, and because in the line of the Southern kings, who had worshipped the Three Jewels, dPal bKra-śis Dar-rgyas Legs-pa'i rgyal-po, who had distinguished himself by the fame of possessing unequal fortune and wisdom (the puṇya and jñāna-saṃbhāra), by his services to all branches of knowledge, and by the spread of the Way of the Doctrine (bsTan-byus), like a stream in summer, when printing this great history of the Doctrine (Čhos-'byuṅ čhen-mo), told us that he "had striven towards this virtuous work (i.e. the printing of this book), keeping in his Mind the command of the Venerable One only (the Life story of bSod-nams rgya-mtsho must have been added to the "Blue Annals" by the editors after the death of 'Gos lo-tsā-ba gŽon-nu-dpal in 1481 A.D.). No one was greater than this lo-tsā-ba (bSod-nams rgya-mtsho) in spreading the fame of our Southern kings and in the discovery of the Path leading towards the abode of perfection. Therefore, on this occasion, you should at least insert a brief account of his life". I did so at his request. In general, the Kālacakra-Tantra (had been translated) by the lo-tsā-ba Gyi-Jo, bLo-gros sñiṅ-po, and others, rMa dGe-ba'i blo-gros, Maṅ-'or Byaṅ-čhub śes-rab, bSod-nams ye-śes, 'A-ža rGya-gar-brtsegs, Tsa-mi Saṅs-rgyas-grags, lDi-ri Čhos-grags, gNam lo-tsā, gÑos lo-tsā-ba of Kha-rag, 'Bro Śes-rab-grags, sTeṅs-pa (40a)
lo-tsā-ba, Roṅ-liṅs lo-tsā-ba, Rwa Čhos-rab, Čhag Čhos-rJe-dpal, Śoṅ-ston rDo-rJe rgyal-mtshan, Yar-kluṅs lo-tsā-ba Grags-pa rgyal-mtshan, dPaṅ lo-tsā-ba bLo-gros brtan-pa, dPaṅ's disciples bLo-gros, the two, and others. The Kālacakra-Tantra was the only book which had so many translators.

The Kālacakra-uttara-tantra (Kg. rGyud-'bum, No. 363) was translated by gÑan lo-tsā-ba (Dharma-grags) and Se'u lo-tsā-ba. Later it was again translated by kLubs lo-tsā-ba bLo-gros-dpal, who added the missing eleven ślokas. The dBaṅ-mdor-bstan (Sekoddeśa, Kg. rGyud-'bum, No. 361) was translated by 'Bro, Rwa, Man-luṅs-pa, sGra-tshad-pa Rin-rgyal, dPaṅ lo-tsā-ba, and Yar-kluṅs lo-tsā-ba. Pu-hraṅs lo-čhuṅ translated the title as dBaṅ-ñer-bstan. The Commentary by Vajragarbha (rDo-rJe sñiṅ-'grel, Hevajrapiṇḍārtha-ṭīkā, Tg.rGyud, No. 1180) was translated by Čog-gru Tiṅ-'dzin bzaṅ-po, gNel-čor Śes-rab-grags, Khyuṅ-po Čhos-brtson, Yar-kluṅs lo-tsā-ba, and dPaṅ bLo-gros brtan-pa. (40*b*)

The Commentary on Saṃvara composed by Vajrapāṇi: I saw its translation by Čog-gru Tiṅ-'dzin bzaṅ-po, which was revised by Śoṅ bLo-brtan, as well as by Khu-dṅos-grub. Regarding the Don-dam-pa'i bsñen-pa (Śrī-Paramārthasevā, Tg.rGyud, No. 1348) I have seen Somanātha's own translation (raṅ-'gyur—without the help of a Tibetan translator), as well as a translation by the Yar-kluṅs lo-tsā-ba.

The lTa-ba'i 'dod-pa mdor-bstan, which has nót formerly been translated into Tibetan, was translated by Kun-spaṅs Čhos-grags-dpal. The Sekoddeśaṭīkā (by Nā-ro-pa, Tg. rGyud, No. 1353) appears to have been translated by the Yar-kluṅs lo-tsā-ba, sGra-tshad-pa and dPaṅ.

The book on Kālacakra. The block print was prepared at the Palace of Čhos-rgyal lhun-po. (41*a*)

BOOK XI.

The Mahāmudrā (Phyag-rgya čhen-po).

Now I shall relate the story of the Mahāmudrā ("Great Seal") doctrine, which seals all the meditative and religious practices, from the Pratimokṣa (doctrine), which is the foundation of the Doctrine of Buddha, to the Guhyasamāja. (While discussing the Path of the Doctrine) there is no need to relate the opinion of ordinary living beings who have no desire to abandon the Phenomenal Existence (saṃsāra, 'khor-ba), and that of the heretical nihilists (rgyaṅ-pan-pa) who do not strive for emancipation. Other heretical schools, as for example the Digambaras (gČer-bu-pa) and others, admitting evil actions to be the root of sufferings of the Phenomenal Existence, attempted to eradicate (evil) actions (through penance). According to the Mīmāṃsakas (sPyod-pa-pa — dPyod-pa-pa) there did not exist a final emancipation (mokṣa, thar-pa) at all, and therefore they strove to get rid of (moral) defilements for the sake of a temporary emancipation only (re-śig-gi thar-pa). The Sāṃkhyas (Graṅs-čan-pa) and the Vaiśeṣikas (Bye-brag-pa) maintained that moral defilement (kleśa, ñon-moṅs-pa) was the root of Phenomenal Existence ('khor-ba). Again the root of moral defilement was Ignorance characterized by the non-understanding of the (nature) of the Self (ātman, bdag). Therefore, they having understood the Self, and having entered concentrated trance, reached various (in all eight stages) stages beginning with the first dhyāna, as far as the Highest Point of meditation (in the sphere of Phenomenal Existence, bhavāgra, srid-pa'i rtse-mo), but they, being caught in the net of an egoistic outlook, were destined to fall (again) into the Avīci hell. In this connection the ācārya Vasubandhu had said: "Is there (another) method of obtaining salvation, than this (Buddhism)? No—and for

what reason? Because the (heretical Teachers) maintain a wrong view on the Self." Buddhist scholars maintain that without abandoning Ignorance, which admits (the existence) of a Self, there is no Salvation. This ātma-dṛṣṭi is of two kinds, that in respect of the individual, and that in respect of the Elements of Existence. The Śrāvakas and Pratyeka-Buddhas having rejected the theory in respect of the individual (pudgala), have obtained a true salvation in which there is no continuity of rebirth. But the wise Bodhisattvas, if they were to obtain salvation for their own sake only, would proceed as described (by Candragomin in his Śiṣya-lekha-dharma-kāvya, ed. by I.P.Minayeff & A. Ivanovsky in Zapiski, IV, p. 77, verse 96: ñe-du 'khor-ba'i rgya-mtsho'i khoṅs-su čhud-gyur-pa /kluṅ-gi naṅ-du lhuṅ-ba lta-bu snaṅ-bžin-du/skye-śi phoṅs-pas ṅo-ma-šes-pa-de bor-nas/gal-te gčig thar-byed-na de-las khrel-bor med—"For there does not exist any one more shameless than he who strives selfishly for salvation, abandoning his family /i.e. living beings/whom he did not recognize as being afflicted by birth and death, sunk into the depth of the Ocean of Phenomenal Existence, as if fallen into a stream"). Therefore one should search for a method of salvation of living beings. There is no one, except
Buddha, who had perceived the entire method of Salvation. (1a)
Therefore it is necessary to reject the theory on the substantiality of the Elements of Phenomenal Existence in order to avoid the defilement of the knowable (jñeya-āvaraṇa). One should strive to abandon this theory. With the help of the theory of Relativity, one will be able to abandon the theory of the substantiality of the Elements of Phenomenal Existence. This last theory will invalidate the first theory because it contradicts the first. Thus one will enter the Ocean of Scriptures (āgama, luṅ) and Philosophy (rigs-pa) in order to establish the theory of Relativity. If the knowledge of Relativity (the author uses the term Phyag-rgya čhen-po ye-śes which here must be understood in the sense of "knowledge of Relativity or Śūnyatā" as in the mDo-lugs

Phyag-rgya čhen-po, the Mahāmudrā according to the Sūtra class) represents an antidote (gñen-po) which contradicts that which should be rejected, it should be considered as an inference (anumāna) obtained by reasoning. If so, then inference must represent a constructive thought (vikalpa, rnam-par rtog-pa). Śrī Dharmakīrti maintained that every constructive thought was ignorance (which must be eradicated), but the knowledge of Relativity which was also stated to represent inference, constructive thought and ignorance, cannot be rejected, and because there does not exist an antidote which could contradict an inference, and because all that which contradicts an inference must be false conceptions, and therefore cannot serve as an antidote.

(The author's conclusion is that one should at first grasp the notion of Relativity in order to avoid moral defilement. Then in its turn the notion of Relativity should be abandoned, but as it represents an ultimate /true/ conception it cannot be rejected with the help of reasoning and theories, and thus it can only be abandoned by intuiting the Mahāmudrā).

Thus the antidote (of this inference, i.e. understanding of Relativity) which is not a mere theory, represents the knowledge of the Mahāmudrā. This (knowledge) can be gained only through the blessing of a holy teacher (i.e. through initiation, and not through reasoning). Thus I have explained the stages of the general Doctrine. In connection with this, the Dharmasvāmin rGod-tshaṅ-pa had said: "In this Doctrine of the Jina Śākyamuni, the great brāhmaṇa Saraha was the first to introduce the Mahāmudrā as the chief of all Paths. The holders of his teaching in India were the Master Śabarapāda, father and son". Accordingly Maitrī-pa accepted the teaching of Śabarapāda (Ri-khrod-žabs), the father, establishing his disciples on the Path of the Mahāmudrā, it spread throughout (the whole) of Jambudvīpa. Now, the followers of the "Upper" school (sTod-lugs-pa) of the Mahāmudrā maintained that Maitrī-pa was born in the year of the Sheep (lug-lo—1007 A.D.), but those of the school of the Lord Ras-čhuṅ-pa maintained that (Maitrī-pa) was born in the year of the Dog (khyi-lo—1010 A.D.), and that he had passed into Nirvāṇa at the age of 78. According to these two schools, Maitrī-pa, who was learned in most of the theories (siddhāntas) of both Buddhists and non-Buddhists, was not satisfied with them, and made numerous attempts to find Śrī Sa-ba-ri dBaṅ-phyug. After having been blessed by him (i.e. initiated), he became enlightened by his teaching, and intuited the meaning of the (Ultimate) Essence. After that he expressed his views (about the Ultimate Essence) in the following words: asmṛti and amanasikāra (dran-pa-med, "that which cannot be remembered", Yid-pa byed-pa med-pa, "that which cannot be imagined"). The great scholar Śānti-pa was not pleased, and debated the matter, and Maitrī-pa won. Henceforth he became known as the Jina Maitrī-pa (Maitrī-pa, the Victor). Though he has had many disciples, the chief among them were: the "Four Great Ones" (čhe-bži), the "Seven Medium Ones" ('briṅ-bdun), and the "Ten Little Ones" (čhuṅ-ba-bču), known as the "Twently Ones". The "Four Great Ones" (were): Na-te-ka-ra, Devākaracandra, Rāmapāla, and Vajrapāṇi—the four. Na-te-ka-ra was a name received (by the disciple) while he was still a heretic. Later (he became known) as Sahajavajra. Devākaracandra: his other name was Śūnyatāsamādhi. He was the author of the Śes-rab ye-śes-gsal-ba (Prajñājñānaprakāśa, Tg. rGyud, No. 2226). Rāmapāla: in Tibetan—dGa'-ba skyoṅ-ba. He was the author of a Commentary on the dBaṅ-ṅes-par bstan-pa (Sekanirdeśa-pañjikā, Tg. rGyud, No. 2253, one of the 'Amanasi' class). Vajrapāṇi was the youngest of the three brothers: Nam-mkha' sñiṅ-po (Ākāśagarbha), Sa'i sñiṅ-po (Kṣitigarbha) and Vajrapāṇi. Introduced by Kṣitigarbha, he requested to be admitted (as disciple) by Maitri-pa. The latter was pleased. Having bound themselves by a piece of cloth, they made the vow not to separate till

they had reached Enlightenment. This Vajrapāṇi (Phyag-na) was born in the Fire-Female-Serpent (me-mo-sbrul—1017 A.D.). From childhood he had a sharp intellect and was learned in all the heretical and Buddhist sciences, as well as in many sections of the Tantras of the Mantrayāna. He especially mastered the Cycle of Dohā (i.e. sÑiṅ-po-skor, Saraha's Dohā). The "Seven Medium Ones": Sāmavajra (mÑam-pa'i rdo-rJe), Atulyavajra (Mi-mñam rdo-rJe), Kha-vajra (Nam-mkha'i rdo-rJe), Lalitavajra (Rol-pa'i rdo-rJe), Dhītiśrījñāna, Abhiyukta, and Jagatpāla. Among the "Ten Little Ones" (čhuṅ-bču): Skandha-pa, Me-go-pa, Rwa-čho, the yogin (Śṛṅgayogin), Ti-pu-pa, Śrī Nālandā-pa, (2b)
Padmamālin (Padma'i phreṅ-ba), Go-čha-ma, Kṛṣṇa (Nag-po-pa), the Junior, Śri Arṇapa, and Balyācārya. Some say that Ka-ro-pa, Phyag-na, Mar-pa, and the Nepālese Śīlabharo were called (his) "Four Spiritual Sons". The followers of the "Upper" school of the Mahāmudrā[1] divided the epoch of the appearance of the doctrine in Tibet into three periods: the early, the intermediate and the last (periods). During the early period the lineage of the doctrine originated with Nirūpa. Then the "upper" and "lower" section of the intermediate period. The "Upper" (sTod-'gyur) translation" was preached by Phyag-na to great teachers, after his arrival in Tibet. The so-called "Lower translation" (sMad-'gyur) was preached by A-su who spent his entire life in dbUs. The so-called "Later translation" (Phyi-'gyur) (originated) with Nag-po Śer-dad, a native of mÑa'-ris. Having gone to India, he met Phyag-na (Vajrapāṇi) who had grown old. Later on his return to Tibet, he preached the doctrine. (The Doctrine) which originated from the Master Mar-pa was called "zur-'gyur" or "additional translation". The early Mahāmudrā: The Great Master (Atiśa) heard from Maitrī-pa the Commentary and the basic text (grantha, gžuṅ) of the Mahāyānottaratantra (Mahāyānottaratantraśāstra, Tg. Sems-tsam, No. 4024; Mahā-

1 Phyag-rgya čhen-po sTod-lugs.

yānottaratantraśāstravyākhyā, Tg. Sems-tsam, No. 4024 by Asaṅga), the Dohā, etc. Later when (Atīśa) was staying at bSam-yas he went for a few days to mČhims-phu, and taught there the Dohā, the Cycle of the Grub-sñiṅ, and the method of following the Samantabhadracaryā (Kun-tu bzaṅ-po'i spyod-pa, name of a Tantric practice) to 'Brom-(ston). 'Brom suspected that these (teachings) might have a bad influence on the morals of Tibetan (monks), and abstained from preaching them much, but there exists a translation of the Jñānasiddhi (Ye-śes grub-pa, Tg. rGyud, No. 2219) by 'Brom (this is the "early" translation of the Mahāmudrā). The Commentary and the basic text of the Mahāyānottaratantra was translated (by Atīśa) at Yer-pa on the request of rṄog Byaṅ-čhub 'byuṅ-gnas. After him the Lord Mar-pa was the "earlier" (who translated the Mahāmudrā Cycle). After him, the "earliest" was that preached by the paṇḍita Vairocanarakṣita who had come to Tibet. After that sKor Nirūpa. After that, the "Upper" and "Lower" schools. After that—Lord Ras-čhuṅ-pa. Finally Nag-po Ser-dad. It should be understood thus. Now the paṇḍita Vairocanarakṣita: he was born in the family of king Sa-tsa-na (Sacana) in the town of Somapurī in the country of Kośala (dakṣiṇa-Kośala) in Southern India. His mother was named sKal-pa bzaṅ-mo (Subhaginī). (3a)
At the age of 12, he attended on his uncle who was a heretical paṇḍita and studied under him. He spent about a year in Western India. Then having gone to Magadha in Madhyadeśa, he met a yogin, and received from him the initiation of Ekavīra-Mañjuśrī (in the Tantras all the chief deities having two arms and without their śakti are called dPa'-bo gčig-pa, ekavīra). After that he accompanied this yogin to Vārāṇasī. The yogin took a wife, and settled there, but Vairocanarakṣita continued his journey to Eastern India. While he was residing at Nālandā, he met a yogin, a native of the country of Bharendra, a kāyastha (yig-mkhan) by caste, a great scholar, named Surapāla, (who possessed the power) of producing a state of unconsciousness in a man by placing

his hand on his head, which lasted till he removed his hand. The yogin admitted Vairocanarakṣita (as disciple), and the latter accompanied him for eight years. He then heard numerous precepts (upadeśas), such as the A-ma-na-si class (the A-ma-na-si'i skor ñer-drug, Tg. rGyud, Nos. 2229-2254), the Dohā and other texts, the Cycle of Mahāmudrā, the system of Maitrī-pa, the precepts of Hevajra, and the precepts of rasāyana (bčud-len-gyi man-ṅag, which consist in abstaining from food, and keeping to a certain diet). For six years he practised penance (dka'-thub) at Jālandhara (Lower Kaṅgrā Valley) in the West. After that he held a Tantric feast (gaṇacakra) in the forest of Nālandā in the company of the yogin Si-ti, the yogin Madana and others. From the paṇḍita Guṇarakṣita of Vikramaśīla he obtained many doctrines, including the Prajñāpāramitā, the "Six Treatises of the Mādhyamaka", the "Father" Tantras, such as the Guhyasamāja and others, the "Mother" Tantras and the Kriyā Tantras. Then from Dhanarakṣita he obtained (many) doctrines, such as the "Domain of Practice" (sPyod-phyogs), the sGrub-thabs bsdus-pa (Sādhanasamuccaya, Tg. rGyud, No. 3400), sādhana of Siṃhanāda (Lokeśvara) together with its rites (kalpa, rtog-pa), the Ārya-Tarakurukulle-kalpa (Kg. rGyud-'bum, No. 437), the sādhana of Seṅ-ldeṅ nags-sgrol (Khadiravaṇītārā-sādhana, Tg. rGyud, No. 3338), the gTum-po'i sgrub-thabs (the sādhana of Vajrapāṇi, Śrī-Vajracaṇḍacittaguhya-tantra, Kg. rGyud, No. 458). From Dharmakīrti he heard the Tshad-ma-'i gtan-tshigs. From Jayākara, a paṇḍita of East Bharendra, the bDe-mčhog bču-gsum-ma (the Thirteen deities of Saṃvara), the Five deities of Phag-mo (Vajravārahī), the Jo-mo U-rgyan-ma (Śrī-Oḍḍīyānatārābhisamayakrama-nāma, Tg. rGyud, No. 1707), etc. He (3b)
obtained several precepts and sādhanas from the paṇḍita Sa-ra-na (Śaraṇa), the head of the assembly of yogins of the town of Somapurī in the East. From the paṇḍita Sudhanagupta he obtained the Ekavīra-Mañjuśrī-Tantra (Siddhikavīra-mahātantrarāja-nāma, Kg. rGyud-'bum, No. 544). From Abhayā-

karagupta he obtained the bDe-mčhog mṅon-'byuṅ (Śrī-Herukābhyudaya-nāma, Kg. rGyud-'bum, No. 374), also the first (upper) part of the Commentary on the Vajraḍāka-Tantra (Śrī-Vajraḍāka-nāma-mahātantrarājavṛtti, Tg. rGyud, No. 1415), a collection of sādhanas, such as the svādhiṣṭha-sādhanas, etc. Though very learned, he hid (his learning), and behaved in a humble way. He visited 24 countries, with the exception of Oḍḍīyāna. He had the intention of going there, and even journeyed towards the South, where he practised Tantric rites, was captured by a king, and thrown into fire, but escaped unburnt. Afterwards he journeyed to Tibet and intended going to Ri-bo rtse-lṅa (Wu-t'ai-shan), but having been appointed chaplain to the king, was not given leave (to go). When Mu-thaṅ-bu of Śiṅ-kun-mkhar (near Liang-chou) harboured ill-feeling towards him, he performed many miracles, but kept them secret. Afterwards he journeyed to China. The king tried to wound him with sword and arrows, but not even a scar appeared on his body. He drank a cup filled with quicksilver, but this also did not harm him. He made the round of two-thirds of Jambudvīpa, and on five occasions visited Tibet. He also visited several upper and lower districts of dbUs and gTsaṅ, but it is impossible to enumerate all the places visited by him. He made a long stay at rGyal of 'Phan-yul, and prepared translations of the Dohā and other works. Since the three Cycles of the Dohā represented his (doctrine), the statement that the "King" and "Queen" Dohā (two books belonging to the Dohā; the series consists of rGyal-po Do-ha, bTsun-mo Do-ha, and dMaṅs Do-ha) were composed by A-su, appears to be untrue. His disciples were: in La-stod—the nirmāṇa-kāya Zla-ba 'od-zer; in gTsaṅ—Rin-po-čhe rGyal-tsha; in dbUs—Žaṅ Rin-po-čhe. Since he had spent a long time in Tibet, it is certain that he had numerous disciples there, but I have not seen any account (about them), and therefore it is impossible for me to enumerate (his other disciples). sKor Ni-rū-pa, who had not performed yet the parakāya-praveśa rite, obtained from him the secret precepts at sÑe-thaṅ. Therefore his coming to Tibet must have preceded that of sKor Nirū-pa. This mahāsiddha showed the manner of entering into Nirvāṇa on the hill-spur of mThar-'on. (4a)

Further, Ka-ro-pa, the disciple of Maitrī-pa: he was born as Maṇigarbha (Nor-bu sñiṅ-po), the middle son of the three sons of father rāja Vāridhāra (Čhu-bo'i rgyun) and mother Candrārkaprabhāvatī (Ñi-zla-'bar), a brāhmaṇī, in the town of Pu-lu-sa-la in the country of Eastern Za-hor. When he was seven, a ḍākinī prophesied (about him), and he was sent to a grammar teacher. In five years he mastered grammar well. Then for four years he studied science with the paṇḍita Kuśalabhadra (dGe-ba bzaṅ-po), a disciple of Śānti-pa. Then for fourteen years he studied (Sanskrit) Grammar with the paṇḍitas Kṛṣṇa (Nag-po) and Balakṛṣṇa (sTobs-čan Nag-po). At that time he had reached the age of 30. At 34, he was ordained by Mitratāra, the great scholar of the Sarvāstivāda at Vikramaśīla. Then he studied the Vinaya (Luṅ-sde bži) with Vimala, the great Vinayadhara. Then, at 39, he studied for four years Nyāya with the paṇḍita Siṃhaguṇa. At the age of 44, he studied with the paṇḍita Sthiramati (bLo-brtan) the Kriyā and Caryā Tantras (Bya-sPyod), as well as the "Father" and "Mother" classes of Tantras (Pha-Ma'i rgyud). Then with the Kashmirian Lakṣmī, the Great, he studied the Mahā-yoga (rÑal-'byor čhen-po, Anuttara-Tantra). At the age of 54, he studied the Prajñāpāramitā with the brāhmaṇa Tha-ga-na. After that he studied the Abhidharma with the scholar Rab-bzaṅ-mdaṅs (Suvarṇa ?) to the west of Vajrāsana. Having met Siṃhatāra, he practised the Ratna-sādhana (Rin-po-čhe'i sgrub-pa) at Vajrāsana till he was 64. After that at the age of 72, he looked like one aged 16. Anxious to expound the doctrine, the source of scholars, he met the yoginī, named Padmanī (Pad-ma-čan), who was meditating on the Prajñāpāramitā, who said to him:

"Pitiable are those living beings,
who, though being Buddhas by nature,

possess no understanding !
Though one may be a scholar in words,
If he does not understand the nature of the Mind, (4b)
He is similar to a beggar, biting chaff,
From which fruit will never be produced.
Though one may obtain the power of longevity,
If one is attached to worldly ways,
One will not be happy, but afflicted by sufferings,
having sunk into the mud of lust and anger.
O Man ! understand your Miṇd !
And meditate on its nature which is non-existent.
Follow the excellent Teacher, and exert yourself in precepts.
Give up the eight worldly doctrines.
Light Bliss !
Seal the Phenomenal Existence with (the Doctrine) of non-origination !"

Then following the prophecy of this yoginī, and that of the two incarnated boys, Ka-ro-pa, taking with him much wealth obtained from his father, proceeded (on a journey), and met a yogin named Nāgapuri, who was staying in the Outer Ocean at a distance of 42 yojanas. He (the yogin) initiated him by holding a Tantric feast (gaṇacakra). Then for three years he practised the sByor-ba-bsum-bču-pa. After that he studied for fourteen years the gŽuṅ-'bum-pa (Prajñāpāramitā in 100,000 verses ?), the rGyud-'bum-pa, the Nam-mkha'-daṅ-mñam-pa'i rgyud (Śrī-Khasamatantrarājanāma, Kg. rGyud, No. 386), the Dam-tshig-gi rtog-pa stoṅ-phrag-phyed-daṅ-bču-gñis-pa'i rgyud, the four Sampuṭi'i rgyud (Sampuṭa-nāma-mahātantra, Kg. rGyud-'bum, Nos. 376; 381, 382), the mKha'-'gro-ma'i sbyor-ba, and the Ñe-bar sbyor-ba'i rgyud. Then again he journeyed towards Vajrāsana. He was told by a fellow student in Grammar, Natekara: "If you like to meditate, the Lord Maitrī-pa possesses the precepts of the "Great Seal", the Unmeditable. Go to him !" Having gone to the Pa-ta monastery, he prac-

tised for seven years (meditation) on the meaning of the (Ultimate) Essence. Then for five years he practised meditation at the cemetery of Keṅ-ri. He then performed various Tantric rites in the Malabar country (Gyad) of the South, at Sa-la-ta-tse, in the town of Kampala, and in Kāśmīra. His other name was Pītakarma. His disciple Dam-pa sKor: He was born in the year Water-Male-Tiger (čhu-pho-stag—1062 A.D.) as the fifth son of father sKor-ston dÑos-grub- (5a)
'bar and mother gÑos-mo gza'-sgron-ma at dGe-tsha on the plain of upper gÑal. Because the (number) five was considered harmful for relatives, his father having performed a magic rite to avert evil, sent him away for study with a monk of dbU-ru. When he was going away, he noticed his sister (srin-mo) scattering dust after him and brandishing a broom (ṅul-mo), and he understood that he was being sent away. He received ordination at Lha-sa, and became known as sKor, the Junior (sKor-čhuṅ-ba). He met two disciples of Atīśa—the Nepālese 'Gyod-pa gsaṅ-ba (Anutāpagupta) and Vairocana. He fell ill. After he had touched some hair from the head of Vairocana, he felt relieved. He asked Vairocana (for instruction) in meditation, and Vairocana bestowed on him a profound meditation (sems-'dzin), and delivered the following prophecy: "You will be blessed by a yogin Śyama". He studied Grammar under 'Gyod-pa gsaṅ-ba and mastered it within one year. As tuition fee he promised three golden sraṅs. After that he journeyed to 'Phan-yul. The wife of a lo-tsā-ba, who had died, presented him with a vivarta (a book written in Vartula or Lañtsa). After that at the age of 10, he became watcher of gold-diggers at gSer-khuṅ-sgaṅ. When his belongings were carried away by a thief, he performed a magic rite, and was successful in it. He gathered much gold and presented it to the Nepālese, as had been promised by him. At the age of 11, he returned to his native place, and read a hundred times the funeral service for his father. Then having stolen a turquoise

hidden by his sister, he proceeded to dbU-ru. At the age of 12, he mastered the exposition of the Vinaya. Having sold his turquoise, he realized 13 golden srańs, one roll of silk gu-liń, and musk worth one golden "žo". At the age of 13, he proceeded to Nepāl in the company of sBa-ston, Dor-śe, and Khoń-ston Rin-čhen. At Ya-gal he studied the Kriyā and Yoga Tantras. (They saw) people going to meet a yoginī at Yam-bu, and the three Tibetans also went there. This yoginī used to live on offerings thrown away by villagers. She proceeded to the vihāra of Mya-ńan-'das-čhuń (the vihāra containing a small image of Buddha entering into Parinirvāṇa). There was also a yogin named Rwa-ru-čan ("with horn") who said to him: "I am the richest man in Nepāl. Let us go to see my residence". He proceeded (5b)
there, and saw inside a brick-built house nothing but some fragments of pottery (gyo-mo), a perforated slate, a goat's horn, and a wooden shovel. He understood that these represented symbols and felt faith born in him. (He then saw) the yoginī sitting on the image of the Teacher lying in Parinirvāṇa, naked, who exhibited her breasts and privy parts, and smiled (at him). He asked her for hidden precepts and the yogin Rwa-ru-čan said to him: "She does not impart doctrines, but only initiations!" He inquired: "How does she initiate?" and Rwa-ru-čan replied: "We have been thirteen merchants. Except for myself, all have died. This yoginī threw some earth on my back, and I asked her what she meant by this. She then told me: 'This is the sand from the Ganges. Now you won't die for 13 days. Otherwise you were to die in seven days! After 13 days you will die.' I then asked what could help, and she replied 'All your wealth and property should be given away to all those who would accept it. Then follow after me. It will help you!' I did accordingly. Then she told me: 'I shall initiate you', and she spat on the palm of my hand. Then by placing her hand on my head a proper concentration of the Mind was born in me. Now I have no need of precepts,

because they have liberated me!" Again Rwa-ru-čan said: "In this country of Nepāl, there are many paṇḍitas, such as the Indian Vajrapāṇi (Phyag-na), Lham-thiṅ-ba, and Bha-ro phyag-rdum (the "One-handed"). They could not help you. But at Ya-gal there is a yogin named mDa'-gžu-čan ("with bow and arrow") who shoots arrows at others, and even when an arrow pierces the body, no harm arises. He could help you. You should ask him!" He did so, but the yogin did not give him anything, except several ślokas. He then begged him in real earnest, and offered him all his belongings. The yogin then took him to a cemetery called Tsin-tsi-liṅ in Indian Thaṅ-khab. He kept outside (of the place), amidst jackals, and other animals. Next day the Teacher sent his maid-servant called Kumudarā to the market place with some gold, and she bought many provisions and drinks for a Tantric feast (gaṇacakra). He also sent sKor-čhuṅ-ba to collect flowers. He then bestowed on him the kalaśa-abhiṣeka (bum-dbaṅ), performed the maṇḍala rite made of flowers, and gave him the name of Prajñāśrījñānakīrti. During the same time the Teacher related many stories to him, and he wrote them down on bark, but the Teacher washed them off. Having studied for four years (Sanskrit) Grammar, he mastered the seventeen sections of Sanskrit Grammar (sgra'i-gnas bču-bdun). After that he attended on the Venerable Kumudarā and asked for her blessing. She bestowed on him the kalaśa-abhiṣeka (bum-dbaṅ), which she called the Prajñā-jñāna-abhiṣeka. The Venerable One said to him: "Son, being afraid of life and death, you strove for the sake of the Doctrine. It is wonderful! I shall bestow (on you) the faultless and extraordinary Vajrayāna. You, son, should practise meditation on it!" and saying so, she placed her foot on his head. After that he obtained from her the complete cycle of the utpannakrama degree of the system of the Black Bhairava (gśin-rje gśed nag-po), etc. The flame of Prajñā (wisdom) was lit in him, and he obtained the understanding of all the doctrines, so that his teacher and the

(6*a*)

latter's wife became pleased. Then she told him: "You should complete your initiation", and saying so, she promised to bestow it on him, but, since he did not possess the necessary implements, he proceeded to Nepāl. (His) two friends who had faith, wished to obtain it also, and told him: "We shall get it!" At the age of 19, he proceeded to Tibet. In the presence of Leṅ lo-tsā-ba of La-stod he bestowed the kalaśa-abhiṣeka on thirteen persons, and was offered a horse. After that he journeyed down (the country), and at Gra-thaṅ, having concealed himself in the residence of the kalyāṇa-mitra Gra-pa mṄon-śes, he preached at night the Saṃvara Cycle according to the methods of Lū-yi-pa and Dīpaṅkara, as well as the two methods of Nā-ro-pa. He offered him half a golden sraṅs. This was the 69th year of Gra-pa. Having obtained in all 13 golden sraṅs, at the end of the year, he proceeded to Tsi-na-tsi-liṅ and spent seven golden sraṅs as an offering to his Teacher who prophesied that in seven years' time fortune would be coming to him. He said (afterwards) that it did come true. With six golden sraṅs he paid the expenses of completing his initiation. After that his Teacher and the latter's wife introduced him to the practice of the yuganaddha (zuṅ-'Jug), and bestowed on him the guhya-abhiṣeka (the second degree of initiation). After that a Nepālese girl named 'Bri-nu became his mudrā. They (the Teacher (6b)
and his wife) bestowed on him the Prajnā-jñāna-abhiṣeka (the third degree of initiation), and also gave him the fourth initiation (dbaṅ-bži) with symbols. After that he studied the entire Grub-sñiṅ Cycle, and felt proud at his ability to understand it. Afterwards he was sent into the presence of one, who had practised secret Tantric rites in the suburb of an Indian town, and he proceeded there. Inside a chapel (mčhod-khaṅ) he found a painted banner (thaṅ-ka) hanging, in front of which were placed the five kinds of offerings. He spent some time there, (and saw) a man dressed as a monk (bhikṣu) holding his alms-bowl and his staff (gsil-byed) coming from the town on a begging round, he (the monk) said to him: "You are

probably the disciple of the yogin mDa'-gžu-'dzin-pa ("Holder of bow and arrow"). Then at night, the monk removed the painted image, behind which he opened a small door, out of which came out numerous mudrās possessing marks and adorned with bone-ornaments. In their company, the monk performed various Tantric rites, and the (feeling) of Bliss increased. In the morning the monk again hid the mudrās, closed the door, and covered it with the painted image (thaṅ-ka). After that the monk went on a begging round and told him: "We Indians practise the secret Tantric rites in this manner". A strong faith was produced in him and for six months he practised secret Tantric rites. When he decided to return to Tibet, the Teacher told him: "In the country of Śrī Oḍḍiyāna there is a jointless skull of a ḍākinī, which has an opening at the forehead. Should it reach your hands, you won't be hindred by any accident. Go to bring it." But he, feeling proud of his understanding of the doctrine (and thus being not afraid of accidents), did not go. The Teacher then said to him: "Well then, take this", and handed him his joint-less skull-cup. At the time of his departure, he felt sad, and on the plain of Tsin-tsi-liṅ he sang the praise of the Venerable Ka-ro-pa. He spent three days circumambulating the Svayambhū-caitya (in Nepāl). A Nepālese alms-giver named Bha-ha said to him: "Please stay on as my house (7a)
priest". He remained there for one month. Now the story of his performance of the rite of parakāya-praveśa (groṅ-'Jug): In the country of India, there was one named the Venerable Ka-ro-pa, learned in the five sciences. After having been a paṇḍita, he became a yogin, in possession of secret precepts handed down by nine Lineages, and possessed of the faculty of prescience. He had many disciples and the chief (among them) was one named Ni-rū-pa-ta'i rnal-'byor-pa (the yogin of Ni-rū-pa-ta). At first (Ni-rū-pa) became learned, and mastered the secret precepts (handed down) by nine Lineages. Having grown old, he attained siddhi at the age of 74, and the Venerable Ka-ro-pa said to him: "O Ni-rū-pa! You

should go to Tibet!" Again on one occasion, Ka-ro-pa said to him: "If you go to Tibet, you will benefit living beings". Ni-rū-pa then said to him: "Would it be possible for me to do something of benefit to living beings?" Again on one occasion the Teacher said to him: "One day you will benefit living beings in Tibet. Go in any case to Tibet!" He inquired: "How shall I go there?" The Teacher said: "From here you should go to the island of rDo-čhu (stone river, or frozen river, the name often designates the gTsaṅ-po, the Sītā, and the Tārīm). You won't be harmed by the dangers of the frozen river. There exists an island of ḍākinīs, and the ḍākinīs will assist you and bless you". Then Ni-rū-pa following his instructions, proceeded as far as the rDo-čhu. This rDo-čhu whenever it touches (the body) of a living being, causes his death and transforms him into a stone. However it did not harm him. Then the ḍākinīs came out to meet him and honoured him. He presided over a Tantric feast (gaṇa-cakra) which was held on three occasions. Then the ḍākinīs delivered a prophecy which said: "You, go to Nepāl! There you will meet a young Tibetan, possessed of (auspicious) marks, who was ordained in his youth, and is endowed with wisdom. His (7b)
time (i.e. death) having come, you must perform the consciousness-transference (groṅ-'Jug) rite, and then go to Tibet. We shall protect you from accidents, and shall assist you." Then the Venerable Ni-rū-pa proceeded to Nepāl, and there met sKor, the Junior (sKor-čhuṅ-ba), at the residence of the alms-giver Bha-ha. Then Ni-rū-pa entered the body of the deceased sKor-čhuṅ-ba. His former body was cremated, and he then proceeded to Tibet (in his new body). At first he went round as a beggar. The Venerable Ka-ro-pa and his wife having come to Lha-sa, met him. From beyond a sand place the Venerable Ku-mu-da-ra (Kumudarā) addressed him, saying: "Prajñākīrti!" He asked her: "How did you get here?" The woman said: "The Venerable Ka-ro-pa is also staying here. We came here because an accident is due to happen to you". He saluted (them), circumambulated

round them, and placed their feet on his head. The Teacher (Ka-ro-pa) blessed him. He used to say: "Because the Teacher had blessed me, when Gye-ru Śe'u-čhuṅ-pa had decided to kill me, the accident did not take place". While in Lha-sa on one occasion he listened to the exposition of the dBaṅ rnam-ṅes (Abhiṣekanirukti, Tg. rGyud, No. 2476). Then he saw his Venerable Teacher and his wife off to Guṅ-thaṅ in Maṅ-yul. Having returned, he put on the dress of a paṇḍita of Zaṅs-gliṅ, and proceeded (on his journey), and thus became known as the "Indian of Zaṅs-gliṅ (in the Vinaya designates Ceylon. According to others—Tāmralipti) who had come to Tibet". Then he put on a Tibetan dress, and preached the Tantric doctrine for 21 years to disciples, including thirteen monks and others, bestowed initiations, and prepared his own translations (without the help of lo-tsā-bas) of numerous Tantric texts. He also preached numerous works belonging to the Tantric class and many texts (belonging) to the class of hidden precepts, and thus helped to spread the profound Tantras of the Holy Doctrine, as well as the essential teachings. In general, from the age of five till the age of 21, he continued his studies. At the age of 20, he proceeded to Tibet. From the age of 21, he expounded the essential meaning (of the doctrine) and passed (8a)
into Nirvāṇa in the year Water-Male-Horse (čhu-pho-rta—1102 A.D.), aged 41. He taught the Doctrine to Čhaṅ-ra Śes-rab seṅ-ge. The latter to (his) son Ye-śes seṅ-ge. The latter to gLaṅ-ston of Khams. The latter to the bla-ma Brag-pa čhen-po. The latter to the bla-ma Myaṅ-čhen-po. The latter to Saṅs-rgyas Jo-sras. The latter to the ācārya Śāk-śe. The latter preached it to the bhikṣu Ratneśvara. Though this sKor had been a great siddha and had spent a considerable time in Tibet, the present day kalyāṇa-mitras do not attach great importance to him. Therefore I have written (his) life story at some length. Again, when the Indian Vajrapāṇi (Phyag-na) went for Tantric practice, and was begging in Nepāl, he was wonder-

ing whether he would be able to spread the Doctrine in Nepāl He thought that he would be able (to do so). Later when he reached the age of 50, he came to Ye-raṅ and settled there (1066 A.D. See S. C. Das: Life of Sum-pa mkhan-po, JASB./1889/, p. 42). He was met by Tibetan scholars, such as 'Brog J̌o-sras and others who asked him to preach the Doctrine to them. He bestowed on them the following doctrines: the basic text of the Grub-sñiṅ (Cycle of Dohā) together with addenda, the nine "bits" (brul-tsho) which followed on the Sūtras, the nine "bits" of precepts which followed on the Tantra of the "Father" class (Pha-rgyud), the nine "bits" which followed on the Tantras of the "Mother" class (Ma-rgyud), in all 27, and bound them with the four mudrās i.e. the karma-mudrā (las-kyi phyag-rgya), the dharmamudrā (čhos-kyi phyag-rgya), the mahāmudrā (The Great Seal), and the samaya-mudrā (dam-tshig-gi phyag-rgya). He also preached them the six "links": the theory accompanying tradition and reasoning, meditation accompanied by experience, practice suitable for the present time, results producing benefit to others, the Path accompanied by the signs of the Inner Heat, and Initiation accompanied by precepts. Among the chief texts were: the "Seven Classes of Realization" (grub-pa sde-bdun), the gSaṅ-ba grub-pa of mTsho-skyes (Saroruha, Padmavajra), the rGyud ma-lus-pa'i don ṅes-par skul-bar byed-pa (Sakalatantrasambhavasañcodanī-śrīguhyasiddhi-nāma, Tg. rGyud, No. 2217), the Thabs-daṅ śes-rab grub-pa of Yan-lag-med-pa'i rdo-rJe (Anaṅgavajra; Prajñopāyaviniścaya-siddhi, Tg. rGyud, No. 2218), the Ye-śes grub-pa of Indrabhūti (Jñānasiddhi-nāma-sādhana, Tg. rGyud, No. 2219), the gÑis-med grub-pa of Lakṣmīkara (Advayasiddhi-sādhana-nāma, Tg. rGyud, No. 2220), the Lhan-čig skyes-grub of Ḍombhī Heruka (Śrī-Sahajasiddhi-nāma, Tg. rGyud, No. 2223), the gSaṅ-ba čhen-po'i de-kho-na-ñid grub-pa of Dā-ri-ka-pa (Dārika, Tg. Śrī-Oḍḍiyānavinirgataguhyamahāghyatattvopadeśa, Tg. rGyud, No. 2221), and the dṄos-po gsal-ba'i rJes-su 'gro-ba'i de-kho-na-ñid (8b) grub-pa composed by the yoginī Tsi-to (Cintā, Vyaktabhāvānugatattva-siddhi, Tg. rGyud, No. 2222). The Essential: the three Dohās: the "King" Dohā, the "Queen" Dohā, and the "Subjects" (dmaṅs) Dohā. Further, the dBaṅ-ṅes-bstan (Sekanirdeśa-nāma, Tg. rGyud, No. 2252) composed by Maitrī-pa. Lesser texts, such as the bDag-med-ma gsal-ba and others (Nairātmya-prakāśa, Tg. rGyud, No. 1308), the De-kho-na-ñid bču-pa'i 'grel-pa composed by Sahajavajra (Lhan-čig skyes-pa'i rdo-rJe, Tattvadaśaṭīkā, Tg. rGyud, No. 2254), the gNas-pa bsdus-pa (Sthitisamuccaya, Tg. rGyud, No. 2227), the rDo-rJe'i tshig-'byed (Vajrapāda-nāma, Tg. rGyud, No. 2255) composed by Phyag-na (Vajrapāṇi), the bLa-ma brgyad-pa'i rim-pa (Guruparaṃparakramopadeśa-nāma, Tg. rGyud, No. 3716), the Śes-rab ye-śes-gsal-ba (Prajñājñānaprakāśa, Tg. rGyud, No. 2226) composed by Devākaracandra, the dBaṅ-ṅes-bstan-gyi 'grel-pa (Sekanirdeśapañjikā, Tg. rGyud, No. 2253) composed by Rāmapāla, the Phyag-rgya bži rJes-su bstan-pa (Caturmudrāniścaya, Tg. rGyud, No. 2225) composed by the ācārya Nāgārjuna. The above were known as the "Cycle of Lesser Texts." After that 'Brog J̌o-sras having invited the bla-ma Vajrapāṇi (Phyag-na) to Tibet, the latter while residing at Čhu-sgo of gTsaṅ, preached extensively the Mahāmudrā doctrine to Tibetan scholars. Among his disciples were: Śe-sṅon Byaṅ-'bar, Žaṅ-sṅa Riṅ-mo, Khams-pa rGwa-ston, sPu-hraṅs Nag-po Śer-daṅ, 'Brog J̌o-sras rDo-rJe-'bar, 'Or-brgyad sTon-čhuṅ, kLuṅ-śod-pa Khyuṅ-khri, Khyi'u brtson-'grus, Ba-reg Thos-pa dga' (a famous scholar), Braṅ-ti bLo-gros dbaṅ, Bra'o 'Bum-la-bar, Brag-pa dKon-grags, Se-ston sGra-gčan-zin, mTshur-'dbyig-gi rgyal-mtshan, the four disciples lo-tsā-bas – Nag-tsho Tshul-khrims rgyal-ba, rMa-ban Čhos-'bar, gÑan Dharma-grags, and mČhuṅ Ye-śes 'byuṅ-gnas. One could increase the number of the above disciples by saying the "Thirty Tibetan scholars." When 'Brog J̌o-sras invited Vajrapāṇi (Phyag-na), he promised him eighty golden sraṅs. During the performance of the funeral rite for his father, he presented him with 50 golden sraṅs packed together as eighty sraṅs. (9a) bLa-ma Phyag-na's attendants having weighed the package, discovered that there were only fifty (sraṅs). The bLa-ma became displeased and said: "It is improper for 'Brog J̌o-sras to tell me lies! If so, his father (meaning his Teacher) also could not be a genuine (teacher), for it is said: 'The father's behaviour will be manifested by the son'." Saying so, he suddenly slashed his belly with a razor. His attendants were frightened, and began to weep, but he said to them: "If you don't like it, nothing will happen," and passing his hand over the wound, he caused it to disappear without leaving even a scar. He then continued his journey towards India and Nepāl (Lho-Bal). The eight signs of his miraculous power (grub-rtags brgyad): (1) when a venomous snake attacked him, he drove it away with the help of the Yamāntaka-yoga spell (gśin-rJe gśed-kyi rnal-'byor), (2) when he came across a mad elephant, a ḍākinī assisted him in driving the animal way. This ḍākinī then uttered a prophecy, and he acting accordingly proceeded to a town, where lived an old brāhmaṇa with a ḍākinī as wife. The two kings of Oḍḍiyāna were waging war against each other. The king A-bhram who was a "seven-born" (skye-ba bdun-pa, means one who had been reborn seven times as a brāhmaṇa. Should any one partake of the flesh of a "seven-born" brāhmaṇa, he would attain miraculous powers/siddhi/. A man who is a "seven-born" possesses seven shadows. In Tibet there exist special pills called sKye-bdun believed to contain pieces of flesh of famous "seven-born" brāhmaṇa) was killed by the other king's minister Moṅ-rtse Moṅ-ga. He hit him with a diamond-pointed arrow between the eye-brows. The corpse of the king was then torn to pieces by ḍākinīs. The wife of the old brāhmaṇa secured the head (of the dead king), and brought it to her house. The brāhmaṇa rebuked her. She told him: "Because of a karmic bond (las-'brel), I attended on you. Now, if you don't need me, I can go," and saying so, she presented the head (of the dead

king) to Vajrapāṇi, and herself passed out. Vajrapāṇi hid the skull underground. Then a sound resounded in the sky and he understood that (the skull) possessed miraculous powers (3). He again took it out from underground. He kept it carefully and obtained miraculous powers. He used to pour a little wine into it, and kept it inside a vase, which became filled with wine. While walking along the bank of the Ganges, two ḍākinīs presented him with a meditative string (sgom-thag) made of stones without joints (4). He manifested the face of Vajra-yoginī to his disciples performing the "homa" offering of Vārahī "with three vases" (Phag-mo bum-gsum-pa—some maṇḍalas of Vajravārahī have triangles, (9b)
in each of which is represented a vase or skull-cup) (5). He gathered the dung of a red cow before it had fallen on the ground, placed it in a pot made of precious substances, then placed fruit on it, and having blessed it, produced fruit without end (6). On the bank of the river Ganges even kings used to be attacked by robbers, but he was able to render the robbers, bodies rigid, with the help of the Yamāntaka-samādhi (trance of Yamāntaka, i.e. he represented himself as Yamāntaka) (7). When J̌o-sras rDo-rJ̌e-'bar offered him gold, he cut his stomach with a razor and this was said to have been his eighth accomplishment (miracle). Also there existed a story that when Zla-ba 'od-zer (Gyi-J̌o lo-tsā-ba), son of 'Khon-phu-ba, came to Nepāl, he perceived many wonderful signs of siddhi performed by Vajrapāṇi. The disciple of Vajrapāṇi—the Kashmirian Dharmaśrī, called the "One-eyed", accompanied the Teacher (on his journey to Tibet). He preached extensively the Cycle of Mahāmudrā. Having consulted his Tibetan disciples, he composed a Commentary on the Śatasāhasrikā Prajñāpāramitā (Tg. Śer-phyin, No. 3802; 'Bum) and the "Key to Sañcaya" (sDud-pa'i lde-mig, Prajñāpāramitākośatāla-nāma, Tg. Śer-phyin, No. 3806). Again among the disciples of Vajrapāṇi (Phyag-na) we find: La-stod gTsaṅ-śod-pa, Śer-sgom Dar-seṅ, J̌o-btsun Me-'bar, Žaṅ-ded-po luṅ-pa, Go-luṅ-pa Grub-

thob btsun-pa, mÑa'-ris Čhaṅ-čhuṅ-pa, La-stod Na-zlum-pa, mKhan-po sÑiṅ-po rgyal-mtshan, mKhan-po rGyal-mtshan-'od, the upādhyāya Kam-mkha' rgyal-mtshan, 'Jam-dbyaṅs rin-čhen bzaṅ-po, and Mi-ñag Śes-rab bzaṅ-po. From the Venerable Ri-mi 'babs-pa (i.e. "one who did not descend from the mountain", one who stayed continuously in meditation in the mountains), I obtained the guide-book composed by Mi-ñag-pa.' Thus the Doctrine which had originated from Vajrapāṇi and his disciples became known as the "Upper" school (sTod-lugs) of Mahāmudrā.

A-su: his grandfather was a paṇḍita, who had come from India, and was the house-priest of the Bha-ros in Nepāl. His son, who was uneducated, became the servant of Bha-ro. A-su was the latter's son. From his childhood he possessed a very sharp mind, and was distinguished by wisdom. He (10a)
used to carry goods as far as the frontier of India (rGya) and presented them to his master Bha-ro who was pleased, and told him: "Now I shall give you a house". A-su told him: "I don't want a house! I prefer religion. Please permit me to enter religion". Bha-ro gave him his permission. At first he obtained many initiation rites and Tantric commentaries, as well as hidden precepts, from a Nepālese paṇḍita named Dze-hūṃ or Śāntibhadra. After that he obtained secret precepts from Vajrapāṇi, realized the Truth, and became a saint (yaṅ-dag-pa'i skyes-bu). He had the intention of going to China and spent some time at Sum-'phreṅ of 'Phan-yul. While he was preaching to many disciples, he married the lady of 'Brom ('Brom-mo gza'), and a son named Grags-pa seṅ-ge was born to him. On seeing his son's face he gave up the idea of going to China, and spent a long time at rLuṅ-śod (near Nag-čhu-ka). rMa-sgom Čhos-kyi śes-rab met A-su at rLuṅ-śod. Later (A-su) was invited by the alms-giver kLu-phyug and stayed at Upper 'Brom. Here he preached his own doctrine, such as the Cycle of Vajravārahī, the Dohā, and the Mahāmudrā, to an assembly of 10,000 monks. At that time the Dharmasvāmin Ras-čhuṅ-pa also

met him and made the request that he might be instructed in the Doctrine. A-su told him: "I have to support my wife and children. Go and beg, and present me with some barley!" Ras-čhuṅ-pa having collected much barley offered A-su twenty donkey loads of grain. A-su had four sons: Grags-pa seṅ-ge, Čhos-kyi grags-pa, Indu, and dBaṅ-ṅe. (His) daughters were named: Lha-mo, 'Dre-mo, and Mi-mo. Altogether he had seven children. The Venerable Grags-pa seṅ-ge mastered the theories of his father, and an understanding of the Mahāmudrā, lofty as sky, was born in his Mind. He perceived all worldly objects as a dream and illusion. He was a yogin who had obtained the two kinds of siddhis. Čhos-kyi grags-pa: In general, he was learned in the characteristics common to all things (sāmānya-lakṣaṇa), and in the (10*b*)
particular essence of the elements of existence (sva-lakṣaṇa). In particular, he became very efficient in the (practice) of the doctrine of the Mahāmudrā. Indu and dBaṅ-ṅe were not able to continue the Spiritual Lineage (of their father). Grags-pa seṅ-ge's son was the siddha mGon-po, his younger brother was Saṅs-rgyas sgom-pa. Then Seṅ-ge-grags. The youngest was the ācārya Bal-po 'Jig-rten. Now the siddha mGon-po: He studied the doctrine of the Mahāmudrā and meditated on it. He became a great scholar, and propitiated the tutelary deity (yi-dam) Vajravārahī, and had a vision of the goddess. As his servants he employed loka-ḍākinīs. The dharmapāla Nātha (Mahākāla) and the eight classes of gods and demons offered him their life-mantra (srog-sñiṅ). He became a yogin possessed of two kinds of siddhis (mčhog-gi dṅos-grub and thun-moṅs-dṅos-grub). Saṅs-rgyas sgom-pa: having no attachment towards the lofty seat of his forefathers, he cast (it) away as spittle. Having cut off his attachment towards food and drink, he practised austerities, subsisting on water (only). The understanding of the Mahāmudrā was produced in him. He was a man whose individual practice did not contradict his religious beliefs. The ācārya Bal-po 'Jig-rten ('Jig-rten dbaṅ-phyug = Lokeśvara): Because of

accumulated former good fortune, he was born as son of a nephew of benevolent forefathers. He gladdened his elder brothers and grasped the thoughts of former teachers. From the high seat of his forefathers, he taught the precepts of the Mahāmudrā, similar to a shining sun, and removed the darkness of living beings. He had visions of tutelary deities, and employed ḍākinīs as servants. He used to hold discussions and give orders to the Dharmapāla lČam-dral (Mahākāla and Ekajaṭī) and Dam-čan pho-mo (Vajrasādhu and rDo-rJe gyu-sgron). Those who had been the spiritual disciples of the bla-ma sKye-med: the "Four Pillars of Meditation" (sGom-ka-ba-bži), the "Six Beans" (gDuṅ-drug), the "Three sons of gYor-po-ba," dMag-pa sgaṅ, and others. The "Four Pillars": sGom-tsho of rGyal, sGom-tsho of Grab, sGom-tsho of Upper Bya-ma-luṅ, and sGom-tsho of kLags. The "Six Beams" (gDuṅ-drug): Rwa lo-tsā-ba, Ba-tshab lo-tsā-ba, Dol-po ye-śes, the kalyāṇa-mitra gÑan, and others. Among the three sons of gYor-po: Rog-pa dMar-ba rDor-seṅ, Žaṅ-bra'o Brag-rtsa-ba, rLuṅ-ston rDo-rJe bla-ma; more- (11a)
over mṄa'-ris Par-pu-ba, sGaṅ-ston 'od-'bar, sPaṅ-ston Čhos-'bar, and others. It was (incorrectly) stated that among them Rog rDor-seṅ taught Saṅs-rgyas brtsag-son. The ācārya rLuṅ-ston pleased his teacher with the three kinds of joy, and an understanding of the Mahāmudrā was born in him. He collected the essence of the Mind of Bal-po sKye-med. He excelled the other disciples, and acquired the faculty of preaching the Dohā in detail. The siddha mGon-po and Saṅs-rgyas sgom-pa obtained the doctrine from him. Bal-po 'Jig-rten obtained the Doctrine from him, and his brother. Dol-pa Jo-sras obtained it from the latter. Again, the one named the bla-ma mṄa'-ris-pa was ordained in his youth, and conducted extensive studies. He especially preached on about fourteen occasions the Vinayamūlasūtra (Pratimokṣa-sūtra). Having heard that the bla-ma Vajrapāṇi possessed a miraculous hidden precept of the Venerable dbU-bčad-ma (Vajravārahī with several heads), he proceeded to ask for it. The bla-ma

Vajrapāṇi said to him: "Do you desire the sublime or the ordinary realization (mČhog-gi dṅos-grub and thun-moṅs-kyi dṅos-grub)?" mṄa'-ris-pa replied: "I desire the sublime realization." Then the Teacher said: "Well! You have grown old. I possess hidden precepts which were not given by me to any one else previously. They are called 'The Cycle of Phyag-rgya čhen-po rde'u' (this method of preaching exists nowadays. The instruction is carried out with the help of pebbles). In it the Method (thabs, upāya), and the Wisdom (śes-rab, prajñā) are combined, and are used as a Path of Spiritual Training. The number of stages between the cause and Effect of Phenomenal Existence (Saṃsāra) and the Sahaja-jñāna was counted with the help of 175 pebbles. It represents a commentary on the three basic texts (i.e. the Three Sections of the Dohā) in which not a single word had been added or omitted from the time of the great Brāhmaṇa (Bram-ze čhen-po—Saraha) over three (i.e.India) to the present time. There was no contradiction in regard to the meaning, and it was not defiled by persons who had broken their vows, and it was not intermixed with any other kind of method of salvation (preached by other Teachers). I shall bestow it on you!" Then having obtained the understanding from the (11b)
Teacher, he stilled his Mind. Afterwards he proceeded to dbU-ru 'Brom-pa. Because Teacher Bal-po had acquired great fame, (mṄa'-ris-pa) was of the opinion that he (Bal-po 'Jig-rten) possessed a Mahāmudrā doctrine which did not require even meditation, and so heard (its exposition). He then found out that the bla-ma Bal-po was preaching the basic texts combined with the theory, but used to leave out the Method (upāya). mṄa'-ris-pa told him: "Bla-ma Vajrapāṇi formerly gave me the 'Cycle of the Pebbles' (rDe'u-skor) in such and such a manner. But why do you, great Teacher, preach in this manner?" Bal-po replied: "Tibetans prefer this sort of exposition, shallow and detailed. For this reason I have abstained from preaching the rDe'u-skor. But I shall preach it to you!" He then prepared a Tantric feast (gaṇa-

cakra), presented his request, and received the (teaching). He then discovered that it was not different from the former which he had obtained from the bLa-ma Vajrapāṇi. Later rLuṅ rDo-rje bla-ma went in search of these hidden precepts. He bestowed on him (the precept) that corresponded to about 150 pebbles, and which followed on former precepts. bLa-ma mṄa'-ris-pa for eight years acted as household priest of Bal-po ('Jig-rten). His disciple was Gru-śul-ba. mṄa'-ris-pa went to Gru-śul, but the elder (sthavira) did not admit him. While he was staying inside an empty enclosure, Gru-śul invited him inside, but he declined. When snow started to fall, he was again asked to come in, and entered (Gru-śul's house). On seeing the painting (thaṅ-ka) representing the Spiritual Lineage (of the Mahāmudrā doctrine), he inquired: "Have you faith in it?"—"Yes, I have", Gru-śul-ba replied. "Do you know their precepts?"—"I don't know", Gru-śul replied. "Well, I have them", and saying so mṄa'-ris-pa bestowed on him the complete precepts during 18 days. Gru-śul-ba presented to him five "žo" of gold "la-thub" (a sort of gold), and mṄa-ris-pa said: "I do not need it," and did not accept it. mṄa'-ris-pa said: "Next year you should come to Čhu-bo-ri on a certain date". Then having fixed the date, mṄa'-ris-pa departed. When the time came for him to return, Gru-śul-ba went to Čhu-bo-ri, and discovered that the Teacher had reached there five days earlier. (12a)
He (Gru-śul-ba) spent there one month and practised secret observances (gsaṅ-spyod), and nobody knew where he went, and where he died. The scholar Par-pu-ba bLo-gros seṅ-ge obtained from him the Mahāmudrā of the Cycle of the Dohā. He (Par-pu-ba) also composed eight text-books (yig-sna), such as the "Summary of the three sections of the Dohā", its commentary and a running commentary ('brel-'Jug), etc. These text-books spread throughout all quarters. His disciples were: sGyer-sgom čhen-po, Saṅs-rgyas dbon po, bla-ma Brag-'bur-ba, Śug-gseb ri-pa, the Dharmasvāmin bLa-ma Dam-pa, Mi-ñag Śes-rab bzaṅ-po, and the Dharmasvāmin

"Who did not descend from the mountain" (Čhos-rJe Ri-mi-'babs-pa) bSod-nams rin-čhen. The latter bestowed on me the Dohā according to the system of Par (Par-pu-ba). The Cycle of A-su became known as the "Lower" school (sMad-lugs) of the Mahāmudrā. Again, the "Later" translation (Phyi-'gyur): When Vajrapāṇi became old, Nag-po Śer-dad mÑa'-ris stayed with him in Eastern India, and obtained (from him) the Ten texts of the Mahāmudrā[2], the "large" and "lesser" recensions of the Dohā (Dohākośagīti, Tg. rGyud, No. 2224 Dohākośa-nāma-caryāgīti, Tg. rGyud No. 2263), the sKu'i mdzod 'čhi-med rdo-rJe (sKu'i mdzod 'čhi-med rdo-rJe'i glu, Kāyakoṣāmṛtavajragīti, Tg. rGyud No. 2269), the gSuṅ-gi mdzod 'Jam-dbyaṅs rdo-rJe (gSuṅ-gi mdzod 'Jam-dbyaṅs rdo-rJe'i glu, Vākkoṣarucirasvaravajragīti, Tg. rGyud, No. 2270), the Thugs-kyi mdzod skye-med rdo-rJe (Thugs-kyi mdzod skye-med rdo-rJe'i glu, Cittakoṣāja-vajragīti, Tg. rGyud, No. 2271), the sKu-gsuṅ-thugs yid-la mi-byed-pa'i mdzod (sKu-gsuṅ-thugs yid-la mi-byed-pa žes-bya-ba, Kāyavākcittamanasākāra-nāma, Tg.rGyud, No. 2272), the sGom-rim drug-pa (Bhāvanākramaṣaṭka-nāma, Tg. rGyud, 2299), the 'Čhi-kha-ma'i gdams-ṅag ('Phags-pa 'Da'-ka ye-śes žes-bya-ba theg-pa čhen-po'i mdo, Ārya-Ātajñāna-nāma-mahāyānasūtra, Kg.rGyud-'bum, No. 122), the rÑog-pa med-pa'i rgyud (rGyud-kyi rgyal-po rÑog-pa-med-pa žes-bya-ba, Anāvila-Tantrarāja, Kg. rGyud-'bum, No, 414 and its commentary Śrī-Anāvilanāma-tantrapañjikā, Tg. rGyud, No. 1204). He (Nag-po Śer dad) was the disciple of 'Gos lo-tsā-ba. Later he founded a monastery behind gŽuṅ-gru sna, and became an official at Lhaṅ-tsho. His death was caused by poison administered by the monks. bLa-ma So heard the hidden precepts from him, and sKor-čhuṅ-ba. He especially spent six years in the presence of Nag-po (Śer-dad). When So became old, he gave (these precepts) to Myaṅ-ston rtsags-se. The latter gave them to the bla-ma Rog-bde. The Lineage of

2 Phyag rgya čhen-po'i čhos-bču.

Teaching (bKa') of the Grub-sñiṅ, as well as that of the "Lesser" texts (26 A-ma-na-si), are not extant at present, but the Lineage of Authorization (luṅ) is as follows: Śa-ba-ra, Maitrī-pa, rGya-gar Phyag-na (Vajrapāṇi), Braṅ-ti, gTsaṅ Yaṅ-dog-'bar, Phyag-zuṅs-skyabs, rTsaṅs-'byuṅ-se, lČe-ston mDo-seṅ, the bla-ma sTon-Śāk, lČe bLo-ldan seṅ-ge, Kun-mkhyen 'Phags-'od, Bu-ston Rin-po-čhe, the lo-tsā-ba Rin-čhen rnam-rgyal, and thus to the Venerable Grags-pa rgyal-mtshan. From him I obtained the "Seven Sections of Grub-pa" (Grub-pa sde-bdun, Tg. rGyud, Nos. 2217-2223) only, the mūla and the commentary of the De-kho-na ñid-bču-pa (Tattvadaśaka-nāma, Tg. rGyud, No. 2232; Tattvadaśakaṭīkā, Tg. rGyud, No. 2254; See. B. Bhattacharyya: Advaya-vajrasaṃgraha, Gaekwad's Oriental Series, Vol. XL/ Baroda, 1927/p. 9). From the birth of rGya-gar Phyag-na (Vajrapāṇi, 1017 A.D.) to the year Fire-Male-Ape (Me-pho-spre'u—1476 A.D.) 460 years have elapsed.

The Book on the (doctrine) of the 'Great Seal' (Mahāmu-drā), handed down by the Jina Maitrī-pa. (13*a*)

BOOK XII.

The Early, Later and Intermediate (sṅa-phyi-bar-gsum) Lineages of Ži-byed (Ži-byed brgyud-pa sṅa-phyi-bar-gsum-gyi skabs).

The story (tshul) of the Lineage of the Holy Doctrine, called sDug-bsṅal Ži-byed. Why was it called "sDug-bsṅal Ži-byed?" Most of the secret precepts and instructions which reached Tibet, helped to protect disciples from sinful actions and purified the defilements of their Minds. This Doctrine brings a speedy alleviation of the sufferings of those who, by the influence of their former lives, are afflicted in body, tormented by diseases, poverty-stricken, tormented by devils, and enables them to practise Yoga—for this reason it was called sDug-bsṅal Ži-byed or the "Alleviator of Sufferings". It was also so named after the "Mantra which alleviates all sufferings" uttered by the Buddha (sDug bsṅal thams-čad rab-tu ži-bar byed-pa'i sṅags, Bhagavatīprañāpāramitā-hṛdaya, mDo-maṅs, vol. I, Śer-sñiṅ, fol. 375. Lalou, "Catalogue du Fonds Tibétain de la Bibliothèque Nationale", p. 40, No. 101). The Master of this Doctrine: Dam-pa Saṅs-rgyas. He was a great master of spiritual realization (siddheśvara), and endowed with countless perfections. Out of the Four Attractions (bsDu-ba'i dṅos-po-bži), mentioned in the Scriptures as methods of leading disciples by a Teacher (sbyin-pa, sñan-pa, don-dpyod and don-'thun), the don-dpyod was the method of preaching by which a teacher guided his disciples on the Path. The fourth "Attraction" (don-'thun-pa) meant that the teacher himself followed the Path, shown to the disciple. Thus Dam-pa (Saṅs-rgyas), when guiding disciples, used to lead them in three stages: (1) ordained with the help of the three vows, (2) the Path of penance, and (3) results beneficial to others. Therefore it is necessary

to state the manner in which Dam-pa had himself passed through these stages. Now the native country of Dam-pa: he was born as a son of a father named brTson-'grus go-čha (Vīryavarman), who belonged to the caste of jewel merchants (nor-bu rin-po-čhe'i len-pa'i rigs-čan), and mother named Ba-ra-sa-ha, who belonged to the caste of incense-makers, and was expert in the offerings to the Jewel (Ratna), in a place where dwelt numerous devotees, in a district called Khron-pa'i glin (Kūpadvīpa) in the province of Carasiṃha in the (1a)
country of Be-ba-la in Southern India. He was born with all his teeth out. When he was taken for examination to a brāhmaṇa astrologer, the latter made the following prophecy: "This boy may become either a paṇḍita, or a yogin. In any case he will be endowed with excellent faculties, such as prescience. Being a 'seven-born' (skye-ba bdun-pa), he will be free from sins, and will be by nature attracted to virtuous deeds." In his childhood he mastered all the sciences, such as the science of Grammar and other branches of knowledge. This was a perfection (developed) through his extraordinary nature (gotra). Later he was ordained by the upādhyāya Kṣemadeva (dGe-ba'i lha), and became learned in the Vinaya of the Holy Doctrine, and excellent (in the observance) of the Pratimokṣa vows. An extraordinary Mental Creative Effort towards Enlightenment was produced in him by his guru gSer-glin-pa (Dharmakīrti), and his observance of vows became similar to a great surging wave. He obtained initiations into maṇḍalas from numerous teachers. He possessed the perfect vows and precepts of a Vidyādhara (a Tantric vow). This was the perfection of his personality (rten), observing the three vows (rten-sdom-pa gsum), i.e. the manner in which Dam-pa passed through the first stage. After that he obtained the profound precepts from 54 siddhas, males and females. His eleven Teachers in the field of Sūtras and Grammar were: kLu-grub (Nāgārjuna), Prajñābhadra (Śes-rab bzan-po), Guṇaprabha (Yon-tan-'od), Dharmakīrti (Čhos-grags), Ākarasiddhi, Śaṅkara, Jñānagarbha (Ye-śes

sñiṅ-po), Asaṅga (Thogs-med), Āryadeva, Śāntideva (Źi-ba-lha), and the guru gSer-gliṅ-pa (Dharmakīrti). His eleven gurus who taught him the Tantras belonging to the "Father" class (Pha-rgyud gyo-ba-rluṅ), and the yogic exercises of breathing were: Vāgīśvara (Ṅag-gi dbaṅ-phyug), Buddha-gupta, Go-dha-rī, Karmavajra, Dza-ba-ri-pa (Javari), Jñānapāda (Ye-śes-žabs), kLu byaṅ (Nāgabodhi), Ānanda, Kṛṣṇapāda (Kṛṣṇa-pa), Vasudharin, and Padmavajra. His eleven gurus, who taught him the Tantras belonging to the "Mother" class (Ma-rgyud), and the experience of Beautitude (bDe-ba ñams) were: Anaṅgavajra Saroruha (mTsho-skyes rdo-rje), Indrabhūti, Ḍombhī-pa, Vajraghaṇṭa (rDo-rje dril-bu-pa), Tillipa, Kṛṣṇapāda (Nag-po'i žabs), Līlāvajra (sGeg-pa rdo-rje), Lū-yi-pa, Vi-rū-pa, Ānandagarbha (Kun-dga' sñiṅ-po), and Ku-ku-ri-pa. His eleven gurus who taught him the symbol of the Mahāmudrā were: Saraha, Caryā-pa, Gu-ṇa-ri, Koṭali (Tog-tse-pa), Ko-śa-pa, Śa-ba-ri-pa, Maitrī-pa, Sāgara- (2a)
siddhi, Ravigupta (Ñi-ma sbas-pa), Ākarasiddhi, and Ratnavajra. His ten gurus who introduced him to his own Mind were (rig-pa ṅo-sprod-pa): Śabari (Ri-khrod-ma), Dri-med-ma (Vimalā), Padmapādā (Pad-mo-žabs), Ku-mu-ḍā, Sukhākarā (bDe-ba'i 'byuṅ-gnas), Gaṅgabhadrī (Gaṅga bzaṅ-mo), Tsi-to-ma (Cintā), Lakṣmī, (Vṛkṣa) parṇī (Śiṅ-lo-ma), and Sukhasiddhī. Having obtained from the above all the Sūtras (Phyi-mtshan-ñid) of the "Outer" Doctrine and all the hidden precepts of the "Father" and "Mother" classes of the "Inner" Doctrine, he practised meditation. He recited the name of his Teacher at Śeṅ-ge-rdzoṅ, and an impartial understanding shone in him. For six years he practised meditation at Eastern Seṅ-ge-rdzoṅ, for 15 years at Vajrāsana, for four years at the Svayambhū-caitya (Raṅ-byuṅ mčhod-rten), for five years at the Mount Ku-ru-ku-lla, for five years on the banks of the Ganges, for five years in the jungles of Eastern India, for five years at the cemeteries of Southern India, for seven years at the cemetery of Śītavana (bSil-ba'i tshal), again for three years at Vajrāsana, and for ten years in the country of Ābhīra

(mṄon-par dga'-ba's yul). He had innumerable visions of tutelary deities, such as the twelve tutelary deities: Mañjughoṣa, Avalokiteśvara, Vajradhara (rDo-rje-'dzin), Tārā Khasarpaṇa (a form of Avalokiteśvara represented as Śiva), Yamāntaka, Raṅ-byuṅ rgyal-mo (name of Ekajaṭī), Sarvanīvaraṇa-viśkambhī (rGrib-sel), 'Od-zer-čan (Marīci), Samantabhadra (Kun-bzaṅs), Vārahī, and Acala. Further, Vairocana (rNam-par snaṅ-mdzad), Hayagrīva (rTa-mgrin), Saṃvara, Hevajra, and other deities. He had also visions of innumerable mantradharas, such as the 36 gurus belonging to the Heavenly abode of ḍākinīs (khecara, mkha'-spyod) and others. Among the ordinary siddhis, he obtained the eye medicine (añjana, mig-sman), applying which one could see treasures underground, the medicine which enabled one to cover the distance of 100 yojanas daily (rkaṅ-mgyogs), magic pills (ril-bu, gulikā), the faculty of passing through earth (sa-'og), the power of employing a yakṣī as one's servant (gnod-'byin-mo), a tongue of a vetāla (ro-laṅs) transformed into a dagger (ral-gri) which enables one to fly through space, moving through sky (mkha'-spyod, Khecara). In respect of the Sublime Realization (mčhog-gi dṅos-grub) he obtained the darśana-mārga or the Path of Illumination (mthoṅ-lam) and the knowledge of the Mahāmudrā (Mahāmudrā-jñāna).

(His) results which were beneficial to others: he performed Tantric rites in all the localities of the 24 countries, etc. Famed as one possessed of spiritual realization, he was known by different names.

Now the manner of his labours for the benefit of others in Tibet: in all he visited Tibet on five occasions. The (2b) first (visit): He journeyed to Tsa-ri via 'Brin-thaṅ and requested the goddess Rematī (to grant) him the power of covering great distances (rkaṅ-mgyogs). Having penetrated as far as sKoṅ-yul and Sum-yul, there was no district in the three regions of sMad (Lower) Khams, which he did not tread with his feet. Though at that time there was no receptacle which he could fill with his teaching, he prophesied that in future times in these localities the Doctrine would spread. The second (visit): having left Kāśmīra, he proceeded towards mṄa'-ris and bestowed several precepts on Žaṅ-žuṅ-gliṅ-kha-pa and on the Bon-po Khra-tshar 'brug-bla.

The third (visit): When he was coming from Nepāl, having befriended some merchants, he met rMaṅ-ra ser-po of Yar-kluṅs. The latter accompanied him, and in gTsaṅ he bestowed many hidden precepts of gČod on sKyo bSod-nams bla-ma and rMaṅ-ra ser-po. The fourth (visit): Having reached Śa-'ug stag-sgo, he stayed at gÑal. He purified the moral defilements of his mother. Later having gone to dbUs, he laboured for the benefit of rMa, So and others. The fifth (visit): He proceeded to China and spent 12 years there. Then again he returned to Diṅ-ri. Once Kun-dga asked him about the number of disciples initiated by Dam-pa in Tibet and who had scattered throughout the country, saying: "How many disciples have you had in Tibet to whom you have given precepts?" Dam-pa replied: "Are you able to count the stars in Heaven above the plain of Diṅ-ri?" (He said so,) because the sky over Diṅ-ri is wide and it is difficult to count the stars on it. These disciples had scattered, and therefore were unable to continue the Lineage. It is difficult for people to know about them. Thus, because he possessed innumerable disciples, he must have had also numerous hidden precepts. (His) famous Lineages are the "Early", the "Intermediate" and the "Later." Now the first Lineage: the doctrine (of this Lineage) was represented by the sādhana of Yamāntaka and the three Cycles of Ži-byed sGrol-ma which were preached by Dam-pa to the Kashmirian Jñānaguhya. They were taught by Dam-pa and Jñānaguhya to Oṅ-po lo-tsā-ba. The latter taught them to Lo-btsun-čhuṅ and bLa-čhuṅ 'od-zer. Now Lo-btsun-čhuṅ: he proceeded to (3a)
India to practise meditation and did not return. bLa-čhuṅ 'od-zer taught (the doctrine) to 'Čhus-pa Dar-brtson. The latter to 'Čhus-pa brtson-seṅ. The latter (taught it) to Rog Śe-srab-'od. Again the Kashmirian Jñānaguhya taught it to sPu-

hraṅs lo-čhuṅ. The latter to dMar-ston Čhos-rgyal. The latter to the kalyāṇa-mitṭa Yol-mo. The latter to gŚen-ston Nam-mkha'. The latter to Kyi-tshaṅ Žig-po. The latter to Rog Śes-rab-'od. The system of Oṅ-po lo-tsā-ba had no sādhanas. The Chapter about the first Lineage.

The "Intermediate" Lineage: The chief precepts were those of rMa, So and sKam, the three, as well as the "lesser" precepts. For three years Dam-pa served on the monastic congregation at sÑed-gro of gÑal, and then proceeded to Čhos-sgro. On his way to Yar-stod, he met gÑags lo-tsā-ba and bestowed on him (the sādhana) of Saṃvara-ekavīra (bDe-mčhog dpa'-bo-gčig). Said Dam-pa to Khu lo-tsā-ba: "Your (Tantric) vows have been defiled", and did not admit him (into his presence). After that he met rMa. This Dam-pa rMa was born in the year Wood-Female-Sheep (śiṅ-mo-lug—1055 A.D.) as son of one named rMa sMon-lam at sKyer-sna of Yar-stod. This Wood-Sheep year (Śiṅ-lug—1055) follows on the year of the passing of Atīśa, during which Pu-to-ba had reached the age of 13. rMa was ordained in his youth, and was given the name of Čhos-kyi Śes-rab. He obtained from his father the Pad-ma dbaṅ-čhen (a rÑiṅ-ma-pa form of Hayagrīva). Then he studied the "Domain of Practice" (sPyod-phyogs), the Mādhyamaka system, the Dohā according to the "Upper" school, and the Grub-sñiṅ (the Cycle of Dohā). At the age of 19, in the year Water-Female-Ox (čhu-mo-glaṅ—1073 A.D.) he met Dam-pa. When bla-ma rMa, having fallen ill, was living in the upper storey of his own house, he once saw a black a-tsa-ra (<ācārya) carrying a single garment on his shoulder. The fierce dogs (of the house) did not bark at him, but circled round him waging their tails. rMa was surprised, and sent a servant to have a look at (the stranger). The servant came back and said that there was an a-tsa-ra (ācārya). rMa then (3b) understood that the a-tsa-ra was an extraordinary man. Then he invited him inside, and the a-tsa-ra entered without being shown the door. rMa then asked for the a-tsa-ra's blessing, and as soon as the a-tsa-ra had blessed him, his illness disappeared. rMa then asked the a-tsa-ra to bestow a secret precept on him. The a-tsa-ra said: "I shall bestow precepts on you because of a karmic link (las-'brel) (between us) which has lasted through many rebirths." Then the a-tsa-ra asked him: "What Doctrine do you know?" rMa replied: "I know the Tantras of the 'Father' class (Pha-rgyud) and the Mahāmudrā". The a-tsa-ra said: "Yours is the Mahāmudrā of Words, but now I shall expound (to you) the Mahāmudrā of Meaning". He then introduced him to the basic doctrine (mūla), basing himself on such words as "the stage in which the eyes remain open and the mental (flow) ceases, in which breath is stopped. This can be obtained with the help of a holy teacher (dpal-ldan bla-ma)" (the stage referred to in the above śloka represents the stage when iḍā and piṅgalā/vital breaths/ sink into the ava-dhūti, and the yogin is said to be able to contemplate the Absolute, i. e. the Mahāmudrā. See M. Shahidullah: "Textes pour l'Etude du Bouddhisme tardif" (Paris, 1928), p. 150: mig-ni mi-'dzums sems-'gog-daṅ/rluṅ-'gog-pa-ni dpal-ldan bla-mas rtogs/). A special experience was born in rMa. Then, after the lapse of 18 days, Dam-pa said: "Now I shall be going!" rMa begged him to stay on, but Dam-pa did not agree. He tried to follow after Dam-pa, but the Teacher forbade him to come along. rMa then said: "In any case you will keep me in your grace", and Dam-pa replied: "This time you must go back, but next winter you may come to 'Phan-yul". rMa practised meditation and his faith grew stronger. In the winter, having taken So-čhuṅ-pa as his servant, he journeyed towards 'Phan-yul. At Byen-yul he was able to clear his doubts regarding the precepts at the feet of Dam-pa, who bestowed on him instruction with the help of "pebbles" (rde'u) arranged in 64 ways. rMa spent three months at the residence of Dam-pa. At that time he met A-su who was staying at rLuṅ-śod. Then rMa returned to his native place, and gave up his servants and property, and became a devotee (sādhaka). He spent one year at the cave of rMa. After that he proceeded to mTsho-rdzoṅ of Koṅ-po Brag-gsum, and spent nine years there. When a great internal feud afflicted the locality, the local deity advised him to mediate in the matter (gña'-mdzad-pa). He said: "I wouldn't be able". But the local deity told him: "I shall help you". rMa had faith in the deity's words, and went towards the place where fighting was taking place. When people resumed fighting, he spread his religious robe between the two contending parties and exclaimed: "Here I shall meditate! Whosoever will disobey, may the nine (4a) kinds of misfortunes fall on him," and saying so, he went off. Wherever he went, he was followed by a great black whirl-wind. The soldiers having become helpless by (the storm) ceased fighting. He then thought: "Now I shall be able to help living beings!" He gathered numerous followers at Dags-po rdzoṅs-kha and proceeded towards Yar-kluṅs. rMa spent three years at Kyi-tshaṅ. Then having gathered numerous disciples, he stayed wherever he was asked to preach the Doctrine. He had five great "Sons" (disciples): Gaṅ-par-gśen, Śud-phu lo-tsā-ba, bla-ma Śe'u, Sog-po mDo-sde, and Žaṅ dGa'-ldan-pa.

Here Sog-po mDo-sde: (He was) a native of Śo-skyam. The eldest of the three brothers was Lha-rJe Sog-sman. The middle one was Sog-po mDo-sde. He was an expert in both medicine and religion. Being a disciple of the father of Dam-pa rMa, he went to attend on Ma-sgom, who was staying at the cave of sKyer-sna. rMa told him: "Having met a siddha from India, I was benefitted by it, otherwise 'on the bed of a great scholar, the corpse of an ordinary human being will be found'".[1] He then asked the siddha to tell him the story of his meeting with (him). He felt faith born in him and asked for hidden precepts. rMa said that "because he had been a former disciple of his, he had to

1 i.e. he would die as an ordinary human being ignorant of religion.

bestow precepts on him." rMa introduced him to the exposition, and bestowed on him the complete hidden precepts. Sog-po also felt faith born in himself, and having abandoned all worldly occupations, became a devotee (sādhaka). Later rMa left Dags-po, and Sog-po went to Yar-mda (Lower Yas-kluṅs) to pay his homage to rMa. He then asked rMa: "O Teacher! What sort of Doctrine have you preached?" rMa replied: "I have preached the way of the Cittotpāda, called the sToṅ-mthun kha-dor mthar-rgyas (Summary, miscellany, extensive)". He thought that rMa must have possessed doctrines which he did not bestow, and therefore made his request. rMa replied: "I have given you the teachings of the Indian Dam-pa without adding or omitting even a single word. This present exposition which I am preaching consists of a few parts of the Teaching of Dam-pa and I have given them separate names, according to country and individuals." Sog-po mDo-sde while residing at bTsan-thaṅ met (4b)
a man, aged 19, who obtained from him the complete hidden precepts. Rog Śes-rab-'od obtained them from that man. Again rMa' disciple Žaṅ dGa'-ldan-pa: (he belonged to the clan) of mČhims-žaṅ, and was born at gTsaṅ-žal of Yar-stod. He obtained the Mahāmudrā doctrine from Dam-pa sKor Ni-rū-pa, as well as the four initiations. Then he followed after rMa to rGyas-sman sTag-rtse. He bestowed spiritual guidance in the Juniper forest of sṄon-čhuṅ-gnas of Byar, and removed doubts from his mind. Among his disciples were: gÑal-ston dGa'-čhuṅ-'bar, sKyog sGom-pa-gtan, Khu-sgom Jo-dga', rGya-dar-seṅ, and 'Čhus-pa Dar-brtson. rGya-dar seṅ-ge: he was born as son of rGya-lon Čhos-'bar at Gra-phyi-phu. At the age of 30, an arrow struck his leg, and he proceeded to the hot springs of Čhu-tshan-kha, and there met Ras-pa Kha-kyog rDo-rJe seṅ-ge, and obtained from him the Mahāmudrā. While Žaṅ was residing at sMan-mo, he obtained precepts from him, and became a yogin endowed with a heavenly understanding. His great "sons" were: Dol-pa dBaṅ-rgyal and Śes-rab me-čhuṅ, called the "Two Jo-sras-spun of sTod."

Žaṅ-ston J̌o-spu and the bla-ma sLob-čhuṅ-ba were called the "Two brothers of gÑags-tsha" in sMad. His Lineage was continued by sMyon-čhuṅ of rGya in the Middle Region (Bar). The latter was born in Lower rGyal (rGya-smad) in Čhu-bo-ri-khra-sna. His name was rGya-tsha-'bar. At the age of 24, he met Gri-khu gdoṅ-pa, who had come to Čhu-bo-ri to meditate, and became his disciple. rGya-smyon taught the doctrine of this Lineage. Three ḍākinīs introduced him to his own Mind, and an understanding, which did not differ from experience, was produced in his Mind. He was given the name of sMyon-pa Don-ldan. He taught (the Doctrine) to Ri-khrod-pa. Again Khu-sgom J̌o-dga', who dwelt in the valley of kLu-mda'-tshe, had numerous disciples. He taught it to rGyal-ba dKon-mčhog-skyabs of sTod-luṅ gŽoṅ-pa-steṅ. The latter preached the doctrine to Rog Śes-rab-'od.

Śes-rab-'od obtained at that place the understanding of the Mahāmudrā. Again Žaṅ-btsun rGyal-ba bKra-śis taught (5a)
it to 'Čhus-pa Dar-brtson. The latter taught it to 'Čhus-pa brtson-seṅ. The latter taught it to Rog Śes-rab-'od. Now there have been two Lineages in the school of rMa: that of the Word, and that of the Meaning. The exposition of the Meaning (don-khrid) included 16 lag-khrid or practical guides. The Lineage of the Word contained the cittotpāda, a summary (stoṅ-thun), a miscellany (kha-'thor), that "which hits the mouth and the nose" (khar-phog snar-phog), meaning criticism of the point of view of others, and the "extensive" (exposition, mthar-rgyas). The Chapter on the school of rMa.

The School of So: When a great famine took place in that region, a family of natives of Ra-mo came to beg for food. There were two brothers. The elder brother, because of his small stature, was called So-chuṅ-ba (So, "the Little One"). The younger being tall was called So-riṅs, or "So, the Tall One". So-čhuṅ-ba (So-čhuṅ dGe-'dun-'bar, also called Dam-pa So) was born in the year Water-Male-Tiger (čhu-pho-stag—1062 A.D.). When he was about ten, they went to Yar-stod sKyer-sna on a begging round. rMa-sgom said to them: "Let this elder boy follow me! I shall give him food and clothing". So they left him with (rMa-sgom). The family proceeded to Yar-kluṅs. There rMa-sgom ordained So, and gave him the name of dGe-'dun-'bar. At the age of 11, he saw for a brief moment the face of Dam-pa, who had come to meet rMa. Some years after Dam-pa's departure, rMa-sgom felt slightly indisposed, and thought of following after Dam-pa. Having taken So-čhuṅ-ba with him, he proceeded there. When the two were staying in the lower valley of Rag-ma, and Dam-pa was staying at Bye-khud of 'Phan-yul, So-čhuṅ-ba happened to visit that place (on a begging round). Dam-pa also came there. From the distance of three fields, Dam-pa shouted: "O! how happy I am! My boy (tsi-lu) has come here!" and he ran towards So-čhuṅ-ba. Grasping the hand of So-čhuṅ-ba, he said: "You have been my disciple during three rebirths! Now you must follow after me!" and saying so took him to Bye-khud. There after a mere introduction to his own Mind (ṅo-sprod means to introduce one to his own Mind. In ancient Tibet religious instructions always began with the introduction of the disciple to his own Mind, that is, explaining to the disciple the nature of his Mind) (his understanding) became similar to Dawn. So-čhuṅ-ba thus obtained a great and immaculate understanding. After his return there, rMa and he, the disciple, were once grinding corn, and So-čhuṅ-ba having left the handle of the grinding stone, remained staring for a considerable time. rMa said to him: "What has happened to you? Did Dam-pa bestow precepts on you?" rMa thought that Dam-pa must have given him (the precepts). Then the Teacher (rMa) and disciple (So-čhuṅ-ba) proceeded to the residence of Dam-pa, and Dam-pa bestowed again several hidden precepts on rMa, who said: "Now we, Teacher and disciple, should return to (our) native place." But So-čhuṅ-ba replied: "I shall ask Dam-pa for one hidden precept." rMa said to him: "The precept can be given by me. You had better return." Then So-čhuṅ-ba replied: "You, Teacher, should

(5b)

go first. I shall follow after you in about a month's time." So-čhuṅ-ba did not go. Then Dam-pa bestowed on him the complete precepts of the Lineage of Meaning (don-brgyud). He attended on Dam-pa wherever the latter went, and Dam-pa bestowed on him the hidden precepts of the 54 male and female siddhas. He asked (Dam-pa's) permission to commit these to writing, and on receiving the latter's permission, wrote them down on the margins of a Prajñāpāramitā ('Bum) which belonged to dTar-kha rDo-rJe-grags. Then he attended on Dam-pa during the latter's journeys, and, when they had reached Kha-rag, Dam-pa said to him: "You must return!" and he replied: "I shall serve on you wherever you go!" Dam-pa said: "You won't be able to follow after me!" and Dam-pa disappeared within a moment. This was the time of Dam-pa's going to China. So-čhuṅ-ba returned. In order to test the power of his Mind (rig-pa'i tshad lta-ba, to test one's own mind), he meditated on the tongue of a bell at the J̌o-khaṅ of Lha-sa, and the bell began to ring by itself. He conducted many similar tests (tshad-lta). He then proceeded to Yar-kluṅs, and thinking that he should present the precepts to rMa, went to rMa's residence at dbU-ra. He said to him: "Now this Mind of mine is not hindered by anything." rMa replied mockingly: "You would do better to feed your parents who are begging." So-čhuṅ-ba (6*a*)
obtained a clear vision of the demons and various ailments which were afflicting sick men, and performed many rites of subduing demons ('dre-'dul). He collected large fees (for these rites) and thus acquired much property with which he bought some landed property at Yar-mda' (Lower Yar-kluṅs), and settled his parents and brother on it. Again at sÑon-čhuṅ of Byar he married his brother So-riṅs-pa, and kept the other at Yar-mda'. He entrusted the book containing the precepts of the 54 male and female siddhas to (his mother) Śud-mo Śāk-sgron, but she damaged the book, and in this manner (the precepts) of eight Lineages were lost. Others were then discovered giving minute details, probably written down

by So-čhuṅ-ba himself. Later 'Čhus-pa Dar-brtson put them into verse and called them the "Three Holy Persons—the Senior, the Middle One and the Junior (Dam-pa skyes-mčhog čhe-'briṅ-čhuṅ-gsum)." So-čhuṅ-ba having heard that Dam-pa was residing at Diṅ-ri, took with him three golden sraṅs, and a good horse, which he had received for curing an invalid, and went to Diṅ-ri. (He found) Dam-pa amidst a crowd, and he threw the three golden sraṅs on the lap of Dam-pa. Then overpowered by joy, he jumped on the lap of Dam-pa and pulled out one of the latter's hairs. People shouted: "Beat him! Beat him!", but Dam-pa said: "Don't beat him! He possesses a good protector (meaning So-čhuṅ-ba was protected by many dharmapālas)." The gold was snatched away by a woman, some said that it was taken away by Sukhasiddhī as payment for a Tantric feast (gaṇacakra) to be held by ḍākinīs. Then (So-čhuṅ-ba) raising himself from the lap of Dam-pa, sang a song, and all present recognized in him a siddha. At that time Dam-pa bestowed on him the 51 precepts removing doubts (mtha'-sel lṅa-bču-rtsa-gčig). After that he journeyed to dbUs. On one occasion Dam-pa was asked about his successor, and said: "If So-čhuṅ-ba were to take it over, (in this country) quartz (dkar-goṅ) would change into butter, bricks into meat, and artemisia (mkhan-pa) into barley, but he feels attached to a piece of dog's (6b)
excrement, and won't stay here." The story of the meeting of the hermit (sgom-čhen) sMon-lam-'bar with So-čhuṅ-ba: This Śa-mi belonged to the clan of Śa-mi. He was born in the valley of upper Guṅ-thaṅ mgon-po in the year Wood-Female-Ox (śiṅ-mo-glaṅ—1085 A. D.). He obtained precepts from sKor Ni-rū-pa who had come to rGya-sman, and a slight (a-to) concentration was produced in him. So-čhuṅ-ba also came there, and met him. So-čhuṅ-ba said: "This meditation of yours is similar to a lump covered by snow! I don't know whether this is a lump of earth, or a stone. But I possess a genuine precept of Dam-pa Saṅs-rgyas. Will you follow me?" Śa-mi said;

"I am ready to go." Thus he attended on So-čhuṅ-ba while the latter was wandering through gÑal and other districts, and carried on his back the presents received by So-čhuṅ-ba. He attended on him for a considerable time, but did not get precepts. On one occasion when the Teacher and disciple were journeying from 'Phan-yul, the Teacher having filled an empty packet of brown sugar with stones, loaded it on Śa-mi, saying: "This brown sugar should be eaten by us, Teacher and disciple, after reaching sTod-luṅs from this place". He carried it and felt tired. So-čhuṅ-ba asked him: "Aren't you tired?" He replied that he was. So-čhuṅ-ba then said: "Well, I shall rest", and saying so, So-čhuṅ-ba sat down cross-legged on a meadow. He felt slightly relieved. When they had reached the summit of the Pass, So-čhuṅ-ba said: "This will be of no use", and he threw away all the stones (contained in the packet). Then, when the Teacher and disciple were staying in the house of a native of sTod-luṅs, Śa-mi thought in the evening that this man had surely no precepts, and that he should go to another teacher. About midnight another thought came to him: "Sometimes this man seems to know some of my thoughts, so perhaps he possesses some precepts."

At dawn Śa-mi decided that he would attend on him, and would see whether he would give him precepts. In the
morning So-čhuṅ-ba said: "O sMon-lam-'bar, your thought (7a)
in the evening was of no use, but that of mid-night was better, and that of Dawn was right". So he remained with So-čhuṅ-ba. On one occasion So-čhuṅ-ba having eaten his food privately, said to Śa-mi: "This morning a man is offering food to the Teacher and disciple. Let us proceed there!" When they had reached the door, (the Teacher said): "This isn't the house", and (going further) the Teacher again said: "This isn't the house," so that the whole day was spent by Śa-mi without food. Going back Śa-mi felt angry. Again on one occasion, when Śa-mi had come back from work on behalf of So-čhuṅ-ba, he (found) a stranger with So-čhuṅ-ba.

(Śa-mi heard) So-čhuṅ-ba telling (that man) in a low voice: "sMon-lam-'bar has come! Hide your things, he might steal them!" Śa-mi thought to himself: "I have been attending on him for such a long time, and have acted honestly, and still he says such things about me!" A violent anger rose in him, and taking out his dagger he dashed towards So-čhuṅ-ba. So-čhuṅ-ba escaped to the store-room and locked the door (behind him). When Śa-mi had come against the door, So-čhuṅ-ba said from inside: "O sMon-lam-'bar! Your Mind is now filled with anger. Look at it!" sMon-lam-'bar had a look at his own Mind, and a pure understanding of the unveiled nature of the Mind was produced in him. Great was his joy, and grasping with both hands the flaps of his coat, he began to dance and sing: "O you Merciful One (So-čhuṅ-ba)! Ya'i!

O you skilful in method! Ya'i!

O you wise one! Ya'i!"

So-čhuṅ-ba then opened the door, and came out saying: "Formerly I attemped to provoke your anger by various means, but the anger did not grow strong." Then he bestowed on him the complete hidden precepts. He followed on So-čhuṅ-ba till the latter's death in the year Earth-Ape (sa-spre—1128 A.D.) at the age of 67. He thus served on him for 34 years without interruption (bar-med). He then built himself a hut (7b) at bZaṅ-groṅ tshugs-kha, and made his bed on the roof (of the hut). Inside the hut he placed goats. He spent his time merely gathering cowdung and playing with children throwing stones, but because of his great inner perfection, his fame became great. He passed away at the age of 87 in the year Iron-Hare (lčags-yos—1171 A.D.). Though I had seen the life-stories (rnam-thar) of his three disciples 'Čhus-pa Dar-brtson, Mel-ka-ba-čan-pa and mThiṅ-gaṅ-ba Ser-tshul, I did not see the "Life-stories" of the others, such as Lug-ro Žig-po and others. When Śa-mi was residing in the lower part of Tod-luṅs, 'Čhus-pa Dar-brtson came to ask him for secret precepts. He sent in word that he had come to ask for precepts, but the Teacher did not even permit him to enter inside. 'Čhus-pa stayed for several days in the vicinity of (Śa-mi's) house and patiently waited (for a chance to meet the Teacher). Once an alms-giver came to invite Śa-mi to attend a religious festival (čhos-ston) in the company of several kalyāṇa-mitras. Śa-mi said: "I shall not go. The ācārya Tiṅ-'dzin will be coming, and will get angry (at seeing me there)", but his wife said: "You should accept the invitation. If you were to take the monk who stayed outside our house, he might be a match for him (meaning Tiṅ-'dzin)." "Well," said (Śa-mi), "ask him!" She then said to 'Čhus-pa: "If you were to go as attendant of the Teacher to-day, would you be able to contest with an ācārya named Tiṅ-'dzin?"—"It can be done," replied Śa-mi. Then the Teacher and disciple started on their journey, and reached the alms-giver's house. Soon after the ācārya Tiṅ-'dzin also came there accompanied by about five disciples. Tiṅ-'dzin said: "O sMon-lam-'bar has also come here! (Imagine) a man like him at the head of the assembly row". 'Čhus-pa said: "His (my Teacher's) constructive thoughts (Vikalpa) have been destroyed, (therefore) my Teacher will not deliver a discourse on the Doctrine. (Instead) I shall try to give a fairly pleasant discourse on religion". Tiṅ-'dzin said: "Let us have it! I am in the habit of not asking questions from others. You put questions to me". 'Čhus-pa having mastered previously the "Six Treatises of the Mādhyamaka system", put him the following question: "Well, according to the Mādhyamaka doctrine (i.e. the Prasannapadā) there cannot exist a common ground for discussion (between) those who have understood the real nature of the Mādhyamaka (i.e. the notion of Śūnyatā), and those who did not understand it. What is (the meaning) of this (rule)?" (In the first chapter of the Prasannapadā, Candrakīrti explained this absence of common ground in a discussion with the ācārya Bhāvaviveka. According to Bhāvaviveka there must exist a common ground, but Candrakīrti rejected this point of view. This was the main point of disagreement between the Svātantrikas and the Prāsaṅgikas. Tsoṅ-kha-pa stated that this rule was the most difficult of all to understand. Lam-rim čhen-po, fol. 289a). Tiṅ-'dzin was unable to reply anything. sGom-smon (Śa-mi) then suddenly rose from his seat and shouted: "You take it! You eat it!" and danced about. At this moment the alms-giver came in; and seizing 'Čhus-pa by the collar, he shouted: "This wretched monk has caused a quarrel between my two teachers. I shall drive him out. sGom-smon (Śa-mi) said: "You have admitted his five disciples, and if you will not keep my only disciple, I shall also be going". The alms-giver then said: "Well then, stay on!" After finishing the religious festival, they started on their return journey, and sGom-smon told 'Čhus-pa: "Your discourse pleased me more than the offering of a full measure ('bre) of gold-sand. I shall bestow precepts on you", and saying so he took him inside his house. For many days they slept keeping their heads together, and carried on extensive religious discussions. Śa-mi bestowed on him the complete secret precepts. 'Čhus-pa taught (the Doctrine) to his own son 'Čhus-pa brTson-'grus seṅ-ge. The latter taught it to the great scholar Rog Śes-rab-'od. Again So-čhuṅ-ba taught it to his younger brother (So-sku-riṅs). The latter taught it to the bla-ma sPaṅ of Byar. The latter taught it to 'Čhus-pa, father and son. Again So(-čhuṅ-ba) taught it to Śa-mi. The latter to the kalayāṇa-mitra lDe'u. The latter taught it to rGyal-ba dKon-skyabs, who taught it to Rog. Again, Śa-mi taught it to mThiṅ-gaṅ-pa. The latter taught it to sPaṅ bzaṅs-pa Ba-ri sgom-čhen. The latter taught it to 'Phraṅ-kha J̌o-btsun. Though I was unable to establish the dates (lo-graṅs) of these three, (it is known) that Śa-mi had passed away in the year Iron-Hare (lčags-yos—1171 A.D.) at the age of 87. The first three years from the year Water-Dragon (čhu-'brug—1172 A.D.) to the year Water-Male-Horse (čhu-pho-rta—1222 A.D.) seem to have been the time of these three Teachers.

Now, the Dharmasvāmin of gÑan-po—'Byuṅ-gnas ye-śes was born in the year Earth-Male-Horse (sa-pho-rta—1198 A.D.) and lived for 67 years, till the year Wood-Male-Mouse (śiṅ-pho-byi-ba—1264 A.D.). Saṅs-rgyas sgom-pa Byaṅ-čhub rdo-rJe was born in the year Fire-Male-Mouse (me-pho- (8b)
byi-ba—1216 A.D.) and lived for 66 years, till the year Iron-Female-Serpent (lčags-mo-sbrul—1281 A.D.). Now the Dharmasvāmin of rGya-brag—Ye-śes-gžon-nu: he was born in the Fire-Female-Serpent (me-mo-sbrul—1257 A.D.) and died at the age of 71 in the year Fire-Female-Hare (me-mo-yos—1327 A.D.). The puruṣottama (skyes-mčhog) bSam-gtan dpal-pa was born at Yar-'brog bran-mda' in the year Iron-Hare (lčags-yos—1291 A.D.) and lived for 76 years, till the Fire-Male-Horse (me-pho-rta—1366 A.D.). Having been ordained, while he was staying among the inmates of Jo-stan tshogs-čhen-mo, he went on one occasion as attendant of the mahā-upādhyāya Čhos-kyi rgyal-mtshan-pa. The mahā-upādhyāya died, having fallen from his horse. He felt great sadness, and having gone away, he associated himself with the upādhyāya gŽon-rin, and visited the rGya-brag Dharmasvāmin Ye-śes gžon-nu, who was residing in the upper part (phu) of Lan-pa in 'Phan-yul. As soon as they had reached the lower part of this valley, he felt the wonderful scent of morality (pervading it). He asked: "Friend gŽon-rin, do you feel it?", and the latter replied: "I don't feel it, but it is probably the scent of the rose-bushes".

As soon as he saw the face (of Ye-śes gžon-nu), a great devotion was born in him. After that he received an introduction into the teaching of the "Lineage of Meaning" (don-brgyud). Soon after an excellent understanding was produced in bSam-gtan-dpal. He also had a vision of the Teacher as Buddha. After that, without practising much penance, he became a Lord of Yoga (rnal-'byor-gyi dbaṅ-phyug, Yogeśvara), and wherever he went, numerous disciples flocked to him. He amassed a large property. He proceeded to Tsa-ri, and there had countless pure visions (dag-pa'i snaṅ-

ba). In every hermitage, where he stayed, he practised the method of Profound Teaching. Later he founded on the same day the Yab-čhos-sdiṅs and the sGo-mo-čhos-sdiṅs monasteries, in which countless male and female yogins gathered. A mere recital of hymns caused all to be filled with understanding. At the foot of the mountain, the place was filled with small huts, which could accommodate one hermit only. Though there was hardly a kind of property which did not reach his hands, he personally did (9a)
not own even a single needle and thread. He did not discriminate between those who offered him a thousand žos and those who offered him a needle with thread, and received all of them with tea and entertainment. All the teachers and disciples subsisted on begging rounds only, and did not own even a field of the size of a blanket for the upkeep of the monastery. In the beginning, though he did not engage in extensive studies, (his) wisdom shone forth from inside him, and he was able to preserve the Lineages of many scholars. He became famous, and when he received an invitation to the Imperial Court, he ignored it, and remained at his own residence. When the Dharmasvāmin, the All-knowing (kun-mkhyen) J̌o-naṅ-pa came to Lha-sa, he said: "You have come here! Let us discuss the Doctrine." But he replied: "I have removed all my doubts regarding the Cause, the Path and Effect of Enlightenment in front of my teacher, the Buddha. It is not necessary for me to put any questions to any one", and so he did not go. After this all the inmates, including the gu-ru dKon-gžon and others, followed the example of this Teacher. They did not keep any monastery lands for the upkeep of the above two monasteries (in Tsa-ri), but gained their livelihood by begging for alms. However they were able to distribute food to not less than a hundred hermits observing the annual seclusion (lo-mtshams-pa). (These hermits) having given up (worldly) life, practised meditation, and did not refute even a single word in the teachings of the religious schools. They used to regard all

those whom they happened to meet, as holy men, even laymen, not to speak of monks. Such was their religious behaviour. The disciple of the puruṣottama (skyes-mčhog-pa bSam-gtan dpal-pa)—the Dharmasvāmin 'Phel-gyag-pa bSam-gtan lhun-grub was born in the year Wood-Female-Hog (śiṅ-mo-phag—1335 A.D.). He lived for 71 years, till the year Wood-Female-Hen (śiṅ-mo-bya—1405 A.D.). The number of teachings that belong to the system of So (-čhuṅ-ba) is as follows: two Lineages, that of the Word, and that of the Meaning; in the "Lineage of the Word" there were two Lineages: the "Senior" Lineage (brgyud-pa čhen-po) and the "Junior" Lineage (brgyud-phran). The "Senior Lineage" included a number of sections which were named after 54 great holy men (dam-pa skyes-mčhog-čhe-ba); 32 intermediate sections named after 32 holy men ('briṅ-so-gñis); 17 short sections named after 17 holy men (dam-pa skyes-mčhog). Each (section) con- (9b)
tained the life-story of one siddha (after whom the section had been named), his main precept, and method of guiding disciples, in all 54 Lineages. Otherwise, it can be divided into 103 Lineages, and for this reason it was called the "Senior" Lineage (brgyud-pa čhen-mo). The "Junior" Lineage (rgyud-phran) included: the Don-skor lṅa-ma (the five sections of Don-skor /Cycle of Meaning/), the Rim-pa bži-ma (Four Stages /of meditation/, bSam-gtan-gyi thun-čhe-čhuṅ, (meditation requiring long hours and short hours), the Grags-pa brgyad (name of a book), the Yab-sras gsum-ma (Teacher and disciples, the three), the sKyon-čan (name of a book) and the sKyon-med (name of a book), and others, in all 32 sections of the Doctrine. In the "Lineage of the Meaning" (don-rgyud): there were two Phyogs-su lhuṅ-ba (partial) and ma-lhuṅ-ba (impartial) branches. The first (consisted) of 54 "Lineages of the Meaning" of the 54 male and female yogins, the 32 "Lineages of the Meaning" of the 32 teachers, the 17 "Lineages of the Meaning" of the 17 holy men. Now, in the "Impartial" branch (Phyogs-su ma-lhuṅ-ba) there were

o sections, that of Mig-'byed skor (Opening the Eyes) and at of mKha'-'gro-ma (mKha'-'gro-ma'i skor). In the first anch (Mig-'byed) there were four "sons" and one "mother", all five. These were known as gŽuṅ-sbas-pa Mig-'byed[1], ; branches Dus-daṅs dus-phran-la gdams-pa, 116 ṅo-sprod, e Ma-'gags rnam-dag (Eternal purity), and the rDo-rJe sems-a'i gsaṅ-lam (the "Secret path of Vajrasattva." These are e four "bu" or sons). In the group of the ḍākinīs (mkha'-ro-ma) were included the four great skor-mgo (sections) of So 'huṅ-ba), the mČhog-sgrub-pa-la brda'-skor (the Series of mbols revealing the Sublime), the Formula of the Four etters expressing the method of securing ordinary realization hun-moṅ sgrub-pa-la yi-ge bži-pa'i skor; in the Tantra the pression yi-ge-bži usually stands for "Evaṃ mayā," or Anuttara"), the Cycle of Dza'-ga-ta (rite of blessing wine), d the Thun Cycle (Thun-skor) which served to obtain both e realizations. The Cycle of Symbols (brda'-skor) contain-l: The Series of Symbols of Heruka (He-ru-ka'i brda'-skor), e Series of Symbols of the Sugata (bDe-bar gśegs-pa'i brda'-or), the Series of Symbols of Vajraghaṇṭa, and the miscella-eous symbols of Dam-pa. The ordinary realization (Thun-moṅ-grub-pa) included: the dMar-mo-gsuṅ-gi sgrub-pa (Propi-ation of Speech of the Red Vārahī), and the sādhana of Nag-o (the Propitiation of the Mind of the Black Vārahī). The st named included: Vārahī-dharma-kāya-sādhana, the (Vāra-ī)-Saṃbhoga-kāya-sādhana, and the (Vārahī)-nirmāṇa-kāya-sā-hana. The Cycle of Dza'-ga-ta included the gTum-mo 'khor-gčig-pa (Eka-caṇḍalīcakra). The Cycle of Thun consisted of sort of karma-yoga (sPyod-lam-gyi ñams-skyoṅ). The oot of the above (system was) the Lineage of Meaning of Mra-ba'i seṅ-ge (Dam-pa rGya-gar) which contained terms (10a) greeing with those of the Tantras, and the Lineage of the Meaning, known as the Fourth Lineage, in which (the

1 The "Mother, opening the Eye of the Hidden"; a book is often called nother", and notes on the book are frequently called "sons" (of the book).

philosophic) terms did not correspond to Tantric terms, and which were not generally known. Then the Ma-tshaṅ mdor-bsdus (Summary of the Essence of the Missing Chapters), and the Rig-pa sraṅs-'Jug (The Weighing of one's own Mind) of So. These were the four Oral Traditions (sñan-brgyud).

The story of Mal Ka-ba-čan-pa initiated by Dam-pa sMon-lam: He was a native of Bye-čan of gYe in the village of Mal rTe'u-ra-pa. His father was Mal Dar-ma-mgon. His mother was Hab-brdal-gza'-mdo-ba. He was the second (lit. the middle one) of their three sons, and was born in the year Fire-Female-Horse (me-pho-rta—1126 A.D.). (In his childhood) he was very naughty and mischievous. He married a very wealthy widow, who (once) said to him: "If you were to enter religion, I would give you provision! If you do not, we had (better) separate." So he entered the gates of religion. At 'Ol-kha he obtained the system of rMa from the ācārya Dar-ma-grags. Having obtained the doctrine of Nā-ro-pa and the sādhana of Bya-rog-ma (a form of Mahākāla—bDud-mgon Bya-rog-ma) from Mal-spos-ka-ba sMon-lam-btsan, he went on a begging round (ldom-bu byed-čiṅ yod-pa-la), and when he had reached Tshi-ra-sgaṅ, (he found the inmates) preparing to partake of tea at the memorial service for So (-čhuṅ-ba) ('das-mčhod). At the head of the row sat a yogin wearing an eye-shade made of bear-skin (dom-ra) who looked at him sternly, and said: "Will you partake of tea?", and handed him his own cup with some tea left in it. Again the yogin inquired: "Would you like some flour? Take it!" and, saying so, he poured out all the flour from a bag, and then walked away. Mal Ka-ba-čan-pa was anxious to meet Dam-pa sGom-smon (Śa-mi) because of the latter's fame, and asked the monks who were present (at the service): "Where is Dam-pa sGom-smon?" One said: "You are stupid! Was he not the man who gave you tea and barley flour just now?" Mal Ka-ba-čan-pa then went in search of Dam-pa sGom-smon, and saw the yogin preaching the Doctrine to a yogin and a monk on the border of a field. Mal Ka-ba-čan-pa saluted

Dam-pa sGom-smon, and faith was born in him. Mal's eyes were filled with tears, and with eyes wide-open, his Mind became devoid of thought. sGom-smon then said to him: "When you capture a man, you may get ransom for him, but having cognized your Mind, you won't get a ransom. What use is there? Set it free!" Then a mental concentration was born in him. Mal Ka-ba-čan-pa spent one night there, and next day went again in search of the Teacher, but was told that (the Teacher) had gone to La-ba 'phraṅ (gorge). So he proceeded there, and met the Teacher, while the latter was preaching religion to a monk. He made the request for secret precepts on the Intermediate Stage (bar-do) and (the Teacher) bestowed them on him. Mal Ka-ba-čan-pa asked: "Shall I attend on you!" The Teacher replied: "I have a wife, resembling a she-devil," and he did not allow Mal (to attend on him). Mal then journeyed to gYor-po, and with the barley which he had obtained on his begging rounds, he bought some fat, and again visited the Teacher. The latter reproached him, saying: "A yogin must be like a dog, which when sold, shouldn't return". Mal Ka-ba-čan-pa made the following request: "Lo-ro Žig-po told (me) about the "Lineage of Meaning" (Don-brgyud) of sMra-ba'i seṅ-ge, and I came to ask for it." (The Teacher exclaimed): "Who said this? I haven't such precepts!' Mal Ka-ba-čan-pa replied: "It was Lo-ro Žig-po!" The Teacher then rebuked Mal and said: "He (Lo-ro Žig-po) had broken his Tantric vow (dam-ñams). All those who met him, will go to Hell". But Mal Ka-ba-čan-pa repeated again and again his request, and finally the Teacher bestowed on him the complete precepts of the "Lineage of Meaning' (don-brgyud). Later the Teacher said to him: "You should become like Lo-ro Žig po!" Then the Teacher made him take the vow of practising meditation for 12 years, (and not to preach the Doctrine to others), saying: "After this you will be relieved of this vow." Mal Ka-ba-čan-pa used to say that the tea and flour given to him by the Teacher were in place of initiation. (10b)

At the age of 35, he met Śa-mi and followed after him for twelve years (for eleven years, Śa-mi having died in 1172). Mal Ka-ba-čan-pa meditated for forty years. He spent two months at the residence of the alms-giver Ge-rgod. Except for this, he never entered a village after he began the practice of meditation. He passed away at the age of 86 in the year of the Sheep (lug-lo—1211 A.D.), and many relics were left behind.

Mal Ka-ba-čan-pa was born in the year Fire-Male-Horse (me-pho-rta—1126 A.D.), when 'Gro-ba'i mgon-po Phag-mo-gru-pa was seventeen, and Śa-mi forty-two. In the following Fire-Female-Sheep year (me-pho-lug—1127 A.D.) rTen-ne (rGyal-ba rTen-ne) was born. sÑe-mdo-pa smra-ba'i seṅ-ge (11a)
was born in the year Fire-Male-Horse year (me-pho-rta—1186 A.D.) which is the 61st year of Ka-ba-čan-pa. The ācārya Kun-bzaṅs having met Ka-ba-čan-pa, obtained from him the "Lineage of Meaning" (Don-brgyud). He was also said to have obtained the "Lineage of Meaning" from the wife of Ka-ba-čan-pa and from the latter's son (J̌o-sras).

The story of the ācārya Kun-bzaṅs: it can be found in the chapter on the Lineage of rDo-rǰe zam-pa. dGyer-sgom (dGyer-sgom tshul-seṅ/Tshul-khrims seṅ-ge/), the Great, was initiated by Ka-ba-čan-pa. His story: he was born in the year Wood-Male-Mouse (śiṅ-pho-byi-ba—1144 A.D.) to father dKon-mčhog-skyabs, a military commander (dmag-dpon), and mother Princess (rGyal-tsha-ma) mDo-sde-rgyan. He belonged to the Be-gu clan of the two dGyer Be-gu-pa and Ne-gu-pa in Yar-kluṅs gśoṅ-pa. He belonged to the Khaṅ-gsar-pa family, and was a descendant of the royal family of Khra-'khrug-pa. He was given the name of Čhos-kyi seṅ-ge. This Čhos-seṅ, who was the eldest of the two brothers, the youngest being the military commander Čhos-rdor, received ordination at the age of 11, and was given the name of Tshul-khrims seṅ-ge. He became the overseer (dpon-gñer) of Khra-'brug. He received the secret name of rDo-rǰe rgyal-po after being initiated into the Samāja Cycle by The kalyāṇa-mitra Hor. From the latter he obtained the basic text (mūla) and the commentary on the Samāja (Guhyasamāja-Tantra, Kg. rGyud-'bum, No. 442; Pradīpodyotana-nāma-ṭīkā, Tg. rGyud, No. 1785), and other texts. Because of the very great fame of dPal Phag-mo-gru-pa, at the age of 19 he proceeded to mTha'-rtsa. As soon as he saw the monastery, an extraordinary faith was born in him. When dPal Phag-mo-gru-pa was coming to the assembly-hall, some monks spread on the ground their shirts (phyam-tshe), others spread (their) religious robes. dGyer being a newcomer, spread on the edge of the road his shirt (phyam-tshe), and Gro-mgon made a special detour to pass over it. Having put his foot on the shirt (phyam-tshe), Gro-mgon looked at him, and said: "The monk (bhikṣu) Vajradhara is very wonderful!" dGyer replied: "I am a novice!" but Phag-mo-gru-pa again said: "You are a novice, but the monk (bhikṣu) Vajradhara (rDo-rje 'dzin-pa) is very wonderful!" dGyer attended the preaching of Phag-mo-gru-pa and perceived him as a Buddha, and an (11*b*) extraordinary experience of a blissful and clear meditation unaccompanied by constructive thought (bde-gsal mi-rtog-pa) was produced in him by itself. He then studied briefly the hidden precepts of the upāya-mārga of the "Six Doctrines" (of Nā-ro-pa) and others. Having returned to his native place to fetch provisions, he found his father carried away by enemies, and he was forced to fight. In the meanwhile, dPal Phag-mo-gru-pa passed away and a great sadness overcame him. He thought that he had to go into the presence of an experienced teacher. Once a scholar said to him: "It is rumoured that there exists an extraordinary one named rNal-'byor Čhos-gyuṅ, a disciple of Dags-po". As soon as he heard the name, devotion and reverence were born in him, and he went to see him. On reaching the lower part of l J̌aṅ, he heard that there was a siddha named Mal Ka-ba-čan-pa living in the upper part of the Valley, and he went to visit him. On meeting the siddha's wife, he asked her to introduce him (to the Teacher). But the Teacher said: "I hate the company of monks! Don't let

him in!" Having borrowed a vessel, from which dogs were fed, he boiled some tea in it without cleaning it. When the Teacher heard about this, he exclaimed: "He can become a yogin!" and became very pleased. He admitted him with the words: "I am glad you came! I can be of benefit to you!" He spent about one month there, and they slept placing their heads together. The (Teacher) bestowed on him many doctrines, such as the mental precepts (thugs-kyi man-ṅag) of the "Lineage of Meaning." They discussed at great length the Doctrine. The Teacher said to him: "Others require repeated explanations, but you are able to master after a single explanation. You are a man endowed with excellent qualities and belong to those who are able to grasp (a subject) spontaneously". He then practised meditation in a cave at Ka-ba-čan, and one evening there appeared (before him) a ḍākinī afflicted by an impure illness (grib-phog-pa). The Precious One introduced her to her own Mind, and the ailment disappeared. The ḍākinī then offered him a skull-cup full of amṛta, and he experienced an undefiled bliss. He offered to Ka-ba-čan-pa and his wife, with about 50 adult monks, 103 valuable presents, which included three horses and a Prajñāpāramitā in 20,000 ślokas, and after the Teacher (12a)
had released himself from his vow (from the 12 years' vow), he asked him to preach the "Lineage of Meaning" to the assembly of disciples. The Teacher preached the doctrine during the fifth month.

The Teacher said: "You, as the Master of the Doctrine, should preach it to those whom you will find fit (to receive it)." dGyer then taught it (this sentence may also mean that dGyer preached it after the 15th day of the same month) to a group which did not exceed fifteen. After that he met rNal-'byor Čhos-gyuṅ at 'Ol-kha, and told him that he had realized the non-origination of the (elements of existence) while staying with Mal. But rNal-'byor Čhos-gyuṅ told him: "This is still not enough!" and bestowed on dGyer the Mahāmudrā system, as well as the complete exposition of the initiation of

the Two-faced Venerable One (Vajravārahī), the "Six Doctrines" of Nā-ro-pa, and others. He liberated him from the bondages of the eight worldly dharmas (čhos-brgyad). dGyer having requested the Teacher's permission to become an itinerant monk (rgyal-khams-pa), proceeded to certain undefined localities. He subdued many fierce demons, such as Mal-gro gzi-čan (name of a nāga) and mKhar-nas of sÑe. Having come to Par-phu, he obtained the complete commentary on the three Cycles of the Dohā (rGyal-po'i Do-ha, gTsun-mo'i Do-ha, dMaṅs-kyi Do-ha) together with their exposition. At that time he reached the age of 30. After that they spent five years at Phreṅ-kha-brag of sTod-luṅs, the alms-giver Ñe-'bum acting as his supporter. dGyer composed numerous texts on auspicious rites, such as the "rTen-'brel rgya-mtsho yaṅs-pa". He proceeded to Oḍḍīyāna on an invitation received from ḍākinīs, having assumed another body (sku-lus-kyi bkod-pa mdzad-pa). He obtained hidden precepts from five siddhas, who included Indrabodhi and others. He had visions of many tutelary deities, such as Saṃvara and others, and was initiated by them. At the age of 38, in the year Iron-Female-Ox (lčags-mo-glaṅ—1181 A.D.) he founded the monastery of sÑe-phu śug-gseb. He spent 24 years there and laboured extensively for the benefit of others. He had three disciples from sTod (Western Tibet): rGya, dMar-mdzod-ma-ba, and 'Dzeṅ. From sMad (East Tibet): the three "Wise Ones". He initiated and guided countless other disciples. He passed away at the age of 61, in the year Wood-Male-Mouse (śiṅ-pho-byi-ba—1204 A.D.) at sunrise of the 14th day of the month of dbYug-gu (9th month of the Tibetan year) amidst numerous miraculous signs. In this Wood-Male-Mouse year (12*b*)
(śiṅ-pho-byi-ba—1204 A.D.) the Kha-čhe paṇ-čhen came to Tibet. After dGyer dPal rGya-mkhar-ba acted as abbot.

Saṅs-rgyas-dbon, initiated by dGyer. His story: his father was the military commander Čhos-rdor, the younger brother of dGyer-Žig, and his mother—rLan-čhuṅ-ma. They had five sons. The eldest Rin-čhen sñiṅ-po was sent in his youth by his mother to dPal rGya-mkhar-ba to enter religion at Śug-gseb. dGyer having perceived this, said: "To-day Rin-čhen sñiṅ-po will be coming! You, monks, go out to meet him! He will excel me." He was received by the monks on the road from sTag-luṅ, and all the monks liked his behaviour. He took up residence at the monastery, and met dGyer. On ordination, he received the name of Rin-čhen dbaṅ-phyug. From dGyer he obtained the three doctrines of sÑe-phu-ba, such as the rTen-'brel and others, as well as the exposition of the three Dohās. After the death of dGyer, dMar-bu brag-pa undertook to support the nephew and invited him to mDzod-ma. While he was supporting him, they put in order the books of sÑe-phu-ba. He bestowed on him the "Oral Tradition" (sñan-brgyud) of bDe-mčhog, the system of Lus-med mkha'-gro (Śrī-Vajra-ḍākaniṣkāyadharma-nāma, Tg. rGyud, No. 1527; a doctrine preached by Ras-čhuṅ-pa, containing nine sentences). After the death of rGya-mkhar-ba, he acted as abbot of sÑe-phu, and maintained with the help of precepts monks and disciples. He passed away amidst wonderful signs at the mansion of Śug-gseb dbUs-gliṅ.

The story of his disciple Brag-'bur-ba: Daṅ-re, the second of the five sons of the military commander Čhos-rdor, had three sons: Saṅs-rgyas rdo-rje, Čhos-kyi bla-ma of Tsa-ri, and Brag-'bur-ba. Brag-'bur-ba in his youth became a disciple of Saṅs-rgyas-dbon. On ordination, he received the name of Rin-čhen-'bum. He practised diligently the precepts of the upāya-mārga at the hermitage of rDo-'on, and a wonderful understanding and experience of bliss, and of the (13a)
"Inner Heat" (bDe-drod) was produced in him. He became abbot of Śug-gseb. When 'Gro-mgon 'Phags-pa was proceeding to the Imperial Court, the Masters of the Doctrine (čhos-dpon) of dbUs came out to meet him, and he was pleased with the signs of the "Inner Heat" of the Precious One (Brag-'bur-ba), and ('Phags-pa) listened to his exposition of hidden precepts. From the Rin-po-čhe 'Bras-dkar-ba he

obtained the three Cycles of the Dohā and their commentary. His disciples, who laboured extensively for the welfare of others, were: dGyer-dbon-ri-pa, the eldest of the two sons of mGon-po, the fourth son of Čhos-rdor, Ṅams-śod Rin-po-čhe, the eldest son of Saṅs-rgyas rdo-rJe, the bla-ma Žaṅ-ston Kun-dga' rgyal-po, the bla-ma Ri-pa, and many scholars and bhadantas (btsun-pa), who benefitted the Doctrine. His (chief) disciple was Śug-gseb Ri-pa. Here is his story: his native place was Lower mKhar-čhu of Ṅams-śod. He belonged to the clan of kLubs. He was born as son of father sKyid-pa-dpal and mother bKra-śis-ldan. He received the name of gŽon-nu rdo-rJe and became a disciple of Brag-'bur-ba at Śug-gseb. On ordination, he received the name of gŽon-nu rin-čhen. He took up the final monastic ordination before the upādhyāya Zul-phu-ba, the karma-ācārya dbUs-khaṅ-pa, and the Secret Preceptor Ka-ba-phu. From Brag-'bur-ba he obtained the Cycle of Ži-byed, such as the "Lineage of Meaning" (don-brgyud) of sMra-ba'i seṅ-ge and the four Zab-don ("Four Profound Meanings"), the Cycle of rTen-'brel, such as the rTen-'brel yid-bžin nor-bu (a text on magic rites), and other texts, the Oral Tradition (sñan-brgyud) of Saṃvara, the three Cycles of the Dohā, according to the Par system (of Par-phu-ba) together with their respective commentaries, the bLa-ma 'brel-'Jug (name of a book), and the Ye-śes 'khor-lo, the basic text (mūla) and commentary, as well as its summary (piṇḍārtha). Further, he obtained numerous initiations, precepts, Sūtras, Tantras, and sādhanas from many teachers, who included 'Gro-mgon 'Phags-pa, 'Gar-čhuṅ-pa gŽon-nu byaṅ-čhub, Čhu-bzaṅs-pa, the ācārya Laṅ-ka Li-pa, and others. He practised meditation at various hermitages, such as Tsa-ri, gLaṅ-ma of Din-ri and others. Later he became abbot of Śug-gseb. With his (13b)
preaching of the Doctrine he satisfied each of the inmates (of this monastery), as well as his numerous disciples. His disciple was 'Ba'-ra-ba rGyal-mtshan-dpal. Having come to Lha-sa, he visited sÑe-phu. On the way he experienced

difficulties because of snow. He met the bla-ma Ri-pa who said in a loud voice during an assembly: "The Teacher of gTsaṅ-pa who is sitting at the head of the row, is an extraordinary person." When he came there to be admitted into religion, he was placed at the head of the row of all (the monks present), and (Ri-pa) bestowed on him the complete precepts of Śug-gseb-pa, such as the "Lineage of Meaning" (Don-brgyud) of the Ži-byed, the three Cycles of the Dohā, the rTen-'brel, and others. When he was going away, he (Ri-pa) arranged a high seat (for him), and honoured him greatly. Ri-pa said: "Ācārya rGyal-mtshan dpal! You, who have obtained all the teachings of our Śug-gseb-pa, guide those who ask for guidance, and preach to those who ask for an exposition (of the Doctrine)." He repeated this earnest request three times. Again the Dharmasvāmin bLa-ma Dam-pa bSod-nams rgyal-mtshan-pa obtained the Dohā according to the method of Par from this bla-ma Ri-pa. gTsaṅ-pa bLo-bzaṅs-pa obtained the Cycle of the "Lineage of Meaning" of Mal Ka-ba-čan-pa from 'Ba'-ra-ba. The mahā-upādhyāya Śākya grags-pa obtained (it) from him. Mal Ka-ba-čan-pa having been born in the year Fire-Male-Horse (me-pho-rta—1126 A.D.), 351 years have elapsed since then till the present Fire-Male-Ape (me-pho-spre'u—1476 A.D.) year. The Chapter on the School of So-(čhuṅ-ba).

The School of sKam: sKam was a disciple of the kalyāṇa-mitra Gra-pa. He was a monk learned in the Prajñāpāramitā (14a)
doctrine, and associated with one named Khams-sgom Tshul-khrims rgyan, a disciple of Gra-pa. He acted as attendant of the kalyāṇa-mitra Gra-pa to kLags-pa-lam. There Gra-pa bestowed the initiation of Phyag-na rdo-rje bha-ba-ma on an alms-giver, who was afflicted by leprosy (sa-gdon). After finishing the initiation rite the two disciples offered a hundred homa-offerings, but the demon became angry. sKam-sgom became afflicted by a tumour in the abdomen (skran), and Khams-sgom became afflicted by dropsy, and later was carried away by leprosy. About that time Dam-pa was

attending for a considerable time on the monastic congregation of rGyal ('Phan-yul). There he made a stove which is even nowadays known for its remarkable way of kindling without blowing. Once when he was carrying a large load of straw, he placed it on the threshold of a door, and nobody was able to move it from there. Dam-pa shouted: "The door of Faith, which leads towards religion, is blocked for my monks of rGyal!" and saying so, he left for China. Thus when Dam-pa made a lengthy stay at rGyal, one day he went for a walk along the edge of the marsh of rGyal. sKam-sgom was also there, suffering from pain (but did not show it). Dam-pa asked him: "O Venerable ascetic! Are you not ill?" "I am not ill! Are you, yourself, not ill?" replied Khams-sgom. Next day the two met again, and Dam-pa asked Khams-sgom the same question. Khams-sgom replied: "Yes, I am ill! Do you have a way to cure me?" Dam-pa replied: "You are a man who prides himself with (his) perfection, but haven't you the means to cure your disease?" Faith was born in Khams-sgom, who said: "At any rate, bestow some hidden precepts on me!" Then Dam-pa bestowed on him the precepts of the Prajñāpāramitā (this term was frequently used to indicate the gČod rites and the Ži-byed system), and all of a sudden Khams-sgom's ailment was cured, and he was filled with amazement. He sent a message to his brother, the bla-ma sKam, saying: "Here there is an Indian teacher, an extraordinary siddha. He cured my illness. You should invite him." sKam sent his elder brother, and invited Dam-pa. (14b)
Dam-pa was performing a consecration rite of the Śatasāhasrikā-Prajñāpāramitā for the alms-giver rTsi rDor-bstan, and did not accept (the invitation). Again the brother pleaded, and Dam-pa inquired: "What is his name?" The brother replied: "His name is sKam Ye-śes rgyal-mtshan." Dam-pa then said: "Well then, I can benefit him! I shall be coming in the morning of the day after to-morrow." Then the brother returned to the house of sKam, and told him: "This Teacher is indeed a wonderful man! He is coming the day

after to-morrow. We should prepare for it!" On that day there was a snowfall. Next morning, at daybreak, an a-tsa-ra (ācārya) entered the house. "Are you the Teacher?"—they inquired, and Dam-pa replied: "Yes—I am!" They said: "We thought you were coming to-morrow." Dam-pa answered: "I was afraid an accident might happen (to you), and therefore came this morning". They asked: "Were you handicapped by snow?" Dam-pa replied: "My feet did not touch snow." They said: "We did not open the door (how did you enter?") Dam-pa said: "The walls are no obstacles for me!" and saying so, he sat down. Then the relatives saluted and honoured him. Dam-pa preached to them the symbolical introduction, and sKam grasped its meaning, and thought to himself: "Alas! (He said too much) in the midst of a crowd". Dam-pa said: "Symbols can be seen by those who have eyes, but not by those who have no eyes", and sKam discovered that the others had not understood it. Dam-pa spent 14 days there and for five days they carried out discussions. During nine days he set aside special hours for preaching, and preached the Doctrine. On the first occasion he introduced him to his own Mind with the help of two methods: by introducing him to the nature of the ailment, and to the nature of meditation. On the second occasion he preached the Four Noble Truths, the Refuge, and various other teachings. After 14 days, he said to him: "I am going!" They begged him to stay on, but he did not grant (their request). They then begged to be allowed to meet him again, and Dam-pa replied: "I shall stay with a jñāna-ḍākinī on the Wu-t'ai-shan of China (Ri-bo-rtse-lṅa in Shan-hsi Province of China). You should address your prayers over there". Then sKam asked him: "Whom should I ask, when feeling uncertain, after you had gone?" Dam-pa replied: "The best kalyāṇa-mitra is your own Mind! A Teacher, able to remove doubts, will emerge from within your own Mind. The second kalyāṇa-mitra is an Ārya (the scriptures of the Buddha), therefore you would read the ajñāpāramitā (mDo-rgyes-'briṅ-bsdus: the Śatasāhasrikā, e Pañcaviṃśatisāhasrikā, and the Aṣṭasāhasrikā-Prajñāpāra-itā). Verily the lowest kind of kalyāṇa-mitras is the indi-dual. But you will not meet me again. You can discuss ith the brothers who had experienced meditation. Meditate r eight years! Then you will obtain the faculty of prescience. fter that you can begin preaching the Prajñāpārami-s." sKam replied: "I had no opportunity to practise editation. Inside my body there were nine tumours in the domen, and Gra-pa had prophesied that I was to die in ree months". Dam-pa replied: "Those who practise editation on the Prajñāpāramitā will not suffer even from adache" (in a passage of the Prajñāpāramitā it is said that ose, who recite its text will suffer much from headaches, :., and by this the karmic influences will be removed, t in the present passage Dam-pa said the opposite). Saying Dam-pa departed. Then sKam practised meditation and e tumours (in his abdomen) became cured. In eight years e faculty of prescience was produced in him. He preached e mÑon-rtogs brgyad-ka (the aṣṭau-padārthāḥ, or dÑos-po gyad, the eight principal subjects of the Abhisamayā-ṃkāra). Besides the Sañcaya (Ārya-Prajñāpāramitā-icayagāthā, Kg. Śer-phyin, No. 13) he used to preach oting from the Śatasāhasrikā-Prajñāpāramitā and the ñcaviṃśatisāhasrikā-Prajñāpāramitā. His disciples, who lowed these teachings, became known as the "Upper neage" and the "Lower Lineage". The "Upper Lineage" s transmitted through 'Khun-'dzi Yaṅ-ḍben-pa dBaṅ-phyug -rJe and rGyams Śes-rab bla-ma. These two were invalids, l introduced themselves to their own Minds by way of ess. They preached as the basic text—the sKabs-daṅ-po e first chapter of the Abhisamayālaṃkāra), as precepts—the ır (Noble) Truths, and various methods (lag-len thor-bu-. Both 'Khun and rGyams preached it to dBon-po Jo-n. The latter to 'Gos. The latter to (his) son 'Gos -ma. The latter to Rog-ston btsan-po. The latter to

Rog Ŝes-rab-'od. Again Lha-rJe-sPrad (obtained) it from sKam. The latter taught it to 'Gos Dar-ma. From him gTsaṅ-pa rṄog obtained it. The latter taught it to rGyal-ba dKon-skyabs. The latter taught it to Rog. Again sKam taught it to the bla-ma Čhag-brag dmar-ba. The latter to the bla-ma gÑos. The latter to the bla-ma sGog-luṅ-pa. The latter taught it to the bla-ma Žaṅ-ston Ŝes-rab. The latter taught it to the bla-ma gŜen. The latter to sKye-med Žaṅ. sKye-med Žaṅ composed a text-book (yig-čha) on the "Oral Precepts," known (15
as the "Nine Groups of Four" (bži-tsho-dgu).

Again sKam taught it to the kālyāṇa-mitra 'Khun. The latter to Čhug-brag dmar-ba. The latter to Thaṅ-čhuṅ-pa, the incarnation of La-stod gTsaṅ-so. The latter to rGya-ston gŽon-nu seṅ-ge. The latter to Sag-ston. Again sKam taught it to rGyams. The latter to Ke-ke Hor-grags. The latter to the bla-ma gÑos. The latter bestowed it on rGya-ston gŽon-nu seṅ-ge. The latter having read the lDen-bži of Ācārya Deva (Āryadeva), had faith born in him. He attended on three teachers, but did not feel satisfied and proceeded to La-stod gTsaṅ-so. He met the nirmāṇa-kāya Thaṅ-čhuṅ-pa and obtained precepts from him. An understanding removing doubts was produced in him. Since there did not exist a text-book (on the doctrine) till the time of Thaṅ-čhuṅ-pa and gÑos, rGya-ston gŽon-nu seṅ-ge wrote a large text-book on the precepts of the sKam school. Its title was "Ŝer-phyin thugs-rgyud lag-len sñan-rgyud Rin-čhen phreṅ-ba Rigs pa'i gtan-tshigs-'phrul-gyi lde-mig" ("The Miraculous Key of Logic; The Garland of Precious Stones of Oral Tradition; The Practice of the Mental Lineage of the Prajñāpāramitā"). Again sKam taught it to rGya-gar Jo-sras. The latter to Ras-pa Lha-ri-pa. The latter to the two brothers Sum and sGom. Again Ŝaṅs-pa Ke-ke Hor-grags followed on sKam for nine years and obtained from him hidden precepts. Later he attended for three months on 'Khun Yaṅ-dben-pa. Ke-ke taught it to the Rin-po-čhe rGyal-tsha. The "Lower Lineage": its (teachings) was handed down by sGro. Not being an invalid

his means that he was not introduced to his own Mind by
sing his illness as a means of spiritual advancement), he used
expound the essential meaning and the Abhisamaya (mṄon-
ır rtogs-pa), differentiating between disciples who were charac-
rized by a gradual development, and a spontaneous develop-
ent (čig-čhar). He commented on Sūtras with the help of
ur different explanations of the principle of Relativity. The
Lower Lineage" was a line which handed down precepts
rough meditation. This sGro was a native of Upper 'Phan-
l. He was the elder brother of the three brothers and
sters born to father sGro-ston 'Phan-rgyal and mother
e-mo bKra-śis, and received the name of sGro Čhos-brtson.
e was ordained in his youth. While he was studying the
ajñāpāramitā with the kalyāṇa-mitra rJe rGan-'bum-pa, the
tter fell ill, and nothing could help him. His retinue said:
One should invite sKam." rJe rGan said: "Both of us are
arned in the Prajñāpāramitā, it would affect my fortune,
I were to show him respect." The monks said: "We
all invite him privately", and rJe rGan replied: "Do it!"
hey accordingly invited sKam to a house which stood apart,
d asked him for hidden precepts. sKam said: "You
dn't invite me to your house, but brought me here. How
that?" rJe rGan replied: "I was afraid it would affect my
rtune, and so invited you privately." sKam was very
spleased, and (his precepts) did not bear any fruit. He
oceeded to the mansion of rJe rGan. Inside it he saw
ages, some more beautiful than the others, some better
an the others, in front of which stood offerings. sKam
rew dust at the painted images and threw the offerings
own. Later when rJe rGan came in, he inquired: "Who
d it?" and felt angry. sKam said: "You had shown
artiality towards the Buddhas, and therefore have fallen ill!"
fter that rJe rGan was more careful, and the precepts bore
uit. His illness was cured, and faith was born in him.
Gro quietly listened to the precepts preached by sKam,
d wondered. Later he asked rJe rGan to visit the resi-

(16a)

dence of sKa. rJe rGan said: "It is to be done! He is a wonderful Teacher. Go there!" So sGro went to (visit) sKam. sKam introduced him to the "Essential Meaning" (sñiṅ-po'i don) and the Abhisamaya. He also introduced him to the Śatasāhasrikā, the Pañcaviṃśatisāhasrikā and the Aṣṭasāhasrikā-Prajñāpāramitās, which he used as precepts. sGro was filled with wonder. About that time Dam-pa (Saṅs-rgyas) was said to be residing at Diṅ-ri. sGro said to sKam: "Shall I go and meet him?" "Well, go!" said sKam, "but my Teacher has hands and feet bigger than those of others" (by this he meant Dam-pa, but did not know whether that Teacher was Dam-pa). He practised meditation on the Prajñāpāramitā and the ūṣmagata-jñāna (drod-kyi ye-śes, the first stage of the four stages of prayoga-mārga) was produced in him. Dam-pa extricated insects from his body (Abhisamayālaṃkāra, IV, 42). Because of this he had many moles (sme-ba) on the upper part of his body, and one mole on his left foot. On the crown of his head there was a hole inside which the (16
big finger could be introduced. bLa-ma sGro then arranged for provisions, and journeyed towards gLaṅ-'khor. About midday of the day on which he was supposed to arrive (do-nub sleb-pa'i ñin-phyed-tsa-na), he heard the voice of Dam-pa. In the evening he went to see Dam-pa whom he found in the midst of a crowd. He saluted him and offered him a present, but Dam-pa refused to accept it. bLa-ma sGro had a piece of pink-coloured silk. He cut a piece, and tied it to the hair of Dam-pa, who became pleased. Then sGro cut the silk into pieces, and tied them all over the blanket worn by Dam-pa, and his hair. This pleased Dam-pa. Then Dam-pa gave him a packet containing some medicinal mixture, as an auspicious token, as well as a shin-bone tied with tendons. Then he gave him a pair of scales (bre-sraṅ) which he placed on a brass plate. sGro did not understand the symbolical meaning of these presents. He asked Kun-dga' (Dam-pa's chief disciple), who said to him: "The first indicates (that you will obtain) the understanding of the

Oneness of Flavour (ekarasa) of all the Elements of Existence. The second (indicates) that you will hold the foot of the Lineage. The third (indicates) that you will be able to measure all the doctrines." When sGro was about to divide the medicine, Dam-pa said: This belongs to yourself!" and handed it over to him. Then he (Dam-pa) ordered five monks to escort him as far as Phuṅ-mkhar. The four companions said to him: "We are unable to obtain precepts", and went to trade to sÑe-nam. (Dam-pa) said to sGro: "Come!" and he followed on him. Dam-pa inquired: "What request have you?" and sGro asked Dam-pa about many theories of scholars which he had studied formerly. Dam-pa said: "You should take these questions before their respective Masters". Kun-dga' told sGro: "You should put questions about the precepts of the Teacher and about your own experience". So sGro put questions on the Prajñāpāramitā doctrine, saying: "sKam Ye-śes rgyal-mtshan-pa had told me this and that". (Dam-pa) was pleased, and inquired: "Are you a disciple of sKam? Is sKam Ye-śes rgyal-mtshan well?" Then sGro understood that he (Dam-pa) was the Teacher (mentioned previously by sKam). sGro then asked Dam-pa for hidden precepts and for his permission (17a)
to remain there. Dam-pa said in the assembly: "I require a copy of the Ārya-Aṣṭasāhasrikā-Prajñāpāramitā. Who has one?" The chaplain (mčhod-gnas-pa) So-hor-'bar and his brother replied: "We shall copy it, and present it to you". Dam-pa said: "Let the copy be (written) in printed characters, or in the cursive script. Let it be completed within one month, and bring it here!" (After one month) Dam-pa said: "Now, where is the Aṣṭasāhasrikā?" They replied: "It isn't yet finished!" and Dam-pa became highly displeased, and said. "You have defeated the a-tsa-ra without showing him consideration. Now I must change my residence!" and saying so, he retired to his ascetic cell (dka'-thub khaṅ-pa). "What will you do with the Aṣṭasāhasrikā?" inquired they, and Dam-pa replied: "I shall introduce it

inside a brass trumpet, and shall blow the trumpet towards the East". After that Dam-pa practised penance for seven days, and then passed away. They (the inmates) gave sGro provisions to last 27 days during which to perform penance. Having cremated Dam-pa's body and collected the relics, sGro proceeded towards his native place, and met sKam. sKam asked him. "Is he my Teacher, or not?" sGro replied: "He is!" sKam then exclaimed: "Alas! (e-su) I should have gone with you on a horse!" He (sGro) spent two years with sKam, who then passed away. After that sGro practised meditation for 29 years amidst the rose-bushes of Lan-pa ('Phan-yul). He had a vision of Avalokiteśvara, and his understanding reached perfection.

Since the age of 72, he preached the Doctrine, and died at the age of 75. He was visited by 'Čhus-pa Dar-brtson. The latter's father was 'Čhus-pa Gaṅ-po. His mother—Khu-mo sGron-ne-lčam. They had three children. After ordination, the boy studied numerous basic texts (gžuṅ) and hidden precepts. He especially became known as a scholar who conducted detailed investigations in the Ži-byed method. After completing the precepts of rMa and So-(čhuṅ-ba), he came to sGro, and heard the precepts of the Prajñāpāramitā. sGro said to him: "You should perform (17b)
penance for 12 years, and then continue the Lineage". 'Čhus-pa then returned to his native place, and engaged in penance for seven years. A ḍākinī prophesied to him about the sPyi-de dgon-pa. During the laying of the foundation, a quarrel arose, and he had to break his penance. But he succeeded in completing his intention, and had a vision of the Tārā and her retinue. Dam-pa appeared (to him) five times in a dream, and the ḍākinīs hoisted 13 parasols (over him). He laid the foundation of the Doctrine in the four districts (ru) of dbUs and gTsaṅ. At the age of 79, he said one day at harvest time: "Now I shall be going home! and went back. After that, his wife went home to fetch provisions for the harvesters, and Čhus-pa said to her. "I

shall die now!" The wife replied. "This cannot be true! Should you however die, what is to be done with your remains?" 'Čhus-pa replied "You should place them in the corner of this house, and cover them with stones". The wife replied. 'If we do like this, worms may eat them." 'Čhus-pa replied. "Worms aren't fortunate enough to eat my body! Never mind! My dead body will once sit erect. There will be trouble at that time", saying so, he passed away. After the lapse of many years, his dead body sat erect (in the corner). When soldiers of dPon-čhen rGyal-bzaṅ came to Yar-kluṅs, they opened the grave and carried away whatever parts of the body they found. His son was 'Čhus-pa brTson-'grus seṅ-ge. Rog Śes-rab-'od obtained the system of sKam from him at Chiṅ-khyim.

At the time of Dam-pa's death, sGro was 40. He was 42 when sKam died. He was 71 when he finished his meditation. Then for four years he preached. He was born in the year Earth-Male-Horse (sa-pho-rta—1078 A.D.). He was the senior of sGam-po-ba by one year. 'Čhus-pa Dar- (18a)
brtson was born in the year Fire-Female-Hen (me-mo-bya—1117 A.D.; according to the Re'u-mig of Sum-pa mkhan-po /JASB. 1889, p. 14/in 1118 A.D.) during which Dam-pa passed away. 'Čhus-pa died at the age of 76 in the year Water-Male-Mouse (čhu-pho-byi-ba—1192 A. D.). This 'Čhus-pa was 7 years younger than dPal Phag-mo-gru-pa. From the birth of 'Čhus-pa to the present Fire-Male-Ape year (me-pho-spre'u—1476 A.D.) 360 years have passed. The Chapter on the school of sKam.

The schools of Gra-pa, lČe and lJaṅ were branches of the "Intermediate Lineage" (bar-du byin-ba'i rgyud). The hidden precepts of the nine "Źi-byed sGron-ma" were bestowed (by Dam-pa) on the kalyāṇa-mitra Gra-pa: the Man-ṅag sku'i sgron-ma (Upadeśakāyapradīpa-nāma, Tg. rGyud, No. 2315), the Theg-pa gsuṅ-gi sgron-ma (Yānavākpradīpa-nāma, Tg. rGyud No. 2316), the gSaṅ-ba Thugs-kyi sgron-ma (Cittaguhyapradīpa-nāma, Tg. rGyud, No. 2323), the Yaṅ-dag lta-ba'i sgron-ma (Saṃdarśanapradīpa-nāma, Tg. rGyud, No. 2317), the Rin-po-čhe sgom-pa'i sgron-ma (Ratnapradīpa-nāma, Tg. No. 2318), the Byaṅ-čhub spyod-pa'i sgron-ma (Bodhicaryāpradīpa-nāma Tg. No.2321), the mÑam-ñid gži'i sgron-ma (Samatāvastu-pradīpa-nāma, Tg. rGyud, No. 2319), the rNal-'byor lam-gyi sgron-ma (Yogapatha-pradīpa-nāma, Tg. No. 2322), and the dṄos-grub 'bras-bu'i sgron-ma (Koṭiniṣṭha-phalapradīpa, Tg. rGyud, No. 2320). When Dam-pa was visiting Gra-thaṅ, Gra-pa thought: "This is an ordinary a-tsa-ra", and did not honour him. In the morning they observed that the reeds, which the a-tsa-ra used as his mat, were not crushed (by the weight of his body). They reported the matter to the kalyāṇa-mitra Gra-pa, who thought: "He must be Dam-pa Saṅs-rgyas", and ran after him. He overtook him at Lower Gra-phyi, and offered him some gold. Though Dam-pa did not accept it, he promised to visit (Gra-pa) later. Having returned to Gra-thaṅ, he (Dam-pa) preached the "Nine Cycles of Sgron-ma." The kalyāṇa-mitra Gra-pa bestowed them on Sum btsun-čhuṅ on the rock of Srin-čhu. The latter bestowed them on Myaṅ-ston Do-pa at Do-ri. The latter on bLa-čhuṅ 'od-zer of Śab. The latter on 'Čhus-pa Dar-brtson at Śaṅs. The latter composed a commentary and precepts, and taught it to 'Čhus-pa brTson-seṅ, who taught it to Rog Śes-rab-'od.

The School of lČe: There lived a father named kalyāṇa-mitra lČe-pa of bZaṅ-yul and his son. 'Tshur-ston dbaṅ-ṅe was the teacher who introduced them first (to the doctrine). (18b)
After that the Kashmirian Somanātha came to Tibet to spread the doctrine of the Kālacakra. lČe, father and son, acted as his supporter in the translation (of the Kālacakra) by gÑos lo-tsā-ba, and supplied him with adequate provisions. They offered him 30 golden sraṅs as remuneration for the translation, and other articles worth 30 sraṅs. He completed the translation within one year, and became an expert in (the doctrine). Finally, when Dam-pa Saṅs-rgyas came to lČe Dal-sgaṅ, lČe-pa was staying in seclusion, and they did

not meet. His son Ẑla-ba grags-pa was born in the year Fire-Male-Dog (me-pho-khyi—1046 A.D.) when the kalyāṇa-mitra Gra-pa was 35. He was ordained and practised penance. He also possessed an excellent knowledge of the Mantrayāna. He was in sorrow at the absence of Dam-pa, and inquired about his whereabouts. He heard that Dam-pa was residing at Yer-pa. He also heard a prophecy uttered by ḍākinīs in the sky: "O son of good family! The Venerable Kamalaśrī is a yogin observing the three vows (the Pratimoksa vow, (2) the Bodhisattva-vow, (3) the Tantric vow). He knows the true thought of the Buddha. As he possesses the three precepts of the Meditative Lineage transmitted from the ācārya Ārya Nāgārjuna, father and son (Āryadeva), ask him for instruction in the Doctrine." During that time Dam-pa was supported by an ascetic named Ñi-khri at Yer-pa. The ascetic Tshul-grags, uncle of the bla-ma lČe, and a disciple named Kon-sgom of Khul-bu were sent to invite Dam-pa. The ascetic Ñi-khri said to them: "I am old and broken down. I am unable to go and attend on the Venerable One! Should the Venerable One depart, my fortune would be lost. Though it is not proper to say such things to a great man like your Teacher lČe, but I can (19a)
say it, as he is somewhat younger than I. I am able to support him, therefore please ask him to come here", saying so, he prevented the Venerable One from going away. When they gathered all the gold owned by lČe Dal-sgaṅ-pa, father and son, they even took away the golden vajra, which served as ornament on his mother's belt, and the fur-lined silk garment of his father, as well as several rolls of woollen cloth, and proceeded to Yer-pa. In front of the Venerable One, they placed a golden maṇḍala, the garment and the woollen cloth, but the Venerable One did not even look at the things but the two rejoiced and seemed happy, as if they were mother and son. The Venerable Kamalaśrī put some questions to lČe Candrakīrti on the vow (Praṇidhāna) of the bodhicitta, on the practice of the bodhi-

citta ('Jug-pa), and on the meaning of the Prajñāpāramitā. After that he put questions on the meaning of the four initiations of the Tantras, as well as many questions about the ultimate meaning of the Mantrayāna. lČe gave his replies on the expression of intention (of developing) the bodhicitta, its practice, the meaning of the Prajñāpāramitā, and on the meaning and symbols of the four initiations of the Mantrayāna, and their ultimate meaning. Their voices sounded louder and louder, and those who happened to be in the neighbourhood came in to listen. The Venerable One (Dam-pa) said: "Now it is time to stop", and saying so, entered the cave of Zla-ba. The ascetic Ñi-khri asked Dam-pa: "How much does this kalyāṇa-mitra lČe know?" Dam-pa replied: "This dog is indeed a good one! But he needs a good stick!" Then he said to him: "I shall preach to you the hidden precepts! Come to the mountain of Lha-ri sñiṅ-po." He proceeded there. At first Dam-pa asked him about the training of the Mind, and then he obtained precepts on it. After that (Dam-pa) preached to him the precepts of the ordinary path (lam thun-moṅ-pa'i gdams-ṅag) of the (19b)
Prajñāpāramitā. Then he taught him the precepts of the extraordinary Prajñāpāramitā (Phar-phyin thun-moṅ-ma-yin-pa'i gdams-ṅag). After that he taught him the common precepts of the Tantra, and the extraordinary precepts of the Tantra. On the whole he taught him during nine months 108 different precepts. Then lČe asked Dam-pa permission to follow after him wherever he would go. Dam-pa then manifested him the symbol of pouring from a vessel filled with water into an empty one, and said: "You and I have become equals! You need not follow me! Should you follow after me, your parents will become displeased. Go to your native place and practise meditation." lČe having returned to his native place, concentrated himself on meditation following the instructions given by Dam-pa. Dam-pa also saw the Ma-ṇi-padma of Lower Yer-pa (probably a famous rock-cut inscription made by some famous teacher). Ñi-ma byaṅ-

čhub, the cousin of lČe, who was studying under Ba-ri-pa, met Dam-pa at Diṅ-ri. Except for some symbols, the Teacher did not give him any teachings in words. Though faith was born in him, Dam-pa did not instruct him with the help of words. Therefore he returned to his native place, and presented a horse to lČe Candrakīrti, and requested for precepts. He bestowed on him several extraordinary precepts of the Mantrayāna, such as the sKu-gsuṅ-thugs (name of a section of Dam-pa's precepts), the Sems-ñid gčig-pu (name of a section of Dam-pa's precepts), the Phyag-rgya gčig (name of another section) and the Phyag-rgya bži, the Rim-lṅa, the Sems-la gros-'debs, and other precepts. He preached only a few precepts to his father, to Sa-then, to sGom-čhen Brag-po, and others, who had asked him about precepts bestowed by Dam-pa. The ācārya Rāhulavajra, an attendant of lČe Candrakīrti, received ordination at the age of 17. He did not separate from the bla-ma Candrakīrti, even for one night, till the latter's death, and received from him the complete hidden precepts of the Venerable One (Dam-pa). Candrakīrti said: "You should meditate like myself, but do not preach it to others! You should eat the whole carcass of the sheep yourself (that (20a)
is, keep the Doctrine to yourself—sa-gzug raṅ-zo, a famous proverb frequently quoted by the writers of the bKa'-gdams-pa). You should drink melted butter and wipe your mouth with a lump of earth (i.e. act, as if you did not get precepts)," saying so, he imposed on him a vow. From him the monk Byaṅ-čhub ye-śes heard the Doctrine. At first he studied much the precepts of the bKa'-gdams-pas and the "Domain of the Practice" (sPyod-phyogs) under the kalyāṇa-mitra Yaṅ-gaṅ-pa, dGe-goṅ-pa, and others, and mastered them. Then he learned numerous texts of the Abhidharma and the Mādhyamaka. He then studied many "Old" and "New" Tantras. From Ñi-ma byaṅ-čhub, who died at sPaṅ-dug-mo, he obtained the complete precepts of Dam-pa. After that he studied the list of precepts which had been taught by Dam-pa to lČe, and obtained the precepts from Rāhulabhadra.

Having understood that the essence of the Doctrine was contained in the precepts of Dam-pa, he stayed in the meditative cell of Candrakīrti. He showed great devotion (towards him), and in his dream saw Candrakīrti as he had seen him before, sitting in Heaven and preaching precepts. He thought whether the dream was due to his faith (in Candrakīrti), or that it represented an illusion created by dPe-dkar. In the morning the ācārya sent a messenger to him and told him to come there. Having gone there, the ācārya Rāhulavajra smiled at him and gave him whatever remained of his food, saying: "Last night I received a prophecy from the bla-ma Candrakīrti, which said that "he will be able to master my entire Doctrine. Offer it to him! Now I have brought all the books, and have placed them in front of you, offering them to you." After finishing tea, he presented him with the ancient books of precepts, and told him not to give them to those who had broken their vows, and to those who were unfit to receive them. The monk Byaṅ-čhub ye-śes taught the Doctrine to Čhus-pa, father and son. They taught it to Rog Śes-rab-'od. This doctrine was known by the name of "The Precepts of the combined Sūtras and Tantras," (20*b*) because these precepts were identical in meaning with the verses of the Sañcaya[2] and the Nāmasaṅgīti, thus they contained precepts which belonged to the Prajñāpāramitā, and the Tantric precepts of the 58 male and female siddhas.

The lǰaṅ system: (Dam-pa) bestowed the precepts of the "unwritten" Prajñāpāramitā (Śer-phyin yi-ge med-pa) on lǰaṅ bKa'-gdams-pa of 'Čhims-yul. lǰaṅ preached them to lǰaṅ-čhuṅ-ba. The latter taught them to 'Čhus-pa, father and son. They taught them to Rog Śes-rab-'od. (It is said) that there had been only one method of revealing the moral faults of disciples (by pointing them out to them). The Chapter on the "Lesser" Lineage (brgyud-phran).

2 (Prajñāpāramitā-sañcaya-gāthā, mDo-maṅs, 108/Cat. du Fonds Tibétain de la Bibliothèque Nationale, par M. Lalou, Paris, 1931/).

The "Separate" Lineage (brgyud-pa-thor-bu-ba): (Dam-pa) imparted on 'Bro-sgom the mTshan-brJod gser-gyi thur-ma (seems to be an explanation of the Nāmasaṅgīti); to 'Gu-sgom he imparted the Las-rgya'i gdams-pa (precepts on Tantric sexual practices); to Čhu-sgom the precepts of sÑiṅ-gtam lhug-pa ("Frank instructions"); to sGom-pa dmar-sgom the precepts of Čhig-čhod-gsum; to gÑags lo-tsā-ba the precepts of the Ekavīra Saṃvara; to lČe-mo dpal-sgom the sixteen sections of the mystic experiences of siddhas; to Ṅor-rJe sgom-pa of Upper gÑal the Lhan-čig skyes-sbyor; to gNas-brtan 'byuṅ-grags of Čhu-bar the precepts of Śes-rab sñiṅ-po (i.e. the Prajñāpāramitā-hṛdaya /mDo-maṅs, Cat. du Fond Tibétain, by M. Lalou, p. 70, No. 101/); to sÑags-bśad Śes-rab rgyal-mtshan the precepts of the Kālacakra; to Śaṅs-pa dbU-sdebs the precepts of Yi-ge-bži-pa (the formula "evaṃ mayā"); to rGya-ston skye-rtsegs of sÑe-mo the precepts of Hevajra; to Žaṅ-sog čhuṅ-ba the guhyasādhana (gsaṅ-sgrub) of (Vajra) vārahī; to the bla-ma dGon-dkar-ba the precepts of Vajrapāṇi; to 'Ban-guṅ-rgyal of sKyi-śod (Lha-sa) the Oral Tradition of Saṃvara; to Ma-gčig Labs-sgron the precepts of gČod; the above (mentioned precepts) belong to the "Intermediate" Lineage (brgyud-pa bar-ma). When Dam-pa proceeded to China, he met on the road leading to Wu-t'ai-shan (rTse-lṅa'i ri) an old sage (ṛṣi), carrying a staff made of ratan wood (čhu-śiṅ). This was a manifestion of Mañjusrī, who said to him: "In this country there are many epidemics. At Vajrāsana there exists a dhāraṇī of Vijaya (rNam-par rgyal-ma). If you bring it to-day, the epidemics in this country will disappear". Dam-pa inquired: "Vajrāsana is far off. From where could I get it to-day?" The sage replied: "Inside a certain cavity in a rock (brag-khuṅ) there is a hole (bug-pa). Go there and bring it here". Dam-pa went towards this cavity, and within an instant was transported to Vajrāsana, and back. Having obtained the dhāraṇī, he pacified the epidemics. After that he again met the Venerable Mañjughoṣa ('Jam-dpal-dbyaṅs). The picture (21a)

depicting his journey to Vajrāsana was drawn by Chinese (artists), and printed copies (of it) have found their way to Tibet. Dam-pa spent 12 years (in China), preached and propagated the doctrines of the Ži-byed. It is said that his precepts and (his) Meditative Lineage exist there (in China) to the present day without interruption. Some maintain even that Dam-pa had died in China. Having come to Tibet, Dam-pa reached Diṅ-ri in the year Fire-Female-Ox (me-mo-glaṅ—1097 A.D.), and while he was staying in the centre of the plain of gLaṅ-'khor, several elders of that place came (to him) saying: "It is improper for a man from the border country to settle in this place!", and expelled him. Dam-pa said: "Let us see who was first to come to this country, you or I? When I first came to this country, such and such was its appearance. Later it became so. Again later it became so." The elders unable to answer, withdrew. His coming to Diṅ-ri is called the "Fifth occasion." The Doctrines which were taught by him since then are called the "Later" Lineage (brgyud-pa phyi-ma). He resided there, subsisting on wild peas (gro-ma). The first to see Dam-pa's face was lČog-ro sMyon-pa (name of a famous Tibetan siddha. A manuscript Life-story/rnam-thar/ (21*b*)
of this siddha is said to exist in Tibet). (Dam-pa's) blessing entered inside him, and by meeting Dam-pa he obtained emancipation. Later he stayed at sKyi-śod (the ancient name of the district of Lha-sa. In the Central Asian Tibetan historical chronicles sKyi-śod often stands for Lha-sa). It is said that even rGya-ma-pa dbOn-ston was unable to defeat him (in the art of magic). The next to see Dam-pa was kLog-skya Ral-pa-čan. On seeing the face of the Teacher a concentrated trance which enabled him to dispense with food and cloth (lto-gos mi-dgos-pa'i tiṅ-ṅe-'dzin) was born in him. Though he did not even know the alphabet, he was able to answer all questions on the Doctrine (put to him). The next after him to see Dam-pa was 'Bro Zla-'od. He was free from the notion of the reality (of Phenomenal Existence), and freed

from the eight worldly dharmas. The next to see Dam-pa was Sum-pa Khu-tshab who developed the notion of not-differentiating day and night, and darkness did not hide objects (for him) (i.e. he was able to see in the dark). The bla-ma Phyar-čhen was the first to build a house (for a monastery). He was the son of the king (mṅa'-bdag) rTse-lde (King of Guge, c. 1076 A.D.). This monastery was considered auspicious because its foundation was laid by a person of royal blood. The first nun, into whose hands Dam-pa had entrusted auspicious objects, was dGe-'dun-skyid, the lady of Čug-mo-za. After her there have been many (nuns) in whom meditation was produced by auspicious objects entrusted by Dam-pa. The first man to honour Dam-pa was rJe Khri-pa. He had spent his life independently, without engaging in agriculture or cattle-breeding. The first to receive precepts from Dam-pa, was Phyar-čhuṅ-ba. After him many head teachers (dbu-čhe) appeared. In the East—Dam-pa Phyar-čhen. In the South—Vajrakrodha. In the West—Phyar-čhuṅ. In the North—the Bodhisattva Kun-dga' (this was the chief disciple of Dam-pa). These were known as the "Four yogins guarding the Gate" (sGo-pa'i rnal-'byor-pa-bži). There were 108 excellent head disciples (bu-čhen); 26 disciples who had removed illusions, and 12 disciples who were able to control their mats (i.e. who did not raise from their meditative mats; gdan-non-gyi slob-ma, a common expression meaning one able to keep to his meditative mat. A common saying says: rta'i goṅ-non-pa sla/gdan-gyi goṅ-non-pa dka'/"it is easy to sit on a horse,/but/difficult to sit on a/meditative/mat." The expression also means sometimes a disciple "fit to sit on his Teacher's/meditative/mat.") On them Dam-pa bestowed precepts separately according to the character of each of them, therefore they cannot be included in a single Lineage of Precepts. Dam-pa introduced the bla-ma Phyar-čhen to the Prajñāpāramitā, which could be meditated upon, and that which could not be meditated upon (i.e. which was beyond meditation). He removed (22a) his doubts with the help of the bKa'-čho-lu ("Lesser Instructions"), the mDo-sbyor ("Classification of Sūtras"), and Don-sdebs ("Summary of Meaning"). Phyar-čhuṅ was introduced by Dam-pa to the precepts which did not differentiate between Tantra and Prajñāpāramita He set his mind in equilibrium with the help of the four seva-sādhanas (bsñen-sgrub-bži). Dam-pa used to say: "Vajrakrodha is fit for the Path of Blessing", and made him pray continuously. Dam-pa said: "The Bodhisattva Kun-dga' belongs to the type of individuals of gradual (spiritual) development". He imparted to him the "Purification of the Mind" (bLo-sbyoṅ), and made him practise the five kinds of penance. Dam-pa said: "The bla-ma rDzoṅ-pa belongs to the type of individuals of spontaneous (spiritual) development". He introduced him to the single initiation (dbaṅ gčig-mo) of the Mahāmudrā, and established him on the Path. He established the bla-ma rGya-sgom-pa on the immaculate Path (dri-med sraṅs) and imparted the precept called "The identification of the Mind" (rig-pa ṅos-'dzin). To the bla-ma Čug he imparted the precepts of the Path of the Four Initiations, explained by symbols, and established him on the Path of the Four Initiations to serve as antidote. To dbUs-pa sGro-ston after the "sÑiṅ-po'i don" ("The Meaning of Essence") and the mṄon-rtogs, he gave an exposition of the characteristics of both the types of individual, that of the gradual (spiritual) development, and that of the spontaneous (spiritual) development. In order to remove his doubts, he preached the "Three Lineages of Meaning" (Don-rgyud-skor-gsum). To the bla-ma Ye-gzi 'bar-re he taught (the Doctrine), basing himself on (his) bLo-bral sems-kyi ṁe-loṅ, and introduced him to the subject of Mahāmudrā. He introduced Ža-ma, sister and brother, to both the types of individual, that of the spontaneous and that of the gradual (spiritual) development, basing himself on the main text of the Dohā. Thus most of his precepts were practised by individuals, who obtained emancipation, but were not generally known. Dam-pa spent 21 years at Diṅ-ri, from the year

Fire-Female-Ox (me-mo-glaṅ—1097 A. D.) till the Fire-Female-Hen (me-mo-bya—1117 A.D.) year. Having benefitted many belonging to different races, he passed away.

The Bodhisattva Kun-dga', one the four "yogin gate-keepers", wrote on about three pages the teaching of Dam-pa, and called it the "bKa'-čho-lu'i skor". The bla-ma Phyag-čhuṅ wrote one and half pages which he called the "Dum-dum khrigs-kyi skor" ("uncomplete, but exact"). (22b)
Phyar-čhen wrote one page called the "bKa'-mdo-sbyor-gyi skor. Vajrakrodha wrote half a page entitled "Rin-po-čhe Don-sdebs-kyi skor". In this manner they collected the teaching of Dam-pa. Of the above (disciples), the Bodhisattva Kun-dga' was the one to whom (Dam-pa) entrusted the "Single" Lineage (čhig-rgyud), saying: "The flood (śwa-čhu) hould be directed towards Kun-dga'!".

The story of the 24 nuns (ma-Jo), who had faith in Dam-pa, as related by the Bodhisattva Kun-dga': Saṅs-rgyas: her native place was Čhu-bzaṅs of Śrī-ri (near Šel-dkar rdzoṅ). She was the beloved danghter of her parents, who possessed Sūtra books. In the company of eight or nine girls she visited Dam-pa. She practised meditation for nine years without returning to her native place, and a yogic insight was produced in her. Dam-pa having perceived her death, said: "O Kun-dga', to-day not far from you, a person, who had seen the Buddha, will pass away! Do you know this person?" Kun-dga' replied: "Is this Dam-pa yourself? "Dam-pa said: "It isn't! But one who is like me". After a short while (en-tsam-na), the lady Saṅs-rgyas passed away. After the cremation of her remains, the sky was filled with rainbows.

gSer btsun-ma: her native place was Ža-ma pha-drug. She asked her father's advice, saying: "I shall be visiting Dam-pa." The father said: "The yogin and nuns belong to different sects. Don't go!" She went however, and asked Dam-pa for hidden precepts. Dam-pa revealed her true name, and she mastered the precepts. She showed great diligence in meditation and used to say often: "The thief will be coming!" (i.e. death is approaching). She lived for a hundred years. After her death, the sky was filled with rainbows. (On her cremation) many relics were left behind, including an image of Vajrasattva.

The lady kLan-čhuṅ: Her native place was La-stod sTag-sde. She obtained precepts from Dam-pa and Kun-dga', (23a) practised them, and obtained spiritual realization. After the death of Dam-pa, she settled in gLaṅ-'khor. She died at the age of 81. Numerous relics were left behind.

The lady 'Bar-ma: her native place was Upper Myaṅ. She became the wife of Dam-pa Čug and obtained precepts from Dam-pa. For three years she wandered like a deer in the mountains, practised meditation and a yogic insight (rtogs-pa) was born in her. She passed away at Tshes-spoṅ of Upper Myaṅ, and numerous relics were left after her.

The lady Ri-ma: she was a native of rTsaṅ-roṅ snar-pa. She married, but separated, because her husband proved to be a wicked man. She accompanied some merchants and met Dam-pa. She obtained hidden precepts from him and practised them for seven years. A yogic insight was born in her. After her death, Dam-pa circumambulated her tomb many times, and all were surprized at this. Many relics were left behind.

The lady Ye-śes lčam: her native place was Maṅ-yul Guṅ-thaṅ. She was an attendant (ñe-gnas-ma) of a female siddha, named the lady rJe-mo, who died at the age of 101. She was expert in the worship of the Teacher, and had a special reverence towards Dam-pa. A yogic insight was born in her. She passed away at Guṅ-thaṅ. (On her cremation) many sounds, lights and rainbows were observed.

The lady Čhos-sgron: she was a native of La-stod lDog-pa. She was the wife of Bodhisattva Kun-dga'. Once when Kun-dga stayed too long in the presence of Dam-pa, she grew angry, and having caught him by the hair, dragged him out. Kun-dga' however respected her, and did not reprove her, but only said: "Proceed slowly! Now aren't you pleased?" The woman suffered pains at the time of her death, because of the infringements of her vows. For this reason she is the most insignificant (ṅan-śos) among the 24 nuns.

The lady Ma-gčes: her native place was La-stod Maṅ-gar. She was taken as wife by Kun-dga', and obtained precepts from both father and son (i.e. Dam-pa and Kun-dga'). She practised meditation with diligence and obtained spiritual realization. She died in this Northern La-stod. After her cremation, an image of Vajrasattva and many other relics were left behind.

The lady Čhos-skyabs: her native place was Khu-le of Upper Myaṅ. Faith having been born in her, she proceeded towards gLaṅ-'khor. She renounced her considerable wealth, and for 12 years subsisted on water only (čhu-'thun-byed-pa). She practised meditation and a yogic insight was born in her. At the time of her death, many relics were left behind.

The lady Čhos-skyid: her native place was Ya-'brog khob-le. She was married, and though she got children and gathered wealth, she used to say that she was going to embrace religion. Her brother the kalyāṇa-mitra gÑal-ston said: "If you have decided to do nothing else, but follow religion, then go to Dam-pa Saṅs-rgyas who resides at Diṅ-ri in La-stod." She went to gLaṅ-'khor (near Diṅ-ri) and spent a long time there. She passed away two years after Dam-pa's death. There were many relics left after her.

The lady sGur-mo: she was a native of Čhu-bzaṅs of Śrī-ri in La-stod. She spent ten years at gLaṅ-'khor and passed away at that place. There were many relics left after her (cremation).

The lady Lha-mo: her native place was sTod-luṅs Ri-ma. Her family name was 'Ber. Having abandoned her native place, she spent six years at gLaṅ-'khor. After the death of Dam-pa, she returned to (her) native place, and stayed there for three years. Later she proceeded to Diṅ-ri, and spent a long time there. She died there, and on her death rainbows and lights were observed.

The lady Myaṅ-mo: she was a native of Tsha-roṅ of Śab. Faith having been born in her, she met Dam-pa. After spending ten years at gLaṅ-'khor she passed away. (On her cremation) an image of the two-faced Vārahī (žal-gñis-ma) was left behind, and many rainbows and lights were observed.

The lady dBaṅ-phyug lčam: she was a native of sTod-luṅs stoṅ-khuṅ. She went to visit Nepāl and met Dam-pa. After spending 11 years at gLaṅ-'khor, she died. Her cremation was accompanied by many auspicious signs.

The lady rDo-rje rgyan: her native place was Diṅ-ri gDoṅ-pa. She was of a very attractive appearance. She had faith in the teaching of Dam-pa and spent 15 years at gLaṅ-'khor. Later she destroyed her illusory visions ('Khrul-žig-tu (24a) soṅ-ba, this expression is applied to those siddhas who having attained a higher stage, appear to be mad to outsiders). At the time of her death, after completing all preparations for the cremation, all saw her led by a luminous body proceeding towards the summit of the northern mountains. This was said to have been prophesied by ḍākinīs. Next day, at dawn, they carried (the body) to the Northern Mountains, and the light preceded the body. All men saw during seven days the luminous shape vibrating without disappearing.

The lady Nam-mkha'-gsal: she was a native of 'Ol-kha in dbUs. She was endowed with a clear understanding, and a fair complexion. She spent six years with Dam-pa, obtained instruction in the Doctrine, practised meditation, and obtained spiritual realization. After the death of Dam-pa, she lived for four years more, and (her) urine was transformed into honey. After that she journeyed to dbUs, and passed away at Byaṅ at the age of 84. All her mortal remains changed into relics.

The lady sGro-ne: she was fond of pomp, was distinguished by liberality to the poor, and was surrounded by a numerous retinue. Because of her proud nature, Dam-pa used to rise (from his seat) whenever he acknowledged her salutation, and exclaim: "O!" (u-lags). He used to honour her in this manner. She held Dam-pa in reverence and received his blessing. She then dismissed all her retinue and entered meditation. Later she became a devout.

The lady 'Phan-mo: her native place was 'Phan-yul. She lived with one attendant at gLaṅ-'khor (near Diṅ-ri), and both died at the same time. (At the time of her death) the valley was filled with medicated perfume (sman-dri), and many auspicious signs were observed. All were filled with wonder.

The lady rJe'u-ma: her native place was Oṅ-po. She was an expert weaver, was obedient, and attended on Dam-pa. She spent many years at Diṅ-ri. She died, having spent many years at Guṅ-thaṅ. Her body was carried to the mountains, and an image of Tārā was (afterwards) recovered on the place where the body had been left.

The lady Ro-zan-ma: her native place was Guṅ-thaṅ. She was the bride of rGya sGom-ma. Dam-pa spoke beforehand of her coming. A yogic insight (rtogs-pa) was born in her, and she obtained spiritual realization. She overcame constructive thoughts. She passed away at Guṅ-thaṅ. During her cremation smoke turned into light. (24b)

The lady Śaṅs-čhuṅ-ma: her native place was Śaṅs-pa. When she was going to see a local fair, she met Dam-pa. Filled with reverence for Dam-pa, she entered the gate of religion. She spent six years at gLaṅ-'khor, and after the death of Dam-pa she settled at Śaṅs. On the cremation of her body, many relics were recovered.

The story of Ža-čhuṅ-ma (Ma-gčig Labs-sgron-ma) was related above. gŽon-nu-ma, a girl from Diṅ-ri-gdoṅ: Her native place was Mar-ma of Upper dbU-ru. Once she came to trade with her father, and met Dam-pa. She felt faith in his teaching, and was blessed by him. A yogic insight was born in her. She used to keep silent, pretending to be dumb. She practised meditation, but died soon afterwards. At the time of her death, Dam-pa said: "To-morrow morning in this place of ours a siddha will pass away." They inquired: "Will Dam-pa pass out?" Dam-pa replied: "Not I! There is a girl longing to go to Oḍḍiyāna." Next morning she died, without being ill.

The female alms-giver (ña-ma) Khyim-pa-mo: she was known as the alms-giver rDor-gsal of Boṅ-śod. She amassed children, husband and wealth, as well as faith, diligence, and reverence. She was compassionate and charitable. At the time of her death, the valley was filled with rainbows and lights. (Her mortal remains) were changed into relics, and all were filled with wonder.

The chapter about the 24 nuns (ma-J̌o, lady).

The Bodhisattva Kun-dga': Throughout five former existences he had been adopted by Dam-pa. In this life, he was born in the year Water-Male-Tiger (čhu-pho-stag—1062 A.D.) as son of father sTod-pa Khri-bzaṅs and mother J̌o-mo Dar-ma (the lady Dar-ma) at Tsha-guṅ, east of Diṅ-ri. When he was called sTod-čhuṅ 'Bum-me Byaṅ-ra, he cried, saying: "I am Kun-dga' ", and so became known by the name of Kun-dga'. He married the lady sKyur-mo gza', and a (25a)
son, gSer-'od, was born to them. He gave up all worldly occupations, and his wife and son were obliged to beg after his means had come to an end. When he was 39, in the year Iron-Dragon (lčags-'brug—1100 A.D.), which was the third year since the coming of Dam-pa to gLaṅ-'khor, he deceived his wife by saying to her: "I am going on a raid towards sÑe-nam la-kha", but instead went to gLaṅ-'khor to interview Dam-pa. Early that morning, Dam-pa's voice resounded: "Inmates of the monastery, listen! To-day the hero rDo-rJe is coming! Let all sweep (the compound), prepare offerings and go to receive him with music". They followed his instructions, and kept watch over all quarters, but no one came. Later in the day, a man of evil appearance, dressed in rags, poorly armed, carrying a small quantity of flour as provisions, came in meekly. Laughing scornfully, all went out to receive him. Dam-pa, pleased, advanced

to meet him, with the words: "I am delighted at the coming here of the (dpa'-bo) hero rDo-rje!", and ordered Phyar-čhuṅ to arrange a high seat for hero rDo-rje (dpa'-bo rDo-rje). As the latter did not understand this symbolic word, Dam-pa himself gathered a heap of ashes on the top of which he placed four intercrossed arrows, saying: "O son, pleasing to all (Kun-dga'-ba'i bu)! If you were to sit on it, it would be good!" Then the Guru Bodhisattva having grasped (with his hand) Dam-pa's garment, inquired. "Of what nature is this Phenomenal Existence?" Dam-pa replied: "Verily it is an insect amidst the excrements of a dog, O Kun-dga' !" Again Kun-dga' inquired: "Living creatures born in this (World) are they possessed of a chance to obtain Bliss?" Dam-pa replied imitating with his fingers the joints of a chain: "The suffering is like the rings of a chain (which follow one after another)". Kun-dga' again inquired: "Does there exist a time during which one can obtain liberation from it (i.e. the suffering)?" "The entry on the Path (25b) of Emancipation is not joined to the narrow gorge of the subjective and objective" (i.e. such time does not exist in the case of a person who differentiates between the subjective and objective). Kun-dga' had faith in these words, and without thinking of his native country, he practised penance.. He spent all his time praying before the Teacher and the latter's blessing entered him. He was thus able to grasp the root of virtue. Dam-pa was pleased, and said: "I shall make you, the hero who had come from Tsha-guṅ, victorious in battle!" Kun-dga' inquired: "But how should I wear my armour?" Dam-pa replied: "Sleep in a cave which can accommodate one person only, and wear a ragged garment, barley sufficient to protect you from evil. Live on food, barely sufficient to keep you alive. Practise meditation till you feel hatred towards it. Associate with men without becoming intimate with them (these are your armours)." Kun-dga' inquired: "How should I meditate?" Dam-pa replied: "You should meditate gazing upwards, this being

an auspicious posture peculiar to the Prajñāpāramitā". Kun-dga' practised meditation, and the power of his wisdom spread without limits. He understood the meaning of Dependent Origination, and Dam-pa was very pleased. "Come here Kun-dga'," exclaimed Dam-pa. When Kun-dga' came into his presence, Dam-pa asked him: "Do you have sufficient weight to press down this seat, if anointed as a royal prince? Are you in good form and unshaken to climb this miraculous ladder? Are you able to rule the four continents, if compared to a cakra-varti-rāja ruling a thousand (Worlds)?" The Guru Bodhi-sattva replied: "I have no knowledge of worldly acts, and I shall not be able to do it! I shall not do it! Also I did not do it. But I possess sufficient diligence and understanding of this divine teaching of Dam-pa." Dam-pa was very pleased, and said: "First, we should steal the king's treasure-house! (i.e. one must first understand the hidden nature and keep many hidden precepts), and keep many keys. After that we should light lamps inside a dark house (one should (26a)
remove the darkness of our mind, and develop higher wisdom. One should ferry the living beings across the ocean of Saṃsāra, and develop a method to help others). For this purpose keep a tinder-box in your bag. Finally, we should act as boatmen during the crossing of the river, and we should prepare inflated-bags." (Dam-pa) entrusted to him the "Lineage of the Meaning" of the Prajñāpāramitā, having divided it into five kinds of Paths and three kinds of penance. He also bestowed on him the book of the "Four teachings" (bKa'-bži) and the "Stream of Initiation" (dBaṅ-gi čhu-bo), together with the "Oral Tradition" (sÑan-brgyud). (Dam-pa) said: "Kun-dga' is the only man equal to me! A river is the only thing constantly flowing down and the Sun and the Moon are the only things which rise (constantly) in the sky." Later at the time of Dam-pa's passing into Nirvāṇa, he said: "I have seen in a dream that the Sun had set in the middle of the sky, and that wicked men had abandoned their works

without completing them. This dream presages a misfortune to a border a-tsa-ra (ācārya)." Kun-dga' said: "Well, we should perform an auspicious ceremony." Dam-pa said: "It is then necessary for you, Kun-dga', to take my place. Come here!" Kun-dga' having approached him, Dam-pa touched him with his hand, making the sign (mudrā) of the combined five Dhyānī-Buddhas, the five centres of Kun-dga's body, and said: "Though the Sun will set, the Moon will rise instead." (Kun-dga') accompanied Dam-pa for 18 years. After that, for four years, he (Kun-dga') bestowed hidden precepts on Pa-tshab sgom-pa. He lived for three years more, and in the year Wood-Male-Dragon (śiṅ-pho-'brug—1124 A.D.) proceeded to the Heavenly Abode (mkha'-spyod—abode of heavenly ḍākinīs). At the time of his death, he recited the following ślokas amidst an assembly of head monks on the summit of gTsug-gtor sgaṅ:

"The Wise One, who has avoided the defilement of
Ignorance, who has mastered the (teaching) of the
entire Lineage of Preaching,
Who has reached the limit of the three kinds of penance,
which belonged to the Lineage of Meditation, etc..."

During the same night he left for the Abode of Heavenly ḍākinīs. His disciple was Pa-tshab sgom-pa. He was born in the year Fire-Female-Serpent (me-mo-sbrul—1077 A.D.) as the son of father Pa-tshab-ston 'Bum-grags and mother Yas-mo dpal-'dren in gYuṅ-po of Lower 'Phan-yul. At the age of 12, he received ordination in the presence of sGro čhuṅ-ba, a disciple of Po-to-ba, at Deb-goṅ gnas-čhuṅ. He studied the Vinaya under the Vinayadhara of gYas. At the age of 19, he took up the final monastic ordination before him. (26b)
After that he came to Po-to-ba and a Mental Creative Effort towards Practice was born in him. He studied the Lam-rim of the bKa'-gdams-pas. From sTod-luṅs rGya-dmar he obtained the Mādhyamaka, the Pramāṇa (Logic) and the Sphuṭārtha ('Grel-čhuṅ). From the Pa-tshab lo-tsā-ba he obtained the "Five Treatises of Maitreya" and the "Domain of Vows" (bsLab-

phyogs). From the Bodhisattva 'Brom he obtained the Abhidharmasamuccaya (mṄon-pa goṅ-ma). From Yoṅ-ge dBaṅ-phyug-grags he obtained the Saṃvara Cycle according to the system of Zaṅs-dkar (lo-tsā-ba). Then he thought: "Now, these studies are enough! I should now practise meditation. Who is the greatest in precepts?" They replied: "sKam-sgom is great". He then recollected that Po-to-ba had once mentioned that there was a guru sKam who was in possession of perfect precepts of the Prajñāpāramitā. The basic text of the Prajñāpāramitā having been explained with the help of the Abhisamayālaṃkāra, similar to the opening of the eyes, he thought that there must exist in connection with it a subtle precept like a mantra. He proceeded to the residence of sKam, who imparted to him the introductory precepts of the eight chapters (of the Abhisamayālaṃkāra) which could be meditated upon during a single sitting, and it was like the lighting of a lamp in darkness. He felt faith produced in him, and inquired: "Who was the Master of this Doctrine?" sKam replied: "This (Doctrine) has been obtained by me from a siddha, named Dam-pa Saṅs-rgyas. He has gone to China. It is said, he might have come back to Diṅ-ri. Being old, I am unable to go there. But you, being young, may meet him, should you go there". Pa-tshab having sold his father's field for some gold, turquoises and silk, proceeded there (to Diṅ-ri), but was delayed on the way, as he was travelling without companions. On the night of his arrival in Diṅ-ri he stayed at Tsha-khuṅ. He resumed his journey early next morning, and when he had reached the summit of gTsug-tor sgaṅ, he saw a large crowd assembled below, and thinking that Dam-pa must be there, he descended in haste. Before reaching the market place, (27a)
he saw a bluish smoke rising, and asked a woman beggar standing nearby: "What was it?" and she replied: "This is the smoke from the funeral pyre of Dam-pa." Stricken by grief, Pa-tshab fell senseless. On awakening, he discovered that the woman beggar had placed his head on her lap. As he was

weeping, the woman beggar told him: "O Teacher and scholar! Do not weep! Though Dam-pa is dead, there exist many elders equals of Dam-pa himself. You will fulfil your purpose. There, towards the East, resides one named Dam-pa Phyar-čhen-po, who is very much like yourself in character. Go there!" Slowly he went there. The woman beggar ran after him, saying: "Scholar from dbUs! You aren't the son of Phyag-čhen. You are a spiritual son of Kun-dga', therefore go to that stone hut over there!" So he went there. At the door (of the hut) he recited the Refuge formula and prostrated himself several times. Then Kun-dga' opened his closed eyes and gazed at him, saying: "O Son of gYas-mo dpal-'dren! Aren't you tired after the journey?" Pa-tshab understood that Kun-dga' was endowed with the faculty of prescience, and a great faith was born in him. At the same moment (the Teacher's) blessing entered him. He then presented to the Bodhisattva a golden maṇḍala, and said: "Because of my insignificant fortune, I was unable to meet Dam-pa. You, Teacher, have compassion towards me!" Kun-dga' said: "To make ripe a raw individual, initiation is necessary. Do you have the necessary provisions?" Pa-tshab then presented Kun-dga' with a golden sraṅs and a roll of silk. Kun-dga' said: "These (presents) are auspicious! You should spend the night in the cave Sa-phug dkar-po. To-morrow come here!" When he came there next day, he saw a book placed (on the table), and Kun-dga' sitting in meditation. Then Kun-dga' bestowed on him the initiation by placing the book on his head. After finishing the initiation, the Guru Bodhisattva said: "Out of the two Mantrayāna (27b)
and the Prajñāpāramitā, the initiation of the Path of Ripening (sMin-lam) should be performed first according to the Mantrayāna. After which the Path of Salvation should be preached. But this (initiation performed by me) bestows the Path of Ripening and Emancipation at the same time (smin-grol—initiation and emancipation), and remains unknown to others up to the present time. It was a peculiarity (khyed-čhos) of

the black a-tsa-ra (i.e. Dam-pa Saṅs-rgyas) who had merged the four streams of initiation into one. Is this not enough?" Pa-tshab replied: "It is enough!" After one year he completed the "Purification of the Mind" (bLo-sbyoṅ), and asked permission to go to dbUs, but Kun-dga' said: "You must arrange for your provisions and spend one year in seclusion." Kun-dga' preached to him the doctrine of the "Five Paths" (Lam-lṅa: tshogs-lam, sbyor-lam, mthoṅ-lam, sgom-lam, mi-slob-lam), and after finishing it, he said: "O son! You must have surely been a scholar before! Now also you came here after a difficult journey. All the hiden precepts were given to you. Have you attained understanding through your practice and an improvement in yogic insight after coming here? If so, tell it to me!" Pa-tshab replied: "When I was living down there, I understood all the elements of Phenomenal Existence to be devoid of heterogeneity, but that understanding was gained with the help of inference. It was like touching a thing in darkness with one's hand. But here the Nature has shown itself to my sense-faculties, and I reached the limit of yogic insight." Kun-dga' approved of it. A package of paper was hanging above Kun-dga's head, and Kun-dga' said: "In it there used to be some salt of good quality. But in La-stod there is no one able to taste it," saying so, he gave the package to Pa-tshab, and said: "Open it at Thel of sNa-mar." Pa-tshab having gone there, opened the package, and found inside the "Nine Questions and Replies on the Doctrine of the Root first-planted" (Thog-mar zug-pa'i rtsa-ba'i čhos-sde žus-len dgu), the three sections of the Lineage of Meaning, the Doctrine of the Tree ('gril-ba sdoṅ-po'i čhos-don rgyud-skor), and under them—the Symbols (mtshon-dpe) and Fragments (brul-tsho) of the Doctrine of Open Branches (gyed-pa yal-ga'i čhos), the Sixteen Doctrines of Leaves (Lo-'dab-kyi čhos-sde bču-drug), the "Five Doctrines of Beautiful Flowers" (mDzes-pa me-tog-gi čhos-sde lṅa), the Indian alphabet of the Outer, Inner and Hidden which represented the "Doctrine of Fruit" ('bras-bu'i čhos-sde Ā-li-Kā-li-phyi-naṅ-gsaṅ-gsum). Then he returned them to his Teacher who said: "You, yourself should chew this salt," and saying so, he handed him the books and paper to copy them. For one year he studied the "Black Guide" (nag-khrid or written explanation of a text; dmar-khrid, an explanation based on experience; originally a medical term meaning the dissecting of a corpse). He revised them and wrote them down in the form of questions and answers, naming them "'Phra-tig" ("Conclusion"). He also used to discuss with other great disciples, and wrote down these discussions, which he called "'Phra-gčod" ("Revised Conclusions"). Pa-tshab then asked Kun-dga' for permission to stay on at Diṅ-ri, but Kun-dga' said: "It is better for you to return to your native place. Your mother is weeping, saying: 'My son must be dead.' You had better go there!" Pa-tshab then gave him the promise to practise meditation for twelve years. Kun-dga' then placed him in an auspicious house, and gave him all the books, saying: "Take these books with you! The owner of these books will come from the right bank of a large river. Give them to him!" Pa-tshab then offered Kun-dga' three golden sraṅs which remained with him after paying off his expenses. Kun-dga' said: "The follower of an a-tsa-ra needs no gold! But in order to increase your merit, I shall accept them," and saying so he threw them skywards. At his departure, Pa-tshab made the following request: "May I avoid hindrances during the journey and in the practice of meditation!" Kun-dga' then gave him a stone called Thiṅ-ril (bluish in colour /rdo-nag-po/. This may represent the name of a precept) which had the power of subduing demons, and a black stone which had the power of driving away devils, and said: "Don't separate from your bodhicitta, and pray to your Teacher." Kun-dga' then saw him off. When Pa-tshab came down from mountains, he searched for three years for the doctrines of the "First Lineage" and the "Intermediate Lineage", and amassed the requisites for practising meditation. Before that date and after that date he prac-

(28a)

tised meditation for 13 years. After finishing his meditation, he laboured for the welfare of others. Because of the wide renown of his precepts, he gathered round him a large retinue. He bestowed hidden precepts on one named Byaṅ-pa dBon-sgom, who had been an assistant preacher, while he was studying philosophy. After that (Byaṅ-pa dBon-sgom) went to gNam-tsho and there departed to the abode of heavenly ḍākinīs. He bestowed hidden precepts on Pa-tshab sgom-nag who then proceeded to China, and died on the Sino-Tibetan border. There exists a caitya (sku-'bum). Bu-śoṅ sgom-pa, who had a jointless skull (there exists several signs indicating the jointless nature of the skull of a living (28b)
person. Among them, an extra tooth between the two upper incisors, etc.), received precepts from him. He then became the chaplain (mčhod-gnas) of the King of Mi-ñag. Thanks to him the Cycle of Nag-khrid žus-len spread over the entire Northern region. A certain Žaṅ-ṅa rnal-'byor-pa who was himself a Master of Hidden Precepts, when he met Pa-tshab sgom-nag, felt in himself a strong quest for the Doctrine. Pa-tshab bestowed on him the hidden precepts, and he became a saint (siddha). He lived for 118 years. Among his learned disciples, Čhu-mig Rin-mo-ba rGya-grags-bsod was the greatest in religious learning, Thaṅ-sag sTon-tshul was the greatest as monk, Žaṅ-rgyu sGro-lhakhaṅ-pa was the greatest among the nobles, and rṄog Ge-ser was the greatest in wisdom. After he had bestowed precepts on them, they removed their illusions. Among the disciples, who came to him during his old age, there was one named gŚen sgom Re-thul-čan. He bestowed on him precepts and removed his illusions. He proceeded to Khams and passed away without leaving behind his physical body. He (Pa-tshab) bestowed on 'Bro-sgom bSod-nams byaṅ-čhub the sādhana of mKha'-gro-ma bDud-rtsi-bum-pa. He obtained emancipation. He was carried away by ḍākinīs to the Abode of the Heavenly Ḍākinīs. One named U-rgyan ras-pa, who was learned in the precepts of Mantrayāna, preached the doctrine of the

three Paths (lam-gsum). He was endowed with a clear mind, and had grasped the meaning of the formula of Dependent Origination (Pratītyasamutpāda). He was able to deliver presages. Ten-ne was one possessed of the complete precepts of the "Single Lineage" (Čhig-brgyud). Pa-tshab continued his studies to the age of 37 in the year Water-Female-Serpent (čhu-mo-sbrul—1113 A.D.). After that he entered meditation beginning with the year Wood-Male-Horse (śiṅ-pho-rta—1114 A.D.). At the age of 41 in the year Fire-Female-Hen (me-mo-bya—1117 A.D.) he proceeded to Diṅ-ri. For four years he received precepts from the great "sons" of Dam-pa Saṅs-rgyas, such as the Bodhisattva Kun-dga' and others. In the year Iron-Female-Ox (lčags-mo-glaṅ—1121 A.D.) he journeyed to dbUs, and practised meditation for 13 years. According to Žib-mo Dar-rtsags he (practised meditation) for 15 years. When Pa-tshab was 74, in the year Iron-Male-Horse (lčags-pho-rta—1150 A.D.), Ten-ne visited him. When Ten-ne was 32, Pa-tshab passed away (294)
in the year Earth-Male-Tiger (sa-pho-stag—1158 A.D.) at the age of 82. His disciple rGyal-ba Ten-ne (also written Gyal-ba rTen-nas-pa): a certain J̌o-sras-skyabs moved his esidence from Śab-sgo-lṅa of gTsaṅ, and settled at Čhu-'khor f Western Lower Yar (Yar-mda'). In the year Fire-Female-Sheep (me-mo-lug—1127 A.D.) a son was born to him and nother 'Tshur-mo-gza' Maṅ-skyid. At the age of three, the oy was able to recollect his previous existences and used to ay: "I have been Mal brTson-'grus bla-ma!" They asked or blessing So-sku-riṅs who had come to Lower Yar (Yar-nda'). The latter said: "The son of this lady will become great saint (siddha). I shall make him the holder of my piritual Lineage!" He then bestowed on him the Thugs-Je čhen-po'i rdzogs-rim and the permission (luṅ) of the Maṇi-mantra (Oṃ Maṇi padme hūṃ). At the age of five, Ten-ne met Ras-čhuṅ-pa at Ra-mo sMan-čhu-kha, who also aid that he was to become a saint (siddha), and that he vould make him the holder of his Lineage. He bestowed on

him the Dohā according to the method of Ti-pu. At the age of 7, he met sGam-po-pa at Lower Yar (Yar-mda'), who said: "This boy will become a saint (siddha). When he will grow up, send him to me!" He bestowed on Ten-ne the Mahāmudrā. At the age of nine, he asked for the permission (luṅ) to recite the prayer of the Tārā from the ācārya sGom-pa, a nephew of Nag-tsho, The ācārya said: "There exists a karmic link (las-'brel) between us", and bestowed on him the prayer with its lesser branches, and the precepts of Atiśa. Before he had reached the age of 15, he mastered (his) father's doctrines—the Ma-gŚin-Phur-gsum (Ma-mo / Ekajaṭī and others/, gŚin-rJe, and Phur pa) and the dPe-Srog-gČaṅ-gsum (dPe-gtad, the entrusting of books; Srog-gtad—the entrusting of the 'life'-mantra / srog-sṅags/; gčaṅ ?). Then for three years, till the age of 18, he acted as minister of Jo-bo Lha-čhen-po of Bya-sa and Lha-btsun sṄon-mo. He also mastered by heart several nītiśāstras (lugs-kyi bstan-bčos), such as the sKye-bo gso-thigs (Nītiśāstrajantupoṣaṇabindu-nāma, Tg. No. 4330). At the age of 25, he developed a desire to visit the countries of his former existences, and journeyed to Yar-'brog. He came across two other ascetics who asked him: "Where are you going?" He replied: "In a former existence my native place was the gorge (roṅ) of Lho-brag. I am going to see it." The two said to him: "At the monastery of Yar-'brog glaṅ-bu over there, there lives one named sPrul-sku Se Jo-sras who has four mad chaplains (mčhod-gnas). Among them there is one named 'the Mad' rGyal-le-lčam who is able to make prophecies. Let us go to see her!" The monastery (29 was situated on the summit of a hill. Then the three reached the foot of the hill, they noticed an old woman wearing a ragged cloak who was running downhill. She grasped the hand of Ten-ne, and exclaimed: "O! you are my brother! You are Ten-ne! Suck from this breast of mine! Don't go to Lho-brag-roṅ! sNaṅ-khaṅ has been destroyed by War. It isn't good there! In Northern dbU-ru lives the son of gYas-mo dpal-'dren who is longing (to see you). Go there!" Up-to this time his name was 'Jig-rten-grags, but since then he became known as Ten-ne. The two other ascetics also put questions to the woman, but failed to get any answer (from her). He (Ten-ne) having returned to his native place, made preparations to proceed to dbU-ru, but his father did not allow him. This caused displeasure in his mind, and he sang a song, and then became a singer in the company of the minstrel Gal-te-dgos (the minstrel was most probably named so after a refrain in his song—"Gal-te dgos", meaning "if /you/ want"). He then took the upāsaka vows in the presence of 'Briṅ-čha Ru-ba (a famous Teacher) and obtained the bsTan-rim (bsTan-rim, a famous bKa'-gdams-pa text composed by Gro-luṅ-pa. The Lam-rim čhen-mo of Tsoṅ-kha-pa is based on this text) according to the method of the ācārya Gra-thaṅ-pa, and the bDen-gñis (name of a book), according to the method of Dam-pa Čhos-sgro-ba. He then fled secretly from his father, having taken with him a kom-thil (a leather sole), some Dar-śam silk, and a skull-cup (thod-phor). He spent the night at Gra-thaṅ, and felt great mental satisfaction. About mid-night while he was staying at the foot of the Sandy Pass (Bye-ma'i la) a thought occurred in his mind that "it wasn't certain whether the words of the old female ascetic were true, or not. Even if they were true, I have wasted two years. How shall I find the son of gYas-mo dpal-'dren among the numerous priests of dbU-ru? It would be better to return to my native home." Then for seven times he recited the stotra of the Tārā, and lay down. Half asleep he suddenly heard a voice coming from above: "O son of noble family! Don't change your mind! Go there! You will fulfil your purpose." When he awoke from his sleep, he looked up towards the sky and saw the letter Tāṃ (the first syllable of the name Tārā with the anusvāra) of blue-green colour, standing out clearly, like a star. He understood it to be a prophecy by the Tārā. Pa-tshab also perceived it. He then thought: "If I were in need of a Teacher, I should proceed to the residence of the Teacher named sPyan-śwa-re-bo, who is very learned (304a) in the doctrine of the Żi-byed, and is residing at sTod-luṅs." Again a thought came to him: "I must at first take the book which contains the method of sending the power of gTsaṅ-btsan (name of a god) now in the possession of a painter of Bran-ka, named kLu-btsan-grags, who had been the disciples of my father and was now residing in Lower 'Phan-yul. After that I must search for a teacher." Thinking thus, he journeyed towards Lower 'Phan-yul. (He found) the painter Bran-ka drawing a painted image of the Tārā for the lady Ma-gčig. This lady said to him: "Ĵo-sras gYu-ru! Do you recognize the gods, besides the chief goddess in the centre (of the painting), riding on geese?"—"Yes, I know them well", he replied and he recited the rNam-dag gtsug-nor (a śloka containing the names of the gods forming part of the parivāra of the Tārā). Ma-gčig said: "Your recitation is beautiful! You must teach me!"—"I haven't time to teach you! I must go to the bla-ma who preaches the Żi-byed doctrine at sTod-luṅs." She replied: "I have an uncle who is learned in the Żi-byed doctrine. I shall take you there, but you must teach me the śloka." Then he inquired: "What system of Żi-byed (is your uncle preaching)?" Ma-gčig replied: "It is the system of the Bodhisattva Kun-dga'" "Do you know the name of his mother?" Ma-gčig replied: "I know, I know it well, she was called gYas-mo dpal-'dren." He rejoiced in his mind and simultaneously blessing entered him. That night he saw in his dream that a ball of light of the size of a bean had appeared on his tongue. He tasted it, and the taste was excellent. He then swallowed it, and his entire body turned into light, and emitted rays which spread over the ten quarters. Next morning the lady Ma-gčig came to show him the monastery. The bla-ma perceived (his coming), and came down to meet him. The bLa-ma said: "Ĵo-sras of Yar-mda', by coming to-day you have pleased me. But you could have come the year before last!" He asked the Teacher to bestow on him the hidden precepts according

to the method of Dam-pa Kun-dga'. "Your coming is auspicious! I shall bestow instruction on you". Then the Teacher added: "According to the method of the Bodhisattva (Kun-dga') the juice of perfection does not stick on those who did not develop their minds, therefore one should bestow the initiation of the Ā-li Kā-li. Do you have the necessary provisions to enable you to receive this initiation?" He replied: "Now I have come in search of a teacher. I shall collect provisions from my native place, and shall then return again". The bLa-ma replied: "Hesitation is the greatest among the creations of devils! One should perform it (the (30b)
initiation) right now! Are there no provisions at all?" He then offered the Teacher the skull-cup (thod-phor) having placed it on the leather sole, and having introduced the corner of a piece of silk into a needle, and placed the needle into the skull-cup. The Teacher said: "According to the omens of the presents made by Jo-sras gYu-ru-ba, you are fit to master profound doctrines (the offering of the skull-cup). You will also be able to guide the faithful ones (the present of the needle with a piece of silk introduced into the needle's eye), but you will fail in amassing a large worldly fortune (the present of an empty skull-cup)". He then placed the book (on his head) and blessed him, and simultaneously an excellent understanding of the undifferentiated samāhita-jñāna (mñam-bžag ye-śes, the intuitive knowledge of the saint at the time of intense concentration) and the pṛṣṭha-labdha-jñāna (rJes-thob ye-śes, the knowledge of the saint acquired after trance) was produced in him. The bla-ma said: "This is the very insight into Nature, but you must also possess the sign and perfection of the Path. For seven days you must obtain the permission (luṅ), must realize the sign, and manifest the three kinds of efforts". (Effort of Body, Mind and Speech/ lus-kyi 'bad-pa, sems-kyi 'bad-pa, ṅag-gi 'bad-pa/). (Handicapped by the lady Ma-gčig for eight months) he was unable to complete the "Purification of the Mind" (bLo-sbyoṅ). He then asked the Teacher: "Does there

exist something like a book on this doctrine?" The Teacher replied: "The a-tsa-ra (Dam-pa Saṅs-rgyas) used to introduce (his disciples) to the Immaculate State of the Mind (rig-pa dri-med), and they concentrated on meditation on it. Therefore books weren't necessary! But you must seek for the Teacher's method (phyag-bžes)." When he went Northwards (towards Nub-Hor), he obtained only two bundles of blue-paper and six female dzos (a crossbreed between a yak and a domestic cow), and offered them to the Teacher. Two dzos he kept for himself. Then for one year he practised the "Guide of the Five Paths" (Lam-lṅa, Lam-lṅa'i khrid), and received initiation. He then wrote down all the saying of his Teacher, and called (his notes) the Žib-mo Dar-tshags. After that he divided the Doctrine into four chapters or sections: (1) bKa'-babs (Authorization), (2) Dri-med (The Immaculate), (3) sÑan-brgyud (Oral Tradition), (4) the Cycle of Dohā (Do-ha'i skor). The Teacher then gradually entrusted the books to his care. Opening a book which belonged to the Cycle of rTen-'brel (rTen-'brel gyi čhos-skor, name of a book by Dam-pa Saṅs-rgyas), the (Teacher) said: "This one was called the 'Cycle of various miracles' (sNa-tshogs rdzu-'phrul-gyi skor). You, yogins, needn't practise it! The corners of the book having been damaged by mice, we cannot use it!" and did not bestow it. He spent one year in correcting the text of the nag-khrid, or written xposition, and conducted numerous debates (on the subject). Then he asked the Teacher's permission to go to his native country, (31a)
but the Teacher did not give it, and said to him: "Still you must complete the corners of the hidden precepts (i.e. you should continue your studies), and arrange them according to order. Also you must get acquainted with the former teachers of this Lineage". He spent another year (doing it). Then Gal-te dgos (the minstrel) came, and asked for hidden precepts, but he did not give them. In order to please him, he proceeded to sTod-luṅs, and asked for religious instruction sMon-lam-'bar and sPyan-śwa-re-bo. He also obtained ins-

uction in the Doctrine from both sÑags čhuṅ-ba of 'Phan-l and Žaṅ-ṅe sGom-čhen. After the lapse of four years, e Teacher said: "Ĵo-sras gYu-ru-ba's path led him well rough the first gorge of penance! Now it is time to proceed gTsaṅ-kha of Yar-mda." The elders having gathered, the eacher said that "he will live for 121 years and that many ints (siddhas) will appear among his sons, nephews and eces." He then made a seven years' vow of penance and editation (dKa'-thub-kyi dam-bča'). He also offered on ven occasions the resolve to impart religion to all those who ould ask him for it. The Teacher said: "There will be no rm, if you were to continue the observance of your vow of editation for a longer period. Should you be unable to ntinue it, you could preach extensively the ordinary doc-ines. But don't impart the hidden precepts of the bKa'-bži those who are unable to become masters of the Doctrine, d don't impart the auspicious rites (rTen-'brel) on those ho are unable to labour for the welfare of others in this life. they do not offer the vow of meditation, do not introduce em to the 'House of the Auspiciousness' (seems to be the me of a Tantric ceremony—rTen-'brel-gyi khaṅ-pa). Should ese disciples become extremely impudent, then guide their inds with the help of the 'Cycle of the Precious Mahā-udrā' (Phyag-rgya čhen-po rin-po-čhe'i skor). In old age ou will be happy. Till then, should you find it difficult to tain provisions and clothing, perform auspicious religious remonies. In general, you shouldn't become the master of ore than four retinues (of disciples), but you must act as a cret yogin, and concentrate your efforts on meditation." en-ne then proceeded towards Yar-mda' and imparted on e old monk (ban-rgan) sGom-grags of rTses-thaṅ the recita-on of the bLo-sbyoṅ (bLo-sbyoṅ-gi bzlas-luṅ). The signs the purification of sins having appeared in him (sGom-grags), e became pleased and promised to support him (Ten-ne). or seven years he practised meditation in a tower at rTses-aṅ. After two years, he heard that Pa-tshab had died.

and visited for a short while (the Teacher's) monastery. (31b
Then for two years he stayed immured, except for a short period during which he attended the funeral service for his deceased father.

For three years he practised meditation and acquired all the merits (obtainable) on the Path. He used to say: "Though my fame as a saint (siddha) was great, in reality the benefit accrued to my disciples from me was insignificant. This seems to have been due to interruption on three occasions in my meditation and penance. Though he did acquire the merits accruing from the sign of the Path, he did not disclose most of it to others. He imparted some (of it) to Žig-po. He (Ten-ne) acquired (the power) of the transference of the vital principle (groṅ-'J̌ug, parakāya-praveśa), and made an exhibition of the transference of the vital principle at the religious college (čhos-ra) of rÑog J̌o-sras. Then in order to practise certain Tantric rites, he became a minstrel, and for six years (went about) singing songs. Then on the advice of J̌o-bo Lha-čhen-po of Bya-sa, Lha-btsun sṄon-mo and J̌o-bo Bye'u čhuṅ-pa, he again put on the monastic robes, and was nominated ācārya of the monastic college. Most of his time was spent in seclusion, during which he composed numerous commentaries (bśad-'bum) on the sayings of Dam-pa (Saṅs-rgyas). He decided to entrust his Lineage to J̌o-sras Nam-mkha', but the latter died young. One named gŽon-pa Ya-tshe was carried away by his desires. Having gone to Koṅ-po, he passed away. Because of his fame of possessing important precepts, numerous leading personalities of dbU and gYor addressed requests to him. But he kept the injunction of his Teacher, and abstained from imparting precepts. The disciples on whom he imparted precepts were: the six kings (gtsad-po) of Ṅam-śod, the six queens and the six princesses (yum-bu), the six kalyāṇa-mitras, the six Tantrics, the six house-holder devotees, and the six merchants trading in the Doctrine (čhos-'tshoṅ-ba'i tshoṅ-dpon-drug) who did not keep the injunction of the Teacher (not to impart precepts), in all

36. The first thirty did not possess the Lineage of Word, the last six did not possess initiation and permission. Therefore no one of the 36 were fit to be masters of his doctrine. Then the Master of the Doctrine Rog Śes-rab-'od, who was indicated in the Teacher's prophecy, came to Yar-kluṅs and made a request for an exposition of the Doctrine. Later, when ha was invited to J̌aṅ and requested to preach the Doctrine, Ten-ne imparted (precepts) on both Žig-po Ñi-ma seṅ-ge and his brother, and appointed them as Masters of the Doctrine. He thought that the abbotship at the monastic college at Yar-kluṅs was a source of hindrance to him, and he (32a) gave it up. After that he dressed as he pleased. Having gone to Yar-stod, he hid some books on the mountain of Bos-mo. He received an invitation from one named the kalyāṇa-mitra of gNas-čhuṅ, and took up residence at gNas-čhuṅ and gSer-lha. There he also hid books on the rocks of Śan-thog. He also hid several books (dpe-gter) in the mountains of Goṅ-bo and Śam-bu. Žig-po while wandering about the country, heard that Ten-ne was residing at gSer-lha, and went there to pay homage to him. Ten-ne said to him: "The coming of Žig-po is welcome! I was invited here by the gNas-čhuṅ kalyāṇa-mitra, but he didn't give me food, and left me to die from hunger! Now you must take me to Gra," and saying so, Ten-ne shed tears profusely. Žig-po replied: "I have been wandering about the country for a long time, I do not know what has happened to my home. I must first go to my home, and arrange for your coming. I shall then come to invite you, Teacher." Ten-ne said: "Son, being careful in the keeping of your vows, I know, you will keep your promise. But it would be better if you were to take me there at the present time." Žig-po then went to his home, sold a good field for butter and barley, and returned to invite the Teacher. When they came to Gra, the Teacher spent his time at various places and used to reproach him sometimes for food, sometimes for clothing, but Žig-po remained contented, felt faith born in himself and endured the reproaches.

At the end of his life Ten-ne became blind. He passed away at the age of 91 in the year Fire-Female-Ox (me-mo-glaṅ —1217 A.D.) at Brag-sgom čhen-mo. They built a caitya and placed the remains inside it. The caitya and remains have been preserved till the present time without damage. When rTag-tu-ṅu (Sadārodana, "Constantly weeping") was searching for Čhos-'phags (Dharmocca? rTag-tu ṅu and Čhos-'phags are the names of two Bodhisattvas mentioned in the last chapter of the Aṣṭsāhasrikā-Prajñāpāramitā. The first was so called because he constantly wept when hearing the Prajñāpāramitā recited. He once made the attempt to sell his heart to a merchant in order to acquire offerings for presentation to the Prajñāpāramitā. The daughter of a rich merchant told him that it was unnecessary to sell his heart, and that she would give him the necessary expenses. They then proceeded in search of Čhos-'phags who was said to possess a complete text of the Prajñāpāramitā. The city of Ch'êng-tu in Ssŭ-ch'üan Province in China is believed to be the residence of the Bodhisattva Čhos-'phags), he found the volumes of the Prajñāpāramitā sealed with seven seals. Because of this omen this Lineage: became a 'Single' Lineage till the seventh teacher of the Lineage: Asaṅga, Vasubandhu, the brāhmaṇa Āryadeva, Dam-pa (Saṅs-rgyas), Kun-dga', Pa-tshab, Te-ne (Ten-ne). His disciple Žig-po and his brother (32b)
propagated the complete precepts towards the ten quarters.

His (Ten-ne's) eulogy by Žig-po:

"Outwardly, as if consumed by strong desires,
Inwardly—a Teacher who had exterminated desires.
Outwardly, as if a very stupid man,
Inwardly—a Teacher of great resignation.
Outwardly—difficult of approach,
He was a Teacher longed for by others, when separated from him.
Outwardly—a man of ordinary body and speech,
Inwardly—a Teacher of steadfast virtue.
Outwardly—reclining without meditating,

Inwardly—a Teacher opening the numberless gates of meditation.

Though in general, he did not study much,
Inwardly (he was) a Teacher aflame with the wisdom born of meditation.

Outwardly—a miser in religion,
Inwardly—a Teacher spreading widely the Meditative Lineage.

I pray to this Lord King of the Hidden (sBabs-pa'i rgyal-po) in human form!" The Chapter on the three classes of teachers of the hidden "Single" Lineage.

Those, on whom the mahāsiddha (grub-čhen) Jina Te-ne (—Ten-ne) had entrusted fully the Lineage of the Doctrine, were the two brothers Rog. Now during the period of the Early Propagation of the Doctrine (bstan-pa sña-dar) there had been one named Nam-mkha' ye-śes, the monk of Rog who possessed knowledge and supernatural powers. His descendants became excellent mantradharas. The 24th in the Line was one named Rog Śes-rab bla-ma, a disciple of Go-rub Yaṅ-dag and dPal Lha-ri-ba. He practised meditation on Vajrakīla, and was successful in the rite of exercising dead bodies. It was foretold that there will be eight great men among his descendants. He was born in the year Iron-Male-Horse (lčags-pho-rta—1090 A.D.), and passed away in the year Water-Female-Serpent (čhu-mo sbrul—1173 A.D.) at the age of 84. His son was bKra-śis grags-pa. He was a mantradhara, who had acquired his father's knowledge, and was born in the year Earth-Male-Horse (sa-pho-rta—1138 A.D.), This Earth-Horse year is the year of the birth of rGya-ma dpon-ston. He passed away at the age of 49. (33a)
Among the three brothers who had incarnated for the welfare of others, and who were born to him and mother Čhos-kyi-dge, the eldest Śes-rab-'od was an incarnation of the East Indian mahā-paṇḍita, named Śes-rab-grub (Prajñāsiddha). He was born in the year Fire-Male-Dog (me-pho-khyi—1166 A.D.). At the age of five his grand-father Śes-rab bla-ma

taught him writing and arithmetics. At the age of 7, he became an expert in reading and was able to recite during one day the Prajñāpāramitā in 25,000 ślokas (Ñi-khri, Pañcaviṃśatisāhasrikā). The father did not believe it, and made him recite the text in his presence. The father joined the palms of his hands in devotion. Till the age of 10, he studied the doctrines of the Tantra with his father and grand-father. The father then thought that one should teach the boy the art of magic. He made him stay in seclusion from the age of 10 to 13, propitiating Vajrakīla. Many signs of miraculous power were observed. Especially, he obtained a clear vision of the complete image of Vajrakīla. He said: "I have completed the propitiation of Kīla. Now my body has become similar to a solid piece of iron. Now if I were surrounded by a thousand demons, they wouldn't be able to harm even my retinue, not to speak of myself." At the age of 13, at the request of Rog-ston btsan-po to his father, he was sent to him for study. For two years he studied, and became master of the mDo (a section of the rÑiṅ-ma Tantra) class, the Cycle of Māyā and of the "Domain of the Mind" (Sems-phyogs), according to the method of So, the sGrub-thabs rnam-gsum, the A-ro gsaṅ-skor, the Vimala (a rÑiṅ-ma book), and the precepts of the "Upper" Lineage of the Ži-byed system, and became learned. From Rog-ston kLu-sbyin he obtained numerous sādhanas of the Kriyā (Tantra). Somewhat later he obtained from him the new translation of the Nāgārjuna system (Guhyasamāja), as well as the Cycle of Saṃvara according to the method of Mar-Do (Mar-pa Dopa). At the age of 15, he obtained from Lha-bdres-ma goṅ-ba the Cycle of mDo, the Cycle of Māyā, according to the method of sKyo, and the "Tantras of Scriptures" (Luṅ-gi rGyud, a class of rÑiṅ-ma Scriptures), called the "Six Little Sons" (Bu-čhuṅ-drug), the Five Tantras of the "early" translation (sṅa-'gyur-gyi rgyud-lṅa belonging to the rÑiṅ-ma-pa sect), the Cycle of Amṛta according to the system of Khams, the rTa-mgrin lha-bži, the sGron-sbrul, and other texts. At the age of 16, he broke one of his teeth, and an iron tooth was put in its place, and thereafter he became known as the "Scholar with an iron tooth" (lčags-so-čan). With the ācārya Yam-śud dŃos grub he studied with great assiduity the Cycle of mDo and the Cycle of Māyā according to the method of Zur, from the age of 16 to the age of 20. No one was able to defeat him in philosophical debates. Formerly he was called rGya-mon, but Yam-śud named him Śes-rab-'od. At the age of 17, he heard from sKyaṅ-po Dar-ma-grags the "Four Doctrines" (č̣hos-bži) of 'J̌am-dpal sgeg-pa, and the "Six Doctrines" of Smṛti (Smṛti'i čhos-drug). At the age of 18, he composed a commentary on the Lam-rim (rÑiṅ-ma'i Lam-rim) of the Cycle of Māyā and a summary (stoṅ-thuṅ) of gŽi-lam. At the age of 19, he journeyed to gTsaṅ. At first he visited So Dar-seṅ in Lower Lhan. As soon as he met him, great faith was born in him. He obtained from him the Doctrine of Yaṅ-dag (a rÑiṅ-ma doctrine), the Cycle of Amṛta, the rDzogs-čhen sgaṅ-dril (a rÑiṅ-ma system), the mDo-sgyu mtshan-ma (a rÑiṅ-ma work), the branches of Abhidharma, and the "Domain of Practice"(bsLab-phyogs). From the latter's assistant preacher Laṅ-ston J̌o-pad (he obtained) the Abhidharmasamuccaya (mŃon-pa Kun-las-btas) and the Cycle of (Vajra)kīla according to the method of sKyi. Grom rGya bSod-nams-'bar at Myaṅ-stod (Upper Myaṅ) he obtained the Cycle of Amṛta according to the method of rGya. From the bla-ma rGya Seṅ-dkar in the Western Gorge of Lho-brag he obtained the Cycle of Amṛta (bDud-rtsi). From Myaṅ Nag-mdo-po he obtained the Cycle of mDo and the Cycle of Māyā. From the ācārya dPon-zlos he obtained the Phyag-rgya čhen-po mdzod. From the ācārya J̌o-dar he obtained the rDzogs-čhen kLoṅ-čhen a (rÑiṅ-ma book). From gTsaṅ-nag brTson-'grus seṅ-ge he obtained the Tshad-ma bsdus-pa (this seems to be a Tibetan work), the Sañcaya (sDud-pa, Prajñāpāramitāsañcayagāthā, mDo-maṅ, fol. 3456; See M. Lalou: "Les mDo-maṅs", Paris, 1931, p. 42, No. 108), according to the method of 'Bum-pa. From the siddha dŃos-grub he obtained the three (33b)

Cycles of the Mahākāruṇika (Avalokiteśvara). Later, while he was residing at the residence of Lha-rJe So, his father who had come to bring some provisions, was suddenly stricken with paralysis, and died. He suffered from deep sorrow, and spent what remained of the provisions in memory of his father. He then proceeded towards dbUs and came to Gra-thaṅ. His father dead, his mother and brother destitute, he (34a) felt sad and thought of going to Khams. But all his relatives advised him not to go there, and installed him (as preacher). From the age of 21, he used to study and preach at the same time. Since then he obtained from numerous teachers (the exposition of the Doctrine). From the kalyāṇa-mitra mTha'-bži he obtained the Prajñāpāramitā, the Mādhyamaka and Logic. Having mastered the upāya-mārga of Nā-ra-pa, an extraordinary experience was produced in him, which removed (his) doubts concerning hidden precepts. At the age of 24, he suspected that he had contracted leprosy. Then Gru rNam-grags, a nephew of Gru go-čha, came to visit bSam-yas, he obtained from him the hidden scroll (sog-dril zab-mo) of Gru, and stayed in seclusion at mKhar-ru-sgaṅ. He succeeded in checking the beginnings of leprosy. Then having gone to sTod-luṅs to ask Ba-ri for instruction in the teachings of the "Lineage of the Meaning" (Don-rgyud), he found that the latter was staying in seclusion. Then having gone to the residence of rGyal-ba dKon-skyabs at Žoṅ-pa steṅs, he asked for the "Lineage of the Meaning (Don-rgyud)" of sMra-ba'i seṅ-ge. At first sKon-skyabs was somewhat reluctant to preach hidden precepts. One day when the Teacher and his disciple were engaged in discussing religious terms, Jo-sras 'Brog-po said: "This kalyāṇa-mitra is the most famous religious scholar below the Sil-ma La of gTsaṅ. How will you be able to defeat him, Teacher?" The Teacher then said to him: "I didn't know you were such a man! Pray excuse me!" and saying so, he imparted to him the complete hidden precepts. He then obtained many precepts of the Ži-byed system, such as the "Precepts of sKam" (sKam-gyi gdams-pa), the Thun-bčud of rMa, and the mTshan-brJod gser-thur (belongs to the Ži-byed system) of 'Brom Ye-śes-'bar. This benefitted also his illness. He spent three months there. The following year, on the night of the full-moon of the month of Pauṣa-pūrṇimā (rGyal-gyis ña-ba, December-January), aged 25, while practising according to the method of Thun-bčud, an incontrovertible Wisdom of cognizing Truth (rtogs-pa'i ye-śes) was born in his Mind. All the Elements of the Phenomenal Existence (čhos thams-čad) and the Nirvāṇic state were understood (by him) to be mere names. He then obtained from Ṅam-śod rGya-ras the exposition of the Mahāmudrā, the teaching of the "Lineage of Meaning" of Ka-ba-čan-pa, the Thabs-lam (Upāya-mārga) in verses (tshigs-bčad-ma), and the (34b) upāya-mārga of mGul-sgom. At that time, whenever strong emotions arose in him, he was able to clarify (his mind) by a mere reflection on the meaning of the basic text (mūla) (of precepts). However he was unable to lead his dull mind along the path. He was also unable to lift his mind from its primary state. When he had reached the age of 28, 'Čhus-pa Dar-brtson passed away, but he heard that the latter's son 'Čhus-pa brTson-'grus seṅ-ge was equal to his father in the possession of hidden precepts and yogic insight. So he proceeded to Čhaṅ-khyim disguised as a beggar (ldom-bu-ba). During the first year, he obtained the permission (luṅ) of rMa, So and sKam, and practised these methods with diligence. He found out that 'Čhus-pa did not differ in his interpretation of the basic text from rGyal-ba dKon-skyabs, but that he was more expert in his manner of exposition and in his method of practice. 'Čhus-pa proceeded to Gra to preside (gral-dpon byed-pa) over the funeral ceremony of the kalyāṇa-mitra Bag-čhags rJes-med. (Rog) entertained all the disciples and supporters (of his Teacher) with his share of the feast, and 'Čhus-pa was pleased and said: "I shall entertain you with what remains of the Doctrine of last year. Come to see me off!" Rog went along to attend on him. At that time (da-res) he obtained the remaining precepts. He especially showed great

diligence in the (study) of the method of So (čhuṅ-ba). The Teacher then entrusted him with the Lineage of the Prajñā-pāramitā and made him promise to do penance for 3 years. Rog was of the opinion that the system of So contained some profound precepts which he did not obtain before, and asked for them, but at that time (the Teacher) did not impart them to him. Later he received a message which read: "a yogin is coming from sKyi-śod. Help him!" Rog arranged a reception for this ācārya-yogin and accompanied him to the residence of the Teacher. The Teacher imparted precepts to him (Rog). He also obtained all the hidden precepts of the Cycle of Ži-byed sgron-ma, the nine Cycles of sGron-ma, the method of lČe and the system of lǰaṅ. The Teacher said to him: "Now there isn't the slightest difference between you and me in the knowledge of the Ži-byed system". He then thought that he should practise the method of sKam for three years. He gave up all (his worldly) possessions, and did not keep anything, not even a tea-cup (gsol-žal, a cup). The ācārya Yam-śud disapproved of it somewhat, but Rog sang a psalm, and the Teacher shed tears. He (Rog) then spent three years immured in the central house of rTse-pa-sgaṅ, (35a)
lived on nectar (rasāyana, 'tsho-ba bčud-len), wore rags, and kept the vow of silence. He practised meditation and obtained the signs of the Path, which were similar to the contact between a stone and a bone (lam-rtags-daṅ rdo-rus phrad—a famous saying often quoted in religious texts, meaning that if one wishes to eat the marrow of the bone, one should crush the bone with a stone. In meditation there is need of a direct contact between the Mind and the Doctrine). The stream of obscuration then came to an end (this sentence may also mean the stoppage of urine as a result of the bčud-len practice). Within one month he developed the notion of the absence of day and night. In general, he first had a vision of the tutelary deity. Secondly, he received prophecies uttered by ḍākinīs. Lastly, he was able to use yakṣas (gnod-sbyin) as his servants. At the age of 30, he met sGyi-tshaṅ.

Žig-po, who was of extreme old age, and was supported on both sides by two female-ascetics (sgom-ma). He used to pass urine and then drink it. He possessed a beautiful body and a smiling countenance. As soon as Rog saw him, all his usual thoughts became transformed. He felt uncertain how to salute and honour the elder. Then sGyi-tshaṅ Žig-po gave him the remaining nectar (i.e. his urine) to drink, which he did, and a feeling of well-being filled his body. He (Rog) then asked several questions on the Doctrine, though he felt uneasy. The Teacher said: "First I had studied the Doctrine. Then I had mastered it, and then I had practised it. Now for me there doesn't exist any difference between religion and non-religion. You do not possess the ear of listening to the Doctrine. I don't know how to preach it to you! But you take this much!", saying so he gave him a nail of his left hand, on which appeared the image of (Vajra) vārahī (the Yoginī, rNal-'byor-ma). Then he discarded all constructive thoughts which differentiated between virtue and sin, between that which was to be abandoned and the antidote (gñen-po), and between mystic trance (samādhi) and knowledge acquired after the trance (pṛṣṭha-labdha-jñāna). When he was formerly residing at the residence of 'Čhus-pa, he heard that Te-ne was in possession of precepts. When J̌o-bo rNal-'byor of Bya-sa had invited the Dharmasvāmin of 'Bri-khuṅ and rGya-ma Rin-čhen sgaṅ-pa, he went to meet them, and about that time met Te-ne. Te-ne bestowed on him the three "Immaculate Lineages of the Ordinary" (Thun-moṅ-gi brgyud-pa dri-med-gsum), and said: "In this Doctrine there are many initiations, etc. You should invite me to your native place, and I shall then complete them. There exists a karmic link between me and you". Rog replied: "I am a yogin and possess no landed property, and am therefore unable to invite you!" Te-ne said: "No one else will come there, except me. In any case you should invite me! The ḍākinīs, guardians of the Doctrine, had also told me about it. I shall complete (the exposition) of the Doctrine". They (35b)

then fixed the time of the invitation in the month of Ña-drug (Kṛttikā, sMin-drug). After that he journeyed to sKyi-tshaṅ and obtained the Nāmasaṅgīti according to the system of Dam-pa (Saṅs-rgyas), etc., as well as the Six Sections (Brul-tsho) of gČod. Formerly the Teacher had given to others three sections only, but now he bestowed on Rog the complete "Six Sections". The Teacher being very aged, he obtained the minutiae from his daughter sKal-ldan. After that when he came to rTse-sgaṅ, he bled from his nose for seven days, due to the non-observance of a former vow of penance. Medicines and rites were of no avail. In general, he honoured and prayed to Teachers. He especially cherished the memory of So Dar-ma seṅ-ge. He saw Dar-ma seṅ-ge wearing a blue mantle (ber) and walking through the space in front of him. Then he (Dar-ma seṅ-ge) touched with his hand (his forehead) between the eye-brows and the bleeding stopped, like a channel changing suddenly its course. After the death of Rog-ston btsan-po and the performance of the funeral rites, he had to postpone the time fixed for the invitation of Te-ne. While he was staying at Baṅ-rims he saw in a dream a woman adorned with cowries who told him: "rGyal-ba Te-ne is waiting for your invitation." He then sent four men to invite the Teacher. The men met the teacher at the house of the alms-giver lČags-'bar in Lower 'On. Te-ne was pleased. The same evening he sent the necessary books with the messengers, and came himself next morning. While Ten-ne was bestowing an initiation for the benefit of Yar-čhen Re'u at rGyabs, Žig-po also came there. Priests and supporters, about 40 in all, obtained the 'A-li Ka-li' initiation. After that they proceeded to Baṅ-rims, and he obtained during three months the ordinary doctrines, such as the bKa'-babs dri-med, and others. Te-ne came again later, and told Rog: "Now prepare a Tantric feast (gaṇacakra). I have to tell you something about the Doctrine." He then bestowed on him the extraordinary precepts (Thun-moṅ ma-yin-pa'i gdams-pa) (36a)
together with the summary (stoṅ-thun) of the Tantra, the

nitiation together with the explanation of the Path (dbaṅ-am-khrid-daṅ-bčas-pa). The Teacher said: "Though I ossess these profound precepts which were unknown pre-iously, I have no right to bestow them on others (sbyin-lbaṅ), (my) Teacher having forbidden it, except (the precepts) f the Single Lineage. Ban-rgan sGom was fit to be entrus-ed with the (precepts) of the Single Lineage (čhig-brgyud), ut he died, and some auspicious signs and merit were bserved. The son, however, isn't fit for the work (las-su-ıa-ruṅ), so having entrusted the Single Lineage to you, don't ivulge its precepts till my death. After my death you can ct according to your own discretion." He then entrusted › him all the books as well as the 16 smaller volumes. ater when Te-ne came again, Žig-po, sGom-pa sMan-gčig-a sTon-pa Nam-mkha' and others also obtained some pre-epts. Further, he bestowed on them the Dohā according › the method of Ža-ma, the Cycle of the short teachings of hyar-čhen (Phyar-čhen-gyi bka'-čho-lu'i skor), the Cycle of njunctions of Phyar-čhuṅ (Phyar-čhuṅ-gi bKa'-rgyas-pa'i kor), the Cycle of the Summary of Vajrakrodha (Vadzra-rodha'i bsdus-pa), and the method of rMa by Sog-po mDo-le. At the time of his death, Te-ne felt attracted towards Rog aore than towards his other disciples, who asked: "Who ossesses the complete doctrine of the Teacher?" The Tea-her (Te-ne) replied: "Who else, if not the ācārya Śes-ıb? He searched inside (for the Doctrine) as for a lost ow. He joined together ends of the ten beams (i.e. 'en kinds of hindrances), and having passed below them, onoured me." In this manner he obtained precepts, but ıey did not help him to develop a sudden trance, besides the ne which he possessed formerly, but the point of the ıought of the Master Dam-pa rGya-gar penetrated into him, ıd all his mental doubts were removed. At the age of 32, e invited the ācārya Robha of Gra-phyi, and obtained from im the bDe-mčhog lha-bču-gsum-ma (The 13 deities of the aṃvara Cycle), the Dohā of Tiṅ-pu (the Dohā according to

Ti-pu), the bŽi-čhos of Lo-ro-ba, the 'Pho-bsre (name of a system), the Thun-'Jog (a section of the Ži-byed), the sÑan-brgyud yum-skor, the rNam-'Joms according to the method of sNur, the "Four Scrolls" (sog-dril bži) of 'Tshur, and other texts. At 33, he built a lane for / public/ benefit. At the age of 35, he obtained from Dar-sgom Žig-po of sÑe-thaṅ the initiation and the precepts of the Cycle of Thig-le sbraṅ-'Jib (name of a book) of rGya-gar Śānti-pa. At the age of 36, he journeyed to mKhar-čhu and had a vision of the maṇḍala of Khrag-'thuṅ (a form of Heruka). At the age of 39, Dam-pa (Saṅs-rgyas) manifested to him his form, and preached to him the sNams-snan-ma (name of a book). At the age of 40, having accepted the present of sÑe-mdo, offered by rGyal-tsha mDo-dbaṅ, he entrusted the monas tery to sMra-ba'i seṅ-ge. At the age of 42, during the performance of the Amṛta rite at rTse-sgaṅ, the nectar ran down, and almost drenched the clothes of the Teacher and disciples. At the age of 48, he developed the faculty of prescience of the Divine Eye (divya-cakṣu, lha'i spyan) at Mu-tig. Then while residing at Tshe-po-luṅ, he visited a village where he met rDo-rJe-grags, son of Ye-śes-grags of mṄa'-ris, who possessed the sÑan-brgyud-yab-skor (belongs to the Ži-byed Cycle), and they exchanged their respective Yab-skor and Yum-skor. After the age of 49, he looked after the welfare of others. Te-ne having passed away, he became free from the (Teacher's) injunction. The kalyāṇa-mitra Khams-pa Śes-rab brtson-'grus having prepared numerous offerings and a Tantric feast (gaṇacakra), Rog taught the "special" precepts. After that (his life) became endangered through it, but later from the age of 65 that danger receded gradually. At the age of 68, he revolved the Great Wheel of the Law at the great monastery of Sum-bču till the middle of the month. At the age of 79, he passed away in the year Wood-Male-Dragon (śiṅ- pho-'brug—1244 A.D.). After the cremation of his remains many relics were left hehind, such as an image of Saṃvarasahaja (bDe-mčhog lhan- (36b) yes) and that of Vajra-yoginī (rDo-rje rnal-'byor-ma, ājravārahī).

His younger brother the Dharmasvāmin Žig-po: In s former life he had been a king of Oḍḍiyāna named harmadeva (Čhos-kyi lha) who had attained spiritual alization through the practice of a secret mantra (gsaṅ-sṅags ıb-mo). From that country he was reborn here in the ar Iron-Female-Hare (lčags-mo-yos—1171 A.D.). At the ;e of 3, he recollected the sufferings of the Saṃsāra and astered well the alphabet. At the age of five or six, (37a) s mother taught him reading. Since the age of 7, he used follow hidden practices and pretended to be dumb. At e age of 12, he heard that the preaching of the Doctrine Kha-rag-gra-pa 'Dul-ba-'od had caused many to develop editation in the compound of the monastic college. As was sent by his mother to another place, he was unable enter the compound of the monastic college, but after aring the above story, he proceeded to the monastery mpound during the night, and said weeping: "Why dn't I come here to-day?" He then paid homage to the ligious people of the Ten Quarters, and a kind of pure state at produced in him. At the age of 16, his father died. e abandoned his secret practices, and supported his mother performing rites in villages. At the age of 18, while siding alone in a cave called Bya-mo spre-ltag, he heard e cry of the owl and at first his mind became uneasy, then pondered over the cause of this uneasiness of (his) mind, d realized the nature of the Mind being devoid of indepen-nt nature. After that he obtained from his elder brother any doctrines and precepts. Further, he wandered through any countries in search of precepts, attending on every mous teacher. At the age of 25, he preached the Prajña-ramitāsañcayagāthā (sDud-pa) to a religious assembly. e discovered that his hearers were not too pleased (with s exposition), and fled to sMan-gčig. On the way experienced some accidents caused by the Evil One

(Māra), but was unharmed. A local goddess received him, and supported him while he was staying at Nam-mkha'-rdzoṅ. At the age of 26, he received a letter from his elder brother which said that the great teacher Te-ne had come to rGyabs and would be bestowing initiations, and that he should come there. He was very pleased, proceeded there, and obtained initiation. Then the Teacher told him that he should practise the method of guidance, and for 23 days he practised the "Purification of the Mind" (bLo-sbyoṅ), and even did not have time to partake of food. He realized all the signs and merits. Then having gone into the presence of the Teacher, he related his experiences to him. The Teacher rebuked him much, and said: "You don't even possess the smell of your father's marrow-bone, and the smell of your mother's fat!" He did not realize that his Teacher was testing the degree of his Purification (37b
of the Mind, and thought that the Teacher was finding excuses for not giving him the precepts. So he sang a song:

"O Venerable Precious Teacher!
Be gracious to your devoted disciple!
In general there are few perfect teachers!
Even rarer are suitable disciples.
I, a beggar of sad mood, irreligious thoughts never come to my mind,
but this time I have broken the vow of residing in a hermitage.
I grasped the foot of the famous Master!
I have earnestly practised the Accumulation of Merit (puṇya-saṃbhāra).
During (the study) of the "Purification of the Mind," which is the Path,
I manifested the three kinds of diligence.
This time there appeared three signs of purification,
Which were difficult to remove.
All the signs of the Path, described in the Tantra,
Were now produced without meditation.

The dream, though it is (caused) by the influences of former existences,
I saw six dreams about which I am afraid even to speak.
I, a beggar who had abandoned existence, writing isn't necessary to me.
O Father ! Show me the presents of the Oral Tradition! "

Thus he sang, and the Teacher could hardly bear his song. The Teacher pretended to have awakened from sleep, and said: "In general, there exist many who follow the Holy Doctrine, but there are very few who obtained the complete hidden precepts of the Meditative Lineage (sgrub-brgyud). Even if he would find the precepts, he wouldn't be able to follow the complete exposition and would be anxious to consult written records. In this manner he missed an auspicious circumstance, and thus I was unable to find one to whom I could entrust the Lineage. I had known previously that you possessed signs and merits, but this isn't yet the reason for completing (the practice). Even if you had completed it, I do not know whether I should bestow precepts of the Oral Tradition on you. Besides myself there is also another Master of this (Doctrine). I must consult (him)!" and saying so, he sang the following song:

"From the mother (yum) the devī Nairātmā
and to the gracious father Pa-tshab,
These precepts were handed down a single Lineage (i.e. transmitted through one disciple only).
The bridge of the Lineage of holders of yogic insight remained unbroken.
The stream of practice did not change its course. (38*a*)
All of them (yogins) obtained signs and merits.
Though I possess a permission, I have no right to transmit it to others, but to a single individual.
Formerly there had been many desirous to obtain it,
I promised them, but then postponed it.
There does not exist even a single disciple in harmony with the Teacher.

I sat continuously observing yogic rules and never accepted blessings from devils,
I never prayed to (gods), and never recited hidden words with my mouth,
I never preached secret doctrines to people.
May this kingly Treasury of Precepts meet a worthy son !
In general I have been famous for my strictness in preaching".

He (Žig-po) used to say: "I myself had faith in his Teaching and thought him to be a matchless Teacher. I also offered him the vow to practise meditation. I also revered him according to existing customs. The Teacher was pleased with me and bestowed on me all the complete Doctrines." Though he had many teachers, he considered Te-ne to be his true teacher (rtsa-ba'i bla-ma or root-teacher). The Dharmasvāmin 'Bri-khuṅ-pa asked him to continue his Lineage, but he replied: "I have to continue the Lineage of the yogic teacher" (Te-ne). At the age of 31, he proceeded to 'Bri-khuṅ. The local deity (gnas-po) having taken possession of a man, went out to receive him. He met the Dharmasvāmin who attended the assembly (of monks). He took up the final monastic ordination in the presence of the abbot dPal-čhen Gur-ba, the ācārya gTsaṅ-pa 'Dul-'dzin, and the Secret Preceptor lČags-ri-pa. He was given the name of Rin-čhen śes-rab. The Precious One himself invested him with the divine vestments and looked at him from right and left, from the back and from the front, saying: "It looks very well!" and stroked his head with his hand. Further, he obtained from sGom-pa sMan-gčig the sKabs-daṅ-po (of the Abhisamayālaṃkāra) and the Cycle of 'Tshal-pa. From 'Čhus-pa brTson-seṅ he obtained the Middle Lineage (brgyud-pa bar-ma). From So Dar-seṅ the Yaṅ-dag-ma-gčig. From 'Čhar-bu rgya-ras he obtained the doctrine of dBaṅ-rab according to the system of So. From Ri-khrod sBug-ston he (38b) obtained the rJe-btsun-ma (prayer to Tārā) according to the method of Pu-hraṅs and the gČod-brul-tsho-drug-pa. From rGyal-ba dKon-skyabs he obtained the method of So. From

Rog-ston btsan-po the Ka-ga-ni, the rNam-'Joms, and the bDud-rtsi čhen-mo. From Rog-ston kLu-sbyin the Guhya-samāja-Tantra proper. From Žig-po bDud-rtsi the rDzogs-čhen sñan-brgyud (the Oral Tradition of the rDzogs-čhen school). From Kha-rag sKyi-ston the Cycle of 'Tshal-pa, such as the "gZer-lṅa" and other texts. From Śaṅs-pa Rom-bhe the 'Pho-ba sPyi-brtol (a text on the transference of the vital principle). From Lo-sgom and gLan sñiṅ-po the initiation of bDe-mčhog bču-gsum-ma. From Rog Śes-rab zla-ba the gSaṅ-ba phur-gčig (name of a rÑiṅ-ma book), and the bDud-rtsi bum-gčig (a rÑiṅ-ma work). From his father the Oral Tradition of the Mahāmudrā (Phyag-rgya čhen-po sñan-brgyud) and other texts. From Lhab-dres-ma goṅ-pa the 'Jam-dpal bśes-gñen-ma (a rÑiṅ-ma book), etc. Having left 'Bri-khuṅ, he felt attracted towards meditation and devoted himself solely to meditation at Tsa-ri, mKhar-čhu, Śambhu, Mu-tig, Pho-ma, and Gaṅs-bzaṅ. Afterwards he mostly laboured for the welfare of others. The gods of the locality came out to receive him. At the age of 37, he took up residence at a hermitage. He gathered round him a retinue of good, bad and mediocre disciples. There also he prepared a copy of the teachings of his Lineage (bKa'-brgyud) written in gold. It was of the size of the Avataṃsaka (Phal-čhen). At the age of 40, he journeyed to Diṅ-ri. Ḍākinīs, possessing wings of wind of the Sun and Moon, received him. After reaching the bank of the 'Oṅ-čhu, he saw both the Precious Dam-pa (Saṅs-rgyas) and the Bodhisattva (Kun-dga') coming to meet him, saying: "Your coming is good!" In the night of his coming to gLaṅ-'khor, he saw a dream that he was going to a land of precious stones, which indicated that he was destined to labour for the welfare of others. He made extensive offerings to the image of the Mahābodhi and to other images. He paid homage and pleased numerous male and female yogins. He used to tell many stories about gLaṅ-'khor, and the inmates of the monastery thought that he was (39a)
a manifestation of Dam-pa. Though he was asked to become

the abbot (of gLaṅ-'khor monastery), he returned. At the time of his departure (from the monastery) he worshipped the sKu-gduṅ Ka-ru (name of Dam-pa's caitya), and the caitya shook thrice. Numerous relics fell out. He caused a shower of Religion to fall on the disciples. He wrote many treatises, such as the Great and Short Lam-rim, the bŚad-'bum and other texts. In the end he attained Nirvāṇa on the 22nd day of the first winter month of (dgun-zla ra-ba) the year Wood-Female-Serpent (śiṅ-mo-sbrul—1245 A.D.) at the age of 75. On the 18th day of the month rGyal (rGyal-gyi zla-ba, December-January) he sat on the lion's throne, erect in body, as if he had no pain. His retinue gathered round him, and he uttered the following words: "From the outset I had but little attraction towards this life. Because of this, I was afraid to become a teacher of the people of the Iron-Age (sñigs-ma'i sems-čan-gyi slob-dpon). However I was compelled to become one. The flower of the pure Mind had to blossom forth, and I was able to benefit living beings. It seems to me that there exist a profound karmic link and votary link between us, Teacher and disciples. You also held me very dear and showed your reverence. I also loved you, and thus, we, father and sons, became happy in harmony with the Doctrine. We stayed together for a long time. It is difficult for one to spend his entire life without harm to one's reputation. Our fame linked to the Doctrine, spread towards all Quarters. Now I am to enter into Parinirvāṇa! Don't be sad, for we are one in Spirit. We shall not remain apart. After my death it won't be necessary for an ascetic, who had reached the stage characterized by the absence of constructive thoughts, to possess the miraculous signs. The ḍākinīs are sweeping (the floor) and arranging a seat. This indicates that there will be an object of worship. You must pray earnestly!" He even gave instructions how to cremate his mortal remains. He also said that "in this monastery all should practise meditation, and that good will result after three years", with these words, (39b) he passed out. As indicated by him, numerous wonderful relics were left behind (after his cremation), and they are preserved till the present time at (his) hermitage.

After him dBon-po Śes-rab dbaṅ-pa occupied the abbot's chair, but died within one year. After him, (his) younger brother 'Dag-'byar-pa was nominated (abbot). He also passed away within one year. Thus it became known that no one was able to occupy the chair, because of its sanctity. However 'Khrul-Źig-pa occupied it for a considerable time.

The scholar sMra-ba'i seṅ-ge: In his former life he had been a heretic, a follower of the Sāṃkhya system in the country of Kāśmīra. He delighted in philosophical debates. He visited East India and defeated (in debates) numerous scholars. Later the paṇḍita Prajñāsiddhi (Śes-rab grub-pa) refuted (his point of view), and defeated him. After that he accepted Prajñāsiddhi as his teacher, and obtained from him the Yamāntaka initiation. He was given the secret name of 'J̌igs-med-rtsal. The Teacher and disciple, proceeded towards Oḍḍiyāna to the palace of king Dharmadeva (Čhos-kyi lha), protecting the Doctrine. At the king's request, Prajñāsiddhi (Śes-rab grub-pa) presided over an assembly, and 'J̌igs-med-rtsal acted as karma-ācārya, and held a Tantric feast (gaṇacakra). They expressed the solemn wish to meet again in all future existences. Because of this, this 'J̌igs-med rtsal was reborn here (in Tibet) in the year Fire-Male-Horse (me-pho-rta—1186 A.D.). At the age of eight, he mastered grammar and astrology, which he was able to learn after glancing over the text once. At the age of 13, he developed both mentally and physically. At the assembly held by Gra, Dol and gŽuṅ, he was noted for his looks. At the age of 14, he preached the Summary of gŽi-lam (a Źi-byed doctrine) while staying immured. Monks and ascetics were filled with faith, and all shed tears. At the age of 15, he studied under rNal-'byor seṅ-ge at 'Čhos-čhaṅ-khyim the Six Treatises of the Mādhyamaka (dbU-ma rigs-tshogs drug). He was able to contend with the Precious One in philosophical debates. At the age of 17, he made an extensive study of numerous grammatical śāstras (of the Sanskrit language) under the ācārya Žaṅ-ston dKon-mčhog of Gra-phyi rta-lam-po. At the age of 20, he visited the scholar J̌o-pad at Kha-rag. Within two years he mastered the mDo, the Māyā, and the "Domain of the Mind" (Sems-phyogs). Then he went on a debating tour through gTsaṅ. At bZaṅ-ne'u-kha he defeated many scholars. One named Ru-mtshams-pa bSod-rin, who was learned in the Abhidharma and Tantras, and who had become the spiritual brother (mčhed-grogs) at the residence of So-pa, said (about him): "He was of an alert mind, but often contradicted his own words (ltag-čhod). He reminded me of my brother the kalyāṇa-mitra Śes-rab in the manner of speech." After that he conducted a debate during the religious assembly held after the death of the kalyāṇa-mitra Bra-bo čhen-po. His opponent was one named Yar-ston Hrul-mo (the "Ragged Scholar" of Yar-kluṅs) whom the kalyāṇa-mitra Śāk-bsam and others were unable to defeat. The subject of the debate was whether one could sharpen once intellect naturally. On several occasions he defeated him, and his fame as a scholar became great. He became known as the "Lion of Speech"(sMra-ba'i seṅ-ge). His real name was brTson-'grus seṅ-ge. At the age of 22, he was installed (čhe-'don mdzad-pa) at sÑe-mdo. He was entrusted with the books and the religious conch (čhos-duṅ). Because he did not finish his studies, his two brothers took charge of the monastery. After that he was again requested to take charge of the monastery, but he did not agree. The Precious One erected a temple at sÑe-mdo, and Žig-po promised him to fill it with religious books. He took charge of the monastery (gnas-gži) and recollected the grace of his two Teachers which was manifested in (their) Worldly actions and in the Holy Doctrine, and due to which it was not necessary for him to look for religious instruction elsewhere, and which helped him to realize his Mind to be a Buddha. For their sake he performed many works, such as the preaching of

(40a)

the Doctrine, mediating in disputes, etc. Some saw him as a worldly human being. When he was 23, J̌o-pad of Kha-rag passed away. In order to carry out the will of the deceased, he made numerous presents (on the occasion of the funeral ceremony). At the age of 31, he practised the "Five Path" (lam-lṅa), and perceived the signs, of purification of defilment as the Cause, and the signs of (40*b*) the control of the five kinds of Vital Breath (prāṇā) as the Path, and the sign of pure vision as the Fruit. He perceived these signs as did his previous Teachers. He did not distinguish between day and night, and a wall was no hindrance for him. Besides the removal of doubts concerning the meaning (of the teaching), his spiritual experience was characterized by beautitude and lucidity, which rose in him like a flame. He danced about oblivious of all, and was unable to stop tears of joy. At the age of 33, he meditated on the (Mañjuśrī)-nāmasaṅgīti, and had a vision of the 'J̌am-dbyaṅs lha-bdun (the seven deities forming the retinue or parivāra of Mañjuśrī) inside the stalk of a lotus flower. At the age of 35, he proceeded to Lha-sa to convey offerings, and saw a light similar in share to the lotus (ku-mu-ta, Skrt. kumuda) flower, emanating from the heart of Avalokiteśvara which afterwards disappeared above the crown of his head. At the age of 38, he accompanied Dus-gsum mkhyen-pa, who was a relative of the Precious One. He also went in the retinue of Žig-po when the latter came to bSam-yas to make offerings. He saw a light emanating from the heart of Hayagrīva similar in shape to a broken piece of coral, and afterwards again disappearing into his heart. At the age of 40, he practised immurement at sÑe-mdo, and during that time saw a red light similar to a coral which then transformed itself into Hayagrīva, the red light filling Ṅams-śod. The neighing of a horse was heard thrice, and on the first occasion it was heard throughout the four districts (ru) of gTsaṅ and dbUs. On the next two occasions it was heard even beyond them. He said: "It was the sign of the coming of fame to

the All-Knowing". At the age of 41, he was guided by ḍākinīs on the way to mKhar-čhu. At sMyoṅ-kha-dga' or mTsho Hūṃ-sgra-sgrogs-pa (The Lake emitting the sound Hūṃ) he performed propitiations of Yaṅ-dag, and the requisites for the propitiations filled a vase, and a shower of nectar fell. At the age of 44, he held a religious assembly on the occasion of the installation of the All-Knowing. Those who sat in the back rows of the crowd which filled the hall of preaching, could not hear the words of the kalyāṇa-mitra, but his words could be heard by those sitting in the back rows. At the age of 58, he came to 'Bri-khuṅ and visited the Lord sPyan-sṅa to convey presents. He saw sPyan-sṅa as Mahābodhi, who said: "Previously your mind had reached the state of heaven, but now I shall change it into that of great heaven". He bestowed on him the Mahāmudrā. Then a thought came to him that he could not improve further his understanding of non-differentiation either in the Past, Present or Future (meaning that he had reached the highest (41*a*)
goal). At the age of 59, he performed a funeral rite, and had a vision of Ye-śes mgon-po "with a smiling face" (Ye-śes mgon-po bžad-pa'i žal-čan, a form of Mahākāla). Then at the age of 62, he passed away on the 8th day of the 11th month (mṛgaśīra) of the year Fire-Female-Sheep (me-mo-lug—1247 A.D.) amidst many extraordinary signs. After his cremation, many relics were left behind. Later when they were offering a water oblution to his image erected as Vajrasattva, the water became filled with relics. When they gilded the image, a shower of relics fell like snow. Thus the three brothers, who were similar to the Rig-gsum mgon-po, had numerous disciples, on whom they bestowed the Stream of Teaching, but the chief repositories of the Family Lineage (gduṅ-rgyud) were 'Khrul-žig Rin-po-čhe and the All-Knowing One.

Now 'Khrul-žig Rin-po-čhe: His father bDe-gśegs čhen-po Śes-rab-'od and his mother, a yoginī of mKhar-čhu, named Byaṅ-čhub-sgron, who had received a prophecy from the

ḍākinīs. She went from mKhar-čhu into the presence of bDe-gśegs čhen-po and told him about the prophecy. He agreed, and after holding a Tantric feast (gaṇacakra), he had intercourse with the yoginī. When she became pregnant, she saw many holy visions, and the child was born in the year Water-Female-Sheep (čhu-mo-lug — 1223 A.D.). He received the name of Dar-ma seṅ-ge. At the age of five, he was able to repeat the rNal-'byor ma'i mon-rtogs and the rNal-'byor-gsum (a sādhana of Vajravārahī) which were constantly recited by his mother. At the age of seven, he mastered numerous rites. In the same year he was sent to sÑe-mdo into the presence of bDe-gśegs čhen-po. The mother asked the latter to teach (the boy) the Cycle of Ritual (phrin-las). bDe-gśegs replied: "What could he do now?" The boy then recited all that he had learnt by heart, and for the first time the father was pleased with his recitation and reading. He then taught him the rite of Vajrakīla. On one occasion, when the boy was sitting on the corner of his father's mat, he ate the remains of his father's food. His step-mother became angry and came to thrash him. He ran (41*b*)
away towards the edge of sNe-'og (n. of precipice). He was caught, and the woman was about to throw him over the precipice, when she was prevented from doing so by the ācārya Lhag-mthoṅ, who sent the boy to 'Od-ma. sMra-ba'i seṅ-ge then said to his wife: "You shouldn't do such things! He should study!" but his step-mother did not allow him to study, and sent him to graze horses and cattle. When he was gathering cowdung, the ācārya rTa'u-sgaṅ-pa broke his basket into which he was gathering cowdung. He then took the boy to the step-mother, and said: "This boy is the son of a saintly teacher (siddha), and will become the object of worship of countless disciples. How is it possible to make him do this sort of manual labour?" Thus the ācārya scolded the step-mother. Since his childhood he understood all the elements of Phenomenal Existence to be dreams and illusions.

He did not get attached to any one, and used to give away food and clothing to all who asked for it. Though his mind was not attracted to (outside) objects, he had a constant feeling of well-being, and all outside objects seemed unreal to him. Nothing was real to him, and because of this he was given the name of 'Khrul-žig, or "Remover of Illusions". At the age of 12, So-pa was invited, and he obtained the initiation into the mDo Cycle (mDo-dbaṅ, mDo is a section of rÑiṅ-ma Tantras). His father said: "To practise religion from inside one's heart, one must complete the recitation of a mantra of a tutelary deity", and bestowed on him the initiation of the "upper" section of the Vajrakīla ritual (the rites of the wrathful deities of the rÑiṅ-ma-pa school contain two sections: the sTod-las, or "upper" rites, which consist of meditations and offering rites /sgom daṅ mčhod-pa 'bul-ba/, and the sMad-las, or the "Lower" rites which consists of magic practices). After having gathered all requisites for propitiations, his father made him perform propitiation rites. The father placed three pills into a vessel in order to examine the omens of the initiation rite. (After examining the omens) he found that the three pills had become nine, which indicated longevity (for his son). The father then told him to labour for the welfare of others, and that to do so one had first to work for one's own benefit. He tried hard to recite the mantra of Vajrakīla, and observed extraordinary signs. He then studied extensively the system of Vajrakīla and the ritual describing the use of a poisoned magic black dagger. At the age of 15, he obtained at Čhaṅ-khyim of 'Čhos the Abhisamayālaṃkāra, the system of rMa, etc. from the kalyāṇa-mitra Kun-dga' and the siddha sPyi-de-ba. At the age of 17, he studied with great assiduity the dGoṅs-'dus (the bLa-ma dGoṅs-'dus, a treatise belonging to the rÑiṅ-ma school). Further, his (father) bDe-gśegs čhen-po bestowed on him the exposition of the complete doctrines possessed by him. When they brought J̌o-'bum, he exclaimed: "I don't need a wife!" and turned away. His father said: "You will need a female assistant (rig-ma) endowed (424a) with (proper) signs for the practice of the Mahāyānic Tantras! This girl possesses the required signs." Then again the girl was brought in. He then obtained the complete Cycle of the Ži-byed system and a sudden experience was produced in him. At the age of 21, he was given the teaching of all the three Lineages of the Ži-byed system, the "Early", the "Later" and the "Intermediate" ones, passessed by bDe-gśegs čhen-po himself. While performing the propitiations (bsñen-pa, seva), he observed all the signs of the Cause, Path and Effect. Then the father told him: "Go to the hermitage and make the request for the complete set of doctrines of Žig-po." When he came to Žig-po, the latter said to him: "I can entrust my Doctrine to this one! This one is capable of becoming a Master of the Doctrine! Death is a possibility (lit. mi-res bus-mo-la 'bab-pa, "a man may become a knee-bone", i.e. he may die). We must do it to-night!" He bestowed on him the complete teachings of the three, the "Early", the "Later" and the "Intermediate" Lineages, and principally the "Later" Lineage. During his initiation into the maṇḍala of the bDe-mčhog nam-mkha' dan mñam-pa (Śrī-Saṃvarakhasama-tantra-rāja-nāma, Kg. rGyud-'bum, No. 415), an extraordinary faith was produced in him, in which he did not differentiate between the Teacher and the principal deity (of the maṇḍala). The Teacher transformed himself into a body of light and his mind, realizing the nature of non-substantiality and matter (snaṅ-ba) became blissful, lucid and free from constructive thoughts. Then the Teacher led him into the "House of auspicious signs" (rTen-'brel-gyi khaṅ-pa, a Tantric rite), and entrusted to him the Spiritual Lineage. At the age of 22, at the time of the death of bDe-gśegs čhen-po, he felt a strong sadness, and the latter said: "You mustn't grieve at the death of the Yogin. Though you didn't train your mind in the method of Logic (rTog-ge'i rigs-pa), you are endowed with the ability for inner investigations. Therefore practise assiduously mental concentration and great benefit for living beings will arise." On the day

of the funeral, though oppressed by strong grief, he saw an extraordinary dream during the night. Following it, during the cremation rites, an image of Avalokiteśvara and the heart (of the Teacher) left unburnt, were recovered by him. They were snatched away by his step-mother, but he did not feel hurt. Because of persistent talk by the Dharmasvāmin Žig-po that he was to die soon, he journeyed to 'Bri-khuṅ to convey numerous presents, which included a sToṅ-dṅu-'thul turquoise and seven horses. On his return he erected a (42
tomb. Before he had finished it, sÑe-mdo-ba also passed away. At the age of 26, he succeeded in finishing the tombs. He then sent Ras-pa rDo-rje-dpal to India and Nepāl (Lho-bal) to make a golden parasol and a gañjira. After completing the work, he sent it, and himself proceeded to Oḍḍiyāna (U-rgyan) and became known as U-rgyan ras-pa. At the age of 29, he settled at rTse-ba-sgaṅ and looked after numerous disciples, who included Thaṅ dbUs-pa and others. The Teacher and the inmates of the three monasteries (dgon-skor-gsum) held frequent consultations. In the end, they decided that 'Khrul-Žig-po was to become abbot. sÑe-mdo, the All-Knowing told him: "You should stay in a hermitage and spread the Meditative Lineage (sgrub-brgyud). Whereas I shall stay at sÑe-mdo and spread the Lineage of Preaching (bśad-brgyud)." But the monks of rTse-sgaṅ and the lay-supporters did not approve of this arrangement. The alms-givers brought presents to him and when their spokesman addressed him, he said instead of "Please don't go!", "Please go!", and all laughed (at his mistake). He exclaimed: "This is an auspicious omen!" At the age of 30, he settled in the hermitage and occupied the abbot's chair. At the age of 31, the two saintly scholars proceeded to Yar-kluṅs to meet the paṇḍita Dānaśīla When they were performing the homa offering, they observed that the fiery signs were somewhat unfavourable. The paṇḍita said: "This won't harm you!" On this occasion (de-res) he obtained from Dam-pa-gar at Thaṅ the Cittotpāda rite (Thugs-bskyed čhen-mo) and

the lesser precepts of observing morality (bsruṅ-sdom-čhuṅ). At the age of 32, he came to 'Bri-khuṅ and received ordination in the presence of sPyan-sṅa and Lha dKon-mčhog-'phel. He made numerous presents. He bestowed on them the complete exposition of the Doctrine. During the same year he made them enter the "Auspicious House" (rTen-'grel khaṅ-pa) where they obtained the complete guidance and initiation of the Five Paths (Lam-lṅa). At the age of 41, he journeyed to sTod-luṅs and mKhar-čhu, and laboured for the welfare of others. Those endowed with clairvoyance saw him as Dam-pa (Saṅs-rgyas). At the age of 42, he proceeded to Phag-mo-gru to convey presents. rGyal-ba Rin-po-čhe was pleased, and even returned his salutation. He obtained (43a) a detailed exposition of the Doctrine, and received numerous presents. At the age of 43, he satiated with precepts the siddha Me-loṅ rdo-rJe (Me-loṅ rdo-rJe, a famous rÑiṅ-ma siddha, b. 1242 A.D., died in 1303 A.D. according to Sum-pa mkhon-po, JASB, /1889/, N.2, p.57), and others. At the age of 44, he invited his own son a sādhaka (sgrub-pa-po) from Phag-mo-gru, and appointed him as abbot of the hermitage. At the age of 45, he proceeded to gÑal to consecrate the image of rDza-dmar-ba. On route and in the vicinity of gÑal he appeased diseases and quarrels. During that year sPyan-sṅa dPal-čhen was appointed by the All-Knowing One (sÑe-mdo-ba) to the chair of rTse-sgaṅ. When he was 48, Dus-gsum mkhyen-pa was sent to Lho-brag. When he was 49, sPyan-sṅa 'Tshal-pa was appointed to the hermitage. From the age of 51, for 31 years he practised solely meditation at Zur-stod. He passed away at the age of 81 in the year Water-Female-Hare (čhu-mo-yos—1303 A.D.). He was reborn from a lotus flower in Sukhāvatī, and became known as the Bodhisattva rDo-rJe mi-zad-pa (Vajrākṣaya). All the relics left behind after the cremation, were placed inside an image (naṅ-rten).

The eldest of his five sons, the sādhaka (sgrub-pa-po) Saṅs-rgyas rin-čhen (lived) between the year Wood-serpent (śiṅ-sbrul—1245 A.D.) and the year Water-Tiger (čhu-stag—1302 A.D). He died at the age of 58. The second son sPyan-sṅa dPal-čhen lived between the year Fire-Sheep (me-lug—1247 A.D.) and the year Wood-Ox (śiṅ-glaṅ—1325 A.D.), for 79 years. The third son Dus-gsum mkhyen-pa lived for 71 years, between the year Water-Mouse (čhu-byi—1252 A.D.) and the year Water-Dog (čhu-khyi—1322 A,D,). The fourth son sPyan-sṅa 'Tshal-pa Śākya rgyal-mtshan lived for 73 years, between the year Earth-Horse (sa-rta—1258 A.D.) and the year Iron-Horse (lčags-rta—1330 A.D.). The fifth (son) the mahā-upādhyāya Tshul-khrims rgyal-mtshan lived for 75 years, between the year Earth-Serpent (sa-sbrul—1269 A.D.) and the year Water-Sheep (čhu-lug—1343 A.D.).

Now Dus-gsum mkhyen-pa: He was born as son of 'Khrul-Žig-pa and lady 'Bum-rgyan. He was ordained by the upādhyāya of Zul-phu named Byaṅ Na-bza' 'phred-gsol. He became a disciple of the younger brother of 'Bri-khuṅ-pa. A yogic insight was produced in him. He obtained many doctrines, and received the final monastic ordination from the upādhyāya Mi-ñag and the ācārya Yon-tan-'od. gCuṅ ('Bri-khuṅ-pa) presented him with his own vestments and sent him away. He obtained the Doctrine from his father with gTsaṅ
Brag-nag-pa. Together they listened to (the exposition) of the (43
complete Cycle of the "Later" Lineage and of numerous Cycles belonging to the rÑiṅ-ma (Tantras). He also obtained numerous doctrines from the elder brother, the sādhaka. He also gained most of the science of sÑe-mdo-ba, the All-Knowing. From the age of 34 till the age of 43, he practised exclusively meditation at the monastery of Lho-brag sTeṅs-čhen-po. At the age of 50, he erected the tombs of the Precious 'Khrul-Žig-pa and of the Sādhaka after their passing, and occupied the abbot's chair. He looked after numerous disciples. The three sons of dPyan-sṅa dPal-čhen: The first (was) sPyan-sṅa Kun-rgyal (who lived for) 35 years, between the year Earth-Serpent (sa-sbrul—1269 A.D.) and the year Water-Hare (čhu-yos—1303 A.D.). The second (son) Yon-

an rgyal-mtshan (lived for) 54 years, between the Iron-Horse lčags-rta—1270 A.D.) and the year Water-Hog (čhu-phag—323 A.D.). The youngest son Drin-čan-pa (lived for) 63 ears, between the year Water-Bird (čhu-bya—1273 A.D.) nd the year Wood-Hog (śiṅ-phag—1335 A.D.). 'Tshal-pa's on the great ascetic (bya-bral čhen-po) Kun-dga' rgyal-mtshan lived for) 76 years, between the year Earth-Hog (sa-phag—299 A.D.) and the year Wood-Tiger (śiṅ-stag—1374 A.D.). Drin-čan-pa's eldest son—the hermit (ri-khrod-pa) Ye-śes zaṅ-po (lived for) 42 years, between the year Iron-Mouse lčags-byi—1300 A.D.) and the year Iron-Serpent (lčags-brul—1341 A.D.). The youngest gTsug-rgyan Yid-bžin or-bu Kun-dga' lhun-grub (lived for) 72 years, between the year Water-Ox (čhu-glaṅ—1313 A.D.) and the year Wood-Mouse (śiṅ-byi—1384 A.D.). His eldest son mKhas-btsun Don-grub rgyal-mtshan (lived for) 42 years, and was born in the year of the Ox (glaṅ-lo—1337 A.D.). The youngest son Rin-po-čhe Čhos-rgyal-ba: he was born at rTse-sgaṅ in the year Iron-Male-Dragon (lčags-pho-'brug—1340 A.D.). From childhood he was characterized by brighter faculties than others. He recollected the work he had performed (in his former lives), and manifested a great power of mind. Without paying attention to difficulties, he became one possessed of all (branches) of knowledge. From the age of 8, he mastered without difficulty (religious) dances, rites (phrin-sgrub), astrology (Indian tradition), and other branches of (knowledge). From the age of 9, he mastered by heart the Guhyagarbha-Tantra (gSaṅ-sñiṅ) and the Cycle of (Vajra)kīla (Kg.rGyud-'bum, No. 832). He also learned by heart the (above) Tantra, its subdivisions (sa-gžuṅ), its commentary and summary (khog-dbub), together with notes (mčhan) on it and verbal commentaries (gsuṅ-sgros). At the age of 12, he became abbot. He used to preach without interval throughout the summer and winter semestres (dbyar-čhos and dgun-čhos). He studied assiduously with his father the initiations, expositions and precepts of the three Lineages of the Ži-byed system, the "Early", the "Later" and the "Intermediate", together with their permissions (luṅ). He also studied extensively the "Old" and "New" Tantras, and preached from memory the large texts. When a bride was brought (44a) (to him) after consultation between all (his relatives), he felt afflicted, and in company with three disciples, four in all, fled away, having heard of the fame of sKyes-mčhog Rin-po-čhe. He met sKyes-mčhog-pa, who was residing at rGya-brag, and an extraordinary faith was born in him as soon as he had seen the Teacher's face. "From where did you come?" inquired sKyes-mčhog-pa. He replied: "From the hermitage of Gra". "O! You are the nephew of Žig-po Rin-po-čhe", saying so he joined the palms of his hands before his chest. "Take from this house whatever you need", said the Teacher. He felt very pleased. He then listened to (the exposition) of the meditation of the Lineage of the Meaning, and attended lectures (tshogs-čhos). After two or three months he was asked to return, and came back. Then he obtained from his father all the secret precepts in the manner of a vase filled to the brim. From the "Great Hermit" (Bya-bral čhen-po) he obtained the Phyag-bžes (method) of 'Khrul-Žig-pa, the Cycle of doctrines of the Dags-po bKa'-brgyud, the initiation into the Vajramālā, and other texts, which were not found at rThe-sgaṅ. He also obtained from the guru A-mogha-pa numerous initiations of the "New" Tantras and many permissions (luṅ) from gTsaṅ-pa Luṅ-maṅ-po, beginning with those of the bKa'-'gyur. Then at the age of 18, he proceeded to sMan-čig and propitiated Phyag-rdor bDe-khros. After that he worshipped many tutelary deities of the "New" and "Old" Tantras. He practised the method of rMa which belonged to the "Intermediate Lineage" (of the Ži-byed), and an understanding of the Mahāmudrā was produced in him. After that, for two years he performed the propitiation of the Lam-lṅa ("the Five Paths"), and observed many extraordinary signs. Then for one year he practised the meditation of the "Three Paths" (lam-gsum, belongs to the Ži-byed). About

at time, when meditating at Dawn, he had a vision of
: Guru of the Lineage (rten-rgyas bskyed) on whose
ages he had concentrated assiduously. His faith then in-
:ased in power, and as soon as he had prayed earnestly,
any doors of mystic trance were opened (before him). For
months he practised the sādhana of dBaṅ-gčig-ma, and
v in a dream his body transformed into a luminous form,
d then absorbed into the heart of the Teacher. He prac- (44b)
:d occasionally the (method) of the "Early" Lineage, as
ll as the method of So. Thus he hoisted the banner of
:ditative ascetics. The Sun of yogic insight shone inside
n, and the darkness of Ignorance vanished. Then the
ters of the differentiation into subject and object (gzuṅ-
:in) fell off, and his power of love and commiseration in-
:ased. He developed the faculty of faith (dad-pa'i dbaṅ-po)
all the devotees (his disciples). He thus took his place
iong his predecessors (in the Lineage). Even the daily
ours of this great man, could not be grasped by mind.
Dawn he used to begin (with the recitation) of the Refuge
mula (skyabs-'gro) and the Cittotpāda (sems-bskyed), and
ditated on the "Five Paths" (lam-lṅa) till day-break. Then
recited the mantras of rTshe-sgrub (the mantra of Ami-
ha), the rNam-'Joms (the mantra of Vajradhara), the sMe-
segs (Kuṇḍalī; the first insures longevity, the second—
noves defilements, the third—purifies the body). After
t he used to arrange offerings (mčhod-pa), recite praise,
yers, offer confession (rgyun-bśags), and offer a gtor-ma
de of white butter (dkar-gtor), etc. After finishing his
rning tea, he recited the Prajñāpāramitā (mdo-sgrub) and
pared many kinds of gtor-ma offerings. Then he recited
prayer of the Lineage called Dus-gsum-ma, and retired
his morning meditation.

After finishing his mid-day meal, he recited the Na-
Doṅ-sprugs (name of a rÑiṅ-ma rite, well-known in
:kim), and the dhāraṇī of gZa'-yum (Rāhula and his śakti).
ter that he retired for the evening meditation. In the

evening he recited 21 times the stotra of the Tārā. At dusk he performed a hundred prostration, the Seven branches (Yan-lag bdun-pa), made a general confession (spyi-bśags), and made offerings to the Religious Protector. After it got dark, he recited the Nam-mkha' sgo-'byed (name of a gČod ceremony), and offered gtor-mas to sKyed-dbuṅs (name of a deity). He also constantly meditated during the day according to the method of sKam and the sPyod-yul (gČod). Such were his usual daily labours. In the above manner he practised exclusively meditation, and observed many extraordinary signs. One night, when he was performing the sKoṅs-brgya-rtsa (a hundred offerings), he saw in a dream that much puss and blood had come out from his body, and that his flesh became emaciated. Then he saw his flesh detached from the bones which assumed a greyish colour. During his propitiation of bDe-khros, (he saw) himself sitting on (the summit) of (45a)
Mount Meru (Ri-bo mčhog-rab), then he got a vision of the three thousand worlds, and his body grew very large. During his initiation into the Cycle of the Venerable One (rJe-btsun-ma—Vajravārahī), he saw the Teacher as the Venerable One. During his propitiation of (Vajra)kīla, a red light of the size of an offering lamp, emanating from the magic dagger, was observed for many days. In a dream (he saw) himself holding with his hand (two) opposite mountain peaks, and beating them like cymbals (čha-laṅ). During his propitiation of Tshe-bdag (a form of Yamāntaka), he saw in a dream that he drank out all (the water) of the gTsaṅ-po. During the offering of the 14th at bSam-gtan-gliṅ, Legs-ldan Nag-po (Kṛṣṇa) came down from the roof of the house and appeared in front of him. All saw him (Kṛṇṣa) descending. At the time of an eclipse of the Moon, when he was performing an offering rite to bDe-khros, and had finished the rite to the Mundane deities, and was about to begin the rite to the Supermundane deities, his body became luminous, fire lit up, and stood out clearly for a considerable time. After finishing the rite, he expressed his satisfaction. When he was asked

about this he said that at the time of the manifestation of (the deity) in front of him, the tutelary deity was seen clearly entering the fire. He was able to offer the homa offering to the (god), in the manner of a man giving it to another. Later there appeared ḍākiṇīs and Religious Protectors, and partook of their shares. bDe-khros and (Vajra)kīla had been the tutelary deities of the previous teachers (of the Lineage). During the initiation rites, these two were the greatest in manifesting their blessing. During the initiations a sick man had his disease cured. They also restored the power of speech to dumb ones. During the performance of medicinal rites, the quantity of medicines increased and numerous were the signs of blessing. He used to perform his usual work in the manner of previous teachers (of the Lineage). He spent all his property (in payment) as soon as received for the memorial services ('das-mčhod) for previous teachers (of the Lineage), erected images, distributed provisions to the poor, and presented offering lamps in the Upper and the Lower (45*b*)
Chapels. Five years after Rin-po-čhe gTsug-rgyan-pa's death, he bestowed the initiation and the exposition of the "Five Paths" (lam-lṅa) on a small number of disciples, who included the latter's son, the bLa-ma 'Od-zer, and others. Then he preached every summer and winter the initiations and the expositions of the Three Lineages of the Ži-byed system, the "Early", the "Later", and the "Intermediate." The benefit for living beings increased. His fame spread over the surface of the Earth. Many kalyāṇa-mitras became his disciples, and the most excellent among them was sKyes-mčhog Rin-čhen bzaṅ-po. He himself admitted that he was an incarnation of Indrabhūti. He had also numerous disciples, such as the bla-ma Grags-don-pa, gTsaṅ-pa bLo-bzaṅs-pa, rTogs-ldan Grags-lhun-pa, and others. At the age of 70, from the autumn of the year Earth-Female-Ox (sa-mo-glaṅ—1409 A.D.) his health became impaired. They applied themselves with diligence to rites, etc. One day he gave instructions to each of his sons, pointing out to them their respective monas-

teries and works. "You, Śes-rab bzaṅ-po, should look after these books in the book-case. You shouldn't abandon the hermitage of sMan-gčig and should foster the interest of living beings according to your abilities." Having imparted instructions as above, he passed away into the Pure Sphere (Dag-pa'i dbyiṅs). He had seven sons: Byaṅ-čhub bzaṅ-po, Dar-ma rin-čhen, 'Od-zer rgyal-mtshan, the sGrub-pa-po (sādhaka) 'Jam-dbyaṅs, Byaṅ-čhub dpal-ldan, Kun-dga' bśes-gñen, the Dharmasvāmin Rin-po-čhe Śes-rab-bzaṅ-po. The Dharmasvāmin Śes-rab bzaṅ-po was born in the year Fire-Male-Tiger (me-pho-stag—1386 A.D.). In childhood he obtained the complete precepts from his father He also knew the rituals. At the age of 24, he bestowed the exposition (of precepts) on sGo-mo Rin-po-čhe Ye-śes-dpal-ba and others, and became a Teacher. After that he constantly laboured for the welfare of others at both Lho-brag and Gra. He was endowed with the understanding of the Mahāmudrā, and was strict in (46a)
the observance of the pure moral code of a monk. From this Master of the Lineage of Teaching, we ('Gos-lo) obtained the Three Lineages of the Ži-byed system, the "Early", the "Later", and the "Intermediate". Rin-po-čhe Byaṅ-bzaṅs-pa's son the bla-ma Kun-dga' rdo-rje was born in the year Wood-Male-Horse (śiṅ-pho-rta—1414 A.D.). In his childhood he studied extensively with his father the method of Māyā (sGyu-'phrul) of the "benign" (Ži-ba) and "wrathful" (khro-bo) aspects, the Cycle of Vajrakīla, and other systems. He also heard much from his father and the Rin-po-čhe Śes-rab bzaṅ-po the complete Cycle of the Ži-byed system. Even now this (Teacher) is still alive, benefitting numerous disciples. The eldest son of the three sons born to sMra-ba'i seṅ-ge, known as the "All-Knowing" (Thams-čad mkhyen-pa), had been a paṇḍita in the South of India, named Lokyatrinātha. By the power of his learning in both the Tantras and Sūtras, he was able to overcome others in philosophical disputes. He had about six excellent disciples. He was reborn as the great Sa-skya-pa Kun-dga' sñiṅ-po. After that he became a paṇḍita

named Prajñāmatiśrī in Jālandhara, endowed with some miraculous powers. With the help of his miraculous powers he visited the country of Oḍḍiyāna. There he visited the Svayambhū-caitya (Raṅ-byuṅ-gi mčhod-rten). On the four sides of this caitya, four great paṇḍitas in turn bestowed on him the initiation of the vase (kalaśa-abhiṣeka) and the other degrees of initiations. At that time he was blessed by the Tathāgatas who filled the entire Sky. He was bathed by Locanā (sPyan-ma, name of a devī) and other deities. He was worshipped by gZugs-rdo-rJe-ma (Rūpavajrī) and other goddesses. After that he proceeded to various cemeteries, such as the Padmakūṭa cemetery (Pad-ma-brtsegs) and others, to perform Tantric rites. Due to the shortness of the time spent by him in meditation, these Tantric rites endangered his life, and he passed away at the age of 49. From there he came here, (46b) such is his story told by himself. He was reborn in the year Fire-Male-Mouse (me-pho-byi-ba—1216 A.D.). When he was nine months old, his mother took him to the place where Te-ne had been cremated at Ri-khrod, and he recollected fully all the circumstances of the cremation. At the age of 7, he mastered reading and grammar, after a single explanation by the Teacher. He also learned from gÑags-ston rNal-'byor-'bum grammatical treatises (śāstras), such as the Rig-bklag and others.

After having studied for seven days, he was able to read with ease the printed script. Later he was able to distinguish between the styles of scripts, paintings and images of India, China, Oḍḍiyāna, and other countries. At the age of eight, he was able to perform the rite of the bKa'-brgyad (name of a rÑiṅ-ma ritual). He offered to his parents the food that remained after the Tantric feast (gaṇacakra) accompanying the rite, and pleased them. At the age of ten, he joined his father in propitiating (their) tutelary deity, and a mystic trance, during which he did not distinguish between day and night, was born in him. Thus this (Teacher), who was endowed with the nature of a Bodhisattva (rigs-ldan) and had

obtained a mass of merits as his birth right, attended, in general, on more than 16 teachers, and especially secured from rGya, the "All-Knowing", the light of the boundless scriptures. From Lhag Ru-ba he obtained an excellent discriminative understanding. From a great Indian paṇḍita he obtained the foundation of the true meaning (yid-čhes don-gyi gnas). From 'J̌i Ri-pa he obtained the rite of the "external" and "inner" maṇḍalas (Phyi-naṅ dkyib-'khor; the naṅ dkyib-'khor belong to the Anuttara-Tantra; the "External" to the other Tantric systems). From lDum-ra-ba he learned the (habit) of earnest study which purified the symbolical and individual streams (dpe-rgyud). From 'Bri-khuṅ-pa he learned the manner of labouring for the welfare of others. From Ri-khrod-pa he obtained the "heat" of blessing by which he was able to subdue demons. From Baṅ-rim-pa he obtained the vital power (gnad-kyi mtshan) of hidden precepts. From the kulapati (rigs-bdag—his father) he himself obtained the understanding of the theory. Because he was able to master a subject by merely reading about it, or merely hearing about it, he became known as "All-Knowing". His real name was bSod-nams-dpal. He also composed numerous śāstras on the "Old" (rÑiṅ) and "New" Tantras, and on many other branches of knowledge. From lDum-ra-ba he obtained especially the sayings of the scholar Tre-bo mGon-po and became an expert in the system of Tre-bo. Through meditation, he obtained many realizations in the Tantras. He (47*a*)
passed away at the age of 62 in the year Fire-Female-Ox (me-mo-glaṅ—1277 A.D.). The eldest of the three sons of the "All-Knowing" (was) Kun-dga' bzaṅ-po: The Dharmasvāmin rGod-tshaṅ-pa, the Great, having passed away in the year Earth-Male-Horse (sa-pho-rta—1258 A.D.), was reborn in the same Horse year (rta-lo—1258 A.D.) at sÑe-mdo as son of sÑe-mdo-ba, the "All-Knowing", who was then aged 43. Till the age of six, the child used to repeat frequently: "I am rGod-tshaṅ-pa!" He also used to say that he had been Mid-la. He pretended that he could not speak till he

was three. From the age of four he mastered reading and writing. From the age of seven, he used to preach to the retinue. Till the age of 12, he obtained from his father many sādhanas and Tantras of the rÑiṅ-ma school, mastered them, and preached them to others. He also taught ritual. At the age of 12, he gathered disciples from different parts, and erected a religious seat. His father entrusted to him all the books and taught him Sūtras, Tantras, Āgamas, and Logic (Pramāṇa). At the age of 13, he taught the Śrī-Guhyasamāja-Tantra, and his father was pleased with the manner of his preaching. At the age of 14 and 15, he stayed in seclusion and had a clear vision of Vajrakīla. He manifested some miraculous powers. Together with Śaṅs-pa Tshul-śe he listened to numerous teachings of the Guhyagarbha and to those of the Three Lineages of the Ži-byed system, the "Early", the "Later", and the "Intermediate". From Śaṅs-tshul himself he obtained several sūtras, such as the Samādhirāja-Sūtra (Kg. mDo, No. 127) and others. From Maṅ-yul (Diṅ-ri) came the ācārya Nam-mkha' ye-śes to visit his father, and to be initiated into the great initiation of the Māyā (sGyu-'phrul) and others. The son assisted in the rite as karma-ācārya. At the age of 16, Ba-ri-ba admitted him to be an incarnation, and dBon-po Čhos-kyi gzi-brJid was sent to offer him numerous presents. After that sPyil-dkar-ba himself having come, they taught each other numerous doctrines. From his father he received the initiation into the Kālacakra. At the age of 17, he met 'Tshal gSer-khaṅ-pa on the way (47b)
to 'Bri-khuṅ, and obtained (from him) many doctrines. He then went to worship the image of Śākyamuni (Jo-bo) in Lhasa, and after that journeyed to 'Bri-khuṅ, and took up ordination. At the age of 18, he listened to numerous expositions by his father at sÑe-mdo. His yogic insight broadened. He accepted his father as his matchless first Teacher (mūla-guru, rtsa-ba'i bla-ma). His 19th year he spent in a similar manner. In the year Fire-Mouse (me-byi—1276 A.D.) the troops of the prince (rgyal-bu) A-rog-čhe (Aruγči) arrived.

In the year Fire-Ox (me-glaṅ—1277 A.D.) his father went to mKhar-čhu. He was invited by the Dharmasvāmin Ba-ri-ba, and proceeded to La-stod (near Diṅ-ri). During the year his father died at mKhar-čhu. On his return from gTsaṅ, he performed pompous funeral rites. In the year Iron-Serpent (lčags-sbrul—1281 A.D.) he met the siddha Seṅ-ge-grags at sÑe-mdo, who imparted precepts to him. At the age of 25, in the year Water-Horse (čhu-rta—1282 A.D.) he met U-rgyan-pa. At Čhu-lug, gYam-bzaṅs and 'Dod-mkhar he heard twice the Mahāsiddha (Grub-čhen-pa, U-rgyan-pa) reciting the commentary on the Kālacakra-Tantra (the Vimalaprabhā). At the age of 36, in the year Water-Serpent (čhu-sbrul—1293 A.D.) he obtained from bČom-Ral (bČom-ldan Rig-ral) the basic text of Śa-ba-ri (Mahāmudrā-vajragīti-nāma, Tg. rGyud, No. 2287), and other texts. In the year Earth-Dog (sa-khyi—1298 A.D.) he invited the lo-tsā-ba Grags-pa rgyal-mtshan (the Yar-kluṅs lo-tsā-ba) and obtained from him the Hevajra, the Nā-ro 'grel-čhen (Vajrapādasārasaṃgrahapañjikā, Tg. rGyud, No. 1196), the Commentary on the Sekoddeśa (Paramārthasaṃgraha-nāma-Sekoddeśaṭīkā, Tg. rGyud, No. 1351), the Upadeśa-mañjarī (Man-ṅag sñe-ma, Śrīsampuṭatantrarājaṭīkāmnāyamañjarī-nāma, Tg. rGyud, No. 1198), the Ka-la-pa (Kalāpasūtra, Tg. sGra-mdo, No. 4282), and many other Indian and Tibetan grammatical works. Later he obtained the Acala-Tantra (Kg. rGyud-'bum, No. 432) and the Bya-ba btus-pa (Kriyāsaṃgraha, Tg. rGyud, No. 2531). When he was 43, in the year Iron-Male-Mouse (lčags-pho-byi-ba—1300 A.D.) Ba-ri-ba passed away. He passed into the Sphere of Great Peace (Ži-ba-čhen-po'i dbyiṅs), the Dharmakāya, in the year Fire-Dragon (me-'brug—1316 A.D.) at the age of 59. The middle son Kun-dga' mgon-po (lived) for 56 years, between the year Wood-Ox (śiṅ-glaṅ—1265 A.D.) and the year Iron-Ape (lčags-spre—1320 A.D.). The youngest son—Kun-mkhyen Kun-dga' don-grub (lived) for 61 years, between the year Earth-Dragon (sa-'brug—1268 A.D.) and the year Earth-Dragon (sa-'brug—1328 A.D.).

The Dharmasvāmin Žig-po's disciple named Saṅs-rgyas ras-pa: he was born at Žiṅ-tshigs of Phu-thaṅ 'khun-pa-sa, and belonged to the 'Briṅ clan. He was the last of the three sons of father mKha'-'gro and mother Sruṅ-skyid, and was born in the year Earth-Female-Hog (sa-mo-phag—1203 A. D.). In this year the 'Bri-khuṅ Dharmasvāmin reached his 61st year. This appears to be the year which preceded the coming to Tibet of the Kha-čhe paṇ-čhen (Śākyaśrī). From his childhood he remembered nothing but death. In his youth he met for a short while rGyal-ba Te-ne. He obtained the lÑa-ldan (name of a system of 'Bri-khuṅ-pa) from rJe sPyan-sña of Phag-mo-gru. When he saw Žig-po on the road, returning from Tsa-ri, he felt faith born in him. At the age of 23, he came to him, and offered him all his possessions. Having taken up the upāsaka vows, he received the name of Rin-čhen smon-lam. (Žig-po) foretold him that in future he would gather about a hundred disciples. He received the final monastic ordination (upasampadā) in the presence of the ācārya sTon-pa, a disciple of Zul-phu-ba. He was then given the initiation and the exposition of the Ži-byed system. For six months he performed the meditation of the "Purification of the Mind" (bLo-sbyoṅ), and all the signs were complete. The spiritual merits of the different degrees having been properly produced in him, his Teacher became pleased. (48a)

He attended on his Teacher till the age of 21. After that he obtained (their respective) precepts from the following teachers: his elder brother the ācārya sTon-pa, the ācārya sTon-pa of Mon-'gar-ba, the ācārya Yon-btsun of bSam-yas, dbOn Rin-po-čhe at 'Bri-khuṅ, Khams-sgom Žig-po at Ru-mtshams čhu-bzaṅs, Ko-brag-pa, Khro-phu-ba, Seṅ-yes, the siddha of Ti-se (Kailāsa), the ācārya Gur-ston at Lho-brag, the ācārya Ri-khrod-pa at mKhar-čhu, sPyan-sña Gaṅs-dkar-ba, Śākya dGe-sbyoṅ, the ācārya dPon-sgom, Gra-pa sTon-gžon, the ācārya sDe-snod-pa of Gru-śul Lha-ri, the ācārya sGom-pa of dMyal, the ācārya kLu-sgom, and the bla-ma bZaṅ-mo-ba. The manner of his meditative practice: he was bound by a vow (given) in the presence of his Teacher, to practise meditation for 12 years. He practised it for three extra years. The localities where he practised meditation (sgrub-pa'i gnas): Gaṅs-dkar Ti-se (Kailāsa), a holy rock-cave in sPu-raṅs, the cave of sPa-gro sTag-tshaṅ, Gaṅ-bzaṅs, J̌o-mo Kha-rag, (48b) La-yag, Gaṅs-phug, mKhar-čhu, the Snows of Čha-luṅ, the Snows of gŽan-lha-mda', gYag-mtsho of Mtsho sna, and Luṅ-stoṅ (desert valley) of Sa-'ug sTag-sgo. Having crossed the Pass of La-čhen in Mon (La-čhen in Sikkim), he arrived at a place called "The valley of Revatī" (Revati'i luṅ) and the lake Mu-le-goṅ which was said to be the residence of Revatī. In its neighbourhood there was great danger from wild animals. Then he saw the river Gaṅgā, and visited an Indian grass-hut village (rtsa'i spyil-po-čan), and felt that it had been the place of his former birth. (He also visited) Dags Lha-sgam-po, sKyo-zur, situated near to his own village, and dGon-dkar. He had an unattached mental attitude towards his own merits. He was able to subsist on one breath per day, move through the Sky in a cross-legged posture, and cover long distances during his journeys. His other attainments he kept secret and did not speak about them (to others). In other words, he (had visions) which could not be described by words. Later he spent some time in looking after the welfare of others at the monastery of Čhar-ma. He manifested the appearance of passing into Nirvāṇa at the age of 78, in the year Iron-Male-Dragon (lčags-pho-'brug—1280 A.D.). The above information I have condensed from his Life-story (rnam-thar) composed by his personal disciple named Myaṅ 'ban-po Dharmasiṃha. The Doctrines which belonged to the "Later" Lineage (of the Ži-byed) were called "Phyag-rgya čhen-po dri-med thigs-pa phyag-bžes-kyi skor", or "The Cycle of Methods of Drops of the Immaculate Mahāmudrā". (Here the term) Mahāmudrā denotes the Mahāmudrā doctrine of Maitrī-pa, because Dam-pa Saṅs-rgyas had been a personal disciple of Maitrī-pa. (The term) "Immaculate" means the sayings of Dam-pa (Saṅs-

rgyas). (The word) "method" means the methods of the precepts which differed slightly from those of the other doctrines. These precepts by their nature belong to the Prajñāpāramitā, but follow the Tantric system. In the Commentary on the De-kho na-ñid bču-pa (Tattvadaśaka-nāma, Tg. rGyud, No. 2236) by Maitrī-pa the system is explained as though it was (494a)
a Prajñāpāramitā doctrine, but had much in common with the Tantras in its practice, as mentioned in the Hevajra-Tantra. He (Maitrī-pa) said: "These precepts are not based on the meditation on deities, and do not follow the system of the four mudrās" (Dharma-mudrā, karma-mudrā, samaya-mudrā and mahā-mudrā. Advayavajrasaṃgraha, ed. by Haraprasad Shastri, Gaekwad's Oriental Series, No. XL, p. X: dharma-mudrā—Absolute Nature; Karma-mudrā—female associate; samaya-mudrā—a deity mentally created/or the Tantric vows/; Mahā-mudrā—the Wisdom of the Absolute). For this reason it is not classified in the Tantra. This agrees with the above statement by Maitrī-pa. This definition includes only the precepts known to the general public. Otherwise it is said that Dam-pa bestowed the initiation into the Kālacakra system on Phyar-čhen and 'Ban Gun-rgyal (this means that he preached the precepts basing himself on the meditation on deities), and that he had also bestowed on many/others/the precepts of the karma-mudrā (i.e. he preached all the four mudrās). Therefore it is wrong to say that the Doctrine of sDug-bsṅal Źi-byed of Dam-pa (Saṅs-rgyas) does not contain Tāntric precepts. Having been described as following on the Tantras, the "Ā-li Kā-li" initiation and other rituals (should be considered) as imitating the Tantras. But because they are not genuine (Tantric rites) one should not mistake them for true Tantras. The "Ā-li Kā-li" initiation should be considered to be similar to the exposition of the dhāraṇīs of 42 letters mentioned in the Prajñāpāramitā-sūtra (which is not a Tantric work). In this system which consists of two sections—the section of the ordinary doctrines (thun-moṅ) and that of the extraordinary doctrines (thun-moṅ-ma-yin-pa'i čhos), the section of "ordinary"

doctrines contains the mDo, the Tantra together with their rituals, the bKa'-babs with the "Oral Tradition," the "Immaculate" (Dri-med) together with the Phra-tig, and the Dar-tshags together with the bŚad-'bum. Firstly, here mDo means the sPyi-mdo (General sūtra)-Čhu-kluṅ mṅon-par rol-pa'i mdo, and the dGos-mdo (Special sūtra)—the Śes-rab sñiṅ-po (Bhagavatī-prajñāpāramitā-hṛdaya, "Catalogue du Fonds Tibétain. Les mDo-maṅ", by M. Lalou,/Paris, 1931/p. 40, No. 101 The "General" Tantra—the sDe-snod gsal-byed; the "Particular" Tantra, or sGos-rGyud-Čhu-kluṅ čhen-po; the Ritual (phyag-len): the Great and Medium dBaṅ-'khor (dBaṅ-'khor čhe-'briṅ); the three Lam-rim, great and small; the bKa'-babs sñan-brgyud known as the Four bKa'-babs (bKa'-babs-bži), and its Lam-sloṅs sñan-brgyud-bži (Four Oral Traditions of Practice). The Dri-med Phra-tig: the Dri-med contains Six Cycles which include the "Root on which the Doctrine is established" (Čhos-zug-pa rtsa-ba). The Phra-tig represents replies by Kun-dga' in answer to Pa-tshab's question about malevolent hindrances (ma-bde-ba'i gegs). The Dar-tshags bśad-'bum consists of 18 Cycles of Dar-tshags žal-gdams bdud-rtsi and others. It represents occasional talks ('phral-gtam) by Pa-tshab, committed to writing by Te-ne (rGyal-ba Te-ne). The bŚad-'bum contains the exposition written (49b)
down by Te-ne, Žig-po, sÑe-mdo-ba, and others. Among the class of "extraordinary" doctrines (Thun-moṅ ma-yin-pa'i čhos-sde) one finds the Tantra and its compendium, the dBaṅ-lam ("Initiation and Path") and its exposition, the "Three Treasures of the Hidden" (gSaṅ-mdzod-gsum), and the Eight Be'u-bum (Booklet). Among the "Three Hidden Treasures": The "Hidden Treasure of the Teacher" (bLa-ma gsaṅ-mdzod), the "Hidden Treasure of the Tutelary deity" (Yi-dam gsaṅ-mdzod), the "Hidden Treasure of the Ḍākinīs (mKha'-'gro gsaṅ-mdzod). The Five Cycles of the Path (Lam-skor-lṅa) (contain): 1. the "Cycle of the Path of the Four Gates of the upāya-mārga of Bi-ru-pa (Bi-ru-pa'i thabs-lam sgo-bži'i lam-skor), 2. the Cycle of the Path of the Four spheres of the

Jpāya-mārga of Saraha (Sa-ra-ha'i thabs-lam yul-bži'i lam-skor), 3. the Cycle of the Eightfold Path of gSer-gliṅ-pa (gSer-gliṅ-pa'i lam-skor brgyad-pa), 4. the Cycle of the Eightfold Path of Āryadeva (Ā-rya-de-ba'i lam-skor brgyad-pa), 5. the Cycle of the Path of the four yoga-arūḍhas of Nā-ro-pa (Nā-ro-pa'i zuṅ-'Jug bži'i lam-skor). The Eight Be'u-bum (Booklets): the Be'u-bum of the Initiation of the Hidden (Zab-mo dbaṅ-gi be'u-bum), the Be'u-bum of the Root of Identification (Ṅo-sprod rtsa-ba'i be'u-bum), the Be'u-bum of the exposition of the Oral Tradition (sÑan-brgyud-khrid-yi be'u-bum), the Booklet (be'u-bum) on the main points of the Four Gates (sGo-bži gnad-kyi be'u-bum), the Booklet of various miracles (sNa-tshogs rdzu-'phrul gyi be'u-bum), the Booklet of Hidden Mantras (Zab-mo sṅags-kyi be'u-bum), the Booklet of the Ḍākinī protecting the Doctrine (bKa'-sruṅs mkha'-'gro'i be'u-bum), the Booklet of the three Royal Precepts (Man-ṅag rgyal čha-gsum-gyi be'u-bum). These are the classes of the "extraordinary" doctrines possessing an injunction (bKa'-rgya-čan).

The Chapter on the "Later" Lineage of the Ži-byed (System).

(50a)

BOOK XIII.

The (system) of gČod-yul, and Kha-rag-pa.

Now I shall relate the (history) of the Lineage of the "gČod-yul of the Demons" (bDud-kyi gČod-yul) of the Prajñāpāramitā (so called because the adepts of the gČod-yul adhered to the philosophic doctrine of the Prajñāpāramitā). Lord Maitrīpāda (Maitrī-pa) had said that even in the Prajñāpāramitā mention was made of practices which imitated those of the Tantras. Because of this, the system was (originally) called sPyod-yul (Tibetan sPyod corresponds to Skrt. gocara, practice. The orthography gČod is a corruption of the first word. Both words are pronounced čöd—čö in modern Tibetan). How can it (i.e. gČod) be similar to the Tantra? Because it agrees with the standpoint of the Hevajra-Tantra (sNar-thaṅ bKa'-'gyur, rGyud-'bum, Vol. I /Ka/, fol. 316b: "Meditation is said to be fruitful at the foot of a solitary tree (a solitary tree, growing in a deserted plain, is popularly believed to be the abode of demons. Because of this wide-spread belief solitary trees are never felled in Tibet, and are often worshipped by the local population), in a cemetery, in an empty cave (mātṛ-gṛha, Tib. ma-mo'i khyim), at night, in a solitary place, or in the neighbourhood of a village (bas-mtha')". Again it is said in the Hevajra-Tantra (sNar-thaṅ bKa'-'gyur, rGyud-'bum, Vol. I /Ka/, fol. 315b: "Having given up (his) physical body, he (the adept) should afterwards practise the rite". And again it is said (Vol. I /Ka/, fol. 315b): "Verily, should an asura, even one equal to Indra, walk in front of you, you should not be afraid of it, and should walk on in the manner of a lion" (Hevajra-Tantra, Vol. I/Ka/, fol. 315b, has brGya-byin-lta-bu yin-na yaṅ). (The system) was also called the "Prajñāpāramitā cutting (the influence) of demons" 'ha-rol-tu phyin-pa bDud kyi gČod-yul; gČod-yul means ıe "act of cutting asunder"). Again, because it is said in ıe Prajñāpāramitāsañcayagāthā (sDud-pa tshigs-su bčad-pa, ıDo-maṅs, Vol. II, fol. 435a; sDud-pa, fol. 27a): "A odhisattva endowed with the power of learning (mkhas-obs-ldan) cannot be overcome or shaken by four demons, ecause of four reasons: because he abides in the Void toṅ-par gnas-pa), because he has not abandoned living eings, because he acts according to his word, and because e is endowed with the blessing of the Sugata." The ıllowers of the gČod-system observe the above four religious ıjunctions, that is, they (accept) the theory of abiding in ıe Void, they (cultivate) compassion by not abandoning ving beings, they (observe) the moral rule of the Bodhi-ıttvas of acting according to one's word, and they strive ɔr the blessing of the Sugata. These are the four (injunc-ions) which constitute the foundation of their spiritual aining. The (injunction) of striving for the blessing of he Sugata (means) the taking of Refuge (skyabs-su'gro-ba), nd the offering of prayers to the Teacher and the Spiritual .ineage. The acting according to one's own word, (means) o abstain from harsh actions (tho-čo ma-yin), and (to abstain) rom breaking the vows, which were taken at the time of he manifestation of the Mental Creative Effort towards :nlightenment. The non-abandoning of living beings, (14) neans a practice characterized by a great compassion and bstention from doing harm to demons (amanuṣya, mi-ma-yin) nd others, by which one becomes free from any sort of ill-vish towards living beings, and makes them enter on the 'ath of Enlightenment. The theory of abiding in the Void, r Śūnyatā, (means) firstly, the abandonment of the view vhich maintains the substantiality of the aggregate (of the lements), which constitute the individual stream (santāna, aṅ-rgyud), and secondly, the non-acceptance of the notion f the reality and substantiality of other living beings. Now, n what ground is such a practice called gČod-yul? In the

Abhidharmakośa V, 34: Phra-rgyas spaṅs-pa ma-yin-daṅ/ yul-ni ñe-bar gnas-pa daṅ /tshul-bžin ma-yin yid-byed-las/ ñon-moṅs rgyu-ni tshaṅ-ba yin. Abhidharmakośa, translated by L. de la Vallée Poussin, V, 34 p. 72 /Paris-Louvain, 1925/) it it said: "Defilement (kleśa) originates from attachments (anuśaya, phra-rgyas), the presence (pratyupasthāna, ñe-bar gnas-pa) of external objects, and a wrong conception of them." That which is to be cut (is) Defilement (kleśa, ñon-moṅs). If these Defilements have originated from attachments, external objects, and wrong conceptions of them, the yogin, as soon as he contacts an external object and rouses (in himself) past inclinations (vāsanā, bag-čhags), should remove (lit. cut asunder) the Defilement, which was preceded by a wrong conception (of the external object). For this reason this system was called gČod-yul (lit. object-cutting).

The secret precepts of the system were handed down from Dam-pa. The (precepts) which were handed down by sKyo bSod-nams bla-ma and Ram-par ser-po of Yar-kluṅs, were called Pho-gČod, or "Male gČod." Those handed down by Ma-gčig (Labs-sgron-ma) were called Mo-gČod, or "Female gČod." Dam-pa Saṅs-rgyas used to say that he had given three words of friendly advice (sñiṅ-gtam) to Ma-Jo mChod-gnas-ma at the residence of Rog-pa of Yar-kluṅs. Through them she attained emancipation. She herself used to say that she had obtained emancipation through them. She, a natural yoginī, preached numerous secret precepts of her own. Now, why is it that one and the same thing was called by two different names: sPyod, or "practice", and gČod, or "cutting asunder?" Such is the case of other texts also. For instance, the Lord of Wealth (Nor-gyi bdag-po) was sometimes called Vaiśravaṇa, which means "Son of Learning" (rNam-thos-kyi bu), and sometimes called Vaiśramaṇa, which means "Son of Rest" (Ṅal-sos-kyi bu). Also one and the same person was sometimes called Nāgabodhi, meaning "The Enlightenment of a Nāga" (kLu'i byaṅ-čhub), and sometimes called Nāgabuddhi, which means "Nāga's wisdom" (kLu'i-blo). In particular, in the Śrī-Sampuṭatantrarājaṭīka-mnāyamañjarī-nāma (Man-ṅag sñe-ma, Tg. rGyud, No. 1198) the word pīlaba (this seems to be a corruption of the Sanskrit pīṭha) is explained by two words: 'thuṅ-spyod, or "drink and practice", and 'thuṅ-gčod, or "drink & cut" (Thuṅ-gčod is a term used to designate a group of sacred places in the list of 24 Sacred Places: 'Thuṅ-gčod, ñe-ba'i 'thuṅ-gčod, žiṅ, ñe-ba'i žiṅ, groṅ-mtha', ñe-ba'i groṅ-mtha', etc. See Bu-ston gSuṅ-'bum, vol. VI /Cha/, fol. 29a.). One should understand (sPyod and gČod) in a similar manner.

Labs-sgron: her native place (was) Khe'u gaṅ. She was born to father Čhos-bla and mother kLuṅs-mo 'Bum-lčam. It is said that she was the sister of the lo-tsā-ba Khe'u-gaṅ 'Khor-lo-grags. She received ordination in her childhood in the presence of Gra-pa mÑon-śes. She was an expert reader, and for a considerable time acted as reader of the Prajñāpāramitā for Gra-pa. As a result of reading the Prajñāpāramitā a clear vision of the Void (Śūnyatā) was produced in her.

About that time she met Dam-pa. She being an expert reader, came once to 'Dam-bu to read (a sacred text). A native of gČer-groṅ named Thod-pa 'Ba'-re (Thod-pa Bhadra. See Ži-byed Čhos-'byuṅ, fol. 25b), who belonged to a family in which some 23 kalyāṇa-mitras had appeared in succession, came there to perform a rite. She had intercourse with the man, and they became husband and wife, and the two went to Koṅ-po. People used to abuse her by calling her Jo-mo bKa'-log-ma (a "nun who had violated her vows") (See Ži-byed čhos-'byuṅ, fol. 27a: "Unable to stand it, they went to Koṅ-po"). A daughter was born to them, who received the name of Koṅ-lčam ("Lady of Koṅ-po"). En route to La-bar another daughter was born to them, who received the name of La-lčam ("Lady of the Pass"). When they came to gYe, three sons were born (to them) at Gaṅs-par sPel-čig-ma: sÑiṅ-po grub-pa, Grub-čhuṅ and Yaṅ-grub. Later she again dressed as a nun, and shaved her head. She obtained the initiation of the Cycle of Māyā from sKyo bSod-nams bla-ma, who was returning from a visit to Khams. While she was sitting in the assembly during the initiation, a yogic insight was produced in her. She stopped listening to the remaining portion of the initiation rite, and went outside. Then others said: "She didn't complete her initiation!" But the Teacher said: "She went away having obtained the initiation of the meaning, but you have obtained the initiation of the word only!" Later she received ordination, and stayed at various places according to her desire, preaching hidden precepts to her disciples. In particular, she made a long stay in the (2b) cave of Zaṅs-ri Khaṅ-dmar (in Lho-kha, nowadays the name is written Zaṅs-ri mKhar-dmar. The place is famous for a beautiful image of Ma-gčig Labs-sgron-ma) attended by the Lady gYag-mo. In this manner she filled the country of Tibet with the hidden precepts of gČod, and passed away at the age of 95.

When Dam-pa (Saṅs-rgyas) visited Tibet, four black birds flew round Dam-pa. When they were seen coming, they transformed themselves into four ḍākinīs: Labs-sgron of gYe, Ma-Jo Byaṅ-čhub of Upper gÑal, Žaṅ-mo rgyal-mthiṅ of gTsaṅ, and sMyon-ma (the "Mad One") of Lha-sa. Jo-mo Byaṅ-čhub of Upper gÑal (possessed) a clear understanding of the (Ultimate) State of Nature. With the help of her benevolent mind she greatly spread the Doctrine of the Buddha.

Žaṅ-mo rgyal-mthiṅ: She being afflicted by grief after her husband's death, Dam-pa bestowed (on her) the precepts which teach the absence of a link ('brel-med) between mind and object (dṅos), and she obtained emancipation.

Lha-sa'i sMyon-ma (the "Mad One of Lha-sa"): she used to settle disputes among the followers of the Doctrine, and is said to have been the person who had shown the King's Will (rGyal-po'i bKa'-čhems) to Atīśa (in the "Stotra of Atīśa", composed by 'Brom-ston, it is said: gaṅ-du rgyal-po'i bKa'-čhems gter tu sbas /mKha'-'gros gter-kha-phyes-nas khyod-la gtad/Śākya-mu-ni'i 'Ja'-sa khyod-khyi drin/). The great "Sons" on whom precepts were bestowed by Labs-sgron: from Upper Yar (kluṅs)—sÑags-pa rgyal-mtshan; from Lower Yar (-kluṅs)—An-ston Rin-čhen-'bar; from Middle Yar (-kluṅs)—Dre-na J̌o-sras and Śud-bu lo-tsā-ba—the Four; rGyal-ba Grub-be, rTogs-ldan rDol-po, Saṅs-rgyas gÑan-čhuṅ, and mNo-sgom čhen-po—the Four; Bya-ston kLu-sgrub, Khu-sgom Čhos-seṅ, sNubs-mo Nam-mkha'-gsal, Gra-pa Hag-ston, Śa-ston rDor-'dzin, sPo-ba sGom-čhen, Ṅag-gi dbaṅ-phyug of Dags-po tshoṅ-sde, rTsi-rgyal-ba of 'Phan-yul, and many others.

(Her) son Grub-čhe: In the beginning he was very mischievous, and became known as "Grub-be, the Enemy of Goats", Ra-dgra grub-ba (because he used to steal all the goats of the villagers). On one occasion he stole a goat belonging to the magician of sTeṅs-ka-ba. After he had heard that the magician had performed a magic rite directed against him, and that many of his friends had died from it, he thought that his mother possessed the means to prevent the harm, and so went to his mother's residence. The mother said to him: "You should be dead!" and saying so, she ran away. She then went to circumambulate the Mount Tsha-thaṅ. When she returned at dusk to her cave, Grub-be was looking for (his) mother. The mother and son met in the cave, and the mother said: "You are not without luck!" She then imparted precepts to him, and said: "Now you should lie down under the table with the offerings of the sorcerer. When he will place the offerings on the table, eat them!" He did so, and the magic power struck back at the sorcerer. At the age of 42, he entered the Gate of the Doctrine. After that he practised meditation and penetrated the meaning of the Ultimate Essence (čhos-ñid, the Absolute). He composed the following verse: (3a)

Mother, who first created my body and mind,
Mother, who provided me with victuals,
Who at last introduced my mind,

I salute and praise the gracious Mother!" (The quotation is found in the Ži-ba Lam-bab, a famous book on gČod).

Later he stayed at the monastery of gYe-čhuṅ gLaṅ-luṅ, free from all hypocrisy, and became a žig-po, or "mad ascetic". He was able to subdue demons by his blessing. He was able to produce wisdom in all his disciples. He passed away at the age of 89. He had three sons: Tshe-dbaṅ, Khu-byug and rNal-'byor-grags (born of his first wife). Kham-bu yal-le was born of another wife. Of Tshe-dbaṅ's three sons, rGyal-ba sTon-gzuṅs lived in Ri-mo-mdo of Dags-po, as foretold by his uncle. Thod-smyon bSam-grub (Śam-po-gaṅs in Yar-Kluṅs, Śam-po, n. of Śiva) was known as the "Snow-man (gaṅs-pa) residing on Śam-po-gaṅs" (Śam-po-gaṅs-la bžugs-pa'i gaṅs-pa). sKye-med 'od-gsal dwelt at A-'o-mdo in Upper gÑal. Thod-smyon bSam-grub fought in his youth in gYe and Yar-Kluṅs, and could not be defeated by any one. Having fallen ill with leprosy, he practised meditation in the snows of Ba-yul. He was cured of leprosy, as a snake sheds its skin. He slept naked on the snow of Śam-po, and when the snow melted, his (body) sunk deep into it. People threw yak tails to him, and he used them to make a garment and mat for himself. He also wore a tail as his hat. The fashion of the black hat of Gaṅs-pas originated with him. He subsisted on water only. Later at Čhu-rgyud-mkhar he partook of (3b)
carrion. At Draṅ-pa, having found scars on the nose of a leper, he sucked them, and his eyes filled with tears. Since that time his fortune increased. He presided over a Tantric feast held by ḍākinīs at Ha'o-gaṅs and Ĵo-mo Kha-rag. He prohibited the killing of wild animals and fishing in the hills, from Sil ma-la-kha as far as Koṅ-daṅ-la. He built a hospice and provided food, protected the Doctrine, and became a matchless saint (siddha). He had 21 male and female disciples, and 18 daughters-siddhas among them: Gaṅs-pa dMu-yan was a matchless one. At the age of 14, when he wished to go to Tsa-ri, he was told by the ma-mo

bDe-ldan: "Stay on the snow-peak of Śam-bu, and imitate (your) father!" He remained. When he was going to Khra-ye-gaṅs, his garments were drenched by a poisonous shower. After fording a river, he felt a violent stomach-ache. He lay down, pressing his stomach against a cold stone, and fell asleep. At once he was cured of the illness. He acted as mediator between Tibet (Bod) and gSer-gyu. He accepted from nomads ewes only (in order to free them. A common practice among Tibetan lamas). It is said he had more than a thousand shepherds, wearing quivers. Thus he became the wealthiest man. He introduced the custom of the continuous recitation of the bKa'-'gyur. After his cremation, numerous relics were left behind. His son (was) Gaṅs-pa Lhun-grub. He spent nine years at Śam-bu in meditation, unseen by men. He made a round of 108 dangerous places, and did away with the apprehension (of demons). It is to be noted that he wore white sleeves (not a religious vestment). At the time of his death many relics were recovered (from the ashes). His son Saṅs-rgyas bstan-bsruṅs: When he was three, he accompanied his father. From the age of 12, he was installed by gods, demons and men. He mastered the sPyod-yul and rDzogs-čhen, such as the Yaṅ-bdag (a rÑiṅ-ma deity, one of the bKa'-brgyad), the Gab-pa (Gab-pa-mṅon-phyuṅ, name of a rÑiṅ-ma book), and the Cycle of Avalokiteśvara, such as the Thugs-kyi ñiṅ-khu, the gSaṅ-ldan ('Jam-dpal gsaṅ-ldan, Ārya-Mañjuśrīnāma-saṅgītisādhana, Tg. rgyud, No. 2579), and other Cycles of Yoga. He mastered the Tshe-bdag (a rÑiṅ-ma deity; n. of a propitiation rite), and other texts, and obtained the fame of one able to conjure and create storms. He also established (4a)
an uninterrupted preaching in the lower part of the Valley, a meditative school in the upper part of the Valley and a monastic college in the middle part of the Valley. He protected the doctrine of his father and grandfather, and became its master. After his death, numerous relics were recovered (from the ashes). Saṅs-rgyas bston-bsruṅs had

four excellent sons: rTogs-ldan Rin-čhen seṅ-ge, the siddha Čhos-sgro ras-pa, 'Khrul-žig dGe-bśes byar-po, and rGyud-'dzin rdo-rje. He latter on reaching the age of 3. developed the faculty of prescience. At the age of 5, he mastered meditation, and was able to preach the Doctrine. At the age of 15, he performed a funeral rite, and took over the chair of his forefathers. At the age of 16, he held a religious assembly at Lho-rgyud (Southern region), and became famous as a learned man. He preached the Doctrine extensively. At the age of 17, he practised meditation on the snow-peak of Śam-bu. Among his numerous Lineage-holders (rGyud-'dzin) was his son Gaṅs-khrod ras-pa. His name was sKal-ldan rdo-rje. From the age of 3, he mastered the religious practice (spyod-lam). When he was 7, his father died, and he journeyed to gSal-rje-gaṅs in company of sPrul-sku sKyid-'bum. At the age of 11, he obtained many expositions of the (nature) of the Mind, headed by the A-ro Khrid-mo-čhe (The Great Exposition of A-ro/a rÑiṅ-ma book/). He practised asceticism and self-immurement. At the age of 13, he was nominated to the abbot's chair of his father. From the age of 15 to 26, he stayed at Śam-bu-gaṅs. From the age of 26, for 12 years, he secured many Teachings, hidden doctrines and mastered them. He laboured greatly for the welfare of others, and passed away in the year Water-Female-Ox (čhu-mo-glaṅ) at the age of 71.

Among Thod-sMyon's sons and daughters: Zlos Nam-mkha'-rgyan, Gaṅs-pa Mu-yan, and sTon-'tsher. sKal-ldan-pa became a disciple of the three, brothers and sister. 'Ban-po Myaṅ Čhos-kyi seṅ-ge became his disciple. Then Sa-ston rdor-'dzin, Saṅs-rgyas Myaṅ-ston, and sKal-ldan-pa; further Dur-khrod-'og-pa rTogs-ldan dol-po, and gTsaṅ-pa (4b) Maṅ-gro-ba, who preached to gYe-ston Saṅ-rgyas of Lho-brag sribs-mo ser-phug. The latter taught it to sGom-pa gŽuṅ-čhuṅ-pa. Ma-gčig's disciple Khu-sgom čhos-seṅ: he was a native of sÑe-mo-khu, and listened (to the exposition of the doctrine) of the "Great Achievement" (rDzogs-čhen), and practised solely meditation. Later he obtained from Ma-gčig the Cycle of Meditation of the Ḍākinīs (mKha'-'gro ñams-kyi skor). When Ma-gčig grew old, he used to massage her feet, and seeing that she was not to live long, he asked her to impart to him the complete doctrine (of gČod). Accordingly she imparted to him the precepts of the Meaning of the Lineage of the Teaching. She also foretold him that he would benefit others. Ma-gčig said: "You should give this to Don-grub (Son of Ma-gčig) also". He thought that he had to preach them to the latter, but the latter did not wish to listen (to the precepts), and for this reason it is said that Don-grub did not possess the meaning of the "Lineage of Teaching". He fell ill with leprosy, and proceeded to perform the gČod rite at a spring called Čhu-mig nag-po mthoṅ-ba dug-zin. After three days, he saw a vision that his heart was taken out, and carried away. After six days he saw that it was given back (to him). On the seventh day the leprosy was completely cured. He passed away at the age of 50.

His disciple Dol-pa Zaṅ-thal: he was a native of 'Tshur-phu. His clan (was) Dol. He was the youngest of four brothers. In his youth he studied under the kalyāṇa-mitra Khyuṅ for eight years the "Six Texts of the Mādhyamaka". He was hoping that he would be given a new exposition (of the doctrine), and when this did not happen, he felt disappointed. He then presented his Teacher with his books, and images, and put on the white dress (of a layman). He then thought that he should practise meditation in a hermitage. He met Khu-sgom, and obtained from him the precepts of gČod. He used to visit places infected with dangers, and his yogic insight became equal to the Sky. He was the victor in debates. People used to say about him: "there was a man wearing the grey clothes (of a layman), possessing a penetrating mind". He became known as "Dol-pa, the Penetrating One" (Dol-pa Zaṅ-thal). In his later life he stayed in Lower Lugs, preached the Doctrine, and passed away at the age of 56. (5a)

His disciple rGya-nag gčer-bu: he was a native of Khra-sna. On the whole, he studied extensively the (exposition) of the Doctrine. During his exposition of the doctrine of gČod at the monastery of Yar-kluṅs skya'o, Dol-pa Zaṅ-thal came there and listened (to his exposition), but only confusion arose. Later he discovered that Dol-pa Zaṅ-thal was more learned (than himself), and said: "I used to sell whey in the country of curds (i.e. I had preached to you who are more learned than me). Now, pray give me all of yours!" Then he obtained the complete Cycle of gČod of Ma-gčig. He used to visit places infested with dangers and performed gČod rites at the spring (čhu-mig) of sBal-'dra of Yar-kluṅs. Though struck thrice by lightning, it did not harm, and he was freed from his illness. He subdued with the help of the gČod rite the Black 'Ba'-ra (n. of a demon). In later life he laboured for the welfare of others at Chu-bo-ri. At the age of 70, he said: "When one wishes to merge one's own mind into the Absolute, one should do it in this manner," saying so, a light having emerged suddenly from the crown of his head, he passed out. His disciple was Saṅs-rgyas rab-ston, a native of bZaṅ-phu brag-dmar. He possessed an extensive knowledge of all the Tantras of the "New" and "Old" classes. Later he obtained from rGya-nag gčer-bu the hidden precepts of Ma-gčig. Having given up life in his thought, he used to visit hermitages only, and passed away at the age of 80.

His disciple Saṅs-rgyas dge-sloṅ: he was a native of rÑog-čan, and belonged to the Ba-śī clan. He was ordained in his youth, and through study removed (his) doubts. From Saṅs-rgyas rab-ston he obtained the Cycles of gČod. He wandered about hermitages and perceived clearly the Ultimate Essence (Čhos-ñid). He looked after numerous disciples, and passed away at the age of 55. His disciple (was) Sum-ston ras-pa who was a native of Gra-phyi, of the village of Bya-rog-tshaṅ. His father (was) the priest (mčhod-gnas) dKon-mčhog and his mother Moṅ-re. He was the elder of his sister. His name (was) Byams-pa. At the age of six, he obtained the initiation into transic meditation from the bLa-ma Žaṅ at Gra-thaṅ, who said about him: "This one will be of benefit to living beings!" At the age of 15, his parents (5*b*) died. He was afflicted with grief and took up ordination at Čags-ri, and received the name of bSod-nams śes-rab. He was also called Dharmavajra. He followed on more than forty teachers, who included the ācārya bKa'-gdams-pa, mÑan-'čhad-pa, Žaṅ lo-tsā-ba, Zaṅs-ri rGyā-ras-pa, the paṇ-čhen Śāk-śrī (Śākyaśrī), Kham-bu Yal-le, Bra'o lo-lsā, Rog Śes-rab-od, father and son, and others. He studied much the Tantras and Sūtras. Before he had completed the study of minor trades (rigs-pa phran-tshegs), he followed on 151 teachers, and mastered the trades, even that of a goldsmith. After that he followed on the bla-ma Do-pa, and at Gye-re a deep yogic insight was produced in him, by which he overcame the differentiation between that which is to be avoided and that which avoids. He also studied all the secret precepts of the gČod system. His disciple was Saṅs-rgyas ston-pa. The latter's disciple—mKhas-btsun gŽon-nu-grub. The latter's disciple—gSer-gliṅ-pa bKra-śis-dpal. The latter's disciple—Brag-po čhe-pa rDo-rJe-dpal. The latter's disciple—Čhos-sgo-ba Čhos-kyi rgya-mtsho. The latter's disciple—rGod-phṛug ras-pa. His life-story was given in the Book on Ni-gu. The Dharmasvāmin rGod-phrug ras-pa gave the instructions to me. Further, rTsi Dar-ma of 'Phan-yul taught ('the gČod system) to Mi-bskyod rdo-rJe. He also wrote treatises. The Doctrine was handed down by him. dPal mKha'-spyod-pa also wrote a treatise on the hidden precepts (of gČod) as well as preached them extensively to others. The Dharmasvāmin Raṅ-byuṅ-ba bestowed them on A-mes Byaṅ-čhub rdo-rJe. The latter bestowed them on his son the Dharmasvāmin Ri-ma-'babs-pa ("One who does not come down from the mountain") bSod-nams rin-čhen. The latter bestowed them on me. The above is (just) one branch.

Again, one named Dam-pa dbUs-pa was learned in the

texts and precepts of both the "Old" and "New" Tantras. He also possessed the precepts of the Źi-byed, the "Great Achievements" (rDzogs-čhen), and others. At first he obtained the hidden precepts of gČod from Ma-gčig. After the death of the Mother (Ma-gčig), he attended for 18 years on (her) son rGyal-ba Don-grub. He also composed a treatise on precepts and became a Master of the Doctrine. He bestowed the precepts (of gČod) on the bLa-ma rDo-rJe bde-ba. The latter was affected by a magic rite (gtad—a magic rite which consists of placing an image of the person against whom the rite is being performed underground) performed by the magician (sṅags-pa) Naṅ-rgyas, as a result of which his body became emaciated. Having heard about the fame of Dam-pa dbUs-pa, he obtained the precepts of gČod and practised them. He resided in a rock cave haunted by demons. He saw in a dream that at first he was fighting a black man, and that he remembered Śūnyatā, and was able to defeat him. After that a snake came out of his nose, and a severe bleeding followed. Immediately after that a yogic insight into (the Ultimate) Nature was produced in him. His body (acquired the power) of moving faster than a horse. He bestowed the precepts on sGom-pa gŹon-nu ye-śes. The latter, though possessing many precepts, was afflicted by illness, and obtained the precepts of gČod from rDo-rJe bde-ba. He used to visit many localities infested with dangers and overcame his ailment. A yogic insight was born in him. He cured many of tuberculosis (gčoṅ-čan). He imparted the precepts (of gČod) to the bla-ma Mi-bskyod rdo-rJe. The latter was born at sÑe-mo mkha'-ru. He was a Tantric. He was harmed by a rite over a dead corpse (bam-sgrub) which did not succeed, and his body became afflicted with tuberculosis. He met the bla-ma gŹon-nu ye-śes, obtained the precepts of gČod, practised them, and restored his health. He also cured many who were suffering from tuberculosis. He bestowed the precepts (of gČod) on the bla-ma Saṅs-rgyas ston-pa, who was a native of Ko-ru of sGoṅ-ma. He was ordained at Gro-sa and became learned in the Prajñāpāramitā, the bDen-gñis and in the systems of rMa, So, and sKam. From Mi-bskyod rdo-rje he obtained the precepts of gČod and heard the complete (teaching) of the Lineage of Meaning (Don-brgyud) of all these (systems). A yogic insight was produced in him. He bestowed (the precepts) on the bla-ma Luṅ-phran-pa čhen-po. He was also learned in the Kālacakra and the Prajñāpāramitā. He heard the precepts (of gČod) from Mi-bskyod rdo-rje, and practised them in a thorough manner. He bestowed them on the bla-ma sTan-gčig-pa gŽon-nu tshul-khrims, who was also called Jo-stan Thaṅ-pa. He first proceeded to Thaṅ-sag and received ordination. He studied the Prasannapadā (dbU-ma tshig-gsal, Tg. dbU-ma, No. 3860), the Mādhyamakāvatāra and the Tantric Cycles by Nāgārjuna under Gri'i lum-pa. From the bla-ma Thar-pa-ba and dPyal lo-tsā-ba he obtained the Abhidharmasamuccaya and the Abhidharmakośa (mŇon-pa goṅ-og), the Prajñāpāramitā and Logic together with the bsDus-gra,[1] the Sādhana, commentary and precepts of the Kālacakra, the "Six Doctrines" of Vārahī (Phag-mo dPyal-gyi čhos-drug) according to the system of dPyal. Also many Tantras and Sādhanas, such as the gŚed-dmar (Śrīmadraktayamāritantrarājanāma, Kg. rGyud-'bum, No. 475). While staying at Jo-stan tshogs-pa he fell ill with tuberculosis. He obtained the precepts of gČod from the bLa-ma Luṅ-phran-pa and meditated in a cemetery. Formerly he used to fall ill, whenever he felt cold, or hot. There he pressed his stomach against a cold stone, drank ice-cold water, and slept naked. He gave up himself saying: "Illness (is) joy. Death (is) pleasure". He practised (the precepts of gČod) and on the eleventh day a foul odour came out of his mouth. On the 12th day, about midnight, he vomitted out all his ailments. About midday he was completely cured. Within half a month he succeeded in completing the study, overcame his disease, and (6b)

1 A course of Eristics.

a mystic trance was produced in him. Whenever he came across fever, plague, cancer (lhog), thogs-bčas and thogs-med-kyi bdud (means physical and mental hindrances), he gave himself up with the words: "Illness (is) joy. Death (is) pleasure!" He intentionally contacted these diseases (thog-'gel drag-po byed-pa) and practised (gČod). All ailments and demons used to vanish by themselves. Great was the benefit to living beings. He resided at gSer-luṅ of sKyam. He bestowed the precepts (of gČod) on the bla-ma bSam-gtan-dar, whose native place was upper Zim-śi of gYe. He was born to father sPo-ra dBon-seṅ and mother J̌o-mo bSam-me. From his childhood he was endowed with faith, commiseration and wisdom. He received ordination at the residence of the bLa-ma J̌o-stan-pa. He made a thorough study of the Guhya-samāja according to the method of Nāgārjuna, the Great Commentary ('Grel-čhen) by Nā-ro-pa (Vajrapādasārasaṃgrahapañjikā, Tg. rGyud, No.1186), the Prasannapadā, the Mādhyamakāvatāra, the Śūnyatāsaptatikārikā-nāma (sToṅ-ñid bdun-bču-pa, Tg. dbU-ma, No.3827), the three Cycles of the Dohā, and the Bodhicaryāvatāra (sPyod-'J̌ug). He obtained the Ṣaḍaṅga (-yoga) according to the method of Thar-lo, the Pañcakrama (Rim-lṅa dmar-khrid-skor), the Thugs-rJe čhen-po'i dmar-khrid (name of a book, the system of Tshem-bu-pa or Tshem-bu dmar-khrid), the Phyag-čhen Gaṅgā-ma, the bLo-sbyoṅ (Mind Purification), the gČod-yul la'u-lag (n. of a gČod text), the gNaṅ-thems-bka'-rgya-ma, and other Cycles of gČod. He practised according to each of them. During his study of the Doctrine at gSer-luṅ, he suddenly fell seriously ill. He told (people) to carry him to a mountain valley, where he could perform the gČod rite. His friends carried him to a place infested with dangers. There he performed the gČod rite, and a trance was produced in him. When the khri-dpon (commander of 10,000 men) of gYam-bzaṅs came from the North, and sent him an invitation, he thought that he should go and meet him. On the way to Śugs he had a stroke (gnam-gdon) and was unable to proceed further. His attendant carried him to a hermitage by the roadside. He showed his pulse to a medical practitioner (lha-rJe) who said that if he would persevere in the treatment, he would perhaps remain alive. But he answered: "I don't want any treatment! I shall carry on religious work!" After that they carried him to a rock-cave near Gri-mdo. There also a doctor was invited, who said that he failed to make him take the medicine. "Don't stay near me!" said he, and asked them to go away. Then he gave himself up (to the practice which was expressed by the words): "Illness (is) joy! Death (is) pleasure!" (na-dga' śi-skyid). From the next morning he began to feel himself slightly better. After the lapse of 3 or 4 days, Khri-čhuṅ-'od of gYam-bzaṅs came there having taken with him a doctor and three or four carcasses (of sheep). The doctor examined his pulse and declared: "The disease has been cured! What a great wonder!" His health became even better, than before his illness. From Thar-pa gliṅ-pa he obtained the sGrol-ma dkar-mo'i tshe-sgrub (the longevity rite of the White Tārā) and the Khrid-čhen brgyad (dKar-čhag Tshig-gi me-tog, fol. 7b). From the bla-ma bLo-gros-dpal he obtained many Tantras, such as the Guhyasamāja, the Rakta-Yamāri, the initiation of the rDo-rJe 'phreṅ-ba, the sByoṅ-rgyud (Sarvadurgatipariśodhanatejorājasya-Tathāgatasya-Arhato-Samyaksambuddhasya kalpaikadeśa-nāma, Kg. rGyud-'bum, No.485), and other texts. From the bla ma Rin-čhen seṅ-ge he obtained the complete initiation into the Kālacakra, the initiation of Hevajra and Nairātmā, the Path & Fruit doctrine (Lam-'bras), together with its branches. At the age of 31, he occupied the chair of the bla-ma Jo-stan-pa. For twenty years he preached without interruption throughout (7b) the four seasons. He made a round of localities infested with dangers, such as the "Black Lake" (mTsho-nag) of dMar-ro, Yar-lha Śam-bu, etc., and practised gČod. When an internecine war broke out between gYa'-(bzaṅs) and Phag-(mo-gru), he felt slightly afflicted in his mind, and founded the (monastery) of lDan-mkhar dGa'-ldan. He obtained from the bla-ma Čhos-dpal mgon-po the complete initiation into the Kālacakra, the Sadaṅga-yoga (sByor-drug) according to the method of J̌o-naṅ-pa, and the Sevasādhana of U-rgyan-pa. From Druṅ Čhos-rJ̌e-pa he obtained the Ṣadaṅga-(yoga) of the mahā-upādhyāya Bu (-ston), the system of Sron, the initiation into the Guhyasamāja, its exposition and precepts (bśad-bka'), and the detailed (dmar-khyid) expositions of the Pañcakrama. From the bla-ma rTogs-ldan-pa he obtained the Ri-čhos-skor (belonging to the "Hermit" doctrine of Yaṅ-dgon-pa, the Sevasādhana, and the Cycle of the upāya-mārga. Whenever he felt ill, he never performed rites or took treatment, but practised solely gČod. He lived in a hermitage without coming down from the mountain. His fame encompassed the Ten Quarters. The Dharmasvāmin Mi-ñag-pa Rin-čhen rgyal-mtshan obtained (the gČod doctrine) from him. sMen-'dor-ba of Thel-čhos-sgo (also) obtained (it) from him.

The Chapter on the "Female" gČod (Mo-gČod).

The (Line) known as "Male" gČod (Pho-gČod): —

Though sMar-ra ser-po of Yar-kluṅs had visited Eastern and Western India, he did not succeed in obtaining the doctrine as desired by him. He then befriended some traders, and on the way to Tibet, came across an A-tsa-ra (ācārya, Indian ascetic). He did not know whether the man was a heretic, or a Buddhist. As his companion he had a kalyāṇa-mitra named dṄos-grub, who possessed a staff made of black wood (čhu-śiṅ) with numerous ornaments carved on the four sides. The Indian ascetic said to him: "Let me have it!" and he gave it away. Then the ascetic said: "This is a heretical weapon with which to perform miraculous deeds! Though I know (how to work it), it is useless", and saying so, he broke the staff. sMa-ra ser-po then asked the ascetic's companion: "Who is it?" and the latter replied: "It is
Dam-pa!" They (sMa-ra ser-po and the kalyāṇa-mitra) then (8a
felt faith in him, and asked for instruction in the Doctrine. To dṄos-grub, (Dam-pa) imparted precepts, and among them the one entitled "External vision should not be taken inside,

tc." (meaning that the Mind should be kept away from outside impressions). dṄos-grub having been convinced, accepted Dam-pa) as his mūla-guru (rtsa-ba'i bla-ma). Then sMa-ra serpo requested instruction in the Doctrine, and Dam-pa told him: "A Doctrine, desired by you, is coming to you in the future." sMa-ra ser-po followed after Dam-pa and reached Dog-stag- ris. Dam-pa took up residence in a hospice, and many people came to ask for his blessing. In particular, many who were blind and deaf were cured on the spot. When sKyo ākya-ye-śes came to a religious assembly, there happened to come also two sons of a rich man of Upper Myaṅ (Myaṅ-stod) who were showing the first symptoms of leprosy. The two were entrusted to the care of sKyo. But the latter was only seeking wealth, and the health of the children did not improve. sKyo heard that Dam-pa had the power of curing instantly diseases. So he asked Dam-pa: "I have two boys, the debris of a demon's feast (meaning that their elder brothers were killed by demons). Pray bless them!" Dampa replied addressing himself to sMa-ra ser-po: "Now the Doctrine desired by you has come!" He then imparted to Kyo, his two disciples and sMa-ra ser-po, the four, the precepts of gČod. (These precepts) sMa-ra ser-po committed to writing and called them "Khrul-tsho-drug-pa" (should read Brul-tsho—Six Groups of Precepts/of gČod/). He did not commit to writing the verbal precepts. The two boys also practised them and were cured of their disease. Both became devotees (sādhaka). sKyo did not preach the precepts to others, but practised them himself. Then being afraid that the Lineage may come to an end, he bestowed them on bOn-po bSod-nams bla-ma only. sKyo having gone to Khams, bestowed on his return journey the four Sections of the "Khrul-tsho" (groups) on Labs-sgron. sMa-ra serpo also abstained from preaching them to others, and constantly practised the method of (Vajra) Vārahī of Had-bu, as well as that of gČod. In his old age, he bestowed them on (8b) his attendant sMyon-pa Be-re, with the words: "Practise

them yourself, but don't bestow them on any one else." At that time both lČe-ston and Phug-ston happened to stay at the monastic college (gra-sa) of Śa-ston rDor-'dzin in Phu-thaṅ. lČe-ston fell ill. He knew that Be-re knew the gČod rite and told about it to Śa-ston, who said: "Go and ask him for the precepts!" Ri-khrod Phug-ston inquired: "How will you, Teacher, go, without completing your studies here? I have been a hermit, and he might impart them to me. I am going there to make the request." rDor-'dzin said: "Well, you might ask my friend lČe-ston to present the request. You can tell him that he possesses an incontrovertible precept of the Prajñāpāramitā handed down from Dam-pa (Saṅs-rgyas), and ask for it." Phug-ston acted accordingly, and made his request. The bla-ma Be-re sMyon-pa said: "No one knows that I possess this doctrine! Did a demon tell it to you?" Again he asked: "Do you really intend practising it?"—"Yes, I want to practise it!" Be-re then imparted to him the gŽuṅ-brul-tsho-drug (The Six groups of Texts on gČod) with the introduction and precepts. While he was practising them at sKyi-tshaṅ, the ācārya Śa-ston sent a man, and Phug-ston came to Phu-thaṅ and preached three of the Brul-tsho. He bestowed the Brul-tsho-drug on a Khams-pa scholar, whose copyist also wrote them down. Later when Rog Śes-rab-'od came to the residence of Ri-khrod Žig-po, and was listening to the recitation of the Nāmasaṅgīti and the (Vajra)vārahī system according to the method of Dampa (Saṅs-rgyas), he asked the yogin-copyist to be his host. From him he found out about the origin of this precept, and requested Phug-ston, who said: "Connection with One (means) a connection with all. When revealed to one, it is revealed to all! Prepare the requisites (for initiation)!" He then bestowed on him the first "Brul-tsho", or group (of texts). He then asked the Teacher: "Does this doctrine include other sections as well?"—"It does", replied the Tea- (9a
cher, "but I didn't disclose more than three to Śa-ston rDor-'dzin at Phu-thaṅ. If I were to preach to you the complete

'recepts, he might become displeased."—"But why did you ıot give him the complete precepts?" inquired Rog Śes-rab-od. The latter replied: "Because the precepts were too rofound! There were many men at his residence and all ould have copied them, therefore I didn't give them. Also hey do not respect their Teacher and simply look after books. Therefore I did not give it to them!" He (Rog) asked that e might be given the complete precepts. The Teacher eplied: "Because you will be of benefit to living beings, I hall impart them to you." He then bestowed on him the "Six Groups" (Brul-tsho drug-pa) together with the "Oral Pre-epts," and said: "Now, outside of these I haven't even a ingle precept! Do not commit the 'Oral Precepts' to vriting," saying so, he imparted them to him gladly. The atter (Rog Śes-rab-'od) bestowed them on Sum-ston ras-pa. The latter on bLa-ma gÑan-ston. Again Ri-khrod Phug-ston (bestowed) them on the daughter sKal-ldan. The latter on gTsaṅ-ston sKyi-tshaṅ-ba. The latter on gÑan-ston. The latter on dbOn-po Čhos-sdiṅs-pa Dar-ma śes-rab. The latter on sGrig-ston Saṅs-rgyas. Again Sum-ston ras-pa bestowed them on Saṅs-rgyas ston-pa. The latter on mkhas-btsun gŽon-nu-grub. After this one, (the succession) continued as in the previous (Lineage). In general the gČod system spread widely. As regards the Life-stories (of its teachers), I have written only about those which had been seen by me.

The Chapter on the "Male" gČod (Pho-gČod).

The natives of the Snow (Country, i.e. Tibet) possess a crown ornament and two ear-ornaments. The crown ornament (is) Padmasambhava. The first ear ornament (is) Kha-rag sGom-čhuṅ. The second (ear ornament) is the Venerable Mid-la. Kha-rag sGom-čhuṅ: He benefitted of two streams
of precepts, and was a yogin who practised meditation only. (9b)
Here one of the streams of these precepts, which originated from A-ro Ye-śes 'byuṅ-gnas: A-ro had been an incarnation. He assumed the appearance of a small boy concealed in the sand near the Riṅ-mo spring. A royal nun saw him there,

having come there for a walk, she thought that "people might start gossiping, if I were to take the child with me out of mercy". She reported the matter to an official of the locality, who said to her: "Well, poor thing! Take him!" She took the child. He lay down like a corpse, and emitted the sound of "A-A", because of this he was called 'A-ro' ("A-corpse". This seems to be a later explanation of the name. Originally it must have been a corrupt form of a Sanskrit word). Later when the child learned to walk, he went inside an enclosure (kun-dga'ra-ba) where monks were telling their prayers. The monks asked him: "A-ro! What are you doing here?" The child replied: "I shall also recite prayers!" "Do you understand the Doctrine?" they inquired, and the child replied: "I know well many doctrines!"—"Well then, do you know this also?" and they handed him a volume of the Bodhicaryāvatāra, and he recited it in a proper manner. "I also know some doctrines unknown to you!" said A-ro, and recited several names of precepts belonging to the system of A-ro. All the monks became amazed, saying: "A-ro is A! He is the origin of knowledge!" Thus he became known as Ye-śes 'byuṅ-gnas. He had a long life, and guided disciples with the help of profound precepts. He also laboured for the welfare of living beings. His disciples were: Ya-zi Bon-ston of Khams, Bru-śa rgyal-bu of Kha-rag, Grum-śiṅ śes-rab-smon-lam of dbUs, Čog-ro Zaṅs dkar mdzod-khur of gTsaṅ. Of the above, Ya-zi Bon-ston proceeded to dbUs and gTsaṅ, and preached the Doctrine to Gru-gu kLog-'byuṅ of Upper gTsaṅ-rgyan. The latter taught it to gLan-sgom Tshul-khrims sñiṅ-po of Bras Chu-bar. The latter used to say: "If I were to preach the Doctrine into the ear of a corpse, the corpse would move. If I were (104)
to teach meditation to a bird of the Sky, it would succeed (in it)". He taught it to rBa-sgom bSod-nams rgyal-mtshan, who belonged to the clan of 'Ju of sBas in 'Phan-yul. Having met Atīśa, he offered him his understanding (of the Doctrine), and the latter became pleased, and said: "Now these (pre-

cepts) of your should be supplemented by love and mercy. Then meditate! Should you experience difficulties in your meditation, Maitreya and Avalokiteśvara will appear to remove them." Atīśa after seeing several Tibetan writings, was not too pleased (with them), but when he saw the Mahāyāna-Yoga (A-ro'i Theg-čhen rnal-'byor) by A-ro, he exclaimed: "These words are full of poetry, and possess an excellent meaning", and became pleased. rBa-sgom was the household priest of the father of Pu-to-ba. Pu-to-ba before going to Rwa-sgreṅ asked him for precepts on meditation. He said: "The meditation of those who didn't study even a little, is even shallower than an arm-pit." Later when Pu-to-ba became a great kalyāṇa-mitra, he thought: "What sort of doctrine rBa-sgom possesses?" After that he had a remarkable dream, and said: "This doctrine of rBa-sgom is a perfect one!" His (rBa-sgom) disciple was Kha-rag sGom-čhuṅ. In a place called Duṅ-žur in Upper gTsaṅ there was a hermit named dKon-mčhog-rten. He had three sons: Bal-po dBaṅ-rdor, after him—Śwa-dbaṅ-rwa, after him—the hermit dBaṅ-phyug blo-gros. dBaṅ-phyug blo-gros was full of faith since his childhood. He resolved to take up ordination. He obtained many precepts of the "Great Achievement"(rDzogs-čhen) from one named Ye-śes of Be'u-klu, a native of Thod-phu. While he was practising meditation in the meditative cell of 'Phyil-phu, Bal-po dBaṅ-rdor acted as his attendant. When rBa-sgom was residing at Brag-dkar rtsi-čan people used to say: "There is a good Master possessing secret (10b)
precepts." Bal-po dBaṅ-rdor went to see him, and when they met, they held a conversation on religion. He understood that the Teacher was endowed with secret precepts, and reverence was born in him. dBaṅ-rdor told this story to gTsaṅ-bu, and added: "Let us go to his place!" (The brother) replied: "But we have no presents (to offer him)!" dBaṅ-rdor replied: "We have a piece of butter. We could offer it. So they went together. As soon as gTsaṅ-bu and rBa-sgom met, their minds became one. gTsaṅ-bu asked for

precepts, and the Teacher said: "You should take up ordination!" He was then ordained in the presence of Mar-sgom at Lab-so. After that he obtained from rBa-sgom the "Three Cycles of Precepts" (gDams-ṅag skor-gsum, probably the Kha-rag skor-gsum). There were others also, who had come to ask for instruction in religion. The Teacher dismissed others, and kept gTsaṅ-bu near himself. rBa-sgom went into seclusion for seven days, and had a vision of Yamāntaka. During this time rBa-sgom wrote out precepts on a slate (gya'-ma), and threw them out of his cell. gTsaṅ-bu read them. Then an alms-giver offered him two loads of flour, and rBa-sgom said: "The Evil One (Māra) has come!" (meaning that he had received worldly things as a present) and ran away. gTsaṅ-bu followed after him. The Teacher and (his) disciple reached Rwa-sgreṅ. (They found) that 'Brom-ston-pa had died, and that rNal-'byor-pa was preaching to a class. gTsaṅ-bu felt reverence towards the hermits of Rwa-sgreṅ. rBa-sgom said: "They are like a sack of wool! (big to look at, and small when pressed down). We, Teacher and disciple, stand higher than they in meditation." They went back and journeyed via 'Dal-ma-luṅ of Yar-'brog. They proceeded to the land of the Lho-la yag-pa nomads. When he was about to start for mKhar-čhu, he received a message saying that his mother had fallen ill. He proceeded to his native place, and found that his mother had passed away. (The relatives) performed the funeral rite (gśid) and killed a cow. Filled with sadness, rBa-sgom went back. (11a)
gTsaṅ-bu helped them in the performance of the funeral rite, and then followed after rBa-sgom. When he reached the monastery of U-skyu-'gul of gŽu, he noticed traces of a cremation. He asked: "Whose are these?" They replied: "The late rBa-sgom's". (gTsaṅ-bu) wept bitterly, and then proceeded towards Rwa-sgreṅ, and for seven years followed on dGon-pa-ba and rNal-'byor-pa. dGon-pa-ba said to him: "Your Teacher has entered seclusion for seven days, and had a vision of Yamāntaka." He understood dGon-pa-ba to

possess the faculty of prescience. Then for a long time he practised meditation in the cave of gŽu-mkhan-brag ("Archer's rock"). Pu-to-ba, teacher and disciple, also happened to stay at the same time on the "Archer's Rock" (gŽu-mkhan-brag). Pu-to-ba said: "This young hermit gTsaṅ-bu is greatly addicted to meditation. Because of lack of study, can he enter the Path? (gTsaṅ-bu) overheard him saying it, and went to see Pu-to-ba. He related to him about (his) understanding of the four blo-ldog ("Turning points of the Mind". The four "Turning points of the Mind" or blo-ldog-bži are: meditation on the value of birth in human form, on the uncertainty of death, the sufferings of Saṃsāra, on Karma, Cause and Effect. /'Čhi-ba mi-rtag-pa, Las-rgyu-'bras,'khor-ba'i ñes-dmigs, thal-'byor rñed-dka'/). A sthavira named rGyal-se said: "Now you, kalyāṇa-mitra, ought to reply to him!" Pu-to-ba said: "I cannot reply to it now!" This gTsaṅ-bu became a sKyes-bu smra-ba'i seṅ-ge ("Lion of Speech among Men"). Pu-to-ba used to send him the best portions of offerings received by himself. Pu-to-ba praised him greatly, saying: "This Doctrine (čhos) which he (gTsaṅ-bu) was able to practise during one day, we, Teacher and disciple, couldn't accomplish within one year." On one occasion rNal-'byor-pa Be'u-kLu'i ye-śes sent him a message: "On account of my illness, come here in the name of our vows!" gTsaṅ-bu went to take leave of Pu-to-ba. Parting was difficult for both, and both shed tears. During his journey to rGyal in 'Phan-yul, he received many requests for religious instruction and offerings. He visited the bla-ma Kha-rag, and for a short time attended on Be'u kLu'i ye-śes. He practised meditation at Kha-rag phug-pa nag-po, (11*b*)
and his fame encompassed all quarters. About a thousand students (tshogs-pa) gathered round him. After a short while he felt this to be a hindrance, dismissed his students, and left only a small number of disciples. Thus he lived for many years. In the end he held a pompous feast and said: "This will be (my) last food!" And added: "After

my death, convey this body to the summit of a mountain, and don't erect memorials after me!" saying so, he passed away. His remains were then carried to the summit of Kha-rag. A yogin having severed with a knife one of his hands, died on the spot. Kha-rag's two disciples: Lho-pa Dharma-skyabs and rDul-ston rDo-rJe rin-čhen.

Lho-pa was a native of La-ya smon-mda'. He obtained many doctrines from Roṅ-pa Čhos-bzaṅ. He took up ordination in the presence of Ba-dkar 'Briṅ-ston, and obtained from him the bsLab-phyogs (Domain of the Vows), the Doctrine of Maitreya, and many others. Also he obtained from Yol Čhos-dbaṅ many hidden precepts. Having visited Kha-rag-pa, he offered him a bag of butter and asked for precepts. (Kha-rag) at once shut the door and said to him: "There are many who possess hidden precepts! You can ask them!" After that Lho-pa spent three years at the residence of Bal-po dBaṅ-rdor (Kha-rag-pa's brother). gTsaṅ-bu said: "Did Lho-pa go away?" (When told that he was still there) he said: "Then, bring him here!" He imparted to him the complete precepts and associated with him for five years. He also became very famous and had numerous disciples who included such great scholars as Yar-sregs rgye-dman and others, Myaṅ sGom-rgod-po, Myaṅ sGom-dkar-po, and Myaṅ sGom-Žig-po Čhos-se, known as the "Three Brothers Myaṅ-sgom" (Myaṅ-sgom mčhed-gsum). rDul-ston, who knew numerous precepts, met Kha-rag-pa and overheard him saying: "This scholar can enter into Religion." rDul-ston then thought: "What does he mean by this? For I have studied numerous doctrines". Later, (12a)
after he had obtained the precepts of the Three Cycles of Kha-rag (Kha-rag skor-gsum), and had practised them, he realized that (Kha-rag-pa's) first words were true. From Kha-rag he proceeded towards Yar-'brog. Thus one of the streams of precepts was that which flowed from Rwa-sgreṅ and consisted of the precepts handed down from Atīśa. Kha-rag-pa combined the two (streams) and named them the "Puri-

fication of the Bodhicitta" (Byaṅ-čhub-sbyoṅ). They were also known by the name of the "Three Cycles of Kha-rag" (Kha-rag skor-gsum). They spread widely. Now the Spiritual Lineage of A-ro himself: rBa-sgom transmitted (the Doctrine) to Dam-pa 'Dzi-sgom of gTsaṅ-roṅ. The latter to Ba-ra sgom-čhen of Yar-'brog. The latter to the lady Myaṅ-mo of Yul-čhos. The latter to the doctor (Lha-rJe) Lha-khaṅ-pa of sKyi-mkhar. The latter to sTon-Śāk of dbUs. The latter to Žig-po bDud-rtsi. In this manner the Lineage spread widely. The Chapter on Kha-rag-pa.

BOOK XIV

The Cycle of the Mahākaruṇika (Thugs-rJe čhen-po'i skor), and that of the Vajrāvali (rDo-rJe phreṅ-ba).

Just as the Bodhisattva Mañjuśrī took over China, in the same manner the Bodhisattva Mahāsattva Ārya Avalokiteśvara protected this country of Tibet. By his blessing the sound of the 'Maṇi' resounds in the mouths of men, women and monks, even children. One can obtain blessing by praying to a tutelary deity, therefore for us (Tibetans) the quickest way to obtain blessings is to follow after Avalokiteśvara himself. The sacred images and monasteries (vihāras) erected by Sroṅ-btsan sgam-po, a manifestation of Avalokiteśvara in the form of a king, are the chief places of worship for the Tibetans. The mountain, on which has been built the Palace where the king resides, received also the name of Potala (the Abode of Avalokiteśvara). It is known that many had attained the realization of Yamāntaka and other deities adhering to the precepts of the mantra, enunciated by the king. Though the Commentary by a teacher, who had followed on this Doctrine enunciated by the king, does not exist at present, there still exist parts of the book on propitiating rites (sādhanas). The saint (siddha) dṄos-grub discovered the hidden book on the Sādhana of Avalokiteśvara. Rog Śes-rab-'od obtained (them) at the monastery of sPa-rnams. He gradually handed them down to his own son, and disciples. Further, the nirmāṇakāya Myaṅ-ston obtained (them) from the saint (siddha) dṄos-grub. He (Myaṅ-ston) transmitted (the Doctrine) to the bLa-ma Ras-pa Mi-bkyod-rdo-rJe, the bLa-ma Śākya seṅ-ge bzaṅ-po, the doctor (lha-rJe) dGe-ba-'bum (the builder of the golden roof over the Lha-sa gTsug-lag-khaṅ), the sister (lčam-mo) Ye-śes-mčhog, Byaṅ-sems čhu-sgom, mTha'-bži bya-bral, bSod-nams seṅ-ge, bKra-śis rgyal-mtshan, and the bLa-ma bLo-gros rgyal-mtshan. From the (last) two—the bLa-ma bSod-nams bzaṅ-po. The latter to rGod-phrug grags-pa 'byuṅ-gnas. The Lineage of Thugs-rJe čhen-po rGyal-ba rgya-mtsho (a form of Avalokiteśvara): sNaṅ-ba mtha'-yas (Amitābha), Thugs-rJe čhen-po (Mahākaruṇika), Padmasambhava (Pad-ma 'byuṅ-gnas), Phag-mo of Bhaṅgala, (up-to) Ti-pu-pa, Ras-čhuṅ-pa, Zaṅs-ri ras-pa, Saṅs-rgyas ras-čhen, sPom-brag-pa' Karma pa-śi, the mahāsiddha U-rgyan-pa, Raṅ-byuṅ rdo-rJe, Khams-čhen rGan-lhas-pa, sTag-ston gŽon-nu-dar, Bag-ston gŽon-tshul-pa, the mahā-upādhyāya Śes-rab rdo-rJe, Čhos-sgo-ba Čhos-dpal śes-rab, rGod-phrug-pa Grags-pa 'byuṅ-gnas, and many others. The rite and initiation of the Kulalokanātha sādhana (Tg. rGyud, No. 2133: Kulalokanāthasādhanāloka-nāma) originated with the Yar-kluṅs lo-tsā-ba Grags-pa rgyal-mtshan. He bestowed its Tantra of 53 ślokas (Kg. rGyud-'bum, No. 436: Kulalokanātha-pañcadaśaka-nāma) together with its Commentary (Tg. rGyud, No. 2134: Lṅa-bču-pa'i bśad-pa, Pañcāśikāṭippaṇī) on the lo-tsā-ba Dus-'khor-ba bSod-śe, from whom a numerous Lineage originated. The Cycle (čhos-skor) of Padmajāla (Pad-ma-dra-ba, Kg. rGyud-'bum, No. 681: Ārya-Avalokiteśvarapadmajāla-mūla-tantrarāja-nāma; Padmajālodbhavasādhana, Tg. rGyud, No. 1750) which was expounded to Bu-ston by the Kashmirian paṇḍita Sumanaśrī, also belongs to the Cycle (čhos-skor) of the Mahākaruṇika (Avalokiteśvara). The manner of transmitting the Doctrine preached by the "Man who had attained spiritual realization" (grub-pa thob-pa'i skyes-bu), an emanation of Avalokiteśvara: There existed a method of taking a vow through the rite of the Mental Creative Effort towards Enlightenment, as well as the degree of transic meditation according to the Mādhyamaka system written by the Bodhisattva Candradhvaja, an indisputable manifestation of Avalokiteśvara. (1a)

The Degree of propitiating Ārya Avalokiteśvara by performing the rite of fasting was preached by the nun Lakṣmī (dPal-mo) personally blessed by Ārya Avalokiteśvara.

She taught it to the paṇḍita Ye-śes bzaṅ-po (Jñānabhadra), blessed by her. He to Bal-po (the Nepālese) Pe-ña-ba, blessed by him. They all were saints (siddhas). The Bodhisattva Candradhvaja obtained (the Doctrine) from him (Pe-ña-ba). The story of his recognition by other people as the Bodhisattva Avalokiteśvara himself: In the temple of Saṃvara (bDe-mčhog lha-khaṅ) in Nepāl many ḍākinīs (2a)
gathered. The temple keeper saw (them) and inquired: "From where did you come? What are you doing here?" The ḍākinīs replied: "We have come from Puṇḍravardhana (Li-khar-śiṅ-'phel, Malda and Dinajpur). Avalokiteśvara of Puṇḍravardhana himself is residing here. We have come to make offerings to him". The keeper continued: "Who is he?" The ḍākinīs answered: "He is the Bodhisattva Candradhvaja!" When the Oṅ-po lo-tsā-ba was sleeping in the Temple of Ārya wa-ti (also known as 'Phags-pa Wa-ti or sKyi-groṅ, Phags-pa. See Vasilyev: "Geography of Tibet" /in Russian/p.11), Wa-ti himself foretold that Candradhvaja was Ārya (Avalokiteśvara) himself, and now many people accepted (him as Avalokiteśvara). Many legends exist, such as for example the following: When Candradhvaja was searching for something which could benefit the purification of sins of living beings, he discovered that by fasting once in the presence of Ārya Avalokiteśvara, one was able to remove a great sin, and obtain (rebirth) in a human form, and that in the end such a person was to go to Sukhāvatī. But I did not cite them here. The bLa-ma Sa-čhen (Kun-dga' sñiṅ-po) acted for a long time as attendant of Candradhvaja. This establishes the time of the appearance of (Candradhvaja). (Candradhvaja) was also the Teacher of 'Gro-ba'i mgon-po dPal Phag-mo gru-pa (1110-1170) and of the siddha La-gyag-pa. The siddha Ñiṅ-phug-pa obtained from him (Candradhvaja) the sādhana of Avalokiteśvara. His parents were natives of Žaṅ-žuṅ. He was born in the year Wood-Male-Dog (śiṅ-pho-khyi—1094 A.D.) in the valleys of sTag-bde seṅ-ge, after they had come to La-stod

gTsaṅ province). His parents fearing that he might lose
is caste, took him in childhood to sPu-raṅs. At the age of
even, he felt faith in Karma and retribution. At the age of
4, he proceeded to dbUs, and came to the residence of the
aṅs-dkar lo-tsā-ba who was then building the Bo-doṅ monas-
ery. He was ordained by Khyuṅ and received the name of
hos-kyi grags-pa. For one month he studied the Doctrine
ith the Lord (rJe) 'Bum-phrag gsum-pa (Sthirapala /brTan-
yoṅ/). He stayed for six years in the presence of Zaṅs-
kar (lo-tsā-ba), and obtained the Cycle of Saṃvara, etc. He
as fed at Čhu-mig riṅ-mo. He received ordination from
Ṅa'-ris 'Jam-dbyaṅs, when the latter came to Lho-brag.
e obtained the Prajñāpāramitā from 'Bre Śes-rab-'bar. He
eached it on 15 occasions. He studied the teachings of the
lyāṇa-mitra dKon-mkhar with the latter's assistant preacher.
om Khyuṅ he obtained the Mādhyamaka system and the
yāya. Further, he obtained the Teaching of rGya-dmar from
e latter's assistant preacher. From the great Ṅur-smrig-pa (he
tained) the Abhidharma. It is said that he obtained the Doc-
ne of Maitreya from Mar-pa lo-tsā-ba of sTag-tshal. This
ust have been (Mar-pa) Do-pa. From the kalyāṇa-mitra
aṅ-ra-ba he obtained the Doctrine of Maitreya according to
e system of bTsan. From sPa-tshab lo-tsā (he obtained) the
Treatises of Mādhyamaka (dbU-ma rigs-tshogs drug).
om the kalyāṇa-mitra gŚen—the Six Doctrines of Tsa lo-tsā-
(Tsa-mi Saṅs-rgyas grags-pa, the famous Sanskrit scholar?).
om mṄa'-ris sKyi-ston—the Cycle of Saṃvara according to
-hraṅs lo-čhuṅ. From rṄog gŽun-pa—the Hevajra-(Tan-
). From dPyal Kun-dga' rdo-rJe and sNubs Phag-mo luṅ-
—the Hevajra-(Tantra) and the Cycle of (Vajra)-Vārahī.
m mTha'-bži—the Tantra (sṅags) and the Vinaya. In the
ervals, he attended on the Bodhisattva Candradhvaja, and
ained from him many doctrines. He also obtained many
trines from rGya-čhu-mig-pa bLa-ma Lho-pa. From 'Khon-
-pa Kīrti, he obtained the exposition of the Pañcakrama.
m Lha-rJe gTsaṅ-śod-pa—the Mahāmudrā. From the

Nepālese A-su-the Cycle of Phyag-čhen sñiṅ-po. Under sNe'u-zur-pa (he studied) the bKa'-gdams-pa doctrine. From Dags-po Lha-rJe (he obtained) the Six Doctrines of Nā-ro-(pa). From Phar-sgom, an attendant of Se mKhar-čhuṅ-ba, he obtained the "Path and Fruit" Doctrine (Lam-'bras). In general, he did not study texts of the rÑiṅ-ma school, and used to say that there did not exist texts belonging to the "New" (Tantras) which he had not studied. He spent eight full years in the snows of rTa-sgo, then six years during which time he spent either the winter or the summer in meditation, in all he spent 14 years in meditation. He developed the faculty of prescience. The local divinity (lha-btsan) of rTa-sgo asked him for religious instruction. He offered his "Life-mantra" (srog-sñiṅ). During his residence there, Ĵo-pad attended on him. After that he journeyed to lDog. The ācārya lDog asked him: "Do you possess the faculty of prescience?" He, thinking that it was improper to tell a lie to his own Teacher, answered: "Yes, I do." The Teacher asked him further: "What are the villagers doing?" and "What is in my hand?" He gave correct replies, and the ācārya being convinced said: "You must recite the Prajñāpāramitā." When he read the sentence "the nature of the sphere of Heaven is limitless" (nam-mkha' khams-kyi raṅ-bžin-de-yaṅ pha-mtha'-med. This passage (34
is found in the Prajñāpāramitāsañcayagāthā, mDo-maṅ, Vol.II, fol. 413b: dmigs-pa-rnams-kyi raṅ-bžin-de-ni pha-mtha'-med /sems-čan raṅ-bžin gaṅ-yin-de-yaṅ pha-mtha'-med/ nam-mkha'i khams-kyi raṅ-bžin-de-yaṅ pha-mtha'-med/'Ĵig-rten mkhyen-pa'i śes rab-de-yaṅ pha-mtha'-med." "The nature of objects is limitless. The nature of living beings is limitless. The nature of Heaven is limitless. The wisdom of Buddha is limitless"), an extraordinary trance was produced in him. After that he did not differentiate between the Intuitive Knowledge of a Saint and the Knowledge of the Saint acquired after the state of concentrated trance (samāhita-jñāna and pṛṣṭha-labdha-jñāna). After that he stayed at Ñiṅ-phug.

He constantly practised fasting and recitation (of sacred texts). At that time he and others saw countless holy visions. He laboured extensively for the welfare of others, and passed away at the age of 93 in the year Fire-Male-Horse (me-pho-rta—1186 A.D.). His disciple Sru-pa rDo-rJe rgyal-po: he was a native of Sru-yul-sgaṅ. From the age of seven, he mastered writing and reading. Once an upāsaka who had gone for fasting to Ñiṅ-phug, gave him some food which was left by the Teacher and some holy water for ablution. The boy was filled with a desire to go and proceeded into the presence of Ñiṅ-phug-pa. The later said about him: "This child will become the successor of the son of the Jina." He then took the boy on his lap and seemed pleased. Then he ordained him, and bestowed on him the vows, from the upāsaka vows up to those of the final monastic ordination. He then mastered the Vinaya-Sūtra (mDo-rtsa by Guṇaprabha). Afterwards he requested that he might be permitted to fast till his death. The Teacher became pleased, and presented him with an image of Avalokiteśvara made of crystal on which Candradhvaja used to meditate. He continued his fast and meditation for five full years, and had a vision of Ārya Avalokiteśvara. One night he saw in a dream himself alone surrounded by many Buddhas and Bodhisattvas, who included Amitābha, Bhaiṣajyaguru and others, speaking among themselves: "We shall adopt as son one who is the most pleasing among us." Among the retinue there was a young child of white complexion who said: "During seventeen existences he had established a Karmic bond with me. He is my son!" He then saw rays of light filling him, and woke up from his dream. When he was about to die, Žaṅ-ston dGra-'Jigs took over the abbot's chair, and he passed away. After the cremation, many images of the Great Merciful One (Mahākaruṇika), and many other relics were recovered (from the ashes).

His disciple was Žaṅ-ston. He was a native of Srug-n-pa. His birth was accompanied by a strong thunder, (3b) lightning and earth tremours. They (the family) had an enemy who remarked: "Such things were taking place that I became afraid!" Because of this the child became known as "Enemy's Terror" (dGra-'Jigs). At the age of seven, he learned writing. He was ordained by Sru-pa. He was a very strict (monk). At the age of 23, after studying the "Seven treatises on Logic"[1] at Sa-skya, he went on a round of monastic colleges to conduct philosophical debates, and became famous as a learned man.

After that he studied the "Five Treatises of Maitreya" (Byams-čhos-lṅa), the Five Stages (Sa sde-lṅa, the Bodhisattva-bhūmi, Tg. Sems-tsam, Nos. 4035-37; 4038-4042), the Abhidharmakośa, and the Abhidharmasamuccaya (mṄon-pa goṅ-'og). After that he proceeded to the residence of the kalyāṇa-mitra Žiṅ-mo čhe-pa, who asked him to become an abbot, and to labour for the Doctrine. He then became abbot and great was the benefit for the Doctrine. He used to preach the Vinaya-āgama by heart and gathered (round him) about 500 monks. He held the Bhaiṣajyaguru and the Tārā as the chief objects of his mental concentration, but on advice of a Bodhisattva that "this doctrine of Avalokiteśvara (the rite of fasting) was beneficial for this 'Dark Age' (Kali-yuga), and that he should practise it", he practised it and had a vision of the Tārā. About midnight he saw a vision of Bhaiṣajyaguru, and at Dawn he had a vision of the one-thousand-armed and one-thousand-eyed Avalokiteśvara. They initiated him, and uttered prophecies. Then he requested Sru-pa to allow him to go to a solitary place, but the latter told him: "You should occupy the chair for three years more!" and presented him with a crystal image of Avalokiteśvara. Then after the

1. Tshad-ma sde-bdun: The Pramāṇavārtikakārikā (Tg. Tshad-m No. 4210), the Pramāṇaviniścaya (Tg. Tshad-ma, No. 4211), the Nyāyabin (Tg. Tshad-ma, No. 4212), the Hetubindu) (Tg. Tshad-ma, No. 4213), t Sambandha-parīkṣāprakaraṇa (Tg. Tshad-ma, No. 4214), the Vādanyāya (T Tshad-ma, No. 4218), and the Santānāntarasiddhi (Tg. Tshad-ma, No. 421

apse of three years, he entrusted the chair to the kalyāṇa-nitra Byaṅ-yes and proceeded to the upper part of the valley, owards a rocky mountain called Rin-čhen spuṅs-pa, and here practised fasting for three months without being seen y any one. For seven months he performed nightly the ite of gČod. In the morning he used to fly over to the Western mountains, and there stay in the Sun, in the vening he flew back to the slope of the rock of Sru. He locked the river of Sru for half a day with his walking taff and performed (other) miracles, similar to those men-ioned above. At the hour of death he said: "My heart vill remain unburnt. Send it to Ga'-roṅ. My tongue v... (also) remain behind. Send it to Don-mo-ri (name of well-known monastery)." He died at the age of 61. After his cremation, a full measure (bre) or relics was ecovered (from the ashes). He bestowed the Doctrine on he mahā-upādhyāya rTsi-'dul-ba Thugs-rJe byaṅ-čhub. The (4a) atter was ordained in his youth. He was learned in the Doctrine in general, and in particular (he was learned) in he Prajñāpāramitā. Having become very famous through is learning, strictness, and goodness, he built vihāras and ounded monastic communities. He supported monks and pheld the moral code, and gathered round himself over a housand monks. Though in general he was learned in all he doctrines, he especially studied the Vinaya and possessed he perfect fragrance of morality. He held as the chief objects f his meditation Bhaiṣajyaguru and Tārā. One night he saw n his dream a woman who told him: "Son of good family! Avalokiteśvara being the essence of all the Buddhas of the Three Times, make a request to Žaṅ-ston dGra-'Jigs at lDog-oṅ, who was to preach next morning the rite of the Mental Creative Effort. Benefit for all living beings will arise!" and aying so, the woman disappeared. He met Žaṅ-ston and equested that he might be given the rite of the Mental Creative Effort towards Enlightenment. The latter then estowed on him the permission (luṅ) to read (the rite) of the

Eleven-faced Avalokiteśvara together with its (meditative) practice, its sādhana and propitiation (bsñen-tshad means the exact number of mantras required for the propitiation of a deity). He became very pleased and made the vow to fast on a thousand occasions. On his 300th fast, on the 16th day of the Sa-ga month, he saw a vision of the Great Merciful One (Mahākaruṇika), who spoke to him. After that he had again and again visions (of the Bodhisattva), and helped the emancipation of living beings. After that he bestowed (the Doctrine) on lDog-loṅ-pa Śākya byaṅ-čhub whose native place was Lower lDog. At the age of seven, he received ordination. At the age of 15, he mastered the Prajñāpāramitā, the Vinaya, and preached them both. He was especially learned in the Vinaya. He made Bhaiṣajyaguru and the Tārā the objects of his meditation. He had a vision of the Seṅ-ldaṅ-nags-sgrol (the Tārā of the Acacia grove; khadira, Acacia Catechu), who foretold the erection by him of the monastery of lDog-ltod, and advised him to proceed to the residence of (4b)
rTsi-'dul, and request the latter (to teach him) the sādhana of Ārya (Avalokiteśvara). Following this advice, he started at sun-rise, met the Teacher, and obtained from him the permission (luṅ). The Teacher said to him: "You should recite the required number of mantras for 21 times at my place". Accordingly, he took up residence there. After that his fortune increased, and he had yearly about 21 disciples who were able to teach the Prajñāpāramitā and the Vinaya. He also made the vow of observing 5000 fasts. On the occasion of his 300th fast, in the night of the main rite (dṅos-gži) a white beam of light appeared in front of him. He grasped it with his hand and was carried away, and reached Potala. Ārya Avalokiteśvara said to him: "Son of good family! Your coming (here) is welcome!" and a white beam of light penetrated (his) heart, and his body was filled with bliss. Again (Avalokiteśvara) said to him: "Till death, labour for the welfare of living beings! After your death, I shall send for you!" and he woke up from his

'eam. During the day he used to preach the Piṭaka and each the Doctrine to individuals according to their desires. t night, he listened to the Doctrine at the feet of Ārya Avalo-iteśvara. He practised numberless meditations. His disciple as the mahā-upādhyāya Byaṅ-čhub-'bar of Čhu-bzaṅs. He as born at Ṅaṅ-dkar of Mus. At the age of 11, he received ie upāsaka vows from lDog-loṅ-pa. After that he took ordination, and studied the Bodhicaryāvatāra and the Iādhyamaka system. At the age of 20, he took up the nal monastic ordination. One night he saw in his dream a hite man, who said to him: "Because you and I have a armic bond (las-'brel), ask lDog-loṅ-pa, who isn't different om me, to bestow on you the permission (luṅ) to read a cred text and the sādhana (of Ārya Avalokiteśvara)," and ying so the man disappeared. Next day he went into the esence of lDog-loṅ-pa and told him about the dream.)og-loṅ-pa said: "It is the Lord! I take Refuge in Him! also had a dream" and saying so, he imparted to him the ermission" (luṅ), together with the sādhana and its rite. yaṅ-čhub-'bar said to him: "After completing a hundred sts, I am going to bDe-ba-čan". The Teacher said: Wait once more for a vision of Avalokiteśvara!" Again he id: "Now a long time has passed. I shall go". The eacher said: "You are different from other people! Quick, editate!" Thus on the occasion of his 300th fast, after idnight of the 15th day, his whole cell became filled with ;ht, and he thought that it must be an eye deception. (5a)
e then saw Avalokiteśvara surrounded by teachers of the Ka'-gdams-pa Lineage. Next morning he prostrated him-lf before lDog-loṅ-pa, who spoke to him: "O son! Were u happy last night?" He replied: "My mind became e from thought constructions." Then the Teacher id to him: "Now you may go to wherever you desire, d labour for the welfare of living beings."

After that he proceeded to Mus, and his fortune increased. ich month he used to perform a great fasting rite and had

visions of many tutelary deities. He passed away at the age of 88. After his cremation, many images of gods and relics were recovered (from the ashes). He bestowed (the sādhana of Avalokiteśvara) on sÑag-phu-pa bSod-nams dbaṅ-phyug. The latter was born at Mus Daṅ-ma-gliṅ-skya. At the age of 5, he became an upāsaka and studied reading and writing. At the age of 11, he was ordained in the presence of the mahā-upādhyāya Śākya-mgon and the ācārya 'Od-zer rtse-mo. At the age of 13, he studied the Vinaya-sūtra (of Guṇaprabha) at lDog-loṅ with the mahā-upādhyāya Kun-rgyal, and the assistant preacher Žaṅ-ston 'Gyur-med-dpal. In the presence of Mus-čhen-pa he studied the "Five Treatises of Maitreya". From the ācārya Byaṅ-seṅ (he obtained) the (Pramāṇaviniścaya). From the ācārya Śes-rab ral-gri—the Pramāṇavārtika and the Bodhisattva-bhūmi (sa-sde). He also made a round of monastic colleges for the purpose of conducting philosophical debates. Once in a dream a woman told him: "You will not live more than seven days!" The mahā-upādhāya Čhu-bzaṅs-pa said to him: "Fasting is the best of the life-preserving ceremonies!" Accordingly he fasted and his life was prolonged. He received final monastic ordination from the mahā-upādhyāya Čhu-bzaṅs-pa and obtained many bKa'-gdams-pa doctrines at Mus-gle-luṅ. He occupied the abbot's chair of Gro-mo-čhe for five years. From the Dharmasvāmin Ñan-čhen-pa he obtained the "Path and Fruit" (Lam-'bras) doctrine and the Cycle of the Doctrines of Dam-pa (Saṅs-rgyas). From the ācārya Grags-tshul he obtained many sādhanas of the maṇḍalas belonging to the "Outer" and "Inner" Tantras (phyi, or outer means the three classes of Tantras; naṅ, or Inner means the Anuttara class). For three years he observed a fast during the month of Vaiśākha. After that his supporters built the monastery of sÑag-phu and presented it to him. He considered the following to be his "root-teachers" (mūla-guru, (5b)
rtsa-ba'i bla-ma; mūla-guru means the personal Teacher of a disciple; rGyud-pa'i bla-ma means the Teachers of the Spiri-

tual Lineage to which the disciple belongs. Mūla-guru is also used to designate the chief Teacher of a disciple/gTso-bo bla-ma/): Ñan-čhen-pa, Čhu-bzaṅs-pa, Mus-čhen-pa, and rGyal-mtshan-dpal. Further, he was the disciple of 42 teachers. Wishing to spread the deeds of Avalokiteśvara, he resolved to observe 10,000 fasts (this seems to mean that he paid people to make them observe fasts). After finishing the 2000th fast, (he found) that all his means had become exhausted. But then following an auspicious dream, his means again increased. He completed his fast within three years. He also spread the practice of fasting. Numerous other persons saw him as Avalokiteśvara in their visions. He passed away at the age of 68 in the Hog year (phag-lo—1371 A.D.?). His disciple was the Precious mahā-upādhyāya bSod-nams bzaṅ-po. The facts about his parents, his ordination and final monastic ordination, their dates, his pecuniary situation in his youth, are to be known from other sources.

After his ordination, he became, in general, the chief among the holders of the moral code till his death, and, in particular, he observed throughout his life the vow of staying on one mat (i.e. taking food without rising from one's seat), and abstaining from meat, without complaining of old age. As regards his knowledge, he attended on many scholars, such as Ña dbOn-po Kun-dga'-pa and others. He became very learned in the Piṭaka of the Sūtras, headed by the Vinaya of the Holy Doctrine. In the Tantras, (he was especially) learned in the Śrī-Kālacakra-Tantra. The Master of philosophical debates and great scholar gYag-brugs Saṅs-rgyas-dpal, and others were unable to defeat him. He had vision of numerous tutelary deities and was endowed with a transic meditation of the Sampannakrama degree of the Ṣadaṅga-yoga, and others. He was the chief disciple of the Dharmasvāmin Phyogs-las rnam-par rgyal-ba (the Bo-doṅ paṇ-čhen). At the age of 80, signs of death having manifested themselves, he practised prāṇāyāma (breath control, rluṅ-sbyor) for one month and succeeded in prolonging his (64) life. The year of his birth was the year Iron-Female-Serpent (lčags-mo-sbrul—1341 A.D.). He passed away painlessly at the age of 93 in the year Water-Female-Ox (čhu-mo-glaṅ—1433 A.D.). His disciples included the Dharmasvāmin De-bžin gśegs-pa, mThoṅ-pa Don-ldan and others. Numerous scholars gathered round him, similar to bees around a flower. Among them sMra-ba'i seṅ-ge Roṅ-ston and others. His (present) wealth: Vaiśravaṇa used to assist him at will. All great men, such as dBaṅ-grags-pa rgyal-mtshan, used to place his foot on their heads. Śrī Vanaratna (Nags-kyi rin-čhen) siddheśvara (grub-pa'i dbaṅ-phyug) used to say: "He is the best yogin in Tibet!" Such a great kalyāṇa-mitra bestowed the precepts of Ārya Avalokiteśvara on bSod-nams-dar the mahā-ārya-sthavira. He also observed the pure vows of an ordained monk. A Mental Creative Effort towards Enlightenment was born in him. He was the chief among those who are satisfied with little and lived contentedly. He used to propitiate continuously Ārya Avalokiteśvara. There were many monks who followed after him. Nowadays they are divided into two groups known as the dbUs-'phags (Saints of dbUs) and gTsaṅ-'phags (Saints of gTsaṅ). Small groups consisting of ten or fifteen monks, the smallest consisting of five, were found in Dags-po and Koṅ-po, at dbUs and gYor, in south and north La-stod. They benefitted greatly the Doctrine. The Chapter on the Lineage of the system of dPal-mo (Lakṣmī) of the Cycle of Avalokiteśvara.

Now the Lineage of the Sādhana (propitiation) of Ārya Amoghapaśa ('Phags-pa Don-yod-žags-pa): a paṇḍita named E-ra-pa-ti (Elāpatra) who was a native of Southern India, came to a vihāra called Bhaktibala (Dad-pa'i stobs) in (6b)
Southern India, and was ordained. He became a great paṇḍita who mastered all the branches of science. On his return to his native country, he preached the Doctrine to his mother. Once when he was walking on the roof of a house, he caused a piece of brick to fall down on his mother's

head, which caused her death. Such an action did not represent a true murder, for as the ācārya Āryadeva had said in his Cittāvaraṇaviśodha (Tg. rGyud, No. 1804, Sems-kyi sgrib-sbyoṅ): "A monk who had asked his aged father to go quickly, and pushing him on, caused the father's death, was not found guilty of a pārājika sin" (this passage refers to a well-known story, contained in the Vinaya-vastu: Once a monk and his father after having received ordination, proceeded to Jetavana. When they had reached the place, they heard the sound of the bell. The monk thought that this was the call for the ceremony of distributing presents, and urged his aged father to go quickly. The aged man fell on the ground, and died. The monk told the Buddha about his committing a sin which involved expulsion (pārājiko), but the Buddha told him that it was not such a sin). Since he did it amidst evil circumstances, he propitiated Amogha-paśa during six months in order to purify the sin, but no signs manifested themselves. He performed the propitiation rite for a second time, and again no signs were observed. Again he performed the rite for a third time, and again no signs were observed. While he was holding in his hand a sandal rosary and was repeating the mantra "Hrī Trailokya......", he fell asleep and the rosary fell from his hand. When he awoke, he saw that all the place was filled with shades and lights, and that a shower of flowers and scented water was falling. He gazed in all directions but failed to see anything. He then looked up the tree, at the foot of which he was sitting, and saw the five deities of the parivāra of Amoghapaśa appearing clearly on the trunk. He said: "O Ārya! Why did you not manifest yourself? Are you small in commiseration, or am I great in defilement?" The Ārya replied: "I have never parted from you!" and he imparted to him many doctrines. Since then he was able to listen to the Doctrine at will. He then thought of going to another country and to spread there the Doctrine of Ārya (Avalokiteśvara). People, however, continued to call him the

"Sinner who had killed his own mother" (Ma-bsad-pa'i sdig-čan), and did not listen to his preaching. Many siddhas such as Śrī Virūpa and others gathered and listened to his preaching of the Doctrine. The king of that country said to the siddhas: "Though you are siddhas, how can you listen to the preaching by such a sinner?" The siddhas replied: "He is the chief of all the siddhas ! All his previous actions have been miracles performed by Ārya (Avalokiteśvara)". After that the king repented and all were filled with faith. He had a servant upāsaka. At the latter's request he composed the sādhana of Amoghapaśa. Elāpatra (E-ra-pa-ti) bestowed it on a yogin of low caste in the South. This yogin attained spiritual realization (siddhi) and when a boatman refused to ferry him across the Ganges, he struck the river with his mendicant staff, and the Ganges stopped flowing. From him the Doctrine was obtained by the paṇḍita Don-yod-rdo-rĵe (Amoghavajra) known as rDo-rĵe gdan-pa. Further, the paṇḍita Dharmakapāla obtained it from Mahākaruṇika (The Great Merciful One). He expounded it to the great bSod-sñoms-pa (Paiṇḍapātika), the siddha of Saṃvara. The latter taught it to Don-yod rdo-rĵe. Don-yod rdo-rĵe was the name of rDo-rĵe gdan-pa, the Senior. He preached it to the teacher Ba-ri. Further, in the vihāra of Khasarpaṇa, Bo dGe-bsñen was worshipping Ārya Avalokiteśvara in order to invite the Ārya. After his death, there was another upāsaka of the Ārya to whom it was prophesied: "You should take up ordination!" He then appointed another upāsaka to attend on the Ārya (Avalokiteśvara) and proceeded to Vikramaśila, took up ordination, and then the final monastic ordination. His name was Śīlākara. He preached the sādhana to the paṇḍita Vairocana. The latter taught it to Ba-ri. Then again a paṇḍita named Chos-ston worshipped Ārya Avalokiteśvara at Khasarpaṇa, and Avalokiteśvara used to preach him the Doctrine in his dreams. Later he instructed him personally. The latter preached it to the paṇḍita Don-yod rdo-rĵe (Amoghavajra). The latter taught it to Ba-ri.

(7a)

Ba-ri: he was a native of Khams-pa sDom-tshaṅ and was born in the year Iron-Male-Dragon (lčags-pho-'brug—1040 A.D.). The Venerable Mid-la was born in the same year. A paṇḍita from Kāśmīra having come to Khams, he heard from him the Abhidharma (mṄon-pa) and the Lesser recension of the Žal-gñis-ma (Vārahī). He had the intention of going to India. Having obtained about seventy golden sraṅs, he took the gold with him and proceeded towards dbUs. At the age of (7b)
15, he met Atīśa at sÑe-thaṅ and requested his blessing. (Atīśa) fortold him: "Go to the residence of rDo-rje gdan-pa! Accidents will not befall you". Having gone to La-stod dPal-thaṅ, he came across about a hundred sheep which were led away to be slaughtered. He felt pity towards them and bought them off paying for each one golden žo. He presented them to the monastery on the condition that they were to be kept alive. Having come to Nepāl, (he had to choose) between the two roads (leading to India), the short but dangerous road, and the long, but safe road. His tutelary deity indicated him to proceed by the short road, and that danger would not present itself. He had a vision of Avalokiteśvara in his dream in the night preceding the crossing of the Ganges. At Kośalakrama (the ferry of Kośala) he met Tsa-mi (Saṅs-rgyas grags-pa). He twice offered him a golden žo, Tsa-mi showed him an image, which had been consecrated by the Buddha and fashioned by Viśvakarman. The image proved similar to the one he had seen in his dream. On seeing the image, an excellent transic meditation was produced in him. During his stay in India, Ārya Avalokiteśvara appeared constantly, and delivered to him many discourses. He also saw the vision of a yoginī who advised him to return. He also saw Ārya Avalokiteśvara in tears and asked: "What was the affliction?" The Bodhisattva replied: "Śiṅ-stan-čan has captured sixty prisoners who are tormented in a prison pit by snakes and frogs, and are weeping from pain." In the morning he ascertained the fact, and having presented a golden sraṅs to the king, begged him to set the prisoners free. The

king said: "Unless I get one golden srans for each prisoner, I shall not release them!" He freed the captives after paying the sixty golden srans. He also called a medical practitioner to treat their wounds inflicted by snakes and torture. He paid him one golden srans, and thus acquired the great fame of a Bodhisattva. Again he saw Avalokiteśvara in tears, and (8a)
when he asked: "What was the affliction?" the Bodhisattva replied: "Bandits carried away the gold which belonged to rGyus lo-tsā-ba, and the latter is full of grief". Following this indication, he proceeded in the morning to the house of rGyus-lo and inquired as to what had happened. The lo-tsā-ba said: "Such is my sad fate!" He gave him two golden žos and pleased him. When he was preparing to go to Tibet, he saw in a dream numerous pretas who said to him "O great lo-tsā-ba! On your way to Tibet, dangers will not befall you! Present an offering to us, and then go!" He then offered a gtor-ma and rice comprising eleven men's loads. With the remaining gold he entertained numerous natives of mṄa'-ris (who had come to India). They said (to him): "The paṇḍita Parahita has come to mṄa'-ris and is preaching the 'Five Treatises of Maitreya' (Byams-čhos sde-lṅa), and the 'Six Treatises of the Mādhyamaka system' (dbU-ma rigs-tshogs-drug)." He journeyed to Guṅ-thaṅ via Nepāl. Then from Lower Gro he proceeded to sPu-hraṅs and obtained the "Six Treatises of the Mādhyamaka" system from the paṇḍita (Parahita). After that he went to worship (the images) of Avalokiteśvara (Mahākaruṇika), Mañjuśrī and Tārā, which were formerly brought by the lo-tsā-ba Rin-čhen bzaṅ-po. That night in a dream he was told that he should repair the big toe on the foot of the Tārā. He brought a (piece of) gor-śi-śa (<Skrt. gośīrṣa, a kind of sandal wood) with gold, and repaired the damage. After that he again journeyed to India and obtained from rDo-rJe gdan-pa (Tsa-mi) numerous doctrines, such as the Cycle of Avalokiteśvara and others. Then he again returned to Tibet. He laboured for the welfare of living beings in many upper and

lower countries. He had numerous disciples to whom he imparted the Cycle of Avalokiteśvara. In particular he preached the Cycle of Avalokiteśvara to sNubs Phag-mo luṅ-pa, Ñe-gnas lho-pa and mKhaṅ-pa Thaṅ-pa of Guṅ-thaṅ. The siddha Žaṅ-žuṅ obtained (it) from the above three. sKye-ma Grags-tshul obtained it from him. The latter (preached it) to kLu-sgrub. The latter to the bLa-ma dKa'-bži-pa. The latter to Don-žags-pa Śes-rab brtson-'grus. The latter to Don-žags-pa Saṅs-rgyas rin-čhen. He became the upādhyāya of Si-tu dGe-blo-ba at 'Tshal. Because of this he became known as the mahā-upādhyāya Saṅ-rin-pa. He met rGyal-tsha, the upādhyāya of sPyan-yas. At sPyan-yas he looked after disciples with the help of the Cycle of Ārya Avalokiteśva- (8b) ra (i.e. by preaching to them the Cycle of Ārya Avalokiteśvara). After that he travelled through the upper and lower regions. Later at the time of his passing into Nirvāṇa, he said: "Convey me to sPyan-yas, the strictest monastic college." On reaching sPyan-yas, he passed out. His remains are preserved until the present day inside a clay stūpa. The ācārya gŽon-nu smon-lam obtained from him the Cycle of Amoghapaśa. From him the mahā-upādhyāya Saṅs-rgyas 'bum-dpal obtained (it). His uninterrupted Lineage exists to the present day. Again, one named Dā-Bodhisattva, who was a nephew of Atīśa, and was a Bodhisattva of this Bhadrakalpa, personally obtained (the Doctrine) from Ārya (Amoghapaśa). There was a scholar named paṇḍita Śrīdhana, who used to worship the Mahābodhi (image) during the day, and at night used to meditate in a cemetery. When he received an invitation to Nepāl, the lo-tsā-ba 'Phags-tshul of mṄa'-ris, and Byaṅ-sems zla-rgyal obtained from him the initiation and blessing, as well as the Cycle of Ārya (Avalokiteśvara). He offered seven golden sraṅs, having borrowed them from other people. The paṇḍita said: "This will do (for one journey)." He then proceeded with the lo-tsā-ba to India. From the Bodhisattva he obtained the Doctrine of the siddha Žaṅ-žuṅ-pa. From him sKye-ma grags-tshul. From the latter the bLa-ma 'Jam-dpal rgyal-mtshan. From the latter Žig-po kun-grol. From the latter Lo-mo-ba Saṅs-rgyas ston-pa. From the latter Saṅs-rgyas dbon-po. After him gŽon-nu blo-gros. Then Grags-pa rgyal-mtshan. Then Grags-pa bzaṅ-po. Then the bLa-ma rDo-rJe rgyal-mtshan. He called his chief doctrine Amoghapaśa. He benefitted many laymen and monks, and became famous. Again from Byaṅ-sems zla-rgyal—Ñiṅ-phug-pa, sKye-ma grags-tshul, the siddha dKon-mčhog-grasg, Saṅs-rgyas 'Jam-rgyal, Thugs-rJe rgyal-mtshan, Čhos-kyi rgyal-mtshan, sKyes-mčhog kLu-sgrub, dKa'-bži-pa dKon-mčhog gžon-nu, 'Jam-dbyaṅs Thugs-rJe śes-rab, Kun-mkhyen (9a) Yon-tan mgon-po, the Bla-ma gŽon-nu byaṅ-čhub, and Śaṅs-pa Kun-mkhyen. Again, Graṅ-po luṅ-pa, bLa-čhen-pa, 'Čhims Nam-mkha'-grags, bSod-nams ye-śes, the upādhyāya Grags-pa gŽon-nu, the mahā-upādhyāya bSod-nams-grags, rGyal-sras Thogs-med-pa, the Dharmasvāmin rGya-ma-ba, Yon-tan-'od, and Kun-mkhyen Śaṅs-pa. The latter bestowed it on me.

The Lineage of the Rigs-gtad (n.of an initiation ceremony) of the five gods of the parivāra of Amoghapaśa: Avalokiteśvara, Śīlākara, Vairocanarakṣita, Ba-ri lo-tsā-ba, sKye-ma grags-tshul, the ācārya Don-žags-pa of sNar-thaṅ, the mahā-upādhyāya sKyo, Byaṅ-čhen-pa bSod-'phel, Bag-ston-pa, the bLa-ma Tshul-rgyal-ba, and Kun-mkhyen Śaṅs-pa. The latter bestowed it on me. He bestowed on me the Rigs-stad (n.of an initiation rite) and the initiation of the Eleven-faced Avalokiteśvara transmitted through this Lineage. The detailed exposition (dmar-khrid) of the Cycle of the Great Merciful One (Mahākaruṇika) according to the system of Byaṅ-sems zla-rgyal (Thugs-rJe-čhen-po'i dmar-khrid Byaṅ-sems zla-rgyal lugs): sKyi-tsha 'od-'byuṅ having heard of the fame of Byaṅ-sems proceeded into the latter's presence, and perceived him as Avalokiteśvara. Again, on another occasion, he saw him as his teacher. Again, whenever a strong feeling of reverence filled him, he saw the Teacher as Avalokiteśvara. Byaṅ-sems said (to him): "Through your Doctrine benefit will arise for living beings", and imparted it to him. From him Žaṅ-dbu-dkar-ba heard it. The latter obtained the power of the Maṇi of the rite, and was able to command gods and demons. He obtained the power of the True Word (dben-tshig, a faculty of obtaining the fulfilment of one's own words). With the help of this doctrine he caused great benefit to others. He preached the doctrine to Žaṅ lo-tsā-ba Mya-ṅan med-pa'i sa-dpal. In his dreams he had repeated visions of the Mahākaruṇika and was able to listen to his preaching. He imparted it to the upādhyāya Byaṅ-čhub rin-čhen. The latter was well qualified for religious studies and great was the benefit for the living beings. Among his disciples there were many who had visions of Avalokiteśvara. He preached (the Cycle (9b) of Avalokiteśvara) to lČe-sgoms Śes-rab rdo-rJe. The latter preached it to the siddha Hūṃ-'bar. The latter had visions of tutelary deities, and amanusyas (demons) used to appear in person to accept (his) offerings. He preached (the Cycle) to the mahā-upādhyāya Byaṅ-čhub-dpal, who had visions of Vajrapāṇi and Mahākāla (mGon-po). He was endowed with a boundless faculty of prescience. He imparted (the Cycle) to dPal rGyal-ba grub-pa, who after reciting the number of mantras prescribed for the propitiation of the five deities (of the parivāra of Amoghapaśa) at the sacred place of Thugs-rJe-rdzoṅ, acquired many merits, such as visions of the Eleven-faced One (Avalokiteśvara), etc. He imparted (the Cycle) to the mahā-upādhyāya 'Jims-čhen-pa, who had visions of his tutelary deity and developed a yogic insight. He preached (the Cycle) to the ascetic (kun-spaṅs) Ri-khrod-pa, who had visions of many tutelary deities. Ri-khrod-pa bestowed it on the mahā-upādhyāya gŽon-nu-'bum. The latter bestowed it on the Dharmasvāmin Čhu-tshan-kha-pa Śes-rab-dpal. The latter bestowed it on sKyes-mčhog Nam-mkha' bzaṅ-po.

The Chapter on the Cycle of Amoghapaśa. The detailed exposition (dmar-khrid) of the method of Zla-rgyal (zla-la rgyab-mtshan). The origins of the Cycle of the Great Merciful One (Mahākaruṇika), which originated with La-stod dMar-po: The Buddha Amitābha, and the ḍākinī Guhyajñānā (gSaṅ-ba ye-śes). She preached it to La-ba-pa or sPyod-pa-pa. The latter to Dur-khrod-pa or Bi-ru-pa (Virūpa). The latter to rDo-rJe gdan-pa, the Senior. The latter to La-stod dMar-po. His native place was 'U-yug. He was born as son of father, the ascetic (sgom-čhen) Lha-brtan and mother Ar-mo siṅ-ṅa. He belonged to the Ram clan. When he was a child, he with six children stoned to death a mad dog. Then they, imitating a homa ceremony of the Tantrics, burnt the dog's corpse inside some shrubs, and thus contacted some Nāgas. His playmates died within one year, and he himself suffered from the disease (leprosy). He (10a) learned the method of meditating on Acala (Mi-gyo-ba) from his uncle, who was a kalyāṇa-mitra, and repeated a few of the mantras, but had no faith in them. He used to imitate his uncle and the latter became displeased, and said to him: "How true is the saying that a relative is a poor teacher! You had better proceed to someone else". Then a thought came to him: "Well! I shall die. I had better go to India". He had a wealthy aunt, who possessed a turquoise called dMar-rkaṅ-tshogs. He borrowed it from her, and told her that one of his cousins was getting married, and that she wished to wear it during the ceremony. Instead, he placed the turquoise inside a split bamboo stick and carried it away towards La-stod. He spent one day at Diṅ-ri. After having gone a little distance from that place, he discovered that he had left the stick behind, and returned. Dam-pa Saṅs-rgyas gave him the stick. On reaching Khab Guṅ-thaṅ, he met one named Mar-pa lo-tsā wearing a black garment and leading a black dog, who was going towards India. He requested him to guide him on the Path. Mar-pa said: "You should exchange this turquoise, which cannot be disposed off in India or Nepāl, for gold". He then returned to La-stod and sold the turquoise, realizing 46 golden sraṅs. This Mar-lo (Mar-pa lo-tsā-ba) was a worshipper of Mahākāla and he obtained from him the sādhana of Mahākāla. When he had reached the Plains of India, he saw in his dream that the Sun had merged into him, and that he was holding the Moon in his hand, and was flying through space. When he awoke, he felt an apprehension rising in him. He reported the matter to Mar-lo who said: "Don't be alarmed! The merging of the Sun into you is a sign that you will penetrate the profound doctrine. The holding of the Moon in your hand is a sign that you will be of benefit to others. The flying through space is the sign of your ability to master the minds (of others)". When he came to rDo-rJe gdan-pa, he presented him half of the gold and asked him to bestow the method with which he could remove hindrances in this life, and obtain Enlightenment in the next. rDo-rJe gdan-pa imparted to him the meditation mantra of the Great Merciful One (Mahākaruṇika), and (to stress its secret nature) he introduced a bamboo tube into his ear, and through it repeated "Oṃ maṇi padme hūṃ". He thought in himself: "This mantra is repeated throughout Tibet by all old men, women and even children. This doctrine seems to be a common one". The Teacher perceived (his doubts) and gave him back the gold. His face darkened, and he related the story to Mar-lo. Mar-lo said to him: "The Teacher (10b) was displeased with you! You had better confess (your fault)! Ask the Teacher for the rite of confession". He accordingly asked the Teacher, who said: "Eat excrement and urine!" He did so. Then the Teacher bestowed on him the initiation into the method of meditation, and he practised meditation. For one month he repeated the "Six letters Formula" (Oṃ Maṇi-Padme-hūṃ), and saw in his dream that many scorpions and snakes had come out of his body, and that his bed was filled with snakes. He felt lightness and serenity. His wounds and sores disappeared, and he began dancing up and down. Next morning he went into the presence of the Teacher and presented him with a golden srang. The Teacher then imparted to him the Tantra of the

Great Merciful One (there exist several Thugs-rJ̌e čhen-po'i rgyud) together with the sādhana (propitiating rite) and precepts. He practised meditation at Vajrāsana. In his dream the Tārā advised him to go to Śītavana (bSil-pa tshal). He asked rDo-rJ̌e gdan-pa, but the latter advised him not to go. Then again he had a clear vision of the Venerable One (Tārā) who again told him to go. He again related the matter to rDo-rJ̌e gdan-pa, who said: "Now you know (more than I). Go there!" He stayed at the foot of the Nyagrodha tree in the "Cool Grove" (Śītavana) and a large black snake entwined itself round him and the tree, so that he was unable to breathe. After practising meditation, he was immediately freed and the snake transformed itself into Vaiśravaṇa, who offered him his Life-mantra (sñiṅ-po) and promised to execute all his wishes. He then held a contest in magic powers with some heretics on the banks of the Ganges. The heretics were defeated and he converted them to the Doctrine of Buddha. His doctrine consisted of the following: the teachings imparted to him by rDo-rJ̌e gdan-pa, those taught to him by ḍākinīs while he was staying at Śītavana, such as the Precepts ransoming death ('Čhi-la bslu-ba'i gdams-ṅag) in order to remove misfortunes to his physical body, the Lam-sbyor-ba-lṅa, with the help of which one was able to cross the five Paths simultaneously, the dBaṅ-bži-khug-pa (the Combination of the Four Initiations) which removed defilements from sins and helped to acquire power, and the Precepts of merging the 18 kinds of relativity (stoṅ-pa bčwo-brgyad) into the essence of the Merciful One with the view of practising all the doctrines simultaneouly. Following the advice of rDo-rJ̌e gdan-pa, he practised for six years (11
secret Tantric rites and then for seven years he practised meditation in the cave of sTag-tshaṅ seṅ-ge (in 'Brug-yul, Bhuṭān). Many signs of spiritual realization were manifested to him. He was able to cover the distance of fifteen days in half a day, and arrived in lČog-ro 'briṅ-mtshams. Because he was wearing a red mantle and a royal turban on

his head, he became known as Dam-pa dMar-po. He settled at rGya-ma ñe-kha, and visited (the country) as far as Si-rib and gLo-bo.

When (the country) was threatened by the troops of the Gar-log (Qarluq), he shot an arrow into a large boulder and pierced it. The troops having seen it, retired. At 'Briṅ-mtshams, he erected a white tent on the shore of the lake during the period of fishing, and spent some time at Bre-čhuṅ. All saw that a lake nymph offered him "water sheep" (mtsho-lug). Endowed with such powers and precepts, he laboured for the welfare of others for a long time. In the end, a disciple of his gave him some poison at Myu-gu-luṅ. Though forewarned, he partook of it, and died. After the cremation (of his remains) a few bones and many relics were recovered (from the ashes).

Kar-ma pa-śi maintained that he had been Dam-pa dMar-po. This cannot be grasped by thought. Of his two sons—the scholar bSod-nams rin-čhen, aged 12, proceeded to the residence of 'J̌aṅ-pa sTon-skyabs without his father's permission, and studied under him. After the lapse of one year, his father brought him about 16 donkey-loads of provisions, and said: "After completing your studies, you should remove all (your) doubts." He also made a long stay at the monastic college of Žaṅ-e-pa. From the age of 12 to the age of 32, he continued his studies, and mastered all the treatises belonging to the Tantra and Sūtra classes. The effects of his studies became manifest in mid-life, and numerous kalyāṇa-mitras appeared (among his disciples). He did not give up his studies to the very end, and throughout this time his transic meditation was perfect. Having become very learned, he wrote treatises, such as the "Mirror of Karma" (Las-kyi me-loṅ), etc., and benefitted others. After the cremation (11b)
(of his remains), an image of Saṃvara in the yuganaddha attitude (yab-yum) and many other relics were recovered (from the ashes). The youngest (son) Bha-ru: when he was 17, his father said to him: "The time for my departure has

come! I shall impart precepts (to you)." In the cave of lČim-čhu-rdo he bestowed on him the Cycles of the Ḍākinīs. At Maṅ-kar-mda' he bestowed on him the basic text of the Cycle of the Great Merciful One (Mahākaruṇika) together with its exposition. At gDan-sa ñe-kha he bestowed on him the propitiating rites (sādhanas), and told him: "You should mainly practise meditation. The power of benefitting living beings will arise." He practised meditation, and his yogic insight became similar to the Sky (in loftiness). He followed the practice which consisted in imitating insanity, and laboured for the welfare of living beings.

sMyon-pa lDom-čhuṅ (there exists a manuscript Life-story (rnam-thar) of sMyon-pa lDom-čhuṅ): he was the son of one named rGya-gar, the chief of Upper Myaṅ. In his childhood he went as attendant of Dam-pa dMar-po, and obtained precepts (from him). Having developed yogic insight, he lived as a beggar. He spent some time at various places in gTsaṅ, Lha-sa and bSam-yas. Later he journeyed to 'Phyos, built a small hut, and settled there. Because of envy shown by the local inhabitants, he had to destroy and rebuild it several times. After that he proceeded to the monastery of Ri-bo, and there laboured extensively for the welfare of living beings. He passed away there. He bestowed the hidden precepts of dMar-po on the ācārya dKon-gñer. The Lineage of Permission (luṅ) to read these precepts still exists.

The Chapter on La-stod dMar-po (also called sPrul-sku dMar-po).

The story of the doctrines taught by the Venerable Mitrayogin (Mitra-dzo-ki).

The Venerable Mitra: he was born in the great city of the country of Ra-dha (Rāḍha in Mayūrabhañja in Orissa) in Eastern India. He was accepted (as disciple) by Lalitavajra (Rol-pa'i rdo-rje), a direct disciple of Tilli-pa. For 12 years he meditated at Kha-sar-paṇa. Avalokiteśvara surrounded by his retinue manifested himself to him, and (12a) ‹pounded the Doctrine to him, and he attained spiritual ·alization (siddhi) (this is his first miracle). His name was ‹jitamitragupta (Mi-pham bśes-gñen sbas-pa). Ekajaṭī ‹ught him the upāya-mārga, and he was able to realize all ‹s wishes, by praying to her and placing in front of him- ·lf a wooden tray. This was (his) second miracle. There ‹ere 12,000 monks at Otantapurī, and there was discord ‹mong them. One of the parties was supported by the ‹uṅ-śiṅ king who led his troops against the monastery. Mitra) threw his mace, and the troops terror stricken ecamped. No harm resulted to the monks and the vihāras. ·his was (his) third (miracle). During the reign of king ‹iṅ-ltad khan (Sultān khan) troops from Vārāṇasī, the dust aised by (their marching feet) almost shrouding the Sun, ‹ttempted to destroy the Doctrine of Buddha in Magadha. Mitrayogin), naked, shouted (at them) and the Earth shook, ‹nd all men and animals stood motionless. The king ‹egged to be forgiven, and he relieved them from torpor. This was (his) fourth miracle. The king Yaśas (Grags-pa) ‹nvited the monks of the four schools (sde-bži) Mahāstha- ·iras, Sarvāstivādins, Mahāsaṃmitīyas and Mahāsaṅghikas ‹s witnesses, and declared: "Should heretics be able to ‹nove my wooden throne, I would give them a thousand golden srańs and would convert all Buddhists to the doctrine of the heretics. Should they fail, I would convert all heretics to the Buddhist doctrine". In the centre of a wide plain he erected his wooden throne. (Mitrayogin exercised his powers) and the heretics were unable to move the throne even a little. Then the heretics were converted to Buddhism. This was (his) fifth miracle. King Upatra (Udbhaṭa?) covered a pit with cloth and invited the Teacher to sit on it. The Teacher fell (into the pit). The king then covered the opening of the pit with wood and stones, but the Teacher was able to reach the market place, and said: "I should have been invited to the Palace by the king." The king felt remorse and placed the Teacher's foot on (his) head. This was (his) sixth miracle. Again the king ordered wood to be piled up, and placed the Teacher on top of it. For three days he set fire to it, but the Teacher remained unburnt. This was (his) seventh miracle. When he was preaching the five profound ślokas to the king of Vārāṇasī, a shower of flowers fell from the Sky, and he showed him the vision of a devaputra offering him a vase filled with nectar. This was (his) eighth miracle. When the king requested that he might be initiated, Mitra told him: "You must draw (12b) the outline of the rāja-maṇḍala with jewels." The king thought that the yogin was deceiving him, and regretted his request for initiation. Mitrayogin then showed himself sitting amidst clouds in the Sky. This was (his) ninth (miracle). Filled with shame, the king worshipped him for seven days, and the yogin came down on a pond, and sat there. This was (his) tenth (miracle). Then the king presented him a town of 1,600,0000 families to support him. The Teacher built there a hospice (sbyin-gtoṅ-gi khaṅ-pa), and distributed alms for three years. After the lapse of three years, he disappeared without anyone knowing where he had gone. This was (his) eleventh miracle. Then in the vicinity of the Kuru-vihāra (Ku-ru bi-ha-ra) of the South, there were two yakṣas who used to devour an old and a young man of the town each day. He subdued them and built a temple. This was (his) twelveth miracle.

In order to kindle the faith of the monks, he cast a magic glance (upwards), and all the birds of the sky came down on his hand and obeyed his words. This was (his) thirteenth miracle. Though he did not preach the Doctrine to the 84 chiefs of Vārāṇasī, by a mere mental projection he caused them to meditate on skeletons (Keṅ-rus-sogs-kyi 'du-śes), etc. They proceeded to a forest, and emancipated their minds from the notions (peculiar) to worldly beings. This was (his) fourteenth miracle. Then the king Jayasena and the paṇḍita Ānanda mistrusted him and made an attempt on his life. He placed them in the mudrā (posture) of intense mental concentration and concentrated his mind on the meaning of

a śloka, and following this they attained emancipation without rising from their seats. This was (his) fifteenth miracle. He uttered a prophecy to a king of Vārāṇasī, which said: "Because of your doubt in me, you will not obtain spiritual realization in this life, but will obtain it in the Intermediate Stage." This was (his) sixteenth miracle. The king of Vārāṇasī thinking in himself: "I shall not let this Teacher go to another place", made him stay in a vihāra, and sealed its gate. Thereupon the Teacher was seen playing on the top of a large boulder, lying outside the vihāra, and simultaneously sitting inside the vihāra. This was (his) seventeeth (134a)
miracle. Then when he was living inside the house of an ascetic (tapasvin), two monks drove away two figures resembling him which appeared outside and inside the house, and when they peeped through a hole inside the house, they saw him preaching the Doctrine to the eight classes of gods and demons. This was (his) eighteenth miracle. The above are called his "18 wonderful stories." According to the twentieth story (nineteenth?), he was admitted by Devaḍāki to Venudvīpa ('Od-ma'i gliṅ) and there met Avalokiteśvara who told him: "Son of good family! You should bestow for the sake of the living beings of future times the initiations of the four classes of Tantras at one time." This was (his) nineteenth miracle (or story). The king of Vārāṇasī worshipped him for seven days, and was given the initiations of all the classes of Tantras in a single maṇḍala at one time. This was (said to be) (his) twentieth miracle. When the lo-tsā-ba Byams-pa'i dpal (Khro-phug lo-tsā-ba), who was studying the Doctrine with the paṇḍita Buddhaśrī, heard that this great siddha, endowed with such miraculous powers, had come to 'Phags-pa Śiṅ-kun (Svayambhū-nātha caitya), he took with him some leaves of piper-betel (tāṃbūla, tāmbo-la), and presented them to Mitrayogin, inquiring about his health. The latter gave him a friendly answer. As the yogin was sitting with his face turned towards Tibet, a thought occurred to the lo-tsā-ba: "he may perhaps go to Tibet," and he

asked the yogin to visit Tibet, but the latter did not promise. He then obtained from him a short summary of the cittotpāda rite. After that the lo-tsa-ba was attacked by fever, and almost passed out. The great siddha (Mitra) proceeded to India, and the lo-tsā-ba followed after him, as soon as his health, which was not quite restored, permitted him to do so.

He found him residing in a fort of the border country, which was guarded by fierce-looking soldiers of Tirahuti (Tīrabhukti, the modern Tirhut in Bihār), who had collected to guide (the siddha). An'a-tsa-ra (ācārya) who was known to him, took him inside and he met the siddha on the roof of the fort. He again asked him about his coming to Tibet, and again (the siddha) made no promise. The lo-tsā-ba thought to himself: "Death is better, than to return to Tibet without inviting this siddha, after having met him". He then made a solemn wish to become the siddha's disciple in his next life, and without hesitation, jumped down from the top of the fort. But the mahāsiddha seized him with (13b)
his hand and exclaimed: "Ha-ha! Don't do such things?" and kept him in his presence. The siddha said: "To enable me to go to Tibet, you should remove your defilements! This fever of yours removed many of your defilements. This time you made an attempt on your own life for my sake, and this has completely removed your defilements. Now I shall go to Tibet." Having promised, the siddha proceeded to Tibet and spent 18 months in Upper gTsaṅ, and preached the Doctrine to many scholars and monks. He also blessed the foundation of the chief vihāra and the great image of Khro-phu (Khro-phu Byams-čhen, the large image of Maitreya at Khro-phu). The lo-tsā-ba attended on the siddha as far as the Pass of Maṅ-yul. Mitrayogin having packed the gold received by him in Tibet in two packages, hung them on his shoulder, and proceeded away, like a falcon chasing his prey. The branches of the Doctrine (the collection of his teachings is well-known by the name of Mi-tra brgya-rtsa and are used in initiation) taught

by him were: the Cycles of the Ordinary Doctrines preached as branches of science, the Cycle of different practices taught as method of inner meditation, the Cycles of the Special Doctrine preached as an introduction to hidden initiation. The first Cycle: it was divided (into the following sections): the bsTan-pa' gru-bo 'čhiṅ-ba rnam-grol (the Boat of the Doctrine which frees from bondages), the rNal-'byor bdun-gyi lam rnam-par-ṅes-pa (The Ascertainment of the Path of the seven Yogas), the Yid-bžin nor-bu (Cintāmaṇi), the bSre-ba bži'i gdams-ṅag and the Rin-čhen phreṅ-ba (the Garland of Jewels). The second Cycle was divided into: (1) the Sādhana of his tutelary deity the Great Merciful One (Mahākaruṇika), and (2) the methods of benefitting others and himself by it. The first (the Sādhana) was divided into twenty mūla-sādhanas (rtsa-ba'i sgrul-thabs) and twenty sādhanas of realization (dṅos-grub sgrub-pa), forty in all. The first: the Yid-bžin nor-bu'i sgrubs-thabs-lha-ñis-stoṅ-sum-bču-ma (the 2030 gods of the sādhana of the Wish-granting Gem), the Ye-śes 'khor-lo-lha lṅa-bču-rtsa-lṅa-ma (the 55 gods of the Jñānacakra), the 'Gro-'dul-lha-sum-bču-rtsa-dgu-ma (39 gods of the maṇḍala of 'Gro-'dul), the 'Khor-los bsgyur-ba-lha-gsum-bču-rtsa-gsum-ma (32 gods of the Cakravartin), the Po-ta-la'i ri'i rtse-mo-lha-ñi-śu-rtsa-lṅa-ma (the 25 gods of the Summit of Mount Potala), the rṄa-sgra-lha-bču-gsum-ma (belongs to the Cycle of Amitābha), the Luṣ-kyi 'khor-lo 'bar-ba'i sgrub-thabs-lha-bču-gčig-ma (the Eleven Gods of the sādhana of Lus-kyi 'khor-lo 'bar-ba), the Rigs-lṅa'i sgrub-thabs (the Sādhana of the Dhyāni-Buddhas), the mKha'-spyod-kyi sgrub-pa (the sādhana of mkha'-spyod), the Tshad-med-bži-sgrub-pa (the sādhana of the catvāryapramāṇāni), the bsKal-bzaṅ-gi sgrub-thabs phyag-stoṅ-pa (the Bhadra-kalpa-sādhana of the Thousand-Armed One), the Žal-bču-gčig-pa (the Sādhana of the Eleven-faced), the 'Jig-rten sgron-ma Yi-ge drug-pa (The Six Letters Formula—"The Lamp of the World"), the Khasarpaṇa tshigs-bčad bži-pa (the four verses of Khasarpaṇa), the Khasarpaṇa 'Jig-rten dbaṅ-phyug (the Khasarpaṇa-Lokeśvara), the Don-žags (Amoghapaśa), the Seṅ-ge sgra (Siṃhanāda), the Draṅ-sroṅ-gi sgrub-pa (Ṛṣi-sādhana), and the Loṅs-sku sku-gsum-gyi sgrub-pa (the Sādhana of the Trinity of Saṃbhoga-kāya). (14a)

The second (dṅos-grub sgrub-pa'i sgrub-thabs): the Loṅs-spyod mi-bzad-pa'i sgrub-pa (the Rite of obtaining inexhaustible wealth), the Nam-mkha' mdzod (Gaganagañja, the Treasury of Heaven), the dPag-bsam śiṅ-čan (Kalpadru-ma, the Wishing Tree), the Cintāmaṇi (Yid-bžin nor-bu), the Bum-pa bzaṅ-po (Kāmaghaṭa, the Pot of Fortune), the 'Dod-'Jo'i-ba (Kāmadhenu, the cow of plenty), the rDo-rJe rin-po-čhe (Vajraratna), the gTer-čhen-po (Mahānidhi, the Great Treasure), the Ñi-zla 'bar-ba (the Shining of the Sun and Moon), the Ral-gri rin-po-čhe (khaḍgaratna, the Precious Sword), the bDud-rtsi'i bum-pa (Amṛtakalaśa, the Vase of Nectar), the Ma-rmos lo-thog (Akṛṣṭoptātaṇḍula-phala-śālī, Mhvpt, No. 5310), the Khrus-kyi rdziṅ-bu (puṣkariṇī, the Swimming Pool), the sMan-gyi bčud-len (Rasāyana), the dṄos-grub ril-bu (Siddhigolā, the Miracu-lous Pill), the Draṅ-sroṅ rig-byed (Ṛṣiveda, Astrology), the rDzogs-ldan-gyi sprin (Satyayuga-megha, the Cloud of Golden Age), the gSer-'gyur-gyi rtsi (Substance changing metals into gold, alchemy, Rasa), the Čaṅ-śes-kyi rta (Ajāneyahaya, the Wise steed), the Balavajra-sādhana (sTobs-kyi rdo-rJe'i sgrub-thabs), the ten 'preceding' doctrines (belonging) to the svārtha class (raṅ-don-la sṅon-'gro'i čhos-bču), the dṄos-gži'i bču-gñis (the Twelve main doctrines), the 'Čhi-ba-la dgos-pa'i čhos-bdun (the Seven doctrines required at death). From among these 29 books; the first: the Dam-tshig gso-ba (Restoration of Vows), the bLa-ma sgrub-pa (the propitiation of the Teacher), the Byin-rlabs mi-bzad-pa (the inexhaustible blessing), the sToṅ-ñid sgom-pa (the Meditation on Relativity), the Khro-ba spaṅ-ba (the Removal of Anger), the sÑiṅ-gi dug sbyaṅ-ba (the Removal of Heart poison), the Ži-gnas bskyed-pa (the Birth of

Quiescence of the Mind), the Tiṅ-'dzin myur-du bskyed-pa (the quick method of producing Mind-concentration), the Zuṅ-'brel-gyi gnad (the Main point of the yuganaddha), and the Ye-śes 'bar-ba (Kindling of knowledge). Among the second: the "Six Books illucidating the Degree of Utpanna-krama" (bsKyed-rim gsal-bar-byed-pa'i čhos-drug), the Padma-sdoṅ-bu-čan-gyi sgrub-pa (the Sādhana of the One holding the Lotus stalk), the Me-tog-gdan-čan-gyi sgrub-pa (the Sādhana of the One Sitting on the Flower), the Me-tog-la brten-pa'i sgrub-pa (Flower Sādhana), the gZugs-brñan-gyi bsgrub-pa (the Sādhana of the Image), the Dri-ma med-pa'i sgrub-pa (the Sādhana of the Immaculate), theYe-ge med-pa'i sgrub-pa (the Sādhana of the Unwritten). The Six Books of the Sampanna-krama degree: the 'Khor-lo-gsum bsgom-pa (Meditation on the Three Cakras), the 'Khor-lo-bčiṅs-grol (the Binding and the unbinding of Cakras), the Ye-śes 'bar-ba (the Kindling of Knowledge), the 'Khor-lo 'bar-ba (the Kindling of Cakras), the 'Khor-lo rnam-dag (Purification of Cakras), and the rDor-Je 'bar-ba'i bsruṅ-ba (the Protection of the flaming Vajra). The third: Raṅ-bsruṅ-pa (Self-protection), the Nad-gsal-ba (Healing of Ailments), the 'Čhi-ba blu-ba (the Ransoming of Death), the 'Groṅ-'Jug (parakāya-praveśa, the Transference of the life-principle), the 'Pho-ba rdo-rJe skar-mda' (the Shooting diamond star of the transference of the life-principle), the rMi-lam dri-med (Immaculate dreams), and the sKye-ba bsdams-pa (Restriction of Rebirth). Among the texts of benefit to others (gžan-don): the sŃon-'gro'i čhos-bču (the Ten preceding Books), and the Twelve Main Books (dṅos-gži'i čhos-bču). The Seven Books especially required by a disciple: the first: the Grags-pa spel-ba (Increase of Fame), the gZi-byin bskyed-pa (Increase of Lustre), the Sems-čan-'gu-byed (Gladdening of living beings), the Ṅag-gi mthu-bskyed-pa (Production of the Power of Speech), the gŚaṅ-sṅags myur-'grub (the "Quick realization of Mantras"), the sMon-lam dbaṅ-du byed-pa (the Control of Wishes), the Dregs-pa ži-ba (14*b*)
(The Subduing of Pride), the Sems-brtan-par-byed-pa (the

Steadying of Mind), and the Sems ṅal-so-ba (the Resting of the Mind), the Yid-'gyod-pa bsal-ba (the Removal of Mental Afflictions). Among the second (group): the gDug-pa 'dul-ba'i čho-ga (the Rite of subduing demons), the gŽan-las rnam-rgyal (the Defeat of Others), the gNod-pa bzlog-pa (the Repulsion of Harm), the sDe-gžom-pa (the Destruction of Enemies' Troops), the dBaṅ-du bya-ba (the Control of Others), the Ṅag-mnon (Causing enemies to become dumb), the bKra-śis-kyi čho-ga (Auspicious Rite), the gŽan-bskyab-pa (Protection of Others), the Mi-'Jigs-pa sbyin-pa (the Gift of Courage), the Nad gso-ba (the Removal of Diseases), the kLu-nad gso-ba (the Curing of ailments caused by Nāgas), the Tshe-'das sbyoṅ-ba (funeral ceremony), and the Ro-bsreg-gi čho-ga (the Rite of Cremation). The third: the rMi-lam rab-brtan (Indications contained in dreams), the rMi-lam ṅan-bzlog (the Removal of Evil Dreams), the Śes-rab bskyed-čhog (the Rite of Producing Wisdom), the Byaṅ-čhub sems-dpa'i byin-rlabs (the Blessing of Bodhisattvas), the Raṅ-byin-rlabs (Self-blessing), the Tiṅ-ṅe-'dzin-gyi dbaṅ-bskur (Initiation into Samādhi), and the Ye-śes dgug-gzug-gi byin-rlabs. The 24 books required ordinarily (Thun-moṅ-du dgos-pa'i čhos), and among them the "Twelve Merit Accumulating Books": the sKu-gzugs-kyi čho-ga (the rite of erecting images) named sKu-gzugs rin-po-čhe'i las, the mČhod-rten-gyi bsñen-bkur (the Worship of a Stūpa), the bSam-mi-khyab-kyi mčhod-pa (the Unconceivable Worship), the Maṇḍala'i čho-ga (the Rite of the Maṇḍala), the Čhos-spyod yan-lag-bži-pa (the Four Branches of the Dharmacaryā), the Čhos-spyod brgya-rtsa (The Hundred /forms/of Dharmacaryā), the Zas-kyi rnal-'byor (the Yoga of taking food), the Lus-sbyin-pa (the Offering of one's own body), the gTor-ma'i čho-ga (the Rite of Offering), the Čhu-sbyin (Water Offering), the Čhu-gtor (Water Libation), and the sByin-bsreg (homa). The five 'Gal-rkyen-spaṅ-ba (the Five removals of accidents): the Čhom-rkun bčiṅ-ba (the Binding of robbers), the Nad-bsruṅ-ba (Protection from Diseases), the mDze-gso-ba (Curing of leprosy), the Čhar-bzlog (the Stopping of Rain), the 'Čhi-ba bsruṅ-ba (Protection from Death). The five sādhanas of 'Thun-rkyen (favourable causes), the Rab-gnas (consecration rite), the bSruṅ-'khor (charms), the Sruṅ-skud (holy thread), the Sri'u gso-pa (Protection of children), and the Čhar-dbab-pa (the Production of rain). Thus 20 mūla-sādhanas (rtsa-ba'i sgrub-thabs), and 20 sādhanas for the attainment of siddhis, in all 40. 29 doctrines of self-benefit, 29 doctrines of benefit to others, in all 58. 22 "common" doctrines. In all 120 sādhanas of practice. The initiation of bDe-čhen ral-gčig (Mahāsukha—Ekajaṭī) and the precepts of Avalokiteśvara in 25 ślokas formed part of the Special Cycle, expounding the Introduction to the Hidden Blessing. The Chapter on the Spiritual Lineage of Khro-pu-ba. (15*a*)

Further, the Phyag-rgya čhen-po 'Khor-ba rgyun-gčod (The Mahāmudrā which cuts the stream of Saṃsāra): A group of five ḍākinīs came forth from the miraculous great Kun-snaṅ (Samantābhāsa) caitya of the country of Dharmagañja (Čhos-kyi mdzod) in Oḍḍiyāna, and preached this doctrine to Śrī Saraha, who taught it to Mitra. The latter bestowed the Čhiṅs-gsum (the "There Summaries"), the "Five Specials" (Khyad-par lṅa), and the Twenty Commentaries ('grel-pa ñi-śu) ending with the bsṄo-ba (Good Wishes), to Ma-gčig Saṅs-rgyas Re-ma. She imparted it to mTshan-ldan 'Khrul-žig čhen-po on the Mount Don-mo. He was a native of Zaṅs-ri, and was ordained in his youth at Thel. He practised meditation in many sacred places, such as the Kailāsa (Ti-se), and others. He stayed at Jo-naṅ, and there met Ma-gčig, who bestowed on him the precepts of the rGyun-gČod (or 'Khor-ba rgyun-gčod). He also met Mitra and developed excellent merit. He lived for more than eighty years. He imparted the doctrine to the siddha Žwa-dmar-ba Grags-pa seṅ-ge, who bestowed it on mKhas-grub-rgyal-ba. The latter on the Dharmasvāmin mKha'-spyod-pa, and wrote a Guide (on the doctrine).

Further, 'Khrul-žig-pa expounded it to mDzes-ma at 'On. mDzes-ma was born in Upper gTsaṅ. She met many sid-

dhas. In her youth she came to Gaṅs-dkar čhu-kha in 'On. Being an expert in the prāṇāyāma (rtsa-rluṅ), she could not be tempted. Whenever some one attempted to tempt her, she would draw all his well-being into herself, and her complexion would assume a shining appearance, while the other would look like a dying man. She composed many books on her mystic experience, and passed away at the age of about seventy. (After the cremation of her remains), her heart and both the eyes were left unburnt. One of the eyes was (preserved) at Gaṅs-dkar, the other at rGya-gar of Do-po-sgaṅ, and the heart was preserved inside the Pad-spuṅs caitya at dPal-ri. mDzes-ma bestowed (the Doctrine) on Bya-bral čhen-po, who was a native of Yar-kluṅs. Most of the time he stayed in Koṅ-po. He died at 'On. In the beginning he used to be a very cleanly person, and disliked others, but afterwards he achieved emancipation independently (of others), used to eat his own excrement and applied it to his body. At times he offered it to the Ratna, at times to demons (of the rGyal-po and 'goṅ-po class), and imitated insanity (smyon-spyod). He was a priest of Thel. He met (15b)
Mitra at Śar-brag. He also met Lha-rJe (Dags-po Lha-rJe) at sGam-po. He met Mid-la at 'Ol-kha. He passed away at mTsho-phyi maṅ-khaṅ of 'On, aged seventy. He bestowed (the Doctrine) on Saṅs-rgyas Ri-pa, whose native place was Yar-kluṅs. At the age of 20, he met sPyan-sṅa Čhos-bži-pa and followed after every good Teacher. He heard the 'Khor-ba rgyun-gčod (the doctrine of Mitra). He acted as Vajradhara for five years at Kailāsa. He became the Teacher of dbOn-po dPal-ldan-grags and of Upper Hor (sTod-Hor, Moghulistān), and received the title of "Imperial Preceptor" (Ti-śrī<Ti-shih). Having come to Koṅ-po he practised the 'Khor-ba rgyun-gčod at the monastery of Śar. He founded a monastery on the summit of sPe-ra in 'On, and called it dPal-ri. He had numerous visions of tutelary deities. He died at the age of 79, and was reborn in gTsaṅ. He bestowed (the Doctrine) on sPrul-sku bLo-ldan, who was born at Yar-kluṅs rnam-rgyal.

He was ordained by Čhos-bži-gsar-ma-pa in his youth. At the age of 20, he successfully propitiated Vajrapāṇi. From the age of 20 to 24, he laboured for the welfare of others, and then proceeded to the Alakāvatī (lČaṅ-lo-čan, the Paradise of Vajrapāṇi, originally Vajrapāṇi was believed to have been the son of Vaiśravaṇa residing in Alakāvatī on the southern slope of Mount Meru). The latter bestowed (the Doctrine) on the bLa-ma bDag-pa, who belonged to the Śud clan. He was born as the son of a Tantric. Endowed with great faith, he promised in the presence of Kar-ma-pa to recite a 100,000,000 times the Maṇi formula. Till twenty, he lived the life of a householder. Between twenty and fifty, he made a round of hermitages, and practised meditation. At the age of 22, he took up ordination under Kun-spaṅs-pa. At the age of 35, he took up the final monastic ordination in the presence of the mahā-upādhyāya bKra-śis seṅ-ge, and listened to about a hundred expositions (of sacred texts), such as the Doctrine of the "Great Achievement" (rDzogs-čhen), and others. He visited about a hundred hermitages, including Čhu-bar and others. In brief: he was born in the year Earth-Female-Sheep (sa-mo-lug—1199 A. D.). At the age of 16, he met Kar-ma-pa. At the age of 20, he took up the upāsaka vows in the presence of Lho-pa Rin-po-čhe. He died at the age of 82 in the year Iron-Dragon (lčags-'brug—1280 A.D.). There appears to exist a numerous Lineage. The Spiritual Lineage of the yoginī named Čhos-ldan-'bum seems to exist in the East and West. This (doctrine) must be recognized as being profound. The Chapter on 'Khor-ba rgyun-gčod. (16*a*)

Further, the mahāsiddha Mitra came to Tibet, after having performed the Yoga called Balarasa. Now the Lineage of the mKha'-spyod bsñen-sgrub preached by him (a book belonging to the Kar-ma-pa sect): The ācārya mTsho-skyes rdo-rje (Saroruha, Padmavajra) bestowed it on Pad-ma'i myu-gu (Padmāṅkuravajra) who was a paṇḍita learned in the five sciences. After having obtained these precepts, he developed an immortal Vajrakāya (mystic body). He bestowed (the Doctrine) on the yogeśvara Mitrayogin. The latter preached to Žwa-dmar čod-paṇ-'dzin-pa Grags-pa seṅ-ge the Cycle of Precepts of Prāṇāyāma, including the Srog-thig rnam-'Joms (of a book), and other texts, as well as many lesser precepts. In particular, he imparted to him the precepts of the mKha'-spyod bsñen-sgrub, its basic text, together with its initiation, branches and exposition. The latter preached all the precepts of the "Oral Tradition", in the manner of a well-filled vase, to the hermit (ri-khrod-pa) Dar-rgyal-ba. The latter preached to dPal mKha'-spyod dbaṅ-po, and also composed a text-book. Again, Grags-seṅ-ba (Gras-pa seṅ-ge) preached it to 'Jam-dbyaṅs Čhos-dor-ba, who also composed a large text-book.

The Chapter on the mKha'-spyod bsñen-sgrub.

Again, Mitra bestowed the precepts of the Six Doctrines (čhos-drug) on the paṇḍita Śāriputta. The latter imparted them to Mi-ñag Grags-pa rin-čhen. His Lineage continues to exist to the present day, and its (teachings) are followed at sMyug-tshal of Lho-brag, There appear also to exist preachers (of this doctrine).

The Lineage of the Initiations known as Mitra brgya-rtsa: rDo-rJe-'čhaṅ (Vajradhara), Avalokiteśvara (sPyan-ras-gzigs), the siddha Mitrayogin. The latter imparted it to the paṇḍita Amoghavajra (Don-yod rdo-rJe). He came to bestow the initiation and its exposition on gČan 'Od-sruṅs mgon-po of gSar-mda' khra-luṅ. At the time of his going to Lower Khams (mDo-Khams) he appears to have bestowed once more all the initiations at Ge-kha-brag. But in later times when the Lineage of Initiations appeared to have come to an end, several kalyāṇa-mitras from Lower Khams (mDo-khams) passed through sGyi-smad khra-luṅ in search of the Lineage. People said: "The lay-brother (upāsaka) named mGo-Khom Jo-sras, a disciple of gČan 'Od-sruṅs mgon-po who lives at 'Phan-yul rGyal, perhaps possesses the Lineage." The kalyāṇa-mitras proceeded to 'Phan-yul in search of him. Byams-pa seṅ-ge, a kalyāṇa-mitra of rGyal, came to gSaṅ-phu to hear the "Doctrine of Maitreya" (Byams-čhos). They met him and inquired about mGo-khom J̌o-sras. Byams-pa seṅ-ge replied: "He was my countryman! But I doubt that he possesses the Hundred Initiations. He used to be an old Tantric, good-natured and pious. With you, I shall also ask for them." Then it is said that he obtained them. Those who did not believe the statement of Byams-pa seṅ-ge (about his obtaining precepts), instead met mGo-khom J̌o-sras himself and obtained the initiations from him. Byams-pa seṅ-ge and Ba-lam-pa Rin-śe exchanged the Initiation and the Vajramālā (rDo-rJe 'phreṅ-ba) of Abhaya. gYun-ston rDo-rJe-dpal obtained it from Ba-lam-pa Rin-śeat-mTshur-phu. rDo-rJe-dpal bestowed it on Bag-ston gŽon-tshul. The latter imparted it to the bLa-ma Tshul-rgyal of sNar-thaṅ. The latter bestowed it on the bla-ma mGon-po-drug. The latter on the Paṇ-čhen 'J̌am-dbyaṅs ral-gri. The latter on Kun-mkhyen 'Dzam-gliṅ Ṅi-śar. The latter on the Dharmasvāmin sTan-gčig-pa Śes-rab bzaṅ-po. I gave here an account of only one Lineage, but (the teaching) was handed down through many other Lineages also.

The Chapter on the system, which originated from the Mahāsiddha Mitra.

The doctrine known as the "Clear Exposition of the Siddha Tshem-bu-pa" (Grub-thob Tshem-bu-pa'i dmar-khrid) also belongs to the Cycle of the Great Merciful One (Mahākaruṇika). Nairātmā bestowed it on the siddha gÑan Tshem-bu-pa named Dar-ma 'od-zer. He was born at Śad-sgo-dar. He did not accept the monastery of sTon-mo-luṅ, and others which were offered to him by rṄog bTsun-dkar-mo, practised meditation only on the mountain of gYas-ru, and attained spiritual realization. He had six disciples to whom he imparted precepts. He bestowed them on a kalyāṇa-mitra of (17a)
'Briṅ-mtshams lčim-luṅ and on the scholar of the Yul-la monastery. These two also attained spiritual realization, and later sent on three occasions offerings to him. He also

bestowed (precepts) on his younger brother sPyil-po dBaṅ-phyug-grags and on his attendant Čhe-brag-pa, as well as on rṄog bTsun-dkar-mo. These also attained spiritual realization with the help of this doctrine. sPyi-bo-lhas-pa Byaṅ-čhub-'od studied many sūtras and śāstras, but he did not know how to practise them combined. He therefore went to Lha-sa to pray to the Lord (J̌o-bo), and there he met gÑan Tshem-bu-pa, and understood him to be a siddha. He made his request to him, and the Teacher understood him to be a suitable vessel (snod-ldan) and bestowed on him the Phyi-theg-pa Lam-rim spuṅs-kyi don-khrid and the Naṅ-gsaṅ-sṅags-kyi dmar-khrid. He practised according to them, and attained spiritual realization. He imparted them to Byaṅ-čhub tshul-khrims, the upādhyāya of sTag-bde brag-dmar. The latter bestowed them on the Bodhisattva Lha-btsun-pa, the upādhyāya of Phyi-'brum dgon-gsar. The latter on Žaṅ Kun-spaṅs-pa. It became one of the great guide-books of the J̌o-naṅ-pas. This (Doctrine) spread in all directions, and great was the benefit. Some of the methods of exposition appear to agree with those of Mahāmudrā. In other texts it was described as agreeing with the pratyāhāra (restraining the organs, sor-sdus) of the Ṣadaṅga-yoga. Also there existed a Lineage of the dmar-khrid (detailed exposition) of the Cycle of the Great Merciful One (Mahākaruṇika). The nun Lakṣmī (dGe-sloṅ-ma dPal-mo) imparted it to dPal-gyi bzaṅ-po (Śrībhadra). The latter on Rin-čhen bzaṅ-po (Ratnabhadra), who imparted it to Atiśa. The latter bestowed it on Yol Čhos-dbaṅ. The lattet on Rog-ston. The latter on rTse-ston J̌o-sras. The latter on Žaṅ-ston Čhos-dbaṅ. The latter on Phra-ston Žig-po. The latter on rNal-'byor skyabs-se. The latter on Rin-po-čhe Ne-mig-pa. The latter on the upādhyāya Rin-byuṅ. The latter on the upādhyāya Saṅs-gžon. The latter on the bla-ma Kun-brsod-pa. The latter transmitted it to mKhasgrub Čhos-dpal, father and son. The Chapter on the dmarkhrid (detailed exposition) of the method (lugs) of Tshem-bu-pa. The Chapter (17b) on the Cycle of the Great Merciful One (Mahākaruṇika).

Among the lČags-ri-bas and the sÑan-čhad-pas there
as a precept called Nar-mkha' skor-gsum. It represented
pratyāhāra precept which served as a Path (of spiritual
:velopment), based on the doctrine of Śūnyatā. It was
excellent precept transmitted from the ṛsi Sūryaratha
Ñi-ma'i śiṅ-rta, a ṛsi of Śambhala) to Kālacakrapāda,
e Senior and Junior, Abhiyukta, the Nepālese Kāyaśrī, the
ārya Kan-pa-ba, and others. The Lineage of the great
:e of the maṇḍala called Kṛyāsamuccaya (Vajrācāryakṛyā-
muccaya, Tg. rGyud, No. 3305), composed by the siddha
med Dar-paṇ (Darpaṇa-ācārya), whose teeth had changed
venty times and who had lived for a thousand two hundred
ars, through which the initiation was transmitted:
ajradhara (rDo-rJe-'čhaṅ), Jñānaḍāka (Ye-śes mkha'-'gro),
arpaṇa-ācārya, Samantabhadra, Jñānajyoti, Śrī Hanumat, Śrī
Iañjubhadra, Śrī Lakṣmībhadra, Dharmajyotirbhadra, Mano-
'abhadra, So-tram Śrībhadra, Śrī Vijayabhadra, Śrī Madan-
hadra, Śrī Lakṣmībhadra, Gaganabhadra, Udayajīvabhadra,
ī Harṣabhadra, Abhāgabhadra, the Nepālese paṇḍita of Ye-
ṅ—Jagadānandajīvabhadra, his son the paṇḍita Mahābodhi,
bzaṅ 'Phags-pa gŽon-nu blo-gros (also known by the name
Ma-ti paṇ-čhen), the Dharmasvāmin Kun-dga' bzaṅ-po, and
ıus) to the Dharmasvāmin dMar-ston rGyal-mtshan 'od-zer.

The origin of the Doctrine: Since in former times there
l not exist translations of it into Tibetan, 'Jam-dbyaṅs Don-
d rgyal-mtshan of dPal-ldan Sa-skya obtained the Sanskrit
κt of the Samuccaya from a Nepālese merchant (this very
py is preserved at the Ṅor monastery in gTsaṅ. Verbal
mmunication by Rev. dGe-'dun Čhos-'phel). This book
ıs then found in the possession of Kun-spaṅs Čhos-grags-
al-bzaṅ-po. It was translated at the latter's request and
th his assistance by Mañjuśrī, a great paṇḍita of Vikrama-
ı, and the Tibetan translator (lo-tsā-ba) Sa-bzaṅ-pa bLo-
)s rgyal-mtshan. While they were unable to find any one
m whom they could obtain its initiation and "permi-
on" (luṅ) to read it, they heard a report that mṄa'-ris-pa

rDo-rJe-dpal had obtained the initiation of the Samuccya at Ye-ran (Kāṭhamāndu). 'Phags-pa gŽon-nu blo-gros with his disciples, seven persons in all, proceeded to Ye-ran in Nepāl, and there obtained the complete initiation and "permission" (luṅ) to read the Text from the paṇḍita Mahābodhi. It spread widely. Again, the Blessed gŚin-rJe mthar-byed (Yamāntakṛt), Virūpa, Ḍombhī-pa, the brāhmaṇa Śrīdhara (dPal-'dzin), Matigarbha, Darpaṇa-ācārya who bestowed on gLo-bo lo-tsā-ba the gŚin rJe gśed-dmar-po'i gzuṅ with its exposition and precepts. The lo-tsā-ba bestowed it on bLo-čhen Saṅs-rgyas. The latter on the lo-tsā-ba mČhog-ldan. The latter on bKa'-bču-pa gŽon-nu seṅ-ge. Also following another Lineage, it was practised by Bu-ston Rin-po-čhe and others, and numerous living beings were nourished by it. The Chapter on Dar-paṇ (Darpaṇa-ācārya). (18a)

The ācārya Abhaya who was endowed with a mind free of illusions in regard to any of the systems of the Prajñāpāramitā or Tantra. from the Lesser sciences (rig-gnas phra-mo) to the Anuttara-yoga-Tantra. Because he had recited the mantra of Vajra-yoginī in his former life, in this life Vajra-yoginī in the form of an ordinary woman appeared before the ācāryā Abhaya. Because of his steadfast attitude of a strick monk, he did not admit this woman. (His) great teachers, such at Kā-so-ri-pa and others, told him that he had acted wrongly by not availing himself of the method through which one could realize the sahaja-jñāna. On many occasions he prayed to Vajra-yoginī. The goddess appeared to him in a dream, and said: "Now, in this life you will not be united with me. But, if you were to compose many commentaries on profound Tantras and many rites of Maṇḍalas, you would soon become (18 a fortunate one." Following her instructions, he composed the Śrīsampuṭatantrarājaṭīkāmnāyamañjarī-nāma (Tg. rGyud, No. 1198), the Śrī-Buddhakapālamahātantrarājaṭīkā-abhayapaddhati-nāma (Mi-'Jigs-pa'i gžuṅ-'grel, Tg. rGyud, No. 1654), and the Vajrāvali-nāma-maṇḍalasādhana (dKyil-'khor-gyi čho-ga rDo-rJe phreṅ-ba, Tg. rGyud, No. 3140). Now, it is said that when the mahā-paṇḍita from Kāśmīra (Śākyaśrībhadra) bestowed on three occasions the initiation of the Vajrāvali (rDo-rJe phreṅ-ba), on the first two occasions he performed all (the maṇḍala rites) accompanied by rites of the Anuttara-Tantra (only), and on the last occasion he said: "The Tibetans are very suspicious! Had I not divided (these maṇḍalas) according to the different classes of Tantras, they would not accept the initiations (through their suspicious nature)." Therefore he divided them according to the classes of Tantras and thus bestowed the initiations.

Chag lo-tsā-ba Chos-rJe-dpal[1] heard it from Ravīndra. He maintained the point of view, that by being initiated into the twenty-eight maṇḍalas one could obtain (the initiations) of all the others. The lo-tsā-ba Grags-pa rgyal-mtshan (the Yar-kluṅs lo-tsā-ba) obtained it from Bhūmiśrī, the mahā-paṇḍita of Kāśmīra. He used to bestow initiations, having arranged them into 45 maṇḍalas. His Holiness Śrī Vanaratna, the mahā-paṇḍita of Eastern India, bestowed on two occasions the initiation of Vajrāvali at the royal palace of sNe'u-gdoṅ. He used to bestow all these initiations according to the system of the Anuttara-Tantra. Some remarked that it was not proper to initiate according to different classes of Tantras, but he replied: ("It would be good to divide them". They again inquired:) "Well then why did you not perform them in accordance with this method?" He replied: "Did I not bestow on you the initiation according to the method of Abhaya? Abhaya did not divide the initiations according to the different classes of the (Tantras), why should I do so?". The Vajrāvali having been translated by many lo-tsā-bas, there exist many differ-

1 A famous Tibetan pilgrim to the Sacred Places of India. The author of a well-known description of Mahābodhi. Born 1197 A.D., died 1265 A.D. A well-known Sanskrit scholar. His biography (rnam-thar) exists in Tibetan. His description of the Mahābodhi is found in the Tibetan collection in the Patna Museum.

ent versions (of it). Nowadays most people favour the translation by Čhag (lo-tsā-ba). Now, the ācārya Abhaya composed a maṇḍala rite belonging to the Sampannakrama-yoga, basing himself on the Tantric text (Guhyasamāja) which said: "One should know the three classes of Yoga, that of blessing, that of imagination (Yoṅs-brtags) and that of the complete manifestation of form." There were many (194)
who used to think: "If one would not propitiate according to the methods of different sādhanas, preached by various teachers, and (expounded) in different Tantras, the propitiations would not be complete. If so, a fully-enlightened (Buddha) cannot propitiate even a single maṇḍala, because he is free of constructive thought. Can you avoid this contradiction! Such people should be initiated according to different rites, and not according to the Vajrāvali belonging to the system of Abhaya. Similarly also one should not speak slightingly of those who bestowed initiations according to the 'Ocean of Sādhanas' (sGrub-thabs rgya-mtsho), transmitted through Abhayākaragupta, Puṇyākaragupta (dGe-ba'i 'byuṅ-gnas sbas-pa), the siddha gLoṅ-žabs, the paṇḍita Kīrticandra, and the lo-tsā-ba Grags-pa rgyal-mtshan, because one is unable to establish whether one is fit or not to enter into this great mystic sphere (dkyil 'khor čhen-po). One should class similarly the sGrub-thabs brgya-rtsa ("Hundred Sādhanas") and other texts transmitted by rDo-rje gdan-pa to Ba-ri lo-tsā-ba. The Chapter on the origin of Vajrāvali (rDo-rje phreṅ-ba) and other texts. I have written the above account of Tantric and Sūtra doctrines, basing myself on that which had been seen by me, heard (by me) from my Teachers, obtained (by me) in the biographies of other (teachers), and read in histories, but, because of my feeble mind, I was not able to relate it all. There have been countless books, some of them believed to have been imparted by gods, such as the many profound doctrines taught by the guhyapati Vajrapāṇi to the mahā-upādhyāya Las-kyi rdo-rje, and the numerous teachings bes-

owed by the Venerable Mañjughoṣa on the teacher dbU-ma-pa.[1] Some of these books have been composed in the style of the Tantras by those endowed with the Yoga of the Ultimate Essence (Tattvatā, bdag-ñid de-kho-ñid). There (19b) exist also numerous psalms expounding (mystic) practices. One should not speak slightingly of them, because of their faulty composition, etc., unless they contradict the three moral precepts (śikṣā ; higher morality, higher thought and higher learning).

Because, as stated in the Vimalaprabhā :

"Even through spoken idiom and broken words,
One, possessed of Yoga, is able to grasp the meaning,
Just as a swan knows how to suck out milk mixed with water.

Great Ones often place no confidence in words,
When investigating the foundation of the Absolute.
If one is able to grasp the meaning with the help of a spoken language,
What use is there of a classical language (i.e. Sanskrit)?"

I have also heard that the inmates of Ri-bo-čhe possessed the exposition of many sādhanas and the Hevajra-Tantra preached by one called the siddha Jñāna to sTag-luṅ Saṅs-rgyas-dbon. During the period preceding the coming of Atīśa to mÑa'-ris, a certain a-tsa-ra dMar-po (the "Red One") also named Śes-rab gsaṅ-ba, a paṇḍita from Oḍḍiyāna, who had become the disciple of Ratnavajra, the Kashmirian, propagated the Tantras belonging to the Cycle of Thig-le (Tilaka), such as the Phyag-rgya čhen-po thig-le and others, together with their commentaries and branches, and these were of benefit to the Tibetans (Śrī-Mahāmudrātilaka-nāma-mahāyoginītantra-rājādhipati, Kg. rGyud-'bum, Nos. 420-422; A-tsa-ra dMar-po was held responsible by some historians for the corruption of certain mystic practices belonging to the Anuttara-yoga-

1. dbU-ma-pa was the teacher of rJe Tsoṅ-kha-pa. He was said to have been the transmitter of Mañjughoṣa's commands and teachings to Tsoṅ-kha-pa.

Tantra. Atiśa came out with a condemnation of these practices. rGyal-ba lṅa-pa'i rgyal-rabs, fol. 48b :] "But Las-čhen Kun-rgyal-ba/a famous historian of the Sa-skya-pa sect, author of a large history of Buddhism in Tibet/says: 'The 'Red' ācārya who had translated the gSaṅ-sṅags Thig-le skor, and compelled many monks to become laymen, was a preacher of a heretical doctrine'. It is true, that some monks who were not his equals in understanding, misunderstood the essence of the Tantras, thus defiling their morality. But who would dare to call such a great siddheśvara as the paṇḍita Śes-rab gsaṅ-ba/in the text Gsaṅ-ba śes-rab/, a heretical teacher, thus causing himself to fall into the bottomless Hell ? Therefore all wise men should abstain from it.") This paṇḍita having again visited Tibet in a later period, became the teacher of the Sa-čhen. Though it is known that the precepts of the sampannakrama degree transmitted through him, continue to exist to the present day, I have not seen books on them. An excellent practice of mystic trance, named gČig-śes Kun-grol (Knowledge which reveals all), which was imparted by a tutelary deity to the Great Venerable Man-luṅs-pa, who had obtained a great Light in the Doctrine, was bestowed by the latter on the Yar-kluṅs lo-tsā-ba Grags-pa rgyal-mtshan. He bestowed it on sÑe-mdo-ba Kun-dga' don-grub. The latter (204)
bestowed it on the bKa'-bču-pa gŽon-nu seṅ-ge. The latter bestowed it on Hūṃ-čhen Nam-mkha' rnal-'byor. It was then handed down to the Guṅ-thaṅ rab-'byams-pa Śes-rab rgyal-mtshan of the present day. The Cycle of the Tārā transmitted by Ravigupta (Ñi-ma sbas-pa). It is said that in the country of Kāśmīra there had been an image of the Ta'u Tārā endowed with miraculous powers (siddhi) in the Temple of Raṅ-byuṅ lha-lṅa. Lepers after worshipping the image were cured of their ailment. About that time the ācārya Ravigupta (Ñi-ma sbas-pa), who was learned in the five sciences and especially in the Tantra, was attacked by leprosy (klu'i gnod-pa). He built a hut for himself to the west of the vihāra, and prayed for three months. Then the

temple's gate moved (by itself) westwards, and the Tārā said: "What is your wish?" and the ācārya replied: "I wish to be cured of leprosy." In that very moment his entire body, except for a small sore on his forehead, assumed its former appearance. He asked: "What was the reason for not curing the sore on the forehead?" The Tārā replied: "Formerly you were born as a hunter, killed animals and in the end set fire to a forest. In consequence of this, you were reborn in Hell and this is your last rebirth of the 500 rebirths in Hell", and saying so, she bestowed on him the sādhana, accompanied by a stotra (which was recited as mantra). The Tārā said "With their help, one may perform any kind of magic rite. I shall grant you miraculous powers (siddhi)". After that the ācārya composed a magic rite which corresponded to the twenty-one sādhanas, as well as general rites and their branches. He taught it to Candragarbha. The latter to Jetāri. The latter to Vāgīśvara (Ṅag-gi dbaṅ-phyug). The latter to Śraddhākara. The latter to Tathāgatarakṣita. The latter to Dānaśīla, who bestowed it on Mal-gyo lo-tsā-ba. In the translation by Mal-gyo the sādhanas and the magic rites were arranged in separate sections, but in the translation by the Khro-phu lo-tsā-ba the magic rites were added in the end of each of the propitiation rites (sādhana). 20b

Its Lineage: the Tārā, Ānanda (Kun-dga'-bo), the arhat Madhyantika (dgra-bčom Ñi-ma-guṅ-pa), Śānavāsin (Śā-na'i gos-čan), Kṛṣṇavāsin (Kṛṣṇa'i gos-čan), the Kashmirian Ravigupta (Kha-čhe Ñi-ma sbas-pa), Rāhulaśrī, Vindaśrī, Paṇ-čhen Śākyaśrī (bhadra). The latter bestowed it on Khro-phu lo-tsā-ba, bla-čhen bSod-dbaṅ, Rin-po čhe-pa, Tshad-ma'i skyes-bu and Bu Rin-po-čhe. Mal-gyo preached it to Sa-čhen.[1] The latter to rTse-mo (one of the five great Sa-skya-pa bla-mas). The latter to the Venerable One (rJe-btsun—one of five Sa-skya-pa bla-mas), who composed many

1 Kun-dga' sñiṅ-po, b. 1092 A.D., d. 1158 A.D.

text books on the system, and taught it to 'Čhims Čhos-seṅ, the Dharmasvāmin 'Jam-gsar, Roṅ-pa rGwa-lo, Śes-rab seṅ-ge, dPal-ldan seṅ-ge, the bLa-ma Dam-pa bSod-nams rgyal-mtshan, the mahā-upādhyāya Śes-rdor-pa, Čhos-sgo-ba Čhos-kyi rgya-mtshan, and rGod-phrug Grags-pa 'byuṅ-gnas. I obtained it from the latter. In general, the cycle of the Tārā (transmitted) through different Lineages filled Tibet. The Chapter on miscellaneous doctrines.

The sTeṅs-pa lo-tsā-ba Tshul-khrims 'byuṅ-gnas whose benefit was great for the Lineage of the Recitation of the Sūtras in Tibet: He was born in the year Fire-Female-Hog (me-mo-phag—1107 A.D.) as son of father sTeṅ-pa Tog-'bar and mother mDa'-mo Bu-skyid. At the age of six he peeped through a hole in the Wall and saw numerous countries (filled) with caityas. Later when he came to India, he discovered it to (be the same country seen previously by him). At the age of ten, he recited some mantras of Acala and was able to cure the ailments of others by blowing on the patient. From his childhood he placed confidence in the Ratna. At the age of 13, he proceeded to Dags-po, because of ill-treatment by his step-mother. He conveyed to his father's house all presents received by him for reciting sacred texts, but his father scolded him. He became sad, and again returned to Dags-po. There he cut his hair in the 21a
presence of sKan-mo gnas-brtan, and assumed the appearance of a monk. He had auspicious dreams. At the age of 15, he took up ordination in the presence of rGya-'dul in Upper Myaṅ. He learnt the "Domain of Practice" (sPyod—phyogs) from Čhims, the "All-knowing". He received the final monastic ordination, bTsun-Śul-rgya acting as upādhyāya, dGe-'dun-skyabs of gÑal acting as ācārya, and Tshul-'phags of sKyi acting as Secret Preceptor (gsaṅ-ston, gsaṅ-ste ston-pa, raho'nuśāsaka, Mhvtpt, No. 8730). Desirous of going to India, but having no gold (to take with him), he copied two volumes of the Śatasāhasrikā Prajñāpāramitā. For this he received 12 golden žos, which he took with him. When

he reached Diṅ-ri, Ārya Avalokiteśvara in the guise of an old man, showed him the road. When he reached Nepāl, he prayed for a safe journey to 'Phags-pa 'Ja'-ma-li (at Kāṭhamāndu/Nepāl/. Nowadays called by Tibetan pilgrims 'Dzamgliṅ dkar-mo) and other images. Then without regard for his life, he journeyed to India and met in Magadha Tsa-mi Saṅs-rgyas grags-pa. He spent ten years with him and then fell ill with malaria. The Tārā prescribed him an ablution, and he was cured. About that time his younger brother Čhos-'bar sold the field, and realized much gold. He left Dags-po and went inquiring about his brother, and thus arrived in Vajrāsana. He said: "The father has died. I have completed the funeral rites. This gold is your share. Now I shall return to my native place." But (sTeṅs-pa lo-tsā-ba) persuaded him to take up study and he became a learned paṇḍita, but died of fever. About the time of his death, he said: "You should take my bones to dGe-ri". Thrice he made him swear: "I shall proceed to Tibet." After that (sTeṅs-pa lo-tsā-ba) returned (to Tibet) and erected a caitya (a relic holder—gduṅ-khaṅ) for his remains. He completed the copying of twenty volumes of the Prajñāpāramitā begun by (his) father. Then taking with him about fifty golden sraṅs, he again journeyed to India and found that the Teacher Tsa-mi was no more. He offered presents to his mortal remains. He studied extensively the Tantras and Sūtras under thirteen scholars: the mahā-paṇḍita Saṃ-ga-ta virwa (Saṃgatavīra), Daśabalaśrī (in the text Dā-sa-bhā-la-śrī), Candrakīrti, Sudhanagupta, Śīlacandra, Vimalarakṣita, Jayagupta, Siṃhahara, Bhāskara, Śīlaśrī, Vasantatilaka, Ānandadeva, and the (21b) Nepālese paṇḍita Nayaśrī. He invited the paṇḍita Alaṅkadeva (=Alaṃkāradeva), a descendant of the Kasmirian Trilocana (sPyan gsum-pa, a famous grammarian). He collected many man-loads of Indian books (many of his books are still preserved in the monastery of Ṅor. The words "books of Śīlākara" /Tshul-Khrims 'byuṅ-gnas/ are inscribed on the manuscripts. Verbal communication by Rev. dGe-'dun-čhos-'phel). He made numerous translations and revised existing translations: the sGrub-thabs bsdus-pa čhen-po, the 'Dul-ba raṅ-gi rnam-bśad (Vinayasūtravṛttyabhidhāna-svavyākhyāna-nāma, Tg. rGyud, No. 4119), the Ñi-khri gžuṅ-'grel (Ārya-Pañcaviṃśatisāhasrikā-Prajñāpāramitopadeśaśāstra - abhisamayālaṃkārakārikā -vārtika, Tg, Śer-phyin, No. 3788), the Jātakamālā composed by (Ārya)śūra (Tg. No. 4150), the Kālacakramūlatantra (Dus-'khor rtsa-rgyud. Probably the Kālacakra-nāma-tantrarāja, Kg. rGyud-'bum, No. 362), and the Cycle of Nāgārjuna (the Guhyasamāja), according to the method of the paṇḍita Alaṃkāradeva. At that time he spent five years in India. Then having again come to India, he studied for three years the Mahāvibhāṣā (Bye-brag bśad-pa čhen-po; there exists a report that half of the Bye-brag bśad-pa had been translated during the reign of Khri-sroṅ lde-btsan). He brought to Tibet the Sanskrit text of this book. After that he and Alaṃkāradeva translated it, but after finishing two thirds of the text, the paṇḍita passed away.

Instead of a funeral rite, they held a great religious assembly of 48 religious chairs. In general, he possessed a clear vision of the maṇḍala of the sixty-two deities of the Saṃvara parivāra, and of many dharmapālas. He became the teacher of great scholars, such as Gro-luṅ-pa čhen-po and others, and the Master of the Doctrine. He passed away at the age of 84, in the year Iron-Male-Dog (lčags-pho-khyi—1190 A.D.). 82 years had passed since the death of the great lo-tsā-ba bLo-ldan Śes-rab. Many relics and images were recovered (from the ashes).

His disciple Čhag dGra-bčom: he was born in the year Water-Female-Hen (čhu-mo-bya—1153 A.D.) in the village of Čhag as son of Mes bKra-śis-dga', when sTeṅs-pa lo-tsā-ba was 47. He was ordained by Gu-rub čhag-ston, the Great, named Rin-čhen tshul-khrims, the direct disciple of Gro-luṅ-pa. He studied Sanskrit Grammar and the work of a translator with sTeṅs-pa lo-tsā-ba. He also listened to (the exposition) of the Guhyasamāja-Tantra according to the method of Nāgārjuna,

the Kālacakra and other systems. He requested his Teacher (to be given the power of conjuring) the dharmapāla Phyag-bži-pa, and this Religious Protector followed after him. He (224)
took up the final monastic ordination before Ma-gro 'Dul-'dzin, a disciple of Byaṅ-sems zla-rgyal, and his disciple the upādhyāya Dar-brtson. He attended on 15 Tibetan teachers, who included the kalyāṇa-mitra Śāk-grub of gTsaṅ, gTsaṅ-dkar, the Čog-gru lo-tsā-ba Mya-ṅan med-pa'i dpal, Zaṅ lo-tsā-ba, and others. In order to remove dangers during his journey to India, he propitiated Khasarpaṇa (a form of Avalokiteśvara) and observed signs. Then having left Nepāl, he journeyed towards India. Every day he used to buy flowers from the market place, and strew them over the Mahābodhi (image) of Vajrāsana, and the flowers remained (hanging) on the ears of the image. Following this, images of flowers appeared miraculously on the ears of a golden image which he erected in later times as substitute for the Mahābodhi image. He attended on Maitrīcandra, rDo-rje gdan-pa, the Junior, Niṣkalaṅka, Śīlākara, Śākyaśrī, and Buddhaśrī. He was particularly indebted to Maitrīcandra, who had foretold him that after meditating inside a small gandhola (temple) at Nālandā, he would obtain the vision of the sixty-two gods of the Saṃvara parivāra above the initiation vase. When he caught fever at gLo-bo-rin, and was laying in the shade of a Nyagrodha tree, he heard a faint sound of bracelets, and looking up he saw a woman of brown complexion, who was sprinkling some holy water (bum-čhu) over his heart, and the ailment's root was destroyed. He understood the woman to be the Tārā. He also visited eighty self-evolved sacred images of India. On his way to Tibet in company of dPyal lo-tsā-ba, he was attacked by brigands of Śi-skyid (meaning "better death, than meeting such brigands") on the banks of the Ganges. He cast at them his magic glance, and the brigands grew stiff. On his arrival in Tibet, he was offered Čhu-mig, rGyal lha-khaṅ, Thaṅ-po-čhe, and other monasteries. He spent some time in them, but chiefly he

resided at rTe'u-ra. This (monastery) was first founded by sKor-čhen-po, a disciple of sNe'u-zur-pa. After him the succession (of abbots) seems to have been interrupted for a time. After that Čhag lo-tsā-ba took it over. Having (22b) invited Buddhaśrī, he translated the Jinamārgāvatāra (rGyal-ba'i lam-'Jug, Tg. dbU-ma, No. 3964) and other texts. He attended on Śākyaśrī, Thams-čad mkhyen-pa'i dpal, Ratnaśrī, and others, and with their help made many translations. When the Kha-čhe paṇ čhen (Śākyaśrībhadra) was bestowing the final monastic ordination on others, Čhag lo-tsā-ba recited in the Sanskrit language the rite, and pleased the great paṇḍita.

His outer appearance: He had a shaven head, (walked) barefoot and abstained from meat. Being endowed with a perfect fragrance of morality, is fragrance spread far and wide. He died at rTe'u-ra at the age of 64, in the year Fire-Male-Mouse (me-pho-byi-ba—1216 A.D.). At that time Čhag, the "Junior" (Čhos-rJe-dpal), was 20. This was the Fire-Male-Mouse year (me-pho-byi-ba—1216 A.D.) during which the Venerable Grags-rgyal died. During the cremation of his remains, all the gods of the parivāra of Saṃvara appeared on his skull, and the Ā-li Kā-li (signs) on his jaw. They are now preserved in the caitya containing relics which are shown to worshippers (phyi-rten). Ravīndra had indicated to Čhag, the "Junior", that the caitya had fallen in ruins and that he had to build four supports (glo-'bur). He did so. The rite of its consecration was performed by Ravīndra from Nepāl. At rTe'u-ra at the time of the consecration rite, a shower of rice grains fell (i.e. the consecration rite was performed in Nepāl, and during it, a shower of rice grains fell at rTe'u-ra in Tibet). Then lightning struck the caitya, but was flung away, and the caitya became known as Thog-brdugs dkar-po (the "White (caitya) lightning-proof"). After his cremation an image of Khasarpaṇa was recovered from the ashes, and is now preserved (inside) a golden image of Śākyamuni. He had many disciples in India, among them the mahā-paṇḍita Dharmaśrī and others.

His nephew Čhag Čhos-rJe-dpal: he was born in the year Fire-Female-Serpent (me-mo-sbrul—1197 A.D.) as son of the ācārya Dharma 'byuṅ-gnas and (mother) Čhos-'bum. This Fire-Serpent year (me-sbrul) is the 26th year of Khro-phu lo-tsā ba. He studied the Sanskrit and Tibetan scripts, the vocabulary, the "Royal Commands" (bka'-bčad, i.e. the Mahāvyutpatti/Tg. sNa-tshogs, No. 4346/and the sGra-sbyor bam-po gñis-pa/Tg. sNa-tshogs, No. 4347/), drawing, and the science of measurements of maṇḍalas and images, etc.

From the age of eleven to the age of 20, he stayed continuously with Čhag dGra-bčom, and obtained (from him) many precepts of the basic texts of the Tantras and Sūtras. On (234) five occasions he attended the cittotpāda rite. In general, from the age of 17 to the age of 45, he made the vow of not separating from his pen and ink (snag-smyug-daṅ mi-'bral-ba). At the age of 14-15, he recited 26,000,000 mantras of Acala and obtained a vision of the god. At the age of 20, his predecessor (the "Elder" Čhag) fearing that his nephew would proceed to India, advised him to study the Abhidharma. After the death of Čhag dGra-bčom, he made preparation to go to India. He obtained many doctrines from the Sa-skya lo-tsā-ba (Sa-lo) in gTsaṅ, Khro-lo (Khro-phu lo-tsā-ba), Myaṅ-stod lo-tsā-ba, Gro-ston bDud-rtsi-grags, and others. He obtained from Lha-btsun-pa mGon-po-dpal of Guṅ-thaṅ the Abhidharmasamuccaya and the Guhyasamāja-Tantra according to the system of Nāgārjuna, following the method of rṄog. He spent ten years with him. At Śiṅ-kun in Nepāl he met Ratnarakṣita. He acted as translator when Khams-pa sTon-grags and others were being initiated by (Ratnarakṣita). He also obtained the initiation into the Saṃvara Cycle and others. He then studied with the mahāpaṇḍita Ravīndra who was an upāsaka, the Nāgārjuna system (the Guhyasamāja-Tantra), the Vajrāvali, the mDo-rgyud rtog pa bsdus-pa, and other texts. He was given the prophecy which said that benefit would arise for many living beings. In Nepāl he spent eight full years. After

that he proceeded to India. He visited Vaiśālī (Yaṅs-pa-čan) via Tirhut (Bihār. In ancient times the name rGya-gar applied to Magadha/Bihār/only). In a dream he had a clear vision of Vajrāsana. On reaching Vajrāsana, he found that there was no one there, all having fled from fear of Turuṣka troops. For a long time he was unable to see the Mahābodhi image (for the doors of the vihāra were blocked with bricks). Later he saw the image, made offerings to the Mahābodhi, and examined the sacred place. At Nālandā he met the paṇḍita Rāhula Śrībhadra and obtained from him many doctrines. The Gar-log troops (Qarluq; here the name designates Muhammedan troops) arrived there, all the natives and their king fled away. Rāhula said to Čhag: "I, being 90 years old, am unable to flee away. (23b
But you, fool, why don't you go away?" Čhag replied: "Even if murdered, I couldn't separate from my Teacher!" Rāhula having found him to be a trustworthy person, became pleased from the bottom of his heart. Having taken his Teacher on his back, he carried him to a temple of Mahākāla (mGon-po) which was feared by the Gar-log troops, and the latter did not harm them. In Magadha he caught fever, and when the fever left him, (his body) became covered with sores. He again caught fever in Tirhut (Tir-hu-ti). Slowly he journeyed to Tibet. In general, he studied the Doctrine (at the feet) of twelve paṇḍitas, four Tibetan lo-tsā bas, 21 learned monks, and others. He was praised by the Sa-skya paṇ-čhen (Kun-dga' rgyal-mtshan) as tha most learned of the translators after the lo-tsā-ba Rin-čhen bzaṅ-po. He was earnestly requested to occupy the abbot's chair of Nag -tsho lo-tsā-ba and spent there four years. He received the keys of eighty monasteries, such as Harimaṇḍa and others. He also received about 300 volumes of sacred scriptures. After that he proceeded to rTe'u-ra. Later at the age of 62, he came to Than-po-čhe. About that time he visited the residence of the paṇḍita Dānaśīla of sTag-tshal, and pronounced many blessings in Sanskrit. The

paṇḍita trembled and the hair on his body stood erect (from amazement). When he was preaching the Doctrine during the summer recess at 'Khor-lo, numerous scholars gathered round him, including Rig-pa'i ral-gri, a famous scholar in the Tibetan language. There were also about a hundred monk-students who had brought their own books. Every day he sounded the conch thirteen times (to gather students for the classes). Then he preached the Doctrine in many monasteries of 'Ju and 'Phyos of Yar-kluṅs, and spent five years in the region of Yar-kluṅs. When the invitation of the Mongol Emperor arrived, the great men of Mongolia and Tibet held a consultation between themselves. as a result of which he was permitted to remain (in Tibet) because of failing health. He was invited to Sa-skya and installed as Teacher by Śar-pa Ye-śes rgyal-mtshan and the dPon-čhen Kun-dga' bzaṅ-po. He became the Master of the (244)
assembly of monks (tshogs-dpon) as well as preached the Doctrine. After that he proceeded to rTe'u-ra and held there a great religious council. He passed into Nirvāṇa at the age of 68, in the year Wood-Male-Mouse (Śiṅ-pho-byi-ba—1264 A.D.). After him dBaṅ-phyug śes-rab of gTsaṅ carried on the burden of abbotship for many years, without being nominated abbot. After him, the bla-ma bsTan-'dzin-dpal, son of Čhag Ñi-ma-dpal, the youngest brother of the "Junior" Čhag, and his younger brother Zla-ba acted as abbots for a short period. In the time of Zla-ba the Sa-skya state (sKya-srid) attacked rTe'u-ra. After the bLa-ma Rin-čhen 'byuṅ-gnas, son of mÑa'-bdag-dpal, the youngest brother of Zla-ba, occupied the chair for 13 years. After him the chair was entrusted to bLo-gros-dpal an official of the bLa-braṅ (Ecclesiastical Palace), aged 74. In the same year he nominated to the abbot's chair Śākya-dpal, an official of the Palace. The year of the death of the bLa-ma Rin-čhen 'byuṅ-gnas and of the nomination of Śākya-dpal is a Fire-Female-Hare year (me-mo-yos—1327 A.D.). Thirteen years later, Śākya-dpal died in the year Earth Female-Hare

(sa-mo-yos—1339 A.D.). Since Čhos-rJe-dpal's death to this Fire-Female-Hare year (me-me-yos—1327 A.D.) of the nomination of Śākya-dpal 64 years have passed. After him the bLa-brań-pa bzań-po-dpal. After him Čhag Čhos-dpal, nephew of Rin-čhen 'byuń-gnas, acted as abbot, but soon died. After him the bLa-brań-pa bZań-po-dpal again became abbot. After that for five years—the Dharmasvāmin Ñi-ma-ba. After him Śākya-dpal acted as abbot for 13 years, and then died. Aftea him the Dharmasvāmin Ye-śes dpal-bzań-po, born in the year Fire-Female Sheep (me-mo-lug–1367 A.D.), came to the abbot's chair at the age of 25. He occupied the chair for 18 years till the year Earth-Male-Mouse (sa-pho-byi- 1408 A.D.). After that, having appointed to the chair the bLa-ma bSam-grub dpal-mgon, he passed away in the year Wood-Male-Dog (Śiń-pho-khyi—1454 A.D.) at the age of 88. bSam-grub dpal-mgon occupied the chair for 25 years, fram the year Earth-Mouse (sa-byi—1408 A.D.) (24*b*)
to the year Water-Mouse čhu-byi—1432 A.D.). After him bSod-blo (bSod-nams blo-gros), born in the year Water-Serpent (čhu-sbrul—1413 A.D.), came to the chair at the age of 20, and occupied it for nine years, from the year Water-Mouse (čhu-byi—1432 A.D.) to the year Iron-Ape (lčags-spre —1440 A.D.). In this very year bLo-bzańs, born in the year Iron-Ox (lčags-glań—1421 A.D.), was nominated to the chair, aged 20. He (bSod-blo) died at the age of 56 in the year Earth-Mouse (sa-byi—1468 A.D.). bLo-bzańs having occupied the chair for 21 years, an Iron-Male-Dragon year (lčags-pho-'brug—1460 A.D.), gave up the chair. He died at the age of 42 in the year Water-Horse (čhu-rta—1462 A.D.). After that Rin čhen čhos-rgyal, born in the year Fire-Female-Hare (me-mo-yos—1447 A.D.), came to the chair in the year Iron-Dragon (lčags-'brug—1460 A.D.), aged 14. Till the present Fire-Male-Ape year (me-pho-spre'u—1476 A.D.) 17 years have passed.

The Chapter on rTe'u-ra.

At gÑal-roń-lins there was a student of the Kālacakra

system, a disciple of Abhaya, named Roṅ-liṅ lo-tsā-ba rDo-rJe rgyal-mtshan. His vihāra called Sags-kha stands undamaged even now. I have not seen his biography, and am therefore unable to go into details.

BOOK XV.

The origin of religious schools, such as the four Tshogs-sde, and others. Queries and replies (concerning the "Blue Annals"; zu-lan). The story of the printing of this edition.

I have already given in brief the story of the origin of the Holy Doctrine in the "Abode of Snows" (Tibet). Now (the story) of the monastic community, which practised this Doctrine: all the Vinayadharas of Tibet belong to the school of the Sarvāstivādins. Among them (one finds) the so-called "Lower" Lineage of the mahā-upādhyāya Śāntarakṣita, handed down by the great bLa-čhen-po (dGoṅs-pa Rab-gsal), the so-called "Upper" Lineage of the East Indian paṇḍita Dharmapāla, who had ordained the three Pālas and others in mṄa'-ris, and the Lineage handed down by the Kashmirian paṇḍita Śākyaśrī (bhadra). Of these three Lineages, the first two have already been mentioned by me. Now I shall ascertain the year in which the great Kashmirian paṇḍita Śākyaśrībhadra, who was destined to become the future Third Buddha Pradyota (Rab-gsal), was born and the year in which he came to Tibet, as well as the manner of his labours for the welfare of living beings. Now the great paṇḍita himself had established the Buddhist Chronology at Sol-nag Thaṅ-po-čhe in the year Fire-Female-Hare (me-mo-yos—1207 A.D.), in which he said: "In the first half of the Kārttika month (October-November), exactly at midnight of the 8th day, when the Moon had set behind the mountains, Munīndra passed into Nirvāṇa. Since then, a thousand seven hundred and fifty years, two and half months and five days have passed:" After dividing these years by sixty, a remainder of ten years is left over. Hence the first (year) of the Buddhist Chronology (as calculated by the mahā-paṇḍita) must have been the Fire-Female-Serpent year (me-mo-sbrul—1197 A.D.).

(One should remember that this calculation was made) three cycles of sixty years after the year Fire-Female-Hare (me-mo-yos—1027 A.D.), which is the first of the period of "current" ('das-lo) years of the Kālacakra scholars. This means that 180 years had elapsed (since the year 1027 A.D.). From the Fire-Hare year (me-yos—1207 A. D.), which had been calculated (by the mahā-paṇḍita) at Thaṅ, to the present Fire-Male-Ape year (me-pho-spre—1476 A.D.) four cycles of sixty years and 30 years have elapsed. Thus (this Fire-Ape year) is the 2020th year after the Nirvāṇa of
the Muni. Such being the Chronology of the Doctrine, the (1a)
birth-year of the mahā-paṇḍita must be the year Fire-Female-Sheep (me-mo-lug—1127 A.D.). For in a stotra composed by the Khro-phu lo-tsā-ba (in honour of the Kha-čhe paṇ-čhen), it is said:

"A thousand six hundred and ninety-two years after the Nirvāṇa of the (Buddha),

the Saint was born as chief of the yellow-garbed monks,

who are the life of the Doctrine of Śākya (the text refers to the pravrajyā or ordination of Śākyaśrībhadra).

Salutation to his feet!" Now, after dividing 1692 by sixty, a remainder of 12 (years) is left over. The 12th year (i.e. the 1692nd year) is an Earth-Male-Dragon year (sa-pho-'brug—1148 A.D.). The word "after" (in the text of the above stotra) means the next year, an Earth-Female-Serpent year (sa-mo-sbrul—1149 A.D.), which is the 23rd year of the mahā-paṇḍita (during which he received his pravrajyā ordination). The above being very clear, the mahā-paṇḍita's 25th year was without doubt an Iron-Female-Sheep year (lčags-mo-lug—1151 A.D.). In this connection it is found stated in the works by sPyi-bo Lhas-pa and others that the mahā-paṇḍita had come to Tibet in his 65th year. However this is a mistake. For the lo-tsā-ba (Khro-phu) has stated that the year of the mahā-paṇḍita's coming to

Tibet was the Wood-Male-Mouse year (Śiṅ-pho-byi-ba—1204 A.D.). This Wood-Male-Mouse year was the 78th year of the mahā-paṇḍita. He spent ten years (in Tibet), till the year Water-Female-Hen (čhu-mo-bya—1213 A.D.). He left Tibet in the year Wood-Male-Dog (śiṅ-pho-khyi—1214 A.D.). In the year Wood-Female-Hen (śiṅ-mo-bya—1225 A.D.) of the next Cycle of Sixty Years (lo-skor) he reached the age of 99. He passed into Nirvāṇa on Saturday, the 5th day of the sGrog-zla (Śatabhiṣā, Aquarii).

The same was stated as follows: "Aged a hundred years, less one, in the year of the Hen (bya-lo—1225 A.D.), in the month of sGrog (Śatabhiṣā), in its first half, on Saturday, the fifth day, the Sun of living beings manifested (his) setting". This Saturday could be clearly calculated with the help of the astrological tables called "lÑa-bsdus" composed by the mahā-paṇḍita himself. In short, the mahā-paṇḍita was born in the year Fire-Female-Sheep (me-mo-lug—1127 A.D.). He was ordained in the year Earth-Female-Serpent (sa-mo-sbrul—1149 A.D.). He came to Tibet at the age of 78 in the year Wood-Male-Mouse (śiṅ-pho-byi-ba—1204 A.D.). He spent ten years in Tibet, till the year Water-Female-Hen (čhu-mo-bya—1213 A.D.). He left Tibet in the year Wood-Male-Dog (2a)
(śiṅ-pho-khyi—1214 A.D.), and laboured extensively for the welfare of living beings in Kāśmīra. He passed into Nirvāṇa at the age of 99, in the year Wood-Female-Hen (śiṅ-mo-bya—1225 A.D.).

The story of his invitation to Tibet and that of his labours for the welfare of living beings: The holy man named Khro-phu lo-tsā-ba (Byams-pa'i dpal) proceeded towards Nepāl and India in order to study the work of a translator, and stopped at sKyi-roṅ. One day he offered one and half silver sraṅ to one named Don-žags-pa čhen-po, a disciple of Rin-po-čhe rGyal-tsha, and requested him to examine the omens of the following three (possibilities): "If I go to India and Nepāl, would accidents befall me? Shall I be able to benefit living beings? Will the good work which I intend doing, be successful?"

Don-žags-pa said: "I couldn't tell whether the three will be successful. I shall examine (the omens) addressing myself to Amoghapaśa". Then the lo-tsā-ba himself having arranged a large offering, examined the dreams. At dawn he saw in his dream an a-tsa-ra (ācārya) with teeth similar to a conch. He inquired: "Who was it?" In reply he heard: "Look at the writing on the back?" He saw the letters Dvi-bhā-śī (Dvi-bhāṣin). Again the a-tsa-ra gave him a leaf of the Bodhi tree on which he found an image of a paṇḍita with a bird-like face. On the back he read: "Mahāmaitrī". Again the a-tsa-ra handed him a mirror in which he saw a paṇḍita who was similar to a god and an inscription which read: "Mañ-juśrī". Then (he saw) the image of a white man, made from the outside of rough woollen cloth, and from the inside of silk, inscribed "Maṇipadme". These four objects influenced his mind greatly, and he thought of keeping them in a temple. He took them there but the a-tsa-ra exclaimed: "Give them back! I shall reverse the order", and added: "Let the lion made of conch run towards all directions! You may leave the leaf and mirror, but take the image of the man made of silk. After you may take the mirror. After that you may take the leaf also." On awakening, he could not understand the dream, though he felt that it was auspicious. At that time he did not understand the meaning of the four inscriptions. (2b)
But later he found out that the lion made of a conch indicated the lo-tsā-ba himself, the white man—the Lord Mitra, the paṇḍita seen in the mirror—Buddhaśrī, the paṇḍita drawn on the leaf—the Kashmirian paṇḍita. (Following these indications) the lo-tsā-ba at first proceeded to Nepāl and the border-country of India. Afterwards he invited the Lord Mitra to Tibet. After that the mahā-paṇḍita Buddhaśrī was invited. On the 7th day of the month of mČhu (the Sixth month) of the year Wood-Male-Mouse (śiṅ-pho-byi-ba—1204 A.D.) of the Chinese chronology the lo-tsā-ba proceeded to invite (the mahā-paṇḍita). He met a kalyāṇa-mitra named rGya who had been a direct disciple of the bLa-ma Žaṅ,

residing at rGyaṅ-ro Guṅ-čhuṅ. Though the latter was staying in seclusion, on hearing about the lo-tsā-ba's coming, he suddenly broke his retirement and went out to receive him. From him the lo-tsā-ba obtained the Cycles of the Doctrine of Žaṅ.

Žaṅ said: "To invite the mahā-paṇḍita it won't do to act humbly and irresolutely! Behave in a noisy manner! The Sun may rise from the West, but you will surely succeed in your purpose." (Journeying) by stages, he (Khro-phu lo-tsā-ba) reached Gro-mo (Chumbi). The natives of Gro-mo showed reverence to him and his provisions increased in quantity. Though he intended going to the Indian market-place of Be-dur (<Vidūra?), he lost the road and wandered about in the forests, which were full of brigands, poisonous snakes, wild beasts, and spirits (mi-ma-yin). Without being harmed by them, he reached the market-place of Be-dur, and sent two Indians, the junior paṇḍita Jayaśrī and Vārāṇasī-pa, accompanied by two Tibetans—J̌o-sras Ñi-ma and Khams-pa Byaṅ-grags, as messengers to convey the invitation to the mahā-paṇḍita at Jagattara (Jagattala) of the East. With them he sent the following letter written in Sanskrit: (3a)

"Salutation to the Buddha Amoghasiddha! To the one who has been born as son of Śākya, in the Doctrine of Śākya, bearing the name of Śākya, the crown of the heads of those who have mastered the five (sciences) and firmly observe the immaculate vows of morality, etc." As presents to accompany the letter he sent a Prajñāpāramitāhṛdaya written in gold, five golden sraṅs, a pair of silk garments and a canopy (bla-re) made of good quality silk of 'J̌u. When the messengers reached a place called La-drug, after a journey of 34 days, the mahā-paṇḍita and his retinue, having been forewarned of the Tibetan invitation, came there in advance. Having failed to find the messengers, they were preparing to return, and were packing their luggage, when the Tibetan messengers arrived and presented to the mahā-paṇḍita the letter and the presents. The mahā-paṇḍita said: "When having had a pre-

monition after that an invitation was due to arrive from Tibet, I came here well in advance of time, we found that the messengers had not arrived and were preparing to return. Didn't I tell you to stay on for a while, for the invitation was surely to come? Now you must advise us what to do," said the mahā-paṇḍita addressing himself to the Junior paṇḍitas. The Junior paṇḍitas replied: "The Dharmasvāmin should himself decide the matter! How are we to understand it with our minds?" The mahā-paṇḍita then said: "I have one to whom I can put a question". He then stayed in seclusion for five days, and asked the Venerable One (Tārā). Then numerous great sthaviras of Eastern India came to beg the mahā-paṇḍita not to proceed to Tibet. They brought with them the images of the Great Merciful One (Mahākaruṇika, Avalokiteśvara) and the Tārā consecrated by the ācārya Nāgārjuna as solicitors (ṅo-čhen). (The Tibetans) bribed the Kashmirian who was in charge of the images, and he pulled out the box of the chariot's wheel and made the images face backwards (in order to create the semblance of a bad omen), and thus helped the Tibetans. The lo-tsā-ba (Khro-phu) having come from Be-dar met the Dharmasvāmin at Vaneśvara. The Dharmasvāmin said: "I thought the lo-tsā-ba knew many doctrines, and was an elderly man endowed with the ability of erecting large images, but he is young. Most probably he will be unable to act as a translator. After I had bestowed on him the cittotpāda rite and several sādhanas, are we, Teacher and disciples, to return?" The paṇḍita Jayaśrī told (the lo-tsā-ba): "The Teacher and (his) disciples despise you, because of your age. You should take measures, and put questions on the Doctrine." At the request of (3b)
Jayaśrī, the mahā-paṇḍita permitted the lo-tsā-ba to ask questions on the Doctrine. Then the lo-tsā-ba put two questions to each of the nine Junior paṇḍitas (of the mahā-paṇḍita's retinue), and they discussed them throughout the evening till midnight. The Dharmasvāmin was pleased, though it interrupted his usual meditation, and said: "It

is wonderful that in Tibet there should exist such speakers on religious subjects!" Then a border king closed the road, and as the Junior paṇḍitas also required litters (doli<ḍolī), this caused great hardships. On arrival at Phag-ri, countless Tibetan monks and laymen gathered there from the four quarters, and attended on the mahā-paṇḍita in every possible way, begged for religious instructions, and the mahā-paṇḍita preached to them numerous kinds of precepts. From rGyaṅ-ro as far as mGur-mo his religious preaching spread and his wealth increased immeasurably. From Tshoṅ-'dus as far as Čhu-mig numerous monks gathered round the mahā-paṇḍita, so that laymen had difficulties in seeing his face. The inmates of Khro-phu arrived in great state at Čhu-mig to receive them. After they had reached Khro-phu, many thousands of learned monks gathered there. The mahā-paṇḍita spent his summer retreat there. There were more than 800 voters (tshul-śiṅ len-pa). In connection with it, the mahā-paṇḍita preached the Aṣṭasāhasrikā-Prajñāpāramitā, as well as the Prātimokṣa and the Sūtrālaṃkāra (Mahāyāna-sūtrālaṃkāra-nāma-kārikā, Tg. Sems-tsam, No. 4040). After that the mahā-paṇḍita proceeded to kLas-mo-čhe of sNar-(thaṅ). There he preached the Commentary on the Pañcaviṃśatisāhasrikā (Prajñāpāramita). When he reached the chapter of the Tathatā-pariccheda, his book of the Aṣṭasāhasrikā-Prajñāpāramitā was taken away by the Tārā who made many offerings to it and proceeded towards the East. The mahā-paṇḍita said: "This indicates that I am to go towards dbUs." (It was said that when the mahā-paṇḍita was reciting the text, a crow, a manifestation of Tārā, snatched away some of the pages of the palm-leaf manuscript, and took them away towards the East. These leaves, believed to have been brought by the crow, were discovered at sPo-khaṅ, and are now preserved in the monastery of sPo-khaṅ). When he had come to the last chapter of the Prajñāpāramitā, he saw a goddess, worshipping this book which was placed inside the maṇḍala of the offerings, and then the goddess proceeded

towards the West. The mahā-paṇḍita said: "This indicated that in my old age I was to go to Kāśmīra. After that the mahā-paṇḍita spent his summer retreat at kLas-mo-čhe of sNar, and spent some time there. After performing the ceremony (dgag-dbye—pravāraṇā) of the end of the rainy (4a)
season (performed at the end of the annual summer retreat), many sthaviras invited him to Čhu-mig riṅ-mo. There he preached the Mādhyamaka-ratna-mālā (dbU-ma rin-čhen phreṅ-ba, Tg. dbU-ma, No. 3901) and the dPe'i-rgyan Dṛṣṭāntamālya, Tg. sPriṅ-yig, No. 4196). After that he was invited by the inmates of Srin-po-ri (near Gyangtse), and then proceeded to 'Tshur-phu and Lha-sa via Upper gŽu-sñe. The mahā-paṇḍita made large offerings to the two images of the Lords (of Lha-sa). Then the mahā-paṇḍita reached Srin-po-ri escorted by numerous horsemen of 'Tshur-phu. The mahā-paṇḍita said to the escort: "At the time of my visit to your monastery, I discovered there were three images of divinities which were mentioned in the Tantra of Saṅs-rgyas thod-pa (Saṅs-rgyas-thod-pa'i rgyud, Śrī-Buddha-kapāla-nāmayoginītantrarāja, Kg. rGyud-'bum, No. 424). Your former Teachers knew them, but had no faith. If I were to introduce you to these gods, and preach to you their precepts, numerous yogins would later appear (among you)." These three gods were: Saṃvara and (his) Śakti in the yuganaddha posture, Śākyamuni in the aspect of Nirmāṇa-kāya with his Śakti Vajra-ḍākinī, and Vajra with the bell (ghaṇṭa) as his śakti (rDo-rJe dril-bu mñam-byor). He spent the summer retreat at Srin-po-ri, and translated the commentary on the Abhidharmasamuccaya by the ācārya Jñānamitra (Ye-śes gśes-gñen; Abhidharmasamuccayavyākhyā-nāma, Tg. Sems-tsam, No. 4054). As general doctrine, he preached the Ārya-Aśokadattavyākaraṇa-nāma (Mya-ṅan-med luṅ-bstan-pa'i mdo, Kg. dKon-brtsegs, No. 46), the dPe-brgya-pa (Gaṅ-po-la sogs-pa'i rtogs-pa-brJod-pa brgya-pa, Pūrṇapramukhāvadānaśataka, Kg. mDo-sde, No. 343), the Las-kyi 'khor-lo bstan-pa (Karmaśataka, Kg. mDo-

sde, No. 340), as well as the Analysis of the Five Treatises of Maitreya and the Six Treatises of the Mādhyamaka (dbU-ma rigs-tshogs). The exposition of the Five Treatises of Maitreya was bestowed by him at the request of the Abbot of Srin-po-ri. gÑal-zaṅs-po-čhe-pa and others practised the rGyal-sras Lam-rim. The mahā-paṇḍita was then invited to bSam-yas by Lha Ži-ba-'od. He journeyed to bSam-yas and 'Čhims-phu. There he met dbOn-ston Rin-čhen-sgaṅ-pa. When the mahā-paṇḍita came to Srin-po-ri, he received an invitation from the inmates of 'Tshur-phu, rGya-ma and 'Bri-khuṅ. Twice he failed to meet 'Bri-khuṅ-pa. On two occasions he visited rGya-ma Rin-čhen-sgaṅ and Rwa-sgreṅ. After that he journeyed to gÑal, Lo-ro and Lho-brag, as well as to 'U-gu-do and Thaṅ-po-čhe. He especially spent a considerable time at Tḥaṅ-po-čhe, and preached there numerous sermons. Up to that time, in order to test the faith of the (4b
lo-tsā-ba (Khro-phu), he acted as an avaricious man, but later he gave away most of his wealth towards the erection of the image of Maitreya at Khro-phu. In the year Water-Male-Ape (čhu-pho-spre'u—1212 A.D.), when the time had come to consecrate the image, they found themselves short of funds, and because of this, the mahā-paṇḍita proceeded again towards dbUs and gYo, gÑal and Lo, and Lho-brag (to gather funds). His entire income was presented to the great image of Maitreya. From the 3rd day till the 13th day of the Dre month (Dre'i zla-ba) of the year Water-Male-Ape (čhu-pho-spre'u—1212 A.D.) the Dharmasvāmin performed the consecration rite of the great image of Maitreya, and numerous wonderful signs accompanied (the rite). After that numerous priests begged him to stay on in Tibet, but he did not agree to that, saying that he had important work to do in Kāśmīra. After that he journeyed through Southern La-stod and benefitted many disciples. The presents received by him, were distributed among the monks of each monastery. On his arrival at Guṅ-thaṅ, he presented 130 golden sraṅs (to Khro-phu lo-tsā-ba), and said: "Give them as remuneration to the

image-makers". After that the lo-tsā-ba escorted him to gLo-bo. One morning he (the mahā-paṇḍita) dismissed his entire retinue, and did not admit any one into his presence, but said: "Lo-tsā-ba come," The lo-tsā-ba having hurried into his presence, the mahā-paṇḍita said to him: "Open your hand!" and then gave him a big package of gold, the lo-tsā-ba's hand almost reaching the ground under its weight. The lo-tsā-ba said: "You have already given me many presents for the image. You had better take this much with you to Kāśmīra." An attendant then told him: "It is better for you to accept the siddhi when given. You may feel regret if this gold gets into the hands of Kashmirian rogues." So he accepted it, and escorted the mahā-paṇḍita to the foot of the mountain pass. On his way to Kāśmīra, the mahā-paṇḍita was twice attacked by robbers, but as he had no gold with him, nothing harmed him. Then he reached Kāśmīra. Though the Doctrine had spread in Kāśmīra, the priests were (5a) few in numbers. The Dharmasvāmin increased the number of priests, and established the right path of the method of the Tantras and Sūtras. The king who had become a heretic, was again established in the Doctrine. The mahā-paṇḍita repaired ruined vihāras and images. Amidst such labours he spent 12 years in Kāśmīra, and passed away in the year Wood-Female-Hen (śiṅ-mo-bya—1225 A.D.) amidst wonderful signs. This great paṇḍita preached numerous doctrines which belonged to the Āgamas and Sciences, Sūtras and Tantras. Great was the number of those whom he established in the vows of the Prātimokṣa, but the two men, who had taken the final monastic ordination in the presence of the mahā-paṇḍita and had taken the vow of a "single mat" (stan-gčig-gi brtul-žugs-'dzin-pa), were rDo-rJe-dpal and Byaṅ-čhub-dpal.

Namo Maitrīnāthāya! Munīndra, Śāriputra, Rāhula, the kṣatriya, Rāhula, the brāhmaṇa, Nāgārjuna, Guṇamati, Ratnamitra, Śrī Dharmapāla, Guṇasāgara, Dharmapāla, Ākaragupta, the mahā-paṇḍita Śākyaśrī, Vajraśrībhadra (rDo-rJe-dpal-bzaṅ-po), Byaṅ-čhub-dpal-bzaṅ-po (Bodhiśrībhadra. The last two seem to be the two disciples of the mahā-paṇḍita: rDo-rJe-dpal and Byaṅ-čhub-dpal. The rest of the Teachers of the Lineage must be Tibetans), 'Od-zer-dpal (Raśmiśrī), Čhos-kyi rgyal-mtshan (Dharmadhvaja), Saṅs-rgyas rin-čhen (Buddharatna), bSod-nams-dpal (Puṇyaśrī), Śes-rab mgon-po (Prajñānātha), Seṅ-ge rgyal-mtshan (Siṃhadhvaja), bSod-nams dbaṅ-phyug (Puṇyeśvara), bKra-śis tshul-khrims (Maṅgalaśīla), Tshul-khrims rin-čhen (Śīlaratna), Saṅs-rgyas blo-gros (Buddhamati), Byaṅ-čhub rgyal-dbaṅ (Bodhijayendra), bKra-śis seṅ-ge (Maṅgalasiṃha), Yon-tan rin-čhen (Guṇaratna), Byaṅ-čhub bzaṅ-po (Bodhibhadra), bLo-gros rgyal-mtshan (Matidhvaja), Don-grub dpal-'byor (Siddhārthaśrībhūti), Byaṅ-čhub grags-pa (Bodhikīrti), and bKra-śis byaṅ-čhub (Maṅgalabodhi). (The above list seems to represent the Lineage of Ordination transmitted by Śākyaśrībhadra. After Vajraśrībhadra it corresponds to the mkhan-rgyud of sNar-thaṅ.)

From the departure of the mahā-paṇḍita from Tibet in the year Water-Female-Hen (čhu-mo-bya—1213 A.D.) to the present Fire-Male-Ape year (me-pho-spre'u—1476 A.D.) 264 years have passed.

The abbots of Tshogs-pa Bya-rdzoṅ:

dKon-mčhog rgyal-mtshan, Thugs-rJe-dpal-pa, Dar-ma dpal-pa, Kun-dga' dpal-pa, gŽon-nu bzaṅ-po-pa, Tshul-khrims dpal-pa, the mahā-upādhyāya Kun-dga'-dpal-pa, Saṅs-rgyas (5b) gžon-nu-pa, Dar-ma bzaṅ-po-pa, Tshul-mgon-pa, bSod-nams 'od-zer, Rin-tshul-pa, bSod-nams śes-rab, Śer-mgon-pa, Grags-bsod-pa, Śer-' phags-pa, Śes-tshul-pa, Rin-śe-pa (Rin-čhen śes-rab), Čhos-dpal-pa, Śes-'od-pa, Kun-śe-pa, Grags-rgyal-ba, dPal-tshul-pa (dPal-'byor tshul-khrims), Rin-grub-pa (Rin-čhen-grub), dBaṅ-śe-pa (dBaṅ-phyug śes-rab), and Zla-rin-pa (Zla-ba rin-čhen).

The abbots of dGe-'dun-sgaṅ:

Lho-brag Byaṅ-čhub-dpal, gTsaṅ-pa dBaṅ-phyug-grags, gŽon-nu byaṅ-čhub, 'Dul-tshad-pa Byaṅ-čhub-bzaṅ-po, 'Jam-dbyaṅs Don-grub-dpal, Yon-tan rgyal-mtshan, dPal-grub-pa, sÑag-phu-ba, Yon-tan blo-gros, brTson-rgyal-ba, Seṅ-ge dpal-pa, Čhos-grub-pa, bLo-gros rgyal-mtshan, Yon-tan lhun-grub, Nam-mkha'-dpal-bzaṅ, and dPal-yon-pa. Also Nam-mkha dpal-bzaṅ, Nam-mkha'-lhun-bzaṅs, and Rab-'byor seṅ-ge.

The abbots of Čhos-luṅ (sPos-khaṅ near Gyangtse):

dbU-mdzad bSod-nams-stobs, after him the mahā-upādhyāya bDe-ba-dpal, Grags-pa gžon-nu, Byaṅ-sems bsod-grags, bSod-nams bzaṅ-po, gŽon-nu mgon-po, Grags-pa rgyal-mtshan, Grags-pa bśes-gñen, Nam-mkha' rgyal-mtshan, Rin-čhen rgyal-mtshan, bŚes-gñen rgyal-mčhog, rGyal-dbaṅ grags-pa, Zla-ba blo-gros, rGyal-ba Phyag-na, bŚes-gñen bzaṅ-po, mGon-po bkra-śis, and Ñi-ma rgyal-mtshan.

The Chapter on the Lineages of Abbots of the four monasteries which belonged to the Lineage of the Kashmirian mahā-paṇḍita, and about the mahā-paṇḍita himself.

More than seven hundred and twenty years after the birth of the religious king Sroṅ-btsan sgam-po, the All-knowing (6a) bLo-bzaṅ grags-pa'i dpal appeared in this World, having been born in the year Fire-Female-Hen (me-mo-bya—1357 A.D.), in the region of Tsoṅ-kha (nowadays the district is called Tsoṅ-thar. A famous mountain near sKu-'bum is still called Tsoṅ-kha'i skyes-ri). In his youth he was introduced into the gates of the Pratimokṣa and Tantra by the great kalyāṇa-mitra Don-grub rin-čhen (he was a native of Amdo and studied in Central Tibet. He founded the famous monastery of Bya-khyuṅ dgon-pa in Amdo /near Pa-yen/, which is considered to have been the first of all the dGe-lugs-pa monasteries), who said: "In the provinces of dbUs and gTsaṅ study this and that" (the Biography/rNam-thar/, fol. 9a, of Je Tsoṅ-kha-pa contains the following passage: "His Teacher wrote down his instructions in ślokas, but when Tsoṅ-kha-pa reached Tibet, he lost the piece of paper /on which the verses were written/ and though he searched for it, he did not find it again. Later he forgot most of the verses, but those which he remembered, were as follows:

"O youthful bLo-bzaṅ grags-pa! You are under the influence
of your virtuous works performed in your former lives.

Verily you were endowed with the faculty of imbibing the nectar of the Good Law in your former lives !...

You will first study earnestly the Abhisamayālaṃkāra which is the ornament of three "Mothers" (the Large, the Middle and the Abridged versions of the Prajñāpāramitā).

If you become learned in it, you will be able to master all the Scriptures.

Keep this advice in a corner of your mind !

Then, as a branch subject, you should study the Mahāyāna Sūtrālaṃkāra which expounds the Path and Practice of the Bodhisattvas, the śāstra Dharmadharmatāvibhaṅga (Tg. Sems-tsam, No. 4023) which describes the Saṃsāra as the foundation of Nirvāṇa, and the treatise entitled Madhyāntavibhaṅga (Tg. Sems-tsam, No. 4521) which preaches the Middle Path, which is without beginning or end, and the Mahāyāna-Uttara-Tantra (Tg. Sems-tsam, No. 4024) which expounds the existence of the Pure Nature of the Mind present in all living beings, and describes it as the Tathāgata-garbha.

You must use these Five Treatises of Maitreya as your "Armour of Knowledge". After that you should study:

The Three body-like śāstras (lus-daṅ-'dra-ba'i bstan-bčos gsum): the large śāstra Pramāṇavārtika, the Pramāṇaviniścaya, the middle-sized, the Nyāyabindu, the Abridged. And the (four) so-called "Lamp-like" treatise ('phros-pa yan-lag lta-bu) comprising the Hetubindu (Tg. Tshad-ma, No. 4213), the Saṃbandhaparīkṣaprakaraṇa (Tg. Tshad-ma, No. 4214), the Santānāntarasiddhi-nāma-prakaraṇa (Tg. Tshad-ma, No.4219), and the Vādanyāya-nāma-prakaraṇa (Tg. Tshad-ma, No. 4218). These "Seven Treatises on Logic" composed by Dharmakīrti are the Light of the Buddha's Doctrine in Jambudvīpa, and are famed as Sun and Moon".

Several verses were forgotten by Tsoṅ-kha-pa. Further he remembered the following:

"You wise one, should feel devotion towards the theory of the absence of Extremes.

You should study the Six Treatises of the Mādhyamaka

composed by Ārya Nāgārjuna and the Treatises based on them.")

At first Tsoṅ-kha-pa attended on many kalyāṇa-mitras at sKyi-śod. Later he attended on the Venerable gŽon-nu blo-gros. He studied most of the Piṭakas. He was of the opinion that except for the practice of wisdom (prajñā), there was no other path of emancipation. Since this doctrine was based on the śāstras of the Mādhyamaka school, he studied it diligently. In the field of Tantras, he found the Śrī-Guhyasamāja-Tantra to be the chief of all the Tantras. He searched for its Essence. In his opinion the All-knowing Bu-ston was the Master of a great number of Tantras (Yoga-Tantra). He studied this class of Tantras with Goṅ-gsum bDe-čhen-pa Čhos-kyi dpal-pa and Khyuṅ-pa Lhas-pa. He held the opinion that the Vinaya of the Holy Doctrine was the basis of the entire Doctrine of Buddha, and studied earnestly the system of the Vinaya under the mahā-upādhyāya sKyor-luṅ-pa. While he was staying among fellow-students of philosophy, though endowed with perfect understanding of the Scriptures (Āgamas) and Sciences (Logic), he avoided such practices, as abusing others, shouting, running, jumping and dancing, and felt very sad and downcast. So I have been told by my Teachers (Some of the ancient Teacher disapproved of the postures and exclamations accompanying debates). After that he chiefly benefitted others by expounding to them the Doctrine. Once, when many wise men had gathered, similar to geese on a lotus pond, among them there was a teacher named dbU-ma-pa (a native of Amdo), who in his childhood had a fleeting vision of the Venerable Mañjuśrī. Later, while engaged in meditation, he obtained a clear vision of the Bodhisattva, and used to inquire about his daily work from the Bodhisattva. Tsoṅ-kha-pa obtained from him (6b)
the initiation of the Venerable One (Mañjuśrī) and recited mantras. Within a short time he obtained a clear vision of the Bodhisattva, and was able to put questions to the Bodhisattva, in the manner of a disciple to his teacher, and obtained

answers. Most of the time he beheld the Bodhisattva, and obtained his instructions. The Venerable One foretold him that should he lead the life of an ascetic he would be able to benefit the Doctrine greatly, more so than in the present state. He did accordingly, and in the company of several companions he proceeded towards 'Ol-kha. There he practised meditation in hermitages, as far as Bum-thaṅ in Mon (Bhuṭān). About that time he studied with the mahā-upādhyāya Čhos-skyabs bzaṅ-po, whose mind had reached the lofty stage by the practice of the bKa'-gdams-pa precepts, and the mahā-upādhyāya Las-kyi rdo-rJe (Karma-vajra), who never abandoned the practice of Bodhisattvas, assisted by the manifestation of the Body, Speech and Mind of Guhyapati, the Lam-rim (Degrees of the Path) composed by Śrī Dīpaṅkarajñāna, and practised it. He spent one day at the foot of the Mo-la Pass of gÑal. There he received a prophecy, which said: "You will become a Buddha in this World. Know it!" His Tutelary deity also prophesied to him that he could benefit others by following the vows of the Vinaya. Following these indications, the Teacher and his disciples wore religious garments which were cut according to the Vinaya rules, as well as the patra and the mat (niṣadana), and other articles (prescribed by the Vinaya). When others saw them, they felt that this was the very manner of ordained priests. Later he introduced to the Vinaya the disciples who wanted to hear from him the Doctrine during a year or a month. And not only that, for (it was said) that the mere hearing of his name from a distance, caused the hair of the body to stand erect. His fame enveloped all quarters and he became a matchless one. Not being (7a)
satisfied with the mere vows of the Pratimokṣa, he developed in his disciples a mental yearning towards Enlightenment which consisted of a solemn wish and practice (of Bodhisattvas) ('Jug-pa, prayoga). He also composed a śāstra expounding the observance of the vows of the above (the mDo-rtsa'i zin-bris rJe Rin-po-čhe'i bKa'-'bum, vol. II. /kha/, fol. 98a). In

his opinion one could practise the vows of Bodhisattvas for tens of millions of Kalpas (Cosmic Period) but, if one did not possess the wisdom intuiting the Absolute, one would not be able to cross over the Ocean of Phenomenal Existence (Saṃsāra). Therefore he composed a treatise expounding the precepts of the degrees of the Path of the three kinds of individuals, which expounded clearly the above system [the Lam-rim čhen-mo, bKa'-'bum, vol. XIII (pa), fol. 481a. Lam-rim čhuṅ-ba, bKa'-'bum, vol. XIV(Pha)]. In his opinion the degrees of the Path of Enlightenment were almost complete in the above system (expounded in the Lam-rim), but that it was necessary to be initiated into the system of Tantras which enabled one to obtain Buddhahood in this very life. Thus he wrote many śāstras describing the degrees of the Path (of Tantra) (the sṄags-rim čhen-mo, vol. III /Ga/, fol.441a: How to first attend on a /Tantric/ Teacher, then how to practise Tantric vows and precepts bestowed by the Teacher, and how to practise having obtained initiation of the two degrees of meditation of the utpannakrama and sampanna-krama degrees). Especially, he composed precepts and commentaries on the Śrī-Guhyasamāja-Tantra basing himself on the texts by the ācārya Nāgārjuna and the latter's disciples (the sGron-gsal rgya-čher bśad-pa, bKa'-'bum, vol.V /ča/, fol.138a; the sGron-gsal-mčhan-gyi yaṅ-'grel, bKa'-'bum, vol.IV /ṅa/, fol. 476a; the Rim-lṅa gsal-sgron, bKa'-'bum, vol.VII /Ja/, fol.312a). At first he laboured for the welfare of others and visited many different countries. In the beginning of the year Earth-Female-Ox (sa-mo-glaṅ—1409 A.D.) he held the Great Prayer Assembly (sMon-lam čhen-mo), and brought down the light of the Doctrine on those who had gathered. In the same year he founded the monastery of dGe-ldan rnam-par rgyal-ba'i gliṅ. Then in the year Wood-Female-Sheep (śiṅ-mo-lug—1415 A.D.) he proceeded towards bKra-śis Do-kha of 'On, and revolved the Wheel of the Doctrines of the Tantras and Sūtras. He gathered a few Tripiṭakadharas and classified the difficult points of the Doctrine. He spent over two months there. After that having come to dGe-ldan, he built the outer chapel (Phyi'i mčhod-khaṅ), and inside it erected a Tantric maṇḍala made of precious stones (the maṇḍala can be still seen at dGe-ldan. One of the images of the maṇḍala became famous as the "rainbow" image, Khaṇḍa-pa 'Ja'-tshon-ma). In the year Earth-Female-Hog (sa-mo-phag—1419 A.D.) he went to the hot springs of sTod-luṅs (a well-known resort in Tibet). When he was preaching the Śrī-Guhyasamāja-Tantra to numerous kalyāṇa-mitras, who had gathered in the vihāra of dPal 'Bras-spuṅs, he placed his preacher's chair facing dGe-ldan. (7b) After completing the exposition of the ninth chapter (of the Guhyasamāja-Tantra), he proceeded to dGe-ldan. On his way there he performed the consecration rite at gSaṅ-sṅags-mkhar. He received an invitation from Lha-spur Gru-bži-pa. While he was residing there, a loud sound of a divine bell (gaṇḍī, a piece of wood used to gather inmates of a monastery, according to the Vinaya of the Sarvāstivādins. The gaṇḍī and the khakkhara or staff are peculiar to the Sarvāstivādins) resounded from the Sky, and following it he proceeded to the mansion (gzims-khaṅ) of dGe-ldan. On arrival there, he presented to the Dharmasvāmin rGyal-tshab Rin-po-čhe a hat and a mantle which symbolized his appointment to the abbot's chair. When he sat meditating, his face shone like that of a sixteen-years old boy, and this was seen by his disciples. Immediately after it, he passed into the Immaculate Sphere (Dag-pa'i dbyiṅs). The above is a brief story of the deeds of the Venerable All-knowing. By the grace of this Venerable One, even those of the monks who had not seen his face, and were residing at distant places, wore the religious robe (cīvara, čhos-gos) and kept with themselves the (meditative) mat, the alms-bowl (pātra) and the other articles (prescribed by the Vinaya). They discarded the wearing of the hood (sdud-ma) as a cloak, and instead wore the mantle (zla-gam), and changed the colour of their hats to that of gold.

The above is an account of his greatness as seen by ordi-
ıary human beings. Now his intrinsic greatness:

In the story about the instructions given by the guhyapati 'ajrapāṇi to the mahā-upādhyāya Las-kyi rdo-rJe (Karmava-ra), it is said: "Even I, Vajrapāṇi, was unable to grasp the neasure of the merit of Sumatikīrtiśrī (bLo-bzaṅ grags-pa-pal) (rJe Rin-po-čhe'i bKa'-'bum, vol. I (ka), Žu-lan sman-ıčhog bdud-rtsi'i 'phreṅ-ba, fol 10b:—kho-bo Phyag-na do-rJes kyaṅ 'di'i yon-tan dpag-par mi-nus-śiṅ). In the above eliable text (it is stated): "After that he will become the odhisattva Mañjuśrīgarbha ('Jam-dpal sñiṅ-po) in the Heaven f Tuṣita" (See Žu-lan, fol. 12b: dGa'-ldan-du Byams-pa'i ruṅ-du Byaṅ-čhub sems-dpa' 'Jam-dpal sñiṅ-po žes-bya-bar kye). In future he will become the Tathāgata Siṃhāsvara Seṅ-ge'i ṅa-ro)." From the above quotations one under-tands that He has been a being with a straight forward Mind, dwelling on a lofty stage (of spiritual evolution), who ıad come here for the welfare of living beings. His Regent rGyal-tshab) was one filled with aversion towards the entire (84)
Vorld, endowed with an enlightened Mind, unhindered (in he understanding) of all the systems (expounded) in the asic texts of the Tantras and Sūtras. He possessed a per-onality bound by pure undefiled morality, even in case of he smallest transgressions. He showed perseverance in ıeritorious deeds without abandoning them even for a single noment. He acted as abbot for 13 years till the year Iron-'emale-Hog (lčags-mo-phag—1431 A.D.). In this year he ıanded over the abbotship to mKhas-grub dGe-legs-dpal, and ıimself embraced a solitary life, and departed to Potala (i.e. ied) in the year Water-Male-Mouse (čhu-pho-byi-ba—1432 A.D.) at the age of 69. mKhas-grub dGe legs-dpal occupied he abbot's chair for eight years till the year Earth-Male-Horse (sa-pho-rta—1438 A.D.), and then passed away. The Dharmasvāmin Legs-pa rgyal-mtshan (an incarnation of this bbot exists in Amdo, and is known by the name of Žwa-lu-a) was born in the year Wood-Hare (śiṅ-yos—1375 A.D.),

and became abbot (of dGe-ldan) in the year Earth-Female-Sheep (sa-mo-lug—1439 A.D.), at the age of 65. He died at the age of 76 in the year Iron-Male-Horse (lčags-pho-rta—1450 A.D.). Druṅ bLo-gros-pa was born in the year Earth-Female-Serpent (sa-mo sbrul—1389 A.D.), and became abbot in the year Iron-Male-Horse (lčags-pho-rta—1450 A.D.), at the age of 62. He remained abbot till the year Water-Female-Sheep (čhu-mo-lug—1463 A.D.), during which he appointed to the chair Ba-so-ba, aged 62, and himself became an ascetic. After that they asked the Dharmasvāmin bLo-gros brtan-pa to occupy the chair.

He is still alive performing meritorious deeds.

The Chapter on dGe-ldan.

(The above are the first six abbots of the 'J̌am-dbyaṅs gtsaṅ-pa bdun-brgyud).

sMra-ba'i seṅ-ge Roṅ-ston čhen-po (he was the first scholar who opposed the dGe-lugs-pas):

He was a Bodhisattva endowed with the power of solemn wish (smon-lam-gyi mthu-čan). He was born as son of a Bon-po family at the rGyal-mo roṅ (rGyal-roṅ in Eastern Khams) in the year Fire-Female-Sheep (me-mo-lug—1367 A.D.). In his youth he proceeded to dBus and gTsaṅ. He studied the sciences at gSaṅ-phu. At the age of 20, he mastered the Pramāṇaviniścaya and became matchless in philosophical debates (Rigs-pa smra-ba). He took the vows of Pratimokṣa at Gro-sar before dMar-ston čhen-po. He attended on different teachers, and mastered all the Piṭakas. Between his studies he preached the Piṭakas to many wise men in fulfilment of their wishes at many localities in South and (8b)
North La-stod, in Upper and Lower gTsaṅ, and at dbU and gYor. He constantly preached the Abhisamayālaṃkāra and its commentary, following mainly on the method (mdzad-srol) of the mahā-upādhyāya Saṅs-rgyas-dpal. He, held in high esteem the "Later" Lineage of the Zi-byed doctrine which included hidden precepts of the above. He, being endowed with the power of solemn wish (smon-lam), nothing is said

about his clashes with local deities, or about the Teacher and his disciples suffering from epidemics. Thus he did not suffer from any kind of accidents. He did not possess even the slightest attachment towards wealth and property. He used to say: "It is improper for a kalyāṇa-mitra to count the price of one or two measures (of grain) received from his disciples. A kalyāṇa-mitra should know how to establish a concomitance (khyab-pa, vyāpti)." He used to say to his disciples who had purified their Inner Self, that "this bond which has no beginning, is enough for us (meaning that they should not be bound by theories). You may follow any kind of theories conforming to your mind." Outwardly he seems to have concentrated on the preaching of the Doctrine only. Inwardly he practised constantly Yoga, and was able to recognize the different shades of the pañca-prāṇā (rluṅ-lṅa).

When the nail of his big toe fell off, it transformed itself into a pearl shell. In the year Wood-Female-Hare (śiṅ-mo-yos —1435 A.D.) he founded the monastery of Nālandā ('Phan-yul. The monastery maintains a school of philosophy), and said: "Ar Byaṅ-čhub ye-śes died while preaching the Prajñāpāramitā. I shall also make my disciples remove my corpse from the preacher's chair (čhos-khri).' Once the Piṭakadhara dGe-ba rgyal-mtshan told him that he had seen in a dream that a serious accident was to befall him during that year and that he should recite mantras and perform rites (in order to remove the evil influences). He replied: "I am not the subject of the ācārya dGe-rgyal's prophecy. Let any kind of accidents take place! I shall live till the age of 83! True to his words he passed away at the age of 83 in the year Earth-Female-Serpent (sa-mo-sbrul--1449 A.D.). According to his instructions, his corpse was not to be removed from the preacher's chair. Not more than two days must have passed between his last preaching and his death (i.e. he had passed (9a)
away on the chair). In his usual conversation he used to say: "I shall not become a boorish Khams-pa like (the present one). I shall become a devaputra drinking nectar in the heaven of

Tuṣita!'' Therefore now he must be surely residing in Tuṣita. Before his passing into Nirvāṇa, he appointed to the Abbot's chair the Dharmasvāmin bKra-śis rnam-rgyal. This one also laboured extensively for the benefit of the Doctrine, preached, erected large images, etc. He was born in the year Earth-Male-Tiger (sa-pho-stag—1398 A.D.) and passed away at the age of 61. The Dharmasvāmin dGe-ba rgyal-mtshan was born in the year Water-Male-Dog (čhu-pho-khyi--1382 A.D.). He came to the chair at the age of 77 in the year Earth-Tiger (sa-stag—1458 A.D.), and lived till the year Water-Horse (čhu-rta—1462 A.D.) for five years, when he died. bDag-po rGya-gar-ba was born in the year Earth-Female-Sheep (sa-mo-lug—1439 A.D.), and became abbot in the year Water-Horse (čhu-rta--1462 A.D.), at the age of 24. He acted as abbot for five years, till the year Fire-Male-Dog (me-mo-khyi—1466 A.D.). He entrusted (the abbotship) to gLaṅ-thaṅ Rin-po-čhe, who appointed to the abbot's chair the Dharmasvāmin Guṅ-ru, and himself became an ascetic.

The Chaper on the monastery of Nālandā (in 'Phan-yul).

This great monastery of dPal rTses-thaṅ (on the gTsaṅ-po in Lho-kha) was founded in the year Iron-Female-Hare (lčags-mo-yos—1351 A.D.) by Ta'i Si-tu Byaṅ-chub rgyal-mtshan famed in all quarters. A ruined octagonal upper structure (dbu-rtse) erected in the time of kLu-mes stood there. Having begun work in the autumn, (Byaṅ čhub rgyal-mtshan) built the court-yard facing this upper structure. To the West of it, inside the court-yard, he built a temple with its door facing East. The octagonal structure having fallen in ruin, he thought that it might have a bad effect on the prognostication of the omens of the locality (sa-dpyad), and therefore removed it towards the western mountains. He also built about forty large houses to accommodate monks, as well as a high wall. After this, in the year Water-Male Dragon (čhu-pho-'brug—1352 A.D.) he invited there numerous priests from various monasteries in order to give a start to the study of the Doctrine. He endowed (the monastery) with property for the upkeep of preachers. He (9b) also established the distribution of food, tea and soup to the common monks. He appointed to the abbot's chair 'J̌am-pa'i dbyaṅs Śākyargyal-mtshan, aged 13, who was able to recite by heart four of the famous series of five volumes ('Dul-ba, dbU-ma, Tshad-ma, Phar-phyin, and mDzod). For four years he maintained a class (of students). At the age of 26, he retired to the Palace (rtse). Then rGyal-sras Grags-pa rin-čhen, who was born in the year Earth-Female-Ox (sa-mo-glan—1349 A.D.), aged 17, came to the abbot's chair in the year Wood-Female-Serpent (śiṅ-mo-sbrul—1365 A.D). He passed away at the age of 19 in the year Fire-Female-Sheep (me-mo-lug—1367 A.D.). After him the ācārya 'J̌am-snon-pa acted as teacher (bla-čhos gsuṅ-ba) in the year Earth-Male-Ape (sa-pho-spre'u—1368 A.D.). At the end of this year, Rin-po-čhe bSod-nams grags-pa, born in the year Earth-Female-Hog (sa-mo-phag—1359 A.D.), aged 10, came to the chair. He occupied the chair till the year Iron-Ape (lčags-spre—1380 A.D.), and held a religious assembly in Lha-sa. In the year Iron-Female-Hen (lčags-mo-bya—1381 A.D.) he retired to the Palace (rtse). He was replaced by Grags-pa rgyal-mtshan, born in the year Wood-Male-Tiger (śiṅ-pho-stag—1374 A.D.), aged 8, who came to the chair in the year Iron-Female-Hen (lčags-mo-bya—1381 A.D.), and preached the Pramāṇavārtika. At the age of 12, before the end of the year Wood-Female-Ox (śiṅ-mo-glaṅ—1385 A.D.), he retired to the Palace (rtse). In this Wood-Female-Ox (śiṅ-mo-glaṅ—1385 A.D.) he retired to the Palace (rtse). In this Wood-Ox year (śiṅ-glaṅ—1385 A.D.) one named Druṅ Byaṅ-čhub rdo-rǰe, born in the year Fire-Female-Serpent (me-mo-sbrul—1377 A.D.), came to the chair, aged 9. He occupied the chair for 44 years till his death in the year Earth Male-Ape (so-pho-spre'u—1428 A.D.). During that time he made the monastery prosperous and wealthy. From the winter retreat of this year, 'J̌am-dbyaṅs grags-pa 'byuṅ-gnas-pa, born in the year Wood-Male-Horse (śiṅ-pho-rta—1414 A. .), aged 15, acted as abbot. In the sixth month of the year Wood-Male-Mouse (čhu-pho-byi-ba—1432 A.D.) he retired to the Palace (rtse). Then during 12 years there was no abbot, but he supervised the monastery from the Palace (lit. "looked at the monastery out of the corner of his eye"). He built a great image (lha-čhen), a great vihāra and prepared a bKa'-'gyur written in gold, and placed it inside (the vihāra). He did not allow women (10a) and wine within the precincts of the monastery, as well as cared well for the teachers and student-monks. After that, beginning with the Wood-Male-Mouse (śiṅ-pho-byi-ba—1444 A.D.), Druṅ Kun-dga' legs-pa'i 'byuṅ-gnas was appointed civil official (naṅ-so) of rTses-thaṅ. In the year Fire-Male-Tiger (me-pho-stag—1446 A.D.) he ('Jam-dbyaṅs Grags-pa 'byuṅ-gnas) preached a new exposition (bśad-gsar). In the summer of the year Earth-Male-Dragon (sa-pho-'brug—1448 A.D.) he retired to the Palace. From this Earth-Dragon year the Čhe-sa Saṅs-rgyas rgyal-mtshan acted as civil official (naṅ-so) for ten years, without occupying the chair, and passed away in the winter of the Fire-Female-Ox year (me-mo-glaṅ—1457 A.D.). After him rDo rJe rin-čhen dbaṅ-gi rgyal-mtshan occupied the chair in the seventh month of the year Fire-Female-Hog (me-mo-phag—1467 A.D.). This great monastery was a place filled with different monks belonging to different sects, whose preaching and study continued without interruption, as well as a place producing all the wishes of living beings. It was a self refuge for preachers, who wandered about countries. This great monastery was founded in the year Iron-Female-Hare (lčags-mo-yos—1351 A.D.), 126 years having passed since then till the year Fire-Male-Ape (me-pho-spre'u—1476 A.D.). The Chapter on rTses-thaṅ.

Now I shall reply to questions put in connection with the "Blue Annals". There exists a disagreement between the (different) accounts of the "Later" Propagation of the Doctrine. I also find it difficult to make up my mind. I have compiled this chapter basing myself on ancient accounts. In regard to the

teacher from whom kLu-mes received ordination, and the story of his labours in dbUs and gTsaṅ, I believe (the account) composed by Pa-śi gNas-brtan to be (nearest to truth). I followed exclusively on his version, because the author was a direct disciple of kLu-mes. In that chapter I have mentioned his name. As regards the story that these two had different preceptors, I have merely repeated his (Pa-śi gNas-brtan) words. The two (preceptors) seem to have been sBa and Rag, since they belong to one group. I have written about the (group) of the "Ten men of dbUs and gTsaṅ" (dbUs- (10*b*)
gTsaṅ mi-bču) basing myself on accounts by Bu-ston and others. (In this question) it is difficult for me to express my own opinion. According to Bu-ston these "Ten-Men" were: from dbUs—the Five: kLu-mes, Sum-pa, Rag-śi, sBa and 'Briṅ; from gTsaṅ: the Two—Lo and Tshoṅ, the two brothers 'O-brgyad and U-pa-de-dkar. Again according to others there have been eight only: from dbUs—kLu-mes, Sum-pa; from gTsaṅ—Lo and Tshoṅ; from mṄa'-ris—Pa-śi rDzi-dkar-ba—six in all; then sBa and Rag. Again there are some who are of the opinion that 'Briṅ has been 'Bri rDzi-dkar-ba because of the absence of any mention of the existence of written works by 'Bri rDzi-dkar-ba in mṄa'-ris. Thus I have based my account on statements made by others, and I do not give them as my own opinion. It is a fact that in dbUs, kLu-mes, Sum-pa and 'Briṅ have founded monasteries and monastic communities. Ka-ba Śākya dbaṅ-phyug was an able disciple of sBa and Rag, who were mentioned in a group. It is also true that in gTsaṅ the number of monasteries increased thanks to Lo and Tshoṅ. (These facts) I accept. Having compiled numerous accounts, I have mentioned the authors' names, for the sake of investigation. The story that the lo-tsā-ba Rin-čhen bzaṅ-po, aged 13, had been ordained by the upādhyāya Ye-śes bzaṅ-po in mṄa'-ris proper, is found in the biography (rnam-thar) of the lo-tsā-ba composed by one named Khri-thaṅ Jñāna. According to it, the lo-tsā-ba had been ordained in the year Iron-Male-Horse (lčags-pho-rta—970

A.D.). The third year after this event, the Water-Female-Hen (čhu-mo-bya—973 A.D.) is the first year of the Period of the "Later" Propagation of the Doctrine, as stated in the History of the Doctrine by Bu-ston Rin-po-čhe who based (his occount) on a story told by an old woman (Bu-ston Čhos-'byuṅ, gSuṅ-'bum. vol XXIV. /Ya/, fol. 136a; "History of Buddhism," translated by E. Obermiller, II, p. 221).

The year Earth-Male-Tiger (sa-pho-stag—978 A.D), which was the fifth year after the Water-Female-Hen year (čhu-mo-bya—973 A.D.), is the first year of the Period of the "Later" Propagation (of the Doctrine) according to 'Brom-ston-pa. Again in later times Atīśa became the Master of the Doctrine, and all bKa'-gdams-pas agree that the year of (11a)
Atīśa's coming was a Horse year (rta-lo), but there exists a disagreement as to the element (dbaṅ-thaṅ) of the year. After thoroughly examining the biographies of rGya-ma-pa, uncle and nephew, sNe'u-zur-pa, sPyan-sṅa and sPu-to-pa, one can state that Atīśa came (to Tibet) in the year Water-Male-Horse (čhu-pho-rta—1042 A.D.). This was the 61st year of Atīśa. After a minute examination of ancient chronicles, I consider the above account, as well as the history of the Lineage from rJe Mar-pa to rṄog, and that of Mid-la to sGam-po-pa, to be reliable accounts. Similarly there is no mistake in the number of years after mKhon dKon-mčhog rgyal-po in the Lineage of the Sa-skya-pas. There exist also many other (accounts) in which there are no mistakes in the number of years. Further, some of the other accounts were narrated by me according to the statements of other (authors). Again there are other accounts written by me without investigating them, basing myself on statements made by others. In short, I consider the date of the religious king Sroṅ-btsan sgam-po, and the dates of Atīśa, 'Brom and others, as well as that of rṄog, Master of the Doctrine, to be correct. This must be kept in mind. Now I shall give a chapter on the one who has laboured most for the sake of the present work. The patron (of his work)

was the khri-dpon (officer-in-charge of 10,000 families, corresponds to the Mongol tümen-ü noyan) of Bya named bKra-śis dar-rgyas, endowed with the power of extraordinary fortune, adorned with wisdom, faith and generosity. Now I shall relate his story:

In general, in this country of Tibet, people call a country by the name of the clan which occupies the greater part of the region. For instance Rog-pa-sa (a country populated by the Rog clan), dGyer-pa-sa (the country populated by the dGyer clan). The borderland of Ma-yul-rdzoṅ in Lower Yar-kluṅs was called Bya-sa because most of its (11b) inhabitants belonged to the clan of Bya. In this country, filled with all kinds of wishes, lived two brothers—named Čhos-kyi ka-ba, "Pillar of Religion" and his younger brother Thod-pa gYu'i smin-ma-čan, "One with turquoise eyebrows". The younger brother had two sons—the upādhyāya Yon-tan-mčhog and Bya Śa-ka. The one named the upādhyāya Yon-tan-mčhog was ordained at 'Briṅ-sde, and acted as upādhyāya to others. He rebuilt the Gaṅs-par lha-khaṅ and took over the four monasteries: kLogs in gYe, Sa-mtha' in Bya, Dro-mda' in Dags-po, sTin-mo-mig in dMyal, and called them the "Four Sons of Gaṅs-par" (Gaṅs-par-gyi bu bži). Bya Śa-ka had two sons: rDo-rJe legs-pa and rDo-rJe dbaṅ-phyug. In their lifetime they came to dMyal, and founded rGya-mtsho groṅ-mkhar. The Son of rDo-rJe dbaṅ-phyug was Rin-čhen-'od, the great teacher of Bya-nag (the bLa-ma Bya-nag čhen-po). At the age of 41, he met the mahā-paṇḍita of Kāśmīra (Śākyaśrībhadra), and obtained from him many doctrines, such as the twelve maṇḍalas of the Tantra (sByoṅ-rgyud, a branch of the Yoga-Tantra), and others. He also followed on many holy men, such as rGyal-ba Thog-dugs-pa, sKyo 'Od-'byuṅ, gŽaṅ rTa-rmig-pa, and others, and was learned in all branches of Science. He was adorned with spiritual realization. In particular, he was able to employ as his attendants the religious protectors of the Tantras, such as sPu-gri bskor-gsum (three deities of the rÑiṅ-ma school), and others. His fame encompassed the entire Snow Land (Tibet). He had four spiritual sons: in Lower Bya—mTshal-sgom Čhos-la dga'-ba; at Lo-ro—Rab-dga'-ba čhen-po; at Dags-po—Ba-tsho ras-pa; at gTaṅ—'U-yug-pa, the Great.

The four "original monasteries" (rtsa-ba'i sde-bži): at dMyal—Čhos-sgro gaoṅ-mkhar; at gYe—Se-bo; at Dags—Na-mo śod; at Bya—rGya-mtsho lhug-tshaṅ.

The son of A-mi Bya-nag čhen-po—Bya J̌o-sras. His son (was) Bya mṄa'-bdag who had three sons: gČen-pa dGe-sloṅ-pa, Bya Rin-čhen, and Čhos-rgyal-dpal-bzaṅ. These three were known as the Bya-rigs-gsum mgon-po (the "Three Lords of Bya").

dGe-sloṅ-pa's sons were: Rin-čhen-dpal, dBaṅ-phyug rin-čhen, Rin-čhen bzaṅ-po, and Dags-po-pa, gYe, Dags. dMyal, Bya, and Lo-ro were his dependencies, and he owned much landed property. (124) Bya Rin-čhen ruled over gYe, dMyal, Bya, Dags, and Lo-ro. He repelled the Mongol troops, and was recognised as chief of all the above localities. He and the mahāsiddha Ur-brgyan-pa became priest and supporter. His son was Kun-dga' rin-čhen. His descendants were numerous, and owned much landed property. This Kun-dga' rin-čhen met the great official (dPon-čhen) of Sa-skya—Kun-dga' bzaṅ-po. Bya Čhos-rgyal-dpal-bzaṅ made peace with the Mongols. At the age of 12, he met 'Gro-mgon 'Phags-pa. He requested Śar-pa Kun-bsod-pa to become his teacher, and heard from him all the three Tantras (rGyud-gsum) together with hidden precepts, etc. He built the vihāra of Yaṅs-rtse, and prepared a copy of the bKa'-'gyur written in gold. He gathered the tax which consisted of the produce of the kingdom, and kept it at mDzod-nag. He laid the foundation of the Royal law, and introduced perfect order in both religious and secular affairs, which excelled that of other (kings). His sons were: Kun-dga' rgyal-mtshan-dpal-bzaṅ-po, the mahā-upādhyāya sPyil-bu-pa, mṄa'-bdag Čhos-seṅ-'od, Bya lKug-pa-dpal, and others. Kun-dga. rgyal-mtshan proceeded to 'Dam (near Tengri-nūr or gNam-mtsho) and requested the dPon-čhen 'Od-zer sen-ge to grant him an official title. The latter bestowed one on him. The official Čhos-rgyal-dpal-bzan of sGu-rab-pa also revered him. The incident of rTa'u-ra-pa also took place in his time. After him dPal-mgon rdo-rJe and his son Drun bLo-gros ruled over the region. After them, the son of Kun-dga' rgyal-mtshan—rGya-ma-pa Kun-dga' bsod nams ruled over his and the monasteries' subjects. After him mÑa'bdag Čhos-sen, son of Čhos-rgyal-dpal-bzan and the queen of 'Bri-khun, was appointed official of Bya and Dags by 'Bri-khun-pa. His son was the mahā-upādhāya Tshul-khrims bzan-po. When he was acting as abbot of Zans-po-čhe, at the unanimous request of the local inhabitants he mounted the throne of Yans-rtse, and (12*b*) laboured for the good of the Doctrine, and the welfare of living beings. He took under his protection all the monasteries, their serfs and the local inhabitants. After him, his son dKon-mčhog bzan-po, the holder of the religious and secular domains, was appointed official by his father. His son bKra-śis dpal-bzan studied in his youth at rTses-than. He held a perfect festival of preaching. Čhos-rgyal Grags-pa rgyal-mtshan appointed him as khri-dpon (official in charge of 10,000 families) of Bya-pa. His sons were: rGyal-ba bKra-śis, Śākya dpal-mgon, Thub-pa rgyal-mtshan, and others. rGyal-ba bKra-śis proceeded to sNe-gdon. He became an attendant of the superior Grags-pa (Gon-ma Grags-pa 'byun-gnas). From sNe-gdon he was appointed khri-dpon of Bya-pa. His younger brother Śākya dpal-mgon was ordained by the mahā-upādhāya Yon-dban, and conducted studies. Since the time of his appointment as abbot of Zans-po-čhe, he continued to perform virtuous deeds of benefit to the Doctrine of Buddha. The sons of rGyal-ba bKra-śis were: Bya bKra-śis dar-rgyas, Pad-ma blTams-mčhog rgyal-po (also rTa-mčhog rgyal-po), the incarnation of sGo-gčig-pa, Bya Tshe-dban rgyal-po, bsKal-bzans Čhos-kyi rgya-mtsho bSod-nams man-thos dban-po'i sde, and Bya Nor-bu rgya-mtsho. Bya bKra-śis dar-

rgyas married the Princess named rDo-rJe Gos-dkar-ma. Čhos-rgyal Nor-bu bkra-śis mi-'gyur dbaṅ-po'i sde and his brother Grags-pa rgyal-mtshan dpal-bzaṅ-po were born to them. ByabKra-śis dar-rgyas legs-pa'i rgyal-po Phyogs-thams-čad-las rnam-par rgyal-ba dbaṅ-po'i sde: He was appointed khri-dpon of Lho-rgyud (the Southern Region) after (the death) of his father by order of the king rDo-rJe Rin-čhen dbaṅ-gi rgyal-po of rTses-thaṅ. Again, from sNe-gdoṅ (name of the palace of the Tibetan kings) he obtained the official title (bkos) of 'Ja'-sa (<Mongol Jasaɣ) and the official robe. He ruled over the Bya-pas. His deeds and fame were great in both the religious and secular spheres. Each of the khri-dpons of Bya-pa were endowed with great fame. The king (sa-skyoṅ), who enjoyed both the religious and secular spheres, as he would a summer stream, at the suggestion of the dPal-ldan lo-tsā-ba čhen-po bSod-nams rgya-mtsho'i sde, who was a great and all-knowing Lord endowed with a perfect vision before which all the scriptures of the Jina were revealed, a siddheśvara who had realized the sahaja-jñāna, arranged for (13a)
the paying of expenses and labour in a way which did not contradict the Doctrine. In the beginning the copyists (par-yig) were paid by dPal rDo-rJe bde-ma who patronized impartially different religious sects. In Lhun-grub Lha-rtse, a district of dbUs, the holy kalyāṇa-mitra dPal Čhos-kyi rgyal-mtshan, who was a follower of the teaching of the Venerable One (bSod-nams rgya-mtsho'i-sde) and the mahā-sthavira dGe-legs dpal-mgon, endowed with wisdom and characterized by strictness and propriety, corrected (the text), as desired by the Venerable great lo-tsā-ba. Śar Dags-po-pa dPal-phyogs thams-čad-las rnam-par rgyal-ba'i lha who was endowed with the faculty of giving a logical and free interpretation of all the vehicles of the Tantras and Sūtras, supervised the proper execution of the work.

The head copyist (yi-ge'i rig-byed-pa) was Ñi-śar bKra-śis, a native of Dol, which was a source of knowledge (rig-pa'i 'byuṅ-gnas). The chief block-maker (brkos-kyi rig-byed-pa) was one named Grags-pa rgyal-mtshan. The dexterity of his and his disciples' hands showed itself in this virtuous work. They started the work in the year Iron-Female-Ox (lčags-mo-glaṅ—1481 A.D.), and completed it at the great Palace called Čhos-rgyal lhun-po in a district of dMyal, which was the essence of the land and a place where the streams of most excellent prosperity had merged into each other.

By virtue of this may the Precious Doctrine of the Jina live long!
May the Holy Men, holders of the Doctrine, live long!
May the monastic community observe the Holy Doctrine by day and by night!
May the supporters and their retinues rule according to the Doctrine!
May the kingdom live without internal strife!
May we in our next lives meet the Holy Men and the kalyāṇa-mitras!
May we labour extensively for the Doctrine of the Buddha!
The Chapter on the execution of the block-print edition (of the "BLUE ANNALS").
Resting on the golden foundation (gser-gyi sa-gži) of the blessing of the Great Merciful One (Avalokiteśvara),
Surrounded by majestic snow mountains,
Where eternal streams of monks flow from the Anavatapta (Ma-dros-pa) Lake of Morality,
Which had removed the heat of defilement and is filled with jewels of preaching and meditation,
Where the Mount Aśvamukha (n. of an iron range) of scholars is sounding the mighty blast of the Doctrine,
Where lies the source of all goodness,
This Land of Snows (Tibet), similar to a great ocean, deserves to be praised by scholars.
The story of the Immaculate Precious Doctrine of the Jina, handed down from Holy Men to Holy Men,
I have thread on a string of letters,

in order that they may be seen by people endowed with the eye of Wisdom.

By virtue of this, may all living beings drink the nectar of the Doctrine of the Jina!

May the eternal deeds of the Jewel of the All-Knowing, the Treasury of all Merits, enter into them!

As an image of the Buddha, even if made of stone, wood or clay, ought to be an object of devotion,

Even so, the Doctrine, which had become a mere shadow, because of the Iron Age, ought to be worshipped by all living beings (this verse is evidently a paraphrase of the well-known second verse of Nāgārjuna's Suhṛllekha: "As an image of the Sugata, even if only made of wood, is honoured by the wise, so also my poem, even if humble, is worthy to be listened to, based on the exposition of the Good Law". Tg. Phrin-yig, No. 4182; translated by H. Wenzel in the JPTS, 1886, pp. 2-32).

May this cause the Precious Doctrine of the Jina to spread by every means, in all directions, and may it live long!

This History of the spread of the Doctrine and that of the preachers in Tibet was compiled by the monk gŽon-nu-dpal, the preacher, in the year Earth-Male-Dog (sa-pho-khyi—1478 A.D.), the 850th year since the birth of the religious king Sroṅ-btsan sgam-po (here again 'Gos-lo-tsā-ba considers the year 629 A.D. to be the year of Sroṅ-btsan sgam-po's birth) in the (monastery) of Čhos rdzoṅ, the Abode of Happiness, where natural amṛta flows near to the grove of dPal Kun-tu bzaṅ-op (Samantabhadra).

Salutation to the Three Jewels!
Of those things which spring from a cause
the cause has been told by the Tathāgata;
And their suppression likewise
the great Śramaṇa has revealed.
(Ye dharmā hetuprabhavā hetun teṣān Tathāgato hy avadat/
teṣāñ ca yo nirodho evaṃvādī mahāśramaṇaḥ//
Śubhaṃ astu sarvajagataṃ)

May the Whole World be happy!
Oṃ svasti.

This treasury of good words (containing) the history of the great systems of the impartial Doctrine in Āryāvarta and Tibet, the origin of the Doctrine and that of men who followed it, was compiled by the excellent scholar 'Gos-lo gŽon-nu-dpal. This necklace of all wise fortunate ones, is called the "BLUE ANNALS" (Deb-ther sṅon-po).

The printing blocks are nowadays kept at the (monastery) of dGa'-ldan brtan-bžugs čhos-'khor, better known by the name of dbUs-gTsaṅ Kun-bde-gliṅ (One of the four chief gliṅ/gliṅ-bži/of Lha-sa), (situated) in the vicinity of the Government seat to Lha-sa.

May the deeds beneficial to living beings increase till the end of the World.

May the inexhaustible virtue, encompassing a wide area, increase perpetually according to the wishes (of living beings).

The ancient block-print edition of the History, called the "BLUE ANNALS", was preserved at Yaṅs-pa-čan. At the time of the Tibetan-Nepālese War (the War of 1792 A.D.), some of the printing blocks having been lost, we have prepared new ones to replace them. We also replaced by new ones those which had become unclear, in the interest of living beings, and deposited the printing blocks at the (monastery) of dbUs-gTsaṅ Kun-bde-gliṅ. This colophon and the words of the solemn wish (praṇidhi) were composed by rTa-tshag-pa Ye-śes blo-bzaṅ bsTan-pa'i mgon-po.

The total of pages (in this volume)—485.

INDEX

SŪTRAS AND ŚĀSTRAS

SANSKRIT

Advayasamatāvijayākhyā-kalpa-mahārāja, II, 418, n. 4.
Advayasiddhisādhana, II, 856.
Anāvila-tantrarāja, II, 865.
Anāvilanāma-tantrapañjikā, II, 865.
Abhidharmakośa, I, 280, 346; II, 490, 698, 793. 808, 982, 993. 1012.
Abhidharmaṭīkālakṣaṇānusāriṇī, I, 342.
Abhidharmasamuccaya, I, 149, 233, 344, 345; II, 490, 534, 698, 808.
Abhidharmasamuccayavyākhyā, II, 1009, 1012, 1069.
Abhidhāna-uttaratantra, I. 163; II, 533, 729, 825.
Abhiṣekanirukti, II, 855.
Abhisamayālaṃkārakārikāvṛttiśuddhamati, I, 207.
Abhisamayālaṃkāra-nāma-prajñāpāramitopadeśaśāstrakārikā, II, 534, 899.
Abhisamayālaṃkāra-nāma-prajñāpāramitopadeśaśāstravṛtti, I, 180.
Abhisamayālaṃkāra - nāma - prajñāpāramitopadeśaśāstravṛtti-duravabodhāloka-nāma-ṭīkā, I. 70.
Amanasikāroddeśa, II, 833.
Aśokadattavyākaraṇa. II, 1069.
Aṣṭasāhasrikā-prajñāpāramitā, I, 70, 209, 249, 364, 377, 379; II, 899, 902, 903, 938, 1068.
Aṣṭasāhasrikāprajñāpāramitāvyākhyābhisamayālaṃkārāloka, I, 70, 209, 236, 249 249, 349.
Ātajñāna, II, 865.
Ātmasādhanāvatāra, I, 370.
Āryamūlasarvāstivādiśrāmaṇerakārikā, I, 85, 277.
Āryamūlasarvāstivādiśrāmaṇerakārikāvṛttiprabhāvatī, I. 32, 85; II, 736.
Ārya-Yamantaka, I. 40.
Udānavarga, I, 268; II. 810.
Upadeśakāyapradīpa, II, 905.
Oḍḍiyānatārābhisamayakrama, II, 845.
Oḍḍiyānavinirgataguhyamahāguhyatattvopadeśa, II, 856.
Karmaśataka, I, 63; II, 1069.
Kalāpasūtra, II. 786, 798, 974.
Kālacakra-tantra, II, 636, 638 753-838, 1017, 1054.
Kālacakratantrottaratantrahṛdaya, II, 534, 640, 838.
Kālacakrasādhanagarbhālaṃkāra, II, 764.

Kālacakropadeśasūryacandrasādhana, II, 533, 640.
Kāvyādarśa, II, 534, 786.
Kulalokanāthapañcadaśaka, II, 1007.
Kulalokanāthasādhanāloka, II, 1007.
Kusumāñjaliguhyasamājanibandha, I. 415.
Kṛṣṇayamāritantrarājatrikalpa, I, 373.
Kṛṣṇayamāritantrarājaprekṣaṇapathapradīpa-nāma-ṭikā, I, 377.
Kṛṣṇayamārimukhaṣaṭcakrasādhana, I, 377.
Koṭiniṣṭhaphalapradīpa. II, 906.
Kosalālaṃkāratattvasaṃgrahaṭikā, I, 353.
Kriyāsaṃgraha, II, 974.
Khadiravaṇitārāsādhana, II, 485.
Khasama-tantrarāja, II, 832, 848.
Guṇapūrṇi-nāma-ṣaḍaṅgayogaṭippaṇī, II, 764.
Guruparaṃparakramopadeśa, II, 857.
Guhyajambhalasādhana, I, 370.
Guhyagarbhatattvaviniścaya, I, 103, 104; II, 534.
Guhyatattvaprakāśa, I, 358.
Cakrasaṃvaraguhyācintya-tantrarāja, I, 142, 208.
Caturaṅgasādhanasamantabhadri, I, 168, 370.
Caturaṅgasādhanasamantabhadri-nāma-ṭikā, I, 168.
Caturmudrāniścaya, II, 857.
Caturyoginīsampuṭatantra, I, 228.
Catuṣpīṭhaṭikā II, 640
Catuḥśatakaśāstrakārikā. I, 343; II, 808.
Candravyākaraṇasūtra, II, 786, 792.
Caryāmelāpakapradīpa, I, 362; II, 736.
Cittakoṣājavajragīti, II, 865.
Cittaguhyapradīpa, II, 905.
Cintāmaṇidhāraṇī, I, 38.
Jātakamālā, I, 268; II, 533, 636, 810, 1054.
Jñānacakṣusādhana, II, 640.
Jñānatilakayoginītantrarājaparamamahādbhuta, I, 361.
Jñānavajrasamuccaya, II, 832.
Jñānasiddhināmasādhana. II, 844, 856.
Ḍākārṇavatantramaṇḍalacakrasādhanaratnapadmarāganidhi, I, 388
Ḍākārṇavamahāyoginītantrarāja, I, 388, 390; II, 497, 549, 813, 825.
Ḍākārṇavamahāyoginītantrarājavāhikaṭikā, I, 388; II, 497.
Ḍākinīvajrapañjara-mahātantrarājakalpa-nāma, I, 209, 363, 400; II, 667.
Ḍākinisarvacittādvayācintyajñānavajravarāhyabhibhavatantrarāja, I, 188, 375.
Tattvajñānasiddhi, I, 393.

Tattvadaśaka, II, 977.
Tattvadaśakaṭikā, II, 725, 857.
Tattvapradipa-nāma-mahāyoginītantrarāja, I, 361.
Tattvasaṃgrahakārikā, I, 355.
Tattvasaṃgrahapañjikā, I, 293.
Tattvasārasaṃgraha, I, 205.
Tattvāloka, I, 353.
Tattvāvatārākhyāsakalasugatavācasaṃkṣiptavyākhyāprakaraṇa, II, II, 725.
Tantrarājaśrīguhyasamājaṭikā, I, 103.
Tarkamudgarakārikā, I, 334, 343.
Trikāyastava, I. 1.
Triśatakārikāvyākhyāna, I, 86; II, 808. (Triśatikā).
Trisamayarājasādhana, I, 312.
Trisamayavyūharāja, II, 832.
Triskandhaka, II, 713.
Trailokyavijaya-mahākalparāja, II, 355.
Dṛṣṭāntamālya, II, 1069.
Dohākoṣa, I, 72, 142.
Dohākoṣagīti, I, 228; II, 533, 865.
Dohākoṣa-nāma-caryāgīti, II, 865.
Dvikramatattvabhāvanā-nāma-mukhāgama, I, 168, 373.
Dharmadharmatāvibhaṅga, I, 233.
Dharmadharmatāvibhaṅgakārikā, I. 220, 347; II, 1074.
Dhyānottamapaṭalakrama, I, 351.
Nāmasaṅgīti, I, 354.
Nītiśāstrajantupoṣaṇabindu, II, 930.
Nairātmyāprakāśa, II, 857.
Nyāyabindu-nāma-prakaraṇa, I, 201; II. 1012, 1074.
Nyāyasamuccaya, II, 195.
Nyāyālaṃkāra, I, 70.
Pañcakrama, I, 284, 367.
Pañcarakṣā, I, 107.
Pañcaviṃśatisāhasrikā-prajñāpāramitā, I, 233, 236, 377; II, 899, 902-940, 1068.
Pañcaviṃśatisāhasrikāprajñāpāramitopadeśaśāstrābhisamay laṃkāra-kārikā-vārtika, II, 1054.
Pañcaviṃśatisāhasrikāprajñāpāramitopadeśāstrābhisamyālaṃkāravṛtti, I, 209, 249.
Pañcaskandhaprakaraṇa, II, 808.
Pañcaśikāṭippaṇi, II, 1007.
Padmajālodbhavasādhana, II. 1007.
Paramādibuddhoddhṛtaśrīkālacakra-nāma-tantrarāja, I, 204; II. 502.

Paramārthasaṃgraha-nāma-sekoddeśaṭīkā, II, 974.
Paramārthasevā, II, 527, 640, 766, 779, 838.
Piṇḍīkṛtasādhana, I, 366.
Pūrṇapramukhāvadānaśataka, II, 1069.
Prajñājñānaprakāśa, II, 857.
Prajñā-nāma-mūlamādhyamakakārikā, I, 334; II, 679, 808, 809.
Prajñāpāramitākośatāla, II, 859.
Prajñāpāramitāsañcayagāthā, I, 331, 367, 377; II, 525, 712, 899, 910, 941, 981, 1010.
Prajñāpradīpamūlamādhyamakavṛtti, I, 341.
Prajñāśataka-nāma-prakaraṇa, II, 638.
Prajñopāyaviniścayasiddhi, II, 856.
Pratipattisāraśataka, I, 803, 811, 824.
Pratimokṣa, I, 79.
Pratimokṣasūtraṭīkāvinayasamuccaya, I, 77, 192, 238.
Pradīpodyotana-nāma-ṭīkā, I, 228, 342, 357, 363, 364, 367, 400; II, 810, 891.
Prabhāvatī, I, 70.
Pramāṇavārtikakārikā, I, 70, 201, 220, 346; II 698, 773, 807, 1012, 1074.
Pramāṇavārtikavṛtti, I, 70.
Pramāṇavārtikālaṃkāra, I, 325.
Pramāṇaviniścaya, I, 155, 201, 236, 386; II,, 532, 542, 698, 1012, 1074.
Pramāṇaviniścayaṭīkā, I, 326.
Pramāṇasamuccaya-nāma-prakaraṇa, I, 220; II, 532, 808.
Pramāṇasamuccayavṛtti, I, 220.
Pratimokṣa-sūtra, II, 808.
Buddha-avataṃsaka-nāma-mahāvaipūlya-sūtra, II, 654, 825.
Buddhakapāla-nāma-yoginītantrarāja, I, 209; II, 832, 1069.
Buddhakapālamahātantrarājaṭīkā-abhayapaddhati, II, 1046.
Bodhicaryāpradīpa, II, 906.
Bodhipathapradīpa, I, 248, 268.
Bodhisattvacaryāvatāra, I, 268, 332, 33; II, 527, 532, 554, 636, 637, 741, 809, 810, 994.
Bodhisattvabhūmi, 64; II, 1012.,
Bodhisattvāvadānakalpalatā, II, 506, 532, 785.
Bhagavatī-prajñāpāramitā-hṛdaya, II, 192.
Bhagavadabhisamaya, I, 144; II, 735.
Bhaṭṭārakamañjuśrīyamāripūjākramavidhi, I, 377.
Bhaṭṭārakāryajanbhalajalendrasādhana, I, 370.
Bhadracaryāpraṇidhānarāja, II, 770.
Bhāvanākramaṣaṭka, II, 865.
Bhikṣuvarṣāgrapṛcchā, I, 30, 86.

Māñjuśrījñānasattvasya-paramārthanāmasaṅgīti, I, 69, 187.
Mañjuśrīnāmasaṅgītiguhyavadvidhivṛttijñānadīpa I, 356; II, 667, 712.
Mañjuśrīnāmasaṅgītivṛttināmārthaprakāśakaraṇa, I, 204.
Mañjuśrīnāmasaṅgītisādhana, I, 160; II, 987.
Mañjuśrīmūlatantra, I, x, 34, 36, 44; 84;II, 791.
Mādhyamakahṛdayavṛttitarkajvālā, I, 29, 258, 311. 324.
Mādhyamakārthasaṃgraha, I, 334.
Mādhyamakālaṃkārakārikā, I, 338; II, 548.
Mādhyamakāloka, I, 333.
Mādhyamakāvatāra, I, 236, 280, 342; II, 535, 808, 809, 993, 994
Mādhyamakāvatāraṭīkā, I, 334
Mādhyamakāvatārabhāṣya, I, 334, 344.
Mādhyamakopadeśa, I, 259, 325.
Madhyāntavibhaṅgakārikā, I, 233; II, 1074.
Mahāmāyā-tantrarāja, I, 209, 293, 364.
Mahāmudrātilaka-nāma-mahāyoginītantrarājādhipati, II, 1049.
Mahāmudrāvajragīti, I, 974.
Mahāyānasaṃgraha, I, 233.
Mahāyānasaṃgrahabhāṣya, I, 257.
Mahāyānasūtrālaṃkāra-nāma-kārikā, I, 233, 268, 293, 348; II, 502, 1068, 1074.
Mahāyānottaratantraśāstra, I, 347, 350; II, 502, 843, 844, 1074.
Mahāyānottaratantraśāstravyākhyā, II, 502, 844.
Mahāvairocanābhisaṃbodhi-tantra, I, 351.
Mahāvyutpatti, I, 43.
Mahāsaṃvarodaya-tantrarāja, II, 824.
Māyājālamahātantrarāja, I, 352.
Māyājālamahātantrarājaṭīkā-ākhyā, I, 352.
Muktitilaka, I. 370.
Muktitilaka-nāma-vyākhyāna, I, 169.
Mukhāgama, I, 169.
Munimatālaṃkāra, I, 32; II, 534, 636, 637, 830.
Mūlamādhyamakavṛttiprasannapadā, I, 236, 280, 334 342, 344; II, 993, 994.
Yamārikṛṣṇakarmasarvacakrasiddhikara, II, 442.
Yamāritantrapañjikāsahajāloka, I, 374.
Yamāriyantrāvali, II, 755.
Yānavākpradīpa, II, 905.
Yuktiṣaṣṭhikākārikā, I, 236, 342 343, II, 548.
Yuktiṣaṣṭhikāvṛtti, I, 342.
Yogacaryābhūmi, 233.
Yogacaryābhūmiviniścayasaṃgraha, I, 233.
Yogacaryābhūmivyākhyā, I, 233.

Yogacaryābhūmau paryāyasaṃgraha, I, 233.
Yogacaryābhūmau bodhisattvabhūmi, I, 233, 268.
Yogacaryābhūmau bodhisattvabhūmivyākhyā, I, 233, 268.
Yogacaryābhūmau vastusaṃgraha, I, 233.
Yogacaryābhūmau vinayasaṃgraha, I, 233.
Yogacaryābhūmau vivaraṇasaṃgraha, I, 233.
Yogacaryābhūmau śrāvakabhūmi, I, 233.
Yogapathapradipa, II, 906.
Yogamālā. II, 735.
Yogaratnamālā-nāma-hevajrapañjikā, I, 228, 364.
Yogaṣaḍaṅga, II, 639.
Yogānusāriṇi-nāma-vajrayoginiṭikā, I, 375.
Yoginisañcārya, I, 384, 385, 388; II, 549.
Raktayamāntakasādhana, I, 379.
Raktayamāri-tantrarāja, I, 379.
Ratnakaraṇḍodghāṭa-nāma-mādhyamakopadeśa, I, 259.
Ratnapradīpa, II, 906.
Ratnamālā, II, 808, 1069.
Ratnamegha, I, 140.
Rājaparikathāratnamālā, I, 343.
Laṅkāvatāra, I, 22.
Laṅkāvatāra-nāma-mahāyānasūtravṛttitathāgatahṛdayālaṃkāra, I, 23.
Laṅkāvatāravṛtti, I, 23.
Lalitavistara, I, 17.
Lokaprajñapti, I, 12, 13, 14, 17.
Vacanamukhāyudhopama, I, 426.
Vajrakīlayamūlatantrakhāṇḍa, I, 106.
Vajracaṇḍacittaguhya-tantra, II, 845.
Vajraḍāka-nāma-uttaratantra, II, 825.
Vajraḍāka-nāma-mahātantrarāja, I, 228.
Vajradhātumahāmaṇḍalavidhisarvavajrodaya, I, 234, 352, 359.
Vajrapada, II, 857.
Vajrapāṇyabhiṣeka, I, 351; II, 832.
Vajrapādasārasaṃgrahapañjikā, II, 830, 974, 994.
Vajrabhairavakalpa-tantrarājā, I, 165.
Vajramaṇḍalālaṃkāramahātantrapañjikā, II, 534.
Vajramantrabhīrusandhimūlatantra, I, 103.
Vajramahābhairava-nāma-tantra, I, 163, 375, 377; II, 442.
Vajrayoginīhomavidhi, I, 393.
Vajravidāraṇā, I, 128; II, 529.
Vajravilāsini-nāma-vajravarāhīsādhana, II, 824.

Vajraśekhara-mahāguhyayogatantra, I, 227, 354, 355; II, 534.
Vajrācāryakṛyāsamuccaya, II, 1045.
Vajrāmṛta-tantra, I, 127.
Vajrāvali-nāma-maṇḍalasādhana, I, 228, 321; II, 1046.
Vākkoṣarucirasvaravajragīti, II, 865.
Vādanyāya-nāma-prakaraṇa, I, 201; III, 1012, 1074.
Vigrahavyāvartanīkārikā, I, 236; II 548.
Vinayakārikā, I, 79, 82, 87, 277; II, 541.
Vinaya-kṣudraka-vastu, I, 77.
Vinayapraśnaṭikā, II, 798.
Vinayavibhaṅga, I, 26.
Vinayavastu, II, 490.
Vinayavastuṭīkā. I, 77.
Vinayasaṃgraha, I, 85.
Vinayasūtra, II 542, 555, 640, 808.
Vinayasūtraṭīkā, I, 77, 79.
Vinayasūtravṛtti-abhidhānasvavyākhyāna, II, 1054.
Vimalaprabhā. I, 358; II, 502, 639, 753 766, 768, 769, 773 776, 785, 789, 793, 794, 795 802, 1049.
Vistarajambhalasādhana, I, 370.
Vyaktabhāvānugatatattvasiddhi, II, 857.
Śatasāhasrikā-prajñāpāramitā, I, 64, 378; II, 899, 902.
Śatasāhasrikāvyākhyā, II, 859.
Śikṣāsamuccaya, I, 268; II, 535 549. 741, 747, 810, 830.
Śūnyatāsaptatikārikā, I, 342; II, 548, 994.
Śūnyatāsaptativṛtti, I, 342.
Śrāmaṇerakārikā, I, 86.
Śrāmaṇeravarṣāgrapṛcchā, I, 31. 86.
Śrāmaṇeraśikṣāpadasūtra. I, 87.
Śrīguhyasamājatantrapāñjikā II, 415.
Śrīguhyasamājatantrarājaṭikācandraprabhā I, 370, 373
Śrīguhyasamājavivaraṇa, II, 415.
Śrīguhyasamājamañjuśrīsādhana, I, 373.
Śrīguhyasamājamaṇḍalavidhi, I, 370, 416.
Śrīguhyasamājalokeśvarasādhana, I, 250, 373, 374.
Śrīguhyasamājasādhanasiddhisaṃbhavanidhi, I, 168.
Śrīguhyasamājastotra, I. 250.
Śrīcakrasaṃvarapañcakramavṛtti. I, 384; II, 803.
Śrīcakrasaṃvarasādhanasarvaśālā-nāma-ṭikā, I, 380,
Śrīcatuḥpīṭhamahāyoginītantrarāja, I, 204 210. 364; II, 400, 403, 475. 532.
Śrī-Tattvajñānasiddhi, I, 377.

Śrī-tattvaviśada-nāma-śrīsaṃvaravṛtti, II, 824.
Śrī-paramādivivaraṇa, I, 353.
Śrī-paramādya-nāma-mahāyānakalparāja, I, 352, 353 354.
Śrīmadraktayamāri-tantrarāja. II, 993.
Śrīmahāsaṃvarodaya-tantrarāja-nāma, I, 388.
Śrīvajraḍāka-nāma-mahātantrarāja, I. 364; II, 846, 888.
Śrīvajrasattva-nāma-sādhana, I, 375, 377.
Śrīsaṃputatantrarājaṭīkāmnāyamañjarī. II, 974. 983. 1046.
Śrīherukasādhana, I, 370.
Śrīhevajrasādhana, I, 143.
Ṣaḍaṅgayoga, II, 640.
Ṣaḍaṅgayoga-nāma-ṭikā, II, 640.
Ṣaḍaṅgaśaraṇa, I, 191.
Sakalatantrasambhavasañcodaniśrīguhyasiddhi, I, 363; II, 856.
Sakṛtprāveśikanirvikalpabhāvanārtha, I, 192.
Sañcayagāthāpañjikā, I. 367.
Saṃskṛtāsaṃskṛtaviniścaya-nāma, I, 21.
Satyadvayavibhaṅgakārikā, I, 322.
Saddharmapuṇḍarika, II, 473, 490.
Saṃtānāntarasiddhi-nāma-prakaraṇa, I, 201; II, 1012, 1074.
Saṃdarśanapradīpa, II. 906.
Saptāṅga, II, 763.
Samatāvastupradīpa, II, 906.
Samantabhadra-nāma-sādhana, I. 370.
Samayabhedavyūhacakra, I. 30.
Samputa. I, 364, 375, 393; II, 832, 848.
Saṃbandhaparīkṣāprakaraṇa, I, 201; II, 1012, 1074.
Saṃvarakhasama-tantrarāja, II, 961.
Sarvatathāgatakāyavākcittakṛṣṇayamāri, I, 163, 200, 228, 374, 375.
Sarvatathāgatakāyavākcittarahasyaguhyasamāja-nāma-mahākalparāja, I, 205. 209, 353, 356, 358 359, 363 ff., 367; II, 891, 1075, 1077, 1078.
Sarvatathāgataguhyatantrayogamahārājādvayasamatāvijaya-nāma-vajraśrī-varamahākalpādi, I, 417, 426.
Sarvatathāgatatattvasaṃgraha, I, 227, 352, 353; II. 753, 812.
Sarvatathāgatatattvasaṃgrahamahāyānābhisamaya-nāma-tantratattvālokakarī-nāma-vyākhyā, I, 352, 355.
Sarvadurgatipariśodhanatejorājasya Tathāgatasya Arhato Samyaksambuddhasya kalpa, I. 165, 354, 355.
Sarvadurgatipariśolhanatejorājasya Tathāgatasya Arhato Samyaksambuddhasya kalpakadeśa, I, 354; II, 485.
Sarvadharmasvabhāvasamatāvipañcitasamādhirāja, II, 451, 825.

Sarvabuddhasamāyogaḍākinīmāyāsambaratantrāthodaraṭikā, I, 103.
Sarvabuddhasamāyogaḍākinijālasambara-nāma-uttaratantra, I, 165.
Sarvarahasya-nāma-tantrarāja I, 352.
Sarvarahasyanibandharahasyapradīpa, I, 352.
Sarvārthasiddhisādhana, I, 393; II, 832.
Sahajasaṃvarasādhana, II, 735, 754.
Sahajasiddhi, I, 363; II, 856,
Sahajasiddhipaddhati, I, 362, 363.
Sādhanasamuccaya, II, 845.
Siddhikavīra-mahātantrarāja, II, 845.
Sukusuma-nāma-dvikramatattvabhāvanāmukhāgamavṛtti, I, 371.
Subāhuparipṛcchā, I. 351.
Sumagadhāvadāna, I, 25.
Suhṛllekha, II, 470, 808, 1092.
Sūtrasamuccaya, I, 272.
Sūtrālaṃkāravyākhyā, II, 502.
Sekanirdeśa, II, 857.
Sekanirdeśapañjikā, II, 842,, 857.
Sekaprakṛyā, II, 758.
Sekoddeśa, II, 533. 640, 758, 768, 838.
Sekoddeśaṭikā, I, 1; II 764, 814, 838.
Sekoddeśapañjikā, II, 794.
Sthaviropanimantraṇa, II, 814.
Sthitisamuccaya, II, 857.
Svapnanirdeśa, I, 31.
Haribhaṭṭajātakamālā, II, 533.
Hetubindu-nāma-prakaraṇa, I, 201; II, 1012, 1074
Herukābhyudaya, II, 846.
Hevajra-tantrarāja I, 187, 207, 209, 358,. 363; II, 533, 638, 667, 764, 797, 980, 1009, 1049.
Hevajrapiṇḍārtha-ṭikā, II, 765, 824, 838.

PERSONAL NAMES

SANSKRIT

Akṣobhyavajra, II, 809.
Ajita, I, 4, 16.
Ajitagupta, I, 38.
Ajitajit, I, 14.
Ajitamitragupta, II, 1031.
Aṅgaja, I, 269.
Atiśa, I, iii, 25, 61, 68 ff., 83, 88, 93, 105, 161, 204, 220, 233, 242ff., 350, 360, 364, 374; II, 420, 440, 455, 629, 665, 697 732, 739, 843-4, 849, 869, 984. 1001, 1044, 1050, 1086.
Atulyadāsa, II, 437.
Atulyavajra, I, 227-8. 325; II, 729, 843.
Advayavajra, II. 731.
Anaṅgavajra, I, 372; II, 856, 869.
Anantajaya, II, 757.
Anāthapiṇḍika, I, 21.
Anutāpagupta, II, 849.
Anupamarakṣita, II, 761, 764, 800.
Aparājita, I, 12.
Abhaya, I, 226, 342, 371; II, 760, 761, 765, 795-6, 800-1, 1043, 1046.
Abhayākara, II, 760, 763, 801.
Abhayākaragupta, I, 32, 219, 371; II, 846, 1048.
Abhāgabhadra, II, 1045.
Abhāva, I, 14.
Abhijña, I, 360-1.
Abhiyukta, I, 396; II, 761, 843, 1045.
Amṛta, I, 22.
Amṛtā, I, 12.
Amṛtodana, I, 12, 13.
Amoghavajra, I, 163, 396; II 729, 1042.
Aruṇa, I, 15.
Arṇa, II, 843.
Arhat, I, 22.
Alaṃkāradeva, II, 1053-4
Avadhūti, I, 243, 390-1.
Aśoka, I, 15, 24-5, 35.
Aṣṭaratha, I, 16.

Aśvaghoṣa, I, 22.
Aśvajit, I, 20, 33.
Asaṅga, I, 34, 35, 67. 234, 344; II, 490, 810, 869, 938.
Asita, I, 5-8.
Ākaragupta, I, 34; II, 1071.
Ākarasiddha, II, 792, 868, 868.
Ākāśagarbha, II, 842.
Ājāneya, I, 33.
Ādarśamukha, I, 15.
Ānanda, I, 12, 15, 20, 22, 346; II, 869, 1032, 1051.
Ānandakīrti, I 347.
Ānandagarbha, I, 352, 355, 373; II, 869.
Ānandadeva, II 1053.
Ānandavajra, II. 552.
Āraṇyaka, II, 758.
Āryadeva, I, 22,, 360 362-3, 365; II, 603, 731, 803, 811, 830, 869, 938, 6101
Ālokī, I, 368.
Ikṣvāku, I. 8, 9, 13, 16.
Ikṣvāku-Virūḍhaka, I, 8, 9.
Indranāla. I, 103,
Indrabuddhi, II, 553.
Indrabodhi. I, 159, 385.
Indrabhūti, I, 359, 361, 362, 363, 385. 390; II, 553, 856, 869.
Iśvarasena, I, 346.
Udaya, I, 45-7.
Udayajīvabhadra, II, 1045.
Udbhaṭa, II, 1031.
Upakuśa, I, 13, 14.
Upagupta, I, 23-4, 32.
Upacāru, I 4, 12, 14.
Upacārumant, I, 4.
Upabhoja I, 15.
Upavāmaka, I, 14.
Upāyaśrīmitra, I, 163.
Upāsakabodhi, II. 758.
Upoṣadha, I, 3, 12, 14.
Ulkā-mukha, I, 8, 11, 13, 16.
Auduṣṭa, I, 23.
Kanakaśrī, I 382, 384.
Kanaśrī, II, 729.
Kaṇiṣka, I, 25.

Kapāla, I, 13.
Kapijit, I, 21.
Kapila, I, 10.
Kamalakuliśa, I, 372.
Kamalaśīla, I, 41, 192.
Kamalaśrī, II, 907.
Kambala, II, 753.
Kambalapāda, I, 362; II, 731.
Karakarṇaka, I, 8, 11, 13, 16.
Karṇa, I, 342.
Karṇaputra, I, 368.
Karṇika, I, 5.
Karmavajra, II, 869, 1079.
Kalyāṇa I, 3, 12, 14.
Kalyāṇamati, II, 803.
Kalyāṇaśrī, I, 241.
Kasori, II, 401.
Kāmadhenu, II, 474.
Kāyaśrī, I, 395; II, 1045.
Kālacakrapāda, I, 219; II, 755-6, 758-9, 761-6 789, 802, 1045
Kālarātrita, I, 231.
Kāśyapa, I, 5, 12, 20, 22, 25-8 39, 43.
Kukuri, II, 869.
Kukkurarāja, I, 159.
Kumārakalaśa, I, x, 314.
Kumārada, I, 22.
Kumārarāja, I, 198; II, 529, 533, 696.
Kumārasthira, I, 16.
Kumudā, II, 869.
Kulika Vijaya, II, 802.
Kuśa, I, 13, 14.
Kuśalabhadra, II, 847.
Kuśalaśrī, I, 242.
Kusali, I, 243, 361.
Kūrmapāda, II, 754, 803.
Kṛkin, I, 16, 17. 26.
Kṛṣṇa, I, 22. 24, 163, 358; II, 803. 843, 847.
Kṛṣṇapāda, I, 161, 243; 372, 384; II, 869.
Kṛṣṇavāsin, II, 1051.
Kṛṣṇasamayavajra, I, 360.
Kṛṣṇācārya, I, 256, 360, 385; II, 639.

Koṭali, II, 869.
Kośa, II, 869.
Kauṇḍinya, I, 20, 33.
Kaurava, I, 13.
Kauśika, I, 4.
Kṣitigarbha, I, 262.
Kṣetravajra, II, 729.
Kṣemadeva, II, 868.
Khavajra, II, 843.

Gaganapati, I, 5, 16.
Gaganabhadra, II, 1045.
Gaṅgādharā, II, 731.
Gaṅgābhadrī, II, 869.
Gandhamādana, I, 23.
Gayādhara, I, 112, 207.
Gayābodhi, I, 159.
Gayā-Kāśyapa, I, 20.
Guṇapāla, I, 69, 84.
Guṇaprabha, II, 868, 1011, 1016.
Guṇamati, I, 34; II, 1071.
Guṇarakṣita, II, 845.
Guṇaratna, II, 1072.
Guṇasāgara, I, 34.
Guha, I, 11.
Guhyapartṛ (Guhyaparta), I, 368.
Guhyaratha, I, 16.
Gopā, I, 11.
Gomiśra, I, 360.
Goṣṭha, I, 13, 16.
Gautama, I, 5-7, 16.
Gautamaśrī, II, 802.
Ghaṇṭā, I, 389.
Ghaṇṭāpāda, II, 754, 811.
Ghalaśa, I, 22.

Candaniprabhava, I, 372.
Candrakīrti, I, 298, 335, 342, 344, 360; II, 882, 909, 910, 1053.
Candragarbha, I, 241.
Candragomin, I, 297; II, 792.
Candradhvaja, II, 1008-9.

Candraprabhākumāra, II, 451-2.
Candrarāhula, I, 360; II, 758.
Candrārkaprabhāvatī, II, 847.
Caryā, II. 809.
Cāru, I, 4, 12, 14.
Cāruka, I, 12.
Cārumant, I, 4, 12, 14.
Cittavajra, I, 362; II, 553.
Citraratha, I, 16.
Cintā, II, 857, 869.
Celuka, II, 755-6, 761-2.

Jagatpāla, II, 843.
Jagadānandajīvabhadra, II, 1045.
Jagadāśvāsa, I, 362.
Jagadratha, I, 14.
Jayaka, I, 13, 14.
Jayagupta, II, 1053.
Jayasena, I, 5, 14, 231-2, 388; II, 1032.
Jayākara, I, 87; II, 845.
Jayānanda, I, 272, 343.
Jālandhara, I, 385.
Jālandharapāda, II, 754, 803.
Jina, I, 12, 227.
Jinarṣabha, I, 16.
Jinadatta, I, 391-2; II, 415.
Jinamitra, I, 344.
Jinālaṃkāra, II, 802.
Jiṣṇu, I, 45-6.
Jihnu, I, 45.
Jetāri, I, 243.
Jñāna, I, 35; II, 1049.
Jñānakīrti, II, 725.
Jñānagarbha, I, 34; II, 400, 417 868.
Jñānaguhya, II, 871.
Jñānajyoti, II, 1045.
Jñānaḍāka, II, 1045.
Jñānadhara, II, 803.
Jñānapāda, I 168, 170, 353, 367, 372, 373-4; II, 416, 441, 869
Jñānaprajña, I, 91.

Jñānabhadra, II, 1008.
Jñānaśrī, I, 70, 85, 206, 347, 355.
Jñānaśrīmati, I, 243.
Jñānaśrīmitra, I, 346, 372.
Jñānākara, I, 260-1, 361.
Jyotiṣkara, I, 14.
Jvāla, I, 14.
Jvālāmālin, I, 14.
Jvālin, I, 14.

Ḍākisumati, II, 731.
Ḍeṅgi, I, 385.
Ḍombhi (Ḍombī), I, 243; II, 869, 1046.
Ḍombhiheruka (Ḍombiheruka), I, 206; 856.

Tathāgatarakṣita, II, 1051.
Tanujit, I, 14.
Tapaskara, I, 5, 15.
Tilli (Tailipāda), I, 361, 365; II, 401, 520, 751, 754, 764, 803, 869.
Trilocana, II. 1053.
Thagana, I, 372; II. 847.

Daṃṣṭrāsena, I, 67.
Darpaṇa-ācārya, II, 1045-6.
Daśadhanvan, I, 16.
Daśabalaśrī, II, 801. 1053.
Daśaratha, I, 12, 13.
Dānarakṣita, I, 105.
Dānaśīla, II, 729, 758, 962, 1051, 1058.
Dānaśrī, I, 243; II, 458.
Dārika, I, 167; II, 761, 856.
Diṅnāga, I, 346; II, 808.
Diṅmukha, II, 803.
Diśāṃpati, I, 13, 15.
Dīpaṅkara, I, 31, 44 368; II, 732, 858.
Dīpaṅkarabhadra, I, 371-3.
Dīpaṅkarajñāna, Dīpaṅkaraśrījñāna, I, 86, 241 ff., 327; II, 1076.
Duṣyanta, I, 4.
Duḥśilā, I, 368.
Devakumāra, II, 715.
Devacandra, I, 344.

Devaḍāki, II, 1033.
Devadatta, I, 12, 19.
Devadhā, I, 11.
Devavitsiṃha I, 39, 218.
Devākara, I, 396.
Devākaracandra, I, 163, 392-4; II, 842, 857.
Devi I, 40.
Devendrabodhi, I, 346
Devendramati, I, 70-1.
Droṇā, I, 12. 13.
Droṇodana. I, 12, 13.
Dhanarakṣita, I, 159; II. 845
Dhanuḥsthaḥ, I, 16.
Dhanuḥsthira, I, 12, 16.
Dhanvantari, I, 15.
Dharaṇīdhara, I, 15.
Dharaṇīmukha, I, 5.
Dharmakapāla, II, 1020.
Dharmakīrti, I, 201, 244 346; II, 499, 803, 841, 845, 868 869.
Dharmaketu, I, 387.
Dharmagupta, II, 801.
Dharmajyotirbhadra, II, 1045.
Dharmatrāta, I, 346.
Dharmadattā, I, 33.
Dharmadhvaja, II. 1072.
Dharmapāla, I, 34 69, 83-4, 85 86, 372; II, 1062 1071.
Dharmapālanātha, I, 40.
Dharmapālarakṣita, I, 212.
Dharmabodhi, I, 105, 159; II, 435.
Dharmabhadra, I. 163.
Dharmamāla, I. 34.
Dharmarakṣita, I, 243.
Dharmaratna, I, 47.
Dharmaśri, II. 801, 859, 1056.
Dharmākara, II, 761.
Dharmākaramati, I, 262.
Dharmākaraśānti, II, 761, 764, 800.
Dharmottara, I, 346.
Dhītika, I, 24.
Dhitiśrijñāna, II, 843.
Dhuṇdhumāra, I, 15.
Dhṛtaratha, I, 16.

Nagnajit, I, 4 14.
Natekara, II, 729, 842, 848.
Nanda, I 12, 19, 28.
Nandabalā, I, 19-20.
Nandavajra, I, 362.
Nandā, I, 20.
Nayaśrī, II, 1053.
Naradeva, I, 5, 41.
Narayadeva, I, 86.
Narāditya. II, 798.
Narendrabodhi, II, 800.
Navatidhanvan, I, 16.
Navaratha, I, 16.
Nāgadatta, I, 4, 14.
Nāgadeva, I, 5, 14, 37.
Nāgapāla, I, 5.
Nāgapuri, II, 848.
Nāgabuddhi, II. 983.
Nāgabodhi, I, 159, 360, 361; II, 798, 869, 982.
Nāgarakṣita, I, 16.
Nāgarāja, I, 37.
Nāgasena, I, 28.
Nāgārjuna, I, 17, 22, 34-5, 220, 227, 234, 260, 274, 280, 343-4, 358-9, 364-5, 366; II, 416, 429, 425, 441-2, 446, 474-5, 491-2, 548, 566, 599, 600, 601, 641, 753, 768, 763, 832, 857, 868, 940, 1054, 1057, 1071, 1075, 1077, 1092.
Nādi-Kāśyapa, I, 20.
Nāyakapāda, II, 801.
Nārāyaṇadeva, I, 31.
Nāro *v* (Nāḍapāda, Nā-ro-pa), I, 243, 252, 260, 361, 372, 381-2, 383-5, 394; II, 499-1, 405, 472-3, 476, 491, 520, 525-6, 530, 533, 549, 586, 629, 633, 638, 641, 668, 670, 728-9, 730, 735, 754-5, 757, 758, 769, 769, 780, 795, 797, 803, 810, 813, 832, 752, 887, 891 893, 942, 979, 994, 1019.
Nūpura, I, 8, 13, 16.
Nūpurapāda, I, 13.
Nimi, Nemi, I, 5, 13, 15.
Niṣkalaṅka, II, 1055.
Nemisthira, I, 175.
Nyaṅku, I, 13, 14.

Padākrama, I, 45.
Padma, I, 43, 95, 106, 149, 156, 203; II, 491, 805, 821.

Padmagarbha, I, 241.
Padmapādā, II, 869.
Padminī, II, 847.
Padmamālin, II, 843.
Padmavajra, I, 362, 389; II, 552, 801, 856, 869, 1041.
Padmasambhava, I, 31, 43, 57, 102-3, 106, 389; II, 474, 800, 821.
Padmākara, I. 373.
Padmāṅkuravajra, II, 1041.
Parameśvara, I, 163.
Parākrama, I, 45.
Parāhita, I, 87, 344.
Parāhitabhadra, I, 325.
Pāghala, II, 798.
Pārāvatapāda, II, 437.
Pārthiva, I, 15.
Pārśva, I, 22, 25.
Piṇḍo, II, 756-7, 761, 764, 789.
Puṇḍarīka, II, 756.
Puṇyadharī, II, 503, 505.
Puṇyaratha, II, 455.
Puṇyaśrī, I, 242; II, 1072.
Puṇyākaragupta, II, 1048.
Puṇyākarabhadra, I, 394.
Puṇyāvatī, I, 35.
Puṇyeśvara, II, 1072.
Pūrṇabhadra, I, 368.
Pūrṇavardhana, I, 342, 344.
Pṛṣata, I, 3.
Paiṇḍapātika, I, 390-1, 393; II, 400, 1020.
Prajñākaragupta, I, 346.
Prajñākaramati, I, 206.
Prajñākīrti, I, 87.
Prajñāgupta, I, 218; II, 697.
Prajñājvāla, I, 272.
Prajñānātha, II, 1072.
Prajñāpāla, I, 69, 84.

Prajñābhadra, I, 243; II, 868.
Prajñālaṃkāra, II, 474.
Prajñāvarman, I, 36.
Prajñāśrījñānakīrti, II, 851.

Prajñāsiṃha, II, 400.
Prajñāsiddha, II, 939, 955.
Praṇāda, I, 13, 14.
Praṇīta, I, 15.
Pradayālu, I, 14.
Prabhāvatī, I, 241.
Pramudavajra (Pramuditāvajra), I, 384.
Praśānta, I, 14.
Praśāntamitra, I, 437.
Prahasta, I, 159.
Pretākara, I, 85.

Balakṛṣṇa, II, 847.
Balacandra, II, 437.
Balin, I, 372-3.
Balyācārya, I, 243; II 843.
Bahuka, I, 15.
Bahubhuj, I, 22.
Bibhaka, I, 22.
Bimbisāra, I, 20.
Buddhagupta, I, 170; II, 869.
Buddhaguhya, I, 191, 251, 372.
Buddhaghoṣa, II, 797, 799, 800, 801-2.
Buddhajñāna, I, 367, 372-4; II. 803.
Buddhajñānapāda, I, 167, 243, 372.
Buddhadatta, I, 392, 397.
Buddhananda, I. 22.
Buddhamati, II, 1072.
Buddhamitra, I, 22.
Buddharatna, II, 1072.
Buddharakṣita, I, 38.
Buddhaśānta, I, 372.
Buddhaśrī, II, 709, 1033, 1055-6, 1065.
Buddhaśrījñāna, I. 369.
Buddhasena, I, 15.
Buddhākarabhadra, I, 163.
Budha, I, 15.
Budhasena, I, 15.
Bodhikīrti, II. 1072.
Bodhijayendra, II, 1072.
Bodhibhadra, I, 244, 382-4; II, 761, 1072.

Bodhirāja, I, 257.
Bodhiśrībhadra, II, 1071.
Brahmadatta, I, 4, 14.
Bhadanta, I, 385.
Bhadra, I, 4; II 758.
Bhadrapāda, II 754, 803.
Bhadrabodhi, II, 766.
Bhadrasajjāna, II, 729.
Bhadrasena, I, 33.
Bhadrika, I, 20, 33.
Bhadrī, I, 6.
Bharata, I, 13.
Bharadvāja, I. 5, 8.
Bhavabhadra, I, 395.
Bhavaskandha, II, 814.
Bhavya, I. 29, 34.
Bhākrama, I, 45.
Bhāgupta, I. 45.
Bhāgin, I, 13.
Bhāva, I, 14.
Bhāvaviveka, II, 882.
Bhāskara, II, 761, 795, 1053.
Bhāskaradeva, II, 800.
Bhāsvat, I, 45.
Bhīmadeva, I, 388.
Bhīmaratha, I, 13.
Bhūgupta, I, 45.
Bhūtakoṭi, I, 243.
Bhūpati, I, 15.
Bhūbhāsa, I, 45.
Bhṛgupāda, I, 13, 14.
Bhogavant, I, 15.
Bhoja, I, 15, 16.
Bhojana, I, 15.

Mañjukīrti, I, 344; II, 756, 760, 763, 765, 789, 795.
Mañjubhadra, II, 1045.
Mañjuśrī, I, 368; II. 1045.
Mañjuśrīkīrtimitra, I, 372.
Mañjuśrīkumāra, I, 45.
Mañjśrījñāna, I, 163.

Mañjuśrīmitra, I, 369; II, 436.
Mañjuśrīvarman, I, 163.
Maṅgala-guru, II. 628-9, 631-2.
Maṅgala-bodhi, II, 1072.
Maṅgalaśila, II, 1072.
Maṅgalasiṃhā, II, 1072.
Maṇigarbha, II, 847.
Matigarbha, II, 1046.
Matijñānabodhi, I, 243.
Matidhvaja, II, 1072.
Matimant, II, 802.
Madanabhadra, II, 1045.
Madhaṅgarasvāmin, II, 802.
Madhyāntika, I. 23; II, 1051.
Manakaśrījñāna, I, 385.
Manojīvabhadra, I, 1045.
Manoda, I, 22.
Marīci, I, 5, 15.
Mahākaruṇa, I, 355, 361, 375, 378, 382.
Mahākāśyapa, I, 33.
Mahākuśa, I, 13, 14.
Mahājana, I, 87, 243.
Mahādeva, I, 5, 13, 15.
Mahānāman, I, 12, 20, 33.
Mahāpadma, I, 28.
Mahāprajāpatī, I, 33.
Mahāpraṇāda, I, 13.
Mahābala, I, 16.
Mahābuddha, I, 15.
Mahābudha, I, 15.
Mahābodhi, II, 1045-6.
Mahābharata, I, 14.
Mahāmuni, I, 22.
Mahālīlādevī, I, 362.
Mahāvahana, I, 16.
Mahāśakuni, I. 13, 14.
Mahāsagara, I, 14.
Mahāsammata, I, 3, 12, 14, 16.
Mahāsudarśanā, I, 12, 14.
Mahendrasena, I. 5.
Mānavadeva, I, x, 45.
Mānavendra, I, x, 45.

Māndhātṛ, I, 4.
Mālika, I, 12.
Mitra, II, 709, 1030-4, 1041-3, 1065.
Mitraguhya, I, 262.
Mitratāra, II, 847.
Mitrayogin, II, 1031-4, 1042.
Muktipakṣa, II, 800.
Muci, I, 12, 14.
Mucilinda, I, 14.
Mūrdhaja, I, 12.
Mṛṇāla, I, 6.
Meghavegin, I, 360.
Meru, I, 13, 14.
Merumant, I, 14.
Maitrī, I, 209; II, 432, 437, 476, 829.
Maitrīcandra, II, 1055.
Maitrīpāda, I, 227-8, 347, 349, 384; II, 492, 451, 489, 725, 728, 730-1, 841-3, 845, 847, 866, 869, 977, 980.
Mokṣākaragupta, II, 757.
Maudgalyāyana, I, 3, 20.

Yamāri, I, 346.
Yaśas, I, 24.
Yaśodharā, I, 18.
Yuvasthira, I, 16.
Yogendratilaka, II 803.
Yoṣa, I, 360, 361.

Rakṣitapāda, I, 369.
Ratna, II, 503, 644.
Ratnakīrti, II, 801-3.
Ratnagupta, II 755, 767.
Ratnaguru, II, 633-4.
Ratnadevī, II, 730.
Ratnapāla, II, 729.
Ratnabuddhi, II, 801.
Ratnabhadra, II, 1044.
Ratnamaṅgala, II 802.
Ratnamitra, I, 34, II, 1071.
Ratnarakṣita, I, 389; II, 726, 800, 1057.
Ratnavajra, I, 206, 229, 344, 372; II, 729, 869, 1049.

Ratnaśrī, I, 393; II, 762, 1056.
Ratnākara, II, 634, 637-8, 801.
Rantākaraśānti, I, 206.
Rathasāra, I, 5.
Ravigupta, I, 346; II, 869, 1050-1.
Raśmiśrī, II, 1072.
Rājabhadrika, I, 12.
Rājyananda, I, 9, 11.
Rāmapāla, II, 729 842, 857.
Rāhula, I, 12, 13, 20, 22. 46; II, 1071.
Rāhulaguptavajra, II, 732.
Rāhulaguhyavajra, I, 242.
Rāhulabhadra, I, 35, 344, 371.
Rāhulavajra, II, 909.
Rāhulaśrī, II, 1051.
Rāhulaśrībhadra, II, 1058.
Rūpati, I, 36.
Roca, I, 3.
Romaputra, I, 14.
Romaputrin, I, 44.

Lakṣmī, II, 847, 869, 1017, 1018, 1044.
Lakṣmiṅkarā, I, 390; II, 553, 758, 856.
Lakṣmībhadra, II, 1045.
Lalitavajra, I, 367; II 731, 801, 843, 869.
Līlādevī, I, 361.
Līlāvajra, I, 204.
Lūhipāda (Lū-yi-pa), I, 234 385, 389: II, 804, 852, 869
Lokeśvara, II, 861.
Lokyatrināthа, II, 970.

Vajrakrodha, II, 913-5.
Vajragarbha, II, 830, 838.
Vajraghaṇṭā, I, 385; II, 489, 803 869, 887.
Vajraghaṇṭāpāda, II, 754.
Vajradharma, I, 361.
Vajrapāṇi, I, 189, 219, 384, 395-6; II, 521, 842-3, 851, 855, 857-9, 860, 862, 864-6, 1979.
Vajravatī, I, 362.
Vajraśrī, I, 361.
Vajraśrībhadra, II, 1071-2.

Vajrā, I, 362; II, 552.
Vatsaka, I, 45.
Vanaratna, II, 797, 799, 800, 801-3, 811, 815, 819, 820-1, 825-6, 828 833, 1018.
Vara-kalyāṇa, I, 3, 12, 14.
Varendraruci, I, 325, 394.
Vasantatilaka, II, 1053.
Vasiṣṭha, I, 11, 13, 16.
Vasudharin, II, 869.
Vasubandhu, I, 22, 55, 344 346; II, 839, 938.
Vasumitra, I, 25.
Vāgiśvara, I, 384; II, 869, 1051.
Vāgiśvarakirti, I, 206, 227; II, 758, 801.
Vāmaka, I, 13, 14.
Vāridhāra, II, 847.
Vāṣpa, I, 20, 33.
Vikhyātadeva, II, 801.
Vikṣāntadeva, II, 761.
Vigatāśoka, I, 15.
Vijaya, I, 4.
Vijayadhanvan, I, 16.
Vijayapāda, II, 754, 764.
Vijayabhadra, II, 1045.
Vitapāda, I, 168, 371.
Vidyākarasiṃha, I, 331.
Vidyākokila, I, 243.
Vinayadhara, I, 77.
Vinayapāda, II, 803.
Vinayākaramati, II, 757-8, 760.
Vinītadeva, I, 346.
Vindaśrī, II, 1051.
Vibhūti, II, 601.
Vibhūticandra, II, 727, 796, 799.
Vimala, I, 102, 104, 170-1, 191; II, 847.
Vimalatejas, I, 35.
Vimalamitra, I, 106-8, 1591-2, 197; II, 491, 497.
Vimalarakṣita, II, 1053.
Vimalā, II, 869.
Virūdhaka, I, 11, 13, 16.
Virūpa, I, 206, 381, 390; II, 731, 755, 869, 1020, 1046.
Virūpakṣa, II, 798.

Viśukalpa, I, 359.
Viśvamitra, I.
Viśvaratha, I, 16.
Vīravajra, II, 552.
Vīryavarman, II, 868.
Vṛkṣaparṇī, II, 869.
Vṛṣa, I, 45-6.
Vetālakṣema, I, 159.
Vairavajra, I, 362.
Vairocana, I, 104, 108, 168, 170-2, 191; II, 729, 849.
Vairocanarakṣita, II, 844-5, 1024.
Vaiśālya, I, 12.
Vyāsa, I, 17.

Śakuni, I, 13, 14.
Śaṅkara, I, 13, 14, 15; II, 868.
Śaṅkarānanda, I, 346.
Śatadhanvan, I, 16.
Śataratha, I, 13.
Śatrujit, I, 4, 14.
Śabarapāda, II, 841, 866.
Śabarī, II, 869.
Śaraṇa, II, 845.
Śākya, I, 3.
Śākyaprabha, I, 159.
Śākyabodhi, I, 346.
Śākyamitra, I, 310, 359.
Śākyamudra, I, 159.
Śākyamuni, I, 242, 346; II, 624, 973, 1056.
Śākyarakṣita, II, 800, 802.
Śākyaśrī, I, 281, 315, 346; II, 446-7, 608, 634, 710, 726, 975, 782, 799, 797, 1055 1062, 1971.
Śākyaśrībhadra, I, 29, 34-5, 277, 306; II, 599, 604, 761, 794, 1047, 1051, 1056, 1051, 1056, 1063, 1072, 1087.
Śākyasena, I, 77.
Śākyasiṃha, I, 100, 159.
Śākyasiṃhadhvaja, II, 802.
Śānavāsika, I, 23.
Śānavāsin, II, 1051.
Śāntarakṣita, I, 34, 38, 39, 42, 44; II, 648, 805, 822, 1062.
Śānti, I, 373; II, 842, 847.

Śāntigarbha, I, 106.
Śāntideva, II, 869.
Śāntibhadra, I, 261, 360; II, 860.
Śābari (Śa-ba-ri-pa), II, 727, 869.
Śāyanta, I, 22.
Śāriputra, I, 20; II, 1042, 1071.
Śikhin, I, 14.
Śiṣyavajra, I, 360.
Śīlākara, I, 247; II. 1024. 1053, 1055
Śīlācandra, II, 1053
Śīlarakṣita. I, 242.
Śīlaratna, II. 1072.
Śīlaśrī, II, 1053.
Śīlasāgara, II, 799.
Śuklā, I, 12.
Śuklodana, I, 12. 13.
Śuddhā, I, 12.
Śuddhodana, I, 5. 12, 13, 16, 21.
Śubhasu, I, 45.
Śūnyatāsamādhi, II, 842.
Śūnyatāsamādhivajra, I, 392.
Śūnyaśrī, I, 372.
Śūradatta, II, 425.
Śṛṅgayogin, II, 843.
Śraddhākara, I, 373; II, 1051.
Śrīgarbha, I, 241.
Śrīgupta, I, 34, 226.
Śrīdhana, II, 795, 1046.
Śrīdharanandana, II, 800.
Śrīprabha, I, 241.
Śrībhadra. II, 801, 1044-5.
Śrūtasena. I, 15,
Saṅghānanda, I. 22.
Sacana, II, 844.
Sajjana, Sañjana, I, 71, 325. 347-8
Samadarśin, I. 15.
Samantajñāna, I, 86.
Samantaprabha, I, 4.
Samantabhadra, II, 1045.
Samantaśrī, II, 756, 761, 789.
Samantāloka, I, 5.

amayavajra, I, 362.
Samudradeva, I, 15.
Samudrasena, I, 5.
Saraha, I; 72, 233; II, 447, 662, 830, 841, 863, 869, 1039.
Saroruha, I, 388-9; II 474, 856, 869, 1041.
arvakāmin, I, 24.
arvajagannātha, II. 553.
Sarvavid, II, 520.
ahajakīrti, II, 801.
ahajavajra, I, 362; II, 552, 851.
ahajavajrā, I. 362.
āgara, I, 14.
āgaradeva, I, 15.
āgarasiddhi, II, 869.
ādhupāla, I, 69. 84.
ādhuputra, II, 761.
āmavajra, II, 847.
iṃha, I. 22, 25, 168, 191.
iṃhatāra, II. 847.
iṃhadhvaja, II. 757, 760, 1072.
iṃhahanu, I, 12, 13. 16.
Siṃhahara, II, 1053.
iddhipāla, I, 58.
iddhivajra, I, 362; II, 552.
imasthira, 15.
ukhaprakāśa (Sukhaprasanna), I, 159.
ukhasiddhi, II, 731, 742-3, 869, 879.
ugataśrī, I, 318.
ujata, I. 3, 16; II, 800, 802-3.
ujataratna, II, 797.
udatta, I, 33.
udarśana, I, 13, 24-5, 32.
udṛśa, I, 15.
udhanagupta, II. 1053.
unayaśri, I. 226, 228.
uprabuddha, I. 12.
ubhūbhāsa. I, 45.
umati, I, 5. 15. 16.
umatikirti, I, 325, 384; II, 729
umatikīrtiśrī, II, 1079.
umanaḥśrī, II, 1007.

Sureṇu, I, 13, 15.
Sulabha, I, 12.
Suvarṇa, I, 13, 14; II, 847.
Suvṛṣa, I, 45.
Susthira, I, 16,
Sūryaketu, II, 758-9.
Sūryagarbha, II, 730.
Sūryaratha, II, 1045.
Sūryaśri, II, 764.
Sūryaśrijñāna, II, 800.
Sonasati, II, 758.
Somanātha, I, 72, 367; II 755. 758. 760. 765-7. 906.
Skandhapāda, II, 843.
Sthira, I, 16.
Sthirapāla, I, 325. 345-6; II 789. 1009.
Sthiramati, I, 28. 159, 344; II. 847.
Smṛti, I, 102, 204-5 346. 372. 395; II, 417.
Smṛtijñānakirti, I, 160.
Svastika, I. 19.
Haklenayaśas, I, 22.
Hanumat, II. 1045.
Haribhadra, I, 331. 367.
Harṣabhadra, II, 1045.
Hasumati, I. 344.
Hastikaśirṣa, I. 16.
Hastiniyaṃsa, I. 8. 11, 13.
Hūṃkāra, I, 106.
Herukadeva, II, 803.

BOOK TITLES

TIBETAN

Kā-ri-kā, II, 541.
Ka-lā-pa, II, 786, 974.
Kun-tu bzaṅ-po'i don-bsdus-pa, I, 370.
Kun-tu bzaṅ-mo, I, 370.
Kun-'dus, I, 153.
Kun-'dus rig-pa'i mdo, I, 158.
Kun-spyod, I, 375, 384; II, 549.
Kun-spyod rgyud-'grel bDe-mčhog-gi don rab-tu gsal-ba, I, 385.
Kun-byed-mdo, I, 137.
Kun-byed rgyyal-po<Kun-byed rgyal-po'i rgyud, I 145, 172.
Ko-sa-la'i rgyan, I, 353.
Kye'i rdo-rje dkyil-'khor-gyi čho-ga, I, 394.
Kye'i rdo-rje'i rdzogs-rim sñiṅ-po brgya-pa, II, 803.
kLoṅ čhen mdzod-bdun, I, 309.
kLoṅ-rdol gsuṅ-'bum, II, 490, 810, 821.
dKar-čhag Tshig-gi me-tog II, 995.
dKon-mčhog rtsegs, II, 490.
dKyil-'khor-gyi čho-ga ślo-ka bži-brgya-lṅa-bču-pa, I, 370, 371.
dKyil-'khor-gyi bstod-pa, I, 251.
bKa' -bčad, II, 1057.
bKa'-gdams gžuṅ-drug, II, 810.
bKa'-bsdu bži-pa, II, 535, 777.
bKa'-bži, I, 220; II, 781.
sKu-gsuṅ-thugs yid-la mi-byed-pa'i mdzod, II, 865.
sKu-gsum ṅo-sprod, II, 533.
sKu'i mdzod 'čhi-med rdo-rje'i-glu, II, 865.
sKyabs-'gro yan-lag drug-pa, I, 192.
sKyon-čan, II, 886.
sKye-bo gso-thigs, II, 930.
sKyes-rabs brgya-rtsa, II, 502.
sKyes-rabs sṅa-phyis, II, 533.
sKyes-rabs phyis-ma, II, 533.
bsKyed-pa'i rim-pa'i sgrub-thabs Kun-tu bzaṅ-po, I, 370.
Khams-gsum rnam-rgyal, I, 355.
Khog-dbub, I, 149.
Khrid-rim-gyi yig čha, II, 703.

Khrul-tsho drug-pa, II, 997.
Khro-bo-la mṅon-par rtogs-pa rgyas-pa, I, 152.
mKha'-'gro rgya-mtsho'i rgyud, II, 497, 499, 549, 825.
mKha'-'gro sñiṅ-thig, II, 497, 534.
mKha'-'gro-ma'i sbyor-ba, II, 848.
mKha'-spyod bsñen-sgrub, II, 539.
'Khor-ba rtsad-gčod-kyi rgyud, I, 145.
'Khrul-spoṅ, I, 385.
Gaṅ-po-la-sogs-pa'i rtogs-pa-brǰod-pa brgya-pa, II, 1069
Gab-pa mṅon-du phyuṅ-ste man-ṅag sgom-sdebs-su bśad-pa, I, 145.
Gab-pa mṅon-phyuṅ, II, 987.
Gur-rigs-bsdus, II, 535.
Grags-pa brgyad, II, 886.
Grub-sñiṅ, I, 72, 227, 229, 233; II, 833, 856, 866.
Grub-pa sde-bdun, II, 534, 866.
Grol-ba'i thig-le žes-bya-ba, I, 169 370.
gLeṅ-'bum, I, 33.
dGe-ldan Phyag-rgya-čhen-po, II, 725.
dGe-tshul-gyi daṅ-po'i lo-dri-ba, I, 86.
dGe-sloṅ-gi daṅ-po'i lo-dri-ba, I, 30, 86.
dGyes-rdor, I, 187.
dGyes-pa rdo-rǰe'i dka'-'grel, I, 228.
'Gro-mgon bka'-'bum, II, 833.
'Grel-čhuṅ, I, 180, 265, 330, 331; II, 611, 680, 698, 923.
'Grel-čhen, I, 70; II, 994.
'Grel-ṭikā, I, 108.
'Grel-pa don-gsal, I, 330, 340.
'Grel-pa rin-čhen rgyan-drug, II, 477.
rGya-čher 'grel-pa, I, 238.
rGyal-po Kṛki'i luṅ-bstan-pa, I, 31.
rGyal-po Do-ha, II, 846, 893.
rGyal-ba lṅa-pa'i rgyal-rabs, II, 1050.
rGyal-ba'i lam-'ǰug, II, 1056.
rGyal-rabs Bon-gyi 'byuṅ-gnas, I, xii, xx.
rGya'i deb-ther žu-thu han-čhen, I, vii.
rGya'i deb-ther žu-thu-čhen, I, 47.
rGya'i yig-tshaṅ, I, vii, xviii, 47.
rGyud-kyi rgyal-po čhen-po dPal rDo-rǰe mkha'-'gro žes-bya-ba, I, 228.
rGyud-kyi rgyal-po rṅog-pa med-pa žes-bya-ba, II, 865.
rGyud-kyi rnam-bžag, II, 663.
rGyud-kyi rnam-bśad, I, 157, 370, 371.
(→kLoṅ-čhen-pa'i gSaṅ-sñiṅ 'grel-pa).

rGyud-kyi bśad-pa, I, 373.
rGyud-'grel čhen-mo, II, 703, 768, 776.
rGyud-don rnam-ṅes, I, 155.
rGyud-'bum dkar-čhag, II, 417.
rGyud-'bum-pa, II, 848.
rGyud-bla — rGyud-bla-ma, I, 233; II, 777.
rGyud-bla-rtsa-'grel, II, 502.
rGyud-bla-ma mṅon-brjod bla-ma, I, 375.
rGyud ma-lus-pa'i don ṅes-par skul-bar byed-pa, II, 856.
rGyud-la 'Jug-pa'i man-ṅag rin-po-čhe Za-ma-tog kha-'byed-pa, II, 756.
sGom-'grel sñiṅ-gi ñi-ma-drug, I, 145.
sGom-yig čhen-mo, I, 145.
sGom-rim, II, 809.
sGom-rim drug-pa, II, 865.
sGyu-'phrul brgyad-bču-pa, I, 153.
Gyu-'phrul thal-ba, I, 171.
Gyu-'phrul dra-ba'i rgyud, I, 352; II, 489.
Gyu-'phrul gsaṅ-ba sñiṅ-po, I, 107.
Gra-sbyor bum-po gñis-pa, II, 1057.
Grub-thabs rgya-mtsho, II, 527, 1048.
Grub-thab čhen-po, II, 1054.
Grub-thabs bsdus-pa, II, 845.
Grub-thabs mtsho-skyes, I, 143.
Gron-sbrul, II, 940.
Gron-ma gsal-ba, I, 228, 357, 359, 364; II, 651.
Gron-ma gsal-ba'i ti-ka čhen-mo, I, 366.
Gron-ma gsal-ba byed-pa žes-bya-ba'i rgya-čher bśad-pa, I, 342.
Gron-ma rnam-drug, II, 663.
Gron-gsal, I, 367; II, 767, 810.
Gron-gsal rgya-čher bśad-pa, II, 1077.
Gron-gsal mčhan-gyi yaṅ-'grel, II, 1077.
rGyad-stoṅ grel-čhen, I, 265.
rGyad-stoṅ-pa, I, 209, 249, 265, 364.
Ṅan-soṅ sbyoṅ-rgyud, I, 165; II, 532.
Ṅes-don rgya-mtsho, II, 535, 776, 777.
Ṅos-grub 'byuṅ-gter, I, 168.
Ṅos-grub 'bras-bu'i sgron-ma, II, 906.
Ṅos-po gsal-ba'i rjes-su 'gro-ba'i de-kho-na-ñid grub-pa, II, 856.
mṄon-brjod, II, 825.
mṄon-pa kun-btus — mṄon-pa kun-las-btus, I, 149, 344; II, 534.
Ṅon-pa goṅ-'og, II, 490, 993, 1012.
mṄon-par rtogs-pa, I, 250, 385.

mṄon-par rtogs-pa'i rgyan-'grel-pa, I, 70.
lṄa-bču-pa'i bśad-pa, II, 1007.
sṄags-rim čhen-mo, II, 1077.
sṄags-log su-'byin, II, 417.
Čig-čhar' ǰug-pa'i sgom-don, I, 192.
gČod-yul la'u-lag, II, 994.
gČes-pa'i lde-mig, II, 763.
bČud-len phreṅ-ba, II, 533.
Chu-kluṅ mṅon-par rol-pa'i mdo, II, 978.
Čhu-kluṅ čhen-po, II, 978.
Čhu-sbyin dbaṅ-po'i sgrub-pa'i thabs-gsum, I, 370.
Čhos-kyi gtam-dam-pa dGes-pa'i sgron-ma, II, 500.
Čhos-skyoṅ Gri-gug-ma, I, 99.
Čhos-daṅ čhos-ñid rnam-par-'byed-pa'i tshig-le'ur byas-pa, I, 347.
Čhos-bču-bži, I, 371.
Čhos-dbyiṅs bstod-pa, II, 492.
'Čhi-kha-ma'i gdams-ṅag, II, 865.
J̌o-mo U-rgyan-ma, II, 845.
'J̌am-rdor, I, 373.
'J̌am-dpal, I, 377.
'J̌am-dpal sku, I, 106.
'J̌am-dpal sṅags-don, I, 163.
'J̌am-dpal mtshan-brǰod-kyi bśad-'bum, I, 160.
'J̌am-dpal žal-luṅ, I, 168.
'J̌am-dpal bśes-gñen-ma, II, 953.
'J̌am-dpal gsaṅ-ldan, I, 143, 160; II, 407, 987.
'J̌am-dpal gsaṅ-ba'i rgyud, I, 163.
'J̌ig-rten snaṅ-byed zla-ba'i no-pi-ka, I, 160.
'J̌ig-rten dbaṅ-phyug, I, 373.
'J̌igs-byed I, 165.
rJ̌e-rin-po-čhe'i gsuṅ-'bum or bKa'-'bum, I, 340; II, 1070, 1079.
Ñams-snaṅ-ma, II, 948.
Ñi-khri, I, 379; II, 537, 940.
Ñi-khri mdo-'grel, I, 233, 236.
Ñi-khri snaṅ-ba, I, 209, 249, 257, 258.
Ñi-khri gžuṅ-'grel, II, 1054.
Ñi-la sgrub-pa, II, 533.
Ñe-bar sbyor-ba'i rgyud, II, 848.
gÑal-ṭikā, I, 335.
gÑis-med grub-pa, II, 856.
gÑis-med rnam-rgyal, II, 426.
gÑis-med rnam-rgyal čhuṅ-ba, II, 417.

gÑis-med rnam-rgyal čhen-po, II, 417.
gÑis-med rnam-rgyal rigs-bsdus čhen-po, II, 426.
mÑam-ñid gži'i sgron-ma, II, 906.
mÑam-sbyor, I, 103, 165.
Ñiṅ-rgyud dkar-čhag I, 137, 143, 153, 156, 200.
Ñiṅ-ma'i rgyud-'bum, I, 102, 103, 104, 105, 137, 143, 153.
Ñog-pa med-pa'i rgyud, II, 865.
Ñan-ṅag me-loṅ, II, 534, 786.
Ñiṅ-thig ya-bži, II, 533.
See rDzogs-čhen sñiṅ-thig).
Ñiṅ-po brgya-pa, II, 811, 824.
Ñiṅ-po gsum, II, 735.
Ñiṅ-mo rgya-pa, II, 833.
sÑiṅ-rig-pa'i ñi-ma drug, I, 145.
sÑen-sgrub U-rgyan bsñan-sgrub, II, 533, 539, 546.
gTum-po'i sgrub-thabs, II, 845.
gTor-ma mi-nub-pa'i sgron-ma. I, 370.
Ta-mgrin lha-bži, II, 940.
Tog-ge tho-ba, I, 343.
Tog-ge tho-ba'i ṭikā, I, 334.
Togs-brjod lhun-po, II, 586.
Ta-'dod mdòr-bstan, II, 779.
Toṅ-ñid bdun-ču-pa, II, 994.
Tod-'grel, I, 447.
rTag — brTag-gñis, I, 198, 207, 209, 363; II, 405, 412, 533, 549, 585, 587,
(brTag-pa gñis-pa) 588, 722, 764, 779, 797, 828, 829, 830.
rTag-gñis-kyi mtha'-gñis rnam-sel, II, 448.
bsTan-'gyur dkar-čhag, I, 103.
bsTan-pa spyi-'grel, II, 777.
bsTan-rim, I, 331.
Thabs-daṅ śes-rab grub-pa, II, 856.
Thams-čad gsaṅ-ba'i rgyud, I, 352.
Thugs-kyi mdzod skye-med rdo-rje'i glu, II, 865.
Thugs-rje čhen-po'i dmar-khrid, II, 994.
Thugs-rje čhen-po'i rgyud, II, 1028.
Thun-'jog, II, 572.
Thub-pa'i dgoṅs-pa'i rgyan, I, 32.
Thub-pa dgoṅs-rgyan, II, 534.
Theg-bsdus<Theg-čhen bsdus-pa, I, 257.
Theg-pa čhen-po rgyud-bla-ma'i bstan-bčos, I, 347.
Theg-pa čhen-po mdo-sde'i rgyan-žes-bya-ba'i tshig-le'ur byas-pa, I, 348.
Theg-pa gsuṅ-gi sgron-ma, II, 905.

mThar-thug-gsum-gyi gdams-pa, I, 275.
Dag-ldan, I, 207.
Dags-po'i rtogs-čhos, II, 460.
Dam-čhos Pad-dkar, II, 490.
Dam-tshig-gi rtog-pa stoṅ-phrag-phyed-daṅ-bču-gñis-pa'i rgyud, II, 848.
Dam-tshig mdo-rgyas, I, 165.
Dam-tshig gsum-bkod, II, 832.
Dam-tshig- gsum-gyi rgyal-po, I, 312.
Dus-kyi 'khor-lo'i rgyud, II, 753.
Dus-kyi 'khor-lo'i sgrub-thabls sñiṅ-po rgyan, II, 764.
Dus-'khor rgyud-'grel, II, 639.
Dus-'khor rgyud phyi-ma, II, 543. 640.
Dus-'khor čhos-'byuṅ, II. 754.
Dus-'khor rtsa-rgyud, II, 1054.
Do-ha mdzod-kyi glu, I, 228.
Don-grub-ma čhe-ba, I, 393; II, 832.
Don-dam bsñen-pa — Don-dam-pa'i bsñen-pa, II. 527, 640, 766, 838.
De-kho-na-ñid-kyi sgron-ma'i rgyud, I, 361.
De-kho-na-ñid-bču-pa, II, 866. 977.
De-kho-na-ñid-bču-pa'i 'grel-pa, II, 725, 857.
De-kho-na-ñid bsdus-pa, II, 753.
De-kho-na-ñid-la 'jug-pa, II, 725.
De-ñid 'dus-pa, I, 227; II, 812.
De-ñid bsdus-pa'i rgyud, I, 352.
Deb-ther sṅon-po, I, i; II, 1093.
Deb-ther dmar-po, I, vi, 47.
Dril-bu rim-lṅa, II, 803.
Dril-bu rim-lṅa'i rnam-par bśad-pa, I, 389.
gDan-bži, II, 412, 475, 629, 793. 832.
gDan-bži'i 'grel-pa, II, 640, 729.
gDar-śar, I, 138.
gDan-bži'i rgyud, I, 228.
gDoṅ-drug-gi rgyud, I, 377.
bDag-grub-pa, I. 370.
bDag-med-ma gsal-ba, II. 857.
bDag-med-ma'i mṅon-par rtogs-pa, I, 394.
bDud-rtsi, I, 127, 128.
bDud-rtsi bum-gčig, II, 953.
bDun-tshigs gžer-lṅa, II. 448.
bDe-mčhog mkha'-'gro rgya-mtsho'i rgyud I, 388
bDe-mčhog 'khor-lo, I, 359.
bDe-mčhog-gi dkyil-'khor-gyi čho-ga, II, 663.

bDe-mčhog rgyud-brgyad, I, 377.
bDe-mčhog mṅon-'byuṅ, II, 846.
bDe-mčhog stod-'grel, II, 447, 534.
bDe-mčhog sdom-pa 'byuṅ-ba'i dkyil-čhog dri-med čhu-rgyan, I, 386.
bDe-mčhog nam-mkha'-daṅ-mñam-pa, II, 832, 961.
bDe-mčhog rtsa-rgyud, I, 163, 375, 385, 389; II, 533.
bDe-mčhog bśad-rgyud, I, 228, 364.
bDe-bar gśegs-pa'i bstan-pa'i gsal-byed čhos-kyi 'byuṅ-gnas gsuṅ-rab rin-po-čhe'i mdzod, I, viii.
bDen-gñis<bDen-pa gñis rnam-par-'byed-pa'i tshig-le'ur byas-pa, I, 332.
mDo-Dgoṅs-'dus<Do dgoṅs-pa 'dus-pa, I, 104, 153, 158; II, 534.
mDo-sde gdams-ṅag 'bogs-pa'i rgyal-po, I, 158.
mDo-rgyes 'briṅ-bsdus, II, 899.
mDo-sgyu mtshan-ma, II, 941.
mDo-sdud-pa, II, 582.
mDo-sde dkon-mčhog-sprin, I, 40.
mDo-sde-rgyan, I, 233.
mDo-maṅ, II, 541.
rDo-rǰe'i tshig-'byed, II, 857.
mDo-rtsa —mDo-rtsa-ba, I, 321; II, 674, 808.
mDo-rtsa'i zin-bris, II, 1076.
mDo-luṅ-bstan rdo-rǰe, I, 171.
mDor-bsdus daṅ-po'i 'grel-pa mi-gyo-snaṅ-ba, II, 640.
mDor-byas, I, 366.
'Dul-ba mDo, II, 555, 654.
'Dul-ba bsdus-pa, I, 85.
'Dul-ba me-tog phreṅ-rgyud, II, 809.
'Dul-ba 'od-ldan, II, 736.
'Dul-ba raṅ-gi rnam-bśad, II, 1054.
'Dul-ba'i mdo'i rgya-čher 'grel-pa, I, 77.
'Dus-pa mDo, I, 158.
'Dus-pa'i dbaṅ-bskur bži-brgya-lṅa-bču-pa, I, 251.
'Dus-phyi-ma'i 'grel-pa, I, 103.
'Dod-'ǰo, I, 389.
rDo-rǰe mkha'-'gro, I, 375; II, 825.
rDo-rǰe gur, I, 209.
rDo-rǰe 'ǰigs-byed, I, 103, 377.
rDo-rǰe sñiṅ-'grel, II, 534, 762, 765, 824, 838.
rDo-rǰe sñiṅ-po, II, 830.
rDo-rǰe gdan-bži, I, 364.
rDo-rǰe rnam-par sgeg-ma, II, 824.
rDo-rǰe phur-pa rtsa-ba'i rgyud-kyi dum-bu, I, 106.

rDo-rje 'phreṅ-ba, I, 228, 320, 371; II, 411, 448, 499, 507, 542, 776, 995, 1046.
rDo-rje me-loṅ, I, 171.
rDo-rje rtse-mo, II, 534.
rDo-rje zam-pa, I, 171.
rDo-rje sems-dpa'i nam-mkha'-che, I, 143.
rDo-rje sems-dpa'i žus-lan, I, 138.
rDor-dbyiṅs, II, 832.
sDud-pa tshigs-su bčad-pa, ('Phags-pa śes-rab-kyi pha-rol-tu phyin-pa sdud pa tshigs-su bčad-pa), I, 331, 337; II, 941, 949, 981.
sDud-pa'i dka'-'grel, II, 489.
sDud-pa'i lde-mig, II, 859.
sDom-rnam-gñis, I, 233.
sDom-pa rgya-mtsho, I, 390.
sDom-pa 'byuṅ-ba, I, 389.
sDom-'byuṅ, II, 824.
sDom-gsum rab-dbye, II, 607.
sDe-snod gsal-byed, II, 978.
sDebs-sbyor me-tog-gi čhuṅ-po, II, 784.
bsDus-don, II, 777.
bsDus-pa'i rgyud, II 762.
Nā-ro 'grel-čhen, II, 417, 830, 974.
Nā-ro čhos-drug, I, 198, 507; II, 741.
Nag-'jigs, II, 442.
Nag-po'i rgyud, I, 377.
Nag-po'i čhos-drug, I, 375, 377.
Nam-mkha'-čhe, II, 448.
Nam-'mkha'-daṅ-mñam-pa'i rgyud čhen-po, I, 172; II, 848.
Ni-gu'i čhos-skor, II, 549.
Ne-gu čhos-drug, II, 491.
Nel-pa'i čhos-'byuṅ, I, viii, XIV, 53.
gNas-pa bsdus-pa, II, 857.
rNam-ṅes, I, 326; II, 532.
rNam-'joms, I, 142.
rNal-'byor 'jug-pa, II, 663.
rNal-'byor spyod-pa'i sa-las byaṅ-čhub sems-dpa'i sa, II, 64.
rNal-'byor lam-gyi sgron-ma, II, 906.
rNam-par snaṅ-mdzod mṅon-par byaṅ-čhub-pa'i rgyud, I, 351.
rNal-'byor rigs-pa'i ñi-ma, I, 137.
Pad-ma d kar-po'i čhos-'byuṅ, I, xii.
Pad-ma dkar-po'i gsuṅ-'bum, II, 588.
Pad-ma-čan, II, 489.
Pad-ma'i bka'-thaṅ, I, 6, 39.

dPag-bsam 'khri-śiṅ, II, 785.
dPal bkra-śis-kyi rnam-par bśad-pa čhen-po, I, 370.
dPal 'khor-lo sdom-pa'i sgrub-thabs rnal-'byor-bži-ldan, I, 385.
dPal-mčhog, I, 227, 354.
dPal-mčhog-rgyud, I, 352.
dPal-ldan bži-pa, II, 400, 403.
dPal-ldan 'khor-lo, I, 362.
dPal-'dus-pa, I, 358.
dPal Ye-śes thig-le'i rgyud-kyi rgyal-po, I, 361.
dPal gsaṅ-ba-'dus-pa, I, 102.
dPuṅ-bzaṅs, I, 351.
dPe-brgya-pa, II, 1069.
dPe-med tsho'i sbyor-drug, II, 640.
dPe'i-rgyan, II, 1069.
dPyid-kyi thig-le žes-bya-ba, II, 803.
sPaṅ-bkoṅ phyag-rgya-ma, I, 38.
sPar-khab, I, 110.
sPuṅs-skor, II, 534.
sPyan-ma'i ṅan-soṅ yoṅs-su sbyoṅ-ba, I, 394.
sPyan-ras-gzigs-yi-ge-drug-ma, I, 40.
sPyi'i khog-dbub-pa, I, 157.
sPyod-'jug, II, 611, 741, 809, 994.
sPyod-bsdus, I, 354.
sPyod-pa bsdus-pa'i sgron-ma, I, 362; II, 736.
Phag-mo mṅon-'byuṅ, I, 188, 375.
Phag-mo gžuṅ-drug—Phag-mo čhos-drug, I, 390, 395; II, 741, 800.
Phal-po-čhe spoṅ-brgyad-ma, II, 654.
Phur-pa, II, 489.
Phur-pa spu-gri, II, 832.
Phur-pa mya-ṅan-las-'das-pa'i rgyud, I, 156.
Phur-pa rtsa-ba, I, 128.
Phyag-rgya čhen-po ga'u-ma, II, 723.
Phyag-rgya-bži rjes-su bstan-pa, II, 857.
Phyag-čhen thig-le rgyud, II, 697.
Phyag-rdor stod-'grel, II, 824.
Phyag-rdor don-'grel, II, 762.
Phyag-rdor dbaṅ-bskur, II, 832.
Phyag-na rdo-rje bdud-rtsi thigs-pa, I, 143.
Phyag-na rdo-rje dbaṅ-bskur-ba'i rgyud, I, 351.
Phyi-naṅ-gi grub-mtha' bsdus-pa, I, 333.
'Phags-pa 'jam-dpal-gyi rtsa-ba'i rgyud, I, x.
'Phags-pa 'Da-ka ye-śes žes-bya-ba theg-pa čhen-po'i mdo, II, 865.

'Phags-pa śes-rab-kyi pha-rol-tu phyin-pa brgyad-stoṅ-pa, II, 170.
'Phags-lam bkod-pa'i rgyud, I, 147.
'Pho-ba spyi-brtol, II, 953.
Bam-po lṅa-bču-pa, I, 77, 192.
Bu-ṭikā, I, 339.
Bu-ston bka'-'bum, I, vii. See Bu-ston gsuṅ-'bum.
Bu-ston čhos-'byuṅ, I, x, xiii, 331; II; 417, 1086.
Bu-ston gsuṅ-'bum, I, 103, 228, 358, 363, 364, 366, 370, 375, 385, 386; II, 417, 424, 938.
Be-'bum dmar-po, II, 722.
Baidūrya dkar-po, I, xvi.
Bya-ba btus-pa, II, 974.
Bya-yul gtor-čhen, I, 99.
Byaṅ-čhub spyod-pa'i sgron-ma, II, 906.
Byaṅ-čhub lam-gyi sgron-ma, I, 248.
Byaṅ-čhub lam-rim, I, 298.
Byaṅ-čhub sems-kyi thig-le, I, 370.
Byaṅ Śambha-la'i lam-yig, II, 790.
Byams-čhos — Byams-čhos sde-lṅa, I, 270, 318, 326; II, 449, 470, 475, 490, 498; 532, 808, 809, 1012, 1022.
Bye-brag-tu bśad-pa čhen-po, I, 243.
Bye-brag bśad-pa čhen-po, II, 1054.
bLa-ma brgyad-pa'i rim-pa, II, 857.
bLa-ma gñis, I, 153.
bLa-ma gsaṅ-'dus, II, 779.
dBaṅ-ṅes bstan-pa — dBaṅ-ṅes-par bstan-pa, II, 842, 857.
dBaṅ-ṅes bstan-gyi 'grel-pa, II, 857.
dBaṅ-mdor — dBaṅ-mdor-bstan, II, 533, 838.
dBaṅ-mdor bstan-rtsa-'grel, II, 640.
dBaṅ-rnam-ṅes, II, 855.
dBaṅ-rab-byed, II, 758.
dbU-ma sñiṅ-po'i 'grel rTog-ge 'bar-ba, I, 29.
—
dbU-ma rTog-ge 'bar-ba, II, 543.
dbU-ma bden-gñis, I, 332.
dbU-ma rtsa-ba śes-rab, II, 475.
dbU-ma rtsa-ba'i 'grel-pa Tshig-gsal-ba žes-bya-ba, I, 334.
dbU-ma rtsa-śes, II, 679.
dbU-ma tshig-gsal, II, 993.
dbU-ma bži-brgya-pa, II, 475.
dU-ma rin-čhen phreṅ-ba, II, 1069.
dbU-ma-la 'jug-pa, II, 475.

dbU-ma śer-gsum, II, 475.
dbU-ma'i sñiṅ-po'i 'grel-pa rTog-ge 'bar-ba, I, 39. See dbU-ma sñiṅ-po'i 'grel-pa.
dbU-ma'i bsdud-pa, I 334.
dbU-ma'i man-ṅag, I, 258, 325.
dbU-ma'i rigs-tshogs-drug, II, 747, 808, 955, 1022, 1070.
'Bum, II, 414.
'Byuṅ-po 'dul-byed, II, 489.
'Byed-rnam-gñis, I, 233.
sBa-bžed, I, v, 57.
sBa-bžed gtsaṅ-ma, I, v, 39.
sBa-bžed žabs-btags-ma, I, v.
sBas-pa mig-'byed, II, 533.
sByin-bsreg, I, 393.
sByin-bsreg gñis-kyi čho-ga, I, 370.
sByoṅ-rgyud, II, 995.
sByoṅ-rgyud ma-bu, I, 354, 355.
sByor-phreṅ, II, 735.
Ma-ga-dha bzaṅ-mo'i rtogs-pa brǰod-pa, I, 25.
Ma-gśen, II, 489.
Man-ṅag sku'i sgron-ma, II, 904.
Man-ṅag-gi sñe-ma, II, 448.

Man-ṅag sñe-ma, II, 801, 974, 983.
Man-luṅs-pa'i lam-yig, II, 790.
Mi-ǰigs-pa'i gžuṅ-'grel, II, 1046.
Mi-tra brgya-tsa, II, 1034 ff.
Mig-sgron, I, 145.
Mid-la'i mgur-'bum, II, 721.
Mun-pa'i go-čha, I, 153, 160.
Me-tog phreṅ-rgyud, I, 82; II 808.
Mya-ṅan-med luṅ-bstan-pa'i mdo, II, 1069.
dMaṅs-Do-ha, II, 846.
sMan-dpyad yan-lag brgyad, II, 792.
sMra-sgo, I, 165.
Tsandra-pa, II, 793.
bTsun-mo Do-ha, II, 846.
rTsa-ba śes-rab, I, 343; II, 766.
rTsa-ba'i ltuṅ-ba'i rgya-čher 'grel-pa, I, 298.
rTsa-ba'i ye-śes čhen-po, I, 370.
ṇTsa-se, II, 548.
rTsod-pa zlog-pa — rTsod-bz'og, I, 236; II, 548.
Tshad-ma kun-btus<Tshad-ma kun-las btus-pa, II, 532, 808.

Tshad-ma rgyan, I, 70, 325.
Tshad-ma sde-bdun, II, 747, 785, 808.
Tshad-ma bsdus-pa I, 195; II, 532.
Tshad-ma bsdus-pa Yid-kyi mun-sel, II, 532.
Tshad-ma rnam-'grel, I, 346.
Tshad-ma rnam-ṅes, I, 155, 331; II, 698, 741.
Tshad-ma'i bsdus-pa, I, 334. See Tshad-ma bsdus-pa.
Tshad-ma'i bsdus-pa Yid-kyi mun-sel, I, 333. See Tshad-ma bsdus-pa Yid-kyi mun-sel.
Tshig-gsal, I, 334.
Tshigs-su bčad-pa'i mdzod, I, 370,
Tshogs-kyi 'khor-lo'i čho ga, I, 370.
Tshem-bu dmar-khrid, II, 994.
mTshan-brjod, I, 187, 375; II, 534, 712,
'Tshal-pa'i čhos-skor, II, 549.
'Tshal-pa'i deb-ther, I, vi.
'Tshog-'jug, I, 236, 280.
rDzogs-čhen sñiṅ-thig, II, 533.
Dzogs-čhen sems-sde, II, 728.
rDzogs-pa čhen-po'i lta-sgom man-ṅag, I, 165.
rDzogs-rim saṅs-rgyas 'čhar-pa, I, 803.
Žal-gyi luṅ, I, 168.
Žal-gñis-ma, I, 377
Žal-gñis-ma čhe-ba, I, 393.
Žal-luṅ, I, 168, 169, 371, 373. See Žal-gyi luṅ.
Ži-ba lam-bab, II, 986.
Ži-byed čhos-'byuṅ, II, 983.
Žu-lan sman-mčhog bdud-rtsi'i 'phreṅ-ba, II, 1079.
Žus-lan khuṅs-kyi gdab-pa, I, 138.
gŽuṅ-'bum-pa, II, 846.
gŽuṅ-lugs-kyi bye-brag bkod-pa'i 'khor-lo, I, 30.
bŽi-brgya-ba, I, 343.
bŽi-pa-la 'jug-pa thabs-daṅ-bčas-pa, I, 370.
Zab-mo naṅ-don, II, 533, 549, 833.
Zab-mo dbaṅ-gi man-ṅag, I, 171.
Zla-gsaṅ thig-le, I, 102.
gZuṅs-kyi dbaṅ-phyug rgyal-pos žus-pa'i mdo, II, 459
gZuṅs-grwa-lṅa, I, 107.
gZer-lṅa, II, 933.
gZer-bu, I, 145.
'Od-ldan, I, 85; II, 798.
Yaṅ-dag, I, 110; II, 448.

Yaṅ-dag lta-ba'i sgron-ma, II, 906.
Yaṅ-dag rtsa-ba'i luṅ, I, 153.
Yaṅ-phur, II, 488.
Yan-lag bdun-ldan, II, 763.
Yid-kyi mun-sel, I, 333.
Yo-ga rdo-rje 'byuṅ-ba, I, 234.
Ye-śes grub-pa, I, 265, 363; II, 844, 856.
Ye-śes rdo-rje kun-las-btus čhe-ba, II, 832.
Ye-śes spyaṅ-sgrub, II, 640.
Ye-śes gsaṅ-rdzogs-kyi rgyud, II, 534.
Raṅ-byuṅ-ba'i bka'-'bum, II, 548.
Ri-čhos, I, 200.
Rig-bklag, II, 971.
Rig-ñi, I, 145.
Rig-gter, II, 808.
Rig-'dzin-bčhu, II, 726.
Rigs-pa drug-bču-pa, I, 236, 342.
Rigs-tshogs-drug, I, 236; II, 441, 475, 566, 768.
Rin-čhen ljoṅ-śiṅ, I, 386.
Rin-čhen phreṅ-ba, I, 274, 343.
Rin-čhen 'bru-dgu, II, 677.
Rin-po-čhe sgom-gyi lde-mig, II, 797.
Rin-po-čhe sgom-pa'i sgron-ma, II, 906.
Rin-po-čhe 'bar-pa, I, 370.
Rin-po-čhe gsal-ba sgron-ma'i rgyud, I, 147.
Rim-lṅa, I, 367; II, 547.
Rim-lṅa gsal-don, I, 389.
Rim-lṅa gsal-sgron, II, 1077.
Rim-lṅa'i dmar-khrid, II, 424.
Rim-bži, I, 234.
Ro-sñoms skor-drug, II, 668.
Re'u-mig, I, 200, 322; II, 589, 697, 726.
rLuṅ-sems gñis-med, II, 547.
La-dwags rgyal-rabs, I, ix.
Lam-sgron, I, 272; II, 611.
Lam-gyi sgron-ma, I, 268.
Lam-rnam-bkod, I, 171.
Lam-rnam-par bkod-pa, I, 152, 153, 157.
Lam-'bras-bu-daṅ-bčas-pa'i rtsa-ba rdo-rje tshig-rkaṅ, I, 143.
Lam-rim, I, 331; II, 640, 680, 954.
Lam-rim čhuṅ-ba, II, 1077.
Lam-loṅs, I, 234.

Las-kyi 'khor-lo bstan-pa, II, 1069.
Las-brgya-rtsa, II, 629.
Lū-yi-pa, I, 377; II, 472, 613, 735.
Lū-yi-la'i mṅon-rtogs-kyi bśad-pa, I, 389.
Lū-yi-pa'i-lugs rdzogs-pa'i rim-pa rnal-'byor čhen-po ñams-su len-lugs, I, 389.
Luṅ-sde-bži, II, 490.
Luṅ-rnam-'byed, II, 490.
Luṅ-'phran-tshegs, II, 490.
Luṅ-žu-ba, II, 490.
Luṅ-gži, II, 490.
Luṅ-rnam-'byed, I, 36.
Legs-bśad gser-phreṅ, I, 340.
Śer-phyin thugs-rgyud lag-len sñam-rgyud rin-čhen phreṅ-ba rigs-pa'i gtan-tshigs 'phrul-gyi lde-mig, II, 900.
Śes-bya-gži-lṅa'i bśad-pa, I, 333.
Śes-rab-kyi pha-rol-tu phyin-pa 'bum-pa rgya-čher 'grel-pa, I, 64.
Śes-rab 'grel-čhuṅ, II, 698.
Śes-rab sñiṅ-po, I, 192; II, 911, 978.
Śes-rab ye-śes gsal-ba, I, 394; II, 842, 857.
gŚin-rǰe dgra-rgyud, I, 163.
gŚn-rǰe dgra-nag, I, 200.
gŚin-rǰe gśed-kyi 'khor-lo'i gsal-byed, II, 755.
gŚed-dmar, II, 993.
gŚed-dmar rdzogs-rim, II, 534.
bŚad-'bum, II, 954.
bŚad-'bum rdo-rǰe don-gsal, I, 156.
bŚes-sprin, II, 808.
Sa-bčad, II, 777.
Sa-rgyan-gñis, II, 810.
Sa-sde—Sa-sde-lṅa, I, 233; II, 490, 534, 678, 810, 1012, 1016.
Sa'i dṅos-gži, II, 810.
Saṅs-rgyas thod-pa'i rgyud, II, 1069.
Saṅs-rgyas mñam-sbyor, I, 102, 164.
Saṅs-rgyas thams-čad-kyi dgoṅs-pa 'dus-pa'i mdo, I, 105.
Saṅs-rgyas thod-pa, II, 832.
Sum-brgya-pa, I, 85, 277; II, 808.
Seṅ-ldeṅ nags-sgrol, II, 845.
Sems-kyi sgrib-sbyoṅ, II, 1019.
Sems-kyi rdo-rǰe bstod-pa, II, 663.
Sems-ñid ṅal-gso, II, 677.
Sems-sde ma-bu bčo-brgyad, II, 534.

gSaṅ-sñiṅ rgyud, I, 148, 151, 152, 153, 155, 156, 157, 158, 160, 163, 164, 168; II, 534, 965.
gSaṅ-sñiṅ rgyud-phyi-ma, I, 104.
gSaṅ-sñiṅ 'grel-pa Par-khab, I, 155, 157.
gSaṅ-sñiṅ sgrub-pa rgyan-gyi me-tog, I, 104.
gSaṅ-'dus sgron-gsal, II, 629.
gSaṅ-'dus sbyor-drug, II, 640.
gSaṅ-ldan, I, 356; II, 793, 987.
gSaṅ-ba grub-pa, I, 363.
gSaṅ-ba čhen-po'i de-kho-na-ñid grub-pa, II, 856.
gSaṅ-ba sñiṅ-po, I, 103, 104, 108.
gSaṅ-ba sñiṅ-po'i rgya-čher 'grel-pa, I, 158.
gSaṅ-ba thugs-kyi sgron-ma, II, 905.
gSaṅ-ba 'dus-pa'i rgya-čher 'grel-pa, I, 342.
gSaṅ-ba 'dus-pa'i 'grel-pa, I, 103.
gSaṅ-ba rnal-'byor-čhen po'i rgyud rdo-rje rtse-mo I, 227.
gSaṅ-ba spyi-rgyud, I, 351.
gSaṅ-ba phur-gčig, II, 953.
gSaṅ-ba'i de-kho-na-ñid gsal-ba, I, 358.
gSal-sgron, I, 153.
gSuṅ-gi mdzod 'Jam-dbyaṅs rdo-rje'i glu, II 865.
bSam-gtan sñiṅ-gi ñi-ma, I, 138.
bSam-gtan phyi-ma, I, 351.
bSam-gtan mig-gi sgron-ma, I, 136, 199.
bSam-mi-khyab, I, 208.
bsLab-btus < bsLab-pa kun-las btus-pa, I, 332, 333; II, 535, 741, 747.
He-ru-ka mṅon-'byuṅ, I, 375.
Lhan-skyes snaṅ-ba, I, 374.
Lhan-čig skyes-grub, I, 361, 363; II, 856.
Lhan-čig skyes-grub rtsa-'grel, II, 552.
Lhan-čig skyes-pa'i rin-po-čhe'i man-ṅag-gi rgyud, I, 362.
Lhan-čig-skyes-sbyor, II, 460, 559, 681, 723.
Lhan-čig ga'u-ma, II, 533.
Lho-brag čhos-'byuṅ, I, v.
A-ma-na-si, II, 833, 866.
A-ma-na-si'i skor ñer-drug, II, 845.
A-ro khrid-mo-čhe, II, 988.
A-ro'i rgyud-čhuṅ-gi luṅ, II, 534.
A-ro'i theg-čhen rnal-'byor, II, 1001.
U-rgyan bsñen-sgrub, II, 779, 810.

PERSONAL NAMES

TIBETAN

Ka-ba Dar-seṅ, I, 79, 232, 306, 313.

Ka-ba sTon-nam, I, 79.

Ka-ba, I, 255, 262, 386.

Ka-ba rGya-gar, I, 264.

Ka-ba Śākya dbaṅ-phyug, I, 253, 259, 262; II, 1085.

Ka-ba -čan-pa, II, 943.

Ka-ba-phu, II, 895.

Ka-tsa-pa, I, 385.

Ka-bži-pa, I, 80.

Ka-rag sGom-čhuṅ, I, 332.

Ka-ro-pa, II, 843, 847-8, 853-5.

Ka-laṅ-rmal, I, 38.

Kan-pa-ba, II, 1045.

Kam-pa, I, 305, 318, 320.

Kam-pa Śes-rab-'od, I, 311.

Kam Yuṅ-pa, I, 264.

Kar-ma-grags, I, 268.

Kar-ma-pa dKon-gžon, II, 518, 721.

Kar-ma-pa, II, 484-8, 517, 519, 520, 523, 547, 551, 811, 813 (dPal- =), 1041.

Kar-ma pa-śi, II, 487, 494, 499, 517,

518, 564, 582, 1007, 1029.

Kar-ma-pa Pa-śi-pa, II, 772. See Kar-ma pa-śi.

Kwa-'oṅ mČhog-grags-pa, I, xviii, 64.

Ku-ku-ri-pa, II, 730, 869.

Ku-ǰol-pa, I, 292.

Ku-rab-pa, I, 155.

Ku-śa-la-na, I, 385.

Ku-śa-li, I, 361.

Kun-bkras-pa, I, 215.

Kun-mkhyen čhen-po (Dol-pa-pa Śes-rab rgyal-mtshan), II, 756, 782, 785.

Kun-dga', I, 180, 197; II, 409, 413, 871, 902-3, 913-7, 920-3, 925-7, 932-3, 938, 960, 978.

Kun-dga' bkra-śis, II, 641.

Kun-dga' mgon-po, II, 974.

Kun-dga' rgyal-po (čhos-rǰe-) II, 829.

Kun-dga' rgyal-mtshan, II, 589.

(Ti-shih-), I, 308.
(Bya-bral čhen-po-), II, 965.
(Sa-skya paṇ-čhen-), I, 211, 382; II, 722.
Kun-dga' rgyal-mtshan-dpal-bzaṅ-po, I, 213-4; II, 1088-9.
Kun-dga' ñi-ma'i rgyal-mtshan-dpal-bzaṅ-po, I, 214.
Kun-dga' sñiṅ-po, I, 373.
Kun-dga' sñiṅ-po (Tsoṅ-kha-pa), II, 504.
Kun-dga' sñiṅ-po (Sa-čhen), I, 382; II, 869.
Kun-dga' don-grub, II, 408, 490, 518, 703, 974.
Kun-dga' rdo-rje, I, vi, 47, 56; II, 970. (mi'i bdag-po-).
Kun-dga' dpal, I, 281, 345.
Kun-dga' dpal-pa, II, 1072.
Kun-dga' dpal-'byor, II, 672.
Kun-dga'-bo, II, 1051.
Kun-dga' blo-gros, I, 213, 308; II, 413, 520.
Kun-dga' dbaṅ-phyug, I, 330.
Kun-dga' 'bar, I, 211.
Kun-dga' bzaṅ-po, I, 216; II, 413, 972, 1045.
(dPon-čhen-), 582, 1059, 1088.
Kun-dga' 'od-zer, I, 201; II, 542.
Kun-dga' rin-čhen, II, 1088.
Kun-dga' rin-čhen rgyal-po, II, 831.
Kun-dga' rin-čhen don-yod-dpal, I, 217.
Kun-dga' legs-pa, II, 595, 802.
Kun-dga' legs-pa'i rgyal-mtshan dpal-bzaṅ-po, I, 213.
Kun-dga' legs-pa'i 'byuṅ-gnas, I, 213.
Kun-dga' bśes-gñen, II, 638, 970.
Kun-dga' seṅ-ge, II, 633.
Kun-'gro mgon-po, II, 553.
Kun-'gro'i mgon-po, I, 362.
Kun-rgyal, II 511, 1016.
Kun-rgyal-ba, I, 283, 810, 813, 815.
Kun-tu-'od (dBaṅ-phyug seṅ-ge, rNo-ra-ba), I, 387.
Kun-ldan, II, 707.
Kun-ldan gTsaṅ-pa Ras-čhuṅ, II 563.
Kun-ldan ras-pa, II, 564, 708-10.
Kun-ldan śes-rab, II, 489.
Kun-nas 'od-zer, I, 4.
Kun-spans Čhos-grags-dpal-bzaṅ-po (Kun-spaṅs Čhos-grags-dpal) II, 785, 828, 1045.
Kun-spaṅs-pa, I, 214; II, 592, 633, 772-5, 794, 1041.
Kun-spaṅs Lha-ri-ba, I, 91.

Kun-blo (bLa-čhen-), II, 634.
Kun-brtsod-pa, II, 1044.
Kun-bzaṅs, I, 186, 188, 190, 341; II, 890.
Kun-rig, II, 520.
Kun-rin, I, 215.
Kun-śe-pa, II, 1072.
Kun-gsal-ba, II, 581.
Kun-bsod-pa, II, 775.
Ke-ke Hor-grags (Śaṅs-pa-), II, 706, 900.
Ke-rtse-ba, I, 113.
Ke-ru, I, 292.
Ko-khyim-pa, I, 79.
Ko-de-luṅ-pa, I, 269.
Ko-bo Ye-śes 'byuṅ-gnas, I, 345.
Ko-brag-pa (Lha-gdoṅ-pa Čhos-rje Ko-brag-pa), II, 446, 519, 679, 690, 691, 726, 728, 796-7, 975. (Ko-brag-pa bSod-nams rgyal-mtshan).
Ko-śa-pa, II, 869.
Koṅ-kha-pa, I, 354. (Thaṅ-ston-).
Koṅ-lčam, II, 983.
Koṅ-ston-pa, II, 727.
Koṅ-ston Śes-rab rdo-rje, I, 321.
Koṅ-nag Čhos-kyi so-ser, II, 678.
Koṅ-pa Dar-śe, II, 632.
Koṅ-po' Jag-čhuṅ, I, 333.
Koṅ-po-ba, II, 745.
Koṅ-btsun Śes-rab ye-śes, I, 109.
Kon-čhen rGyal-ba-skyabs, II, 571.
Kor-ston Rāja, I, 188.
Kyi-tshaṅ Žig-po, II, 872.
Kyu-ra gŽon-nu 'od-zer, I, 264.
Kyu-ra Rin-po-čhe, II, 645.
Kyu-ra A-skyabs, I, 376.
Kye-ma Grags-tshul, I, 81.
Kṛṣṇa'i gos-čan, II, 1051.
kLaṅ-čhuṅ, II, 916.
kLal-pa Kun-rgyal, I, 100.
kLu, I, 74, 76.
kLu-skyoṅ, I, 5.
kLu-khri, I, 324.
kLu-grub, I, 344, 396; II, 416, 474, 868, 1023.
kLu-dge-'bar-po, II, 610.
kLu-sgom, II, 975.

kLu-byaṅ, I. 324; II, 869.
kLu-mes, I, 34, 61-2, 74-5, 77, 88, 93, 378; II, 1085.
kLu-btsan-grags, II, 932.
kLu'i-byaṅ-čhub, II, 982.
kLu'i-blo, II, 983.
kLuṅ-nam (kLuṅ-nam-phrul-gyi rgyal-po), I, 37, 46.
kLuṅ-śod-pa Khyuṅ-khri, II, 857.
kLuṅs-śod Ral-pa, I, 285.
kLuṅs-mo 'bum-lčam, II, 983.
kLun rDor-po, I, 376.
kLun rGyam-legs, I, 376.
kLun Se-bo Śākya-rgyal, I, 376.
kLubs, II, 761.
kLubs-dkar (kLubs-dkar-ba), I, 277; II, 654.
kLubs-dkar Tshul-khrims-grags, I, 82.
kLubs J̌o-sras, I, 760.
kLubs Saṅghakīrti, II, 760.
kLubs lo-tsā-ba bLo-gros-dpal, II, 838.
kLu'i-sde, I, 28.
kLu'i byaṅ-čhub, I, 360-1; II, 798.
kLu'i-lha, I, 5.
kLus-bsruṅs, I, 16.
kLo-ston, I, 354.
kLog-skya ston-pa, II, 402.
kLog-skya-ba, II, 446.
kLog-skya ǰo-sras, II, 399
kLog-skya Śes-rab-rtsegs, I, 382.
kLog-skya 'Byuṅ-gnas rgyal-mtshan, II, 403.
kLog-skya Ral-pa-čan, II, 912.
kLoṅ-šhen-pa, I, 200, 201, 309; II, 529.
kLoṅ-čhen Rab-'byams-pa, I, 200; II, 723.
(See Tshul-khrims blo-gros).
kLoṅ-rtse-ba, II, 711.
kLog-ston dGe-'dun-skyabs, I, 190.
dKa'-bču-pa, II, 588-9.
dKa'-thub, II, 520.
dKa'-thub-spyod, I, 5.
dKa'-bži-pa, II, 1023.
dKar-sgom ǰo-nag, I, 132.
dKar-po (sKu-yal-ba), II, 621.
dKar-gdum-pa, II, 594.
dKar-po Rin-bzaṅs, II, 549.

dKar-mo, I, 12.
dKon-skyabs, II, 747, 883, 900, 942-3, 952.
dKon-mkhar, II, 736, 1009.
dKon- mčhog, II, 990.
dKon mčhog-skyabs, II, 876, 890.
dKon-mčhog-grags, II, 1024.
dKon-mčhog rgya-mtsho, I, 330.
dKon-mčhog rgyan, II, 750.
dKon-mčhog rgyal-po, I, 210.
dKon-mčhog rgyal-mtshan, II, 500, 565, 1072.
dKon-mčhog-rten, II, 1001.
dKon-mčhog rdo-rje, II, 450.
dKon-mčhog-dpal, I, 332.
dKon-mčhog-'bar, I, 373.
dKon-mčhog-brtsegs, I, 352.
dKon-mčhog tshul-khrims, I, 330.
dKon-mčhog gžon-nu, I, 396; II, 1024.
(bKa'-bži-pa-).
dKon-mčhog bzaṅ-po, II, 451, 1089.
dKon-mčhog rin-čhen, II, 678.
dKon-mčhog-bsruṅs, II, 760
dKon-gñer, II, 1030.
dKon-gžon, II, 784, 885.
bKa'-bču-pa, II, 830.
bKa'-bču-pa gŽon-nu seṅ-ge, II, 1046, 1050.
bKa'-gdams-pa, II, 482, 991.
bKa'-bži-pa, II, 792.
bKra-śis, I, 19; II, 536.
bKra-śis-skyid, I, 301; II, 728.
bKra-śis grags-pa, I, 156; II, 522, 647, 939.
bKra-śis rgya-mtsho-ba, I, 155-6.
bKra-śis rgyal-mtshan (bKras-rgyal-ba), I, 316; II, 1006-7.
bKra-śis sgaṅ-pa, I, 196, 292, 298.
bKra-śis dṅos-grub, I, 195.
bKra-śis dar-rgyas legs-pa'i rgyal-po, I, ii. bKra-śis dar-rgyas, II, 1087
bKra-śis-lde, I, 37.
bKra-śis rnam-rgyal, II, 809, 1082.
bKra-śis lde-mgon, I, 37.
bKra-śis-dpal-ldan, II, 895.
bKra-śis- dpal-ldan-pa, II, 412.
bKra-śis dpal-pa, II, 413, 648.

bKra-śis dpal-rtsegs Ñi-ma'i dbaṅ-po bsruṅ-ba'i go-čha (sTag-luṅ čhos-rje-), II, 593, 637-8, 640, 647-8, 787. (bKra-śis dpal-pa).
bKra-śis dpal-bzaṅ, II, 1089.
bKra-śis-dpal-'od-pa, II, 647.
bKra-śis byaṅ-čhub, II, 1072.
bKra-śis bla-ma, II, 628, 630.
bKra-śis-'bum, I, 128, 303; II, 520.
bKra-śis 'byuṅ-gnas, II, 510.
bKra-śis Tshe-riṅ-ma, II, 435.
bKra-śis tshul-pa, II, 637. (Jo-stan mkhan-čhen-)
bKra-śis tshul-khrims, II, 1072.
bKra-śis bzaṅ-po, I, 335.
bKra-śis-'od, II, 658.
bKra-śis gyuṅ-druṅ, I, 175.
bKra-śis rin-čhen, I, 309; II, 528, 761-2. (bKras-rin-pa).
bKra-śis seṅ-ge, I, 308, 341, 344; II, 585, 1041, 1072.
bKras-luṅ-pa, I, 200.
rKaṅ-gdub-čan, I, 8, 16.
rKaṅ-gdub-čan-žabs, I, 13.
rKaṅ-pa'i 'gros, I, 45.
rKun-po, I, 376.
Kyaṅ, rKyaṅ-mo-kha-pa, II, 670.
Kyaṅ-čhens Pruk-sku, III, 693-4.
Kyaṅ-čhen ras-pa gŽon-nu bsod-nams, II, 693.
Kyaṅ-čhen-pa Śākyaśrī, II, 536.
Kyaṅ-pa Čhos-blo, I, 352-3, 373.
Kyaṅ-mo sPaṅ-kha-ba, II, 477.
Kan-mo gnas-brtan, II, 1052.
Kam, II, 73, 79; II, 896-9, 900, 901-5, 944, 993.
Kam-sgom, II, 896-7, 924.
Kam-sgom Ye-śes rgyal-mtshan, I, 234; II, 897.
Kam-po rDo-rje dpal-rtsegs, II, 479.
Kam Ye-śes rgyal-mtshan, I, 97; II, 903.
Kam gSal-ba'i sñiṅ-po, I, 78.
Kar-čhuṅ-pa, I, 331.
Kar-mda'-gdoṅ, I, 8.
Kal-ldan, I, 13; II, 999.
Kal-ldan rgyal-po, I, 325.
Kal-ldan Čhos-kyi seṅ-ge, I, 199.
Kal-ldan-pa, II, 988.
Kal-ldan Ye-śes seṅ-ge (Zwa-ra'i-), II, 563-4, 652-4.
Kal-pa bzaṅ-mo, II, 844.

sKu-'bum-pa, I, 321.
sKu-yal-ba, II, 523, 623, 627. 629, 647.
sKu-yal Rin-čhen-mgon. II, 621.
sKu-bsruṅs sTon-pa, I. 285.
sKor, I, 318; II, 855.
sKor-čhuṅ-ba, II, 849. 851, 854-5. 865.
sKor Jo-sras, I, 318-9.
sKor-ston dṄos-grub-'bar, II. 849.
sKor-Ni-rū-pa, I, 97, 124; II, 729, 844, 846-7, 875.
sKos, II, 726.
sKya-rgyal Čhos-skyid, II, 532.
sKya-ston Čhos-seṅ, I, 120.
sKya-ston Śāk-yes, I, 122.
sKya-reṅ, I, 15.
sKyaṅ-po Dar-ma-grags, II, 941.
sKyabs-se, I, 373.
sKyi rGyal-ba'i gtsug-tor, I, 64.
sKyi-ston, II, 396.
sKyi-ston Grags-'bum, I, 336. 345.
sKyi-ston Čhos-grags, II, 688.
sKyi-ston 'Jam-dbyaṅs, II, 756. 776.
sKyi-nor Jñāna, I, 352, 355.
sKyi-po Tshul-'phags, II, 734.
sKyi Bye-ma-luṅ-pa, I, 356.
sKyi-tsha 'Od-'byuṅ, II, 1024.
sKyi-riṅs Yon-tan seṅ-ge, I, 237.
sKyid-lde, I, 38, 205.
sKyid-lde Ñi-ma-mgon, I. 37.
sKyid-pa-dpal, II, 895.
sKyid-'bum (sPrul-sku-), II, 988.
sKyid-mkhar-pa, I, 136-7.
sKyil-mkhar Lha-khaṅ-pa, I, 332.
sKyur-mo-gza', II, 920.
sKye-po Tshul-'phags, I, 81.
sKye-po Ye-rdor, II. 462.
sKye-ma Grags-tshul, II, 1023-4.
sKye-med, II, 862.
sKye-med Žaṅ., II. 900.
sKye-med 'Od-gsal, II. 986.
sKye-tshe Ye-śes dbaṅ-phyug, I. 190.
sKyer-sgaṅ-pa. II, 522. 738, 742. 746.
sKyer-sgaṅ-pa Dharma seṅ-ge. II 737.

sKyel, I, 82.
sKyel-nag Grags-seṅ. I, 335-6.
sKyes-mčhog kLu-grub. II, 1024.
sKyes-mčhog Nam-mkha' bzaṅ-po, II, 1025.
sKyes-mčhog-pa, II, 694-5.
sKyes-mčhog Rin-po-čhe, II. 966.
sKyes-mčhog Rin-čhen bzaṅ-po, II, 969.
sKyo, I, 156; II, 1024.
sKyo-ston, I, 273, 306.
sKyo-ston-pa, I, 336-7.
sKyo-ston sMon-lam tshul-khrims, I. 283.
sKyo-ston Rin-po-čhe Byaṅ-čhub zin-čhen, I. 305.
sKyo-ston Śāk-yes, I, 120.
sKyo 'Od-'byuṅ. II, 1087.
sKyo Śākya ye-śes, II. 997.
sKyo bSod-nams bla-ma, II. 871, 982, 984.
sKyog sGom-pa-gtan, II, 875.
sKyogs Śes-rab 'byuṅ-gnas, I. 77.
sKyoṅ, I, 90.
sKyor-mo Dar-rgyan. I, 280.
sKyor-luṅ-pa, II, 1075.
bsKal-bzaṅ, II, 667.
bsKal-bzaṅs Čhos-kyi rgya-mtsho bsod-nams maṅ-thos dbaṅ-po'i sde, II. 1089.
Kha-čhe, I, 98.
Kha-čhe- dGon-pa-pa, I, 219. 232; II. 729.
Kha-čhe paṇ-čhen (Śākyaśri). I, 35, 82, 103, 277, 281, 306, 316, 346, 349, 365; II, 421, 446, 485, 518, 599, 600, 604, 608, 656, 770, 790, 797, 893, 975, 1056, 1063.
Kha-thog-pa Byams-pa-'bum, II. 486.
Kha-rag. II, 957, 1003-4. See Kha-rag-pa.
Kha-rag sKyi-ston, II, 953.
Kha-rag Grags-rgyal-ba, II, 687.
Kha-rag gra-pa 'Dul-ba-'od, II. 715, 949.
Kha-rag sGom-čhuṅ, I. 193, 266, 269; II, 557
Kha-rag sñiṅ-po, I, 156.
Kha-rag sTon-sñiṅ, I, 143, 147.
Kha-rag-pa. II, 687, 736, 1003-5.
Kha-ru-ba, I, 321.
Kha-ru Mes-ston, I, 81.
Kha-li- kha-čhu, I, xix.
Khaṅ-čhen-pa, II, 614-5.
Khaṅ-gsar-pa, I, 128. 230-1.

Khaṅ-gsar-pa Nam-mkha-'od, II, 768-9.
Kham-pa-luṅ-pa, I, 179.
Kham-pa-luṅ-pa čhen-po, I, 265, 318.
Kham-pa Śes-rab rdo-rǰe, I, 355.
Kham-bu Ya-le, II, 656, 986, 991.
Kham-luṅ-pa, I, 284.
Khams-sgam, II, 897.
Khams-sgom Tshul-khrims-rgyan, II, 896.
Khams-sgom Žig-po, II, 975.
Khams-čhen rGan-lhas-pa, II, 1007.
Khams-pa Go-čha, I, 104.
Khams-pa rGwa-ston, II, 857.
Khams-pa sTon-grags, II, 1057.
Khams-ston, II, 744.
Khams-pa, I, 110; II, 465, 748.
Khams-pa Go-čha, II, 571.
Khams-pa rGwa-ston, I, 354.
Khams-pa Byaṅ-gzags, II, 1066.
Khams-pa dbUs-se, II, 462.
Khams-pa Žu-lo, II, 763.
Khams-pa lo-tsā-ba sTon-'bum, II, 734.
Khams-pa Śes-rab rdo-rǰe, I, 356.
Khams-pa Śes-rab brtson-'grus, II, 948.
Khams-pa Sa-phug-pa Śākya rdo-rǰe, I, 373 ff.
Khams-pa A-seṅ, II, 475.
Khu, I, 74, 262, 327, 331; II, 624.
Khu-go-ba, II, 517.
Khu-sgom, II, 574, 989.
Khu-sgom J̌o-dga', II, 875-6.
Khu-sgom Čhos-seṅ (Čhos-kyi seṅ-ge), II, 985, 988 ff.
Khu-dṅos-grub, I, 72; II, 838.
Khu-čhen-po, I, 76.
Khu J̌o-sras Ne-tso, II 333.
Khu-lto-gza' Lan-čig-ma, I, 251.
Khu-ston, I, 96, 255, 262, 324; II, 627.
Khu-ston brTson-'grus-gyuṅ-druṅ, I, 88, 93, 343, II, 404
Khu-dro rTogs-ldan, II, 511.
Khu mDo-sde-'bar, I, 94, 272.
Khu Ne-tso, I, 396.
Khu sPyan-gyas-pa, I, 98, 319.
Khu-ba, II, 657.
Khu Byaṅ-čhub-'od, I, 167.

Khu-dbyug, II, 986.
Khu-mo Khye-'dren-'bum, II, 717.
Khu-mo sGron-me-lčam, II, 904.
Khu-le'i-kha-mo-zer-ston, I, 273.
Khu-luṅ-pa, II, 727.
Khu lo-tsā-ba mDo-sde-'bar, I, 343, 376; II, 872
Khu lo-tsā-ba Ne-tso, II, 706.
Khu Ser-brtson, I, 94, 330.
Khu-lhas-pa, I, 385.
Khe-gad, II, 403.
Khe'u-gaṅ 'Khor-lo-grags, II, 983.
Khoṅ-ston Rin-čhen, II, 850.
Khol-pa, II, 523.
Khol-po-dga', II, 520.
Khya-bza' 'Bum-me, I, 197
Khyi'u brTson-'grus, II, 857.
Khyi-ra ras-pa, II, 435.
Khyim-pa-mo (rDor-gsal), II, 920.
Khyu-mčhog, I, 45-6.
Khyu-mčhog bzaṅ-po, I, 45.
Khyuṅ, I, 127-8; II, 1009.
Khyuṅ Kham-po-čhe, I, 285.
Khyuṅ-po, I, 119-20, 222; II, 439 (gYe-čhuṅ pa, Khyuṅ-tshaṅ-pa), 749.
Khyuṅ Kham-po-che, I, 285.
Khyuṅ-po Grags-pa, I, 93.
Khyuṅ-po Grags-se, I, 70-1, 119-20, 127.
Khyuṅ-po Čhos-brtson, I, 71, 325, 328; II, 838.
Khyuṅ-po 'Čhal-čhen, I, 156.
Khyuṅ-po rTa-čhuṅ Grags-se, I, 121.
Khyuṅ-po Thu-re, I, 376.
Khyuṅ-po Dar-ma-'bar, I, 376.
Khyuṅ-po rNal-'byor, I, 271; II, 728, 752
Khyuṅ-po dbYig-'od, I, 167.
Khyuṅ-po Seṅ-ge, I, 156.
Khyuṅ-po bSod-nams-dpal, II, 676.
Khyuṅ-po Lhas-pa gŽon-nu bsod-nams, I, 366; II, 1075.
Khyuṅ-ma Śāk-dar, I, 198.
Khyuṅ-tshaṅ Thod-dmar-pa, I, 89,
Khyuṅ-tshaṅ-pa, II, 439, 441-4, 446-7, 449, 462, 660, 678. See Khyuṅ-po.
Khyuṅ-tshaṅ-pa Ye-śes bla-ma, II, 435.
Khyuṅ Rin-čhen-grags, I, 326, 332.
Khra-phu-ba 'Od-'byuṅ, I, 284.

Khra-tshar 'brug-bla, II, 871.
Khrag-skyugs-pa, II, 517.
Khri-bKra-śis brtsegs-pa-dpal, I, 37-8, 108, 205.
Khri-sgra-dpuṅs-btsan, I, 37.
Khri-čhuṅ, I, 38.
Khri-čhaṅ-'od, II, 995.
Khri-gñan-gzuṅs-btsan, I, 37.
Khri-thaṅ Jñāna, I, 68; II, 1085.
Khri-thog, I, 37.
Khri 'Du-sroṅ—Khri 'Dus-sroṅ, I, xix.
Khri-lde gtsug-brtan, I, xix, 40, 50-1.
Khri-lde gtsug-brtan Mes-ag-tshoms, I, 37.
Khri-lde gtsug-brtsan, I, xix.
Khri-lde sroṅ-btsan, I, xii, xix, 37, 52.
Khri-pa, II, 733.
Khri Maṅ-slon maṅ-rtsan, I, xix.
Khri-smon-ma 'Bum-skyid, II, 584.
Khri-gtsug-lde-brtsan, I, xix.
Khri-gtsug-lde-btsan Ral-pa-čan, I, 52.
Khri-btsan, I, 37.
Khri-btsan-po 'Od-lde, I, 36.
Khri-btsun, I, 220.
Khri-mdzes-lha-legs, I, 210.
Khri 'U-dum-btsan Dar-ma, I, 37.
Khri-sroṅ lde-btsan, I, v, xix, xx, 37, 40, 46, 51-2, 100, 104, 105, 108, 111, 210, 324, 395; II, 474, 648, 696, 789, 805, 1054.
Khri-sroṅ lde'u-btsan, I, 44.
Khri-mdzes-lha-legs, I, 210.
Khri sroṅ-btsan, I, xi, xix.
Khro-phu-ba, I, 203; II, 744, 791, 975, 1039.
Khro-phu lo-tsā-ba (Tshul-khrims śes-rab, Byams-pa-dpal), I, 195, 306, 387, 396, II, 446, 599, 677, 708, 710-11, 727, 797, 1033, 1051, 1057, 1063-4, 1066-7, 1070.
Khro-phu Rin-po-čhe bSod-nams seṅ-ge, I, 345.
Khro-phu sems-dpa' čhen-po, II, 710-11.
Khro-bo-'ban, II, 581.
Khrom-bžer (Rin-čhen seṅ-ge), I, 292, 305-6, 308, 311.
Khrom-bžer dbOn-po Roṅ-gžon, I, 307-8.
mKhan-pa Thaṅ-pa, II, 1023.
mKhan-čhen-pa, II, 514.
mKhan-po, II, 466.
mKhan-po-ba, II, 467, 623.
mKhan-po Bodhisattva, II, 571.

mKhan-dbon-pa Rin-čhen bkra-śis, II, 630.
mKham-pa-luṅ-pa — mKham-luṅ-pa, I, 302-4
mKha'-'gro, II, 975.
mKha'-'gro dPal-gyi ye-śes, I, 171.
mKha'-spyod-pa (dPal-), I, 151; II, 545, 591, 647.
mKha'-spyod dbaṅ-po (Kar-ma Žwa-dmar-pa), II, 540.
mKha'-spyod dbaṅ-po Ye-dpal, II, 705.
mKhar-rgyal-ba, II, 744.
mKhar-sgo-ba, II, 712.
mKhar-čhu-ba, II, 703.
mKhar-čhen dPal-gyi dbaṅ-phyug, I, 166.
mKhar-thog-pa, II, 584.
mKhar-ba, II, 664.
mKhar-rtse-ba, II, 641.
mKhar-tsha-rgyal, I, 221.
mKhar-luṅ-pa, II, 665.
mKhas-grub Khra-pa, II, 696.
mKhas-grub dGe-legs-dpal, II, 1079.
mKhas-grub rGyal-ba, II, 1039.
mKhas-grub čhen-po, II, 629-30.
mKhas-grub Čhos-rje, II, 750.
mKhas-grub Čhos-dpal-pa, I, 155; II, 779, 1044.
mKhas-grub Dar-rgyal-ba, II, 518, 536, 540.
mKhas-grub Dar-ma rgyal-mtshan, II, 532.
mKhas-grub Darmarāja, II, 518.
mKhas-grub rDo-rje rgyal-mtshan, I, 310.
mKhas-grub-pa, II, 498.
mKhas-grub Byaṅ-čhub rgyal-mtshan, II, 535.
mKhas-grub Rin-čhen rgyal-mtshan, II, 608.
mKhas-grub Śaṅs-ston, II, 747, 749.
mKhas-grub Ahūṃvajra, II, 450.
mKhas-pa Jo-nam, I, 133.
mKhas-pa dBaṅ-rdor, II, 517.
mKhas-btsun Dad-pa-mgon, I, 82.
mKhas-btsun Dad-pa, I, 98-9.
mKhas-btsun Don-grub rgyal-mtshan, II, 965.
mKhas-btsun Don-grub gžon-nu, II, 693.
mKhas-btsun-pa, I, 215; II, 518.
mKhas-btsun Byaṅ čhub, II, 727.
mKhas-btsun gŽon-nu-grub, II, 749, 751, 991, 999.
mKhas-btsun gŽon-nu-'od, I, 310.
mKhas-btsun Yon-tan rgya-mtsho, II, 775-6.

mKhas-btsun Śes-rab-'od, I, 311.
mKhas-btsun bSod-nams 'od-zer, II, 696.
mKhon dKon-mčhog rgyal-po, II, 1086. See 'Khon dKon-mčhog rgyal-po.
mKhyen-rab dbaṅ-phyug, I, 385.
'Khar-čhuṅ, I, 132.
'Khun, II, 900.
'Khun-'dzi Yaṅ-dben-pa dBaṅ-phyug rdo-rje, II, 899.
'Khun Yaṅ-dben-pa, II, 900.
'Khon, II, 418.
'Khon kLu'i dbaṅ-po-bsruṅ-ba, I, 210.
'Khon dKon-mčhog rgyal-po, I, 72-3, 123, 208, 215, 226, 325; II, 405.
'Khon-Gad-pa Kirti, I, 364; II, 416, 418, 426, 1009.
'Khon sGye-čhu-pa, I, 228.
'Khon Jo-sras rtse-mo, I, 333.
'Khon dPal-po-čhe, I, 210.
'Khon-phu-ba, I, 221-2, 225-6, 229, 230-2, 237; II, 859.
'Khor-re, I, 37.
'Khor-re-ba, II, 665.
'Khyam-ma, I, 123.
'Khrul-žig Khams-pa, II, 718.
'Khrul-žig dGe-bśes byar-po, II, 988.
'Khrul-žig Dar-ma, I, 197.
'Khrul-žig Dharma seṅ-ge, I, 197.
'Khrul-žig Nam-mkha' rnal-'byor, II, 672.
'Khrul-žig sNa'u-pa (sNa'u Bya-bral-pa), II, 720, 962.
'Khrul-žig-pa, II, 723, 955, 964, 966, 1039.
'Khrul-žig Rin-po-čhe, II, 958-60.
'Khrul-žig Seṅ-ge rgyan-pa, I, 195-6.
'Khrul-žig bSod-nams-'bum, II, 544, 546.
'Khro-ston Ku-śu-ra-ba, I, 269.
Gas-ston bLa-sgaṅ-pa Śes-rab rdo-rje, II, 610.
Ga-ston bla-ma, II, 627.
Ga-thuṅ, II, 478.
Ga-roṅ lo-tsā-ba, I, 220.
Ga-sraṅ nag-po, I, 75-6.
Gaṅ-ga bzaṅ-mo, II, 869.
Gaṅ-par-gśen, II, 874.
Gaṅ-spel, I, 344.
Gaṅs-khrod-ras-pa (sKal-ldan rdo-rje), II, 988.
Gaṅs-sñan, I, 235.
Gaṅs-pa, II, 517-8, 703.

Gaṅs-pa Ñi-khri, I, 135.
Gaṅs-pa dBaṅ-phyug rgyal-mtshan, II, 519.
Gaṅs-pa dMu-yan, II, 986, 988.
Gaṅs-pa Rin-čhen 'od-zer, II, 519.
Gaṅs-pa Śe'u, I, 227, 230, 326; II, 444.
Gans-pa Śe'u bLo-gros byaṅ-čhub, I, 332.
Gaṅs-pa Lhun-grub, II, 987.
Gan-čhag-pa, II, 705.
Gan-pa Da-re, I, 307.
Gar dPal-gyi sñiṅ-po, I, 170.
Gar-mi Yon-tan gyuṅ-druṅ, I, 345.
Gal-te-dgos, II, 931, 934.
Gu-ne-ru, I, 367.
Gu'i-guṅ-pa, II, 503-4, 506, 509.
Gu'i-guṅ-pa Rin-čhen-dpal, II, 518.
Gu-ri-ba, I, 277.
Gu-ru-legs, I, 37.
Gu-rub Čhag-ston (Rin-čhen tshul-khrims), II, 1054.
Gu-śri čhen-mo, I, 217.
Gu-śri-ba, I, 218; II, 517, 520.
Guṅ mGon-po-skyabs, II, 417.
Guṅ-pa Ye-śes, I, 352.
Guṅ-pa Lha-rje, I, 331.
Guṅ-thaṅ ras-pa, II, 449.
Guṅ-ru (Čhos-rje-), II, 1082.
Guṅ-sroṅ guṅ-btsan, I, 37, 46, 49.
Gur-ston, I, 267; II, 975.
Gur-śiṅ brTson-'grus rgyal-mtshan, I, 352.
Gul-pi-pa, I, 305.
Ge-rgod, II, 890.
Go-čha-ma, II, 843.
Go-ra-ba, I, 190.
Go-rub Yaṅ-dag, II, 939.
Go-rub lo-tsā-ba dge-sloṅ Čhos-kyi śes-rab, I, 162-3, 167.
Go-rub lo-tsā-ba Tshul-khrims rgyal-ba, I, 383.
Go-luṅ-pa, II, 699.
Go-luṅ-pa Grub-thob btsun-pa, II, 859-60.
Goṅ-bu ra-čan, I, 326.
Goṅ-ma Grags-pa 'byuṅ-gnas, II, 1089.
Goṅ-mo-sgaṅ-pa, I, 284.
Goṅ-gsum bDe-čhen-pa Čhos-kyi dpal-pa, II, 1075.
Gya-pa Gaṅs-pa, II, 519.

Gyaṅ-mo-čhe, I, 81.
Gyaṅ-ro Dar-mgon, II, 655.
Gyam-bzaṅs čhos-rje, I, 82.
Gyam-śiṅ, II, 727.
Gyi-jo, I, 207; II, 755, 762, 766, 837.
Gyi-jo, Zla-ba'i 'od-zer, I, 72.
Gyi-ljaṅ, I, 208. (dbU-dkar-ba).
Gyi-ljaṅs-gza' lČam-bu, I, 286.
Gye-ru Še'u-čhuṅ-pa, II, 855.
Gye-re mČhog-skyoṅ, I, 100.
Gyor-po Ke-tu, I, 292.
Gra, II, 955.
Gra-jaṅ-pa Nam-mkha'-'od, II, 715 (Saṅs-rgyas ras-čhen, Lha-ri-ba).
Gra-thaṅ-pa, II, 931.
Gra-'dul, I, 319.
Gra-pa, I, 82, 96-8, 100-1; II, 759, 896, 905-7.
Gra-pa mṄon-śes, I, 72, 75, 77, 93-4-5, 347; II, 405, 755, 765, 852, 983.
Gra-pa sTon-gžon, II, 975.
Gra-pa Hag-ston, II, 985.
Gra-phyi-ba, I, 77.
Gra-mi, I, 82.
Grags, I, 376.
Grags-rgyal-ba, II, 1056, 1072.
Grags-čhen-pa, II, 424.
Grags-don-pa, II, 969.
Grags-rdor-ba, II, 587-9.
Grags-ldan, I, 344.
Grags-pa, II, 639, 1031. (Goṅ-ma Grags-pa 'byuṅ-gnas).
Grags-pa rgyal-mtshan, I, 320, 344; II, 413, 545; 1024, 1073; 1083.
Grags-pa rgyal-mtshan (Goṅ-ma-), II, 644, 721.
Grags-pa rgyal-mtshan (Čhos-rgyal-), II, 1089.
Grags-pa rgyal-mtshan (bla-ma-), II, 741.
Grags-pa rgyal-mtshan (dBaṅ-), II, 509, 641-2, 644-5, 1081.
Grasgs-pa rgyal-mtshan (Ža-lu Rin-po-čhe-), II, 590.
Grags-pa rgyal-mtshan (Yar-kluṅs lo-tsā-ba), I, 281, 379; II, 411, 639, 658, 780, 788, 791-2, 837, 974, 1047-8, 1050.
Grags-pa rgyal-mtshan (Sa-skya-pa, rJe-btsun-), I, 194, 211, 217, 306, 365; II, 633, 866.
Grags-pa rgyal-mtshan-dpal-bzaṅ-po, II, 1090.
Grags-pa mtha'-yas, II, 824, 831.
Grags-pa-lde, I, 37.
Grags-pa-dpal, I, 330; II, 651.

Grags-pa-dpal-grub, II, 517.
Grags-pa 'bum-me, I, 195.
Grags-pa 'byuṅ-gnas (sPyan-sṅa), II, 572.
Grags-pa 'byuṅ-gnas (-pa), (mi-'i) bdag-po, Čhos-rgyal-), II, 412, 594, 704, 799, 800-1, 808-9.
Grags-pa sMon-lam blo-gros, I, 81.
Grags-pa tshul-khrims, I, 396.
Grags-pa gžon-nu, II, 1024, 1075.
Grags-pa bzaṅ-po, I, 320; II, 629, 1024.
Grags-pa 'od-zer (Ti-śri-), II, 711.
Grags-pa ye-śes-pa, II, 581.
Grags-pa yon-tan (Lho Rin-po-čhe-), II, 592, 595.
Grags-pa rin-čhen, I, 38, 281.
Grags-pa śes-rab, I, vi, 283, 388.
Grags-pa seṅ-ge (Bya-), I, 272, (Zem Rin-po-čhe-), I, 301, (Čhos-rje-), II, 538, 860-1.
Grags-pa seṅ-ge (rTogs-ldan-), II, 523, 537, 540.
Grags-pa seṅ-ge (Žwa-dmar čod paṇ-'dzin-pa-), II, 1042.
Grags-byaṅ-pa, II, 727.
Grags-dbaṅ, I, 217.
Grags-'bum, I, 319.
Grags-btsan-lde, I, 37.
Grags-bzaṅ-pa, II, 800.
Grags-'od, II, 583.
Grags-ye, II, 582.
Grags-rin-pa 'Jam-sṅon-pa, I, 346.
Grags-se-ba, I, 198.
Grags-seṅ (Čhos-rje-), II, 539; (rTogs-ldan-), II, 496, 533.
Grags-bsod, II, 579, 1072.
Graṅ-po-luṅ-pa, II, 1024.
Graṅs-'dzin-ma, I, 18.
Gran-bu-ba, I, 376.
Grab-mkhar-ba, II, 712.
Gri-gum btsan-po, I, 36.
Gri'i lum-pa, II, 993.
Gru-gu kLog-'byuṅ, II, 1000.
Gru-gu-luṅ-pa, I, 269.
Gru-gu sTon-pa bLo-gros seṅ-ge, II, 563.
Gru-go-čha, II, 942.
Gru mČhog-gi ye-śes, I, 345.
Gru rNam-grags, II, 942.
Gru-mer, I, 75-6, 88, 94; II, 404.

Gru-mer Tshul-khrims 'byuṅ-gnas, I, 77.
Gru-mer Ye-śes 'byuṅ-gnas, I, 74.
Gru Legs-pa'i sgrom-ma, I, 108.
Gru Śākya-'bum, I, 397.
Gru-śul, I, 334; II, 864.
Grub rGyal-ba'i ye-śes, I, 345.
Grub-čhuṅ-pa, II, 983.
Grub-čhe, II, 985.
Grub-čhen-pa, II, 696.
Grub-thabs-dpon, II, 420.
Grub-thob dKon-mčhog-grags, I, 396.
Grub-pa dPal-bzaṅ-po, II, 446.
Grub-pa'i rdo-rje, I, 362; II, 553.
Grub-be, II, 985.
Grub-pa śes-rab, I, 283.
Grub-śe-ba, I, 283.
Grum Ye-śes rgyal-mtshan, I, xviii, 55, 67.
Grum-śiṅ gLa-čan, I, 167.
Grum-śiṅ gLag-čan, I, 167.
Grum-śiṅ Śes-rab smon-lam, II, 1000.
Gre'i Mi'u-čhuṅ II, 403.
Gro-ston bDud-rtsi-grags, I, 282; II, 1057.
Gro-phu lo-tsā-ba (Gro-lo), II, 745.
Gro-luṅ-pa, I, 314, 326; II, 931.
Gro-luṅ-pa čhen-po, II, 1054.
Gro-luṅ-pa mDo-sde rgyal-mtshan, II, 784.
Gro-luṅ-pa bLo-gros 'byuṅ-gnas, I, 326.
Gro-śol-ba, II, 566.
Grog-pa brTson-seṅ, I, 269.
Grol-grub-pa, I, 376.
Grol-sgom, II, 461.
Grol-sgom Čhos-gyuṅ, II, 468 ff.
Grol-ston Lha-'bum, II, 705.
gLaṅ, I, 270.
gLaṅ-čben-'dul, I, 16.
gLaṅ-ston, II, 855.
gLaṅ-ston Śer-seṅ, I, 90.
gLaṅ-ston Seṅ-ge-'bum, I, 91.
gLaṅ-thaṅ-pa, I, 73, 236, 270-1, 291.
gLaṅ-thaṅ Žaṅ, I, 271.
gLaṅ-thaṅ Rin-po-čhe, II, 1082.
gLaṅ Dar-ma, I, ix, xiv, xvi, 60, 88.

gLaṅ-po-čhe-'dul, I, 8.
gLaṅ-pos-byin, I, 4, 14.
gLaṅ dPal-gyi seṅ-ge, I, 104.
gLaṅ-phug-pa, II, 744.
gLaṅ Bya-rab-pa, I, 269.
gLaṅ gTsug-gi rin-čhen, I, 104.
gLaṅ Tshul-byaṅ, I, 88.
gLaṅ-ri-thaṅ-pa, I, 235, 269, 289, 318; II, 732.
gLaṅ-ri-thaṅ-pa rDo-rje seṅ-ge, I, 270-1, 273.
gLaṅ-ri-ba, II, 727.
gLaṅ-luṅ-pa, I, 297, 300, 302; II, 587.
gLan, I, 90, 277; II, 761.
gLan-sgom Tshul-khrims sñiṅ-po, II, 1000.
gLan čhu-mig-luṅ-ṅu-ba, I, 314.
gLan Čhos-kyi dbaṅ-phyug, II, 760.
gLan Čhos dbaṅ, II, 763.
gLan Čhos-'byuṅ, I, 355.
gLan Jo-btsun seṅ-ge, I, 157.
gLan Ña-tshal-pa bSod-nams mgon-po, I, 142, 151.
gLan sñiṅ-po, II, 953.
gLan-ston Śāk-bzaṅs, I, 119.
gLan rDo-rje 'od-po, I, 155.
gLan rTsan-tsha Ñi-ma-lčam, I, 365.
gLan Baṅ-so-ba (Čhos-kyi dbaṅ-phyug), II, 755-6.
gLan-mo-čhe-pa, II, 420.
gLan Tshul-khrims byaṅ-čhub, I, 78, (gLan Tshul-byaṅ), I, 263, 306.
gLan Ye-śes byaṅ-čhub, I, 74-5.
gLan Ye-śes-'bar, I, 74.
gLan Ye-śes śes-rab, I, 77.
gLan Śākya byaṅ-čhub, I, 120, 124.
gLan Śākya-bzaṅ-po, I, 120, 157.
gLiṅ, II, 522, 659, 660, 665, 667.
gLiṅ-kha-pa, II, 442.
gLiṅ-pa, II, 630.
gLiṅ-ras, II, 426, 451, 568, 660-2, 680.
gLiṅ-ras-pa, II, 564.
glen-mi-kho-ba, I, 234.
gLo-bo lo-tsā-ba Śes-rab zin-čhen, I, 379; II, 1046.
gLoṅ-žabs, II, 1048.
dGa'-ldan-pa, II, 727.
dGa'-ba skyoṅ-ba, II, 842.
dGa'-ba'i rdo-rje, I, 362.

dGa'-bo, I, 12.
dGe-skyabs, I, 210.
dGe-skyoṅ, I, 262.
dGe-goṅ-pa, II, 919.
dGe-mčhog, I, 3.
dGe-bsñen-pa. I, 339; II, 693.
dGe-bsñen byaṅ-čhub, II, 758.
dGe-mthoṅ, I, 210.
dGe-dom, I, 74.
dGe-'dun-skyabs. I, 273; II. 563, 1052.
dGe-'dun-skyid, II, 913.
dGe-'dun-grub, I, 33. 339.
dGe-'dun sgaṅ-pa, II, 504, 518.
dGe-'dun čhos-'phel, I, xxi, 30, 372; II, 417, 682, 801. 1045, 1053.
dGe-'dun-brtan, II, 784.
dGe-'dun rin-čhen-pa, II,490.
dGe-sdiṅ-pa. II, 444-6.
dGe-'phel, I. 12.
dGe-ba, I, 3. 12.
dGe-ba rgyal-mtshan (dGe-rgyal), II. 565, 1081-2.
dGe-ba sPaṅ-kha-ba, II, 451.
dGe-ba-'bar, II, 847.
dGe-ba-'bum (Lha-rje-), II, 1006.
dGe-ba rab-gsal, I, xvii.
dGe-ba-gsal, I, xvii, 64.
dGe-ba'i dpal, I, 241.
dGe-ba'i blo, II, 803.
dGe-ba'i blo-gros, I, 70, 262.
dGe-ba'i 'byuṅ-gnas sbas-pa, II. 1048.
dGe-ba'i lha, II, 868.
dGe-brag-pa, I, 341.
dGe-blo, I, 85.
dGe-sbyoṅ čhen-po, I, 269.
dGe-legs-dpal, I, 83.
dGe-legs-dpal-mgon, I, ii, 1090.
dGoṅs-pa rab-gsal. I. xvii, 34. 67.
dGon, I, 292.
dGon-dkar-ba, II, 911.
dGon-pa, I. 215.
dGon-pa Don-grub bla-ma. II, 522.
dGon-pa-pa, I. 233. 258, 284, 311-2, 320-1, 324, 758, 1002, (dGon-pa-pa 'Dzeṅ dBaṅ-phyug rgyal-mtshan), I, 262, 266.

dGon-mer-pa, I, 269.
dGon-gsar-pa (rje-), II, 670, 695.
dGos-pa-btsan, I, 190.
dGye 'Phags-pa śes-rab, I, 170.
dGyen-pa rdo-rje, I, 98.
dGyer-sgom, I, 292-305, 314-5, 317, 565.
dGyer-sgom Tshul-khrims señ-ge (Tshul-señ, Čhos-kyi señ-ge, rDo-rje rgyal-po), II, 890-4.
dGyer-sgom Ri-ba Rin-čhen tshul-khrims, II. 450.
dGyer-sgom Se-po, I, 208.
dGyer-čhen dGon-rgyab-pa, I, 93.
dGyer dPal rGya-mkhar-ba, II, 893.
dGyer dbOn-ri-pa, II, 895.
dGyer-mo-čhe-pa, I, 93.
dGyer-žig, II, 893.
dGra-goñ-ba Dar-ma señ-ge, I, 341.
dGra-bčom-pa, I, 22, 100.
dGra-'dul, I, 4.
dGrol-sgom, I, 180.
mGo-skya-ba, I, 190.
mGo-khom Jo-sras, II, 1042, 1043.
mGo-rgyal, II, 629.
mGo-bya-tsha, II, 688.
mGo blon-pa, II, 507, 514.
mGo-yags, II, 621, 629.
mGon, II, 449.
mGon Gad-pa Kirti, II, 416.
mGon-rgyal-ba (rTogs-ldan-), II. 495, 497, 532, 806.
mGon-po, II, 861-2, 895.
mGon-po bkra-śis, II, 1073.
mGon-po rgyal, II, 581.
mGon-po-drug, II, 1043.
mGon-po ye-śes, I, 310; II, 535-6.
mGon-po rin-čhen, I, 373.
mGon-po sañs-rgyas, I, 93.
mGon-gžon-pa, II, 584.
mGon-yes, II, 676.
'Gar, I, 300, 327, 364; II. 603, 607.
'Gar bKra-śis rin-čhen, II, 408.
'Gar Grags-pa dbañ-phyug, II, 421.
'Gar dGa'-ba, I, 262.
'Gar dGe-ba, I, 262, 380.

'Gar-sgom dkar-po, II, 462.
'Gar-čhuṅ-pa gŽon-nu byaṅ-čhub, II. 895.
'Gar Čhos-kyi śes-rab. I, 364.
'Gar Čhos-sdiṅs-pa, II, 577.
'Gar sTon-btsan, I. 49.
'Gar sTon-btsan nam-mkha', I, 376.
'Gar-ston Tshul-khrims bzaṅ-po, I, 164.
'Gar dam-pa, II, 603.
'Gar dam-pa Čhos-sdiṅs-pa. II, 602.
'Gar-pa, I, 271.
'Gar dBaṅ-grub, I, 333.
'Gar btsun-ma, II, 421.
'Gar Žaṅ-žuṅ-pa, I, 271.
'Gar-srags, I, 75.
'Gar bSod-yes (bSod-nams ye-śes), I, 127.
'Gar A-tsa, I, 376.
'Gu-sgom, II, 911.
'Ger-nag rTogs-ldan Čhos-dpal ye-śes, II, 544-5.
'Go-čhen-po (Ñi-ma), II, 760.
'Go-bya-tsha, I, 118.
'Goṅ-lug, II, 615.
'Goṅs-ston, II, 454.
'Gos, I, 72, 360.
'Gos (Khug-pa Lhas-btsas), I, 72, 327, 360, 363-4, 366, 374; II. 760, 763, 899.
'Gos (of gNas-khaṅ), I, 269.
'Gos (gŽon-nu-dpal), II, 837.
'Gos Khug-pa Lhas-btsas. I, 102, 117, 123, 226, 360.
'Gos-rgan, I, 41-2.
'Gos-ston Byaṅ-'bar, I, 156.
'Gos sTon-btsan, I, 262.
'Gos Dar-ma, II, 899, 900.
'Gos lo-tsā-ba (rTa-nag Khug-pa Lhas-btsas), I. xx, 121, 167, 208-9; II, 425, 556, 865.
'Gos lo-tsā-ba (gŽon-nu-dpal), I, 356; II, 835.
'Gos lo-tsā-ba gŽon-nu-dpal, I, i, ii, iv. 25; II, 810, 812, 837, 1093.
'Gos lo-tsā-ba gŽon-nu-žabs, II. 814, 826.
'Gos Lha-khaṅ-ltag-pa, II, 622.
'Gos Lhas-btsas, I, 165. 354. 360, 366. See 'Gos Khug-pa Lhas-btsas.
'Gyod-pa gsaṅ-ba, II, 849.
'Gro-mgon Dam-pa Śāk-rgyal. I, 171.
'Gro-mgon Žaṅ. II, 522. See bLa-ma Žaṅ.
'Gro-mgon Rin-čhen-mdzes. II, 719.

'Gro-mgon Rin-po-čhe, I, 197.
'Gro Ñi-ma, II, 766.
'Gro-ba dbUgs-'byin-pa, I, 362; II, 552.
'Gro-ba'i mgon-po (Lha-), I, 278-9, 280.
'Gro-ba'i mgon-po 'Phags-pa, II, 422. See 'Phags-pa.
'Grol-pa, II, 468.
rGwa-lo<rGwa lo-tsā-ba (rNam-rgyal rdo-rje), I, 379; II, 469, 475, 555-6, 614, 713-4, 756, 760, 773, 785, 789, 790, 791, 792, 796.
rGaṅ-mtshams, I, 15.
rGan-'bum-pa (rje rGan), II, 901-2.
rGal-gyam-pa, II, 727.
rGod-phrug Grags-pa, II, 704; rGod-phrug Grags-pa 'byuṅ-gnas, II, 451, 1007, 1052.
rGod-phrug čhos-rje, II, 693.
rGod-phrug ras-pa, II, 705, 752, 795, 991.
rGod-tshaṅ-pa (mGon-po rdo-rje, mGon-po-dpal), II, 519, 527, 547 670-2, 679, 680-8, 690, 692, 696, 698-9, 700-2, 725, 841, 972.
rGya (kalyāna-mitra), I, 127, 235. (of Ri-mo-čan) 292; II, 442; 893; 1065.
rGya-gar, II, 1030.
rGya-gar grags-pa, II, 791.
rGya-gar Jo-sras, II, 900.
rGya-gar Phyag-na, I, 72; II, 521, 866.
rGya-gar Bai-ro, II, 474.
rGya Grags-bsod, II, 736.
rGya yags-pa, II, 670-1.
rGya rGyal-tshul, I, 165.
rGya-sgom, II, 445, 480.
rGya-sgom-pa, II, 914, 919.
rGya-sgom rMi-ras, II, 561.
rGya-sgom Ye-śes-'od, II, 517.
rGya-lčags-ri Goṅ-kha-pa, I, 374.
rGya-čhu-mig-pa bla-ma Lho-pa, II, 1009.
rGya čhen-po, II, 554.
rGya-'čhiṅ-ru-ba, I, 154, 329, 331, 335, 341.
rGya-ston, I, 125, (of gTsaṅ), 273, 296, (kalyāṇa-mitra) 706.
rGya-ston sKye-rtsegs, II, 911.
rGya-ston Žig-po, II, 403.
rGya-ston gŽon-nu seṅ-ge, II, 900.
rGya-ston bSod-rin, I, 341.
rGya Dar-seṅ, I, 376; II, 875.
rGya-dur Dar-yes, I, 82.
rGya-drag čhos-rje, II, 751.

rGya-'dul, I, 379.
rGya 'dul-'dzin, I, 270.
rGya 'dul-'dzin dBaṅ-phyug tshul-khrims-'bar, I, 78.
rGya-brda 'dul-'dzin, I, 81.
rGya-nag, I, 126. Lha-rǰe rGya-nag.
rGya-nam, I, 407-8.
rGya Nam-mkha', I, 364, 388.
rGya-nag gčer-ba, II, 990.
rGya-nom-snaṅ, I, 15.
rGya-pa Se-re, II, 463.
rGya-spaṅ-thaṅ-pa, I, 276.
rGya-spaṅs-pa, I, 307.
rGya-phug J̌o-sras, II, 726.
rGya Pho-ba-luṅ-pa, II, 417-8, 426, 449, 451, 517, 524.
rGya-bo-pa, I, 113. See Zur-čhuṅ Śes-rab grags-pa.
rGya-brag čhos-rǰe (Ye-śes gžon-nu), II, 525, 537, 884.
rGya bLo-gros byaṅ-čhub, I, 159.
rGya-dbaṅ Tshur-tsha sPraṅ-dar, II, 485.
rGya-ma bKra-śis rgyal-mtshan, I, 329.
rGya-ma-pa, I, 317; II, 444, 1024, 1086.
rGya-ma-pa bKra-śis-rgyal, I, 308.
rGya-ma-pa dbOn-ston, II, 912. rGya-ma dbOn-ston, I, 35, 305; II, 939.
rGya-ma Rin-čhen sgaṅ-pa, II, 945.
rGya-ma-pa Saṅ-yon, I, 307.
rGya-mo Khye-'dren-dpal, II, 749.
rGya-mon Čhos-grags, I, 355.
rGya-dmar, II, 1009.
rGya-dmar-pa, I, 230; II, 440-1: (sTod-luṅs-), II, 475.
rGya-dmar-pa Byaṅ-čhub-grags, I, 332.
rGya rTsad-skor-ba, I, 127.
rGya-rtse-sbre-ba, I, 285.
rGya brTson-seṅ, I, 127, 245-6, 262. (brTson-grus seṅ-ge).
rGya-tsha-'bar, II, 876.
rGya Tshul-le, I, 345.
rGya-mtsho-grags, II, 406.
rGya-mtsho bla-ma, II, 519.
rGya-mtsho-lha, I, 5, 15.
rGya-zur-po Tsha-ba, II, 664.
rGya Ye-tshul, I, 352.
rGya 'A-ma-čan, II, 406, 688.
rGya Ye-śes mgon-po, I, 155-6.
rGya-ra Ban-smyon, I, 234.

rGya-ras, I, 181; II, 680, 682, 706.
rGya Rin-po-čhe, I, 221.
rGya-ri-ba, I, 292.
rGya-loṅ Čhos-grags, I, 376.
rGya-loṅ Čhos-'bar, II, 875.
rGya Śes-rab-'bar, I, 291.
rGya Saṅs-rgyas dbaṅ-phyug, II, 509.
rGya Seṅ-dkar, II, 941.
rGyaṅ-dkar-ba, I, 314.
rGyaṅ-ro Dar-ma-mgon, I, 345.
rGyaṅ-ro Byaṅ-čhub-'bum, I, 338.
rGyaṅ-ro gŽon-rin, II, 446, 727.
rGyan-thaṅ-pa, II, 563, 565.
rGyams, II, 900.
rGyams Śes-rab bla-ma, II, 899.
rGyal Gro-phu-ba Tshul-khrims-grags, I, 81.
rGyal-čhuṅ, I, 220.
rGyal To-ri loṅ-btsan, I, 37.
rGyal-lde, I, 5.
rGyal-po, I, 110; II, 727.
rGyal-po skyab-po, II, 659.
rGyal-po-dga', II, 409.
rGyal-po dGe-mdzes-'od, II, 657.
rGyal-po Tshe-'phel, II, 749.
rGyal-po bZaṅ-ldan, I, 12.
rGyal-ba, I, 12; II, 489, 568, 581-2, 632.
rGyal-ba bKra-śis, II, 1089.
rGyal-ba Khyu-mčhog, I, 16.
rGyal-ba Gaṅs-pa, II, 487.
rGyal-ba Grub-be, II, 985.
rGyal-ba-čan, I, 227.
rGyal-ba-mčhog, I, 340.
rGyal-ba mČhog-dbyaṅs, II, 474.
rGyal-ba brTen-ne, II, 601, 929.
rGyal-ba Thog-dugs-pa, II, 1087.
rGyal-ba-pa, I, 13, 14; II, 831.
rGyal-ba sPo-ston, I, 180.
rGyal-ba Phyag-na, II, 1073.
rGyal-ba Yaṅ-dgon-pa, I, 200. See Yaṅ-dgon-pa.
rGyal-ba Ye-grags, I, 90.
rGyal-ba gYuṅ-druṅ dbaṅ-phyug, I, 78.
rGyal-ba Rin-po-čhe (Grags-pa brtson-'grus), II, 579, 580-1.

rGyal-ba bzaṅ-po, I, 217.
rGyal-ba Lha-naṅ-pa (gÑos), II, 601-2.
rGyal-ba'i sde, I, 14, 232.
rGyal-ba'i śes-rab, I, 31, 34, 85.
rGyal-ba'i sras-po bDe-'byuṅ-ba, II, 591.
rGyal-bas byin, I, 392; II, 415.
rGyal-bu, II, 583.
rGyal-dbaṅ grags-pa, II, 1073.
rGyal-dbaṅ blo-gros, II, 592.
rGyal-mo 'od-zer, I, 399.
rGyal-mo gYu-sgra sñiṅ-po, I, 170.
rGyal-tsha, I, 94, 99, 100, 278, 396; II, 564, 705, 708-11, 846, 900, 1023, 1064.
rGyal-tsha mDo-dbaṅ, II, 948.
rGyal-tsha Byaṅ-ye, I, 80.
rGyal-tsha Žaṅ-ye, I, 80.
rGyal-tsha gŽon-nu-grags, I, 98.
rGyal-tsha bSod-nams-'phags, II, 697.
rGyal-tsha Ra-mo, II, 413.
rGyal-tsha Rin-čhen mgon-po, II, 408.
rGyal-tshab Rin-po-čhe, II, 1078.
rGyal-mtshan-grags, II, 727.
rGyal-mtshan-pa, II, 727.
rGyal-mtshan-dpal, II, 509, 690, 896, 1017.
rGyal-mtshan-'bum, II, 695, 748.
rGyal-mtshan bzaṅ-po, I, 321, 346; II, 592, 705, 781.
rGyal-mtshan-'od, II, 860.
rGyal-bzaṅ (dPon-čhen-), II, 905.
rGyal-bzaṅ-ba, II, 782.
rGyal-bzaṅs-pa, I, 126, 151; II, 536, 588-9.
rGyal-lug-lhas, I, 76.
rGyal-luṅ-phu-ba čhen-po, II, 426.
rGyal-le-lčam, II, 930.
rGyal-śes, I, 86.
rGyal-se, II, 1003.
rGyal-sras Grags-pa rin-čhen, II, 1083.
rGyal-sras Grags-rin-po, II, 585.
rGyal-sras Thogs-med-pa, I, 310; II, 585, 1024.
rGyal-sras Dri-med-pa (kLoṅ-čhen rab-'byams-pa), II, 723.
rGyal-sras Rin-po-čhe, I, 355; II, 584.
rGyal-srid-dga', I, 9.
rGyal-gsum, I, 126.
rGyas-byed, I, 13.

rGyu-gdags-pa, I, 17.
rGyu-bug-pa (of Śaṅs), I, 272.
rGyud-'dzin rdo-rǰe, II, 988.
rGyus-nag bde-gśegs, II, 697.
rGyus sMon-lam-grags, I, 73.
sGa-sgom Ag-tshoms, I, 264.
sGa-dam-pa bDe-gśegs-śes-pa, I, 158.
sGaṅ-ston 'Od-'bar, II, 862.
sGaṅ Śākya yon-tan, I, 283. (Kham-pa-luṅ-pa).
sGaṅ Śes-rab bla-ma, II, 706.
sGaṅ Ri-bo-čhe-pa, II, 706.
sGaṅ lo-tsā-ba, II, 793.
sGaṅ Indra, I, 376.
sGaṅs-ston Śer-'bum, I, 355.
sGaṅs-pa (Lha-'bri-), II, 573.
sGam-po-pa (bLo-gros-grags Lha-rǰe sGam-po-pa, Dags-po), I, 384; II, 420, 435, 451, 481, 521-2, 558-9, 560, 572, 650, 672, 711, 718, 721, 725, 737, 905, 930, 1086.
sGi-li Čhos-'od, II, 564.
sGur-mo, II, 917.
sGeg-pa rdo-rǰe, I, 204, 367; II, 869.
sGo-gčig-pa, II, 1089.
sGo-maṅs-pa, II, 579. (sPyan-sṅa-).
sGo-mo Rin-po-čhe Ye-śes-dpal, II, 970.
sGo-mo Rin-po-čhe bZaṅ-dpal-pa, II, 643.
sGog-luṅ-pa, II, 900.
sGom, II, 716, 900. Ban-rgan sGom, II, 947.
sGom-grags, II, 935.
sGom-čhuṅ (Śes-rab byaṅ-čhub), II, 462-3, 465, 467. sGom-čhuṅ-ba, I, 266.
sGom-čhen Čhos-'phel, I, 166.
sGom-čhen rDor-'byuṅ, I, 110.
sGom-čhen Brag-po, II, 909.
sGom-čhen sMon-lam, II, 439.
sGom-čhen Śāk-sde, I, 110.
sGom-čhos, II, 439.
sGom-pa (Tshul-khrims sñiṅ-po), I, 199, 271; II, 463-4, 464-9, 471, 475-6, 478, 577, 605-67, 615, 662, 711, 714, 930, 975.
sGom-pa dKon-mčhog-bsruṅs, I, 367; II, 755, 766-7.
sGom-pa Grags-mdzes, II, 463.
sGom-pa Grags-legs, II, 704.
sGom-pa Dad-pa, I, 321.
sGom-pa Dad bla-ma, I, 262.

sGom-pa rDo-rje-mgon, II, 474.
sGom-pa Byaṅ-skyabs, I, 304.
sGom-pa dMar-sgom, II, 911.
sGom-pa sMan-gčig-pa, II, 947, 952.
sGom-pa Tshul-khrims, I, 262.
sGom-pa Ži-mdzes, II, 471.
sGom-pa gŽuṅ-čhuṅ-pa, II, 988.
sGom-pa Ye-śes-ldan, II, 716.
sGom-pa gŽon-nu ye-śes, II, 992.
sGom-pa Rin-čhen bla-ma, I, 264.
sGom-pa Rin-gžon, II, 638.
sGom-pa Śāk-rin (Śākya rin-čhen, 'Bri-khuṅ-), II, 564, 578.
sGom-pa Śes-rab dbaṅ-phyug, I, 311-2.
sGom-ma rNal-'byor-ma, I, 138.
sGom-tshul, II, 471, 475, 479, 706.
sGom-tsho (of Grab), II, 862.
sGom-tsho (of rGya), II, 862.
sGom-tsho (of Bya-ma-luṅ), 862. sGom-tsho (of kLags), II, 862.
sGom Žig-po, II, 481.
sGom-śu, I, 132.
sGom-bsam, II, 619.
sGyi-tshaṅ Žig-po, 944-5.
sGyu-sbyaṅs dbaṅ-seṅ, I, 269.
sGyer-sgom čhen-po, II, 864.
sGra-gčan-zin, I, 12, 16, 344.
sGra gčan-zin bzaṅ-po, I, 371.
sGra-gčan gsaṅ-ba'i rdo-rje, I, 242.
sGra-tshad Rin-čhen rnam-rgyal I, vi.
sGra-tshad-pa (Rin-čhen rnam-rgyal), I,
sGra-tshad-pa Rin-čhen rgyal-mtshan (Rin-rgyal), II, 785, 838.
sGrig-ston Saṅs-rgyas, II, 999.
sGrin mkhan-po Čhos-ston, II, 654.
sGrub-pa Žig-po, II, 688.
sGre-pa, I, 273, 318; II, 458-9.
sGre-mo, I, 126.
sGro, II, 900-5.
sGro Ārya Byaṅ-tshul, I, 262.
sGro-čhuṅ-ba, II, 923.
sGro Čhos-brtson, II, 901.
sGro-ston, I, 113; II, 767.
sGro-ston gNam-la brtsegs, II, 755, 766-7.
sGro-ston 'Phan-rgyal, II, 901.

sGro Dar-seṅ, I, 128.
sGro-ne, II, 918.
sGro-phug-pa, I, 122, 126; II, 706. (Lha-rje čhen-pa sGro-phug-pa).
sGro-sbug-pa, I, 124, 126-8, 130, 149, 156, 171.
sGro-mon-čan-pa, II, 692.
sGro-lag-pa, I, 269.
sGroṅ-ma-ba, II, 705.
sGron-ne, II, 435.
sGrod-luṅ-pa, II, 720.
sGrol-sgom mDo-čhen, II, 409.
sGrol-ma, I, 88.
sGrol-ma-pa, I, 160.
sGrol-ma-'bum, II, 521.
sGrol-ma-'tsho, II, 522.
sGro'i sTag-mgo-ba, I, 269.
brGya-byin, I, 4.
brGya-byin sdoṅ-po, I, 103.
Ṅa-ru 'od-de, I, 135.
Ṅa-len-nu, I, 4.
Ṅag-gi dbaṅ-phyug, I, 384; II, 763, 795, 869, 985, 1051.
Ṅag-gi dbaṅ-phyug grags-pa, I, 206, 227; II, 763. See Pham-thiṅ-pa.
Ṅag-dbaṅ-grags, II, 801.
Ṅag-dbaṅ grags-pa dpal-bzaṅ-po, II, 647.
Ṅag-dbaṅ-ba, II, 807.
Ṅaṅ-phu-ba, II, 604-5.
Ṅaṅ-tshaṅ-pa, I, 292.
Ṅaṅ-tshul, I, 45.
Ṅan-spoṅ, I, 13.
Ṅan Yon-tan-mčhog, I, 108.
Ṅan-lam rGyal-mčhog-dbyaṅs, I, 104. Ṅan-lam rGyal-ba mčhog-dbyaṅs, II, 805.
Ṅan-lam Byaṅ čhub rgyal-mtshan, I, 173.
Ṅab-thuṅ Byaṅ-čhub rgyal-mtshan, I, 109.
Ṅab-mi, I, 364; II, 432.
Ṅab-mi Byaṅ-čhub rgyal-mtshan, I, 364.
Ṅam-rdzoṅ, II, 446, 449, 450.
Ṅam-rdzoṅ ston-pa, II, 435, 437, 449
Ṅam rdzoṅ ras-pa, II, 435.
Ṅam-śod-pa, II, 573-4.
Ṅams-śod rGya-ras, II, 943.
Ṅams-śod Rin-po-čhe, II, 895.
Ṅar-ton, II, 432.

Ṅar-dbaṅ, I, 329.
Ṅar Yon-tan-grags, I, 343.
Ṅu, I, 188.
Ṅu rDo-rje-rgyan, I, 187, 189.
Ṅu-ston Dad-pa brtson-'grus, I, 189.
Ṅu-gčer-bu, I, 187.
Ṅur-ston bSod-nams rgyal-mtshan, I, 93.
Ṅur-pa čhen-po, I, 93.
Ṅur-pa gYuṅ-śe, I, 292.
Ṅur-pa Śes-rab rgyal-mtshan, I, 93.
Ṅur-smrig-pa, II, 1009.
Ṅur-luṅs-pa, II, 678.
Ṅes-'gro, I, 13, 14.
Ṅes-'phel, I, 15.
Ṅo-nag, II, 488.
Ṅo-pa Dar-śe, II, 783.
Ṅog Śes-rab bla-ma, I, 156.
Ṅom-pa, II, 513.
Ṅom-pa Bya-bral-pa, II, 512-3, 515.
Ṅor-rje, I, 186; II, 768.
Ṅor-rje Kun-dga-'od, I, 361, 365; II. 408.
Ṅor-rje sGom-pa, II, 911.
Ṅor-rje ras-pa, II, 603, (Bal-bu goṅ-pa).
dṄal-čhu-pa, I, 232.
dṄul-mo rGyal-le-lčam, I, 181.
dṄos-grub, II, 941, 996-7, 1006.
dṄos Čhos-śes, II, 727.
mṄa'-bdag Čhos-sen-'od (Čhos-seṅ), II, 1088-9.
mṄa'-bdag-dpal, II, 1059.
mṄa'-nag gTsug-tor dbaṅ-phyug, I. 125.
mṄa'-ris sKyi-ston, I. 397; II, 706, 1009.
mṄa'-ris dgra-bčom, I, 81; II. 727.
mṄa'-ris Čhaṅ-čhuṅ-pa, II, 860.
mṄa'-ris 'Jam-dbyaṅs, m-dbyaṅs, II, 1009.
mṄa'-ris-pa, I, 198; II, 465, 481, 643, 863-4.
mṄa'-ris-pa rDo-rje-dpal, II, 1046.
mṄa'-ris-pa Žaṅ-sgom, II, 706.
mṄa'-ris Par-pu-ba, II, 862.
mṄa'-ris rab-'byams-pa Śer-rgya-ba, II, 830, 835.
mṄa'-gsal-ldan, I, 314.
mṄoṅ-gra-ba Rin-čhen rtse-mo, II, 785.
mṄon-pa-ba, II, 518.

mṄon śes-čan, I, 360-1.
rṄa-len-gyi rgyal-po, I, 13.
rṄan, I, 95.
rṄan-čhuṅ ston-pa, I, 96.
rṄul-ston Rin-dbaṅ, II, 733.
rṄo-thog-pa, I, 154. rṄo-thog-pa Čhos-kyi bzaṅ-po, I, 346.
rṄog, I, 76, 220, 262, 271, 324, 350, 356; II, 403-7, 412-13, 430-1, 433, 442, 473, 813, 1086.
rṄog Kun-dga' rdo-rǰe, II, 409.
rṄog sKya-bo, I, 326.
rṄog Ge-ser-ba, I, 354, 364; II, 928. See rṄog dbUs-pa Ge-ser.
rṄog Čhos-kyi rdo-rǰe (Čhos-rdor), I, 356; II, 403-4, 407.
rṄog Čhos-dbaṅ, I, 291.
rṄog J̌o-sras, II, 936.
rṄog J̌o-sras Ra-mo, I, 333.
rṄog Ñi-ma seṅ-ge, I, 365.
rṄog-ston, II, 754.
rṄog Dad-pa-čan, II, 406.
rṄog mDo-sde, I, 376, 396; II, 404, 406-8, 414, 706, 712.
rṄog rDo-rǰe seṅ-ge, I, 194.
rṄog-pa, II, 667.
rṄog Byaṅ-čhub-dpal, II, 809.
rṄog Byaṅ-čhub 'byuṅ-gnas, I, 74, 77, 259; II, 844.
rṄog bLo-ldan śes-rab (rṄog Lo-čhen-po), I, 72-3, 75, 325; II, 698.
rṄog dbUs-pa Ge-ser, I, 364. See rṄog Ge-ser-ba.
rṄog Mun-ne, I, 366; II, 556.
rṄog-btsun dkar-mo, I, 81; II, 1043-4.
rṄog gŽuṅ-po, II, 403, 1009.
rṄog Ye-śes, I, 365.
rṄog Legs-pa'i śes-rab, I, 93, 258, 262, 324, 326, 353; II, 474. rṄog Legs-śes, I, 233.
rṄog lo-tsā-ba, I, iv, 273, 293, 328ff, 339, 341, 348, 379; II, 405, 474. See rṄog bLo-ldan śes-rab.
rṄog Seṅ-ge-kha-pa, II, 563, 565, 603.
rṄog Āryadeva, I, 365.
sṄags-skyes Lhan-čig skyes-pa'i sgron-me, II, 435.
sṄon-po Yon-rdor-ba, II, 699.
sṄon-mo (Lha-btsun-), I, 366, 376.
sṄon-lam-pa (Gra-phu-ba skyes-mčhog-), II, 694.
brṄog brTson-seṅ, I, 235.
Čaṅ-ṅe, I, 123.
Čug, II, 914.

Čuṅ-ston rgyan-ne, II, 439. (gÑal-smad-pa-).
Čog-gru Tiṅ-'dzin bzaṅ-po, II, 838.
Čog-gru lo-tsā-ba Mya-ṅan-med-pa'i dpal, II, 1055.
Čog-ro Čhos-kyi rgyal-mtshan (Čog-ro Čhos-rgyal), I, 383-4, 386ff; II, 408.
Čog-ro kLu'i rgyal-mtshan, I, 345.
Čog-ro Zaṅs-dkar mdzod-khur, I, 167; II, 1000.
gČan 'Od-sruṅs mgon-po, II, 1042.
gČuṅ ('Bri khuṅ-pa), II, 964.
gČuṅ bču-gñis-pa, II, 580.
gČuṅ-po, II, 677.
gČuṅ-po bLo-gros-dpal, I, 94.
gČuṅ Bya-bral-pa, II, 632, 643.
gČuṅ Rin-po-čhe (rDo-rje grags-pa), II, 577-9, 601, 609.
gČen-po dGe-sloṅ-pa, II, 1088.
gČer-ba Waṅ-thuṅ, I, 129.
gČod-pa, II, 513-4.
bČad-po Lha-sgom, II, 462.
bČu-gñis Rin-po-čhe, II, 584.
bČu-gñis-pa (Rin-čhen rdo-rje), II, 579, 580, 586.
bČu-gñis gsar-ma-ba (Grags-pa śes-rab, Grags-se-ba), II, 584.
bČom-ldan Ral-gri, I, 345.
bČom-ral (lČom-ldan Rig-ral, Rig-pai' ral-gri, Rig-ral), I, 337; II, 974.
lČags-'bar, II, 946.
lČags-žiṅ-pa, II, 271.
lČags-ri Goṅ-kha-pa, II, 453.
lČags-ri-pa, II, 952.
lČaṅ-maṅ-phu-ba, II, 486.
lČaṅ-ra-ba, I, 348; II, 1009.
lČaṅ-ra-ba lDum-ston, II, 471.
lČaṅ-ri-ba, I, 90.
lČal-pe ba, II, 727.
lČam-me, II, 413, 435.
lČe, II, 759, 760, 766, 905-9, 944.
lČe bKra-śis, I, 359.
lČe-sgom, II, 711.
lČe-sgom nag-po, I, 193-4, 199.
lČe-sgom Śes-rab rdo-rje, II, 1025.
lČe Candrakīrti, II, 907, 909, 910.
lČe rje-btsun bSod-nams-dpal, I, 397.
lČe-ston, I, 171; II, 998.
lČe-ston mGon-po, II, 677.
lČe-ston rGya-nag, I, 125.

lČe-ston J̌o-gzuṅs, I, 128.
lČe-ston mDo-seṅ, II, 866. lČe-ston mDo-sde seṅ-ge, I, 397.
lČe-ston Saṅs-rgyas, II, 677.
lČe Dal (— Dwal)-sgaṅ-pa, I, 72; II, 906-7.
lČe 'Dul-'dzin, I, 80.
lČe-pa, II, 759, 906.
lČe bLo-ldan seṅ-ge, I, 397; II, 866.
lČe dBaṅ-phyug rdo-rǰe, I, 397.
lČe-mo dPal-sgom, II, 911.
lČe-btsun Seṅ-ge dbaṅ-phyug, I, 192-4.
lČe-žar, I, 353.
lČe Śākya-mčhog, I, 110.
lČog-ro sMyon-pa, II, 688, 912.
Čha-ba, II, 471.
Čhag, II, 1058.
Čhag Khri-mčhog, I, 233, 259, 262, 322.
Čhag dGra-bčom-pa, I, 94; II, 608, 709, 1054, 1057.
Čhag Čhos-rǰe-dpal, I, 366; II, 837, 1056-7. Čhag Čhos-dpal, II, 1060. See Čhag lo-tsā-ba.
Čhag Ñi-ma, I, 82.
Čhag Ñi-ma-dpal, II, 1059.
Čhag Brag-dmar-pa, II, 900.
Čhag mal-pa, I, 292.
Čhag lo-tsā
Čhag Lo-tsā-ba (Čhos-rǰe-dpal), I, 94, 379, 389; II, 417, 699, 727, 757, 765, 1047-8, 1056.
Čhag Seṅ-ge-grags, II, 474.
Čhags-ston Nam-mkha', I, 111.
Čhaṅ-ma sṅon-po, I, 329,
Čhaṅ-ra Śes-rab seṅ-ge, II, 855.
Čhu-goṅ dPal-le, II, 403.
Čhu-sgom, II, 538, 911.
Čhu-sgom-ma bSam-gtan-rgyan, II, 530.
Čhu-čhal Mon-gras, II, 680.
Čhu-bo'i rgyun, II, 847.
Čhu-mig-pa, I, 195, 329; II, 608, 728, 749.
Čhu-mig Riṅ-mo-ba rGya Grags-bsod, II. 928.
Čhu-tsha-kha-pa Śes-rab-dpal, II, 1025.
Čhu-bzaṅs-pa, II, 895, 1016-7.
Čhu-gsol 'Od-ser bzaṅ-po, II, 511.
Čhud-kha-pa, II, 830.
Čhe-btsan-skyes, I, 104-5.

Che-sa Saṅs-rgyas rgyal-mtshan, II, 595, 1084.
Ched-čher Bag-ye sgom-pa, I, 285.
Chen-po Yon rin-pa, II, 592.
Čhes-ston bSod-nams rgyal-mtshan, II, 416.
Čhos-kyi ka-ba, II, 1087.
Čhos-kyi khu-'gyur gsal-ba'i mčhog, I, 173.
Čhos-kyi grags-pa (Ñiṅ-phug-pa), II, 1008.
Čhos-kyi grags-pa (gSer-gliṅ-pa), I, 244; II, 724, 800, 803, 861.
Čhos-kyi grags-pa Ye-śes dpal-bzaṅ-po, II, 831.
Čhos-kyi dge, II, 939.
Čhos-kyi rgya-mtsho, II, 696.
Čhos-kyi rgyal-po, II, 610, 647.
Čhos-kyi-rgyal mtshan, I, 166, 214-5, 276; II, 411.
Čhos-kyi rgyal-mtshan (Gu-śrī-), II, 509.
Čhos-kyi mčhog, I, 346.
Čhos-kyi sde, I, 15.
Čhos-kyi pad-ma, I, 297.
Čhos-kyi dpal-pa, II, 794.
Čhos-kyi byaṅ-čhub, II, 435.
Čhos-kyi blo-gros, II, 417. (Mar-pa-).
Čhos-kyi dbaṅ-phyug, I, 383.
Čhos-kyi brtson-'grus, I, 80.
Čhos-kyi bzaṅ-po, I, 160; II, 706.
Čhos-kyi 'od-zer, II, 520.
Čhos-kyi ye-śes (rDza-dgon Kun-spaṅs-), II, 544.
Čhos-kyi bśes-gñen, I, 166.
Čhos-kyi seṅ-ge (Čhos-seṅ-ba), I, 154-6, 346.
Čhos-kyi lha, II, 949, 955.
Čhos-sku 'od-zer (bDag-med rdo-rje, Chos-kyi 'od-zer), I, 335, 345, 365, 374, 397; II, 407, 422, 756, 770-2.
Čhos-skyabs, I, 97, 324-5; II, 629, 917.
Čhos-skyabs bzaṅ-po, I, 321; II, 1076.
Čhos-skyid, II, 917.
Čhos-skyoṅ mgon-po, I, 40.
Čhos-skyobs, I, 346.
Čhos-'khor sgaṅ-pa, II, 830, 834-5.
Čhos-grags (of gSos-khaṅ), I, 344, 346; II, 833, 868.
Čhos-grags-dpal, II, 534.
Čhos-grags dpal-bzaṅ-po, II, 777.
Čhos-grags ye-śes, II, 551. (Žwa-dmar čod-paṇ-'dzin-pa-).
Čhos-grags rin-čhen-dpal, I, 80.
Čhos-grub-pa, I, 1073.

Čhos-rgyal, I, 356, 383; II, 520, 744.
Čhos-rgyal dpal-bzaṅ (Bya-), II, 1088-9.
Čhos-rgyal-ba, I, 321; II, 965.
Čhos-rgyal bzaṅ-po, I, 321.
Čhos-rgyal bzaṅ-po dbu-nag-pa, I, 321.
Čhos-sgo-ba Čhos-kyi rgya-mtsho, II, 991.
Čhos-sgo-ba Čhos-kyi rgyal-mtshan, II, 105.
Čhos-sgo-ba Čhos-dpal śes-rab, II, 451, 589, 590, 592, 751, 1007.
Čhos-sgo-ba rDo-rje ye-śes, II, 609.
Čhos-sgo-ba Tshul-khrims bzaṅ-po, II, 588.
Čhos-sgro-ba, II, 931.
Čhos-sgro ras-pa, II, 988.
Čhos-sgron, II, 916.
Čhos-lčam, II, 632.
Čhos-mčhog, I, 298. Čhos-mčhog-pa, I, 98.
Čhos-rje-dpal, II, 1060.
Čhos-rje-ba, I, 321.
Čhos-rje Bu-ston, I, 374.
Čhos-rje bla-ma, I, 153; II, 636.
Čhos-ston, II, 1020.
Čhos-mthoṅ, II, 688.
~~Čhos-rdor, II,~~ 410-1, 893, 895.
Čhos-ldaṅ, II, 604.
Čhos-ldan-'bum, II, 1041.
Čhos-sdiṅs-pa, II, 696, 727.
Čhos-dpal mgon-po, I, 345; II, 996.
Čhos-dpal rgyal-ba, I, 321.
Čhos-dpal rgyal-mtshan, I, 201, 330.
Čhos-dpal-pa, I, 94; II, 532, 1072.
Čhos-dpal ye-śes ('Ger-nag rTogs-ldan-), II, 509, 516, 546ff.
Čhos-dpal śes-rab, II, 587.
Čhos-phug-pa gŽon-nu blo-gros, I, 320.
Čhos-'phags, I, 166.
Čhos-'phel, I, 381.
Čhos-byaṅ, II, 520.
Čhos-bla, II, 983.
Čhos-blo, II, 520.
Čhos-dbaṅ (Čhos-kyi dbaṅ-phyug), I, 309; (Rin-po-čhe-), II, 468.
Čhos-dbaṅ (Guru-), II, 445, 542.
Čhos-dbaṅ Nam-bza' 'phred-gsol, I, 80.
Čhos-dbyiṅs-pa (rDo-rje bkra-śis), II, 693, 722-3.
Čhos-dbyiṅs-dbaṅ-phyug, II, 722.

Čhos-'bar, II, 1053.
Čhos-'byuṅ ži-ba, II, 764, 800.
Čhos-'byuṅ rin-čhen, II, 748.
Čhos-sbas, II, 801.
Čhos-sbyin-ma, I, 33.
Čhos-smon-lam, II, 654.
Čhos-bzaṅ, II, 545-6-7.
Čhos-bzaṅ ñi-ma, II, 781.
Čhos-bžad, I, 166.
Čhos-bži-gsar-ma-pa, II, 1041.
Čhos-yags, II, 629.
Čhos-gyuṅ, II, 461; rNal-'byor Čhos-gyuṅ, II, 468.
Čhos-rab, I, 379.
Čhos-rin, I, 189.
Čhos-la dga'-ba, I, 364; II, 408.
Čhos-legs, I, 93.
Čhos-seṅ-pa, II, 779.
Čhos-bsam-'od(mKhar-čhu-ba-), II, 657.
mČhims, II, 791.
mČhims Nam-mkha'-grags, I, 283; II, 727.
mČhims brTson-rgyal, I, 345.
mČhuṅ Ye-śes 'byuṅ-gnas, II, 857.
mČhe-ba'i sde, I, 67.
mČhen Tshul-khrims bla-ma, I, 78.
mČhe'u Dar-re, II, 409.
mČhog-ldan (lo-tsā-ba-), I, 345, 374, 385; II, 785-6, 1046.
mČhog-dbyaṅs, II, 822.
'Čhad-mo Nam-mkha', I, 208.
'Čhan-bu rGya-ras, II, 563, 566.
'Čhad-kha-pa, II, 614.
'Čhad-khaṅ Lha bLo-gros-'od, I, 308.
'Čhar-rgyal, I, 45-7.
'Čhar-bu rgya-ras, II, 952.
'Čhal-čhuṅ, I, 156.
'Čhims. II, 406.
'Čhims Čhen-mo, I, 336,
'Čhims Čhos-seṅ, II, 1052.
'Čhims rDo-rje spre-čhuṅ, I, 94.
'Čhims Nam-mkha'-grags, I, 81; II, 1024.
'Čhud-pa, II, 882-3, 904-5, 910, 945.
'Čhus-pa gaṅ-po, II, 904.
'Čhud-pa Jo-bsod, I, 319.

'Čhud-pa Dar-brtson, II, 871, 875-6, 879, 881, 904-5-6. 943.
'Čhud-pa brTson-señ (brTson-'grus señ-ge), II, 871, 883, 905-6, 952.
Ja-mthoñ, II, 405.
Ja-pa grags-pa, I, 66.
Jam-gsar, II, 678.
Ju-tse btsan-po, I, xix, xx, 52.
Je-bo Yon-tan rgya-mtsho, I, 159.
Jo-bkra, I, 166.
Jo-dga', I, 38.
Jodge. II, 747.
Jo-mgon, I, 110.
Jo-rgyal, II, 744.
Jo-stan (Tsha-roñ-), I, 273. Jo-stan, II, 744.
Jo-stan Nag-po, I, 313.
Jo-stan Nag-po Dar-tshul, I, 79.
Jo-ston, II, 462. Jo-ston Dar-brtson, II, 532.
Jo-ston dBañ-phyug-grags, I, 232.
Jo-brtan, I, 166.
Jo-dar, II, 941.
Jo-bde, I, 365; II, 413.
Jo-rdor, II, 435.
Jo-nañ-pa (Kun-mkhyen-), I, 309; II, 885, 996.
Jo-nañ lo-tsā-ba, I, 350.
Jo-nam, I, 141, 329.
Jo-pad, II, 956-7, 1010.
Jo-bo 'Khon-par-skyes, I, 210.
Jo-bo rNal-'byor, I, 38, 276; II, 945.
Jo-bo Bye'u-čhuñ-pa, II, 936.
Jo-bo 'Tshar-pa snu-pa, I, 365.
Jo-bo-legs, I, 265.
Jo-bo Śākya bkra-śis, I, 38.
Jo-bo Śākya-mgon, I, 38.
Jo-bo Se-btsun, I, 93, 251.
Jo-bo Lha, II, 727.
Jo-bo Lha mGon-po-dpal, I, 366.
Jo-bo Lha-čhen-po (of Bya-sa), II, 930, 936
Jo-bo Lha-btsun, II, 715,
Jo-'bag, I, 38, 278.
Jo-'bar, I, 194-5.
Jo-'bum, II, 768, 960.
Jo-mo sGre-mo, I, 171; II, 409, 439.
Jo-mo Dar-ma, II, 920.

Jo-mo-nan-pa, I, 349.
Jo-mo-ba, I, 177.
Jo-mo Byaṅ-čhub, II, 984.
Jo-mo Myaṅ-mo, I, 128.
Jo-mo Zer-mo, I, 171.
Jo-mo bSam-me, II, 994.
Jo-bstun, I, 278.
Jo-btsun Khyuṅ, I, 379.
Jo-btsun sGom-nag, I, 237
Jo-btsun rTag-pa, I, 366.
Jo-btsun rDo-rje grags-pa, I, 123, 127.
Jo-btsun rDo-rje-'bar, I, 110, 122.
Jo-btsun Me-'bar, II, 859.
Jo-rtse, I, 110.
Jo-rtsegs, I, 166.
Jo-zi-gza' bKra-śis-mtsho, II, 621.
Jo-bzaṅ, I, 166.
Jo-'od, II, 413.
Jo-rin'khor-lo, II, 406.
Jo-śāk, II, 413.
Jo-śo-re, I, 176.
Jo-sras I, 144, 196, 273; II, 442.
Jo-sras Koṅ-po, I, 27
Jo-sras- skyabs, II, 929
Jo-sras 'Jam-dpal, I, 106.
Jo-sras Nam-mkha', I, 3[illegible]6; II, 936.
Jo-sras Ñi-ma; II, 1066.
Jo-sras 'Brog-po, II, 942.
Jo-sras-ma rGya-ma, I, 133.
Jo-sras ma rGya-ma hor, I, 133.
Jo-sras-ma Śākya lčam-mo, I, 122.
Jo-sras-ma mṄa'-mo gtsug-tor-lčam, I, 122.
Jo-sras 'Od-zer, I, 166.
Jo-sras Yaṅ-dag, I, 396.
Jo sras gYu-ru, II, 932-3, 935.
Jo-sras Ra-pe, I, 166.
Jo-sras bSod-nams-dpal, I, 197.
Jo-sras Lhas-spuṅs, I, 166.
Jo-sras A-seṅ, II, 444.
Jo-sruṅs, II, 677.
Jo-bsam, II, 688.
Jo-bsod, I, 141-3; II, 413, 445.

J̌og-po, II, 732.
J̌oṅ-ǰi, II, 641.
J̌oṅ-ǰi bSod-nams rin-čhen, II, 642.
'J̌ag-čhen Byams-pa-dpal, II, 749.
'J̌ag-pa rGyal-mtshan-'bum, II, 748.
'J̌aṅ-pa sTon-skyabs, I, 333, 335; II, 1029.
'J̌aṅ-pa gŽon-byaṅ, I, 233, 345.
'J̌aṅ Bras-stag-pa, II, 556.
'J̌am-rgyal, I, 396.
'J̌am-sgeg, II, 779.
'J̌am-sṅon-pa, II, 1083.
'J̌am-nag, II, 518.
'J̌am-pa'i rdo-rǰe, I, 372.
'J̌am-pa'i dbyaṅs Čhos-mgon-pa, II, 535.
'J̌am-pa'i dbyaṅs Don-yod rgyal-mtshan, II, 786.
'J̌am-pa'i dbyaṅs Śākya rgyal-mtshan, II, 1083.
'J̌am-pa'i dbyaṅs bSam-grub rdo-rǰe, I, 202.
'J̌am-dpal-skyid, II, 638.
'J̌am-dpal grags-pa'i bśes-gñen, I, 372.
'J̌am-dpal rgyal-mtshan, II, 1024.
'J̌am dpal ye-śes, I, 92.
'J̌am-dpal bśes-gñen, I, 168, 369; II, 436.
'J̌am-dpal seṅ-ge, I, 329; II, 643.
'J̌am-dpon seṅ-ge, II, 642.
'J̌am-dbyaṅs (bTsun-pa), I, 337-8.
'J̌am-dbyaṅs (sgrub-pa-po), II, 970.
'J̌am-dbyaṅs grags-pa 'byuṅ-gnas, II, 1083-4.
'J̌am-dbyaṅs Kun-dga' seṅ-ge, II, 671.
'J̌am-dbyaṅs skyi-ston, II, 785.
'J̌am dbyaṅs Gu-śrī, II, 501.
'J̌am-dbyaṅs mgon-po, II, 676.
'J̌am dbyaṅs Čhos-kyi mgon-po-ba, II, 781. (Čhos-mgon-po), II, 782.
'J̌am-dbyaṅs Čhos-kyi rdo-rǰe, II, 541.
'J̌am-dbyaṅs Čhos-mgon-pa, II, 536.
'J̌am-dbyaṅs sTon-gžon, I, 346.
'J̌am-dbyaṅs Thugs-rǰe śes-rab, II, 1024.
'J̌am-dbyaṅs Don-grub-dpal, II, 1072.
'J̌am-dbyaṅs Don-grub 'od-zer, II, 580, 810.
'J̌am-dbyaṅs Don-yod-pa, II, 634.
'J̌am-dbyaṅs Don-yod rgyal-mtshan, II, 1045.
'J̌am-dbyaṅs-pa, I, 267; (mČhims 'J̌am-dpal-dbyaṅs, or 'J̌am-dbyaṅs gsar-ma), II, 775.

'Jam-dbyaṅs bLo-gros seṅ-ge, II, 517.
'Jam-dbyaṅs bLo-gros rgyal-mtshan (sMan-čhu-kha-pa), II, 782.
'Jam dbyaṅs ral-gri (paṇ-čhen), II, 1043.
'Jam-dbyaṅs Rin-čhen-rgyal-mtshan, II, 633.
'Jam dbyaṅs Rin-čhen bzaṅ-po, II, 860.
'Jam-dbyaṅs Rin-čhen seṅ-ge, I, 309.
'Jam-dbyaṅs Rin-rgyal-ba, II, 536, 717, 781, 792.
'Jam-dbyaṅs Śākya gžon-nu, I, 100, 329. 'Jam-dbyaṅs Śāk-gžon, II, 524.
'Jam-dbyaṅs Sa-skya-pa, I, 346.
'Jam dbyaṅs gsar-ma, I, 335; II, 727, 756.
'Jam-dbyaṅs bSam-grub rdo-rje, I, 149, 151, 153.
'Jam rin, II, 542.
'Jam-seṅ, I, 329.
'Jam gsar, I, 335; II, 770, 771, 1052, (Čhos-rje-).
'Jam gsar Śes-rab 'od-zer, II, 769.
'Ji-da-rmal, I, 37.
'Ji-ri-pa, II, 972.
'Jig-rten-grags, II, 931.
'Jig-rten mgon-po, I, 306; II, 565. (Chos-rje-), II, 563, 604-5,607.
'Jigs-med gliṅ-pa, I, 105.
'Jigs-byed śiṅ-rta, I, 13.
'Jigs-med 'byuṅ-gnas sbas-pa, I, 32.
'Jiṅ-pa dGye-luṅ-pa, I, 272.
'Jims-čhen-pa, II, 1025.
'Ju-ga gaṅs-pa, II, 601.
rJe Khams-pa rDor-rgyal, I, 188.
rJe Khri-pa, II, 913.
rJe 'Khon-bubs, I, 167.
rJe-thog-btsan, I, 37.
rJe Dags-po Rin-po-čhe, II, 463.
rJe-mo, II, 916.
rJe-mo bkra-śis, II, 901.
rJe-btsun II, 750.
rJe'u-ma, II, 919.
lJaṅ, II, 905, 944.
lJaṅ bka'-gdams-pa, II, 910.
lJaṅ-tsha Lha-dbon, I, 105.
lJaṅ-čhuṅ-ba, II, 910.
Ña-ga-mo-ba, I, 292.
Ña-dbon. II, 780.
Ña-dbon Kun-dga', I, 340. Ña-dbon-po Kun-dga'-pa, II, 1017.
Ña-dbon-po, I, 345.

Ña-dbon Kun-dga'-dpal, II, 777.
Ñag-mo-ba, I, 227-8.
Ñag-re se-bo, II, 563, 565 (grub-thob-).
Ñaṅ Ñi-ma 'od-zer, II, 542.
Ñaṅ-bran-pa Čhos-kyi ye-śes, I, 332.
Ñan-čhen-pa, II, 1016-7.
Ñan-pa (dGe.bśes-), II, 759.
Ñan Lha-sdiṅs-pa, I, 276.
Ñi-khri, II, 907-8.
Ñi-khri-'bum, I, 128; II, 907.
Ñi-thog-pa, II, 747.
Ñi-po, I, 126, 128.
Ñi-phug-pa, I, 314.
Ñi-'bum, I, 194.
Ñi-ma, II, 727.
Ñi-ma guṅ-pa, I, 23; II, 1051. (dgra-bčom-).
Ñi-ma mgon, II, 692.
Ñi-ma rgyal-mtshan, I, 94, 102, 283; II, 688, 758, 1073.
Ñi-ma 'dul-'dzin, I, 284.
Ñi-ma-dpal, II, 764.
Ñi-ma dpal ye-śes, II, 800.
Ñi-ma spral-nag, II, 727.
Ñi-ma-ba, II, 1060.
Ñi-ma byaṅ-čhub, II, 601, 908-9.
Ñi-ma sbas pa, I, 346; II, 869, 1050.
Ñi-ma seṅ-ge, II, 671.
Ñi-ma'i sñiṅ-po, II, 730.
Ñi-ma'i dbaṅ-po'i 'od-zer, I, 366.
Ñi-ma'i 'od-kyi seṅ-ge, I, 158.
Ñi-ma'i śiṅ-rta, I, 1045.
Ñi-'od seṅ-ge, I, 108.
Ñi-zla-'bar, II, 847.
Ñi-śar bkra-śis, I, ii; II, 1090.
Ñi-seṅ, I, 166.
Ñiṅ-phug-pa, II, 1008, 1011, 1024.
Ñe-ston, I, 125.
Ñe-ston Čhos-kyi seṅ-ge, I, 149.
Ñe-ne, I, 128.
Ñe-gnas Rin-čhen-grags, II, 439.
Ñe-gnas gSal-byaṅ, II, 518.
Ñe-gnas Lho-pa, II, 1023.
Ñe-'bum, II, 893.

Ñe-mal-pa, I, 271.
Ñe-mdzes, I, 4, 12.
Ñe-za, I, 15.
Ñeg-po Čhos-ldan, II, 797.
gÑa-ma-pa, I, 226.
gÑa'-čhuṅ, I, 95.
gÑa'-ne, I, 95.
gÑags, I, 277.
gÑags Grags-tshul, I, 347.
gÑags dGe-ba-'bar, I, 176.
gÑags-sgom, II, 656.
gÑags gČer-phu-ba (rTa-śoṅ ras-pa), II, 439.
gÑags-čhuṅ lo-tsā-ba, I, 318.
gÑags-ston rNal-'byor-'bum, II, 971.
gÑags-nag, II, 462.
gÑags-dmar-po, II, 462.
gÑags gYuṅ-ston Khro-rgyal, II, 427, 429.
gÑags Lo-tsā-ba, I, 318; II, 872, 911.
gÑags-bśad Śes-rab rgyal-mtshan, II, 911.
gÑags Jñāna, I, 170.
gÑags Jñānakumāra, I, 104, 108, 167.
gÑan, I, 155, 271, 274; II, 765, 862.
gÑan-čhuṅ-ras-pa, II, 453.
gÑan-ston, II, 999.
gÑan-ston Tshul-'bar, I, 355.
gÑan-ston Ri-rtse-ba, I, 364.
gÑan-thog J̌o-'bum, I, 387.
gÑan-thog Nam-ye, II, 632.
gÑan Dar-ma seṅ-ge, I, 355.
gÑan rDo-rje seṅ-ge (lDum-ra-sgaṅ-pa-), I, 388; II, 408.
gÑan-sde-gsum, I, 113.
gÑan Dharma-grags, II, 857.
gÑan-nag dBaṅ-grags, I, 110.
gÑan sNa-me-ba, I, 266.
gÑan-po ('Byuṅ-gnas ye-śes), II, 884.
gÑan dPal-dbyaṅs, I, 104.
gÑan Tshem-bu-pa Dar-ma 'od-zer, II, 1043-4.
gÑan-ras, I, 189; II, 489, 517, 568. gÑan-ras dGe-'dun-'bum, II, 490, 568.
gÑan-lo, I, 293, 325, 328; II, 407, 763. gÑan lo-tsā-ba, I, 71, 73, 232, 372; II, 533, 760, 766, 838.
gÑan Lha-khaṅ-sgaṅ pa, II, 483.

gÑal-ston, II, 464, 917.
gÑal-ston-grags, I, 156.
gÑal-ston dGa'-čhuṅ-'bar, II, 875.
gÑal Dar-ma gzi-brǰid (Goṅ-gad-pa-), II, 654.
gÑal rDo-rǰe-'od (Gra-phyi-ba-), II, 439.
gÑal-sde, II, 466.
gÑal-pa, I, 75.
gÑal-pa Gro, II, 768.
gÑal-pa 'Gar Čhos-kyi rdo-rǰe, I, 364.
gÑal-pa rÑog Čhuṅ-ma-čan, II, 406.
gÑal-pa J̌o-sras, II, 481.
gÑal-pa Ñi-ma śes-rab, I, 354-5.
gÑal-pa Dad-pa bzaṅ-po, I, 329.
gÑal-pa Dar-ma 'od-zer, I, 81.
gÑal-pa 'Dul-'dzin, II, 597.
gÑal-pa Byaṅ-čhub-'bum, II, 467.
gÑal-pa Me, I, 314. gÑal-pa Žig-po, I, 331.
gÑal-pa Yon-tan seṅ-ge, I, 333.
gÑal-pa Ra-ston, I, 292.
gÑal-pa Ri-lu, I, 329.
gÑal-pa lo-tsā, II, 727.
gÑal-pa gSuṅ-bčad, II, 446, 449. gÑal-pa gSuṅ-bčad-pa Ñi-ma seṅ-ge, II, 450.
gÑal-pa Hrul-po, II, 797.
gÑal-byuṅ-ba, I, 293.
gÑal-žig, I, 329, 335, 341; II, 769, 783. See gÑal-pa Žig-po.
gÑal Zaṅs-po-čhe-pa, II, 1070.
gÑis-mčhod-pa (Grags-pa rin-čhen), II, 582.
gÑis-pa gÑal-žig (rGyal-ba Ri-khrod seṅ-ge), II, 608.
gÑegs Ri-pa, I, 376.
gÑen, I, 279.
gÑen-sa-phug-pa, I, 237.
gÑos, I, 186, 270; II, 598, 610, 608, 900.
gÑos Grags-pa-dpal, I, 373.
gÑos rGyal-ba Lha-naṅ-pa, II, 601, 608.
gÑos-sgom, II, 446, 448-9, 761.
gÑos sGyi-khuṅ-pa, II, 768.
gÑos Čhu-bo-ri-pa, I, 142.
gÑos J̌o-sras dPal-le, I, 333.
gÑos-ston, I, 273.
gÑos-ston bla-ma, I, 141.
gÑos-ston Žig-po, II, 727.

gÑos Dar-ma-'od, II, 796.
gÑos rDo-rje bla-ma, I, 373.
gÑos-nag Grags-pa-dpal, II, 601.
gÑos dPal-le, I, 373.
gÑos Bra-gor-pa, I, 269, 320.
gÑos 'Byuṅ-po, I, 372-3; II, 759.
gÑos-mo-gza' sGron-ma, II, 849.
gÑos Tshul-khrims rgyal-mtshan, I, 74.
gÑos 'Od-ma, II, 761-2.
gÑos lo-tsā-ba, I, 373; II, 601, 837, 906.
mÑan-'čhad-pa, II, 991.
mÑam-lta, I, 15.
mÑam-pa'i rdo-rje, II, 843.
mÑam-med Grags-pa rgyal-po, II, 652.
mÑam-med 'Dul-ba 'dzin-pa, I, 284.
mÑam-med-pa, I, 155.
mÑam-med Śākya ye-śes, II, 408.
mÑa'-ti Jo-śāk, I, 120, 122.
sÑag-phu-pa bSod-nams dbaṅ-phyug, II, 1016. sÑag-phu-pa, II, 1072.
sÑags, I, 46.
sÑags-čhuṅ-ba, II, 935.
sÑags-pa rgyal-mtshan, II, 985.
sÑan-ston Kun-dga'-dar, I, 373.
sÑan-dpal-dbyaṅs, I, 170.
sÑi-sgom, I, 289, 290.
sÑi-ba, I, 376.
sÑi-ba rgyal-po, II, 453.
sÑiṅ-po grub-pa, II, 983.
sÑug-rum-pa, I, 306, 323-4; II, 453, 458.
sÑe-ston Ñi-ma rdo-rje, I, 131.
sÑe-thaṅ-pa, II, 585.
sÑe-thaṅ-pa, bKra-śis seṅ-ge, I, 341; II, 591.
sÑe-mdo. I, 388, II. 579, 601.
sÑe-mdo Kun-dga' don-grub, I, 197. See sÑe-mdo-ba Kun-dga' don-grub.
sÑe-mdo-ba, I, 156; II, 538, 963-6, 972, 978.
sÑe-mdo-ba Kun-dga' don-grub, II, 537, 736, 962, 1050.
sÑe-mdo-ba sMra-ba'i seṅ-ge, II, 890.
sÑe-phu-ba, II, 894.
sÑe-ma-pa, I, 220.
sÑe-mṅa'-ba, II, 727.
Ta (čhen-po), I, 292.

Ta-mo, I, xix.
Ta'i Si-tu, II, 584.
Ta'i Si-tu Byaṅ-čhub rgyal-ba, II, 498.
Ta'i Si-tu Byaṅ-čhub rgyal-mtshan, I, 197, 202, 217-8; II, 591, 1082.
Ti-pu, II, 948. Ti-pu-pa, II, 437, 843, 1007 (Ti-phu, Ti-phu-pa, Te-pu-pa, Ti-bu-žabs, II, 437).
Ti-śrī Kun-blo, II, 792.
Ti-śri ras-pa, II, 601.
Ti-se-ba Dar-ma rgyal-po, II, 583.
Tiṅ-'dzin, II, 882-3.
Tiṅ-'dzin bzaṅ-po, II; 528, (dboṅ-čhen dPon-po-).
Te-luṅ Se-'bar, I, 345.
Ten-ne, II, 929, 930-1, 935-9, 945-8, 950, 952, 975, 978.
Tog-tse-pa, II, 869.
Tre-bo, II, 408, 517.
Tre-bo mgon-po, I, 307, 364, 376, 388; II, 407-8, 756, 760, 768, 972.
Tre-bo mČhog-gi bla-ma (Tre-bo mČhog-bla), I, 326, 376; II, 474.
gTum-ston, I, 272, 282, 305,
gTum-ston bLo-gros grags-pa, I, 282.
gTer-rgyal-ba, II, 579.
gTer-rgyal Rin-po-čhe, II, 580.
rTa-skod, I, 22.
rTa-sgom, II, 446.
rTa-pa gŽon-nu bzaṅ-po, I, 344.
rTa-ston Jo-yes, I, 141-3, 145-6.
rTa-ston Jo-'bum, I, 141.
rTa-ston dBaṅ-grags, I, 141.
rTa-ston gži-brjid, I, 104, 148.
rTa-thaṅ-pa, II, 664.
rTa-thul, I, 20.
rTa-nag bDud-rtsi, I, 149.
rTa-nag Dharmakīrti, I, 228.
rTa-tshag-pa Ye-śes blo-bzaṅ bstan-pa'i mgon-po, II, 1093.
rTa'u-sgaṅ-pa, II, 959.
rTa-rog, I, 111.
rTa-gsum Śu-bžer, I, 251.
rTag-pa Rin-čhen-grags, I, 365.
rTe'u-ra-pa, II, 835.
rTen-ne, II, 890 (rGyal-ba rTen-ne).
rTogs-čhen, I, 15.
rTogs-ldan dKon-seṅ, II, 727.
rTogs-ldan Grags-lhun-pa, II, 969.

rTogs-ldan sÑo-nal-ma Ye-śes rgyal-mtshan, II, 779.
rTogs-ldan rDol-po, II, 985.
rTogs-ldan Na-khra-ba, II, 696.
rTogs-ldan-pa, II, 996.
rTogs-ldan Mi-ñag sgom-riṅs, II, 563.
rTogs-ldan Śag-śaṅ, II, 696.
rTogs-ldan So-nag rgya-bo, II, 643.
rTogs-ldan bSam-gtan-dpal, I, 310.
rTogs-sde, I, 15.
rTogs-pa, I, 15.
lTaṅ-ba, I, 12.
lTaṅ-zuṅ, I, 13.
sTa-sgra lha-snaṅ, I, 170.
sTag, I, 127.
sTag-dkar, I, 95.
sTag-skye, II, 728.
sTag-mgo-pa, II, 517.
sTag-čhu-pa, II, 523.
sTag-sna khri-sum-rje, I, 67.
sTag-čhuṅ, I, 95.
sTag-ston gŽon-nu-dar, II, 1007.
sTag-ston gŽon-nu-dpal, I, 396.
sTag-del-ba, II, 517.
sTag-sde-ba, II, 784, 786.
sTag-sde-ba Seṅ-ge rgyal-mtshan, II, 783.
sTag-sde-ba brTson-rgyal, II, 784.
sTag-pa Kha-čhe, I, 376, 379.
sTag-pa Lha-po, I, 135.
sTag-rtse-ba, I, 339.
sTag-tshaṅ ras-pa, II, 720.
sTag-tshab, I, 95. See Gra-pa mÑon-śes.
sTag-tshab-'bar, I, 284.
sTag-ri gnaṅ-gzigs, I, 37.
sTag-luṅ Kun-spaṅs Rin-po-čhe, II, 518.
sTag luṅ čhos-rje, II, 651.
sTag-luṅ-thaṅ-pa, II, 518, 522, 561, 563-4, (bKra-śis-dpal), 610, 613-5, 617, 621-5, 627, 629, 642, 646, 649.
sTag-luṅ-pa, II, 570-1, 574, 652, 682.
sTag-luṅ Saṅs-rgyas-dbon, II, 1049.
sTag-lo gŽon-nu brtson-'grus, I, 205.
sTag-lo gŽon-tshul, I, 72.
sTag-lo Zla-sgron, II, 470.

Tag-śam-čan, I, 180.
Tan-gčig-pa gŽon-nu tshul-khrims (Jo-stan Thaṅ-pa, bla-ma Jo-stan-pa), II, 993-5.
Tan-gčig-pa Śes-rab bzaṅ-po, II, 1043.
Tabs-ka-čhen-po, I, 305.
Tabs-ka-ba, I, 284.
Tar-ka dPal-skyid, II, 470.
Tar-ka Bodhirāja, II, 470.
Tar-kha rDo-rǰe grags, II, 878.
Teṅ-pa Tog-'bar, II, 1052.
Teṅs-pa Lo-tsā-ba (Tshul-khrims 'byuṅ-gnas), II, 654, 837, 1052-4.
Toṅ-ñid Tiṅ-'dzin, I, 393-5. sToṅ-ñid Tiṅ-'dzin rde-rǰe, I, 392.
Toṅ-ñid Tiṅ-'dzin rdo-rǰe, I, 392.
Toṅ-na-mo-ba, I, 234.
Toṅ-tshaṅ 'Phags-pa Rin-po-čhe, I, 109.
Toṅ-bžer bču-ston, II, 612.
Tod-čhuṅ 'Bum-me byaṅ-ra (Kun-dga'), II, 920.
Tod-rǰe-ma, II, 726.
Tod-pa Khri-bzaṅs, II, 920.
Tod-pa Dharma, I, 81.
Tod-mo rDo-rǰe-'tsho, I, 208.
Tod-zur-ba, I, 157.
Tod-luṅ rGya-dmar-pa, I, 236 ; II, 923.
Tod-luṅ-pa, II, 518, 728.
Tod-luṅ-pa čhen-po, I, 80, 285, 322. sTod-luṅ-pa čhen-po Rin-čhen sñiṅ-po, I, 286-8.
Ton, II, 680.
Ton-skya, II, 688.
Ton-skyabs, I, 166, 238.
Ton-grub-pa, II, 727.
Ton-rgyal, II, 477, 637.
Ton-čhar, I, 196.
Ton-čhuṅ dbaṅ-mo, II, 413.
Ton-dar, I, 166, 319; 529.
Ton-nag, II, 581.
on-pa, I, 236-7, 322, 325; II, 529, 530, 579-80, 975 (of Mon-'gar-ba).
on-pa 'Khar-re, I, 132.
on-pa Dharmarāja, I, 237.
on-pa Nam-mkha', II, 947.
on-pa bLa- skyabs, I, 131.
on-pa dBaṅ-phyug rgyal-pa, I, 236.
on-pa Tshul-śe, II, 707.

sTon-pa Yaṅ-rab, I, 262.
sTon-pa Saṅs-rgyas-dpal, II, 604.
sTon-ma bDud-rtsi-'bum, I, 133.
sTon-ma-luṅ-pa, I, 374.
sTon-'tsher, II, 988.
sTon-gžon, I, 280; II, 678. See sBas-pa sTon-gžon.
sTon-gzuṅs, II, 986 (rGyal-ba-).
sTon-yes, I, 396; II, 741.
sTon-gyuṅ, I, 166,
sTon-śāk, I, 127, *129*; II, 866, 1005.
sTon-bśod-pa, I, 100
sTon-seṅ, I, 166.
sTobs-čan Nag-po, II, 847.
sTobs-po-čhe, I, 16.
bsTan-pa'i rgyal-mtshan, II, 633, 778.
bsTan-'dzin-dpal, II, 1059,
bsTan-rim-pa, II, 829.
bsTan-gsal-ba, II, 830.
bsTan-bsruṅs, I, 201.
Tha-ga-pa dGa'-ba'i rdo-rje, II, 552.
Thag-ma rDor-gžon, I, 79; II, 602.
Thaṅ-dkar-ba 'Od-zer 'byuṅ-gnas, II, 630,
Thaṅ-skya-pa, II, 629.
Thaṅ-khab, II, 851.
Thaṅ-čhuṅ-pa, I, 381-2; II, 900.
Thaṅ-ston, II, 447.
Thaṅ-ston 'Bum-me, I, 171,
Thaṅ-ston-pa Čhos-kyi-'od, I, 374.
Thaṅ-ston lo-tsā-ba, II, 791.
Thaṅ-'dul, I, 285.
Thaṅ-pa-pa, I, 302. Thaṅ-pa-pa 'Phags-pa-skyabs, I, 397; II, 419.
Thaṅ-po-čhe-ba, I, 269; II, 572.
Thaṅ dbus-pa, II, 962.
Thaṅ-bzaṅs dPal-gyi rdo-rje, I, 170.
Thaṅ-la-bar, I, 15.
Thaṅ-sag sTon-tshul, II, 928.
Thaṅ-sag-pa, I, 344; II, 651.
Thaṅ-sag-pa bSod-nams rgyal-mtshan, I, 344.
Thaṅ-sag gŽon-nu rgyal-mtshan, I, 310.
Thams-čad mkhyen-pa'i-dpal, II, 1056.
Tha'i-skyam čhen-po, II, 512.
Thar-pa-rgyun, I, 197.

Thar-pa-ba, II, 993.
Thar-pa 'byuṅ-gnas sbas-pa, II, 757.
Thar-pa lam-ston (Ye-śes sñiṅ-po), II, 400.
Thar-pa lo-tsā-ba, I, 104; II, 793, 800.
Thar-pa gliṅ-pa, II, 995.
Thar-pa'i phag-sgom, I, 285.
Thar-lo Ñi-ma rgyal-mtshan, II, 792-3. (See Thar-pa lo-tsā-ba).
Thugs-kyi rdo-rje, I, 362. II, 553.
Thugs-rje-skyabs, II, 63[illegible], 634.
Thugs-rje rgyal-mtshan, II, 1024.
Thugs-rje čhen-po, I, 355, 360, 375.
Thugs-rje dpal-pa, II, 1072.
Thugs-rje brtson-'grus, II, 756, 771-2. (Kun-spaṅs-).
Thuṅ-kha-'bar, I, 180.
Thub-pa, I, 324; II, 629.
Thub-pa rgyal-mtshan, II, 1089,
Thub-pa rdo-rje, I, 152.
Thub-pa śes-rab, I, 382.
Thub-pa bSod-ñoms-pa, II, 604.
Thub-med, I, 16.
Thur-ba-pa, I, 397.
Thur-la-ba Tshul-khrims-skyabs, II, 706.
Thur-śe, II, 784.
The-śo-legs, I, 37.
Theg-čhen-pa, II, 704.
Thel-pa, II, 548.
Thel-pa Kun-rgyal-ba, II, 800.
Tho-gar Nam-mkha', I, 159.
Tho-gar gNam-sde, I, 345.
Tho-ston, II, 706.
Tho-tho-ri-gñan-btsan, I, 39, 105.
Thog-kha-pa (rGyal-sras-), II, 579.
Thog-kha-pa Rin-čhen seṅ-ge, II, 609.
Thogs-med, I, 67, 344; II, 869, ('Phags-pa-)
Thog-med-grags, II, 412-3.
Thogs-med-pa, II, 636.
Thod-dkar Nam-mkha'-sde, I, 110
Thod-pa, I, 188.
Thod-pa 'Ba'-re, II, 983.
hod-pa gYu'i smin-ma-čan, II, 1087.
hod-pa bSam-grub, II, 481, 597.
Thod-smyon bSam-grub, II, 986, 988.

Thon-ston grub-pa, II, 706.
Thon-mi Sambhoṭa, I, 218-9, 376.
Thos-pa-dga', II, 427-9, 431, See Mid-la.
Thos-pa'i sde, I, 15.
mTha', I, 376.
mTha'-ston, I, 82.
mTha'-'dul, I, 40.
mTha'-ma Tshul-khrims-'od, II, 517.
mTha'-bži, II, 942, 1009.
mTha'-bži Grags-pa rin-čhen, I, 190.
mTha'-bži-pa So-thaṅ-pa, I, 376.
mTha'-bži brTson-'gru-pa-'bar, I, 79.
mTha'-bži bya-bral, II, 1006.
mThai-bži bya-bral-pa, II, 451.
mTha'-bži-gza' Čhos-sgron, I, 232.
mTha'-bži lo-tsā-ba, I, 232-33.
mTha'-yas rnam-par rgyal-ba, II, 757.
mThiṅ-gaṅ-pa (Ser-tshul), II, 881, 883.
mThoṅ-ba don-ldan-pa (Čhos-rje-), I, 338; II, 512, 548-9, 550, 781, 1018.
'Thon-mi, I, 40.
'Thon-mi Sambhoṭa, I, 39.
Dā-čhen-pō, I, 229, 243; II, 729.
Dags-čhuṅ-pa, I, 132-4, 187.
Dags-po, II, 522.
Dags-po rGya-ras, I, 132.
Dags-po-sGom-čhuṅ, II, 483.
Dags-po sGom-tshul, II, 462, 608.
Dags-po sÑi-sgom, II, 558.
Dags-po 'Dul-'dzin, I, 81; II, 462, 466, 518.
Dags-po-pa, II, 1088.
Dags-po dBaṅ-rgyal, I, 71, 93, 328.
Dags-po gTsaṅ-'dul, I, 273.
Dags-po Rin-čhe (Dags-po Rin-po-čhe), II, 724.
Dags-po lha-rje, II, 261, 528, 1010, 1040.
Dags-lha-sgam-po, II, 548.
Daṅ-spro-mkhan čhen-po, II, 829.
Daṅ-ra-ba Jo-bo-bgres-po, II, 619.
Daṅ-bug-pa, Daṅ-bug-pa sMra-ba'i seṅ-ge, I, 333-4.
Dam-čhos-gliṅ-pa, II, 468.
Dam-pa (Saṅs-rgyas), II, 816.
Dam-pa sKor, II, 849.
Dam-pa 'Gar, II, 962.

Dam-pa rGya-gar, I, 176, 182; II, 706, 887, 947.
Dam-pa sGom-smon (Śa-mi), II, 888-9.
Dam-pa Čug, II, 916.
Dam-pa Čhos-sdiṅs-pa, II, 601 ('Gar-).
Dam-pa dPal-ldan bla-ma, II, 535, 585-6.
Dam-pa Phyar-čhuṅ, II, 706.
Dam-pa dbUs-pa, II, 991-2.
Dam-pa sBor-maṅ, I, 128.
Dam-pa dMar-po, II, 1029, 1030.
Dam-pa rMa (Čhos-kyi śes-rab), II, 872.
Dam-pa sMon-lam, II, 888.
Dam-pa 'Dzi-sgom, II, 1005.
Dam-pa Yo-čhuṅ-ba, I, 129.
Dam-pa Rin-po-čhe, I, 387.
Dam-pa Saṅs-rgyas, I, 35, 72-3, 96, 220, 222-5, 228, 294; II, 435, 488, 538, 694, 733, 867-8, 871-3, 877-9, 896-9, 902-926, 934, 936, 938, 946, 948, 953, 963, 976-7, 982-4, 996-8, 1016, 1025.
Dam-pa Se-brag-pa, I, 130, 135-6.
Dam-tshig-rdo-rje, I, 362; II, 552.
Dar-rgyal-ba, II, 498-9, 1042.
Dar-sgom Žig-po, II, 948.
Dar-rje dPal-gyi grags-pa, I, 108.
Dar-ston, I, 273.
Dar-rdor, II, 666.
Dar-paṇ, I, 379, 380; II, 1045-6.
Dar-blo, I, 314.
Dar-'byuṅ, II, 518.
Dar-ma, gLaṅ Dar-ma dbU-dum-btsan, I, vii, xix, 38, 47, 53, 71; II, 688.
Dar-ma 'U-dum-btsan, I, 63.
Dar-ma bkra-śis, I, 98
Dar-ma-grags, I, 273, 284; II, 888.
Dar-ma mgon-po, I, 198.
Dar-ma sgaṅ-pa, I, 320; II, 489.
Dar-ma-lčam, II, 518.
Dar-ma-brtan, I, 166.
Dar-ma-dpal-pa, II, 1072.
Dar ma-'bum, I, 128.
Dar-ma brtson-'grus, I, 348.
Dar-ma tshul-khrims, II, 541.
Dar-ma bzaṅ-po-pa, II, 1072.
Dar-ma ye-śes, I, 82. See rGya-a-dur Dar-yes.
Dar-ma rin-čhen, I, 341; II, 970.

Dar-ma Śākya, I, 374.
Dar-ma śes-rab, I, 344; II, 481.
Dar-ma bsod-nams, I, 82, 109, 320.
Dar-brtson, I, 314; II, 1055.
Dar-bzaṅ, I, 166; II, 696.
Dar-'od, I, 335.
Dar-yes, I, 99.
Dar Yon-tan grags-pa, I, 233, 236; II, 441.
Dar-rin, I, 273.
Dar-re, I, 182.
Dar-seṅ, II, 728.
Dwags-po bKra-śis rnam-par-rgyal-ba, II, 807.
Diṅ-khri btsan-po, I, 36.
Diṅ-hu dben-dpon, II, 500.
Du-pa-ba, I, 238.
Dug-ge-ma, II, 697.
Dug-čan, I, 14.
Dug-čan-pa'i lha, I, 15.
Duṅ-mtsho-ba, II, 720.
Duṅ-mtsho ras-pa (Śes-rab rgyal-mtshan, Rin-čhen bzaṅ-po), II, 583, 717, 719-20, 722.
Duṅ-luṅ-pa, II, 677.
Dun-ben śa-ba, I, 338.
Dum-bu ri-pa (Zla-ba rgyal-mtshan, Zla-rgyal), I, 292, 305, 314.
Dur-khrod-pa (Virū-pa), II, 1026.
Dur-khrod-'og-pa rTogs-ldan Dol-pa, II, 988.
Dus-kyi 'khor-lo-ba, II, 760, 763.
Dus-'khor-ba, I, 381; II, 758, 761-2.
Dus-'khor-ba bKra-śis rin-čhen, II, 796.
Dus-'khor-ba Ye-śes rin-čhen, II, 785.
Dus-žabs-čhen-po, II, 755-6.
Dus-žabs-pa, I, 219; II, 758.
Dus-žabs-pa čhuṅ-ṅu, II, 755, 766.
Dus-žabs-pa čhe-ba, II, 789.
Dus-žabs-pa čhuṅ-ba, II, 789.
Dus-gsum mkhyen-pa, I, 332, 333; II, 439, 462, 473 (dGe-'phel, Čhos-kyi grags-pa), II, 481-2, 484-5, 513, 517-8, 522-3-4, 530, 540, 542, 599, 957, 963-4.
De-bžin gśegs-pa (Čhos-rje-; Čhos-dpal bzaṅ-po), I, 310; II, 506-14, 520, 543-4 548, 551, 592, 643, 781, 1018.
De'u Śaṅ-rdor, I, 322.
De-śo-legs, I, 36.
Do-khro Yon-tshul, I, 376

Do-pa, II, 473, 991.
Do-pa Dar-śa, II, 632.
Do-pa Dar-ma śes-rab, II, 652.
Do-brag-pa dPon-mo Rin-mtsho, II, 586.
Don-grub, II, 541, 989, 992.
Don-grub kun-dga', II, 788.
Don-grub-dpal, I, 310, 341; II, 499.
Don-grub dpal-pa, (lDum-čhuṅ-ba-), 411-12; II, 541, 811.
Don-grub dpal-'byor, II, 1072.
Don-grub 'od-zer (Gu-śri-), II, 509.
Don-grub rin-čhen, II, 1073.
Don-steṅs-pa, I, 82, 97-8, 318; II, 555. See Čhos-skyabs.
Don-mo-ri-pa, II, 627.
Don-tshul, I, 344.
Don-žags-pa, II, 1024.
Don-žags-pa Śes-rab brtson-'grus, II, 1023.
Don-žags-pa Saṅs-rgyas rin-čhen, I, 99, 100; II 1023.
Don-žags-pa čhen-po, II, 1064-5.
Don-yod rgyal-mtshan, I, 214; II, 636.
Don-yod rdo-rje, II, 1020, 1042 (rDo-rje gdan-pa).
Don-yod-pa, II, 635.
Dom-mgo-pa, II, 517.
Dom-thod-čan, II, 728.
Dom-pa Bya-bral-pa, II, 509.
Dom-tshaṅ-ras-pa, II, 720.
Dom a-tsa-ra dPal Me-tog-sgro, I, 167.
Do'i gze-ba bLo-ldan, I, 384.
Dor-śe, II, 850.
Dol, II, 955.
Dol-pa, I, 270, 273.
Dol-pa Gag-ston, II, 403.
Dol-pa 'Gar-ston dBaṅ-phyug-grub, I, 365; II, 768.
Dol-pa Ñi-śar, I, 397.
Dol-pa dBaṅ-rgyal, II, 875.
Dol-pa dMar-žur-pa, I, 270. See Rog Śes-rab rgya-mtsho.
Dol-pa Žaṅ-thal, II, 989, 990.
Dol-pa Rab-tu dga'-ba'i rdo-rje, I, 186.
Dol-po sGom-čhen, I, 353.
Dol-po-pa, II, 535, 755-6.
Dol-po ye-śes, II, 862.
Draṅ-po-luṅ-pa, I, 314.
Draṇ-ston mṬha'-brel, II, 408.

Dran-ston Šer-seṅ, II, 727.
Dri-'dul, I, 90.
Dri-ma-med-pa'i gzi-brjid, I, 35.
Dri-med-pa, II, 545.
Dri-med-ma, II, 869.
Drin-čan-pa, II, 965.
Drin-čhen mkhas-pa čhen-po, I, 171.
Dril-bu-pa, I, 384-5, 389; II, 489, 833.
Druṅ Kun-dga' legs-pa'i 'byuṅ-gnas, II, 1084.
Druṅ-čhen (čhos-rje-), II, 610.
Druṅ-čhen Kun-dga' rdo-rje, I, vii.
Druṅ-čhen thams-čad-mkhyen-pa dGe-ba'i blo-gros, I, vii.
Druṅ-čhen-pa, II, 411.
Druṅ Čhos-rje-pa, II, 996.
Druṅ Byaṅ-čhub rdo-rje, II, 1083.
Druṅ bLo-gros-pa, II, 1080, 1089.
Druṅ Rin-rdor-ba, II, 585.
Druṅ bŠes-gñen-pa, II, 610.
Druṅ bSod-nams rgyal-mtshan, II, 412.
Druṅ bSod-nams bzaṅ-po, II, 584.
Dre-na Jo-sras, II, 985.
Drod-čhuṅ-pa, II, 690, 696,
Drod-'byor, I, 180.
gDags-khri-btsan-po, I, 36.
gDum (Čhos-rje-), II, 563.
mDa'-mo Bu-skyid, II, 1052.
bDag-čhen 'Jam-dbyaṅs-pa, II, 591.
bDag-ñid čhen-po, II, 633-4.
bDag-pa, II, 1041.
bDag-po rGya-gar-ba, II, 1082.
bDag-po Šāk-rin-pa, II, 587. bDag-po Šākya rin-čhen-pa, II, 589.
bDud-rtsi-dar, I, 133,
bDud-rtsi-dpal, I, 133.
bDud-rtsi-'bum, I, 128.
bDud-rtsi-ma, I, 12.
bDud-rtsi-zas, I, 12.
bDe-čhen seṅ-ge, II, 687.
bDe-mčhog rdo-rje, I, 385.
bDe-mčhog saṅs-rgyas, II, 693.
bDe-ba skyoṅ, II, 435.
bDe-ba-čhen-po, I, 372.
bDe-ba-dpal, II, 1073.

bDe-byed, I, 13, 14.
bDe-ba'i 'byuṅ-gnas, II, 869.
bDe-bzaṅ-pa (rab-'byams-pa-), II, 830.
bDe-gśegs čhen-po, I, 316. bDe-gśegs čhen-po Śes-rab-'od, II, 958-9, 960-1.
mDa'-gžu-čan, II, 851.
mDa'-gžu-'dzin-pa, II, 853.
mDar-skyogs-me, II, 471.
mDo-ston Seṅ-ge rgyal-mtshan, I, 164.
mDo-sde, II, 412ff.
mDo-sde dkar-po, II, 466,
mDo-sde-grags, I, 376.
mDo-sde-rgyan, II, 890.
mDo-sde-dpal, II, 698.
mDo-ba Karma-pa, II, 747.
mDo-ba-pa, II, 742,
mDo-ba ras-pa, I, 197; II, 518.
mDo-luṅ-pa, I, 269.
mDo'i Khyuṅ-po Hūṃ-sñiṅ, I, 165.
mDos-khar-ba, II, 466.
'Dag-'byar-pa, II, 955.
'Dam-pa Žig-po, II, 527. 'Dam-žig, II, 696.
'Dar 'dul-'dzin, I, 79.
'Dar Tshul-khrims rgyal-po, I, 81.
'Dar-'dzin, I, 14.
'Dar-ras, II, 687.
'Du-sroṅ maṅ-po-rje, I, xix, 50.
'Dul-dkar gŽon-nu tshul-khrims, II, 420.
'Dul-Gra-pa, I, 307.
'Dul-ba 'byuṅ-gnas blo-gros, II, 757-8; 'Dul-ba'i 'byuṅ-gnas blo-gros, II, 760.
'Dul-ba 'dzin-pa, I, 267, 274. II, 466-7. See Dags-po.
'Dul-ba-lha, I, 346.
'Dul-tshad-pa Byaṅ-čhub bzaṅ-po, II, 1072.
'Dul-'dzin, I, 271; II, (upādhyāya) 607; 665 (ācārya).
'Dul-'dzin Grub-pa-dpal, I, 81.
'Dul-'dzin dPal-ldan bzaṅ-po, I, 283.
'Dul-'dzin Sal-gur ston-pa, I, 285.
'Dus-sroṅ maṅ-po-rje, I, 37. See 'Du-sroṅ maṅ-po-rje.
'De-čhuṅ Saṅs-rgyas, II, 482.
'Dri-sgaṅ-pa, I, 278.
'Dre-mo khye-'dren-dpal, II, 676.
'Dren-pa'i žabs, II, 801.
rDul-ston, rDo-rje rin-čhen, II, 1004.

rDul-bzaṅ, I, 13, 15.
rDo-rje, II, 552; (bram-ze-mo-), 596; 920-1.
rDo-rje-skyabs, II, 446.
rDo-rje-skyid, I, 182.
rDo-rje khro-bo, II, 448.
rDo-rje Gos-dkar-ma, II, 1090.
rDo-rje-grags, II, 436, 948.
rDo-rje-rgyan, II, 722, 759, 918.
rDo-rje rgyal-po, II, 554, 610.
rDo-rje rgyal-mtshan, I, 156, 320; II, 422-3, 756, 792-3, 795, 1024.
rDo-rje čhos, I, 361.
rDo-rje sñiṅ po, I, 176.
rDo-rje-brtan, I, 166.
rDo-rje gdan-pa, I, 88; II, 729, 731, 1020-2, 1026-8, 1048, 1055.
rDo-rje bde-ba, II, 592.
rDo-rje bde-ba čhen-po, I, 371.
rDo-rje bde-ma, II, 831, 836.
rDo-rje-dpal, I, 34, 150, 361; II, 726, 1071-2.
rDo-rje dpal-rtsegs, II, 481,
rDo-rje dpal-bzaṅ-po, II, 1071.
rDo-rje-bla-ma, I, 373.
rDo-rje-'bum, I, 128, 150.
rDo-rje dbaṅ-phyug, I, 87, 93; II, 405, 1087.
rDo-rje mi-bskyod (gTsaṅ-pa Rin-po-čhe), I, 292.
rDo-rje gtsug-tor, I, 210.
rDo-rje tshul-khrims, II, 608.
rDo-rje 'dzin-pa gŽon-nu rgyal-mtshan, I, 310.
rDo-rje gžon-nu, I, 167, 300, 306, 324.
rDo-rje bžad-pa, I, 103.
rDo-rje gzi-brjid, I, 373. See Saṅs-rgyas ras-čhen rgyal-ba Lha-naṅ-pa.
rDo-rje 'od-zer, I, 333.
rDo-rje rin-čhen, II, 410.
rDo-rje rin-po-čhe, I, 210.
rDo-rje rin-čhen dbaṅ-gi rgyal-po, II, 1090.
rDo-rje rin-čhen dbaṅ-gi rgyal-mtshan, II, 1084.
rDo-rje legs-pa, II, 1087.
rDo-rje seṅ-ge (rDor-seṅ), I, 355; II, 413, 529, 789.
rDo-rje sems-dpa', II, 711.
rDo-rje sra-brtan, I, 373.
rDo-ston, I, 325.
rDo-ston Śes-rab-grags, I, 282.
rDo-pa (gNas-po-), II, 570.

rDor Theg-pa, II, 581.
rDor- blo-ba, II, 718.
rDor-mo, II, 434.
rDor-'dzin Saṅs-rgyas rgyal-mtshan, II, 584.
rDor-se-ba, I, 321.
rDor-rin-pa, II, 580, 609, 610.
lDaṅ-ma lhun-rgyal, I, 192.
lDan-ma dKon-mčhog seṅ ge, I, 333.
lDan-ma Grags-rin, I, 329.
lDan-ma bla-ma Śer-'bal, II, 611.
lDi-ri Čhos-grags, II, 837.
lDum (Čhos-rje-), II, 563.
lDum-ra-ba, II, 972.
lDe-rgyal-po, I, 37.
lDe-rnol-nam, I, 37.
lDe-rnol-po, I, 37.
lDe-sprin-btsan, I, 37.
lDe-'phrul-nam-gzuṅ-btsan, I, 37.
lDe-gtsugs-mgon, I, 37.
lDe-rus-pa, II, 727.
lDe-sroṅ-btsan, I, xix.
lDe'u, II, 883.
lDe'u-sgaṅ-pa, I, 196.
lDog, II, 1010.
lDog Goṅ-kha-pa, I, 354.
lDog-pa Ye-grags, I, 81.
lDog-loṅ-pa Śākya byaṅ-čhub, II, 1014-5.
lDoṅ-ṅar-ba, I, 390-2.
lDoṅ-ston, II, 517.
mDa' Byaṅ-čhub sems-dpa', I, 142.
sDe-snod-pa, II, 975.
sDe-srid Saṅs-rgyas rgya-mtsho, I, xvi.
sDo-tsha Čhos-sku, II, 408.
Dharma blo-gros, II, 732.
Dharma seṅ-ge, I, 98.
Na-ba-kū-ṭi-pa, I, 361.
Na-mo-ba, I, 292.
Na-bza' 'Phreṅ-gsol, I, 212.
Nā-ro-pa, I, 180, 209, 243, 252, 260, 261, 372, 375, 380-5, 395; II, 400-1, 416, 420, 430, 432, 438, 450, 472-3, 478, 520, 526, 529, 641, 670, 710, 728-9, 730, 735, 741, 754-5, 758, 760, 764, 780, 795, 797, 803, 813, 832, 838, 852, 888, 891, 893, 942, 994, 1010.

Nā-ro paṇ-čhen, I, 206; II, 757.
Nag-po, I, 358; II, 847.
Nag-po Dam-tshig rdo-rje, I, 167, 261, 360, 374.
Nag-po spyod-pa-ba, I, 380; II, 602.
Nag-po-pa, I, 360, 385; II, 754, 803, 843.
Nag-po-žabs, I, 243; II, 869.—Nag-po'i žabs.
Nag-po-žabs čhuṅ-ba, I, 372.
Nag-po Śer-dad, II, 843-4, 865.
Nag-mo (A-lan-kho), I., 57.
Nag-tshaṅ-pa, II, 603.
Nag-tsho, I, 242, 245ff, 271, 311, 321, 324, 364-5, 374; II, 930.
Nag-tsho Tshul-khrims rgyal-ba, I, 31, 245, 258, 262; II, 857.
Nag-tsho lo-tsā-ba, I, 88, 247, 328, 380; II, 404.
Nag-śod dPe-ston, I, 272.
Nags-kyi rin-čhen, II, 797, 1018.
Nags-mgo-ba, II, 518.
Nags-ston mtha'-dag, I, 269.
Nags-pa, II, 627.
Nags-luṅ-pa, II, 622.
Naṅ-ston mgon-po, I, 142.
Naṅ-pa, II, 442.
Nam-mkha' grags-pa, II, 536, 749.
Nam-mkha'-rgyan, II, 597.
Nam-mkha' rgyal-mtshan, I, 338; II, 537, 860, 1073. (Ṅom-), II, 512.
Nam-mkha' rgyal-mtshan dpal-bzaṅ-po, I, 213; II, 635.
Nam-mkha' sñiṅ-po (sKyes-mčhog-), II, 652, 705 842.
Nam-mkha' brtan-pa, I, 217.
Nam-mkha bdag-po.—Nam-mkha'i bdag-po, I, 5, 16.
Nam-mkha' rdo-rje, I, 199, 297.
Nam-mkha'-dpal, I, 98.
Nam-mkha' dpal-brtsegs rgyal-po, II, 652.
Nam-mkha' dpal-bzaṅ, II, 1073.
Nam-mkha' dpal-bzaṅ-po (Kun-dga'-bo, Nam-mkha' rin-čhen, Yon-tan rgya-mtsho), II, 635-41, 672, 787.
Nam-mkha'-dpal lo-tsā, II, 727.
Nam-mkha' byaṅ-čhub (gTsaṅ-pa-), II, 659.
Nam-mkha' dbaṅ-phyug, II, 413.
Nam-mkha' gžon-nu, I, 98-9.
Nam-mkha' bzaṅ-po (Lha-ri-kha-pa Čhos-rje-), II, 639, 694-5, 779, 788.
Nam-mkha-'od, I, 384; II, 463, 517, 522, 540, 564, 755.
Nam-mkha' 'od-zer (bKa'-bži-pa-), II, 687.
Nam-mkha' ye-śes, II, 939, 973.

Nam-mkha' legs-pa'i blo-gros rgyal-mtshan dpal-bzaṅ-po, I, 213.
Nam-mkha'-gsal, II, 918.
Nam-mkha' bsod-nams-pa, II, 721.
Nam-mkha' lhun bzaṅs, II, 1073.
Nam-mkha'i rdo-rǰe, II, 843.
Nam dGa'-ldan byaṅ-čhub, I, 64.
Nam-'gag-pa, II, 580.
Nam-naṅ Zla-ba'i rdo-rǰe, I, 345.
Nam-pa 'phan-ne, II, 462.
Nam-legs-pa, II, 635.
Nal-rba sñiṅ-po, I, 121.
Ni gu, II, 641, 991.
Ni-gu-ma, II, 728, 730-1, 747-8, 750, 752.
Ni-rū-pa, II, 853-4.
Ne-mig-pa, II, 1044.
Ne-tso, I, 376.
Ne-riṅs-pa (bDe-legs rgyal-mtshan), II, 686, 688.
Nel-pa paṇḍita Grags-pa sMon-lam tshul-khrims, I, viii, xvi, 61.
Nel-pa paṇ-čhen, II, 751.
Non 'J̌am.dpal, I, 63.
Nor-bu bKra-śis mi-'gyur dbaṅ-po'i sde, II, 1090. (Čhos-rgyal-).
Nor-bu sñiṅ-po, II, 847.
Nor-bzaṅs-dpal, I, 346.
gNam-lde 'Od-sruṅs, I, 37.
gNam-'phar-ba, II, 442.
gNam mtsho-ba Mi-bskyod rdo-rǰe, II. 490.
gNam-mtsho-ba čhen-po, II, 517.
gNam-ri sroṅ-btsan, I, 37, 105.
gNam lo-tsā, II, 837.
gNas-bčas, I, 21.
gNas-'ǰug, I, 13, 16.
gNas-brtan, I, 91, 278.
gNas-brtan 'byuṅ-grags, II, 911.
gNas-brtan Rin-čhen-'od, II, 638,
gNas-naṅ-pa, II, 519-20.
gNos-sel, I, 13.
gNur Ñi-ma, II, 705.
gNel-čor Śes-rab grags, II, 838.
mNo-sgom čhen-po, II, 985.
rNa-ba, I, 16.
rNa-ba-čan, I, 5.
rNam-rgyal grags-pa, II, 788, 831.

rNam-rgyal-žabs, I, 380; II, 754, 764, 803.
rNam-par rgyal-ba'i gžu, I, 16.
rNam-par-ba, I, 322, 329.
rNam-'phar-ba (Ṅaṅ-tshaṅ-pa), I, 292.
rNam-śes-skyid, II, 468.
rNal-'byor, II, 672, 792.
rNal-'byor skyabs-se, II, 1044.
rNal-'byor-grags, II, 986.
rNal-'byor rgyal-tshad, I, 123.
rNal-'byor čhen-po (rNal-'byor-pa čhen-po, rNal-'byor A-mes), I, 233, 262, 264, 322.
rNal-'byor Čhos-gyuṅ, II, 891-2.
rNal-'byor-pa, I, 284, 286, 321, 323; II, 1002-3.
rNal-'byor Byaṅ-seṅ, I, 79.
rNal 'byor dbaṅ-po'i thig-le, II, 803.
rNal-'byor seṅ-ge, II, 955.
rNal Rin-čhen-gliṅ-pa, II, 564.
rNel-gyam-pa, II, 727.
sNa-nam, I, 74-5, 262.
sNa nam J̌o-sras, I, 88.
sNa-nam rDo-rǰe bdud-'ǰoms, I, 104, 166.
sNa-nam rDo-rǰe dbaṅ-phyug, I, 77.
sNa-nam Tshul-khrims byaṅ-čhub, I, 159.
sNa-nam Tshul-khrims śes-rab, I, 156.
sNa-nam Žal-yon-po, I, 159.
sNa-phu-ba (gLiṅ-ras-pa), II, 563, 667.
sNa Tsha-roṅ-pa Śer-gžon, II, 784.
sNaṅ, I, 270.
sNaṅ kha'u-ba, I, 372.
sNaṅ-sgom, II, 587.
sNaṅ-dre'u-lhas-pa, I, 269.
sNam J̌o-dpal, I, 305.
sNa'u-pa, II, 584, 722-3.
sNar-rgya Tshul-khrims yon-tan, I, 81.
sNar-rgya Rin-tshul, I, 81.
sNar-ston Žig-po, I, 396.
sNar-ston Seṅ-ge-'od, I, 157.
sNubs, I, 82.
sNubs-sgom, I, 314.
sNubs-čhen Saṅs-rgyas ye-śes, II, 445.
sNubs mčhod-gnas, I, 292, 306.
sNubs-ston, I, 156, 396; II, 448.

sNubs-ston bag-ma, I, 120.
sNubs rDo-rje btsan-grags, I, 297.
sNubs Nam-mkha' sñiṅ-po, I, 104
sNubs dPa'-brtan, I, 167.
sNubs Phag-mo-luṅ-pa, II, 1009, 1023
sNubs-mo Nam-mkha'-gsal, II, 985.
sNubs Saṅs-rgyas, I, 159.
sNubs Saṅs-rgyas ye-śes, I, 104, 153.
sNubs Śaṅs-po-čhe, I, 177, 180, 182.
sNubs A-la-la, I, 292.
sNur Čhos-'phags, I, 355.
sNur Ñi-ma, I, 376.
sNur Ñi-ma 'od-zer, I 355.
sNur Dharma-grags, I, 342.
sNur-pa, II, 708.
sNur Ye-śes rgyal-mtshan, I, 355.
sNe-mdo, II, 408, 426.
sNe-pho, I, 77.
sNe-pho Grags-pa rgyal-mtshan, I, 78.
sNe'u-gdoṅ-pa, II, 548.
sNe'u-zur-pa, I, 73, 180, 266-7, 271, 284, 297, 299, 311-3, 331; II, 1010, 1085.
Pa-gor bLon-čhen 'phags-pa, I, 108.
Pa-tshab (sPa-tshab,) lo-tsā-ba, Ñi-ma grags), I, 94, 230, 236, 272, 297, 305, 322, 328, 341, 344, 350, 365-6; II, 407, 441, 862, 923-4, 926-9, 931, 935, 951, 978, 1009.
Pa-tshab sgom-nag, II, 928.
Pa-tshab sgom-pa, II, 923.
Pa-tshab ston 'Bum-grags, II, 923.
Pa-ra-ga-ta, II, 471.
Pa-śi, II, 652.
Pa-śi Don-grub seṅ-ge, II, 680.
Pa-śi rDor-rin, II, 591.
Pa-śi gNas-brtan, II, 1085.
Pa-śi rDzi-dkar-ba, II, 1085.
Pa-śi Śāk-'od, I, 149.
Paṅ-ka Dar-čhuṅ, I, 165.
Pad-ma, II, 805.
Pad-ma dkar-po, I, xiii, 358; II, 756-7, 803.
Pad-ma-čan, II, 847.
Pad-ma-rdo-rje, I, 362-3, 389; II, 552, 659 (gLiṅ).
Pad-ma bltams-mčhog rgyal-po (rTa-mčhog rgyal-po), II, 1089.

Pad-ma dbaṅ-rgyal, I, 109.
Pad-ma-'bar, I, 156
Pad-ma 'byuṅ-gnas, II, 1007.
Pad-ma bzaṅ-po, II, 412.
Pad-ma bzaṅ-po-ba (dKa-bču-pa-), II, 781.
Pad-ma'i sñiṅ-po, I. 241.
Pad-ma'i phreṅ-ba, II, 843.
Pad-ma'i myu-gu, II, 1041.
Pad-ma'i rtsa-lag, I, 6.
Pad-mo-žabs, II, 869.
Paṇ-čhen Me-waṅ-ga, I, 346.
Par-tab (<Pratāpa)-rmal, I, 38.
Par gNas-brtan grags-pa, I, 66.
Par-pu-ba, II, 895.
Par-pu-ba bLo-gros seṅ-ge, II, 864-5.
Pi-to-pa, I, 262.
Piṇḍo-pa bSod-sñoms-pa, I, 361.
Pu-to-ba, I, 88, 234-5; II, 872, 1001, 1003.
Pu-hraṅs-pa, I, 220. See sPu-hraṅs.
Pu-hraṅs lo-tsā-ba, I 221, 226; II, 706.
Pur Candra, I, 376.
Pe-ta, II, 435.
Po-to-ba, I, 71, 141-2, 263, 266-7, 270-1, 282, 287, 312-3; II, 405, 454.
Po-to-ba Rin-čhen-gsal, I, 73, 236, 268; II, 474, 830, 923-4.
Po-doṅ-ba, II, 829.
Pom-po-pa, I, 291.
Pra-spaṅ, II, 655.
dPaṅ, II, 787, 838.
dPaṅ bLo-gros brtan-pa, II, 785-6, 792. dPaṅ lo-tsā-ba, I, 345; II, 634, 838,
dPaṅ lo-tsā-ba bLo-gros brtan-pa, II, 534, 837-8.
dPa'-bas-byin, II, 452,
dPa'-bo rdo rje, I, 362; II, 552.
dPal, I, 302.
dPal bkra-śis dar-rgyas legs-pa'i rgyal-po, II, 824, 831, 837.
dPal sKyer-śiṅ ras-pa, II, 687.
dPal mKha'-spyod-pa, II, 991.
dPal mKha'-spyod dbaṅ-po, II, 545, 1042.
dPal'khor-btsan, I., 37, 46, 60,205.
dPal-gyi mgon, I, 37.
dPal-gyi rdo-rje, I, 53.
dPal-gyi Naṅ-tshul-ma, I, 100.
dPal-gyi 'byor-pa, I, 87.

dPal-gyi bzaṅ-po, II, 1044.
dPal-gyi 'od-zer, I, 241.
dPal-grub-pa, II, 1072.
dPal-mgon rdo-rje, II, 1089.
dPal rGya-mkhar-ba (dGyer-), II, 844.
dPal rGyal-ba grub-pa, II, 1025.
dPal sGam-po-pa, I, 73.
dPal Ṅag-gi dbaṅ-po, II, 412, 594.
dPal-lčam Čhos-'bar, I, 182.
dPal-čhen Gur-ba, II, 952.
dPal-čhen Go-bo, II, 409.
dPal-čhen rGwa-lo (dPal-čhen-pa), I, 226; II, 461.
dPal-čhen Čhos-yes, II, 565, 601, 603.
dPal-čhen rDor-gžon, I, 306.
dPal-čhen-pa, II, 734.
dPal-čhen 'od-po, I, 211.
dPal Čhos-kyi grags-pa, II, 412, 813.
dPal Čhos-kyi rgyal-mtshan, I, ii; II, 1090.
dPal-mčhog Dad-pa'i rdo-rje, I, 389.
dPal 'Jigs-med grags-pa, II, 788.
dPal-'dren, I, 277.
dPal rDo-rje bde-ma, II, 822, 1090.
dPal-ldan-gros, I, 81.
dPal-ldan rṄor-gžon, I, 81.
dPal-ldan-mčhog, II, 501.
dPal-ldan rDo-rje rgyal-mtshan, I, 155-6.
dPal-ldan-pa, I, 346.
dPal-ldan 'dzom-pa, II, 806.
dPal-ldan ye-śes, II, 790.
dPal-ldan seṅ-ge, I, 330, 374, 385; II, 785, 1052.
dPal-lde, I, 38, 205.
dPal-dbyaṅs, II, 659.
dPal-'bal, I, 177.
dPal-'bum, I, 217.
dPal-'byor, II, 812.
dPal-'byor rgya-mtsho-ba, II, 808.
dPal-'byor Don-grub-pa, II, 517, 551. (Gu-śri-).
dPal-'byor śes-rab, I, 81, 87.
dPal-sbas, I, 34, 226.
dPal Mar-me-mdzad ye-śes, I, 241.
dPal-mo, II, 1007, 1018, 1044.
dPal-brtsegs (Ka-ba-), I, 102, 331, 344.

dPal-brtsegs rgya-mtsho, II, 652.
dPal-brtsegs bzaṅ-po, II, 652.
dPal-tshul-pa (dPal-'byor tshul-khrims), II, 1072.
dPal-'dzin, I, 107, 168; II, 474, 795, 1046.
dPal-'dzin dga'-ba, II, 800.
dPal-bzaṅ-po, II, 632.
dPal-bzaṅs-pa, I, 321; II, 722, 749.
dPal-yon-pa, II, 1073.
dPal-legs, I, 95.
dPal Śri-ri-phug-pa, II, 607.
dPal Lha-ri-ba, II, 939.
dPal Amogha, II, 829.
dPe-med-'tsho, II, 764, 793, 800.
dPon mGon-po-rgyal, II, 581.
dPon-sgom, II, 975.
dPon Čhos-rgyal, I, 262.
dPon-nag rDo-rǰe, I, 128.
dPon Byaṅ-'od, II, 572.
dPon-zlos, II, 941.
dPon Rin-čhen-skyabs, II, 582-4.
dPon Saṅ-se, I, 198.
dPyal, I, 395-6; II, 659, 791.
dPyal, Kun-dga'-grags, I, 396.
dPyal Kun-dga' rdo-rǰe (Kun-rdor), I, 132, 376, 386, 394-7; II, 706, 1009.
dPyal lo-tsā-ba, II, 446, 727, 993.
dPyal-lo, II, 1055.
dPyal Čhos-bzaṅs, I, 379, 396; II, 519, 797.
dPyal 'Byuṅ-gnas rgyal-mtshan, I, 395.
dPyal-la Zar-ston, I, 396.
dPyal A-mo-gha, II, 797.
sPa, sPa-ri-ba, II, 670.
sPa rgya-mtsho, I, 323.
sPa-ba gLan-ston, II, 678.
sPaṅ, II, 883.
sPaṅ-dkar-ba, II, 696.
sPaṅ-kha Dar-čhuṅ, I, 354.
sPaṅ-gyaṅ bla-ma, I, 376.
sPaṅ-ston Čhos-'bar, II, 862.
sPaṅ-po-ba, II, 744.
sPaṅ-bzaṅs-pa Ba-ri sgom-čhen, II, 883.
sPaṅ 'Od-zer bla-ma, II, 564.
sPaṅs Mi-pham mgon-po, I, 171-3.

sPaṅs Saṅs-rgyas mgon-po, I, 171.
sPar-phu-ba, II, 563, 566-7, 664.
sPu-to-pa, II, 1086.
sPu-ston-'bar-thog, I, 355.
sPu-de guṅ-rgyal, I, 36.
sPu-hraṅs Nag-po śer-dad, II, 857.
sPu-hraṅs lo-čhuṅ, I, 380; II, 555, 581, 838, 871-2, 1009
sPu-hraṅs lo-čhen, I, 382.
sPur-sgom, I, 182.
sPen-phug, II, 739.
sPo-čhuṅ-ba Tshul-khrims śes-rab, I, 325.
sPo-to-ba, II, 615.
sPo-spo bKra-śis seṅ-ge, II, 601, 607ff.
sPo-ba sgom-čhen, II, 985.
sPo-bo Yon-tan seṅ-ge, I, 331.
sPo-ra dbOn-seṅ, II, 994.
sPo lo-tsā-ba, I, 376.
sPon-po-ba bla-ma A-skyabs, II, 611.
sPom-brag-pa, II, 483, 1007. ('Bri-rgyal Dam-pa Čhos-phyug).
sPos-skya-pa Seṅ-ge rin-čhen, II, 671.
sPos-sgaṅ-ba, II, 706.
sPos-wol-pa sTon-čhuṅ, I, 234.
sPyaṅ-tshaṅ-pa Seṅ-ge rgyal-mtshan, I, 355.
sPyan-sṅa, I, 235, 263, 286-8, 290-1, 293, 296, 299, 301, 305, 314, 319; II, (rje-) 571, 574-9, 580-1, 582-3, 604, 607, 609, 690, 692, 746, 958, 963
sPyan-sṅa Kun-dga' rgyal-mtshan, I, 92.
sPyan-sṅa Kun-rgyal, II, 964.
sPyan-sṅa Kun-rdor-ba, I, 92.
sPyan-sṅa Kun-spaṅs-pa, II, 587, 591, 687.
sPyan-sṅa Kun-blo-ba, I, 316.
sPyan-sṅa Kun-bzaṅ-pa, I, 316.
sPyan-sṅa Gaṅs-dkar-ba, II, 975.
sPyan-sṅa Grags-pa-ba, I, 283.
sPyan-sṅa Grags-pa byaṅ-čhub-pa, II, 787.
sPyan-sṅa Grags-pa bśes-gñen-pa, II, 717.
sPyan-sṅa Grags-byaṅ-ba, II, 587-8, 687.
sPyan-sṅa sGam-po-pa, II, 604.
sPyan-sṅa Ṅag-gi dbaṅ-phyug, II, 803.
sPyan-sṅa Čhos-kyi rgyal-po, II, 506.
sPyan-sṅa Čhos-kyi rdo-rje, I, 304.
sPyan-sṅa Čhos-kyi seṅ-ge, II, 642.
sPyan-sna Čhos-tshul-pa, II, 468.

sPyan-sña Čhos-bži-pa, II, 1040.
sPyan-sña sTag-śod-pa, II, 517.
sPyan-sña rDor-rgyal-ba, II, 658.
sPyan-sña rDor-rin-pa, II, 517.
sPyan-sña Nam-mkha' dpal-brtsegs rgyal-po, II, 642.
sPyan-sña rNal-'byor-pa, I, 180.
sPyan-sña dPal-čhen, II, 963-4.
sPyan-sña dPal-ldan bzań-po (Grags-pa blo-gros), II, 587.
sPyan-sña bLo-gros rgyal-mtshan, I, 62, 93, 317.
sPyan-sña bLo-gros rnam-dag-pa, I, 304.
sPyan-sña-ba Tshul-khrims-'bar, I, 236, 284.
sPyan sña 'Tshal-pa (Śākya rgyal-mtshan), II, 963-4.
sPyan-sña gŽon-'od-pa, I, 316.
sPyan-sña Ye-śes grags-pa bzań-po, I, 92.
sPyan-sña Yon-tan rgyal-mtshan, I, 93.
sPyan-sña Rin-čhen-ldan, II, 691.
sPyan-sña Rin-po-čhe, II, 601.
sPyan-sña Rin-po-čhe bSod-nams rgyal-mtshan bzań-po, II, 721.
sPyan-sña Rin-sań-ba, I, 309. (Rin-čhen seń-ge).
sPyan-sña Sańs-rgyas byań-čhub-pa, I, 316.
sPyan-sña gSer-thog-pa, II, 717.
sPyan-sña bSod-nams grags-pa (bSod-grags-pa), I, 92; II, 590, 643.
sPyan-sña bSod-nams bzań-po-ba, II, 588, 644.
sPyan-sña bSod-nams 'od-mdzes-pa, II, 658.
sPyan-śwa-re-bo, II, 932, 934.
sPyan-gsum-pa, III, 1053.
sPyi-ther-ba, II, 400.
sPyi-ther-ba Rin-tshul, I, 81.
sPyi-dpon-pa, II, 622.
sPyi-bo-nas skyes, I, 12.
sPyi-bo Lhas-pa, 314; II, 1063.
sPyi-bo Lhas-pa Byań-čhub-'od, II, 1044.
sPyi-lhas-pa, II, 641.
sPyil-dkar-ba, II, 973.
sPyil Jo-sras Žań-ba-skyabs, I, 187.
sPyil-po dBań-phyug-grags, II, 1044.
sPyil-bu-pa, I, 279; II, 1088. See Se sPyil-bu-pa.
sPra-gańs-pa, II, 601.
sPrin-gyi śugs-čan, I, 360.
sPrul-sku, I, 147-8.
sPrul-sku rgya-mtsho, I, 197.
sPrul-sku blo-ldan, II, 1040.

sPre'u-btul, I, 21.
Pha-rgan lDoṅ-ston, I, 265.
Pha-ǰo dbUs-pa, I, 188.
Pha-gtsaṅ-pa, I, 292.
Pha-rol gnon-ñid, I, 45.
Phag, I, 269, 270.
Phag-ston bSam-gtan bzaṅ-po, I, 344.
Phag-mo, II, 1007.
Phag-mo gru-pa (dPal-), I, 142, 148, 151, 158, 186, 218, 226, 270-1, 305, 328, 332, 334, 386, II, 441, 462, 474, 480, 552-569, 570-1, 574, 580, 590, 595-6, 612-5, 619, 620-1, 623-4, 643, 645-6, 649, 651-2, 655, 659, 663, 705-8, 710-11, 724, 737, 746, 814, 890-1, 905, 1008.
Pham-thiṅ-pa (Ṅag-gi dbaṅ-phyug grags-pa), I, 227-8, 380-1-2, 384, 395, II, 402, 851.
Phar-sgom, II, 1010.
Phu-gu-ru-pa, II, 727.
Phu čhuṅ-ba, I, 235, 263, 267ff, 288, 318.
Phu-čhuṅ-ba gŽon-nu rgyal-mtshan, I, 73, 236.
Phu-thaṅ Dar-dkon, I, 335
Phu-ri-ba, II, 686.
Phu-ri-ba dKon-mčhog rgyal-mtshan, II, 687.
Phu-ri-ba sTon-lo-čhe, II, 727.
Phug-ston, II, 998. (Ri-khrod-), II, 999.
Phug-pa mgon, II, 518-9.
Phug-pa rgyal, II, 518.
Phug-pa dar, II, 518.
Phug-pa-ba, II, 442.
Phur-pa skyabs, II, 722.
Phul-dmar-ba, II, 690.
Pho-brags, I, 148.
Pho-braṅ sdiṅs-pa, I, 269.
Pho-braṅ Ži-ba-'od, I, 354.
Pho-rog mDo-sde-mgon, II, 728.
Pho-rog-pa, II, 727.
Phog-pa, II, 708.
Phoṅ-mdo-ba, I, 321; II, 616-7.
Phya-dar ston-pa, I, 258, 262.
Phyā-pa, I, 298, 332, 334, 343, 349; II, 465, 474, 555, 566, 734. Phyā-pa Čhos-kyi seṅ-ge, I, 186, 329.
Phya-ru 'dul-'dzin, II, 726.
Phya-ru-ba Seṅ-ge-dpal, II, 773.
Phyag-na, I, 212, 219, 384, 395; II, 404, 843, 851, 855, 857-8.

Phyag-zuṅs-skyabs, II, 866.
Phyar-čhuṅ-ba, II, 913-5, 921, 947.
Phyar-čhen, II, 913, 925, 947, 977. (Phyar-čhen-pa).
Phyas-sor-pa, II, 465.
Phyi-luṅ-ba rGya-pa, I, 314.
Phyug-po sGaṅ-dkar-ba, I, 216.
Phyug-mo dpal-le, II, 635.
Phyogs-bdag, I, 13, 15.
Phyogs-grol, II, 800, 803.
Phyogs-glaṅ, I, 346.
Phyogs-pa, II, 779.
Phyog-las rnam-rgyal, I, 329; II, 777-80.
Phyog-las rnam-par rgyal-ba (Bo-doṅ paṇ-čhen), II, 1017.
Phra-ston Žig-po, II, 1034.
Phra-la riṅ-mo, I, 160 (ācārya-).
Phreṅ-ba-čan, I, 12.
'Phags-mčhog-pa, II, 704.
'Phags-mčhog bSod-nams-dpal, II, 703.
'Phags-pa, I, 211, 216, 218, 234-7, 297, 307, 366; II, 420, (gSer-sdiṅs-pa), 421, 423-3, 425, 464, 479, 589-90. 'Gro-mgon 'Phags-pa, II, 581-2, 628, 631-2, 649, 651, 750, 784-5, 791, 894-5, 1088.
'Phags-pa skyes-po, I, 8, 16.
'Phags-pa lČe-sgom, II, 738.
'Phags-pa gDan-sa-ba dPal-bzaṅ-pa, II, 830.
'Phags-pa Yon-tan rgya-mtsho, I, 306.
'Phags-tshul lo-tsā-ba, II, 1023.
'Phags-'od, I, 356, 365, 374; II, 422-3.
'Phags-'od-pa, II, 794, 866.
'Phaṅs Byaṅ-brtson, I, 126.
'Phaṅs dBaṅ-phyug rgyal-mtshan, I, 74.
'Phan, I, 127.
'Phan-mo, II, 919.
'Phan-yul-mdo Thod-lo-pa, II, 728
'Phan-yul-pa rGya, I, 285.
'Phel-gyag-pa bSam-gtan lhun-grub, II, 886.
'Phyar-sToṅ-nag-mo, I, 81.
'Phraṅ-kha Jo-btsun, II, 883.
'Phraṅ-kha Ber-čhuṅ, I, 252, 263, 322.
Ba-dkar 'Briṅ-ston, II, 1004.
Ba-čhar-ba, II, 409.
Ba-tsho ras-pa, II, 1088.
Ba-ra sgom-čhen, II, 1005.

Ba-ri, II, 942, 1020-1.
Ba-ri (Rin-čhen-grags), I, 73.
Ba-ri sPyil-dkar-ba, II, 687.
Ba-ri-ba, II, 446, 727, 909, 973-4.
Ba-ri lo-tsā-ba, I, 73, 186, 211, 293; II, 405, 407, 469, 472, 556, 1024, 1048.
Ba-reg Thos-pa-dga', I, 376; II, 857.
Ba-laṅ-gnas, I, 13, 16.
Ba-lam-pa, I, 292.
Ba-lam-pa Rin-se, II, 1043.
Ba-śi'i gNas-brtan, I, 61.
Ba-so-ba, II, 1080.
Bag-čhags rješ-med, II, 943.
Bag-ston-pa, II, 1024.
Bag-ston gŽon-tshul, I, 396; II, 1007, 1043.
Baṅ-ston, I, 358, 262.
Baṅ-ston Śes-rab rin-čhen, I, 344.
Baṅ-ra-ba, I, 292.
Baṅ Rin-čhen rdo-rje, I, 63.
Baṅ-so-ba, II, 445, 972.
Ban-kar-ba 'Jam-dpal bzaṅ-po-ba, II, 517, 551.
Ban-čhen sKyas-bu, I, 272.
Ban-de-ba Rin-byaṅ, I, 269.
Ban-blon mGo-yags, II, 621.
Ban-blon-'bar-po, II, 610.
Bar-thaṅ-pa, I, 374.
Bar-'brog-pa, II, 727.
Bar-pa, I, 91.
Bar-pu-pa, I, 333.
Bar-bza', II, 547.
Bal-pu, I, 14.
Bal-po, I, 210.
Bal-po 'Jig-rten, II, 861-4.
Bal-po Pe-ña-ba, II, 1008.
Bal-po dBaṅ-rdor, II, 1001, 1004.
Bal-bu goṅ-pa, II, 601, 603.
Bal-bu-čan, I, 4.
Bi-ru-pa (Vi-rū-pa), II, 613, 869.
Bu, II, 794.
Bu-ston Kha-čhe, I, 197, 308, 355, 374.
Bu-ston, I, 2, 82, 102-3, 149, 309, 366, 379, 385-6, 410, 417, 423, 534, 585
705, 755, 782, 812, 833, 996, 1075, 1085.
Bu-ston Grags-seṅ, I, 335.

Bu-ston Rin-po-čhe, I, 60, 150, 217, 304, 331, 338, 345, 374, 389, 396, 532, 584, 658, 711, 750, 754, 756, 781, 793, 800, 866, 104', 1086. See Bu-ston, Bu-ston Kha-čhe, Bu Rin-po-čhe, Bu-ston Rin-čhen-grub.
Bu Rin-po-čhe, I, 335, 356, 366, 379, 385, 410, 422, 425, 763, 1051.
Bu-ston Rin-čhen-grub, I, xx, 81, 158; II, 417, 425.
Bu-ston Seṅ-ge-'od, II, 773.
Bug-pa-čan, I, 96.
Bur-sgom, II, 661, 735.
Bur-sgom Nag-po, II, 439, 556.
Bur-pa Yul-sman, I, 314.
Bul-ba-pa, I, 292.
Be'u, I, 45 6.
Be'u kLu'i ye-śes, II, 1003.
Be-re sMyon-pa, II, 998. See sMyon-pa Be-re.
Benda-pa, II, 400.
Ber-re, I, 110.
Bo dGe-bsñen, I, 1020.
Bo-doṅ Rin-rtse (Rin-čhen rtse-mo), I, 335, 345; II, 699. Bo-doṅ Rin-po-čhe, II, 783.
Bod-rgyal-ba, II, 799.
Bod-čhuṅ-ba (Lha-rje-), II, 616.
Bon-sgom Do-pa, I, 121.
Bon-ston Śer-bzaṅ, I, 330.
Bon-gnas-pa, II, 468.
Bos-ris-ba, II, 654.
Bya, I, 269, 270.
Bya bKra-śis dar-rgyas, II, 1088.
Bya bKra-śis dar-rgyas legs-pa'i rgyal-po Phyogs-thams-čad-las rnam-par rgyal-ba dbaṅ-po'i sde, II, 1090.
Bya lKug-pa-dpal, II, 1088.
Bya-khaṅ-pa bSod-nams rin-čhen, II, 418.
Bya-rgyus-pa, I, 273.
Bya-sgom Grol-sgom, II, 462.
Bya Ṅur-mo, I, 275.
Bya mṄa'-bdag, II, 1088.
Bya-čhen-po, I, 154.
Bya 'Čhad-kha-pa, I, 273ff, 276-7, 282.
Bya Jo-sras, II, 1088.
Bya-ston 'Čhad-kha-pa, I, 273.
Bya-ston kLu-grub, II, 985.
Bya-ston rDo-rje-grags, I, 125.
Bya-'dul, I, 298, 306; II, 409, 441, 555. (Bya-'dul-pa).

Bya 'Dul-'dzin, I, 80.
Bya 'Dul-ba 'dzin-pa, I, 322.
Bya-sder-ba, I, 345.
Bya Nor-bu rgya-mtsho, II, 1089.
Bya-yul dkar-mo, I, 335.
Bya-yul-pa, I, 73, 99, 286-90, 292, 295-8, 304-5, 311, 315, 318; II, 438, 453, 468, 555, 613.
Bya-yul-pa čhen-po, I, 285.
Bya-yul-pa Sańs-rgyas sgom-pa, I, 308.
Bya-yul Rin-po-čhe bLo-gros rnam-dag, I, 310.
Bya Rin-čhen, II, 1088.
Bya-luń-pa Byań-thań ras-pa, II, 601.
Bya-lo Zla-ba 'od-zer, I, 407.
Bya Śa-ka, II, 1087.
Bya-sa, II, 558.
Byań-grags, I, 273, 286,
Byań-gliń-pa, II, 686, 786.
Byań-rgyal-ba, II, 536, 590, 592, 717.
Byań-čhub-grags, I, 272. Byań-čhub grags-pa, II, 1072.
Byań-čhub dge-mdzes, I, 314, 317.
Byań-čhub mgon-po, II, 537.
Byań-čhub rgya-mtsho, II, 550, 646-7, 696-7. (sTag-luń čhos-rje-).
Byań-čhub rgyal-dbań, II, 1072.
Byań-čhub-sgron, II, 958.
Byań-čhub dńos-grub (Lho La-yag-pa-), II, 470.
Byań-čhub-mčhog, II, 696.
Byań-čhub-dar, I, 373.
Byań-čhub 'dre-bkol, I, 203.
Byań-čhub rdo-rje, II, 601.
Byań-čhub rnam-rgyal, II, 830.
Byań-čhub-dpal, I, 34, 98; II, 1025, 1071-2. Byań-čhub-dpal (sPre'u-žiń Rin-po-čhe-), II, 450.
Byań-čhub dpal-ldan, II, 970.
Byań-čhub dpal-pa, II, 411, 413.
Byań-čhub-dpal-bzań-po, II, 717, 1071.
Byań-čhub-dpal-bzań, II, 722.
Byań-čhub-'bar, II, 1015.
Byań-čhub 'byuń-gnas, I, 86.
Byań-čhub rtse-mo (lo-tsā-ba), II, 778-9, 787-8.
Byań-čhub tshul-khrims, II, 1044.
Byań-čhub gžon-nu, II, 696.
Byań-čhub bzań-po, I, 224, 382, 384; II, 970, 1072.

Byaṅ-čhub-'od, I, x, 37, 86, 244, 262, 278, 305, 374. (Lha-btsun).
Byaṅ-čhub ye-śes, I, 330; II, 910.
Byaṅ-čhub yon-tan, I, 196; II, 696.
Byaṅ-čhub rin-čhen, I, 262, 277, 339; II, 1025.
Byaṅ-čhub seṅ-ge, I, 84; II, 703-4.
Byaṅ-čhub sems-dpa', I, 96; II, 741.
Byaṅ-čhen 'Jam-riṅs-pa, I, 374.
Byaṅ-čhen-pa bSod-'phel, II, 1024.
Byaṅ Dar-ma ratna, I, 288.
Byaṅ-rdor, I, 216; II, 775.
Byaṅ Ṅa-bza'-'phred-gsol, II, 964.
Byaṅ-pa, II, 801.
Byaṅ-pa Ta'i-dban-pa, II, 778.
Byaṅ-pa dbOn-sgom, II, 928.
Byaṅ-dpal-pa, I, 98.
Byaṅ-bla, I, 291.
Byaṅ-rtse (Byaṅ-čhub rtse-mo, lo-čhen), I, 345; II, 585-6, 636, 639.
Byaṅ-yes, II, 716, 1013.
Byaṅ-ran-stan-pa, I, 376.
Byaṅ-rin, I, 216.
Byaṅ-seṅ, I, 276, 301; II, 571, 623, 1016.
Byaṅ-sems rgyal-ba ye-śes, I, 153; II, 756, 772, 775. Byaṅ-sems rgyal-yes, II, 526, 634, 775, 783.
Byaṅ-sems čhu-sgom, II, 1006.
Byaṅ-sems-pa, II, 775.
Byaṅ-sems zla-rgyal, II, 1024, 1055.
Byaṅ-sems bsod-grags, II, 1073.
Byams-čhos-pa Byaṅ-čhub rgyal-mtshan, II, 518.
Byams-pa (Sum-ston ras-pa), II, 991.
Byams-pa (of Čhos-'khor-gliṅ), I, 308, 341.
Byams-pa-gliṅ-pa, II, 811, 814-5.
Byams-pa seṅ-ge, II, 1043.
Byams-pa'i blo-gros, I, 262.
Byar-khaṅ-pa, I, 320
Byar-pa Rin-gžon, I, 269.
Byar-po ba, II, 661.
Byar-po-ba Ra-śer-snaṅ, II, 439.
Byi-ba hab-śa, I, 219.
Byi-gza' rgyas-čhuṅ, I, 300.
Bye-skyid-pa, I, 345.
Bye-ma ras-pa, II, 720
Bra-bo čhen-po, II, 956.

Brag-dkar-ba, II, 655.
Brag-dkar-mo-ba, I, 147; II, 477.
Brag-dkar-po-ba, II, 706.
Brag-dkar śes-yes, II, 716.
Brag-dgon-pa, II, 611.
Brag-steṅs-pa, I, 354.
Brag-ston, I, 262.
Brag-nag-pa Čhos-skyoṅ-dpal, II, 774.
Brag-nag-pa (gŽon-nu bsod-nams), I, 396.
Brag-pa, I, 321. See bSod-nams dpal-ldan.
Brag-pa dKon-grags, II, 857.
Brag-pa čhen-po, II, 855.
Brag-pa Rin-čhen, II, 583.
Brag-po-čhe-pa rDo-rje-dpal, II, 751-2, 991.
Brag-'bur-ba (Rin-čhen-'bum), II, 864, 894-5.
Brag-dmar rDo-rje phur-pa, I, 81.
Brag-rtsa-pa, II, 468.
Braṅ-ti, I, 382; II, 866.
Braṅ-ti Dar-ma sñiṅ-po, I, 345.
Braṅ-ti bLo-gros-dbaṅ, II, 857.
Braṅ-pa, I, 376.
Braṅ-śoṅ-ba, I, 314.
Bra'o-pa, II, 728.
Bra'o 'Bum-la-bar, II, 857.
Bra'o lo-tsā, II, 991.
Bran-ka, II, 625.
Bran-ka Jo-btsun, I, 264.
Brab-śi-gza' dGe-sum khro-mo, II, 610.
Bru-śa rgyal-bu, II, 1000.
Bru-śa Rigs-'dzin, II, 575-6.
Bru-śa bSod-nams seṅ-ge, I, 333.
Bre-ston 'Bum-lha-'bar, I, 96.
Bre-bo-ma, I, 12.
Bre-bo-zas, I, 12.
bLa-skyabs rdo-rje, I, 171.
bLa-gaṅ-pa, II, 610.
bLa-čhuṅ 'od-zer, II, 871, 906.
bLa-čhen, I, 215.
bLa-čhen-pa, II, 592, 1024.
bLa-čhen po, I, 65-6; II, 649.
bLa-čhen-po dGoṅs-pa-gsal (rab-gsal), I, 167; II, 1062.
bLa-'dos, I, 138.

bLa-ma dGe-sloṅ, I, 362. See La-ba-pa.
bLa-ma rgyal-mtshan, I, 133; II 546, 551.
bLa-ma Dum-pa, II, 584, 636, 658, 774, 787, 794, 864.
bLa-ma Nag-po, II, 520.
bLa-ma-pa, II, 495-6.
bLa-ma Ye-śes, I, 329.
bLo-grags, II, 405.
bLo-gros, II, 837.
bLo-gros-grags, I, 81.
bLo-gros grags-pa, II, 523.
bLo-gros rgya-mtsho, I, 345.
bLo-gros rgyal-mtshan, I, 156, 214, 317 (sPyan-sṅa-); bLo-gros rgyal-mtshan-pa, II, 800; (bLa-ma-) 1007; 1072; 1073 (of dGe-'dun-sgaṅ). (Gu-śrī-), II, 509.
bLo-gros rgyal-mtshan dpal-bzaṅ-po, II, 548.
bLo-gros 'ǰigs-med, I, 317.
bLo-gros sñiṅ-po, II, 837.
bLo-gros brtan-pa, I, 310, 329; II, (lo-tsā-ba-), 527, 1080 (Čhos-rǰe-).
bLo-gros-dpal, II, (lo-tsā-ba), 776, 995, 1059.
bLo-gros dpal-rin-pa, I, 344.
bLo-gros 'phel-ba, II, 413.
bLo-gros-'bar, I, 329.
bLo-gros 'byuṅ-gnas, I, 331.
bLo-gros mtshuṅs-med, II, 524-5, 532.
bLo-gros bzaṅ-po, I, 5; II, 723.
bLo-gros'-od (Lha-), I, 281-2.
bLo-gros ye-śes, I, 280.
bLo-gros rin-čhen, II, 484.
bLo-gros seṅ-ge, I, 308, 329; II, 498, 671-2.
bLo-čhen, I, 217.
bLo-čhen Saṅs-rgyas, II, 1046.
bLo-brtan, I, 344.
bLo-ston, II, 712.
bLo-ldan (bstan-skyoṅ), I, 73.
bLo-ldan śes-rab, I, 70, 124, 341, 347, 396; II, 1054. See rṄog lo-tsā-ba.
bLo-brag-pa, I, 329.
bLo-bzaṅ, I, 15, 16; (of Čhos-'khor-gliṅ), I, 308-9.
bLo-bzaṅ grags-pa, I, 283 (mahā-upādhyāya-); (Tsoṅ-kha-pa), II, 589, 592, 610, 1073.
bLo-bzaṅ-grags-pa-dpal, II, 1079. See Tsoṅ-kha-pa.
bLo-bzaṅ grags-pa'i dpal, I, 81, 272; II, 1073. See Tsoṅ-kha-pa.
bLo-bzaṅ Mi-'gyur rdo-rje, I, xxi.

bLo-bzaṅs, I, 341; II, 1060.
bLo-bzaṅs-pa, II, 724.
bLo-rin, I, 341.
bLo-sems-'tsho, I, 38,
bLo-gsal-ba, I, 83.
dBa' Saṅ-śi, I, 41.
dBa' gSal-snaṅ, I, 38, 41.
dBaṅ, I, 302, 376.
dBaṅ Kun-dga' legs-pa, I, 214.
dBaṅ Grags-pa rgyal-mtshan, I, 152, 217.
dBaṅ-mgon, I, 110.
dBaṅ-ṅe, I, 110; II, 861.
dBaṅ-ston dKon-mčhog rgyal-po, I, 208.
dBaṅ-phyug-grags, I, 269, 344; II, 616.
dBaṅ-phyug-mgon (Žaṅ-), I, 254.
dBaṅ-phyug rgyal-po, I, 331.
dBaṅ-phyug rgyal-ba, II, 790.
dBaṅ-phyug-lčam, II, 918.
dBaṅ-phyug čhen-po'i sde I, 5.
dBaṅ-phyug-lde, I, 325, 346.
dBaṅ-phyug-dpal, I, 48.
dBaṅ-phyug blo-gros, II, 1001.
dBaṅ-phyug-'bar, I, 265. (sTon-pa-).
dBaṅ-phyug-'bum, I, 133; II, 413.
dBaṅ-phyug brtson-'grus (Lo-ras-pa), II, 673
dBaṅ-phyug gžon-nu, I, 240, 302. See Saṅs-rgyas ǰo-bo.
dBaṅ-phyug ye-śes, I, 280.
dBaṅ-phyug rin-čhen, II, 1088.
dBaṅ-phyug legs-pa, II, 522.
dBaṅ-phyug śes-rab, II, 722, 1059
dBaṅ-ba, II, 610.
dBaṅ-brtson, I, 217.
dBaṅ Ratna, I, 214.
dBaṅ-rin, I, 373; II, 520, (dBaṅ-rin-pa), 782.
dBaṅ-śe-pa, II, 1072.
dBaṅ-seṅ, II, 617
dBaṅ-bsod, II, 584.
dBas rGyal-ba ye-śes, I, 345.
dBas We-na A-dar, II, 553.
dBas Śākya rdo-rje, I, 284.
dbU-rgyan-pa, I, 341.
dbU-ltebs, I, 180.

dbU-dum-brtsan' — U-'i dum-brtan, I, xix.
dbU-ma-pa, I, 99; II, 524, (bla-ma-), 703, 744, 1049.
dbU-ma-pa Śer-'bum, I, 335; II; 773.
dbU-rtse-ba, II, 488.
dbU-ri-pa (Lo-ras-pa), II, 677-8.
dbU-se, I, 299; II, 622.
dbU-gtso-bar-sdiṅs-pa, II, 688.
dbUs-khaṅ-pa, II, 895.
dbUs ston-čhuṅ, I, 314.
dbUs-pa, II, 678.
dbUs-pa Groṅ-po-čhe, I, 208.
dbUs-pa rGwa-sum, I, 364.
dbUs-pa sGro-ston, II, 914.
dbUs-pa J̌o-bsod, I, 131.
dbUs-pa bLo-gsal, I, 337-8. (Byaṅ-čhub ye-śes).
dbUs-pa Śes-rab rdo-rje, I, 397.
dbUs-pa Sa-'thor, I, 120.
dbEn-pa bSod seṅ, I, 396.
dbOn, II, 685, 715.
dbOn-grags-pa, II, 547.
dbOn J̌o-'phan, II, 697.
dbOn-ston sKyer-sgaṅ-pa, II, 737.
dbOn-ston Rin-čhen sgaṅ-pa, II, 1070.
dbOn-ston Rin-po-čhe, I, 315-6.
dbOn Thuṅ-ri-pa, II, 581.
dbOn-po, II, 652, 655.
dbOn-po dKon-mčhog-bzaṅ, II, 747.
dbOn-po Khri-brtan seṅ-ge, I, 82.
dbOn-po Čhos-kyi gzi-brjid, II, 973.
dbOn-po Čhos-dbaṅ, I, 80.
dbOn-po Čhos-sdiṅs-pa, II, 999. (Dar-ma śes-rab).
dbOn-po J̌o-dkon, II, 899.
dbOn-po dPal-ldan-grags, II, 1040.
dbOn po dBaṅ-phyug gžon-nu, II, 693.
dbOn-po 'Byuṅ-gnas rgyal-mtshan, I, 94.
dbOn-po gŽon-nu bzaṅ-po, II, 583.
dbOn-po Rin grub, II, 694.
dbOn-po Śar-gliṅ-pa, II, 579. See Rin-po-čhe Grags bsod-pa,
dbOn-po Śes-rab dbaṅ-pa, II, 955.
dbOn-po bSod-nams bla-ma, II, 997.
dbOn-po Lha-dge, II, 715.
dbOn-po A-dpal, II, 520.

dbOn Bi-či, I, 67.
dbOn-'bum, II, 692.
dbOn-ras Dar-ma sen-ge, II, 671, 683.
dbOn Rin-po-čhe, II, 517, 577, 601, 607, 609, 648, 975.
dbOn Ŝer-'byun, II, 601, 604.
dbOn Ŝes-rab-rgyal, II, 579.
dbOn Sen-ge-rgyal, I, 147.
dbYar Ñi-ma brtson-'grus, I, 336.
dbYig-gñen, I, 55, 344, 346.
dbYig-than ston-pa, I, 305.
dBran-ston Phul-dmar-pa, II, 727.
'Ba-sgom Dig-ma, I, 121.
'Ba'-ra-ba, II, 692-3, 748, 752, 896.
'Ba'-ra-ba rGyal-mtshan-dpal, II, 895.
'Ba'-ri Čhos-sen, II, 524.
'Ba'-ril, I, 292.
'Ba'-rom-pa, II, 462.
'Ba'-le, I, 292.
'Ban, I, 127, 345, 379.
'Ban dKon-mčhog rdo-rje, I, 376.
'Ban Gan-rgyal, II, 911, 977.
'Ban-dha-phug-pa, II, 563.
'Ban-po Čhos-dban, II, 532.
'Ban-po Myan Čhos-kyi sen-ge, II, 988.
'Ban-po bTsun-śāk, II, 533.
'Bab-rom-pa (Dar-ma dban-phyug), II, 469-70.
'Bar-ston Ŝes-rab grags-pa, I, 184.
'Bar-sde, I, 37.
'Bar-ma, II, 916.
'Bal, II, 737.
'Bal-sgom Phyag-na, II, 735.
'Bal-tsha sTag-del-pa, II, 482.
'Bal Tshad-ma-pa, I, 332, 385; II, 740.
'Bu-ban Gans-pa, II, 601.
'Bum-rgod, I, 166.
'Bum-rgyan, II, 964.
'Bum-bstan, I, 166.
'Bum-dpal, I, 166.
'Bum-phrag gsum-pa (brTan-skyon), I, 325, 345-6; II, 407, 789, 1009.
'Bum'bar, I, 166.
'Bum-me, I, 319.
'Be-dkar, I, 273.

'Be sPyan-ras-gzigs, I, 300.
'Be-mo Pad-ma-sgron, II, 733.
'Be-mon-bu čhuṅ-ba, I, 269.
'Be Saṅs-rgyas sgom-pa, I, 306.
'Bon-ston lčags-skyu, I, 125.
'Bom, II, 566.
'Byuṅ-gnas seṅ-ge, II, 728.
'Byuṅ-tshul, I, 96-7.
'Byuṅ-śes, I, 96-7.
'Byuṅ-seṅ, II, 521.
'Braṅ-ri-ba, II, 829.
'Bras, 'Bras-mo-pa, II, 670-1.
'Bras-dkar-ba, II, 894.
'Bri-khuṅ gLiṅ-pa, II, 577.
'Bri-khuṅ gČuṅ Rin-po-čhe, I, 319.
'Bri-khuṅ Čhos-rje, II, 433, 518.
'Bri-khuṅ-pa, I, 264, 387; II, 457-8, 545, 552, 562, 570, 601, 608-9, 625, 627, 655, 681, 724, 741, 746, 829, 952, 954, 972, 975, 1070 1089.
'Bri-sgom gLiṅ-kha-pa, II, 442.
'Bri-sgom Don-grub (gYe-čhen-mo-ba......), II, 439.
'Bri-sgom yaṅ-legs, II, 435.
'Bri-sgom ras-pa, II, 435.
'Bri rDzi-dkar-ba, II, 1085.
'Bri-ri-ba Śākya-'od, II, 715.
'Briṅ, I, 77; II, 1085.
'Briṅ Čha-ru-ba, II, 931.
'Briṅ mČhams-žaṅ, I, 345.
'Briṅ-ston, I, 88.
'Briṅ-gza'-ma Thod-dkar, I, 46. —'Bri-bza' Thod-dkar.
'Brin-mtshams-ma sPa-tshab-gza', II, 435.
'Brin Ye-śes yon-tan, I, 62, 324.
'Bre, I, 127, 330, 332, 379.
'Bre Ko-de-luṅ-pa, I, 266.
'Bre Kha-skyog-pa, I, 376.
'Bre Khro-čhuṅ-pa, I, 110.
'Bre rGyal-ba'i blo-gros, I, 104.
'Bre čhen-po, I, 80, 93-4.
'Bre-ston Lha-dga', II, 430.
'Bre sPal-gyi blo-gros, I, 104.
'Bre Śes-rab-'bar, I, 326, 376; II, 748, 1009.
'Bre A-tsar Sa-le, I, 156.
'Bro, II, 762-3, 785, 792, 838.

'Bro-sgom, II, 910.
'Bro-sgom bSod-nams byaṅ-čhub, II, 928.
'Bro-stag-snaṅ-khri-gsum-rǰe, I, 63.
'Bro-ldog-gza' Gyu-gu-lčam, II, 571.
'Bro-dmar-yu, II, 462.
'Bro Zla-'od, II, 912.
'Bro-gza' Di-paṃ, I, 104.
Bro lo-tsā-ba, II, 755, 760, 766, 784.
'Bro Śes-rab-grags, II, 837.
'Bro-seṅ-dkar-stod-pa Ye-śes bla-ma, I, 78.
'Bro-seṅ-dkar Śākya-'od, I, 72.
'Brog, I, 72, 262.
'Brog čhuṅ-pa, I, 612.
'Brog J̌o-sras, II, 857-8.
'Brog J̌o-sras rDo-rǰe-'bar, II, 857, 859.
'Brog-mi, I, 72, 112, 205-10, 215, 360, 399.
'Brog-mo, II, 540.
'Broṅ-zi-legs, I, 37.
'Broṅs-stoṅs-pa, I, 269.
'Brom, I, 72, 186, 251-4, 263, 282, 284, 326-7; II, 844, 924, 1086.
'Brom-ston, I, xiv, 61-2, 89, 93, 205, 261-7, 344; II, 455, 844, 984, 1002.
'Brom-ston-pa rGyal-ba'i byuṅ-gnas, I, 262, 321.
'Brom-ston Rin-čhen śes-rab, II, 450.
'Brom Do-pa ston-čhuṅ, I, 208.
'Brom-'dul, I, 285.
'Brom-pa, I, 74, 387.
'Brom Ye-śes-'bar, II, 943.
'Brom Rin-čhen-'bar, I, 192.
rBa-sgom bSod-nams rgyal-mtshan, II, 1000-2, 1005.
sBa, I, 77; II, 1085.
sBa-goṅ Ye-śes gyuṅ-druṅ, I, 66.
sBa dGe-mthoṅ, I, 117.
sBa-sgom, I, 174-5, 177-8; II, 1084.
sBa-sgom Ye-śes byaṅ-čhub, I, 175, 182.
sBa-ston, II, 850.
sBa-'dul, I, 273.
sBa-mo Čhos-brtson, II, 406.
sBa Wa-ba-čan, II, 406.
sBa-btsun bLo-gros 'byuṅ-gnas, I, 62.
sBa-yags me-po, I, 301.
sBa Rakṣita, I, 171.
sBa Ratna, I, v, 34.

sBa-ras, II, 491.
sBa-reg, I, 378.
sBa gSal-snaṅ, I, v; II, 789.
sBal-ti, I, 300; II, 602.
sBal-ti J̌o-sras, I, 79.
sBal-bu Dor-la, I, 184.
sBas, I, 300.
sBas-sgom, II, 613.
sBas-ti, I, 319.
sBas rNal-'byor mgon-po, I, 302.
sBas-pa sTon-gžon, I, 280-1, 307.
sBas bLo-gros dbaṅ-phyug, I, 192.
sBug Ye-rgyal, II, 406, 409.
sBo-čhuṅ, I, 77.
sBo-čhuṅ Tshul-khrims 'byuṅ-gnas, I, 78.
sBom-brag-pa, II, 485.
sByin-pa seṅ-ge, I, 345.
sBra, II, 716.
Bha-lde, I, 37.
Bha-ru, II, 1029.
Bha-ro, II, 447.
Bha-ro Phyag-rdum, I, 377.
Bhe-ston rDo-rje śes-rab, I, 74.
Bhu-su-ku, I, 171 (mČhog-gi byaṅ-čhub).
Ma-'gag-pa, I, 12.
Ma-gčig, I, 220-2, 230; II, 932-3, 988-9-90, 992.
Ma-gčig Čhos-sgron, II, 687.
Ma-gčig Driṅ-čan zur-mo, I, 171.
Ma-gčig sprul-sku, II, 743.
Ma-gčig Byaṅ-pa-mo, I, 214.
Ma-gčig Ža-ma, I, 124, 167, 219, 235, 239; II, 436, 557.
Ma-gčig Yaṅ-dgos, II, 440.
Ma-gčig Re-ma, II, 711.
Ma-gčig Labs-sgron-ma, I, 97, 225; II, 481, 706, 811, 982, 984. (Ma-gčig Labs-sgron).
Ma-gčig Saṅs-rgyas re-ma, II, 1039.
Ma-gčig Oṅ-ǰo, II, 443, 446.
Ma-ǰo mČhod-gnas-ma, II, 982,
Ma-ti paṇ-čhen, II, 776.
Ma-thaṅ-pa, I, 271.
Ma-thog Byaṅ-'bar, I, 120, 376.
Ma-thog-pa, I, 120.

Ma-drel-ba, II, 482.
Ma-bdun-pa, II, 687-8. (mDo-bo-čhe-pa).
Ma-ma gYuṅ-druṅ bkra-śis, I, 112.
Ma-žaṅ, I, 40-2.
Ma-śi-ba, I, 22.
Ma-saṅs, I, 210.
Ma-hā-lhun-po, I, 141.
Ma-he-bhā-ro, I, 392-4.
Mag-pa gÑan-čhuṅ, I, 269.
Maṅ-skyid, II, 711.
Maṅ-gur-ba, II, 651. (Maṅgala guru).
Maṅ-naṅ-pa, I, 355.
Maṅ-pos bkur-ba, I, 3.
Maṅ-gza' Dar-skyid, II, 664.
Maṅ-'or Byaṅ-čhub śes-rab, I, 328; II, 837.
Maṅ-ra, I, 266, 288.
Maṅ-ra sGom-pa, I, 285.
Maṅ-ra 'Byuṅ-gnas rgyal-mtshan, I, 322.
Maṅ-ra Seṅ-ge rgyal-mtshan, I, 364-5; II, 418.
Maṅ-sroṅ, I, 46.
Maṅ-sroṅ maṅ-btsan, I, xix, xx, 37, 49.
Mañju-gliṅ-pa, I, 231.
Man-mkhar-ba, II, 557.
Man-luṅs guru, I, 307; II, 425.
Man-luṅs-pa, II, 640, 780, 790, 838, 1050.
Mar-gul guru, II, 644.
Mar-čhuṅ Lho-brag-pa, I, 159, 160.
Mar-ston, II, 677.
Mar-ston Tshul-khrims 'byuṅ-gnas, II, 444.
Mar-ston gYaṅ-'bar, II, 797.
Mar-thuṅ Dad-pa śes-rab, I, 71, 328.
Mar-pa (Dar-ma dbaṅ-phyug, Čhos-kyi blo-gros), I, 72, 88, 95, 97, 123, 208-9, 226, 364; II, 399-433, 477, 604, 606, 724-5, 728, 765, 814, 833, 843-4, 1086.
Mar-pa mGo-yags, II, 401, 403.
Mar-pa Čhom-thaṅ-pa, II, 615.
Mar-pa Čhos-kyi blo-gros, II, 417.
Mar-pa Čhos-kyi dbaṅ-phyug, I, 163.
Mar-pa Do-pa (Mar-Do, Mar-pa Do-pa Čhos-kyidbaṅ-phyug of Yar-'brog), I, 73, 165, 167, 350, 380, 383-6; II, 445, 910. 1009
Mar-pa rDor-yes, I, 334-5.
Mar-pa Phug-pa, I, 319,

Mar-pa Bya-ze-ba, I, 234; II, 403.
Mar-pa dBaṅ-phyug 'od-zer, I, 399.
Mar-pa 'Bar-ba rgyal-mtshan, II, 444.
Mar-pa Mon-nag, II, 414-5.
Mar-pa lo-tsā (Mar-lo), II, 414-5, 1026-6.
Mar-pa lo-tsā-ba, II, 1099.
Mar-pa Śes rab-'od, I, 126, 171.
Mar-pa Seṅ-rdzi, I, 228.
Mar-pa bSod-rin, I, 376.
Mar-pa Lha-sñiṅ, II, 569.
Mar-pa Lho-brag-pa, I, 389, 399; II, 414.
Mar-me-mdzad bzaṅ-po, I, 371-2.
Mar-yul bLo-ldan, II, 453.
Mal Ka-ba-čan (Ka-ba-čan-pa), I, 306; II, 881, 888-9, 890-2, 896.
Mal-gyo, I, 380.
Mal-gyo lo-tsā-ba bLo-gros-grags, I, 382; II, 1051.
Mal-gro bKra-śis sgaṅ-pa, I, 314
Ma-gro 'Dul-'dzin, II, 1055.
Mal-gro-ba gLaṅ-sgom, I, 269.
Mal Dar-ma-mgon, II, 888.
Mal 'Dul-'dzin-pa, II, 409.
Mal Nag-mo, II, 409.
Mal-spos-ka-ba sMon-lam-btsan, II, 888.
Mal-byed tshaṅ-pa, I, 144, 147.
Mal brTson-'grus bla-ma, II, 929.
Mal Yer-pa-ba, II, 408, 439.
Mal Śes-rab sems-pa, I, 262-3.
Mi-bskyod rdo-rje, II, 991-3, 1006.
Mi čhen-po, I, 243.
Mi-ñag, II, 964.
Mi-ñag Grags-pa rin-čhen, II, 1042.
Mi-ñag sGom-riṅs, II, 566.
Mi-ñag 'Byuṅ-gnas, I, 111.
Mi-ñag Žaṅ-žuṅ, II, 426.
Mi-ñag gŽon-nu sñiṅ-po, II, 789.
Mi-ñag Rab-'byams-pa Čhos-kyi grags-pa, II, 830.
Mi-ñag Rin-čhen bzaṅ-po, I, 330.
Mi-ñag lo-tsā-ba, I, 228.
Mi-ñag Śes-rab bzaṅ-po, II, 860, 864.
Mi-ñag-pa Rin-čhen rgyal-mtshan, II, 996.
Mi-pham dpal-ldan, II, 541.
Mi-dbaṅ-blo, II, 800.

Mi'i ñi-ma, II, 798.
Mi'i lha, I, x, 5, 45.
Miṅ-čhen, I, 20, 23.
Mi-thub zla-ba, I, 206.
Mi-pham bśes-gñen sbas-pa, II, 1031.
Mi-srid, I, 14.
Mid-la, I, 73, 109, 226, 261, 314; II, 403, 405, 448-51, 454-6, 458-9, 471, 478, 488, 521, 528, 560, 581, 651, 655-6, 707, 721, 724, 824, 972, 1021, 1040, 1086.
Mid-la ras-pa, II, 403, 427-437, 453, 455, 527.
Mid-la gYuṅ-rgyal, II, 427.
Mid-la Śer-rgyal (Śes-rab rgyal-mtshan), II, 427, 429.
Mu-khyud, I, 5, 13.
Mu-khyud brtan, I, 15.
Mu-khri btsan-po, I, 36.
Mu-thug btsan--po, I, xx.
Mu-ne btsan-po, I, v, xix, xx, 37, 46, 52.
Mu-dbon, II, 478.
Mu-sman-phyar, I, 292.
Mu-zu dGe-ba-gsal, I, xvii, 67.
Mun-čhaṅ, I, xi.
Mun-sel, I, 5, 15.
Mum-me Brag-kha-ba, II, 772-3.
Mus-čhen-pa, II, 1016-7.
Me-go-pa, II, 843.
Me-lče, I, 14.
Me-lče-ldan, I, 14.
Me-lče'i phreṅ, I, 14.
Me-čhar, II, 654.
Me-ston 'Dul-'dzin, II, 786.
Me-dpuṅ, I, 166.
Me-gza' sKyid-de, II, 672.
Me-loṅ rdo-rje, I, 153, 196-7, 199; II, 963.
Me-loṅ-pa, I, 198, 202.
Me-loṅ-žal, I, 15.
Me-lha-khaṅ-pa, I, 233.
Me-lha-khaṅ-sna-ba, II, 426.
Me-lhaṅ-tsher, I, 326.
Meg-čhuṅ dBaṅ-seṅ, I, 118.
Mer-khri btsan-po, I, 36.
Mes-kun-po, II, 405.
Mes-ston Kun-sñiṅ, II, 706.

Mes-ston mGon-po, I, 131, 143.
Mes-ston Čhos-'bar, I, 98.
Mes-ston tshon-po, I, 143.
Mes mDo-sde, II, 409.
Mes rDo-rje rgyal-mtshan, I, 132.
Mes-tshon-po dPyal-se-tsa, I, 73; II, 403, 405, 477.
Mes Ag-tshom, I, 46, 105.
Mo-han rdo-rje, I, 227.
Mon-gra-pa, I, 273.
Mon-ston 'Byuṅ-gnas śes-rab, I, 232.
Mon-re, II, 990.
Mya-ṅan-bral, I, 15.
Mya-ṅan-med, I, 15, 24.
Myaṅ, I, 273, 300, 376; II, 445.
Myaṅ-sgom dkar-po, II, 1004.
Myaṅ bKa'-gdams-pa, I, 193.
Myaṅ-sgom rgod-po, II, 550, 1004.
Myaṅ-sgom sPraṅ-ltag, II, 403.
Myaṅ-sgom Žig-po Čhos-se, II, 1004.
Myaṅ čhen-po, II, 855.
Myaṅ Tiṅ-'dzin bzaṅ-po, I, 107, 167, 192.
Myaṅ-ston, II, 1006.
Myaṅ-ston čhen-po, I, 155.
Myaṅ-ston Do-pa, II, 906.
Myaṅ-ston rTsags-se, I, 132; II, 865.
Myaṅ-stod-pa, I, 314.
Myaṅ-stod lo-tsā-ba, II, 1057.
Myaṅ 'Dul-'dzin, I, 81.
Myaṅ Dharmasiṃha, I, 186, 189.
Myaṅ-nag mDo-po, I, 125, 154; II, 941.
Myaṅ-po Ri-kha-pa, I, 269.
Myaṅ Byaṅ-čhub-grags, I, 173-4.
Myaṅ-bran, II, 555.
Myaṅ-bran Čhos-kyi seṅ-ge, I, 333.
Myaṅ-bran-pa Čhos-yes, II, 734.
Myaṅ-mi, I, 262.
Myaṅ-mi čhen-po, I, 234.
Myaṅ-mi Dar-ma, I, 192.
Myaṅ-mo, II, 918; 1005.
Myaṅ-mo dPal-ldan-'bum, II, 695.
Myaṅ-mtshams Rin-čhen bla-ma, I, 78-9.
Myaṅ 'Tshal-pa, II, 727.

Myaṅ-gza 'dKar-rgyan, II, 427.
Myaṅ Ye-śes' byuṅ-gnas, I, 109-10.
Myaṅ-ral, II, 445 (Ñi-ma 'od-zer).
Myaṅ-ro-pa, I, 273.
Myaṅ Lags-žiṅ-pa, I, 273.
Myaṅ Śes-rab-mčhog, I, 109.
Myaṅ Śes-rab 'byuṅ-gnas, I, 173-4.
Myaṅ gśen-groṅ-pa, II, 563, 565.
dMag-pa-sgaṅ, II, 862.
dMar, II, 706.
dMar Čhos-kyi rgyal-po, I, 382.
dMar Čhos-kyi rgyal-mtshan, I, 382, 388; II, 555 706.
dMar Čhos-rgyal, I, 355, 383.
dMar-ston, I, 83.
dMar-ston rGyal-mtshan 'od-zer, II, 809.
dMar-ston čhen-po, II, 1080.
dMar-ston Čhos-kyi rgyal-mtshan, I, 354.
dMar-ston Čhos-rgyal, II, 872.
dMar-ston 'Jam, I, 142-3, 147.
dMar-ston gŽon-nu rgyal-mtshan, I, 344.
dMar-pa, II, 564.
dMar-po (Śes-rab gsaṅ-ba), II, 1049-50.
dMar-ban Śākyamuni, I, 63.
dMar-bu-brag-pa gŽon-nu śes-rab, II, 450.
dMar mDzod-ma-ba, II, 893.
dMar-gza' Pad-ma, II, 652.
dMar Śes-rab rdo-rje, I, 382.
rMa, I, 73, 239; II, 872-7, 904, 947, 993.
rMa dGe-ba'i blo-gros, II, 837.
rMa-sgom, II, 874-7.
rMa-sgom Čhos-kyi śes-rab, I, 97, 186; II, 860.
rMa-ston, I, 267.
rMa-ban Čhos-'bar, II, 405, 857.
rMa-bya rNa-ra-ba, I, 88.
rMa-bya Byaṅ-brtson, I, 147, 329. (Byaṅ-čhub brtson-'grus), 334, 343.
rMa-bya Byaṅ-ye (Byaṅ-čhub ye-śes), I, 236, 343.
rMa-bya rTsod-pa'i seṅ-ge, I, 333.
rMa-mo Khye-mkhar, II, 440.
rMa sMon-lam, II, 872.
rMa-tsho Byaṅ-čhub rdo-rje, I, 79,80. rMa-tsho Byaṅ-rdor, I, 322.
rMa-gza' Rin-čhen-'bum, I, 232. See mTha'-bži lo-tsā-ba.
rMa-ra Jo-sras rMa-bya, I, 118.

rMa Rin-čhen-mčhog, I, 104, 108, 167, 191.
rMa lo-tsā-ba, I, 71, 219, 220, 232, 240. rMa lo-tsā-ba Čhos-'bar, I, 219.
rMa-se, II, 512,
rMa-se rTogs-ldan, II, 509-10.
rMaṅ-ra ser-po, II, 871.
rMugs-saṅs-pa Rin-čhen bla-ma, II, 537.
rMen-dor-ba, II, 555.
rMe'u-ston-pa, II, 733.
rMog-sgom, II, 614.
rMog-čog-pa, II, 518.
rMog-čog-pa Rin-čhen blo-gros, II, 751.
rMog-čog-pa (Rin-čhen brtson-'grus), II, 446, 463, 733, 737, 738, 746.
sMa-ra ser-po, II, 996-7.
sMan-kluṅs-pa, II, 518.
sMan-tsha-'bar, II, 688.
sMan-žabs, I, 168, 371.
sMan-luṅ-pa, I, 155; II, 581.
sMar Śākyamuni, I, xvii.
sMar-ra ser-po, II, 996.
sMi-ri-ba (Čhos-rje-), II, 783.
sMen-'dor-ba, II, 996.
sMe'u Byaṅ-čhub-'od, II, 517.
sMon-mda'-ba, II, 470.
sMon-lam, II, 439.
sMon-lam-rgyan, I, 237.
sMon-lam rdo-rje, I, vi.
sMon-lam-'bar (Lha-rje-), II, 468, 580, 879, 880-2, 934.
sMon-lam tshul-khrims, I, 331.
sMon-čhuṅ, II, 876 (rGya-smyon).
sMyon-pa lDom-čhuṅ, II, 1030.
sMyon-pa Don-ldan, II, 876.
sMyon-pa Be-re, II, 997.
sMyon-ma, II, 984.
sMra-ba'i seṅ-ge, II, 948, 955-6, 959, 970 (brTson-'grus-seṅ-ge).
Tsa-tra-ra, I, 368.
Tsa-mi, II, 530, 699. (Saṅs-rgyas grags-pa), 761, 795-6, 837, 1009, 1021, 1053.
Tsa-ri sGom-čhuṅ, II, 439.
Tsa-ri sGom-pa, II, 739.
Tsa-ri sÑon-sṅon, II, 498.
Tsa-ri-ba, II, 676.
Tsa-ri ras-pa, II, 720, 744.
Tsaṅs Yaṅ-dag-'bar, I, 376.

Tsi-to, II, 857.
Tsi-to-ma, II, 869.
Tsi-lu-pa, II, 755-7, 761-3, 789.
Tsi-luṅ-pa, II, 597.
Tsoṅ-kha-pa, I, 34, 340, 366, 389; II, 411-2, 425, 504, 586, 588-9, 610, 656, 693, 703, 711, 782, 795, 883, 931, 1049, 1073-5. See bLo-bzaṅ grags-pa, Kun-dga' sñiṅ-po.
gTsaṅ-dkar, I, 329; II, 708-9, 1055. gTsaṅ-dkar-ba, II, 708.
gTsaṅ Kha-bo-čhe, I, 325.
gTsaṅ-gad gÑos-pa, I, 273.
gTsaṅ dGe-brag-pa Tshul-khrims gžon-nu, I, 373.
gTsaṅ-sgom hrul-po, I, 139.
gTsaṅ-ston, I, 303, 314; II, 484, 676.
gTsaṅ-ston dKon-ne, II, 481.
gTsaṅ-ston sKyi-tshaṅ-ba, II, 990.
gTsaṅ-nag-pa, I, 236, 285, 333, 348; II, 420, 465.
gTsaṅ-nag-pa brTson-'grus seṅ-ge, I, 333; II, 941.
gTsaṅ-nag 'Od-'bar, I, 149.
gTsaṅ-pa, I, 198, 271, 295, 297, 299; II, 420, 440, 623, 627, 670, 671-3, 675, 727, 742, 744.
gTsaṅ-pa Khyuṅ-po, I, 277.
gTsaṅ-pa mKhar-po-pa, I, 269.
gTsaṅ-pa Gru-gu, I, 335.
gTsaṅ-pa rGya-ras, I, 300; II, 693. See gTsaṅ-pa Ye-śes rdo-rje.
gTsaṅ-pa rṄog, II, 900.
gTsaṅ-pa Jo-phad, I, 285.
gTsaṅ-pa Jo-nam, I, 335.
gTsaṅ-pa 'Jam-dpal-seṅ-ge, I, 329, 333.
gTsaṅ-pa Drug-po, II, 727.
gTsaṅ-pa 'Dul-'dzin, II, 952.
gTsaṅ-pa dPal-grags, II, 480.
gTsaṅ-pa Byi-ston, I, 149.
gTsaṅ-pa bLo-gros bzaṅ-po-ba, II, 692.
gTsaṅ-pa bLo-bzaṅs-pa, II, 896, 969.
gTsaṅ-pa dBaṅ-phyug-grags, II, 1072.
gTsaṅ-pa Maṅ-gro-ba, II, 988.
gTsaṅ-pa Yaṅ-dag rdo-rje, I, 397.
gTsaṅ-pa Ye-śes rdo-rje, II, 664ff. (gTsaṅ-pa rGya-ras, gYuṅ-druṅ-dpal).
gTsaṅ-pa Ral-gčig-ma, I, 176.
gTsaṅ-pa Sar-spos, I, 236, 343; II, 519.
gTsaṅ-pa Sa-rbo, II, 421.
gTsaṅ-pa Sum pa, II, 439.

gTsaṅ-'phraṅ-pa čhen-po, II, 451.
gTsaṅ-bu, II, 1001-3.
gTsaṅ Brag-nag-pa, II, 964.
gTsaṅ-mi mkhas-pa rGya-nam, I, 384
gTsaṅ-tsha J̌o-tshul, II, 409.
gTsaṅ-žig, II, 608.
gTsaṅ Yaṅ-dag-'bar, II, 866.
gTsaṅ Rab-gsal, I, 63-4.
gTsaṅ So-ba, II, 517, 727.
gTsug-rgyan-pa, II, 969.
gTsug-rgyan Yid-bžin nor-bu Kun-dga' lhun-grub, II, 965.
gTsug-tor-skyabs, II, 519.
gTsug-ru Rin-čhen gžon-nu, I, 108.
gTsug-lag phreṅ-ba, I, v.
gTso-bo rgyal-gyuṅ, II, 726.
bTsad-tsha, II, 665.
bTsad-tsha lčam-me, I, 376.
bTsad-tsha Śāk-rdor, I, 123.
bTsan Kha-bo-čhe, I, 71-2, 177, 186, 293, 328, 347-8, 379.
bTsan-dgon-pa, I, 201, 330.
bTsan-thaṅ-pa, I, 186.
bTsan-thaṅ-pa rGyal-ba-dpal, I, 343.
bTsan-phyug-lde, I, 37.
bTsan-'od, I, 95.
bTsun-čhuṅ, I, 221.
bTsun-čhuṅ-ma, II, 480.
bTsun-ma, II, 596.
bTsun-mo-čan, I, 360-1.
bTsun Śul-rgya, II, 1052.
rTsa-skya dKon-mčhog-grags, I, 355.
rTsags, I, 143, 147; II, 414.
rTsags Dharmarāja, II, 408.
rTsags bla-ma, I. 111.
rTsags dBaṅ-phyug seṅ-ge, I, 329, 333.
rTsags Śāk-riṅs, I, 120.
rTsaṅs 'byuṅ-se, II, 866.
rTsad-tsha Śāk-rdor, I, 171. See bTsad-tsha Śāk-rdor.
rTsi-rgyal-ba, II, 985.
rTsi-sñan, II, 705.
rTsi Dar-ma, II, 991.
rTsi-'dul-ba Thugs-rje byaṅ-čhub, II, 1013.
rTsi rDor-bstan, II, 897.

rTsi-bar-ba (mKhas-čhen-), II, 518.
rTsi-mo Nam-mkha'-gsal, II, 477.
rTsi-luṅ-pa, II, 563, 565.
rTsibs, I, 22.
rTsibs-dgon-pa, I, 314.
rTse-dkar-ba, I, 320.
rTse-sgaṅ-pa, I, 156.
rTse-čhen-pa Grags-yon, II, 590.
rTse-ston Kun-bzaṅs, II, 708.
rTse-ston J̌o-sras, II, 1044.
rTse-lde, I, 37, 70, 325, 328; II, 405, 453, 913.
rTse-pa Kun-dga' gžon-nu, I, 344.
rTse-phrom Byaṅ-dpal, I, 121.
rTse-bor-ba, I, 273.
rTse-mo (bSod-nams rtse-mo), I, 382; II, 1051.
rTsed-pa, I, 272.
brTsod-śe, I, 319.
brTson-'grus go-čha, II, 868.
brTson-'grus rgyal po, I, 321.
brTson-'grus rgyal-mtshan (brTson-rgyal), I, 68, 300, 322.
brTson-'grus rdo-rǰe, I, 382
brTson-'grus dbaṅ-phyug, I, 190.
brTson-'grus-'bar, I, 80.
brTson-'grus gžon-nu, I, 297.
brTson-'grus bzaṅ-po, I, 309-10.
brTson-'grus seṅ-ge, I, 299, 329; II, 744. (Saṅs-rgyas ston-pa).
brTson-rgyal-ba, I, 98; II, 1072.
brTson-rin-pa, I, 309.
brTson-seṅ, I, 345.
Tsha-roṅ-pa, I, 318.
Tshaṅs-byin, I, 4
Tshad-ma'i skyes-bu, I, 331, 345; II, 1051.
Tshan-čhen-thub, I. 14.
Tshan-po-čhe, I, 15.
Tshan-po-čhe-'dul, I, 4.
Tsha'o (Tsha-bo) Saṅs-rgyas-byin, I, 392-3.
Tshar-ston sGo-maṅs-pa, II, 610.
Tshal-pa smon-lam-pa, I, 341.
Tshul-khrims bkra-śis, I, 320.
Tshul-khrims-skyabs, I, 397; II, 419.
Tshul-khrims mgon-po, I, 304-5.
Tshul-khrims rgyal-po, I, 210.

Tshul-khrims rgyal-ba, I, 86.
Tshul-khrims rgyal-mtshan, II, 964.
Tshul-khrims-dpal, II, 462, 521, 543.
Tshul-khrims dpal-pa, I, 344.
Tshul-khrims blo-gros (rDzogs-čhen-pa Thshul-blo, kLoṅ-čhen-pa), I, 309.
Tshul-khrims-'bar, I, 73; II, 785.
Tshul-khrims-'bum, I, 81.
Tshul-khrims 'byuṅ-gnas, I, 262; II, 1053.
Tshul-khrims bzaṅ-po, II, 1089.
Tshul-khrims 'od-zer, I, 314.
Tshul-khrims rin-čhen, II, 491; 1072.
Tshul-khrims śes-rab, I, 304; (gTsaṅ-tsha J̌o-tshul-), II, 409.
Tshul-mgon-pa, II, 412, 1072.
Tshul-rgyan-pa, I, 341.
Tshul-rgyal ('Bri-khuṅ-pa), I, 303; II, 1043.
Tshul-rgyal-ba, I, 100, 155-6; II, 585-6, 588, 1024.
Tshul-'phags, I, 89; II, 1052.
Tshul-bla-ba, II, 637.
Tshul-blo, II, 529.
Tshul-rin, II, 524, 537.
Tshul-la, II, 829.
Tshul-śe, I, 273.
Tshul-śes, II, 747.
Tshe-lčam, II, 463.
Tshe-dbaṅ, II, 986.
Tshe-'dzin, I, 210.
Tshe-la dbaṅ-phyug, I, 210.
Tshem-bu-pa, II, 1043.
Tshes-pa, I, 273.
Tshes-bži rñiṅ-ma-ba, II, 583, 720. (Grags-pa rgyal-mtshan).
Tshes-bži-pa, II, 584.
Tshes-bži gsar-ma-ba (Tshes-bži-pa, Grags-pa byaṅ-čhub), II, 585.
Tshogs-ston-Śāk, II, 744.
Tshogs-pa Čhos-luṅ-pa, I, 150.
Tshoṅ, II, 1085.
mTshan-ldan 'khrul-žig čhen-po, II, 1039.
mTshams-bčad-pa Grags-pa rgyal-mtshan, II, 609.
mTshams-ston Go-čha, I, 165.
mTshams-brtan, I, 15.
mTshal-sgom Čhos-la dga'-ba, II, 1088.
mTshal-pa, II, 682.
mTshuṅs-med Rin-ǧžon-pa, II, 584.

mTshur 'dbyig-gi rgyal-mtshan, II, 857.
mTsho-dkar-ba, II, 586.
mTsho-dkar-mo-ba, II, 518.
mTsho-skyes, I, 389; II, 474, 856. mTsho-skyes rdo-rje, I, 389; II, 869, 1041.
mTsho-sna-ba (Tshul-khrims śes-rab), I, 304, 321.
mTsho-sna-ba Śes-rab bzaṅ-po, I, 320.
'Tshar-dgu gza'-skyid, I, 176.
'Tshar-steṅs-pa, I, 198.
'Tshar-ston, I, 142.
'Tshal-pa Kun-dga' rdo rje, I, 49.
'Tshal-pa dGa'-bde gśegs-pa, II, 525.
'Tshal-min Čhos-kyi grags-pa, II, 835.
'Tshal gSer-khaṅ-pa, II, 973.
'Tshur, I, 66; II, 405, 415, 418.
'Tshur dBaṅ-gi rdo-rje, II, 416.
Tshur-ston Čhos-kyi rin-čhen, II, 549.
'Tshur-ston dBaṅ-ṅe, I, 364; II, 439.
'Tshur-ston dbYig-ge, I, 164.
'Tshur-nag Ye-śes-dpal, I, 170.
'Tshur-phu 'Jam-dbyaṅs go-śri, II, 813.
'Tshur-phu-ba, II, 621-2.
'Tshur-dBaṅ-ṅe, I, 73; II, 403, 414.
'Tshur-mo-gza' Maṅ-skyid, II, 929.
'Tshur Śes-rab-mčhog, I, 66.
'Tshe-mi Čhul-po, I, 376.
'Tshe-mi bSod-nams-'bar, I, 376.
'Tshe'u-bar-ba, II, 408.
'Tsher-ston, I, 285.
Dza-thig-dza-la, I, 368.
Dza-sna-ba, II, 829.
Dza-ba-ri-pa, II, 869.
Dza-hūṃ, I, 384.
Dzam-čan-ne, I, 329.
Dzam-bha-la (Jambhala) Ti-śrī (Ti-shih) mGon, I, vii, 56.
Dze-ta-ri, I, 243.
mDzes-čan, I, 12.
mDzes-ldan, I, 4, 12.
'Dzan-pa Byaṅ-skyabs, II, 444.
'Dzam-gliṅ Ñi-śar (Kun-mkhyen-), II, 1043.
'Dzar dGe-po, I, 376.
'Dzims-pa, I, 77-8. ('Dzims-pa Śes-rab-'od). (Kun-mkhyen-), II, 785.

'Dzims-pa kLog-sñiṅ, I, 81.
'Dzims-pa Mes-ston, I, 81.
'Dzeṅ (Dharmabodhi), I, 175-190, 226; II, 893.
'Dzeṅ Jo-sras, I, 186-191,
'Dzeṅ dBaṅ-phyug-mtshan, I, 266. See dGon-pa-pa.
'Dzob-gza' brTson-'grus-rgyan, II. 493.
rDza-dgon Kun-spaṅs-pa (Čhos-kyi ye-śes), II, 545.
rDza-bor-pa, I, 180,
rDza-ra-ba, II, 736.
rDza-ri-ba Myaṅ-ro-pa, II, 727.
rDza-riṅs-pa Śes-rab-dpal, II, 693,
rDza-gśoṅs-pa Śes-rab-dpal, II, 498.
rDzi-sgom sKyes-se, II, 462.
rDziṅ-kha-pa, I, 262.
rDziṅ-bu-kha-pa. I, 374,
rDzil 'Od-grags, I, 314.
rDzoṅ-mgo-pa, II, 572.
rDzoṅ-pa, I, 387; II, 568, 914.
rDzoṅ-pa Rin-čhen seṅ-ge, II, 517.
Wa-ston, I, 285; II, 663.
Wam-ku Paṇḍita, I, 346.
Waṅ-mo rGya-gar-gsal, I, 133.
Waṅ-mo Žu-ba gŽon-nu-dpal, II, 774.
Wa-brag dkar-ba, I, 269; II, 768.
Wa-Žwa, II, 68c.
War Padma, I, 314.
Ža-čhuṅ-ma, II, 919. See Ma-gčig Labs-sgron-ma.
Ža-ba, I, 289.
Ža-ma, I, 215, 218, 220-40; II, 446, 914, 947.
Ža-ma rGyal-le, I, 220.
Ža-ma rDo-rje rgyal-mtshan, I, 219.
Ža-ma seṅ-ge, I, 220. See Seṅ-ge rgyal-po.
Ža-lu sKu-žaṅ-pa, II, 750.
Ža-lu-ma Ma-gčig gŽon-nu-'bum, I, 214.
Žwa-čhen Rin-'byuṅ, II, 532.
Žwa-dmar rTogs-ldan Rin-po-čhe, II, 724.
Žwa-lu-pa, II, 1079.
Žaṅ (bLa-ma, 'Gro-mgon-), I, 133, 139, 194, 297, 299, 376; II, 406, 469, 479, 549, 568-9, 601, 622, 655, 663, 668-9, 670, 709, 1065-6.
Žaṅ (kalyāṇa-mitra-), I, 227; II, 558.
Žaṅ (kun-spaṅs-), II, 422, 797, 1044.
Žaṅ (ācārya-), I, 277; II, 680, 736.

Žaṅ, II, 659.
Žaṅ (dGa'-ldan-pa), II, 875.
Žaṅ (lo-tsā-ba-), II, 991.
Žaṅ Ka-ma-pa, I, 266.
Žaṅ bKra-śis rdo-rje, I, 193.
Žaṅ-skyabs, II, 629, 632.
Žaṅ-mkhar-ba bSod-nams bzaṅ-po, I, 155.
Žaṅ-gye-pa, I, 331.
Žaṅ dGa'-ldan-pa, II, 874-5.
Žaṅ dGe-ba, II, 709.
Žaṅ dGon-pa, I, 215.
Žaṅ 'Gros-čhuṅ-ba, I, 111.
Žaṅ rGya-ma-pa, I, 230.
Žaṅ rGyal-ba'i yon-tan, I, 108.
Žaṅ rGyal-ma sPaṅ-sgaṅ-pa, I, 364.
Žaṅ rgyu-sgro-lha-khaṅ-pa, II, 928.
Žaṅ-sgom Čhos-seṅ, II, 733.
Žaṅ-sgom-'byuṅ-gnas-'od, II, 717.
Žaṅ-ṅa rnal-'byor-pa, II, 928.
Žaṅ Ṅaṅ-rgyal-ba (gZi-brjid rin-čhen), II, 608.
Žaṅ-ṅe sGom-čhen, II, 935.
Žaṅ-sna-riṅ-mo, II, 857.
Žaṅ-lčam dkar-yal, I, 302.
Žaṅ-lčam-ma, II, 583.
Žaṅ-lčam 'Bum-skyid, II, 653.
Žaṅ čhuṅ-ba, I, 314.
Žaṅ čhen-po, I, 253, 255, 269.
Žaṅ-čhen-po dGe-ba, I, 64.
Žaṅ-stag-dkar-ba, I, 95.
Žaṅ-ston, I, 125, 194; II, 448. 1011.
Žaṅ-ston Kun-dga'-grags, II, 405.
Žaṅ-ston Kun-dga' rgyal-po, II, 895.
Žaṅ-ston dKon-mčhog, II, 956.
Žaṅ-ston dGra-'jigs, II, 1011-13.
Žaṅ-ston 'Gyur-med-dpal, II, 1016.
Žoṅ-ston sGo-mig-pa, II, 615.
Žaṅ-ston sṄags-se, I, 121.
Žaṅ-ston Čhos-kyi bla-ma, I, 282.
Žaṅ-ston Čhos-dbaṅ, II, 1044.
Žaṅ-ston Čhos-'bar, I, 95, 97.
Žaṅ-ston Jo-'khyams, I, 144.
Žaṅ-ston Jo-spu, II, 876.

Žaṅ-ston-pa Grags-sbyor, II, 405.
Žaṅ-ston 'Tshem-ba, I, 90.
Žaṅ-ston 'Od-'bar, I, 236.
Žaṅ-ston Śes-rab, II, 900.
Žaṅ-ston Śes-rab-'bar, II, 469.
Žaṅ-ston bSod-nams grags-pa (Yar-'brog Kha-ba-luṅ-pa), II, 779.
Žaṅ Thoṅ-sag-pa Ye-śes 'byuṅ-gnas, I, 343ff.
Žaṅ Ded-po-luṅ-pa, II, 859.
Žaṅ Dran-pa, I, 95.
Žaṅ mDo-sde-grags, II, 445.
Žaṅ mDo-sde-dpal, I, 335.
Žaṅ-'dul, I, 235.
Žaṅ-nag, II, 435.
Žaṅ sNa-čhuṅ ston-pa, I, 233.
Žaṅ sNa-nam rDo-rje dbaṅ-phyug, I, 76, 100.
Žaṅ-po Mon, I, 235.
Žaṅ Bra'o-brag-rtsa-ba, II, 862.
Žaṅ Bro-sñon, I, 180.
Žaṅ dBaṅ-phyug-mgon, I, 255. See dBaṅ-phyug-mgon.
Žaṅ dbU-dkar-ba, II, 1024-5.
Žaṅ-mo rgyal-mthiṅ, II, 984.
Žaṅ gTsaṅ-'od, I, 376.
Žaṅ-btsun, I, 216.
Žaṅ-btsun rGyal-ba bkra śis, II, 876.
Žaṅ-btsun gÑan, I, 271.
Žaṅ-btsun mDo-sde-dpal, I, 346.
Žaṅ-btsun rDo-rje-'od, I, 282.
Žaṅ-btsun Pu-hraṅs-pa, II, 583.
Žaṅ-btsun dbOn-čhuṅ, II, 707.
Žaṅ-btsun sMon-lam dbaṅ-phyug, I, 387.
Žaṅ-btsun Yer-pa-ba, I, 262, 321.
Žaṅ brTson-grags, I, vi.
Žaṅ Tshul-khrims śes-rab, I, 387.
Žaṅ Tshes-čhuṅ-ba, I, 374.
Žaṅ Tshes-spoṅ-ba Čhos-kyi bla-ma, I, 326, 328, 332.
Žaṅ mTshal-pa, II, 565, 744, 796.
Žaṅ 'Tshal-pa, I, 139; II, 445.
Žaṅ Ži-mdzes, II, 707.
Žaṅ Ži-mdzes śes-rab, I, 81.
Žaṅ-žuṅ (siddha-), II, 1023.
Žaṅ-žuṅ gLiṅ-kha-pa, II, 871.
Žaṅ-žuṅ rGyal-ba'i śes-rab, I, 78.

Žaṅ-žuṅ Yon-tan-grags, I, 167.
Žaṅ-ye, I, 374.
Žaṅ Ye-śes-sde, I, 345.
Žaṅ gYe-ba, I, 94.
Žaṅ Rin-po-čhe (brTson-'grus-grags), II, 517, 711-5, 717, 845, 1055.
Žaṅ lo-tsā-ba (Phur-pa-skyabs), II, 445, 449, 999.
Žaṅ lo-tsā-ba Mya-ṅan med-pa'i sa-dpal, II, 1025.
Žaṅ Śes-rab-'od, I, 82.
Žaṅ Ṣag-pa, I, 376.
Žaṅ Sum-thog-pa, II, 462, 573, 597, 707.
Žaṅ-se-tsha Legs-brtan, I, 95.
Žaṅ Se-gseb, II, 580.
Žaṅ Sog-čhuṅ-ba, II, 911.
Žaṅ bSod-nams-mkhar, II, 405.
Žaṅ bSam-gliṅ-pa, II, 699.
Žaṅ-lha, I, 91.
Žar, I, 147.
Žar-dgon-pa, I, 269, 273.
Žar-čhos, I, 273.
Žal-sṅa-ba, II, 792-3.
Žal-gdams-pa, I, 182.
Žwa-dmar-pa, II, 517, 827.
Žwa-dmar-pa Grags-pa seṅ-ge, II, 1039.
Žwa-ser-ba, II, 517.
Ži-ston bSod-rgyal, I, 121.
Ži-ba-skyoṅ, II, 435.
Ži-ba-dpal, II, 587, 589.
Ži-ba-'tsho, I, 34; II, 822.
Ži-ba bzaṅ-po, I, 360.
Ži-ba-'od—Ži-ba'i-'od, I, 37, 102, 244; II, 431, 575, 1070.
Ži-ba-lha, II, 369.
Ži-byed mgon po. II, 687.
Žig-po (of dbUs), I, 127, 129, 130. (bDud-rtsi), I, 131-4, 137, 139, 141-2, 148, 320; II, 936-8, 946-9, 952, 956-7, 961-2, 966, 975, 978. (upādhyāya of sKyor-mo-luṅ), I, 302,
Žig-po Kun-grol, I, 319; II, 1024.
Žig-po Ñi-ma seṅ-ge, II, 937.
Žig-po bDud-rtsi, I, 131-3, 144-7; II, 655-6, 953, 1005. See Žig-po.
Žig-po Byaṅ-dpal, II, 698.
Žig-po Rin-čhen 'byuṅ-gnas, I, 306.
Žiṅ-gi rdo-rje, II, 729.
Žiṅ-mo čhe-pa, II, 1012.

Žib-mo Dar-rtsags, II, 929.
Žu bKa'-gdams-pa, I, 376.
Žu-ston Hral-mo, I, 329; II, 708,
Žu-don-mo-ri-ba, II, 706.
Žu-byas dṄos-grub, II, 613.
Žu bSod-śāk, I, 159.
Žus-len-pa, I, 322, 365.
Žeṅ-'od, I, 396.
Žo-luṅ-mtsho-kha-ba, II, 782.
gŽaṅ rTa-rmig-pa, II, 1087.
gŽan-gyis mi-thub-pa, I, 16.
gŽi Kun-spaṅs-pa, I, 339.
gŽu-bkra, I, 16.
gŽu-dgu-bču-pa, I, 16.
gŽu-brgya-pa, I, 16.
gŽu-bču-pa, I, 16.
gŽu-pa nag-po, II, 745.
gŽu-ba sTon-yes, I, 79.
gŽu-sa, I, 16.
gŽuṅ, II, 955.
gŽuṅ-pa, I, 302.
gŽus, I, 72, 325.
gŽon-brtan, I, 16.
gŽon-nu-grags, I, 74, 190, 315.
gŽon-nu mgon-po, II, 1073.
gŽon-nu rgya-mtsho, I, 354.
gŽon-nu rgyal-po, I, 198.
gŽon-nu rgyal-mtshan, I, 94, 344.
gŽon-nu-mčhog, I, 87.
gŽon-nu don-grub, I, 202.
gŽon-nu-dpal (ācārya), II, 499, ('Gos-) 1092. See 'Gos lo-tsā-ba. gŽon-nu-dpal, I, 98.
gŽon-nu dpal-pa, II, 541.
gŽon-nu-'phel, I, 310.
gŽon-nu byaṅ-čhub, II, 490, 528, 537, 1024, 1072.
gŽon-nu blo-gros, II, 1024, 1075.
gŽon-nu blo-ldan, I, 329.
gŽon-nu-'bum, I, 196, 316; II, 491, 517, 1025.
gŽon-nu-ma, II, 919.
gŽon-nu smon-lam, II, 1023.
gŽon-nu tshul-khrims, I, 94, (sKar-čhuṅ riṅ-mo), 330.
gŽon-nu-'od, I, 286; II, 422.

gŽon-nu yon-tan, I, 284.
gŽon-nu rin-čhen, II, 748.
gŽon-nu śes-rab, I, 93, 352.
gŽon-nu seṅ-ge, I, 80, 98, 316; II, 671, 774, 789.
gŽon-nu seṅ-ge blo-gros (bKa'-bču-pa-), II, 774.
gŽon-nu gsaṅ-čhol, II, 520.
gŽon-pa-čhe, I, 16.
gŽon-pa Ya-tshe, II, 936.
gŽon-dbaṅ, I, 216-7.
gŽon-dbaṅ-ba, II, 585. 586.
gŽon-brtson (gŽon-nu brtson-'grus), I, 309.
gŽon-tshul, I, 78, 281.
gŽon-'od, I, 317.
gŽon-'od-pa, I, 98; II, 594 (rGya-na Rin-po-čhe).
gŽon-rin, I, 330; II, 884.
gŽon-seṅ, I, 329.
bŽaṅ dPal-gyi rdo-rje, I, 66.
bŽaṅ-riṅs, I, 335.
bŽin-'bar, I, 16.
Za-ṅam Rin-čhen-dbyig, I, 173.
Za ldan, I, 15.
Za-nam Ži-lde, I, 37.
Za-ba, I, 15.
Za-ba-čan, I, 15.
Za-ra-ba, II, 608.
Za-luṅ-pa, I, 196-7; II, 728.
Zwa-ra-ba, II, 653, 655-8. Zwa-ra-ba bDe-legs-'od, II, 658.
Zaṅ-zaṅ Ne-riṅs-pa, II, 538.
Zaṅs-dkar 'Phags-pa śes-rab, I, 354; II, 407.
Zaṅs-dkar gŽon-nu tshul-khrims, I, 354.
Zaṅs-dkar lo-tsā-ba, I, 70, 73, 80, 232, 237, 354-5; II, 924, 1009.
Zaṅs-pa'i 'bro-ras, I, 142.
Zaṅs-po, I, 278.
Zaṅs-po čhe-ba, I, 304.
Zaṅs-tsha, I, 212.
Zaṅs-tsha bSod-nams rgyal-mtshan, I, 211.
Zaṅs-ri rGya-ras, I, 143 147; II, 991. (Zaṅs-ri rGya-ras-pa).
Zaṅs-ri-pa, I, 144, 147; II, 480.
Zar-ston lo-tsā-ba, I, 396.
Zar-pa Jo-btsun, I, 285.
Zar-pa Phag-sgom, I, 286.
Zas-dkar, I, 12.

Zas-gtsaṅ, I, 12, 16.
Zi-ston Ma-ri-tse, II, 444.
Zi-na bKra-śis-skyid, II, 585.
Zi-na Rin-čhen 'dzom-pa, II, 587, 589.
Ziṅs-po Zla-ba, II, 706.
Zim-śiṅ Ye-śes sñiṅ-po, II, 462.
Zug-sgom, II, 680.
Zug-ston, II, 680.
Zug-mo dPal-rgyan, II, 680.
Zur, I, 105, 127, 156; II, 830.
Zur-sgom, I, 113.
Zur-khaṅ-pa, I, 282. See Lha-.
Zur-čhuṅ-ba, I, 132, 154; II, 706.
Zur-čhuṅ Śes-rab grags-pa, I, 111, 114-5, 118-9, 120-4.
Zur-nag 'Khor-lo, I, 110, 125.
Zur-pa, I, 360.
Zur-po, I, 109, 110.
Zur-phug-pa, II, 692, 696.
Zur Byams-pa seṅ-ge, I, 149, 151.
Zur Śākya 'byuṅ-gnas, I, 151.
Zur Śākya seṅ-ge, I, 122-3. See mṄa'-tsha Hor-po.
Zur Śes-rab 'byuṅ-gnas, I, 110.
Zur-mo dGe-'dun-'bum, I, 172.
Zur 'Od-po, I, 110.
Zur-re-ba mTha'-bži, I, 269.
Zur Hur-po, I, 376.
Zul-phu-ba, I, 322; II, 895, 975.
Zem, I, 302, 319.
Zem Tshe-riṅ-mo-ba, I, 307.
Zem Riṅ-po-čhe, I, 301.
Zem Riṅ-mo-ba, I, 304.
Ze'u brTson-'grus grags-pa, I, 283.
Zer-mo dGe-sloṅ-ma mDe-gnas-ma, I, 171.
Ze-zi-gza' gZuṅs-sgron, II, 629.
Zoṅ mČhog-čhos-skyoṅ, I, 66.
Zla-grags, II, 678.
Zla-mgon, I, 72.
Zla-ba, II, 1059.
Zla-ba grags-pa, I, 344; II, 907.
Zla-ba mgon-po, I, 96, 367; II, 755.
Zla-ba rgyal-mtshan, II, 472, 561, 1025.
Zla-ba blo-gros, II, 1073.

Zla-ba 'od-zer, II, 846, 859. (Gyi-ǰo lo-tsā-ba).
Zla-ba seṅ-ge, II, 703.
Zla-ba'i sñiṅ-po, I, 241.
Zla-'od-pa, II, 617, 629.
Zla-rin-pa (Zla-ba rin-čhen), II, 1072.
Zlos Nam-mkha'-rgyan, II, 988.
gZi, I, 74.
gZi-brǰid, II, 410, 451.
gZi-brǰid grags-pa, II, 409.
gZi-brǰid rgyal-po, I, 373.
gZi-brǰid-'bar, I, 166.
gZig-mgo-pa, II, 517.
gZig Ye-śes dbaṅ-po, I, 187, 189, 190.
gZu dGa'-ba'i rdo-rǰe, I, 348.
gZugs-čan sñiṅ-po, I, 20.
gZuṅ-lǰaṅ--mdo-ba, II, 713.
gZuṅs-lčam, II, 633.
gZus, I, 78, 100.
gZus rDo-rǰe rgyal-mtshan, I, 77, 262.
gZus-mo Dar-čhuṅ, II, 659.
gZe-ba, I, 365, 385.
gZe-ba J̌o-bde, I, 385.
gZe-ba Don-grub-mgon, I, 374.
gZe-ba bLo-ldan, I, 385.
bZa'-btuṅ-ldan, I, 16.
bZa'-btuṅ-mod, I, 16.
bZaṅ-sgom Śes-rab rgyal-po, I, 111.
bZaṅ-ston Hor-grags, I, 141.
bZaṅ-ldan, I, 20, 23.
bZaṅ-sde, I, 33.
bZaṅ-pa, II, 669.
bZaṅ-pa Dar-ma-'od, I, 329.
bZaṅ-pa Don-grub, I, 329.
bZaṅ-pa Byaṅ-skyabs, I, 345.
bZaṅ-pa dBaṅ-rdor, II, 441.
bZaṅ-po, I, 4; II, 758.
bZaṅ-po-dpal, I, 94, 213. bLa-braṅ-pa bZaṅ-po-dpal, II, 1060.
bZaṅ-po-žabs, II, 754, 803.
bZaṅ-mo, I, 6.
bZaṅ-mo dKon-ne, I, 208.
bZaṅ-mo-ba, II, 410, 976.
bZaṅ-yul-pa, II, 744.

bZaṅ-len, I, 12.
bZaṅs Mig-po-čhe, I, 110.
bZad-pa, II, 741.
bZod-dka', I, 4.
bZod-pa dka'-ba, I, 14.
bZod-pa-pa (bKa'-bču-pa-), I, 283.
'A-ža rGya-gar-brtsegs, II, 837.
'Al-pa rDo-rje dbaṅ-phyug, I, 66.
'I-li-ji, II, 500.
'U-yug-pa, I, 345; II, 1088.
'U-yug-pa A-mi, I, 285.
'O-brgyad, II, 1085.
'O-thaṅ-pa, I, 292.
'O-phraṅ dPal-gyi gžon-nu, I, 170.
'Od-kyi dkyil-'khor-čan, II, 805.
'Od-skyid-'bar, I, 38.
'Od-čhen-pa, I, 330.
'Od-'jo, I, 267, 299.
'Od-'jo-ba, I, 98, 306.
'Od-ldan, I, 32, 45.
'Od-lde, I, 27-8, 70, 205, 244,
'Od-lde sPu-rgyal, II, 648.
'Od-pho, II, 728.
'Od-byed, I, 14.
'Od-byed-lha, II, 795, 800.
'Od-'bar seṅ-ge, I, 189.
'Od-'byuṅ, II, 532.
'Od-mdzes, I, 3.
'Od-zer, II, 969.
'Od-zer mgon-po, I, 307, 329.
'Od-zer rgya-mtsho, II, 542.
'Od zer rgyal-po, I, 308.
'Od-zer rgyal-mtshan, II, 970.
'Od-zer nam-mkha', II, 507.
'Od-zer-dpal, II, 410, 542, 1072.
'Od-zer-'bum, I, 166.
'Od-zer rtse-mo, II, 1016.
'Od-zer seṅ-ge, I, 217, (dPon-čhen-), II, 1089.
'Od-bzaṅ-ba, II, 829.
'Od-sruṅs, I, 44, 46, 60.
'Od-gsal-ba, I, 99, 302.
'Om-thaṅ-pa, I, 292; II, 659.

'Or-kha-pa, II, 706.
'Or-brgyad ston-čhuṅ, II, 857.
'Or-ston, II, 528.
'Ol-kha-ba, II, 714.
'Ol-kha-ba Grol-sgom, II, 462.
'Ol-rgod-pa, II, 727.
'Ol-sgom, I, 111.
'Ol J̌o-sras, I, 190.
'Ol-pa čhen-po, II, 706.
'Ol-pa Byaṅ-čhub rdo-rǰe, I, 374.
Ya-ṅal dkar-po, II, 743.
Ya-'brog-pa Gu-rub yaṅ-dag, I, 156.
Ya-tse-ba, II, 605, 607.
Ya-zi Dar-ma śes-rab, I, 171.
Ya-zi Bon-ston, I, 167; II, 1000.
Yaṅ-khaṅ bla-ma, I, 120.
Yaṅ-khyed bla-ma, I, 165, 167, 220.
Yaṅ-gaṅ-pa, II, 555, 909.
Yaṅ-grub, II, 983.
Yaṅ-dgon-pa (rGyal-ba-, rGyal-mtshan-dpal), I, 307; II, 451, 577, 579, 686, 688-692, 695, 727, 746, 996.
Yaṅ-'dul, I, 40.
Yaṅ-dben-pa, I, 237-40.
Yaṅ-rtse-ba, I, 330.
Yaṅ-rtse-ba Rin-čhen seṅ-ge, II, 711.
Yan-čhen mGon-rgyal, II, 627.
Yan-lag-'byuṅ, I, 269.
Yam-śud kLu-čhuṅ, I, 354.
Yam-śud rGyal-ba-'od, I, 75, 93, 95.
Yam-śud dṄos-grub, I, 156; II, 941.
Yar-kluṅs-pa, II, 728.
Yar-kluṅs lo-tsā-ba (Grags-pa rgyal-mtshan), I, 350; II, 838.
Yar-khaṅ-pa, II, 580.
Yar-rgyal-ba'i śes-rab, I, 345.
Yar-ston Hrul-mo, II, 956.
Yar-'brog dkar-po, II, 728.
Yar-'brog gŽon-rgyal, I, 329.
Yar-sregs rgya-dman, II, 1004.
Yar-mo dpal-'dren, II, 923.
Yi-ge-pa, I, 372.
Yid-brten-pa, I, 28.
Yu-dam-pa, II, 580.

Yu-pi-ba, II, 680.
Yu-mo, I, 179; II, 634, 755, 760, 766, 768, 787.
Yuṅ-pa Ka-skyog-po, I, 264.
Yul-čhos-pa Lha-bzo, I, 285.
Ye-grags, I, 164.
Ye-mgon, I, 200.
Ye-rgyal-ba, II, 497, 517.
Ye-phug-pa, II, 564, 572. Ye-phug-pa Ye-śes-rtsegs, II, 565.
Ye-gžon-pa, II, 538.
Ye-raṅ-ba, I, 227-8.
Ye-śes, II, 1001.
Ye-śes-mkhar, I, 374.
Ye-śes grags-pa, II, 725, 948.
Ye-śes grub-pa, I, 265.
Ye-śes rgya-mtsho, I, 109, 159; II, 810.
Ye-śes rgyal-mtshan, I, 286, 310.
Ye-śes-lčam, II, 916.
Ye-śes-mčhog (lčam-mo), II, 1006.
Ye-śes sñiṅ-po, I, 34; II, 405, (bDe-gśegs-), 417, 868.
Ye-śes-mdo, I, 191.
Ye-śes rdo-rje, I, 273; II, 789.
Ye-śes-dpal, II, 410, 541.
Ye-śes-dpal-bzaṅ-po, II, 1060.
Ye-śes bla-ma, II, 572.
Ye-śes blo-gros, II, 475.
Ye-śes dbaṅ-po-ma, II, 549.
Ye-śes dbaṅ-phyug, II, 517.
Ye-śes-'bar, I, 311.
Ye-śes 'byuṅ-gnas, I, 212-3.
Ye-śes 'tsho-rgyal, II, 579.
Ye-śes-'dzin, II, 803.
Ye-śes-žabs, I, 233, 353, 367, 372-3; II, 416, 441, 869.
Ye-śes bzaṅ-po, I, 68; II, 965, 1008, 1085.
Ye-śes-'od, I, 69, 83-4, 102.
Ye-śes rin-čhen, II, 635, 672.
Ye-śes bśes-gñen, II, 1069.
Ye-śes seṅ-ge, I, 269, 379; II, 523-4, 855.
Ye-śes bsod-nams rgya-mtsho, I, 92.
Yer-pa-ba, I, 198; II, 713.
Yel-pa, II, 566-8. Yel-pa Ye-śes-brtsegs, II, 566.
Ye dGe-bsñen rDo-rje dbaṅ-phyug, I, 160, 164.
Ye-mi kLu-phyug, II, 468.

Yoṅ-ge dBaṅ-phyug-grags, II, 924.
Yoṅ-btsun, I, 217.
Yon-mgon, II, 784.
Yon-tan mgon-po (Kun-mkhyen-), II, 1024.
Yon-tan rgya-mtsho, I, 108-9, 329, 330.
Yon-tan rgyal-mtshan, II, 965, 1072.
Yon-tan-mčhog, II, 1087.
Yon-tan blo-gros, II, 1072.
Yon-tan dbaṅ-phyug, I, 157.
Yon-tan-'bar, I, 264.
Yon-tan 'byuṅ-gnas, I, 210.
Yon-tan-gzuṅs, I, 128, 132-3, 135.
Yon-tan-'od, II, 816, 964, 1024.
Yon-tan 'od-zer, I, 321.
Yon-tan rin-čhen, II, 1072.
Yon-tan rin-čhen bsam-se-ba, I, 321.
Yon-tan lhun-grub, II, 1073.
Yon-blo-ba, II, 507-9.
Yon-dbaṅ, II, 1089.
Yon-dbaṅ-pa, I, 321.
Yon-btsun, II, 775, 975.
Yol, I, 327.
Yol-lčags, I, 319.
Yol Čhos-dbaṅ, I, 255, 262; II, 474, 1004, 1044.
Yol-ston rDo-rje dbaṅ-phyug, I, 256.
Yol-mo, II, 872.
Yol-rdzoṅ rNal-'byor-pa, I, 264.
gYag-ston paṇ-čhen, I, 150.
gYu-luṅ-pa, I, 292.
gYag-ston Zla-ba 'od-zer, I, 187, 190.
gYag rDo-rje 'dzin-pa, I, 165.
gYag-sde paṇ-čhen, I, 310; II, 518, 532, 536, 722, 781.
gYag-brugs Saṅs-rgyas-dpal, II, 1017.
gYag-mo, II, 984.
gYag-yu, I, 339.
gYag-ru dPal-grags, II, 601.
gYag-ru ras-pa, II, 517.
gYaṅ-skyoṅ-ba rGyal-ba don-grub, II, 450.
gYabs-ston, I, 125.
gYam-bzaṅs Čhos-rje, II, 465, 653.
gYam-bzaṅs sNubs-sgom, I, 319.
gYam-bzaṅs-pa, II, 528-9, 659.

gYa'-ṅos-pa, I, 269.
gYa'-spaṅ skyes-gčig, I, 210.
gYa'-bzaṅ Čhos-rje, I, 186.
gYa'-ras, II, 693.
gYas-mo dpal-'dren, II, 923, 925, 931-2.
gYu, I, 75.
gYu-rgyal-ba, II, 727.
gYu-sgra sñiṅ-po, I, 167.
gYu čan, I, 38.
gYu-ston, I, 125.
gYu-thog J̌o-rgyal, II, 677.
gYuṅ-ston, II, 429.
gYuṅ-ston-pa, I, 109, 149; II, 493, 499, 518, 534, 541.
gYuṅ-ston rDo-rǰe-dpal, II, 493, 1043.
gYuṅ-'druṅ rgyal-ba, II, 728.
gYuṅ-'druṅ brtan-'bar, I, 286.
gYuṅ-'druṅ-'bum, II, 632.
gYuṅ-'druṅ bsod-nams, II, 584.
gYuṅ-phug-pa, II, 797.
gYe, II, 741.
gYe-pa'i sgre-pa, I, 285.
gYe-ston Saṅs-rgyas, II, 988.
gYo dGe-'byuṅ, I, xvii, 63.
gYor-gñan II, 555, 734.
gYor-ston, I, 273, 387.
gYor-po, II, 736, 862.
gYor-po rGya-mo-čhe, II, 733-4.
Ra-thuṅ Śes-rab tshul-khrims, I, 109.
Ra-rdzi ras-pa, II, 435.
Rwa, II, 762-3, 785, 792, 838.
Rwa Khri-bzaṅ-'bar, I, 345.
Rwa-sgom rDo-rǰe rgyal-po, I, 376.
Rwa-čho, II, 843.
Rwa Čhos-rab, I, 377; II, 756, 789, 837.
Rwa J̌o-dar, II, 445.
Rwa 'Bum-seṅ, I, 379; II, 756, 789-90.
Rwa Ye-śes seṅ-ge, I, 379; II, 756, 789.
Rwa ru-čan, II, 850-1.
Rwa-lo, I, 293, 325, 328; II, 407, 442, 756, 765; Rwa lo-tsā-ba, I, 71, 296, 377, 379, 396; II, 659, 755, 862. Rwa lo-tsā-ba rDo-rǰe grags (pa), I, 374 ff.; II, 789.
Rwa Saṅs-rgyas kun-dga', II, 445.
Rag, II, 1085.

Rag-ma-ba, I, 302.
Rag-śi, I, 77, II, 572, 1085.
Rag-śi Tshul-khrims, I, 61-2.
Raṅ-grol, I, 189.
Raṅ-thag mkhan-po, I, 135-6.
Raṅ-byuṅ Kun-mkhyen Čhos-kyi rgyal-po, II, 517.
Raṅ-'byuṅ rdo rje (Karma-), I, 150, 199, 200, 308-9, 389; II, 410, 487, 493-4, 497-8, 502, 517, 520, 524-5, 528, 533, 537-8, 541 2, 548, 582, 696, 722, 751, 775, 796, 1007.
Raṅ-'byuṅ-ba, I, 338; II, 487, 493, 527, 703, 796, 991.
Raṅ-'byuṅ saṅs rgyas, II, 519.
Rab-kha-ba, I, 292.
Rab-dga'-ba čhen po, II, 1088.
Rab-tu sgra-grags, I, 13.
Rab-tu ži-ba'i bśes-gñen, I, 371.
Rab-brtan, I, 16.
Rab-gduṅ-ldan, I, 14.
Rab 'dul, I, 14.
Rab-dbya Jo-sras, I, 376.
Rab-'byor seṅ-ge, II, 1073.
Rab-bzaṅ-mdaṅs, II, 847.
Rab-gsal, I, xvii.
Rab-gsal zla-ba, II, 753.
Ram, I, 270; II, 407-8, 446.
Ram-ston rgyal-ba, I, 121.
Ram rDo-rje btsan, II, 407.
Ram sdiṅ-ma ba, I, 269; II, 705.
Ram bTsan-čan, II, 406.
Ral-rgyags-gza'-lčam-ma, I, 292.
Ral-lčags ston- tshul, II, 477.
Ral-pa-čan, I, xix, 37, 44, 50, 71, 108, 191; II, 648.
Ras-chuṅ-pa (Lo-ro-ba), I, 142-3, 273; II, 435-440, 450-1, 521, 533, 556, 568, 588, 655-6, 660, 868, 678, 739, 842, 844, 860-1, 929, 1007.
Ras-čhen, II, 484. See Saṅs-rgyas ras-čhen.
Ras-ston bsod-rin, II, 532.
Ras-pa (Čhos-rje-), II, 682-3.
Ras-pa (Ti-śri-), II, 470.
Ras-pa Kha-kyog rDo-rje seṅ-ge II, 875.
Ras-pa sGom-thag, I, 181.
Ras-pa Dri-med-'od, I, 196.
Ras-pa rDo-rje-dpal, II, 962.
Ras-pa dBaṅ-ṅe, II, 445.

Ras-pa Ži-ba-'od, II, 435.
Ras-pa lo-tsā, II, 727.
Ras-pa Lha-ri-pa, II, 900.
Ri-khor ras-pa, II, 491.
Ri-khrod-pa (Śa-ba-ri-pa), II, 451, 541-2, 876, 972, 975, 1025.
Ri-khrod-pa dBaṅ-phyug, II, 796.
Ri-khrod sBug-ston, II, 952.
Ri-khrod-ma, II, 869.
Ri-khrod-žabs, II, 841.
Ri-khrod žig-po, II, 998.
Ri-khrod rluṅ-čhuṅ, 180-1.
Ri-goṅ-pa, II, 745.
Ri-mgo-ba, II 518.
Ri-ston bLo-čhen-'od, II, 779.
Ri-dags-dgra (Śa-ba-ri), II 818.
Ri-gdoṅ-pa Śes-rab rgyal-mtshan, I, 155-6.
Ri-pa, II 895-6.
Ri-pa gŽon-nu rgyal-mtshan, II, 692.
Ri-pa Śākya bzaṅ-po, I, 373.
Ri-phug-pa, II, 601.
Ri-bo-sgaṅ-pa, II, 504.
Ri-bo-čhe-pa, II, 513.
Ri-ma, II, 916.
Ri-ma-'babs-pa (Čhos-rje-), II, 546, 860 991.
Ri-mer-ba, I, 302.
Rig-pa'i khu-yug, I, 243.
Rig-pa'i, brug-sgra, II, 694.
Rig-pa'i ral-gri (bČom-ldan-), I, 336, 339; II, 1059. See bČom-ldan-pa, Rig-ral.
Rig-pa'i ral-gri (bKa'-bži-pa-), II, 544, 548, (Rin-čhen bzaṅ-po).
Rig-'dzin Kumārarāja, I, 197; II, 491.
Rig-'dzin sñiṅ-po, II, 789.
Rig-'dzin-pa, I, 201.
Rig-'dzin gŽon-nu rgyal-po, II, 696.
Rig-ral (Rig-pa'i ral-gri), I, 58, 102, 104, 337 (bČom-ldan Ral-gri).
Rig-ral, II, 544.
Rigs-ldan, II, 516, 555-6, 817.
Rigs-ldan rgyal-dka', II, 754.
Rigs-ldan rnam-rgyal, II, 802.
Rin, I, 74.
Rin-skyabs, I, 79.
Rin-grub-pa (Rin-čhen-grub), II, 1072.
Rin-rgyal, I, vi.

Rin-rgyal-ba, I, 396-7.
Rin-čan-pa, I, 314.
Rin-čhen, I, 126, 321; II, 405, 506.
Rin-čhen grags-pa, I, vii, viii, 47, 330, 376; II, 519, 801, 803.
Rin-čhen-grub (Rin-grub), I, 309.
Rin-čhen gliṅ-pa, II, 426, 439.
Rin-čhen-mgon, I, 133; II, (sKu-yal-ba-), 621. 623, (bLa-ma-), 696.
Rin-čhen rgya-mtsho, I, 344.
Rin-čhen rgyal-po (dPon-čhen-), II, 823.
Rin-čhen rgyal-po (Lha-), I, 373; II, 413, 581.
Rin-čhen rgyal-mtshan I, 212; II, 810, 813, 1073.
Rin-čhen rgyal-mtshan-dpal-bzaṅ-po II, 749.
Rin-čhen sgaṅ-pa, I, 314.
Rin-čhen-čhos-rgyal, II, 835. 1060.
Rin-čhen Ĵo-sras, II, 657.
Rin-čhen sñiṅ-po, I, 265, 286, II, 893.
Rin-čhen rdo-rje, I, 206, 229, 344, 378; II, 729, 749. (bKa'-bži-pa-).
Rin-čhen rnam-rgyal, I, 330.
Rin-čhen rnam-rgyal-ba (lo-tsā-ba-), II, 794, 866.
Rin-čhen-dpal I. 59; II, 413; (Emperor) 492, ('I-li-ji) 500; 517; (bla-ma) 520; 599. (Sa-skya-pa-), 659. (U-rgyana-pa) 699, 1088. (bKa'-bži-pa)- II, 509, 545, (Gu-śrī-) 509. (Zur-dgon bka'-bži-pa) 544.
Rin-čhen dpal-pa, II, 638.
Rin-čhen dpal-bzaṅ-po, II, 723.
Rin-čhen-dpal-bzaṅs, II, 608.
Rin-čhen byaṅ-čhub, I, 330.
Rin-čhen blo-gros, II, 608.
Rin-čhen dbaṅ-phyug, II, 894.
Rin-čhen 'byuṅ-gnas, II, 634, 1059
Rin-čhen smon-lam, II, 975.
Rin-čhen rtse-mo, II, 698, 783.
Rin-čhen brtson-'grus, II, 735.
Rin-čhen tshul-khrims, II, 782.
Rin-čhen rdzogs-pa, II, 696.
Rin-čhen gžon-nu, II, 720.
Rin-čhen bzaṅ-po (bka'-bži-pa-), II, 509.
Rin-čhen bzaṅ-po (dPon-), II, 823-4, 831.
Rin-čhen bzaṅ-po (bla-ma-), II, 410-1, 1088.
Rin-čhen bzaṅ-po (Ratnabhadra), II, 1044.
Rin-čhen bzaṅ-po (lo-tsā-ba-), I, 68. 102, 123, 205, 209, 249, 262, 328 351-52, 359, 372-3, 380; II, 417, 472, 432, 1085.
Rin-čhen bzaṅ-po-ba, II, 596.

Rin-čhen-'od (bLa-ma Bya-nag čhen-po-), II, 1087.
Rin-čhen 'od-zer, I, 220; II, 518.
Rin-čhen śes-rab, II, 581.
Rin-čhen seṅ-ge (rTogs-ldan-) II, 988.
Rin-čhen seṅ-ge (Yan-rtse-ba-), I, 385, 396; II, 995.
Rin-čhen seṅ-ge (Lha-), I. 281-2.
Rin-čhen bsam-gtan-dpal-bzaṅ, II. 749.
Rin-čhen lha-mo, II, 730.
Rin-rdor-ba, II, 586.
Rin-rnam-pa, I, 374 (sGra-tshad-pa).
Rin-po-čhe-ba, II, 512, 581, 1051.
Rin-spuṅs-pa, I. 340; II, 692.
Rin-byuṅ, II, 1044.
Rin-smon, II, 532.
Rin-tshul (Rin-čhen tshul-khrims), I. 309; II, 1072.
Rin-gžon (ācārya), I, 308; II, 410.
Rin-gžon-pa (bla-čhen-), II. 588-9. 591, 696.
Rin-bzaṅs dkar-po (Rin-bzaṅs-pa), II. 546, 549.
Rin-śe-pa (Rin-čhen śes-rab), II, 1072.
Ri'u-sgaṅ-pa, II. 518.
Ril-pa, I, 182.
Ru Ānandavajra, I. 166.
Ru-čhe bTsan-skyes, I, 159.
Ru Dharmabodhi, I. 159.
Ru-mtshams-pa bSod-rin, II, 956.
Rug-pa'i rgya-sgom, I. 285.
Rug-pa'i Žaṅ-čhen-po, I, 264.
Rus-sbal-žabs, II. 754, 803. Rus-sbal-žabs-čan, I, 380.
Red-mda'-pa (gŽon-nu blo-gros), I, 336, 339-40. 349.
Red-mda'-ma, I, 213.
Re'u-rmal, I, 37.
Ro-mñam-rdo-rje (Khams-pa Ro-mñam), II. 416, 426.
Ro-mñams, II, 418.
Ro-'bye-gza' bTsun-ne, II. 553.
Ro-zan-ma, II, 919.
Rog, I. 270, 329, 345; II, 943-8.
Rog mŇon-pa-pa (Rog mŇon-pa). I, 270, 376 379; II, 440.
Rog Čhos-kyi brtson-'grus, I. 345.
Rog Čhos-dbaṅ I, 80.
Rog 'Čhims-phu-ba, I. 322.
Rog-ston, II, 678, 1044
Rog-ston kLu-sbyin, II, 940, 953.

Rog-ston bṬsan-po, I, 156; II, 899, 940, 953.
Rog-bde, II, 865.
Rog rDor-seṅ, II, 862. See Rog-pa dMar-pa rDor-seṅ.
Rog-pa, II, 982.
Rog-pa rGwa-lo, II, 1052.
Rog-pa dMar-pa rDor-seṅ, II, 862. See Rog rDor-seṅ.
Rog-pa sar-ma, II, 982.
Rog-po-dga', I, 188.
Rog byugs-se, I, 376.
Rog-dmar-žur-pa, I, 98, 269.
Rog Śākya 'byuṅ-gnas, I, 110.
Rog Śes-rab rgya-mtsho, I, 270. See Dol-pa dMar-žur-pa.
Rog Śes-rab bla-ma, II, 939.
Rog Śes-rab zla-ba, II, 953.
Rog Śes-rab-'od, I, 156-7; II, 871-2, 875-6, 883, 900, 905-6, 910, 937, 991, 998-9.
Roṅ-gliṅ lo-tsā-ba, II, 837. Roṅ-gliṅ lo-tsā-ba rDo-rje rgyal-mtshan, II, 1061.
Roṅ-čhuṅ ras-pa, II, 435.
Roṅ-čhen-pa, II, 516.
Roṅ-ston (sMra-ba'i khyu-mčhog čhen-po-), II, 799, 1018.
Roṅ-ston Kha-bo-čhe, I, 284.
Roṅ-ston čhen-po (sMra-ba'i seṅ-ge), II, 1080. See Roṅ-ston.
Roṅ-ston sMra-ba'i seṅ-ge čhen-mo, I, 340; II, 807, 809.
Roṅ-thoṅ-pa, II, 727.
Roṅ-pa, I, 164.
Roṅ-pa Kun-dga', I, 166.
Roṅ-pa 'Gar-dge-ba, II, 477.
Roṅ-pa rGā-lo—Roṅ-pa rGwa-lo, I, 307, 336, 396; II, 627.
Roṅ-pa rGyal-le, I, 364-5. Roṅ-pa rGya-le, I, 376.
Roṅ-pa Čhos-mgon, I, 374.
Roṅ-pa Čhos-bzaṅ, II, 1004.
Roṅ-pa Jo-bzaṅ, I, 166.
Roṅ-pa Phyag-sor-pa, I, 321, 365, 374.
Roṅ-pa 'Bum-'bar, I, 166.
Roṅ-pa Śes-rab seṅ-ge, II, 756, 785.
Roṅ-pa Ser-seṅ, I, 396.
Roṅ-po dGe-riṅs, I, 387.
Roṅ-ban dPal-gyi rin-po-čhe, I, 165.
Roṅ-ban Yon-tan rin-čhen, I, 160, 167.
Roṅ-ban Rin-čhen tshul-khrims, I, 160, 164-5, 167.
Roṅ-zom, I, 157, 162, 256.
Roṅ-zom Čhos-bzaṅ, I, 226. Roṅ-žom Čhos-kyi bzaṅ-po, I, 160-7, 230, 383.

Rom-po-ba, I, 387.
Rol-pa Lha-mo-čhe, I, 361.
Rol-pa'i rdo-rje (Čhos-rje Kar-ma-pa-), II, 449, 493, 501, 504, 518, 541, 543, 547, 595, 731, 843.
Rol-pa'i rdo-rje (Lalitavajra), II, 1030.
rLaṅs-pa, I, 20, 33.
rLa-čhuṅ-ma, II, 893.
rLuṅ, I, 74, 147.
rLuṅ-ston rDo-rje bla-ma, II, 862. rLuṅ-rDo-rje bla-ma, II 864.
rLuṅ-dam-pa čhen-po, I, 180.
rLuṅ-phyag-dum, I, 144.
rLuṅ-ras, I, 181.
rLuṅs Legs-pa'i śes-rab, I, 77.
La-stod dMar-po, II, 1025-6, 1030.
La-stod gTsaṅ-śod-pa, II, 859.
La-stod gTsaṅ-so, II, 900.
La-drug, II, 409.
La-ba-pa (dPal-, sPyod-pa-pa), I, 362-3, 385; II, 426, 753, 1026.
La-ba'i 'od-zer, II, 352.
La-mo-ba, I, 292.
La-zi Śes-rab sgron-ma, I, 170.
La-yag Jo-sras, II, 462.
La-yag-pa, II, 518.
La-gyag-pa, II, 1008.
Lag-rna, I, 8.
Lag-rna-čan, I, 16.
Laṅ-ka-li-pa, II, 895.
Laṅ-ston Jo-pad, II, 941.
Laṅ-ston Dar-ma bsod-nams, I, 126.
Laṅ-pa sTon-śāk, I, 295.
Laṅ-tsha sTon-nag, I, 376.
Laṅ-za sTon-pa Dar-ma bsod-nams, I, 171.
Laṅ-lab Byaṅ-čhub rdo-rje, I, 156.
Laṅs-ston, I, 171.
Lan-pa, II, 979.
Labs-sgron, I, 180; II, 983-5.
Las-kyi rdo-rje, I, 105; 782, 1048, 1076, 1079.
Las-čhen Kun-rgyal-ba, II, 1050.
Las-čhen Rin-rgyal-ba, II, 645.
Las-stod-pa, II, 678,
Las-stod dBaṅ-rgyal, II, 533.
Li-the-se, I, 38.

Li-bdud rTsi-grags, I, 345.
Li-byin-ha-ra, II, 814.
Li-mo Ye-śes-sgron, I, 284.
Li-ras, II, 568.
Lu-skam ras-pa, II, 435.
Lu-dpon Su-kha-de-va, I, 344.
Lugs-smad-pa, I, 273.
Luṅ-gi-rgya-mtsho (sTan-gčig-pa-), I, 310.
Luṅ-gi dbaṅ-phyug (Lha-), I, 276-8.
Luṅ-phran-pa čhen-po, II, 993.
Luṅ-mo-pa mDo-sde, I, 271.
Lu'i-pa—Lū-yi-pa, I, 143, 380, 385, 389; II, 803-4, 852, 869.
Lus-thub, I, 14.
Legs-skyes, I, 5; II, 800, 803.
Legs-mčhog-pa, II, 749.
Legs-mthoṅ, I, 13.
Legs-ldan-'byed, I, 29.
Legs-pa rgyal-mtshan, II, 1079.
Legs-pa-dpal, I, 217.
Legs-pa-ba, II, 589.
Legs-pa'i śes-rab, I, 352.
Legs-par-skyes, I, 16.
Legs-par rab-gsal, I, 12.
Legs-byin, I, 33.
Legs-mdzes, II, 462.
Legs-bśad-pa (rab-'byams-pa-), II, 830-1.
Legs-se, II, 435.
Leṅ, I, 72, 262.
Leṅ, lo-tsā-ba, II, 852.
Lo (rGyal-ba-), II, 726, 1085.
Lo (Lo-ras-pa), II, 670, 672-3.
Lo-grags-pa, II, 780.
Lo-sgom, II, 953.
Lo-ston rDo-rje dbaṅ-phyug, I, 205.
Lo-thuṅ Śak-rgyal, I, 111.
Lo-be-ba Kun-bzaṅ, II, 733.
Lo-byi-mgo-pa, II, 439, 440.
Lo-mo-ba Saṅs-rgyas ston-pa, II, 1024.
Lo btsun-čhuṅ, II, 871.
Lo-žiṅ-pa, II, 727.
Lo-ras, II, 409, 676, 679.
Lo-ras Čhos-skyoṅ-dpal, II, 691.

Lo-ro gLan byi-mgo-pa, II, 439.
Lo-ro-ba, II, 948.
Lo-ro Žig-po, II, 889.
Lo-ro Ye-mgon, II, 667.
Lo-ro Ras-čhuṅ-pa, 235.
Lo-ro-ras-pa, II, 568, 709. (Ras-čhuṅ-pa).
Lo-rog, I, 111.
Log-phug-pa, II, 421.
Loṅ-po, II, 629.
Śa-gaṅ lo-tsā-ba, I, 104.
Śa Grags-pa seṅ-ge, II, 517.
Śa-ston rDor-'dzin, II, 985, 998-9.
Śa-pa-gliṅ-pa, I, 292; II, 475.
Śa-ba-ri, II, 866. Śa-ba-ri-pa, II, 869. Śa-ba-ri dbaṅ-phyug, I, 380; II, 727, 774, 795-6, 798-9, 821, 842. See Ri-khrod-pa dBaṅ-phyug.
Śa-bo sgaṅ-pa Pad-ma byaṅ-čhub, I, 271.
Śa-dbu-rtse-ba, II, 564.
Śa-mi (sGom-smon), I, 79, 80, 82, 273; II, 879, 880-3, 890.
Śa-mi 'dul-'dzin, II, 466.
Śa-yaṅ-dgon-pa, II, 564.
Śa-ra-ba, i, 267.
Śā-na'i gos-čan, II, 1051.
Śwa-dbaṅ-rwa, II, 1001.
Śāk-grub, II, 1055.
Śāk-mgon, I, 110.
Śāk-'bum-pa, I, 155.
Śāk-'byuṅ-pa, I, 151.
Śāk-gžon, I, 292, 341.
Śāk-'od, I, 110, 138.
Śāk-śe, II, 855.
Śākya bkra-śis, I, 280.
Śākya grags-pa, II, 546, 549, 896. (mKhan-čhen-), II, 693.
Śākya grub-pa, I, 81-2l
Śākya dge-sbyoṅ, II, 975.
Śākya mgon, I, 38; II, 1016.
Śākya rgyal-po-pa, I, 190; II, 405.
Śākya rgyal-mtshan, II, 801.
Śākya gñan, I, 138.
Śākya rdo-rje. I, 82, 171, 353.
Śākya-dpal, II, 1059-60.
Śākya dpal-mgon, II, 1089.
Śākya-blo, I, 70, 346.

Śākya blo-gros, I, x, 210, 262.
Śākya dbaṅ-phyug, I, 331.
Śākya 'bum-pa, II, 716-7, 747.
Śākya gžon-nu, I, 205, 344; II, 490.
Śākya bzaṅ-po, I, 216. (sTag-luṅ lo-tsā-ba-), 310l (Gu-śri-), II, 509.
Śākya-'od, I, 155.
Śākya ye-śes, II, 715-6.
Śākya ras-pa, II, 687.
Śākya rin-čhen, I, 38; II, 807.
Śākya śes-rab, I, 63.
Śākya bśes-gñen, I, 360.
Śākya seṅ-ge, I, 73, 122.
Śākya seṅ-ge rgyal-mtshan, II, 802.
Śākya seṅ-ge bzaṅ-po, II, 1006.
Śākya bSod-nams rgyal-mtshan-dpal-bzaṅ-po (Lha-), I, 282.
Śaṅs-čhuṅ-ma, II, 919.
Śaṅs-pa, II, 727, 733, 735, 742, 746, 751-2.
Śaṅs-pa Kun-mkhyen, I, 151; II, 704, 1024.
Śaṅs-ston, II, 748.
Śaṅs-pa Jo-stan, I, 82.
Śaṅs-pa dbU-sdebs, II, 911.
Śaṅs-pa Mar-ston, II, 445-6.
Śaṅs-pa Tshul-śe (Śaṅs-tshul), 973.
Śaṅs-pa ras-pa, I, 193.
Śaṅs-pa Roṁ-bhe, II, 953.
Śaṅs-pa Śāk-'bum, I, 149.
Śab-kyi brag-rtse so-nag-pa, I, 203.
Śab-pa-gliṅ-pa, I, 305; II, 453.
Śab-mo-lčam-čig, I, 208.
Śab-rtsa-gser-ba, I, 125.
Śab-rtse rGya-gar, I, 353.
Śam-po me-dig, I, 326.
Śam-'bum, II, 727.
Śar-gliṅ-pa, II, 580.
Śar Dags-po-pa dPal-phyogs-thams-čad-las rnam-par rgyal-ba'i-lha, I, ii; II, 1090.
Śar-pa, II, 518.
Śar-pa Kun-bsod-pa, II, 1088.
Śar-pa Ye-śes rgyal-mtshan, II, 1059.
Śar-ba-pa, I, 73, 236, 260, 269, 270-1-5, 282.4, 305, 320, 341, 372; II, 475.
Śar-ba-pa bLo-gros grags, I, 273.
Śar Rin-po-čhe, II, 595.

Śiṅ-mgo-pa, II, 565.
Śiṅ-rta brgya-pa, I, 13.
Śiṅ-rta bču-pa, I, 12, 13.
Śiṅ-rta brtan, I, 16.
Śiṅ-rta sdu-gu-čan, I, 14.
Śiṅ-rta rnam-par sna-tshogs-pa, I, 16.
Śiṅ-rta sna-tshogs, I, 16.
Śiṅ-rta bzliṅ-po, I, 16.
Śiṅ-rta sra-ba, I, 5.
Śiṅ-lo-ma, II, 869.
Śu-ston Mon-sras, I, 132.
Śug-rtsar-ba, II, 563.
Śug-gseb-pa, II, 896.
Śug-gseb-ri-pa, (gŽon-nu rdo-rje, gŽon-nu rin-čhen), II. 692, 864, 895.
Śuṅ-ke lo-tsā-ba Dar-ma rdo-rje, I, 365-6.
Śuṅ-ke śPa-ba-čan, II, 403.
Śuṅ-bu gŽon-nu grags-pa, I, 76.
Śud-phu lo-tsā-ba 'Byuṅ-gnas rgyal-mtshan, II, 407, 874.
Śud-bu lo-tsā-ba, II, 985.
Śud-mo Śāk-sgron, II, 878.
Śe, I, 627.
Śe-rgan sMan-čhuṅ, II, 733.
Śe-sṅon Byaṅ-'bar, II, 857.
Śe-pa-dar-re, II, 617,
Śe'u, II, 874.
Śe'u-ba, I, 128.
Śer-mgon-pa, II, 634, 1072.
Śer-rgyal-ba (mṄa'-ris rab-'byams-pa-), II, 831.
Śer-sgom Dar-seṅ, II, 859.
Śer-don-pa, II, 590-2.
Śer-'phags-pa, II, 1072.
Śer-'byuṅ, ('Prul-sku) I, 133, II, 466
Śer-'byuṅ, (Prajñākaragupta), I, 340.
Śer-seṅ, I, 289.
Śel-brag-pa, II, 705.
Śes, I, 269.
Śes-skor-ba, I, 267.
Śes-rgyal, II, 792.
Śes-rdor-ba, II, 451, 1052.
Śes-tshul-pa, II, 1072.
Śes-'od-pa, II, 1072.
Śes-rab, I, 190; II, 956.

Śes-rab-kyi dbaṅ-po gsal-ba, I, 206.
Śes-ab gu-śrī, II, 501.
Śes-rab go-čha, I, 36.
Śes-rab-grags, II, 464.
Śes-rab-grub, II, 939, 955.
Śes-rab-mgon-po, II, 1072.
Śes-rab mgon-po Saṅs-rgyas legs-pa, I, 93; II, 695.
Śes-rab rgyan, II, 421.
Śes-rab rgyal-ba, I, 95.
Śes-rab rgyal-mtshan, I, 155, 283, (ācārya) 309, (upādhyāya) 320, (abbot of gSaṅ-phu) 329; (Guṅ-thaṅ rab-'byams-pa-), II, 1050.
Śes-rab rgyal-mtshan (Kun-mkhyen-' Čhos-rje Kun-mkhyen čhen-po-, Dol-po-pa-), II, 775-6, 778, 780, 782, 785.
Śes-rab-dar, II, 696.
Śes-rab rdo-rje, 233, 262, 272, 284, 344; II, 475, 751, 1007.
Śes-rab-pa, II, 592.
Śes-rab dpal, II, 489. 619, 663, (Čhu-tshan-kha-pa-), II, 544
Śes-rab dpal-ldan, I, 329.
Śes-rab dpal-ldan (bka'-bži-pa-), II, 807.
Śes-rab dpal-bzaṅs, I, 374.
Śes-rab bla-ma, II, 627.
Śes-rab dbaṅ-po, II, 830.
Śes-rab-'bar, I, 291, 330.
Śes-rab 'bum-pa, II, 783.
Śes-rab 'byuṅ-gnas, I, 66, 262. (Śer-'byuṅ) II, 466, ('Bri-khuṅ-gliṅ-pa) 468. ('Jam-dbyaṅs mgon-po) 676.
Śes-rab 'byuṅ-gnas blo-gros, I, 201.
Śes-rab me-čhuṅ, II, 875.
Śes-rab tshul-khrims, I, 210.
Śes-rab bzaṅ-po (mTsho-sna-pa-), I, 82, (Prajñābhadra) 243-4; II, 868. (Čhos-rje-) 970.
Śes-rab-'od, II, 939, (rGya-mon) 941.
Śes-rab 'od-zer-pa, II, 751.
Śes-rab yon-tan, I, 210.
Śes-rab ral-gri, II, 1016.
Śes-rab seṅ-ge, I, 339, (bla-ma-) 379, (Prajñāsiṃha) II, 400; 672; 791; 1052.
Śes-rab sen-ge-ba, II, 793.
Śes-rab gsan-ba (Śam-thabs dmar-po-), II, 697.
Śo-sgom 'Phags-pa, II, 464.
Śo-sras, I, 181.
Śo-mo-gza' Čhe-lčam, II, 453.
Śo-rom 'Phags-pa, II, 462.

Soṅ, II, 784, 794.
Soṅ-ston, I, 218.
Soṅ-ston rDo-rje rgyal-mtshan, II, 784, 786, 837.
Soṅ-ston Rab-brtan, II, 749.
Soṅ bLo-gros brtan-pa, II, 785.
Soṅ bLo-brtan, I, 345, 379; II, 838.
Sod-bu lo-tsā-ba, I, 180.
Śol-po-ba, II, 409.
gŚen, II, 706, 1009.
gSen-dgon dkar-ba (rDo-rje dbaṅ-phyug), II, 565.
gSen-sgom dkar-ba, II 563.
gSen-sgom Žig-po, II, 448ff.
gSen-sgom Re-thul-čan, II, 928.
gSen-sgom Ros-po, I, 208.
gSen-čhen-po, II, 706.
gSen-ston Nam-mkha', II, 872.
gSen-pa rDo-rje seṅ-ge, II, 4c8, 477.
gSen-sa-bug-pa, I, 236.
gSen-tsha Dar-ma-'od, I, 176.
bSes-gñen rgyal-mčhog, II, 1073.
gSes gñen bzaṅ-po, II, 1073.
bŚes-gñen gsaṅ-ba, I, 262.
Sa-skya-pa, I, 103; II, 556-7, 559, 724-5, 744, 792.
Sa-skya-pa Kun-dga' sñiṅ-po, II, 970.
Sa-skya paṇ-čhen, I, 34, 195, 216, 218, 307, 335; II, 501, 690, 784.
Sa-skya paṇḍita Kun-dga' rgyal-mtshan, I, 103, 212, 232, 306, 346; II, 578, 606-7, 692, 726, 745, 809, 1058.
Sa-skya lo-tsā-ba (Sa-lo), II, 1057.
Sa-khyim, I, 11.
Sa-khrom rGya-mtsho-'bar, I, 165.
Sa-grags-seṅ-ba, II, 58?.
Sa-čhen, II, 558.
Sa-čhen Kun-sñiṅ-(Kun-dga' sñiṅ-po), I, 126, 211, 215; II, 569, 1008, 1050-1. See Sa-skya-pa
Kun-dga' sñiṅ-po.
Sa--ston rDor-'dzin, II, 988.
Sa-ston Lha-riṅ, II, 747.
Sa-then, II, 909.
Śa-dag, I, 15.
Sa-'dres-pa, I, 360.
Sa-paṇ, II, 589. See Sa-skya paṇ-čhen.
Sa-gtso, I, 15.

Sa-'tsho-ma, I, 18.
Sa-'dzin, I, 15.
Sa-bzaṅ 'Phags-pa gŽon-nu blo-gros (Ma-ti paṇ-čhen), 1045-6.
Sa-bzaṅ-pa bLo-gros rgyal-mtshan, II, 1045.
Sa-'od, I, 45.
Sa-'od-bzaṅ, I, 45.
Sa-la sPyod-pa'i dbaṅ-phyug, II, 823.
Sa-sruṅ, I, 45.
Sag-ston, II, 900.
Saṅ-grags, I, 341.
Saṅ-čhos-pa, I, 329.
Saṅ-blo ba, II, 588-9.
Saṅ-bzaṅ-pa, II, 633.
Saṅ-yon-pa, (Saṅs-rgyas yon-tan), I, 316-7.
Saṅ-rin-pa, II, 1023.
Saṅ-śi, I, 41; II, 789.
Saṅgha-rmal, I, 37.
Saṅs-rgyas, II, 623; 915.
Saṅs-rgyas skyabs, II, 435, 612, 695. (Yon-čhen-), 579.
Saṅs-rgyas khrom-ras, II, 687.
Saṅs-rgyas goṅ-la-ba-pa, I, 155.
Saṅs-rgyas-grags, I, 154.
Saṅs-rgyas dge-sloṅ, II, 990.
Saṅs-rgyas mgon-po, I, 98, 100, 170.
Saṅs-rgyas rgya-sgom, II, 657. (dGon-gsar-pa-).
Saṅs-rgyas rgyal-mtshan, I, 98. (Čhe-sa-), II, 412.
Saṅs-rgyas sgom-pa, I, 300-1; of Bya-yu) 304, (of sNar-thaṅ) 319; II, 621, 623; 861-2.
Saṅs-rgyas sgom-pa byaṅ-čhub rdo-rje, I, 884.
Saṅs-rgyas sgom-pa seṅ-ge-skyabs, I, 282.
Saṅs-rgyas Jo-bo, I, 94, 302ff, 308.
Saṅs-rgyas Jo-sras, II, 855.
Saṅs-rgyas' Jam-rgyal, II, 1024.
Saṅs-rgyas gÑan-ston, II, 743, 746. Saṅs-rgyas gÑan-ston Čhos-kyi śes-rab, II, 741.
Saṅs-rgyas gÑan-čhuṅ, II, 385.
Saṅs rgyas gÑan-ras, II, 568.
Saṅs-rgyas gÑal-čhuṅ-ba, II, 557.
Saṅs-rgyas sÑan-ston, II, 737.
Saṅs-rgyas sñiṅ-ston, II, 716.
Saṅs-rgyas ston, I, 132. Saṅs-rgyas ston-pa, I. 303-4, 308, 320; (rTson-'grus seṅ-ge), 743-51, 991, (bla-ma-) 992; 999.

Saṅs-rgyas brtan-pa, I, 98.
Saṅs-rgyas bstan-bsruṅs, II, 987.
Saṅs-rgyas Dags-čhuṅ, I, 132.
Saṅs-rgyas rdo-rǰe, I, 320 (of Čhos-phug). (Dus-'khor-ba-) II, 699, 700, 796; 896.
Saṅs-rgyas-dpal, (gYag-phrug-) I, 339, (mahā-upādhyāya-) 340-1; II, 1080.
Saṅs-rgyas-dpal (sTag-luṅ Rin-po-čhe-), II, 783.
Saṅs-rgyas dpal-bzaṅ-po, II, 633.
Saṅs-rgyas dpal-rin, I, 202.
Saṅs-rgyas-'phel, I, 340.
Saṅs-rgyas blo-gros (Čhos-rǰe), II, 704, 1080; Saṅs-rgyas blo-gros-pa (mahā-upādhyāya-) 535, 592, 482.
Saṅs-rgyas bya-sgom (gÑal-smad-dpal-ri-ba-), II, 657.
Saṅs rgyas-dbon, (of rGya-ma), I, 271; (Grags-pa-dpal) II, 6502; (bla-ma, 696; (abbot of sÑe-phu), 893-4.
Saṅs-rgyas-dbon-po, (of rGyal-steṅs) I, 304; (of Čhos-phug), 320; 864, 1024.
Saṅs-rgyas-dbyaṅs, II, 797, 799, 800.
Saṅs-rgyas-'bum, II, 716.
Saṅs-rgyas 'bum-dpal, I, 98; II, 1023.
Saṅs-rgyas 'bum-me, II, 406, 716.
Saṅs-rgyas 'mi-bskyod rdo-rǰe, II, 689.
Saṅs-rgyas Myaṅ-ston, II, 988.
Saṅs-rgyas gTsaṅ-ston, I, 307.
Saṅs-rgyas brtsag-son, II, 862.
Saṅs-rgyas gžon-nu, II, 716.
Saṅs-rgyas gžon-nu-pa (abbot of Tshogs-pa Bya-rdzoṅ), II, 1072.
Saṅs-rgyas gžon-'od, I, 316.
Saṅs-rgyas bzaṅ-po, I, 93, 1090; II, 634.
Saṅs-rgyas 'od-'byuṅ, I, 316.
Saṅs-rgyas 'od-zer, I, 308.
Saṅs-rgyas yar-byon, I, 307 (of sTag-luṅ) ; II, 523, 629, 630-1, 650-1.
Saṅs-rgyas yar-byon śes-rab bla-ma, II, 627-8.
Saṅs-rgyas ye-śes, I, 160, 171; (ācārya-), 367, 369; II, 803.
Saṅs-rgyas ye-śes-žabs, I, 108-9, 243 (ācārya Buddhajñānapāda).
Saṅs-rgyas yon-tan (Saṅ-yon-pa), I, 316.
Saṅs-rgyas rab-ston, II, 990.
Saṅs-rgyas ras-čhen, I, 374 ; II, 480, 483-4, 690, 1007.
Saṅs-rgyas ras-pa, I, 197 ; II, 975.
Saṅs-rgyas ras-pa čhen-po, II, 517.
Saṅs-rgyas ri-pa, II, 1040.
Saṅs-rgyas rin-čhen, II, 509 ; (sgrub-pa-po-), 963, (Gu-śri-) 1072.
Saṅs-rgyas riṅ-čhen rgyal-mtshan dpal-bzaṅ-po, I, 151.

Saṅs-rgyas rin-čhen-pa, I, 172; II, 779.
Saṅs-rgyas le-sgom (gSer-lta-ba-), II, 657.
Saṅs-rgyas śes-rab, I, 321.
Saṅs-rgyas seṅ-ge, II, 516.
Saṅs-rgyas gsaṅ-ba, I, 170, 191, 351-2.
Saṅs-rgyas lha-sgom (Gor-gdoṅ-pa-), II, 657.
Saṅs-gžon, II, 1044.
Saṅs-rin-pa, II, 716.
Sad-na-legs, I, xx.
Sam-bu lo-tsā-ba, II, 712.
Sa'i sñiṅ-po, II, 842.
Sa'i gdoṅ, I, 5.
Si-tu dGe-blo-ba, II, 498, 1023.
Si-tu dGe-sloṅ-ba, 639.
Si-tu Čhos-rin, II, 693.
Si-tu Rab-bstan-pa, II, 799.
Si-li-ma, I, 210.
Su-ston Zla-grags, I, 121.
Sun-luṅ-pa bSod-nams rdo-rǰe, I, 982.
Sum, I, 74, 76; II, 900.
Sum-ston dGe-'dun, II, 444.
Sum-ston Čhos-dar, II, 439.
Sum-ston Ñi-ma, I, 133.
Sum-ston Ye-'bar, I, 353, 355.
Sum-ston ras-pa (bSod-nams śes-rab), II, 744, 990, 999.
Sum-pa, I, 75, 252; II, 661, 663, 706, 1085.
Sum-pa Khu-tshab, II, 911.
Sum-pa mkhan po, II, 905, 963.
Sum-pa mThu-čhen, I, 262.
Sum-pa Phod-ka-čan, II, 406.
Sum-pa bLo-gros, I, 111.
Sum-pa dBaṅ-phyug, II, 440.
Sum-pa dBaṅ-tshul, I, 111.
Sum-pa Ye-'bar, I, 118.
Sum-pa Ye-śes blo-gros, I, xv, 61.
Sum-pa lo-tsā-ba (Dharma yon-tan), I, 388.
Se, I, 207, 210, 225, 238, 277; II, 760.
Se-mkhar čhuṅ-ba, I, 225; II, 1010.
Se-čhuṅ-ba, I, 289.
Se-čhen, I, 149, 154, 212, 216, 307.
Se-čhen rgyal-po, I, vi.
Se-čhen Nam-mkha' rgyal-mtshan, II, 755-6.

Se Čhos-kyi mṅa'-bdag, II, 760.
Se-ǰig, II, 728.
Se J̌o-sras (sPrul-sku-), II, 930.
Se-ston Kun-rig, I, 208, 215.
Se-ston sGra-gčan-zin, II, 857.
Se-ston J̌o-khro, II, 448.
Se-ston 'Byuṅ-ldan-'od, I, 157.
Se-dur-luṅ-pa, I, 143, 147.
Se-rnol-nam-lde, I, 37.
Se-rnol-po-lde, I, 37.
Se-'Pyil-pa—Se sPyil-bu-pa, I, 275-7. See Čhos-kyi rgyal-mtshan.
Se-ban ston-čhuṅ, II, 435.
Se-ban ras-pa, II, 435.
Se-byaṅ-pa, I, 229.
Se-mig-pa II, 726.
Se-mo-čhe-ba, II, 783.
Se-mo-čhe-ba Nam-mkha' rgyal-mtshan, II, 768-9, 771.
Se-btsun, I, 205, 252, 324, 345. See J̌o-bo Se-btsun.
Se-tsha bSod-nams rgyal-mtshan, I, 335.
Se Ye-śes brtson-'grus, I, 205.
Se-rigs, I, 376.
Se-luṅ-pa, I, 196.
Se lo-tsā-ba (gŽon-nu tshul-khri ms), II, 761-765, 795.
Seṅ-ge-grags, I, xvii, 64; II, 974 (siddha-).
Seṅ-ge-' gram, I, 12, 13, 16.
Seṅ-ge rgyal-po, I, 200. See Ža-ma Seṅ-ge. (bČu-gsum-pa-), II, 671,
Seṅ-ge rgyal-mtshan (of Khu-mdo), I, 262, 310; II, 1072.
Seṅ-ge rgyal-mtshan, I, 220. See Ža-ma seṅ-ge, 329.
Sen-ge rgyal-mtshan (rDor-'dzin-), II, 584.
Seṅ-ge rgyal-mtshan (Siṃhadhvaja), II, 757. (kLog-skya bka'-bži-pa) 518.
Seṅ-rgyal-ba (mahā-upādhyāya-), I, 310; II, 584.
Seṅ-ge-rgyab, I, 197.
Seṅ-ge-sgra, I, 12; II, 409.
Seṅ-ge-dpal, I, 217, (mahā-upādhyāya-) 308, 336 (of Čhu-mig); (dGe-ba'i bśes-gñen-) II, 564; (U-rgyan-pa) 697, 783 (disciple of Yon-tan rgya-mtsho-ba).
Seṅ-ge-dpal-pa, II, 451 (mahā-upādhyāya-), 722; (abbot of dGe-'dun-sgaṅ) 1072.
Seṅ-ge-ba, I, 151.
Seṅ-ge-'bum, II, 411.
Seṅ-ge dbon-po, I, 197.
Seṅ-ge rdzoṅ-pa, II, 727.
Seṅ-ge zil-gnon, I, 81-2.

Seṅ-ge bzaṅ-po, I, 367.
Seṅ-gza' Maṅ-skyid, II, 485.
Seṅ yes, II, 975.
Ser-pa rgyal-mtshan, I, 135.
Ser-ma-pa, II, 727.
So, I, 156.
So sKu-riṅs, II, 929.
So-khri-btsan-po, I, 36.
So dGe-'dun, I, 376.
So dGe-'dun-'bar, I, 97.
So-čhuṅ dGe-'dun-'bar, II, 876-81, 883. (Dam-pa So).
So-čhuṅ-ba, I, 124 186, 234; II, 741, 873, 8?8, 896, 904, 944.
So bsñun-gdaṅs, I, 180.
So-ston, I, 91, 190.
So-ston rDo-rje rgyal-mtshan, I, 364-5.
So Dar-ma sñiṅ-po, I, 157.
So Dar-ma seṅ-ge, I, 157; 665, 946. So Dar-seṅ, II, 941, 952.
So rDo-rje rgyal-mtshan, I, 376.
So-ldan, 15.
So-pa, II, 960.
So Maṅ-btsan, I, 181.
So-tshab 'dul-'dzin, I, 376.
So-zur-pa, II, 727.
So Ye-śes dbaṅ-phyug, I, 108-9.
So-riṅs, II, 876, 878.
Sog, I, 78-80.
Sog-po, Sog-po mDo-sde, II, 874-5. 947
Sog-po dPal-gyi ye-śes, I, 108, 170.
Sog-po-ba, I, 269.
Sog-dbon, I, 330.
Son-pa Kun-rgyal, II, 772.
Sra-brtan rdo-rje, I, 166.
Srags rgya-mtsho, I, 66.
Sraṅ-skya-pa, II, 727.
Srad čhen-po, I, 229.
Srad-ma dkar-po, II, 466.
Srad Ye-gžon, I, 354.
Sri-dkar saṅ-śi, II, 545.
Sri-thar-skyid, I, 303.
Srid-pa, 14.
Sribs-khri-btsan-po, I, 36.
Sru-pa rDo-rje rgyal-po, II, 1011-2.

Sru-gza' sGron-ma-skyid, I, 170.
Sruṅ-skyid, II, 975.
Srul-glen, I, 219.
Sregs, II, 744.
Sro, I, 149.
Sroṅ-ṅe, I, 37, 83, 244.
Sroṅ-btsan-sgam-po, I, iii, ix, x, xi, 37, 39, 40, 44, 47, 49, 53, 71, 105, 218-9; II, 487, 656, 1073, 1086, 1092.
Sron-pa Kun-dga'-rgyal (Sron-pa Kun-rgyal), II, 774.
Sron-pa Čhos-dpal, II, 774.
sLe'u-čhuṅ-pa, II, 829.
sLob-čhuṅ-ba, II, 876.
sLob-pa'i rdo rje, I, 360.
gSaṅ-ston Ye-śes bla-ma, I, 170.
gSaṅ-phu-ba, I, 323.
gSaṅ-ba ye-śes, II, 1026.
gSal-mčhog (mṄa'-ris-pa-), II, 439.
gSal-rje-ba, II, 608.
gSal-ldoṅ-Sor-re, II, 462.
gSal-snaṅ, I, 41-2.
gSal-pa, II, 727.
gSal-ba'i sñiṅ-po, I, 208, 215.
gSal-byaṅ, II, 462.
gSal-yes, II, 462.
gSer-khaṅ-steṅs-pa Kun-dga' rgyal-mtshan, II, 716.
gSer-khaṅ-pa, II, 488, 786.
gSer-gliṅ-pa, I, 361; II, 751, 868.
gSer-gliṅ-pa bKra-śis-dpal, II, 450, 750, 991.
gSer-mdog, I, 13.
gSer-sdiṅs-pa, I, 319; II, 422, 425.
gSer-sdiṅs-pa gžon-nu-'od, I, 397; II, 424, 770.
gSer-btsun-ma, II, 915.
gSer-'od, I, 166.
gSer-luṅ-pa, I, 186, 189.
gSo-sbyoṅ-'phags, I, 4, 12.
bSam-grub, II, 547.
bSam-grub dpal-mgon, II, 1060.
bSam-grub bzaṅ-po-ba, I, 346.
bSam-grub ye-śes, I, 346.
bSam-grub rin-čhen, I, 201.
bSam-gliṅ Rin-po-čhe, II, 518.
bSam-gtan-dar, II, 994.

bSam-gtan-dpal-pa, II, 694, 751, 884, 886, (upādhyāya-) 722.
bSam-gtan rin-čhen, II, 517.
gSam-yas-pa, 471.
bSod-grags-pa, II, 586.
bSod-rgyal, I, 155; II, 446.
bSod-sňoms-gliṅ-pa, II, 601.
bSod-sňoms-pa, I, 390-3; II, 761, 764, 689, 1020.
bSod-nams-grags, II, 697, 1024.
bSod-nams grags-pa, I, 10, 92; II, 774, 1083.
bSod-nams-mgon, II, 536. bSod-nams mgon-po, I, 82; (Khaṅ-gsar-pa-), 385.
bSod-nams rgya-mtsho I, xi; II, 520. (lo-tsā-ba) 803, 805ff.
bSod-nams rgya-mtsho'i sde (lo-tsā-ba čhen-po), II, 805, 837, 1090.
bSod-nams rgyal-po, I, 221.
bSod-nams rgyal-mtshan, (kun-spaṅs-) I, 92, (maha-upādhyāya-) 190, 282, (Čhos-rje bLa-ma dam-pa) 309, 316; II, 424, 591, 634, 639, 645, 692, 703-5, 782, 786, 792, 1052.
bSod-nams rgyal-mtshan dpal-bzaṅ-po, I, 214; II, 424, 499, 589.
bSod-nams mčhog-grub, I, 283; II, 800, 810. (sNar-thaṅ upādhyāya).
bSod-nams-stobs (dbU-mdzad-), II, 1073.
bSod-nams-daṅ-ldan-pa, I, 35.
bSod-nams-dar, II, 1018.
bSod-nams don-grub, II, 493.
bSod-nams rnam par rgyal-ba, II, (of Byams-gliṅ) 412; (sMra-ba'i dbaṅ-phyug) 788, 802-3, 823.
bSod-nams dpal (Puṇyaśrī) I, 242; (of Čhos-'khor-gliṅ) 341; II, 748; (Kun-mkhyen-) 972; 1072.
bSod-nams-dpal-ldan, I, 321.
bSod-nams dpal-'byor, I, 94.
bSod-nams-'phel, I, 329.
bSod-nams blo-gros (Byaṅ-sems-) I, 202, (Ti-śri-) 214; (of rTe'u-ra) II, 1060
bSod-nams dbaṅ-phyug, 374; (ācārya-) II, 634; 1072.
bSod-nams-'bar, I, 234.
bSon-nams-'bum (bLa-ma-), II, 542.
bSod-nams rtse-mo (ācārya-) I, 211; II, 708.
bSod-nams bzaṅ-po (bSod-bzaṅ-po) I, 156 (ācārya-), 213; (dBaṅ-) 214; (mahā-upādhyāya-) II, 507-9, 1017; (Rin-po-čhe-) 781, (bLa-ma-) 1007; (abbot of Čhos-luṅ) 1073 (mTshal-min Rin-po-čhe-), 548.
bSod-nams-'od, II, 541.
bSod-nams 'od-zer (lo-tsā-ba) I, 338; (mahā-upādhyāya-) II, 528, 703; (ācārya-) 699; (vidyādhara-) 836; (abbot of Tshogs-pa Bya-rdzoṅ) 1072.
bSod-nams 'od zer-ba (bLa-ma-), II, 761, 763; (Čhen-po-) 830.

bSod-nams rin-čhen, I, 307; II, 455 (sGam-po-pa), (mkhas-pa-) 1329; (Ri-mi-'babs-pa-) 544, 865.
bSod-nams śes-rab, II, 1072.
bSod-nams seṅ-ge (of Ru-mtshams) I, 331, (Preceptor-) 344, (Rin-po-čhe-), 396; (ācārya-) II, 524, 537; (bKa'-bču-pa-), 592; (Phro-phu Riṅ-po-čhe-) II, 773; 1006.
bSod-nams lhun-grub, I, 282; II, 795.
bSod dbaṅ, II, 711, (bLa-čhen-), 1051.
bSod-gžon-pa, II, 696.
bSod-bzaṅ-ba, II, 780, 782.
bSod-bzaṅs (bKa'-bču-pa-), II, 829.
bSod-bzaṅs-pa, I, 516, 588, 590.
bSod-yes-pa, II, 511.
bSod-rin, II, 537.
bSruṅ-ba'i žabs, I, 368-9.
Ha-mu, I, 394-6.
Ha-mu dkar-po, I, 386, 393-4, 395.
Hwa-śaṅ, II, 611.
Hags, I, 143, 147.
Hab, I, 179.
Hab J̌o-sras 'J̌am-dpal, I, 185.
Hab-brdal-gza'-mdo-ba, II, 888.
Hu-la, II, 580.
Hūṃ-čhen Nam-mkha' rnal-'byor, II, 1050.
Hūṃ-'bar, II, 1025.
Hor, II, 891.
Hor-gza'-mo, I, 297.
Hyendu Kun-dga' rgyal-mtshan, II, 831.
Hyendu Lhun-grub bkra-śis, II, 831.
Lha, I, 189.
Lha dKon-mčhog-'phel, II, 963.
Lha-khaṅ-pa, I, 138 9, 163; II, 583, 1005 (Lha-rǰe-).
Lha-khaṅ-steṅs-pa, II, 658.
Lha-khaṅ bLa-braṅ-pa, 217.
Lha Grags-pa 'od-pa, II, 658.
Lha dGe-'dun sgaṅ-pa, I, 236, 307.
Lha 'Gro-mgon, I, 307. Lha 'Gro-ba'i mgon-po, I. 267, 320.
Lha-rgyal, II, 540.
Lha-sgaṅ-pa, II, 678.
Lha-sgom, II, 718.
Lha-čhen-po, I, 5, 13, 262, 307.
Lha-rǰe, I, 171.

Lha-rje Kun-dga', I, 110.
Lha-rje Kun-rgyal, II, 665.
Lha-rje sKyob-pa, II, 727.
Lha-rje rGya-nag, I, 127, 129-30.
Lha-rje mṄa'-seṅ-ge, I, 154.
Lha-rje lČe-ston rGya-nag, I, 126.
Lha-rje J̌o-'khor, II, 706.
Lha-rje Ña-ri-ba, I, 129, 157.
Lha-rje sÑi-sgom, I, 180.
Lha-rje lDe-gśegs, I, 159.
Lha-rje sNubs-čhuṅ, II, 428-9, 432.
Lha-rje sNubs-smad, I, 138,
Lha-rje sPrad, II, 900.
Lha-rje Phan pa ba-rag, II, 688.
Lha-rje bLa-ma, I, 123.
Lha-rje dBa, I, 376.
Lha-rje sMan-pa, I, 110.
Lha-rje gTsaṅ--śod-pa, II, 1009.
Lha-rje Zur-po-čhe, I, 110.
Lca-rje Zur-po-čhe Śākya 'byuṅ-gnas, I, 110, 114.
Lha-rje Zur-dpal, I, 110.
Lha rje Zla-ba'i 'od-zer, I, 229, 232, 238-9.
Lha-rje 'Ug-pa-luṅ-pa, I, 112-5, 118, 159.
Lha-rje Yaṅ-khye, I, 121-2.
Lha-rje Ra-sman, II, 659.
Lha-rje Ri-ston, I, 365.
Lha-rje Śaṅs-čhuṅ-pa, I, 159, 160.
Lha-rje Śaṅs-pa Nag-po, I, 124.
Lha-rje Śes-rab bzaṅ-po, II, 706.
Lha-rje Se-riṅs, II, 403.
Lha-rje Sog-sman, II, 874.
Lha-rje bSam-gtan, I, 262.
Lha-rje Hūṃ-čhuṅ, I, 109.
Lha-rje Lha-khaṅ-pa, I, 127, 132, 135.
Lha-rje Hor-po, I, 126.
Lha-rje Lha (Yar-kluṅs-pa-) II, 439
Lha-ston Žig po, I, 330.
Lha-brtan, II, 1026.
Lha-tho-tho-ri-gñan-btsan, I, 37-8.
Lha-thog-gza' sGaṅ-lčam Miṅ-'dren, I, 474.
Lha-gdoṅ-pa, II, 579, 691, 695.
Lha-bdres-ma-goṅ-ba, II, 949.

Lha-sde, I, 37, 69, 244.
Lha-sde-btsan, I, 68.
Lha-pa, I, 727.
Lha sPu-gu-do-ba, I, 319.
Lha sPur-gru-bži-pa, II, 1078.
Lha Phyug-mkhar-ba, II, 408, 716.
Lha Phyug-pa Ñi-ma-'od, II, 715.
Lha Brag-kha-pa, I, 280.
Lha bla-ma Ye-śes-'od, I, 244.
Lha-dbaṅ-pa, II, 931. (Tshal-pa naṅ-so).
Lha-dbaṅ-blo, I, 70, 346.
Lha 'Bri-sgaṅ-pa, I, 319.
Lha-mo, II, 917.
Lha-mo-skyid, II, 507.
Lha-mo-skyid, II, 517.
Lha-mo lčam, II, 522.
Lha-mo-dpal, II, 627.
Lha-mo dpal-mo, I, 390.
Lha-btsun sÑon-mo, II, 930, 936.
Lha-btsun-pa, II, 1044.
Lha-btsun-pa mGon-po-dpal, II, 1057.
Lha-btsun Bodhirāja, I, 257.
Lha-btsun Sogs-kha-pa, II, 690.
Lha Zur-khaṅ-pa, I, 280-2, 320.
Lha-gzigs Rin-čhen rgyal-mtshan (Lha-gzigs-pa), II, 544-6.
Lha-bzo, I, 396.
Lha-yul-pa, I, 330.
Lha-ri-dpal, I, 196.
Lha-rig-pa, I, 187.
Lha-luṅ-pa, I, 398; II, 468.
Lha-luṅ dPal-gyi rdo-rje, I, 170, 345.
Lha-bSod-nams 'od-zer-ba, II, 658-9.
Lhag, I, 269.
Lhag-ru-ba, I, 280-1 ; II, 972.
Lhan-skyes-grags, II, 801.
Lhan-gčig-skyes-pa'i rdo-rje, I, 362 ; II, 552, 725.
Lhab, I, 96.
Lhab-dres-ma goṅ-pa, I, 156.
Lhab-mi, I, 365.
Lhab-mi čhen-po, I, 262, 265.
Lhab-mi Śes-rab gyuṅ-druṅ, I, 264.
Lha'i Rig-pa seṅ-ge I, 39, 218.

Lhas-sbas, I, 380.
Lhiṅ-ṅe Yan-thub-bu Tshul-khrims, II, 554.
Lhiṅ-ṅe 'Od-zer rgyal-mtshan, II, 554.
Lhun-sde rab-'byams-pa, II, 829.
Lhun-po, I, 13.
Lhun-po-ldan, I, 14.
Lha-stod-pa, I, 269.
Lho-nag, II, 408.
Lho-pa, I, 82; II, 442, 557.
Lho-pa Grub-seṅ, II, 335; I, 791.
Lho-pa sGog-zan, I, 333.
Lho-pa rTa-sgom, II, 445.
Lho-pa lTo-'ber, I, 147.
Lho-pa Dar-sgom, II, 462.
Lho-pa rDo-rje sñiṅ-po, I, 364.
Lho-pa Dharma-skyabs, II, 1004.
Lho-pa Byaṅ-ston, II, 439.
Lho-pa Rin-po-čhe, II, 1041.
Lho-brag-pa, I, 331; II, 728.
Lho-brag Byaṅ-čhub-dpal, II, 1072.
Lho-brag-luṅ-pa, II, 728.
Lho-tsha bLa-ma-skyabs, I, 132.
Lho-tshaṅ-pa, I, 385.
Lho Rin-po-čhe, II, 518.
Lho La-yag-pa, II, 519.
A-kun, II, 629.
A-rgod-gza', II, 523.
A-'ǰid-rmal, I, 38.
A-stag 'Od-ldan, I, 138.
A-dig, II, 605.
A-nan-rmal, I, 37.
A-pho Čhos-grags, 164.
A-dbaṅ Ye-śes dbaṅ-phyug, II, 519.
A-mi dKon-mčhog-dpal, II, 532.
A-mi Bya-nag čhen-po, II, 1088.
A-mi Byaṅ-čhub 'dre-bkol, II, 571.
A-mi Śer-blo, I, 110.
A-mi Śer-brtson, I, 126.
A-mi Śes-rab bzaṅ-po, I, 110.
A-mi He-ru, I, 110.
A-me Mi-ñag, I, 376.
A-mes rṄog rDo-rje dbaṅ-phyug, II, 518.

A-mes Byaṅ-čhub rdo-rje, II, 991.
A-mes Byaṅ-čhub 'byuṅ-gnas, I, 262.
A-mes sMaṅ-rgan, I, 264.
A-ža rGya-gor-rtsegs, II, 759.
A-ro (Ye-śes 'byuṅ-gnas), I, 167; II, 556, 999, 1000, 1005.
A-la gZi-čhen, I, 121.
A-śog-lde, I, 37.
A-su, II, 843, 860-1, 873, 1010.
A-seṅ (Khams-pa), I, 386, (bla-ma-), II, 556, 734, 746.
Ag-len, I, 216.
An-ston Grags-rin, I, 352, 354.
Ar, I, 330, 332, 386; II, 555.
Ar Byaṅ-čhub ye-śes, II, 1081.
Ar-mo-siṅ-ṅa, II, 1026.
I-śo-legs, I, 37.
U-rgyan-pa (Ur-brgyan-pa, U-rgyan-guru. Grub-čhen-pa), I, 148, 197-8; II, 487-8, 490, 493, 517, 526, 528, 533, 603, 658, 686, 695-6, 698, 700-5, 762, 786, 796, 810, 974, 996, 1007, 1088.
U-rgyan (Pad-ma, I, 198.
U-rgyan ras-pa, II, 928, 962.
U-rgyan Śes-rab gsaṅ-ba, I, 218.
U-pa-de-gsal, I, 170.
U-yug-pa, I, 335.
U-yug-pa mÑa'-bsam-gtan, I, 165
U-yug-pa Sod-nams seṅ-ge, I, 335.
U-rin rgyan-'bar, II, 554.
Un-a-naṅ-ga, I, 104.
E-rgyal, II, 529.
E-śo-legs, I, 36.
Oṅ-po lo-tsā-ba, II, 871-2, 1008.

CHINESE NAMES

Ai-ti, I, 54.
Chao K'uang-yin, I, 55, note 44.
Chao-tsung, I, 54.
Chao-wang, I, 17, 47.
Chao-Yü-ju, I, 56.
Chêng Hua, I, 59.
Chêng-t'ung, I, 59.
Ch'i-li-so-tsan, I, xix.
Ch'i-li-su-lung-lieh-tsan, I, xix.
Ch'i-ni-si-lung, I, xix.
Ch'i-tan Tai-Liao, I, 55.
Ch'i-tsung-lung-tsan, I, xix.
Chien-wan, I, 59.
Chin, I, 56.
Chin-ch'êng kung-chu, I, 51.
Ch'in-shih huang-ti, I, 47, 57.
Ching-t'ai, I, 59.
Chou, I, 17, 47, 56.
Chu-Fa-lan, I, 47.
Chu-wên, I, 55.
Chung-tsung, I, 50, 54.
Han, I, 47-8, 51.
Hou-Chin, I, 48, 57.
Hou-Liang, I, 55.
Hsi-Chin, I, 48, 57.
Hsi-tsung, I, 54.
Hsien-ti, I, 48.
Hsien-tsung, I, 52.
Hsüan-tê, I, 59.
Hsüan-tsang, I, 55.
Hsüan-tsung, I, 51, 54.
Huang-ch'ao, I, 55.
Hung Wu, I, 59, 60.
I-tsung, I, 54.
Jên-tsung, I, 59.
Jui-tsung, I, 50-1.
K'a-li-k'a-tsu—K'o-li-k'o-tsu, I, xix.
Kao-hun, I, 52.

Kao-ti, I, 47.
Kao-tsu, I, 47, 55.
Kao-tsung, I, 50, 56.
Kuang Wu-ti, I, 47.
Lao-chang ch'êng-hsiang, II, 503.
Liang, I, 55.
Li Chih, I, 49.
Ming-ti, I, 47, note 57.
Mu-tsung, I, 52, 54.
Su-tsung, I, 51.
Sui, I, 48.
Ssŭ-ma Chao, I, 48, 57.
Shun-tsung, I, 52.
Ta-mo, I, 53.
Tai-Ming, I, 59.
T'ai-tsu, I, 58.
Tai-tsung, I, 51-2.
T'ai-tsung, I, 49, 50-2, 219.
T'ang Kao-tsu, I, 55.
T'ang Kao-tsung, I, ix, 48-9, 50-1, 53-4.
T'ang T'ai-tsung, I, 48-9, 50-1, 55.
Tê-tsung, I, 52.
T'ien-shun, I, 59.
Ts'ao-ts'ao, I, 48.
Tsu-chieh-tsien, I, xix.
Tu-tsung, I, 56.
Tung-Chin, I, 48.
Wan-yen Hsün, I, 56.
Wang Mang, I, 47, 57.
Wei, I, 57.
Wên-ch'êng, I, xii. Wên-ch'êng kung-chu, I, 49, 50.
Wên-tsung, I, 52, 54.
Wu-tsê-t'ien, I, 50.
Yang-ti, I, 48, 57.
Ying-tsung, I, 58.
Yü-ju, I, 56.
Yun-wên, II, 512.
Yung-lo, I 69, 60; II, 645.

MONGOL NAMES

Alan γoa (A-lan-kho), I, 57.
Altan-qan (Am-tan khan), I, 56.
Aruγči, II, 973. (A-rog-čhe).
A'uǰang-boro'ul, I, 57. (La'u-ǰaṅ bhe-re-'ol).
Ayurparibhadra Buyantu, I, 58. (A-yu-par-pa-ta Bu-yan-du).
Baišingqor-doγšin, I, 57. (Ba'i-śiṅ and Khor-thog-śiṅ).
Bartan ba'ātur, I, 57. (Bar-than ba-dur).
Bata-čiqan, I, 57. (Ba-da čhi-gan).
Bayan čingsang, I, 56. (Ba-yan čhiṅ-saṅ).
Begter, I, 58, note 51.
Belgũtei, I, 58, note 51.
Biker, I, 57. (sBi-khir).
Bondončar mungqaγ, I, 57. (Bo-don-čhār mu-gan).
Borte čino-a, I, 57. (sBor-ta-čhe).
Buyantu-qan, I, 337.
Činggis, I, 56. (J̌iṅ-gir), 58, 60.
Dobun-mergan, I, 57. (Du-ban mer-gan).
Doorda-darqan, I, 91; II, 577-8. (Dor-tog—Dor-ta).
El Temũr, I, 59. (El Thamur).
Erinčin-bal (Rin-čhen-dpal), II, 500.
Gegēn, I, 56. (Ge-gen).
Godan, I, 211; II, 578.
Go-yug Gũyũk, I, 58.
Hő'e-lũn, I. 58. (Hu-lun).
Kúlũg, I, 58. (Go-lug).
Kuśala, I, 50 (Ku-śa-la).
Menen-tudun, I, 57. (Ma-nan Thodon).
Miliči, II, 577. (Mi-li-byi). cf. Mongal personal name: Melči.
Mőngke-qan, I, 58. (Moṅ-gol gan).
Őgedei, I, 58. (O-go-ta).
Őlǰeitũ Temũr, I, 58. (Ol-ǰa-du).
Qabiči, I, 57. (Ga'i-čhi).
Qabul-qan, I, 57. (Ka-bu-la gan).
Qači'un, I, 58, note 51.
Qaidu qan, I, 57. (Ga'i-thu gan).
Qarču, I, 57. (Kha-ǰu).
Qasar, I, 58, note 51.
Qoričar mergan, I, 57. (Čhi-ǰi mer-gan).

Qubilai, I, vi, 56, 58; II, 487, 631, 702. (Go-pe-la).
Rajapika, I, 59. (Ra-khyi-phag).
Sayang Sečen, I, xiii.
Sečen, I, 56, 58, 60 (Se-čhen). See Qubilai. Sečen qan (Se-čhen gan).
Siremün ch'êng-hsiang, II, 503. (Ži-ra-mu čhiṅ-saṅ).
Tamača, I, 57. (Tham-čhag).
Temüge, I, 58, note 51.
Toγ Temür Jayaγātu, I, 59. (Thog Thi-mur 'Ja'-ya-du).
Toγan Temür, I, vii.
Toγon Temür, I, 59, 60; II, 500. (Tho-gan Thi-mur). cf. Toγan Temür.
Tuγluγ Temür, II, 504.
Tumbaγai Sečen, I. 57.
Tumbinai qan, I, 57. (Dum-bi-ha'i khan).
Türegene, I, 58, note 53.
Yeke-nidun, I, 57. (Pas-ka nidum).
Yesügei-ba'ātur, I, 58. (Ye-phur-ga ba dur).
Yesün Temür, I, 59. (Ye-sun The-mur).

A PLACE NAME INDEX
TO GEORGE N. ROERICH'S TRANSLATION
OF THE BLUE ANNALS

The following is an index of the proper names of places occurring in George N. Roerich's translation of the Tibetan historical text *The Blue Annals*, as published in *The Royal Asiatic Society of Bengal Monograph Series*, vol. VII, Part One (1949) and Part Two (1953) at Calcutta.

The second volume of Roerich's translation includes indexes of book titles in Sanskrit and Tibetan, and of personal names in Sanskrit, Tibetan, Chinese, and Mongolian; and it is hoped that this place name index will be a useful addition to those indexes.

The index is arranged according to the sequence of the Tibetan alphabet, and the transcription was made according to the system used by Roerich in his translation. There were not enough Sanskrit place names to warrant a separate indexing, therefore these will be found according to the Tibetan alphabetical sequence. The Sanskrit letters " v " and " ś " are listed under the Tibetan letters " w " and " ś ", respectively.

Although this is primarily a place name index, I have included certain proper names which are not actually *place* names; such as, the names of certain statues, tombs, and chortens. These *non-place* names are printed in italics to render them readily identifiable as such. In addition to the names of major geographical locations and physical structures, I have included the proper names of all places, even though they might be no more than a grove of trees or a huge boulder, in the hope of making this index even more useful to those doing Tibetan research. On the other hand, the names of supramundane locations are omitted unless such names might be of value for a mundane identification. Also omitted are the names of countries as a whole, e.g., Tibet, China, Nepal, etc.; but the names of smaller geographical units, such as U–rgyan, mṄa–ris, etc., are included.

While compiling this index, it became apparent that there were misprints in the published translation, which were not indicated in the *Errata*. Whenever a place name appeared to be misprinted, or varied in spelling upon a subsequent occurrence, it was compared with a copy of the original Tibetan text, kindly loaned to me by Professor Tucci, in order to obtain the correct spelling. Although it would be impractical to list each of these corrections here in the preface, the following are some of the more interesting cases.

The most frequent misprint is due to the omission of the diacritical dot above the "ṅ", which transcribes the Tibetan letter ང, e.g., *bon–gron* (II, p. 448) should read *bon–groṅ*. There are a few composing errors, e.g., *gaoṅ–mkhar* (II, p. 1088) should read *groṅ–mkhar*; and *Phag–mo–thu* (I, p. 198) is, of course, *Phag–mo–gru*.

The contradictory spellings of *sTod–luṅs 'phar–tshȧr* (I, p. 234) and *sTod–luṅs 'phar–tshan* (II, p. 487) proved, under comparison with the original text, to be both wrong; the correct spelling being *sTod–luṅs 'phar–tshaṅ*.

The various spellings of *U–yug*, *U–yog*, and *'U–yug*, all proved to be *'U–yug*, and are therefore listed in the index under the single entry of *'U–yug*.

On the other hand, the various spellings of *lKog–phreṅ* (II, p. 492), *Kog–'phreṅ* (II, p. 496), and *lKog–'phraṅ* (II, p. 543) are all confirmed by Professor Tucci's copy; however, since all three appear to be variations of the same name, they are listed under the single entry of *lKog–'phreṅ*. The suspicious readings of *Dags–po Kroṅs–kha* (II, p. 657) and of *Dags–po rDzoṅs–kha* (II, p. 874) are also confirmed, and are listed as two separate entries.

Lastly, instead of *Be–ba–la* (II, p. 868), Professor Tucci's copy reads: *Be–da–la*, and is most likely the same name as *Be–ta–la* (*Vetala*) (I, p. 391 and p. 394).

In regards to those names which were misprinted in the published translation, only the corrected spellings will be found in the index. It is to be noted, however, that only those names which appeared to be in error were compared with the original text; to have done more would have required more time than the nature of this index would have warranted.

I wish to express my thanks to Dr. Roerich for his kind interest in this index; and my gratitude to Professor Tucci for making its publication possible.

TURRELL V. WYLIE
University of Washington

Rome, March 1st, 1957.

Ka-ka, I, 302.
Ka-chu, II, 826.
Ka-ṭa-ka, II, 762.
Ka-thog, I, 158; II, 484.
Ka-drug, II, 631, 634.
Ka-na-kra-śo-tam, II, 798.
Ka-pe-rdzogs-gsum, I, 158.
Ka-ba-can, I, 197; II, 892.
Ka-ba-sa, II, 304.
Ka-bžhi-steṅs, II, 593.
Ka-ru, II, 691, 954.
Kā-la Duṅ-mtsho, II, 719, 720.
Kwa-chu, I, 75, 77, 78.
Kāilāsa, I, 139, 269; II, 434, 574, 579, 598, 602, 605, 669, 682, 686, 693, 700, 720, 726, 975, 976, 1039, 1040. See Ti-se.
Ka'u-li (Korea), II, 502.
Kāurava, I, 13.
Kāuśāmbī, I, 21.
Kaṅgrā, II, 669, 682, 700, 745, 845.
Kāthmāndu, I, 225, 227, 231.
Kanauj, I, 368.
Kaniṣka-caitya, I, 25.
Kan-mon-śod, I, 278.
Kānyakubja, I, 4, 14.
Kapāla, I, 13.
Kapilavastu, I, 3, 4, 11, 19, 21, 22.
Kāmpīlya, I, 14.
Kam, II, 311.
Kam-kam, II, 305, 306, 307.
Kaṃ-ka-ta, II, 730.
Kaṃ-ko-na, II, 368.
Kam-chu (Kan-chou), II, 503, 504.
Kam-chu-gliṅ, II, 500.
Kampala, II, 849.
Kāmarūpa, II, 693.
Kārttika, II, 485.
Karṇikavana, I, 25.
Kar-ma, II, 490, 492, 494, 500, 505, 506, 507, 510, 512, 514, 550.
Kar-ma-rñiṅ, I, ii.
Kar-ma'i yaṅ-dgon, II, 514.
Kālakuṭa, II, 732.
Kaliṅga, I, 13; II, 798.
Kāśī, I, 21.
Kin-byaṅ-hu (Chin-ch'eng-fu), I, 54.
Ku-yuṅ-sgaṅs, II, 617.
Ku-ru-ku-lla, II, 869.
Ku-ru bi-ha-ra, II, 1032.
Ku-ru-luṅ, II, 679.
Ku-la śam-bu, II, 817.
Ku-luṅ, II, 621.
Ku-śi-ldan, I, 15.
Kuṅ-bzaṅs-gliṅ, I, 197.
Kuṅs dgon-pa, II, 483.
Kupaja, I, 369.
Kun-dga-ra-ba, I, 75, 76; II, 583.
Kun-du-bzaṅ-po, II, 452.
Kun-bde-gliṅ, I, ii.
Kun-snaṅ, I, 5; II, 1039.
Kul-'chiṫ-ru, I, 354.
Kuśanagara, I, 5, 22; II, 663.
Kuśāvatī, I, 15.
Kusumpura, II, 763.

Keṅ-ri, II, 849.
Ko-khyim, I, 78; II, 617.
Ko-brag, II, 727.
Ko-ru, II, 992.
Ko-ron-sa, II, 427.
Koṅ-ka-ṇa, II, 360.
Koṅ-gyo, II, 507, 515.
Koṅ-daṅ-la, II, 986.
Koṅ-po, I, 181, 198, 200, 278; II, 481, 491, 492, 493, 494, 505, 506, 508, 515, 516, 524, 525, 529, 542, 543, 544, 545, 548, 549, 550, 551, 591, 603, 647, 672, 694, 696, 936, 983, 1018, 1040.
Koṅ-po brag-gsum, II, 874.
Koṅ-po-sraṅ, II, 496.
Koṅ-pho, II, 550.
Koṅ-bu-chen, II, 495.
Koṅ-mo'i ri, II, 726.
Koṅ-yul, II, 495.
Kośala, II, 844.
Kośalakrama, II, 1021.
Kyi-tshaṅ, II, 874.
kLags, II, 862.
kLas-mo-che, I, 81; II, 421, 600, 1068, 1069.
kLu-goṅ, I, 310.
kLu-chu (T'ao-shui), I, 53.
kLu-mda'-tshe, II, 876.
kLu-dbyaṅs, I, 13.
kLu'i byaṅ-chub, II, 798.
kLuṅs-śod, II, 468.
kLuṅs-śod 'byin-pa, I, 61.
kLuṅs-śod zur-re, I, 308.
kLogs, II, 1087.
kLoṅ-rdol, II, 668.
dKar-chuṅ, I, 94.
dKar-po chos-luṅ, II, 675.
dKar-ma, II, 543.
dKar-śod, II, 572.
dKor, I, 278.
bKra-śis, 190.
bKra-śis-sgo-maṅ, II, 406.
bKra-śis-ljoṅs, II, 548.
bKra-śis Do-kha, II, 589, 1077.
bKra-śis-dpal-'bar, II, 631.
bKra-śis 'Od-'bar, II, 563.
bKra-śis-gsar-ma, II, 489.
bKra-śis-lhun-po, I, ii, 339.
bKrab-tiṅ, II, 617.
rKyaṅ, II, 722.
rKyaṅ-chen, II, 694.
rKyaṅ-'dur, I, 335; II, 769, 771.
rKyaṅ-mo-kha, II, 670.
lKugs-luṅs, II, 737, 739, 740.
lKog-'phreṅ, II, 492, 496, 543 (see preface).
sKam-skam, I, 90.
sKam-dgon, I, 316.
sKam-dgos-luṅ, II, 566.
sKam-po gnas-naṅ, II, 479.
sKar-chuṅ, II, 759.
sKu-gduṅ Ka-ru, II, 954 (see Ka-ru).
sKu-'bum, I, 65; II, 1073.
sKu-'bum-ltag, II, 644.
sKu-'bum mthoṅ-grol chen-mo, II, 776.
sKuṅs, II, 525.
sKoṅ, II, 642.
sKoṅ-dgon, II, 652.
sKoṅ-yul, II, 870.
sKya-srid, II, 1059.
sKyags, I, 199.
sKyam, II, 994.
sKyam-phu, I, 201.
sKyi, I, 154, 155; II, 438.
sKyi-khuṅ, I, 176, 185.
sKyi-mkhar, I, 126; II, 1005.
sKyi-chu, I, 202, 303; II, 717.
sKyi-smad, I, 288, 289.
sKyi-tshaṅ, II, 438, 946, 998.
sKyi-roṅ (Skyid-roṅ), I, 41, 254, 255, 392; II, 401, 433, 488, 528, 603, 656, 709, 711, 801, 1008, 1064.
sKyi-luṅ, I, 183.

sKyi-śod, I, vi, 294, 373, 384; II, 590, 591, 668, 693, 695, 734, 911, 912, 944, 1075.
sKyid-ru, I, 95, 96.
sKyil-mkhar lha-khaṅ, I, 135.
sKyegs-gnas-rñiṅ, I, 330.
sKyeṅ-luṅs, I, 120 (sKeṅ-luṅs, 124).
sKyer-sgaṅ, II, 738, 740, 743.
sKyer-sna, II, 872, 874, 876.
sKyo, I, 124.
sKyo-groṅ, I, 305.
sKyo-ro-ro, II, 664.
sKyo-zur, II, 976.
sKyor-mo-luṅ, I, 79, 83, 190, 278, 302; II, 410, 673.

Kha-na bar-pa, II, 540.
Kha-ba kluṅs, II, 829.
Kha-bi, I, 367.
Kha-brag-mdo, II, 547.
Kha-rag, I, 207; II, 522, 675, 687, 715, 878, 956, 957, 1000, 1004.
Kha-rag phug-pa nag-po, II, 1003.
Kha-rag Bon-drug, II, 715.
Kha-rag-śar, II, 491.
Kha-rag lha-mtsho, II, 718.
Kha-sar-paṇa, II, 1020, 1030.
Khwa-tse wiṅ-gir, I, 69.
Khaṅ-sṅon, I, 114.
Khaṅ-pa-gnas, I, 274.
Khaṅ-dmar, I, 75.
Khaṅ-gsar, I, 216.
Khaṅ-gsar-gliṅ, I, 217.
Khaṅ-gsar chen-mo-ba, I, 217.
Khab Guṅ-thaṅ, I, 260, 321, 338; II, 436, 1026.
Kham-groṅ, II, 676.
Kham-pa-luṅ, I, 283.
Khams, I, 34, 93, 126, 128, 132, 155, 157, 158, 160, 168, 170, 192, 204, 216, 251, 253, 258, 263, 267, 292, 324, 325, 330, 338, 345, 372, 384, 386, 395; II, 410, 411, 418, 465, 474, 479, 486, 490, 492, 500, 505, 507, 508, 510, 511, 514, 516, 519, 522, 545, 551, 553, 554, 558, 563, 564, 565, 595, 615, 616, 617, 630, 635, 649, 651, 652, 662, 663, 712, 728, 741, 777, 789, 796, 828, 832, 855, 928, 942, 984, 997, 1000, 1080.
Khams-pa sDom-tshaṅ, II, 1021.
Khams-gsum, I, 77; II, 568.
Khams-gsum zaṅs-khaṅ, I, 62.
Khar-chu, II, 438.
Khu, I, 76.
Khu-dron-tsha, I, 76.
Khu-byug dBen-pa-rdzoṅ, II, 527.
Khu-luṅ, II, 518, 665.
Khu-le, II, 664, 917.
Khug-pa, I, 360.
Khuṅs-roṅ, I, 160.
Khul-bu, II, 907.
Khe-naṅ, II, 498.
Khe'u-gaṅ, II, 983.
Khoṅ-rkyaṅ Yaṅ-khaṅ, II, 747.
Khyag-pa dkar-mo, II, 694.
Khyam, II, 786.
Khyams Khaṅ-gsar, II, 806.
Khyuṅ-dkar, II, 684, 686.
Khyuṅ-kha-luṅ, II, 597.
Khyuṅ-po, II, 550.
Khyuṅ-tshaṅ, II, 443.
Khyuṅ-tshaṅ-brag, II, 443.
Khra-sna', II, 990.
Khra-phu, I, 284.
Khra-'brug, I, 40, 319; II, 642, 656, 890.
Khra-tsa, I, 68.
Khra-ye-gaṅs, II, 987.
Khra-śod sPom-brag, II, 484.

Khra–śod sBom–rag–sna, II, 486.
Khrab, I, 177.
Khrab–la–kha, I, 82, 93, 284.
Khrig–mo, I, 199.
Khrims–khaṅ–gliṅ, II, 812, 822, 826, 827.
Khro–phu, I, 335; II, 707, 708, 709, 1034, 1068, 1070.
Khro–phu'i Byams–chen, II, 600, 709, 710, 1034, 1070.
Khron–pa'i gliṅ, II, 868.
Khrom, I, 159.
mKha'–'gro–gliṅ, I, 198.
mKhan–grags, I, 268.
mKhan–pa–gliṅ, I, 197.
mKhan–pa–ljoṅs, I, 197.
mKhar–mgon, II, 722.
mKhar–chu, I, 196, 197, 199; II, 606, 667, 668, 676, 682, 686, 895, 948, 953, 958, 959, 963, 974, 975, 976, 1002.
mKhar–phug, I, 78; II, 789.
mKhar–ru–sgaṅ, II, 942.
'Khon–phu, I, 229.
'Khon–phu rdziṅs, I, 229.
'Khor–lo, II, 1059.

Ga–sgrog–gi steṅs, II, 507.
Ga–chu, II, 501.
Gaṅ–pa–thog, I, 75.
Gaṅ–bzaṅs, II, 743, 953, 976.
Gaṅs–dkar, II, 478, 492, 522, 1040.
Gaṅs–dkar chu–kha, II, 1040.
Gaṅs–dkar Ti–se, II, 976 (See Ti–se).
Gaṅgā (Ganges), II, 441, 667, 850, 858, 869, 976, 1020, 1021, 1028, 1055.
Gaṅs Ti–se, II, 682, 693 (See Ti–se).
Gaṅs–par, I, 179, 187.
Gaṅs–par sPel–cig–ma, II, 983.
Gaṅs–par gser–chu, II, 657.
Gaṅs–par lha–khaṅ, II, 1087.
Gaṅs–phug, II, 976.
Gaṅs–ri thod–dkar, I, 309.
Gad–pa–steṅs, I, 77.
Gad–pas lha–khaṅ, I, 72.
Gad–'phreṅ, I, 195.
Gandhamādana, I, 23.
Gam–pa–byaṅ–thaṅ, I, 256.
Gayā, I, 22.
Gu–ge, I, 37; II, 643.
Gu–laṅ, II, 729.
Guṅ–thaṅ, I, 130, 207, 245, 366; II, 432, 435, 436, 496, 498, 786, 787, 802, 855, 916, 919, 1022, 1023, 1057, 1070.
Guṅ–thaṅ mgon–po, II, 879.
Guṅ–bu, I, 120.
Guṅ–bu–mkhar, II, 741.
Guntur, I, 368.
Ge–kha–brag, II, 1042.
Geya, I, 13.
Go–chen sPaṅ–dkar, II, 493.
Go–roṅ, I, xvii, 64.
Go–la, I, 21.
Go–luṅ, II, 698.
Go–luṅ–phu, II, 698.
Gog–dor, II, 449.
Goṅ–dkar, I, 338; II, 799.
Goṅ–pa–ri, I, 279.
Goṅ–po dBen–tsha, I, 176.
Goṅ–bu, I, 124.
Goṅ–bu–mkhar, II, 741.
Goṅ–bo, II, 937.
Gol–go–luṅ, I, 286.
Govicandra, II, 804.
Gya–ba, II, 519.
Gya–bar, II, 518.
Gyaṅ–pa, I, 298.
Gyaṅ–tse, II, 732, 791, 799, 1073.
Gyad, II, 849.
Gyam, II, 726.
Gyam–rim, II, 726.

Gyur-dmar, II, 694.
Gye-re, II, 991.
Gra, I, 96, 352; II, 654, 671, 715, 822, 937, 943, 966, 970.
Gra-thaṅ, I, 76, 77, 96, 97, 235; II, 823, 852, 906, 931, 942, 991.
Gra-dol, I, vi.
Gra-phyi, I, 75, 78; II, 693, 906, 947, 990.
Gra-phyi khaṅ-dmar, I, 154.
Gra-phyi rTa-lam-po, II, 956.
Gra-phyi-phu, II, 875.
Gra-phyi tshoṅ-'dus, I, 256.
Gra-rabs, II, 653.
Gra'i phu-stoṅ-groṅ, I, 201.
Grags-chen, II, 672.
Grags-tshab, I, 79.
Graṅ-mo, II, 720.
Grab, I, 269, 292; II, 862.
Gri-mdo, II, 995.
Grib, I, 331; II, 738.
Grib-kyi phu, I, 331.
Grib-dgon, II, 546.
Gru-mur, II, 611.
Gru-'dzin, I, 4.
Gru-bži-dgon, II, 478, 479.
Gru-bži-ma, II, 479.
Gru-śul-sgo, I, 303.
Gru-śul lha-ri, II, 975.
Grub-pa'i gnas-bdun, I, 473.
Grum-bu-luṅ, I, 142; II, 411.
Gre, II, 732.
Gro, II, 1022.
Gro-phug, I, 73.
Gro-bo-luṅ, II, 421, 431, 437, 473, 606, 814, 816.
Gro-bo-kluṅs, II, 403, 816.
Gro-mo (Chumbi), II, 710, 732, 1066.
Gro-mo-che, II, 1016.
Gro-luṅ, I, 331.
Gro-śul cha-khrod, II, 657.
Gro-sa, I, 79, 83, 276, 301, 306, 307, 308; II, 571, 993, 1080.
Gro-sa-ba, I, 278.
Grog, I, 305.
Grog-phugs-śaṅ, II, 481.
Groṅ-chuṅ, II, 769.
Grom-pa Sa-skya, I, 338.
Grol, II, 467.
gLa-'khor, II, 691.
gLag, I, 95.
gLag-pa-lam, I, 148.
gLaṅ, I, 155.
gLaṅ-'khor, II, 902, 912, 916, 917, 918, 919, 920, 953, 954.
gLaṅ-chen-gnas, I, 14.
gLaṅ-thaṅ, I, 271, 314; II, 643.
gLaṅ-po-sna, II, 659.
gLaṅ-ma, II, 895.
gLaṅ-liṅ-la, II, 617, 622, 650.
gLan-luṅ, I, 302; II, 695.
gLiṅ, II, 507.
gLe'u-chuṅ, II, 666.
gLes-dgon, II, 565.
gLo-bo, I, 262; II, 643, 1029, 1071.
gLo-bo-rin, II, 1055.
gLoṅ-thaṅ sGron-me, I, 126.
gLoṅ-thaṅ 'Jig-rten-sgron, I, 64.
dGa'-ldan, II, 686.
dGa'-ldan brTan-bžugs chos-'khor, II, 1093.
dGa'-ldan-ma-mo, II, 544, 545.
dGa'-ba-dgoṅ, I, 78, 79, 83, 336.
dGa'-ma-mo, II, 543, 547, 549, 550, 551 (See dGa'-ldan-ma-mo).
dGe-goṅ, I, 110, 275, 319.
dGe-ldan, II, 1078, 1080.
dGe-ldan rnam-par rgyal-ba'i gliṅ, II, 1077.
dGe-'dun-sgaṅ, I, 276; II, 1072.
dGe-ri, II, 1053.

dGe–tsha, II, 849.
dGoṅ–sna, I, 176.
dGon–dkar, II, 976.
dGon–pa–goṅ, I, 312.
dGon–pa Lha–gdoṅ, II, 688.
dGon–rtse, I, 197.
dGon Rin–chen–gliṅ, II, 687.
dGon–gsar, II, 593.
dGyer–pa–sa, II, 1087.
mGar–phug, II, 465.
mGur–mo, II, 1068.
mGo–bo'i ri–bo, I, 23.
'Ga', II, 740.
'Ga'–roṅ, II, 1013.
'Gar, II, 421, 602.
'Gar–brag, I, 235, 238.
'Gur–mo, I, 183.
'Goṅ–de Do–ra, II, 652.
'Gos, I, 327.
'Gos–yul, II, 687.
'Gres–phu, I, 275.
'Gres–phu sGom–chen–sdiṅs, I, 275.
rGaṅ–mo lhas–pa, II, 748.
rGod–dkar–la, I, 258.
rGod–tshaṅ, II, 527, 684, 685, 686.
rGya, I, 80, 81, 185; II, 876.
rGya–mkhar–stod, II, 419.
rGya–gar, II, 1040.
rGya–dur, I, 82, 277; II, 654.
rGya–mda', II, 542.
rGya–pa I, 112.
rGya–phibs, I, 258.
rGya–bo, I, 116, 117.
rGya–bo–dgu–'dus, I, 114, 116.
rGya–brag, II, 643, 966.
rGya–ma, I, 271; II, 600, 789, 1070.
rGya–ma ñe–kha, II, 1029 (See next entry).
rGya–ma ñe'u–kha, I, 174.
rGya–ma Rin–chen–sgaṅ, II, 1070.
rGya–dmar, I, 386.
rGya–smad, II, 876.
rGya–sman, II, 879.
rGya–mtsho groṅ–mkhar, II, 1087.
rGya–mtsho–sgaṅ, II, 548.
rGya–mtsho lhug–tshaṅ, II, 1088
rGya–yags, II, 671.
rGya–ra Gad–logs, I, 141.
rGya–rab–pa, I, 63.
rGya–ri–mo–can, I, 78.
rGya–ro 'Tshal–ma, I, 177.
rGya–sa–sgaṅ, I, 319 (sic! see next entry)
rGya–sar–sgaṅ, I, 99, 277.
rGyaṅ, I, 255.
rGyaṅ–ro, II, 448, 1068.
rGyaṅ–ro Guṅ–chuṅ, II, 1066.
rGyaṇ–ro sPe'u–dmar, I, 352.
rGyabs, II, 946, 950.
rGyal ('Phan–yul), I, 78; II, 649, 846, 897, 1003 (see rGyal–lha–khaṅ) (for rGyal area, see next entry).
rGyal, I, 253, 255, 269, 273; II, 421, 543, 862, 876, 1043.
rGyal–dgon, II, 564.
rGyal–te Thaṅ–kar, II, 773.
rGyal–steṅs, I, 304.
rGyal–po–steṅs, I, 305.
rGyal–po'i khab, II, 814, 829.
rGyal–mo stag–rtse, I, 173.
rGyal–mo–roṅ, I, 170, 340; II, 1080.
rGyal–sman, I, vi.
rGyal–rtse, II, 799.
rGyal–žiṅ, I, 251.
rGyal–bzaṅs, I, 239; II, 812.
rGyal–lug–lhas, I, 75, 76, 88.
rGyal–lha–khaṅ, I, 87, 88, 90, 91, 92, 263, 306, 330, 346; II, 405, 475, 783, 1055.
rGyas–smad stag–rtse, I, 154; II, 875.

rGyas-sa-sgaṅ, I, 319 (see rGya-sa-sgaṅ)
rGyu-sa, II, 696.
sGa-goṅ, II, 443.
sGa-'dra, I, 96; II, 657.
sGaṅ, II, 545.
sGaṅ-gyaṅ śed-luṅ, II, 621.
sGaṅ-chuṅ, II, 545.
sGaṅ-ra, I, 297.
sGam-po, II, 458, 459, 460, 464, 465, 467, 469, 471, 476, 477, 490, 498, 558, 559, 571, 574, 607, 642, 662, 668, 672, 704, 718, 719, 737, 1040.
sGam-po gnas-naṅ, II, 481.
sGu-rab-ba, II, 1089.
sGo, II, 501.
sGo-mo chos-sdiṅs, II, 885.
sGoṅ-ma, II, 992.
sGom-sde, II, 406, 549, 550, 716.
sGos-luṅ, II, 579.
sGyi-smad Khra-luṅ, II, 1042.
sGyel, I, 61.
sGrags, I, 198.
sGrags-kyi Yaṅ-rdzoṅ, I, 174.
sGrags-phu, I, 196.
sGre-mkhar, I, 75.
sGro-phug, I, 113.
sGro-sbug, I, 125.
sGro-lag, I, 268.
sGro-luṅ ser-chuṅ-pa, II, 518.

Ṅa-drug, I, 229.
Ṅaṅ-dkar, II, 1015.
Ṅaṅ-rgyal, II, 569, 608, 752.
Ṅaṅ-phu, II, 604.
Ṅaṅ-'brug, II, 608.
Ṅan-lam, I, 89; II, 805.
Ṅam-riṅs, II, 778.
Ṅam-rim, II, 818.
Ṅam-śod, II, 557, 565, 574, 575, 936 (cf. next entry).
Ṅams-śod, I, 143, 144, 177, 184; II, 438, 570, 895, 957 (cf. preceeding entry).
Ṅal-mda', II, 468.
Ṅur-smrig, I, 80, 378, 382; II, 790.
Ṅer-gom, I, 301.
Ṅo-sgra, I, 280.
Ṅog, I, 109.
Ṅom-chu, II, 550.
Ṅor, II, 1045, 1053.
mṄa'-phu, I, 124.
mṄa'-ris, I, xvii, 37, 93, 123, 204, 205, 207, 208, 215, 220, 229, 244, 247, 251, 252, 253, 267, 314, 317, 325, 352, 355, 380; II, 594, 710, 732, 766, 777, 787, 843, 871, 948, 1022, 1023, 1049, 1085.
mṄar-steṅs, II, 457.
mṄon-dga', II, 591, 829.
mṄon-par dga'-ba'i yul, II, 870.
rṄo-chu, II, 579.
rṄo-thog-thel, I, 154.
rṄog-can, II, 990.
rṄog-chu, I, 252.
rṄod, II, 493, 517.
rṄod A-rig thaṅ, II, 548.
rṄor, II, 778.
sṄar-'dzin, I, 318.
sṄon-chuṅ-gnas, II, 875, 878.
lṄa-ba, II, 777.
lṄa-len, I, 13.
lṄag-stag-ris, II, 427.

Ca-ri-tra, II, 826.
Caitya-giri, I, 22.
Caṅ-in-rtse, I, xvii, 64.

Campā, I, 5, 14.
Carasiṃha, II, 868.
Calakoṭa, II, 819.
Ci-phug, II, 652.
Cuṅ-mchog-dkar, 438.
Cog-ro lha-sdiṅs, II, 449.
Coṅ-tu-mkhar, II, 487.
Com-thaṅ, II, 612.
gCan-chen-sraṅs, II, 464.
gCuṅ-pa Yu-ba-gdoṅ, II, 749.
gCer-groṅ, II, 983.
lCag-ri, II, 991.
lCags-nur, II, 691.
lCags-spyil, II, 675.
lCags-phur-can, II, 668.
lCaṅ-gliṅ gru-bži, II, 642.
lCaṅ-rtsigs, I, 177.
lCaṅ-tshigs, I, 75.
lCaṅ-sar ser-ma-brag-gdoṅ, II, 450.
lCam-be (Campā), II, 693.
lCam-luṅ, II, 435.
lCim-chu-rdo, II, 1030.
lCes, I, 62.
lCog-ro 'briṅ-mtshams, II, 1028.
lCog-la, I, 201.

Cha-luṅ, II, 976.
Chag, II, 1054.
Chag-gi gtsug-lag-khaṅ, I, 88.
Chaṅ-khyim, II, 905, 943, 960.
Chab-tshan-kha, II, 695.
Chab-luṅ, II, 692.
Cham-la-kha, II, 511.
Char-ma, II, 976.
Chu-khyer, II, 430, 432.
Chu-khyer-mda', II, 470.
Chu-'khor, II, 929.
Chu-gle'u chuṅ-ba, II, 663.
Chu-rgyud-mkhar, II, 986.
Chu-sgo, II, 857.
Chu-nyi-ma, II, 544.
Chu-mdo, II, 540.
Chu-bar, I, 120, 124; II, 434, 435, 704, 720, 721, 814, 819, 911, 1041.
Chu-bo-ri, I, 63, 142, 144, 295; II, 479, 668, 670, 864, 876, 990.
Chu-bo-ri-khra-sna, II, 876.
Chu-mig, I, 212, 331; II, 408, 792, 1055, 1068.
Chu-mig dkar-mo, II, 675.
Chu-mig dgon-gsar, II, 536.
Chu-mig sde-skor, I, 81.
Chu-mig nag-po mthoṅ-ba-dug zin, II, 989.
Chu-mig riṅ-mo, II, 688, 788, 1009, 1069.
Chu-mig-luṅ, I, 79, 81, 82.
Chu-tshan-kha, II, 875.
Chu-bzaṅs, II, 915, 917, 1015.
Chu-lug, II, 974.
Chu-śul, II, 759.
Chu-srin byis-pa gsod, I, 21.
Chu-gsol, II, 511.
Chumbi (see Gro-mo).
Ch'eng-tu, II, 938.
Cho-rab, I, 287.
Chos-kyi-mdzod, II, 1039.
Chos-'khor-gliṅ, I, 308, 309, 341; II, 536, 778.
Chos-'khor-sgaṅ, I, 152; II, 830.
Chos-'khor Ta-bo, I, 355.
Chos-'khor-bsam-yas, I, 257.
Chos-rgyal-lhun-po, I, ii; II, 838, 1091.
Chos-sgro, II, 872.
Chos-sgro groṅ-mkhar, II, 1088.
Chos-ldiṅs, I, 138, 139.
Chos-sdiṅs, II, 704.
Chos-phug, I, 320.
Chos-rdzoṅ, I, ii; II, 1092.
Chos-luṅ, I, 109, 110; II, 678, 1073.
Chos-luṅ-tshogs, I, 396.

mChims–phu ('Chims–phu), I, 40, 44, 174, 194, 201, 260, 277; II, 492, 823, 828, 844, 1070.
mChog–dgon, II, 605.
mChod–rten–dkar–po, I, 381.
mChod–rten–dkar–mo, I, 336.
mChod–rten–ri, I, 22.
'Chad–dkar, II, 654, 732.
'Chad–kha–rñiṅ–ma, I, 275.
'Chad–kha–pa, I, 280.
'Chad–kha–gsar–pa, I, 276.
'Chad–po–che, II, 450.
'Chiṅ–ri, II, 450.
'Chiṅ–ru, I, 256.
'Chims, I, 305, 306, 345.
'Chims–phu (see mChims–phu).
'Chims–yul, II, 910.
'Chu–gu, II, 655.
'Chos, II, 960.

Jagattara, II, 1066.
Jaṅ, II, 937.
Jamali (see *Ārya–jamali*).
Jal–gyi–phu, I, 193, 194.
Jālandhara, I, 368, 391: II, 520, 598, 669, 682, 686, 700, 745, 845.
Jetavana, II, 1019.
Jo–khaṅ (Lhasa), I, 44, 258: II, 465, 672, 776, 878, 1006.
Jo–stan tshogs–chen–mo, II, 884.
Jo–stan tshogs–pa, II, 993.
Jo–naṅ, II, 772, 775, 778, 794, 1039.
Jo–mo, I, 179.
Jo–mo Kha–rag, II, 976, 986.
Jo–mo–gaṅs, II, 491, 518, 527, 675.
Jo–mo gLaṅ–bzaṅ–ma, II, 832.
Jo–mo 'Gro–sa, II, 675.
Jo–mo–naṅ, II, 526, 633, 634, 772, 773, 775, 776, 777.
Jo–mo lha–ri, II, 675.
Jog–po, II, 732.
Jya–žur, I, xvii, 63.
Jyekundo, II, 507.
Jvālinī (Dzwa–li–ni'i brag–phug), I, 22.
'Ja–tshon–gliṅ, II, 543
'Jag, II, 748.
'Jam, II, 732.
'Jam–ne, II, 548.
'Jam–lha–khaṅ, I, 338.
'Jal, II, 705.
'Ju, II, 1059, 1066.
'Ju–ma, I, 76.
lJaṅ, I, 190; II, 486, 591, 612, 648, 891.
lJaṅ–nag, II, 545.
lJaṅ–yul, I, 212.
lJaṅ Seṅ–ge–kha, II, 565.

Ña–khan, II, 513.
Ña–mo–kha, II, 466.
Ña–mo–gyur, II, 406.
Ña–ra, I, 126.
Ña–ri, I, 112.
Ñagrodhārāma, I, 21, 22.
Ñaṅ–pa, I, 288.
Ñaṅ–po, II, 645.
Ñan, I, 284, 302, 312.
Ñan–tsho, I, 255, 265, 266.
Ñan–re, II, 829.
Ñan–lha–sdiṅs, I, 276.
Ñi–ma–mkhar, II, 819.
Ñi–zla–sgan, II, 654.
Ñiṅ–phug, II, 1010, 1011.
Ñuṅ–ti (Kūḷu), II, 644.
gÑags, I, 170.
gÑags–tsha, II, 876.
gÑags Lha–byar–ma, II, 463.
gÑan–dkar, II, 707.
gÑan–chen–thaṅ–lha, I, 76 (see next entry).
gÑan Thaṅ–lha, II, 587, 598 (see Thaṅ–lha).

gÑan-po, II, 884.
gÑal, I, vi, 72, 75, 82, 269, 270, 273, 276, 278, 284, 320, 365, 376, 382; II, 403, 439, 440, 481, 577, 608, 656, 657, 661, 672, 709, 720, 849, 871, 872, 880, 911, 963, 984, 986, 1070, 1076.
gÑal-gyi-chos-sgo, I, 62.
gÑal-sgaṅ-thog, I, 326.
gÑal-boṅ-sñi, II, 463.
gÑal-tshan-gsum, II, 658.
gÑal-roṅ, II, 449.
gÑal-roṅ-liṅs, II, 1060.
gÑal Lo-ro, II, 702.
gÑas-gži zaṅs-can, I, 176.
gÑer, I, 288.
rÑog jo-sras, II, 936.
sÑag-phu, II, 1016.
sÑiṅ-khuṅ, II, 491.
sÑiṅ-druṅ, II, 500.
sÑug-rum, I, 285, 322.
sÑe, II, 893.
sÑe-thaṅ, I, 193, 259, 260, 262, 263, 288, 324, 330; II, 673, 794, 847, 948, 1021.
sÑe-mdo, II, 490, 948, 956, 957, 959, 962, 972, 973, 974.
sÑe-nam, II, 449, 648, 903.
sÑe-nam snaṅ-yul, I, 374.
sÑe-nam la-kha, II, 920.
sÑe-phu, II, 894, 895.
sÑe-phu śug-gseb, II, 893.
sÑe-bo, II, 498, 548.
sÑe-mo, II, 478, 526, 731.
sÑe-mo-khu, II, 988.
sÑe-mo mkha'-ru, II, 992.
sÑe-mo ra-maṅs, II, 728.
sÑed-gro, II, 872.
sÑel-ṅe, II, 612.

Ta-ċhien-lu (see Dar-tshe-mdo)
Tā-žig, I, 46.
Tā-la'i phreṅ, I, 5.
Ta'i-tu (Tai-tu), II, 500, 501.
Ta'u Tārā, II, 1050.
Takṣaśīlā, I, 4, 14, 367.
Tabo, I, ix.
Tamākṣaya, II, 741.
Tāmralipti, I, 13, 14, 15.
Tar-mda', II, 615.
Tārīm, II, 854.
Tālamāla (Tālahāra), I, 5.
Ti-sgro, I, 183, 193.
Ti-ra-hu-ti (Tirhut), I, 383; II, 580, 1034, 1058.
Ti-se, II, 433, 579, 669, 686, 700, 720, 726, 975, 976, 1039 (See Kāilāsa).
Ti-se'i lha-naṅ, II, 602.
Til, II, 476.
Tun-huang, I, xi, xii.
Tulakṣetra, II, 400.
Tre (Tre-bo), II, 479, 500.
Tre-śod, II, 474.
Tre-śod-mthil, II, 551.
Tre-śod rNa-rgyan, II, 482.
gTaṅ, II, 1088.
bTaṅ-braṅ, I, 20.
rTa-sgo, II, 1010.
rTa-nag, I, 228, 360; II, 518, 711.
rTa-nag gnas-gsar, I, 151.
rTa-nag-phug, II, 431.
rTa-phug mKha'-'gro-gliṅ, II, 530.
rTa-bar, I, 278.
rTa-bar rgyal-'dzin, II, 495.
rTa-mo, II, 435.
rTa-myog, II, 496, 497.
rTiṅ-ser, II, 612.
rTe'u-ra, I, 94; II, 1056, 1058, 1059, 1060.
sTag-mgo, I, 232; II, 669.
sTag-sgo, I, 196.
sTag-ṅos-mkhar, II, 553.
sTag-can, I, 318, 319.
sTag-bde brag-dmar, II, 1044.

sTag-bde seṅ-ge, II, 1008.
sTag-sde seṅ-rgyal, II, 791.
sTag-ma-phu, II, 543.
sTag-rtse, II, 507, 543, 546, 547, 548, 549.
sTag-rtse-mkhar, I, 170.
sTag-rtse rnam-rgyal, II, 543.
sTag-tshaṅ, I, 214.
sTag-tshaṅ seṅ-ge, II, 1028.
sTag-tshal, II, 440, 1009, 1058.
sTag-tshal gdoṅ-stoṅ, I, 355.
sTag-tshal smon-gro, I, 81.
sTag-luṅ, I, 268, 307, 313, 338; II, 412, 523, 532, 570, 571, 593, 616, 617, 620, 621, 622, 623, 628, 629, 630, 631, 632, 633, 634, 641, 645, 649, 786, 787, 792, 894.
sTag-luṅ-thaṅ, II, 627, 648.
sTag-luṅ 'brag-mgo, II, 643.
sTag-luṅ gtsug-lag-khaṅ, II, 625.
sTag-lha sgam-po, II, 543.
sTabs-ka, I, 284.
sTin-mo-mig, II, 1087.
sTeṅ-khaṅ, II, 611.
sTeṅ-gro, II, 686.
sTeṅ-byaṅ, II, 612.
sTeṅs-ka-ba, II, 985.
sToṅ-khuṅ-roṅ, I, 170.
sToṅ-ra, I, 133.
sToṅ-gsum zil-gnon, II, 631.
sTod, II, 580, 875.
sTod-khuṅ, I, 148.
sTod-sñe-nam 'Dam-phug, I, 232.
sTod-smad, I, vi.
sTod-luṅ rGya-dmar, II, 555.
sTod-luṅ-chu, I, ii.
sTod-lun gŽoṅ-pa-steṅ, II, 876.
sTod-luṅs, I, vi, xvii, 42, 148, 251, 262, 265, 286, 314, 332, 386; II, 441, 464, 544, 557, 587, 734, 880, 881, 893, 932, 942, 963, 1078.
sTod-luṅs-gram, II, 722.
sTod-luṅs gram-pa, II, 519.
sTod-luṅs sToṅ-khuṅ, II, 918.
sTod-luṅs-gnam, II, 737.
sTod-luṅs 'phar tshaṅ, I, 234; II, 487.
sTod-luṅs btsan-'gro, I, 286.
sTod-luṅs mtsho-smad, I, 335.
sTod-luṅs-'tshur, I, 297 (see Mtshur-phu).
sTod-luṅs Ri-ma, II, 917.
sTod-luṅs śo-ma-ra, II, 729.
sTod-luṅs Sa-thaṅ, II, 475.
sTod-Hor, II, 504, 1040.
sTon-mo-luṅ, II, 782, 1043.

Tha-thal, I, 503.
Thag, I, 112, 116, 117.
Thaṅ, I, 354; II, 1063.
Thaṅ-skya, I, 141, 148; II, 611, 617, 622, 634.
Thaṅ-skya lha-khaṅ, II, 610, 634.
Thaṅ-skya lha-thel, II, 611.
Thaṅ-khab, II, 851.
Thaṅ-mgo, II, 615, 620.
Thaṅ-chuṅ, I, 176.
Thaṅ-po-che, I, 93, 94, 257; II, 404, 1055, 1058, 1070 (see Sol-nag Thaṅ-po-che).
Thaṅ-sag, I, 310, 343, 344; II, 993.
Thaṅ-lha, I, 43; II, 486, 490, 492, 522, 536, 538 (see gÑan-chen-thaṅ-lha).
Thaṅ-lha-mdzod, II, 787.
Thar-pa, II, 790, 791.
Thar-pa-Khro-phu, II, 792.
Thar-pa-gliṅ, II, 658, 676, 751, 829.
Thu-gud, II, 423.
Thugs-rje-rdzoṅ, II, 1025.

Thur-la, II, 319, 420.
Thel, II, 577, 584, 586, 642, 644, 645, 752, 926, 1039, 1040.
Tho-liṅ, I, 84, 86, 87 (see Mtho-ldiṅ).
Thod-pa-can, I, 13.
Thod-phu, II, 1001.
mTha'-'dul, I, 40.
mTha'-rtsa, II, 891.
mTha'-luṅ, II, 655, 656.
mThar-thog, I, 268.
mThar-'on, II, 847.
mTho-ldiṅ, I, 247, 249 (see Tho-Liṅ).

Da-luṅ, I, 40.
Dag-sgaṅ, II, 621.
Dag-pa sel-ri, I, 199.
Dags, II, 573, 607, 1089.
Dags-po (Dwags-po), I, vi, 155, 185, 187, 189, 278, 292, 296, 305, 365; II, 453, 498, 516, 548, 572, 602, 603, 672, 718, 723, 824, 875, 986, 1018, 1052, 1053, 1087, 1088.
Dags-po Kroṅs-kha, II, 657.
Dags-po Tshoṅ-sde, II, 985.
Dags-po rDzoṅs-kha, II, 874.
Dags-po Žu-ru, I, 182, 184.
Dags-po la-bar, II, 546.
Dags-lha sGam-po, II, 528, 719, 976.
Daṅ-mo-luṅ, I, 300.
Dad-pa'i stobs, II, 1018.
Dan-tig, I, xviii, 65, 67.
Dantapura, I, 5, 15.
Dan-bag, I, 157, 202.
Dab-phyar sPaṅ-sgaṅ, II, 771.
Dam-pa, II, 797, 811.
Dar, I, 91; II, 615, 617, 618.
Dar-ma-sgaṅ, I, 276.
Dar-tshe-mdo (Ta-chien-lu), II, 411.
Dar-yul, I, 232, 269; II, 477, 635.
Dar-yul Bye-ma, II, 783.
Duṅ-zur, II, 1001.
Duṅ-luṅ, I, 197.
Dum-bu-ri, I, 305.
Dums, II, 673.
Dus-'khor Lha-mo-che, II, 783.
Dhu-ma-ta-la, II, 701.
Diṅ-ri, I, 36, 73, 200, 222, 225, 294; II, 429, 435, 488, 518, 519, 528, 691, 692, 726, 727, 733, 796, 816, 871, 879, 895, 902, 909, 912, 914, 917, 919, 920, 924, 927, 929, 953, 973, 974, 1026, 1053.
Diṅ-ri gDoṅ-pa, II, 918, 919.
Dinajpur, II, 1008.
Deb-goṅ gnas-chuṅ, II, 923.
Derge, I, 202.
Devadhā, I, 11.
Devīkoṭi (De-bi-ko-ṭi), II, 729.
Do-po-sgaṅ, II, 1040.
Do-ri, II, 906.
Don-mo, II, 1039.
Don-mo-ri, I, 82; II, 1013.
Dol, I, ii, 176, 256, 269, 270, 292; II, 414, 415, 480, 667, 760, 1090.
Dol-mda', II, 695.
Dol-mṅar mar-ma-gser-steṅs, II, 667.
Dol-po, II, 776.
Dol bSam-gtan-gliṅ, II, 836.
Dol Lhun-grub lha-rtse, II, 827.
Draṅ-chuṅ-mdo, I, 63.
Draṅ-pa, II, 986.
Draṅ-po-luṅ, I, 82.
Dro-mda', II, 1087.
gDan-sa ñe-kha, II, 1030.
gDan-sa-thel, I, 338; II, 570, 582, 583, 584, 585, 586, 587, 588, 592, 593, 643, 649, 687,

717, 752, 787, 802 (see next entry).
gDan-sa-mthil, II, 561, 563, 564, 571 (see preceeding entry).
gDan-sa Rin-po-che, II, 560.
gDuṅ-khaṅ chen-mo, II, 407.
gDoṅ-sna, II, 627.
bDe-chen, II, 499, 500, 504, 526, 528, 529, 531, 541.
bDe-chen-steṅs, II, 491, 525, 537, 538, 686, 698, 699.
bDe-mchog-raṅ-'byuṅ, I, 381.
bDe-mchog lha-khaṅ, II, 1008.
bDe-ldan, I, 20.
bDe-ba-can, I, 308, 341; II, 542, 670, 737, 1015.
bDe-gśegs, II, 560.
mDo, II, 712.
mDo-khams, I, 213; II, 474, 553, 630, 647, 1042.
mDo-khra lcim-luṅ, II, 449.
mDo-mkhar, I, 94.
mDo-sde-sbug, I, 348.
mDo-smad, I, 386; II, 501, 595, 607, 696.
mDo-luṅ, I, 305.
mDog, II, 775.
mDor-lha-steṅs, II, 612.
'Dam, I, 263, 279, 354; II, 542, 577, 652, 1089.
'Dar-cho, I, 81.
'Dar-'dzin, I, 14.
'Dal-ma-luṅ, II, 1002.
'Dul-gra, I, 306.
'Dul-gro, II, 469.
'Dod-mkhar, II, 974.
'Dol-kha, II, 811.
'Dres-pa'i groṅ-khyer, I, 13.
rDaṅ-khaṅ-dmar, II, 611.
rDo, II, 625.
rDo-rgyus-brag, II, 480.
rDo-chu, II, 854.
rDo-rje-gliṅ, II, 686.
rDo-rje-gdan, II, 701.
rDo-rje-sems-dpa'i khaṅ-bu, I, 116.
rDo-mda', II, 644.
rDo-'on, II, 894.
rDo-raṅ-thag, II, 568.
rDor-thas-phu, I, 148.
lDan, I, 78, 272; II, 505, 510.
lDan-mkhar dga'-ldan, II, 995.
lDan-sga, II, 545.
lDan-stod gTson-du, II, 596.
lDan-rdzoṅ, II, 693.
lDan-yul, I, 202.
lDum-ra, II, 688.
lDog, I, 354; II, 1010, 1014.
lDog-stag-ris, II, 997.
lDog-ltod, II, 1014.
lDod-loṅ, II, 1013, 1016.
lDoṅ, II, 501.
brDa, I, 82.

Na-kra'i gduṅ-khaṅ, II, 468.
Na-mo-śod, II, 1088.
Na-len-dra, II, 809, 822 (see Nālandā).
Nag-chu-ka, II, 860.
Nag-mo, I, 273.
Nag-mo-pa, II, 736.
Nag-mo-ri, I, 120.
Nag-tshaṅ, II, 619.
Nags-phu, II, 492, 494, 497, 529.
Nags-śod, II, 546, 549, 625, 662.
Nāgabodhi, II, 798.
Naṅ-dol, I, vi.
Nātha, I, 170.
Nam-mkha'-rdzoṅ, II, 950.
Nam-ra, II, 401.
Nar-phug, I, 198.
Nālandā (India), I, 229, 367, 382; II, 400, 729, 757, 844, 845, 1055, 1058.
Nālandā ('Phan-yul), II, 1081, 1082 (see Na-len-dra).

Ning-hsia, II, 486, 492.
Ne'u-thog, I, 325, 332, 340, 341; II, 405, 786 (see gSaṅ-phu).
Ne'u-ru, I, 81.
Nor-bu-gliṅ, I, 367.
gNam, I, 262, 263; II, 500, 540.
gNam-thaṅ dkar-po, I, 207.
gNam-par, II, 524.
gNam-rtse-ldan, I, 330.
gNam-mtsho, I, 386; II, 605, 614, 928, 1089.
gNam-rdziṅ-kha, II, 734.
gNas-khaṅ, I, 269.
gNas-mkhar, II, 466.
gNas-sgor, I, 96.
gNas-chuṅ, II, 937.
gNas-rñiṅ, II, 749.
gNas-drug, II, 571.
gNas-naṅ, II, 498, 530, 531, 538, 539, 540, 541, 542, 546, 549.
gNas-mo-che, I, 95.
rNa-rgyan-gyi nags, I, 25.
rNam-rgyal, II, 827.
rNam-thos tshal-gyi-gnas, II, 497.
rNam-par, I, 322.
sNa, I, 77.
sNa-nam, I, 81, 277.
sNa-phu, II, 665, 666, 667, 668.
sNa-phur-dgon, II, 664.
sNa-bo-la, I, 256.
sNa-mo-rdzoṅ, II, 584.
sNa-dmar, I, 199; II, 926.
sNa-riṅs, II, 420.
sNa-śud, I, 96, 253.
sNa'u gaṅs-ra, II, 720.
sNaṅ-khaṅ, II, 930.
sNaṅ-gro, I, 72.
sNaṅ-ra-sgaṅ, I, 284.
sNaṅ-gsal, I, 148.
sNar-thaṅ, I, 81, 272, 282, 283, 305, 319, 336, 337, 338, 339; II, 592, 749, 782, 810, 1024, 1043, 1068, 1069, 1072.
sNar-blas-mo-che, I, 82.
sNi-śaṅ, II, 435.
sNubs, II, 705.
sNubs-yul, I, 183.
sNubs-yul roṅ, I, 292.
sNul-mthso-gliṅ-dgu, I, 193.
sNe-gdoṅ, II, 595, 642, 645, 800, 1089, 1090 (see sNe'u-gdoṅ).
sNe-bo, II, 507.
sNe-'og, II, 959.
sNe'u-mkhar, II, 779.
sNe'u-gduṅ, I, 300.
sNe'u-gdoṅ, II, 586, 703, 1047 (see sNe-gdoṅ).
sNe'u-zur, I, 311, 313.
bsNubs, II, 654, 659.

Pa-gor, I, 131.
Pa-ta, II, 848.
Pa-yen, II, 1073.
Pa'i-mi'i-sa (Pai-ma-ssu), I, 48.
Pāñcāla, I, 13.
Pāṭaliputra, I, 28.
Pad-spuṅs, I, 285; II, 1040.
Pad-ma-brtsegs, II, 971.
Padmakūta, II, 971.
Par-phu, II, 893.
Pārileyyakavana, I, 21.
Pu-rgyal, I, 36.
Pu-thaṅ, I, 336.
Puṇḍravardhana, II, 1008.
Puṇyāvati, I, 35.
Pulahari, I, 382 (see next entry).
Puṣpahari (Phul-la-ha-ri), II, 400, 757.
Peking (Imperial Palace [pho-braṅ]), I, vi, vii, 212, 213, 214, 215; II, 531, 544, 628, 631, 775, 787, 793, 885, 894.
Pe-ri-le-ya'i-nags, I, 21.
Po-rgyaṅ, II, 542.
Po-ta-ri, I, 71, 93.

Potala, I, 4, 5, 8, 10, 14, 15, 16; II, 509, 791, 1006, 1014, 1079.
Po-to dgon-pa, I, 268.
Po-doṅ, I, 147, 273.
Po-re, I, 185.
Prabhāsa, I, 16.
dPa-ri, I, 63.
dPal Kun-tu-bzaṅ-po, II, 1092.
dPal Chu-bo-ri, I, 63.
dPal-thaṅ, I, 255.
dPal-mo chos-sdiṅs, II, 647.
dPal-mo dPal-thaṅ, II, 427, 682.
dPal Myu-gu-luṅ, II, 399.
dPal-ri, II, 1040.
dPal-luṅ, I, 187.
dPuṅs-riṅs, I, 319.
dPe-dkar-gliṅ, I, 257.
dPe-med-lhun-grub gtsug-lag-khaṅ, I, 84.
dPon-po-ri, I, 217.
sPa-gro, II, 421, 478, 672, 692, 800.
sPa-gro sTag-tshaṅ, II, 976.
sPa-rnams, II, 1006.
sPa-tshab, I, 341.
sPa-ri, II, 670.
sPa-ri Byaṅ-chub-gliṅ, II, 670.
sPaṅ-thaṅ-stod, I, 306.
sPaṅ-dug-mo, II, 909.
sPaṅ-po-kha, II, 693
sPaṅ-sa, I, 276.
sPu-gu-dor, I, 154, 277, 280.
sPu-tra, II, 528.
sPu-raṅs, II, 976, 1009 (see sPu-hraṅs).
sPu-hraṅs, I, 37, 68, 251, 342, 352; II, 594, 1022.
sPuṅ-dra, II, 686.
sPuṅ-riṅs, I, 189, 190.
sPe-ra, II, 1040.
sPeṅ-pa, II, 775.
sPel-sgo dgon-pa, II, 484.
sPel-dmar, I, 257.
sPel-bži, II, 410.
sPo-khaṅ, II, 1068.
sPo-bo, II, 481, 506, 548, 550, 603, 694.
sPon-phug, II, 477.
sPom, II, 523.
sPom-po, II, 523, 545.
sPos-khaṅ, II, 1073.
sPyaṅ-luṅ, II, 698.
sPyad, II, 686.
sPyad-luṅs śar-kha, II, 784.
sPyan-gyas, I, 82, 98, 99, 100, 101; II, 1023.
sPyi-de dgon-pa, II, 904.
sPyi-gnas gyo-gu, II, 572.
sPyi-bo, II, 823.
sPyil-bu, I, 276, 279, 280, 281, 307, 320.
sPras, II, 615, 617.
sPras-pa, II, 616.
sPrul-pa'i sde, II, 501.
sPre'u-btul, I, 21.
sPre'u-žiṅ, II, 409, 411, 412, 413.
sPre'u-žiṅ-gliṅ, II, 412.

Pha-drug, I, 219, 220; II, 687.
Pha-boṅ dkar-leb, II, 478, 518.
Pha-boṅ-kha, I, 297.
Pha-woṅ-thaṅ, I, 267.
Pha-li-luṅ, II, 783.
Phag-mo-gru, I, 198; II, 476, 498, 560, 567, 574, 582, 595, 596, 607, 612, 614, 615, 619, 620, 642, 644, 653, 656, 661, 663, 706, 707, 963, 975, 995.
Phag-mo mṅon-'byuṅ, I, 183.
Phag-ri, II, 732, 1068.
Phambī, I, 227.
Phi-ri sTag-luṅ, II, 615.
Phu-chuṅ, I, 288.
Phu-thaṅ, II, 998.
Phu-thaṅ 'Khun-pa-sa, II, 975.
Phu-thaṅ sPyan-gyas, I, 98.

Phug-chuṅ-roṅ, I, 179.
Phug-po-che, I, 75, 76, 93, 174, 177, 180, 182.
Phug-po-che lha-ri, I, 174, 175.
Phug-mo, I, 184; II, 529, 538.
Phug-mo-che, II, 530.
Phu-mo'i brag, II, 527.
Phuṅ-mkhar, II, 903.
Phuṅ-po, I, 174.
Phuṅ-po ri-bo-che, I, 150.
Phur-dgon rin-chen-gliṅ, II, 603.
Phur-moṅ-sgaṅ, I, 132.
Pho-thoṅ, I, xvii.
Pho-braṅ 'Um-bu bla-mkhar, II, 812.
Pho-ma, II, 669, 953.
Pho-mo, II, 473.
Pho-mo lha-khaṅ, II, 473.
Phoṅ-mdo, I, 322; II, 616, 617, 620, 625, 628, 631, 649.
Phoṅ-mdo khaṅ-chen, II, 614.
Phom Lha-khab, II, 683.
Phyā, I, 79.
Phya-yul, II, 469.
Phyag-rje, I, 292.
Phyag-'tshal-sgaṅ, II, 607.
Phyag-la, II, 625.
Phyi-'brum dgon-gsar, II, 1044.
Phyogs, I, 348.
Phreṅ-kha-brag, II, 893.
'Phags-pa 'Ja-ma-li, I, 392; II, 1053 (see next entry).
'Phags-pa Wa-ti, II, 528, 1008.
'Phags-pa śiṅ-kun, I, 230; II, 799, 821, 1033.
'Phaṅ-thaṅ, I, 43.
'Phan-po, II, 783.
'Phan-yul, I, 78, 79, 83, 88, 233, 234, 253, 259, 263, 268, 271, 275, 281, 306, 310, 311, 313, 341, 342, 343, 346; II, 405, 453, 469, 478, 635, 655, 732, 740, 760, 809, 822, 846, 849, 860, 873, 877, 880, 884, 896, 901, 904, 919, 923, 932, 935, 985, 991, 1000, 1003, 1042.
'Phan-yul Rgyal, II, 1042 (see rGyal-lha-khaṅ).
'Phan-yul Stag-mgo, I, 232.
'Phar-tshaṅ, II, 463 (cf. sTod-luṅs 'Phar-tshaṅ).
'Phyil-phu, II, 1001.
'Phyogs-kyi Dog-pa, I, 62.
'Phyoṅ-po, I, vi.
'Phyoṅ-po khe-ru, I, 155.
'Phyos, II, 438, 1030, 1059.
'Phyos-kha-sgiṅ, II, 720.
'Phraṅ-po, II, 663.
'Phraṅ-'og, I, 208.
'Phruṅ, I, 178.
'Phrul-snaṅ, I, 40, 44, 219.

Ba-do, II, 405.
Ba-yags, I, 271.
Ba-yul, II, 718, 986.
Ba-yo, II, 543, 546, 548.
Ba-ri, I, 177.
Ba-lam-śa-tsha, I, 74, 75.
Ba-so-thaṅ, I, 78.
Baṅ, I, 114.
Baṅ-mdo, II, 548.
Baṅ-rims, II, 946.
Bad, II, 625.
Bar-thaṅ, I, 318.
Bar-'brog, II, 691.
Bar-'brog rDo-rje-gliṅ, II, 671, 686.
Bar-yul, I, 76.
Bar-gsar rdziṅ-kha, I, 197.
Bal, I, 354.
Bal-thul-ma, II, 816.
Bal-po rdzoṅ, I, 254, 361.
Bal-bu, I, 175.
Bhaktibala, II, 1018.
Bhaṅgala, I, 360; II, 1007.
Bharendra, II, 844.
Bihār, II, 1034.

Bu–dal, I, 279.
Bu–tshal–gser–khaṅ, I, 62.
Bu–le, II, 690.
Buṅ–śiṅ, II, 1031.
Bum–thaṅ, II, 421, 676, 1076.
Bum–thaṅ Thar–pa–gliṅ, II, 676
Bur, I, 258; II, 556, 670.
Be–ta–la (Vetala), I, 391, 394; II, 868 (see preface).
Be–dur, II, 1066, 1067.
Bengal, I, 390.
Be–ba–la, II, 868 (see preface).
Be–ri, II, 504.
Bo–doṅ, I, 79, 345, 346; II, 679, 787, 1009.
Bo–doṅ–e, II, 698, 786.
Bo–doṅ Rin–rtse, II, 702, 783.
Boṅ–ra, II, 784.
Boṅ–ra–steṅs, II, 621, 627 (see gYaṅ–śod Boṅ–ra–steṅs).
Boṅ–śod, II, 920.
Bodhgayā, I, 369, 394.
Bon–groṅ, II, 448.
Bos–mo, II, 937.
Bya, I, 272; II, 1087, 1088, 1089, 1090.
Bya–lkog, II, 477.
Bya–skyuṅs, II, 668.
Bya–khyuṅ dgon–pa, II, 1073.
Bya–khyi lha–khaṅ, II, 554.
Bya–grags, I, 91.
Bya–rgod phuṅ–po'i ri, II, 669.
Bya Ṅur–mo, I, 275.
Bya–ma–luṅ, II, 862.
Bya–mo spre–ltag, II, 949.
Bya–tshaṅ, II, 688.
Bya–žiṅ, II, 654.
Bya–bzaṅ, II, 478.
Bya–yul, I, 289, 291, 292, 296, 301, 302, 303, 304, 305, 306, 307, 308, 319; II, 438, 543, 612.
Bya–yul Dags–po, I, 289.
Bya–ru dBen–tsha, II, 706.
Bya–ruṅ kha–śor, I, 39, 230.
Bya–rog–tshaṅ, 78; II, 684, 990.
Bya–rog–rdzoṅ, II, 582.
Bya–sa, I, 277; II, 930, 936, 945, 1087.
Byaṅ, II, 918.
Byaṅ Klag–brag, I, 238.
Byaṅ–gliṅ, II, 686.
Byaṅ–chub–gliṅ, I, 95.
Byaṅ–rta–sna, II, 565.
Byaṅ–thaṅ, I, xvii.
Byaṅ–tsam–luṅ, II, 403.
Byaṅ–tsha–kha, II, 669.
Byaṅ–rom–po, I, 271.
Byaṅ–luṅ, I, 278.
Byams–gliṅ, II, 412.
Byams–chen, I, 340.
Byams–pa–gliṅ, I, 338; II, 815, 822, 826, 827, 830, 836.
Byar, II, 439, 875, 878, 883.
Byar–og–og, II, 657.
Byin–phag, II, 692.
Byin–legs, II, 543.
Byur, II, 704.
Bye–khud, II, 877.
Bye–gliṅ, I, 78.
Bye–can, II, 888.
Bye–chuṅ, I, 280.
Bye–thaṅ, II, 677.
Bye–ma, II, 648.
Bye–ma'i, la, II, 931.
Bye–ma–luṅ, I, 75 (see Bye–luṅ).
Bye–ma seṅ–ge, I, 151.
Bye–luṅ, I, 76; II, 540.
Byen, I, 275.
Byen–yul, II, 873.
Byes–can, I, 318.
Bra–gor, I, 279, 284, 320.
Brag–dkar, II, 527, 655.
Brag–dkar rtsi–can, II, 1001.
Brag–kha, II, 774.
Brag–gu Ri–bo–che, II, 477.
Brag–rgya, I, 348.

Brag-rgyab, I, 311.
Brag-sgom chen-mo, II, 938.
Brag-nag, I, 325; II, 810, 813, 828.
Brag-po-che, II, 615.
Brag-phyi, II, 494.
Brag-dmar, I, 229; II, 527.
Brag-dmar-mgrin-bzaṅs, I, 40.
Brag-dmar rdzoṅ, I, 170.
Brag-dmar 'Um-bu-tshal, I, 42.
Brag-ram, I, 335.
Brag-gsum, II, 548.
Brag-lha klu-phug, II, 738, 812.
Brags-rgyab, I, 263.
Braṅ-gis-ñal, I, 4.
Braṅ Ra-mo-che, I, 79, 300.
Bran-ka, II, 932.
Brab-śi sam-pa, II, 611.
Bras Chu-bar, II, 1000.
Brin, II, 449, 454, 456, 458.
Brin sÑe-nam, II, 453.
Brin-las, I, 332.
Bru-mda', II, 607.
Bru-ža, I, 159.
Brud-kyi Dad-mo-steṅs, II, 444.
Brul-gyi Ra-ba dkar-po, I, 288.
Bre-gu, I, 62.
Bre-chuṅ, II, 1029.
Brom-pa Brag-dmar, I, 81.
bLa-mda', I, 278.
bLa-do, I, 193, 384.
bLa-braṅ, I, 330; II, 1059.
bLa-braṅ bKra-śis-'khyil, I, iii.
bLa-braṅ nag-po, II, 617.
bLa-ye-thaṅ, II, 628.
dBaṅ-chen-ri, I, 371.
dBaṅ-po, II, 829.
dBaṅ-po'i phug, I, 371.
dbU, II, 702, 936, 1080.
dbU-stod, II, 542.
dbU-rtse-rigs-gsum, II, 806.
dbU-rtse-lha-khaṅ, I, 379.
dbU-tshal, I, 77.
dbU-ra, II, 878.
dbU-ri, II, 675, 679.
dbU-ru, I, 76, 99, 142, 179, 182, 202, 273, 316; II, 438, 453, 454, 455, 458, 469, 521, 549, 570, 655, 678, 681, 849, 850, 919, 930, 931.
dbU-ru sKar-chuṅ, I, 62.
dbU-ru Ṅan-lam Ral-gsum, I, 173.
dbU-ru 'Brom-pa, II, 863.
dbU-ru-žwa, I, 173, 192.
dbU-ru-luṅ, II, 622.
dbUr-goṅ-ma, I, 75.
dbUs, I, xiv, xv, xvii, xviii, 34, 37, 93, 127, 129, 130, 136, 138, 142, 143, 153, 170, 177, 203, 204, 216, 217, 218, 220, 235, 237, 238, 244, 247, 249, 253, 254, 255, 270, 283, 286, 305, 307, 319, 324, 325, 338, 339, 340, 343, 344, 345, 346, 352, 354, 373, 379, 380; II, 410, 427, 429, 432, 438, 442, 450, 453, 457, 465, 475, 479, 482, 490, 492, 504, 508. 509, 522, 523, 524, 543, 548, 551, 555, 564, 579, 592, 600, 602, 604, 612, 620, 622, 625, 630, 633, 639, 641, 649, 659, 663, 672, 675, 696, 705, 710, 728, 741, 750, 761, 775, 776, 777, 778, 785, 786, 789, 791, 796, 832, 843, 846, 871, 879, 894, 904, 918, 925, 926, 929, 942, 957, 1000, 1005, 1009, 1018, 1021, 1068, 1070, 1073, 1080, 1085, 1090.
dbUs-khu, I, 327.
dbUs-gtsaṅ Kun-bde-gliṅ, II, 1093.
dbUs-sde, II, 445.

dbEn–dmar, II, 790, 791, 792, 793.
dbYar–mo–thaṅ, II, 696.
'Bar'–ri, II, 692.
'Bab–rom, II, 469, 470.
'Bar–ba'i phug (see Jvālinī).
'Bal, II, 740.
'Bum–žiṅ, II, 655.
'Bob–sa dkar–sgaṅ, II, 483.
'Byi, II, 612.
'Bras, II, 457.
'Bras–spuṅs, II, 412, 583, 1078.
'Bras–yul, I, 340.
'Bri, I, 315; II, 599.
'Bri–khuṅ ('Bri–guṅ), I, 217, 281, 308, 309, 387; II, 506, 560, 566, 570, 571, 572, 573, 576, 577, 578, 579, 580, 583, 598, 599, 600, 601, 602, 603, 604, 606, 608, 609, 610, 625, 642; 668; 681, 743, 945, 952, 953, 958, 962, 963, 973, 975, 1070, 1089.
'Bri–khuṅ–Thel, II, 577, 607, 649.
'Bri–lcam, II, 527.
'Bri–chu, I, 158.
'Bri–luṅ dam–pa chos–phyug, II, 485.
'Bri–luṅ–rne–śod, II, 553.
'Briṅ, II, 687.
'Briṅ sña–nam, I, 229.
'Briṅ–thaṅ, II, 870.
'Briṅ–sde, II, 1087.
'Briṅ–mtshams, II, 1029.
'Briṅ–mtshams lcim–luṅ, II, 1043.
'Brug, II, 608, 664, 667, 669, 670, 674, 678, 681, 693.
'Brug–yul, II, 676, 1029.
'Brug Ra–luṅ, II, 672.
'Bre, I, 75, 330.
'Bro–ldog, II, 571.
'Brog, I, 133.
'Brog–yaṅs–steṅs, II, 715.
'Broṅ–bu, II, 714, 723.
'Brom, I, 295; II, 860.
sBa–gor brag–nag, I, 81.
sBa–snams, II, 696.
sBas, II, 1000.
sBal–'dra', II, 990.
sBu–chu, I, 278.
sBuḋ–tra, I, 198; II, 698.
sBom–po, I, 158.
sBraṅ–po 'U–lu, I, 134.
Ma–bkọd, I, 75, 76.
Ma–kha (Mecca), II, 516.
Ma–dros–pa, II, 526, 1091.
Ma–pham, II, 726.
Ma–phebs–'bebs, I, 14.
Ma–mo–gnas, I, 104.
Ma–yul, II, 568.
Ma–yul–rdzoṅ, II, 1087.
Ma–yul–roṅ, II, 568.
Magadha, I, 13, 20, 243, 342, 367, 368, 371, 383, 390; II, 798, 844, 1031, 1053, 1058.
Maṅ–kar–mda', II, 1030.
Maṅ–dkar–sgaṅ, II, 704.
Maṅ–dkar spaṅ–sgaṅ, I, 237.
Maṅ–'gar sgaṅ, II, 560, 569, 570
Maṅ–naṅ, I, 352.
Maṅ–ra, I, 78.
Maṅ–ra gYu–mtsho, I, 64.
Maṅ–yul, I, 42, 44, 207; II, 767, 855, 973, 1034.
Maṅ–yul guṅ–thaṅ, II, 916.
Mativihāra, I, 243.
Madras, I, 368.
Madhyadeśa, I, 33, 393; II, 401, 754, 756, 757, 758, 761, 765, 844.
Maṇibhāga, II, 543.
Maṇḍal nag–po, II, 718.
Manasarovar, II, 526.
Mar–steṅs, II, 544, 550.
Mar–snon, I, 298.
Mar–ma, II, 919.

Mar-yul, I, 37, 130, 352; II, 700.
Mal-gro, I, 193, 275, 286, 305; II, 565, 602, 614.
Mal-gro rGyal-bzaṅs-sgaṅ, I, 239.
Mal-gro gser-thog, I, 234.
Mal rTe'u-ra-pa, II, 888.
Malabar, II, 849.
Malaya, I, 158.
Malda, II, 1008.
Mallas, I, 22.
Mahācaitya, II, 797.
Mahābodi, I, 280; II, 790, 791, 1047, 1055, 1058.
Mahendragiri, I, 371.
Mi-ñag (Tangut Hsi-hsia), I, xvii, 58, 64; II, 501, 502, 503, 510, 511, 928.
Mi-ñag-ga (Ning-hsia), II, 486, 492, 740.
Mi-ñag rab-sgaṅ, II, 501.
Mi-chos, I, 75.
Mithilā, I, 5.
Mid-la'i rdzoṅ-drug, II, 433.
Miśrakapura, I, 13, 15.
Mu-tig, II, 695, 948, 953.
Mu-le-goṅ, II, 976.
Mun-pa mi-bzad-pa, II, 741.
Mus, II, 1015.
Mus-gle-luṅ, II, 1016.
Mus Daṅ-ma-gliṅ-skya, II, 1016.
Me-dge lha-'tsho, I, 386.
Me-tog-khyim, II, 763.
Me-tog ra-ba, I, 214.
Meṅ-ge, I, 232.
Men-žaṅ (Mes-žaṅ), II, 643, 644.
Mer-nag-kha, II, 555.
Mo-ra-'gyel, I, 74.
Mo-la, II, 1076.
Mog-sa, II, 663.
Mon (Lahul), I, 198; II, 478, 602, 676, 976, 1076.
Mon-kha-zer-mo, I, 181.
Mon-grab, I, 320.
Mon-mgar-'gan, I, 74.
Mon-'gar, I, 183; II, 653.
Mon-'gar mgon-po gdoṅ, II, 657.
Mon-'gar rgyal-bzaṅs, I, 238.
Mon-'gar-ba, II, 975.
Mon Ba-gro, I, 150.
Mon Lug-mgo-steṅs, I, 304.
Mya-ṅan-'das-chuṅ, II, 850.
Myaṅ, I, 78, 110, 126, 127, 128, 138, 164, 173, 192, 193, 202, 236, 269, 272, 273, 292, 352, 353; II, 440, 492, 518, 519, 659, 664, 671, 676, 678, 679, 696, 726, 749, 769, 916, 917, 941, 997, 1030, 1052.
Myaṅ-chu, II, 457.
Myaṅ-stod gtsaṅ-po, I, 355.
Myaṅ nag-'ol-po, I, 134.
Myaṅ-po, I, 257; II, 494, 495, 505, 507, 542, 544, 547, 548, 549, 550, 662, 668, 688.
Myaṅ-ro, I, 79, 119, 332, 335; II, 405, 675.
Myaṅ-ro bLa-riṅs, I, 82.
Myu-gu-sna, I, 326.
Myu-gu-luṅ, I, 112, 207, 208; II, 399, 1029.
Mṛgamātṛ, I, 22.
dMag-gis mi-tshugs-pa, I, 4.
dMar-khams, II, 481, 482, 484, 513.
dMar-po-ri, I, 43, 71, 93.
dMar-mo, II, 653.
dMar-tsha-thuṅ, II, 548.
dMar-ro, II, 995.
dMu, I, 78; II, 792.
dMyal, I, ii; II, 975, 1087, 1088, 1090.
rMa, I, 70; II, 874.
rMa-chu (Huang-ho), I, xvii-xviii, 65, II, 777.

rMa-bya'i-gnas, I, 236.
rMog-cog, II, 737.
sMad, I, 305; II, 876.
sMad-khams, II, 870.
sMan-gro, I, 354.
sMan-rgyal, II, 829.
sMan-gcig, II, 949, 966, 970.
sMan-mo, II, 875.
sMan-rtse (Man-tzu), I, 56; II, 502.
sMan-luṅ, I, 155.
sMi-ri, II, 783.
sMyug-tshal, I, 199; II, 1042.
sMyoṅ-kha-dga', II, 958.

Tsa-ri, I, 200; II, 498, 544, 548, 579, 602, 603, 668, 669, 683, 686, 719, 729, 748, 815, 829, 832, 870, 884, 885, 895, 953, 975, 986.
Tsa-ri sgom-po, II, 739.
Tsa-ri-tra, II, 813.
Tsa-ri gYu-mtsho, II, 491, 601 (see gYu-mtsho).
Tsa-ri gsar-ma, II, 543.
Tsa-ri'i gnas-chen, II, 824.
Tsa-rin-chen, II, 543.
Tsa'i naṅ, II, 565.
Tsa'i phu-gaṅs-žur-mo, II, 488.
Tsam-luṅ, II, 401.
Tsi-luṅ, II, 565.
Tsin-tsi-liṅ, II, 851, 852, 853.
Tsoṅ-kha, II, 1073.
Tsoṅ-kha bde-khams, I, xvii, 63.
Tsoṅ-kha'i skyes-ri, II, 1073.
Tsoṅ-thar, II, 1073.
gTsaṅ, I, xiv, xv, xvii, xviii, 34, 37, 136, 144, 153, 160, 174, 176, 177, 182, 185, 187, 203, 204, 207, 216, 217, 218, 238, 244, 255, 262, 269, 270, 273, 284, 292, 314, 318, 321, 325, 339, 342, 343, 344, 346, 352, 374, 378, 379, II, 399, 407, 410, 427, 428, 429, 432, 448, 454, 465, 471, 479, 492, 504, 525, 526, 528, 555, 556, 602, 615, 634, 635, 636, 640, 641, 647, 649, 654, 655, 663, 669, 672, 675, 684, 686, 688, 693, 696, 703, 739, 741, 750, 751, 775, 776, 777, 778, 788, 791, 792, 794, 796, 818, 846, 857, 871, 904, 929, 941, 942, 956, 957, 974, 984, 1000, 1001, 1009, 1018, 1030, 1034, 1039, 1040, 1045, 1055, 1057, 1059, 1073, 1080, 1085.
gTsaṅ-kha, II, 935.
gTsaṅ-'gar, I, 327.
gTsaṅ-rgyaṅ-mkhar, I, 326.
gTsaṅ-rgyan, II, 1000.
gTsaṅ Chu-mig, II, 408.
gTsaṅ-po, I, 112, 256; II, 550, 718, 769, 854, 968, 1082.
gTsaṅ-roṅ, I, 314, 380; II, 402, 405, 428, 664, 723, 1005.
gTsaṅ-roṅ-gyuṅ, I, 80.
gTsaṅ-žal, II, 653, 875.
gTsug-gtor sgaṅ, II, 923, 924.
gTsoṅ-kha, II, 504.
bTsan-gro, I, 302, 304.
bTsan-thaṅ, I, 78, 187, 189, 319; II, 827, 875.
bTsan-brag, II, 492.
rTsaṅ-roṅ snar-pa, II, 916.
rTsi-'or, I, 75.
rTsibs-ri, II, 421.
rTse, II, 585.
rTse-sgaṅ, II, 946, 948, 962, 963, 965, 966.
rTse-pa-sgaṅ, II, 944, 962.
rTse-lha-sgaṅ, II, 507, 508, 516, 544.
rTses-thaṅ, I, 338, 339; II, 413, 585, 586, 587, 588, 590, 592, 593, 642, 649, 749, 779, 781,

799, 800, 802, 808, 822, 828, 935, 1082, 1084, 1089, 1090.
rTses-thaṅ bsam-gliṅ, II, 812.

Tsha-khuṅ, II, 924.
Tsha-guṅ, II, 920, 921.
Tsha-thaṅ, II, 985.
Tsha-sna, I, 255; II, 786.
Tsha-'phraṅ nag-po, II, 501.
Tsha-ba-sgaṅ, II, 481, 490.
Tsha-'ba-yul, I, 134.
Tsha-ba-roṅ, I, 170.
Tsha-mig, I, 75.
Tsha-roṅ, I, 79, 313, 340; II, 560, 612, 918.
Tsha-luṅ, II, 732.
Tshal-pa-gru, II, 711.
Tshi-ra-sgaṅ, II, 888.
Tshur-sgaṅ, II, 515.
Tshe-po-luṅ, II, 948.
Tshe-spoṅ, I, 75.
Tshes, I, 76.
Tshogs-chen-pa, II, 826.
Tshogs-sde, II, 826.
Tshogs-pa, I, 80.
Tshogs-pa Bya-rdzoṅ, II, 1072.
Tshoṅ-'dus, I, 25, 149; II, 454, 642, 679, 1068.
Tshoṅ-'dus mgur-mo, I, 238; II, 448.
Tshoṅ-'dus-gnas, I, 75.
mTshal, I, vi, vii; II, 722.
mTshal-sgaṅ, II, 559, 560.
mTshal-guṅ-thaṅ, II, 717 (see 'Tshal guṅ-thaṅ).
mTshal-pa phyug-po, II, 719.
mTshur-phu ('Tshur-phu) I, 197, 198, 199, 338; II, 467, 480, 485, 486, 487, 489, 490, 494, 498, 499, 500, 504, 506, 508, 510, 519, 524, 540, 544, 549, 600, 742, 810, 989, 1069, 1070.
mTsho-nag, II, 995.
mTsho-sna, II, 656, 702, 976.
mTsho-sna Dril-chuṅ, II, 439.
mTsho-snaṅ, II, 541.
mTsho-phyi maṅ-khaṅ, II, 1040.
mTsho-ma-pham, II, 526.
mTsho-mo-ru khyuṅ, II, 499.
mTsho-rdzoṅ, I, 181; II, 874.
mTsho-luṅ, I, 232, 235.
mTsho Hūṃ-sgra-sgrogs-pa, II, 958.
'Tshar-dgu-luṅs, I, 176.
'Tshar-steṅs, I, 199.
'Tshar-'tshur, I, 176.
'Tshal, I, vi; II, 642, 1023.
'Tshal guṅ-thaṅ, I, vi, 338, 341 (see mTshal guṅ-thaṅ).
'Tshal-chuṅ, I, 74, 79, 288.
'Tshal-pa, II, 410.
'Tshal-dbus-gliṅ, II, 778.
'Tshur, II, 479.
'Tshur-ṅos-bzaṅs, II, 479.
'Tshur-ca-ra, II, 530.
'Tshur-phu (see mTshur-phu)
'Tshur-phu-kuṅs, II, 491.
'Tshur lha-luṅ, II, 464.
'Tshel-min, II, 814.
'Tsho-ña, I, 111.

Dzwa-li-ni'i brag-phug, I, 22.
Dzam-gliṅ dkar-mo, II, 1053 (see 'Phags-pa Wa-ti).
mDzo-ra, II, 616.
mDzod-dge-dgon-pa, I, iii.
mDzod-nag, II, 1088.
mDzod-ma, II, 894.
'Dzaṅ, I, 238.
'Dzin, I, 184.
'Dzims, I, 78.
rDza-dgon, II, 545.
rDza-chu Dar-mo, II, 720.
rDza-spo, II, 694.
rDza-a-ban gaṅs-kyi me-loṅ, II, 506.

rDzoṅ, I, 222.
rDzoṅ-drug, II, 527.
rDzoṅ-pa, II, 478.
rDzoṅ-ri, II, 438.

Wa-seṅ-ge, I. 173.
Wal-sna, II, 536.
Wu-t'ai-shan, I, 184, 220, 227, 336, 381; II, 492, 598, 669, 679, 783, 846, 898, 911 (see Ri-bo-rtse-lṅa).
Vāi-dūr, II, 710.
Vāiśalī, I, 21, 24; II, 1058.
Vajrāsana, I, 19, 228, 242, 246, 247, 360, 371, 372; II, 483, 530, 570, 613, 701, 733, 760, 790, 801, 847, 848, 869, 911, 1028, 1053, 1055, 1058.
Vaneśvara, II, 1067.
Vārāṇasī, I, 4, 5, 14, 15, 16, 20, 23; II, 844, 1031, 1033.
Vikramaśīla, I, 229, 243, 244, 245, 246, 247, 254, 259, 372, 377, 380, 391, 392; II, 758, 763, 845, 847, 1020, 1045.
Vindhya, II, 729.
Vulture Peak, II, 451, 483, 669 (see Bya-rgod phuṅ-po'i ri).
Vetala (see Be-ta-la).
Verañjā, I, 22.
Veluvana, I, 21.

Ža-ma pha-drug, II, 915.
Ža-lu (Žwa-lu), I, 335, 338, 342, 366; II, 417, 423, 794.
Ža-lu khaṅ-gsar, I, 214.
Žaṅ, I, 254.
Žaṅ-gye, I, 331.
Žaṅ-žuṅ, I, 34, 37, 84, 87; II, 1008.
Žaṅ-e-pa, II, 1029.
Žaṅs-chen, I, 82.
Žaṅs-po-che, I, 82.
Žiṅ-mo-che, I, 84.
Žiṅ-tshigs, II, 975.
Žu-ru, I, 182.
Žer, I, 68.
Žo-kha, II, 494.
Žogs, I, 273, 292, 302.
Žogs-steṅs, I, 196.
Žoṅ-pa-steṅs, II, 942.
Žoṅ-žoṅ, II, 732, 733.
Žor-dgon-mo-che, II, 503.
gŽan-lṅa-mda', II, 976.
gŽi-ga-tse, I, 222.
gŽu, I, 75, 76, 251; II, 479, 1002.
gŽu Kun-dga' ra-ba, II, 792.
gŽu-mkhan-brag, II, 1003.
gŽu-sñe, II, 1069.
gŽu-sñe'i bar-rdzoṅ, II, 478.
gŽu-brag-dmar, II, 747.
gŽuṅ, I, 300; II, 406, 672, 673, 674, 694.
gŽuṅ-gru-sna, II, 865.
gŽuṅ-sgra-mkhar, I, 256.
gŽuṅ Ri-bo, II, 404, 430.
gŽeṅs, II, 659.
gŽo, I, 272, 274, 275.
bŽi-thog, I, 217.

Za-chu-'dus, II, 481.
Za-ri-roṅ, I, 78.
Za-luṅ, II, 720.
Za-hor, I, 39, 159, 241, 350; II, 847.
Zaṅs-gliṅ, II, 796, 855.
Zaṅs-chen, I, 320.
Zaṅs-po-che, I, 278, 279; II, 1089.
Zaṅs-phu, II, 816.
Zaṅs-ri, I, 178; II, 476, 662, 663, 706, 1039.
Zaṅs-ri khaṅ-dmar, II, 984.
Zaṅs-ri mkhar-dmar, II, 984.
Zaṅs-ri Lu-gu-sgaṅ, II, 607.
Zaṅs-luṅ, II, 464, 572, 642.

Zam–'tsher, I, 81.
Zar, I, 286.
Zar–po, II, 671.
Zwa–ra dgon, II, 653, 654, 655, 657.
Zi–liṅ–mkhar, II, 551.
Zim–śi, II, 994.
Zuṅ–mkhar, I, 148.
Zur, II, 545.
Zur–khaṅ, I, 225.
Zur–mkhar, II, 720.
Zur–stod, II, 963.
Zur–phud, I, 76.
Zur–maṅ, II, 511.
Zur–ra–ri, I, 174, 175.
Zul–phu, I, 212, II, 410, 964.
Zul–phul, I, 80, 83; II, 555.
Zo–thuṅ, I, 177.
Zla–dgon, II, 579, 582, 663.
Zla–ba, II, 908.
gZad, I, 129, 132, 133, 138, 142.
gZad–phu, I, 140.
gZid, I, 75.
gZo, I, 183, 193.
bZaṅ, I, 269; II, 751.
bZaṅ–groṅ tshugs–kha, II, 881.
bZaṅ– ne'u–kha, II, 956.
bZaṅ–phu brag–dmar, II, 990.
bZaṅ–yul, II, 759, 906.
bZad, I, 141.

'An–'ga–bo, II, 501.
'U–gu–do, II, 1070.
'U–yug, I, 179, 193, 227, 230; II, 739, 768, 1026.
'U–śaṅ–rdo, I, 335.
'Ug–skad, I, 132, 141, 144.
'Ug–pa–luṅ, I, 111, 114, 151.
'Um–phug, I, 79.
'Um–bu bla–mkhar, II, 812.
'Um–bu–tshal, I, 42.
'O–de–guṅ–rgyal, II, 457, 458, 656.
'O–phug, II, 547.
'O–yug, II, 443, 677.
'O–śod mtho–steṅs, I, 198.
'Og–gdoṅ, I, 111.
'Oṅ–chu, II, 953.
'Od–khri, II, 435.
'Od–can, I, 75.
'Od–'jo, I, 284.
'Od–ma'i gliṅ, II, 1033.
'Od–gsal, I, 99, 302.
'On, I, 178; II, 573, 612, 655, 692, 1039, 1040, 1077.
'On–nag–po stod–pa–klad, I, 190.
'On–rmi–sdiṅs, II, 662.
'On tshoṅ–'dus, II, 498.
'On lha–khaṅ ke–ru, I, 257.
'Ol–kha, I, 187; II, 465, 468, 477, 888, 892, 918, 1040, 1076.
'Ol–ka bKra–śis–thaṅ, II, 516, 548.

Ya–'gal (Yam–'gal), I, 231, 392; II, 850, 851.
Ya–rgyal, II, 606.
Ya–thaṅ, II, 622.
Ya–'brog, I, 350.
Ya–'brog khob–le, II, 917.
Ya–'brog–do, I, 324.
Ya–tshe, I, 38; II, 580, 583 (Ya–tse, 787).
Ya–ru gTsaṅ–po, II, 496.
Yaṅ–dkar, II, 684, 686.
Yaṅ–gaṅ, I, 270.
Yaṅ–dgon, II, 530, 617, 619, 628, 630, 745.
Yaṅ–dgon naṅ–so, II, 591, 645.
Yaṅ–'dul, I, 40.
Yaṅ–dben, I, 235, 237, 238; II, 505.
Yaṅs–pa–can, I, ii; II, 1058, 1093.
Yaṅs–rtse, II, 1088, 1089.
Yab, I, 75; II, 694.
Yab–chos–sdiṅs, II, 885.

Yam-bu, II, 850.
Yar-kluṅs, I, 77, 79, 96, 105, 170, 173, 176, 178, 189, 217, 218, 273, 279, 318, 319, 335, 343, 345; II, 427, 429, 438, 458, 480, 481, 565, 577, 584, 607, 656, 657, 778, 787, 796, 799, 802, 871, 874, 875, 877, 878, 904, 937, 956, 962, 982, 985, 986, 990, 997, 1040, 1059, 1087.
Yar-kluṅs skya'o, II, 990.
Yar-kluṅs gcen-pa, II, 717.
Yar-kluṅs-bstan-thaṅ, II, 806.
Yar-kluṅs rnam-rgyal, II, 1040.
Yar-kluṅs Phug-mo-che, II, 477.
Yar-kluṅs bya-sa, II, 657.
Yar-kluṅs rog-pa, I, 97.
Yar-kluṅs-śar, I, 210.
Yar-kluṅs gśoṅ-pa, II, 890.
Yar-khugs, II, 662.
Yar-rgyab, II, 824.
Yar-rgyal, II, 693.
Yar-chab gTsaṅ-po, II, 496.
Yar-stod, I, 76, 348; II, 603, 872, 875, 937.
Yar-stod skyer-sna, II, 876.
Yar-mda', II, 875, 878, 929, 930, 932, 935.
Yar-'brog, II, 465, 606, 678, 788, 831, 930, 1002, 1004, 1005 (see Ya-'brog).
Yar-'brog Kha-ba-kluṅs, II, 829.
Yar-'brog glaṅ-bu, II, 930.
Yar-'brog bran-mda', II, 884.
Yar-lha śam-bu, II, 995 (see Śam-bu).
Yu-gur, II, 501.
Yu-gur-gyi yul (Uighur), I, 49.
Yugs, I, 76.
Yuṅ, I, 273.
Yur-'og, I, 75.
Yul-skyoṅ, II, 607.
Yul-chos, II, 1005.
Yul-la, II, 1043.
Ye-goṅ, II, 548.
Ye-ran, I, 231, 361; II, 447, 789, 856, 1046.
Yer-pa, I, 44, 75, 259, 295, 260; II, 642, 844, 907, 908.
Yer-pa Ba-reṅ, I, 74.
Yer-pa lha-khaṅ, I, 74.
Yer-rtsi-sgaṅ, I, 321.
Yel-pa, I, 297.
Yor-mda', II, 550.
Yol, I, 327; II, 741, 749.
Yol-pa-brag, I, 129.
Yol-phu, II, 745.
Yol-phu gser-gliṅ, II, 750.
Yol-rin-chen-gliṅ, II, 536.
gYa'-snaṅ, II, 781.
gYa'-bzaṅ, I, 134.
gYa'-luṅ, II, 773.
gYag-mkhar sṅon-po, 717.
gYag-sde, I, 269; II, 478.
gYag-sde bye-ma, II, 532.
gYag-mtsho, II, 976.
gYaṅ-śod Boṅ-ra-steṅs, II, 610, 633 (see Boṅ-ra-steṅs).
gYaṅ-hril, II, 592,
gYam-bzaṅs, II, 541, 656, 657, 659, 829, 974, 994, 995.
gYal, I, 200, 296.
gYas, II, 923.
gYas-ru, I, 131; II, 677, 773, 1043.
gYas-ru khaṅ-khri, I, 116.
gYu-sgra, I, 269.
gYu-sgro, I, 75.
gYu-'brug, I, 173.
gYu-ma, II, 546.
gYu-rtse, I, 75.
gYu-mtsho, II, 491, 683, 815 (see Tsa-ri-gYu-mtsho).
gYu-ru, I, 75, 141, 201.
gYu-ru-gra, I, 195.

gYuṅ-po, II, 923.
gYur-spe, II, 608.
gYus-dga'-ldan, II, 792.
gYe, I, 95, 273, 321; II, 566, 718, 888, 983, 984, 986, 994, 1087, 1088.
gYe-chuṅ glaṅ-luṅ, II, 986.
gYe-ru, I, 279.
gYer, I, 318; II, 458.
gYes, II, 481.
gYo, II, 1070.
gYo-ru-gra, II, 566.
gYor, I, 95; II, 693, 695, 702, 936, 1018, 1080.
gYor-stod, I, 63.
gYor-po, II, 656, 736, 759, 885.
gYor-po, bum-gliṅ, I, 78.
gYor-po lugs-smad, II, 706.

Ra-ka-brag, II, 639.
Ra-sgreṅs (Rwa-sgreṅs), I, 186, 233, 253, 263, 264, 265, 266, 267, 269, 272, 279, 284, 296, 306, 312, 313, 323, 325, 330; II, 595, 641, 649, 682, 710, 1001, 1002, 1004, 1070.
Ra-dum-brag, I, 150.
Ra-dha (Rāḍha), II, 1030.
Ra-ba zlum-po, I, 88.
Ra-byaṅ, II, 700.
Ra-ma-do-li, I, 225, II, 804.
Ra-mo, II, 655, 876.
Ra-mo-che, I, 40, 41, 219, 342; II, 591.
Ra-mo sMan-chu-kha, II, 929.
Ra-tshag, I, 75; II, 529, 530.
Ra-luṅ, II, 665, 667, 670, 680, 683, 684.
Ra-sa (Lhasa), I, 79.
Ra-sa-'dzims, I, 78.
Rwa-stod dgon-pa, II, 542.
Rag-ma, II, 877.
Rags-rtsigs khaṅ-pa, I, 257.
Raṅ-byuṅ mchod-rten, II, 869, 971.
Raṅ-byuṅ lha-lṅa, II, 1050.
Raṅ-byon-lṅa-ldan, II, 672.
Raṅs-mtsho, I, 196.
Rājagṛha, I, 5, 15, 20, 21, 22, 360; II, 451, 732.
Ratnakūṭi, I, 315; II, 599.
Ratnagiri, II, 755.
Rab-groṅ, II, 745.
Rab-sgaṅ, II, 501.
Ram-pa lha-sdiṅs, I, 322.
Rāmali, I, 5.
Ral-gsum, II, 544.
Ri-khrod, II, 971.
Ri-goṅ, II, 746, 747, 748.
Ri-rgya-dgon, II, 564.
Ri-steṅs, I, 321.
Ri-thel, II, 622.
Ri Ḍan-tig, I, 65.
Ri-nag, II, 732.
Ri-nag-po, I, 242.
Ri-phug, I, 95.
Ri-bo, II, 403, 473, 1030.
Ri-bo-che, II, 507, 550, 652, 1049.
Ri-bo mchog-rab (Meru), II, 968.
Ri-bo sPos-kyi-ṅad-ldan, I, 23.
Ri-bo-rtse-lṅa, I, 220, 336; II, 492, 669, 679, 783, 846, 898, 911 (see Wu t'ai shan).
Ri-mer, I, 302.
Ri-mo-can, I, 292.
Ri-mo-mdo, II, 986.
Riṅ-mo, II, 999.
Rin-chen-sgaṅ, I, 216, 313.
Rin-chen sPuṅs-pa, II, 560, 1013.
Rin-chen ri-bo, II, 755.
Rin-spuṅs, I, 338; II, 692.
Rin-po-che'i gliṅ, II, 818.
Ru-mtshams, I, 331; II, 522.
Ru-mtshams chu-bzaṅs, II, 975.

Ru–mtshams Pho–ba–luṅ, II, 426.
Ru–mtshams Lug–ra–kha, II, 746.
Ru–bži, I, 162.
Ru–lag, I, 205.
Rug–pa, I, 267.
Re–rgyab, II, 542.
Re–śod, II, 542.
Reb–koṅ, I, 334.
Revati'i luṅ, II, 976.
Rog–pa–sa, II, 1078.
Roṅ, I, 68, 109, 160, 235, 255, 262, 388; II, 430, 615, 617, 618, 773, 789.
Roṅ–skam, I, 78, 100, 319.
Roṅ–mkhar–phug, I, 81.
Roṅ Chu–tshan, I, 126.
Roṅ–snar, I, 193.
Roṅ–po, II, 642.
Roṅ–rtse–dkar, I, 279.
Roṅ–wo, I, 334.
Roṅ–lho–rtsa, I, 78.
rLuṅ–śod, II, 860, 872.
rLuṅ–śod Dar–chos–sdiṅs, II, 603.

La–kha, I, 177, 320.
La–kha–śar, II, 670.
La–chen, II, 976.
La–stod, I, 132, 180, 208, 219, 229, 233, 235, 236, 270; II, 427, 449, 495, 684, 688, 689, 693, 695, 739, 741, 771, 786, 787, 796, 830, 846, 852, 917, 926, 974, 1008, 1018, 1026, 1070, 1080.
La–stod gro–luṅ, II, 489.
La–stod gCuṅ–pa mchog–dkar, I, 227.
La–stod stag–sde, II, 916.
La–stod ldog–pa, II, 916.
La–stod dPal–thaṅ, II, 1021.
La–stod sPu–tra, II, 489.
La–stod maṅ–'gar, II, 917.
La–stod gTsaṅ–so, II, 900.
La–drug, II, 1066.
La–mda'–'bar–bzaṅ, II, 665.
La–phyi, II, 434, 648, 726.
La–ba 'phraṅ, II, 889.
La–bar, II, 983.
La–mo, I, 61, 269.
La–ya smon–mda', II, 1004.
La–yag, II, 976.
La–so, II, 449.
Lag–sor dgon–pa, I, 321.
Laṅ–gro'i 'chad–pa–ltag, I, 193.
Lan–'khar–naṅ, II, 429.
Lan–gro, II, 443.
Lan–chou, I, 227.
Lan–pa, I, 260, 311; II, 458, 884, 904.
Lan–pa sPyil–bu, I, 259.
Lab–so, II, 1002.
Lam, II, 575.
Lam–phug, II, 464.
Las–stod, I, 198, 340, 354, 388; II, 399, 402, 406, 478, 603, 685.
Las–stod chuṅ–pa, II, 440.
Las–stod–byaṅ, II, 812.
Li–khar–śiṅ–'phel, II, 1008.
Li–yul, I, 40, 110.
Lu–chuṅ–gi–khra, II, 680.
Lu–pe śan (Liu pin shan), II, 505.
Lu–ru, I, 238.
Lu–ru'i grag, I, 238.
Lu–ro, I, 273.
Lugs, II, 989.
Luṅ–stoṅ, II, 976.
Lumbinī, I, 17.
Legs–par–snaṅ, I, 16.
Lo, I, 94, 285, 287, 294, 296, 299, 303; II, 1070.
Lo–gya–duṅ bDe–mchog–raṅ–'byuṅ, I, 381.
Lo–chia–t'un, I, 227.

Lo-chuṅ, I, 178.
Lo-naṅ, II, 672.
Lo-mo, I, 174, 178, 320.
Lo-ro, I, 142, 143, 273, 304; II, 439, 469, 476, 661, 663, 672, 1070, 1088.
Lo-ro-'phar, II, 568.
Lo-ro mi-sna, II, 439.
Lo-ro žiṅ-gsar, I, 273.
Log-groṅ, II, 784.

Śa-ston rDor-'dzin, II, 998.
Śa-pho-sraṅ, I, 279.
Śa-'ug, I, 196.
Śa-'ug stag-sgo, I, 72, 319; II, 464, 477.
Śag-rtsa, II, 732.
Śaṅs, I, 79, 111, 115, 120, 171, 193, 199, 272, 354; II, 444, 692, 732, 739, 906, 919.
Śaṅs-pa, II, 919.
Śaṅs-rtse-gdoṅ, II, 792.
Śaṅs-sreg-žiṅ, I, 82, 103.
Śaṅs-lha-phu, I, 126.
Śad-sgo-dar, II, 1043.
Śāntapurī, II, 799, 821.
Śan-thog, II, 937.
Shan-hsi, I, 220, II, 669, 679.
Śab, I, 82, 162, 222, 224, 227; II, 420, 705, 732, 906, 918.
Śab-sgo-lṅa, II, 929.
Śab lcaṅ-ra, I, 79.
Śab-pa-gliṅ, I, 305; II, 464.
Śab-zo-ṅa-ba, II, 518.
Śam-po-gaṅs, II, 986.
Śambhar, II, 792, 793.
Śambhala, II, 516, 699, 753, 756, 757, 761, 783, 814, 825, 1045.
Śam-bu, II, 491, 696, 814, 937, 953, 987, 988.
Śam-bu-gaṅs, II, 988.
Śam-bu-lcal, II, 657.
Śar, II, 1040.
Śar-kha, I, 46, 47.
Śar-sdoṅ ri-khrod, II, 504.
Śar-ba, I, 217.
Śar-brag, II, 1040.
Śar-lho'i-rdzoṅ, II, 565.
Śala, I, 22.
Śi-skyid, II, 1055.
Śiṅ-kun, II, 1057.
Śiṅ-skam, II, 675.
Śiṅ-khun-mkhar (Liang-chou), I, viii; II, 501, 846.
Śiṅ-gi-ri, II, 693.
Śītavana, I, 20; II, 701, 869, 1028.
Śin-cu (Shang-chou), I, 51.
Śirṣaparvata, I, 23.
Śiśumāra-giri, I, 21.
Śug-luṅ spaṅ-kha, II, 743.
Śug-gseb, II, 893, 894, 895.
Śug-gseb dbUs-gliṅ, II, 894.
Śugs, II, 994.
Śud, I, 77.
Śel-dkar, I, 255; II, 684, 686, 696.
Śel-dkar-rdzoṅ, II, 421, 915.
Śo-skyam, I, 187; II, 874.
Śo-dgon, II, 564.
Śo-ma-ra, II, 615.
Śo-ru, I, 189.
Śoṅ-yur, II, 748.
Śrāvastī, I, 21, 22.
Śrī, I, 388.
Śrī Dhānya-kaṭaka, II, 791, 798.
Śrīnagar, II, 400.
Śrīparvata, I, 35; II, 402.
Śrī Phag-mo-gru, II, 663.
Śrī-ri, II, 527, 684, 686, 688, 691, 696, 700, 915, 917.
Śrī-ri gNam-sdins, II, 690.
Śrīsthāna, I, 35.
gŚar, I, 157.
gŚen-groṅ, II, 565.
gŚoṅs, I, 109.

Sa-skor thoṅ-pa, I, 311.
Sa-skya, I, 56, 194, 196, 205, 207, 208, 211, 212, 213, 216, 217, 218, 281, 316, 335, 337, 339; II, 399, 405, 492, 527, 528, 556, 582, 632, 633, 634, 651, 669, 695, 708, 750, 774, 775, 776, 785, 1012, 1045, 1059, 1088.
Sa-skya dga'-ldan, I, 339.
Sa-mtha', II, 1087.
Sa-phu, II, 627.
Sa-phug dkar-po, II, 925.
Sa-dmar, I, 90.
Sa-'ug, II, 669.
Sa-'ug stag-sgo, II, 976.
Sa-la-ta-tse, II, 849.
Sa-śod, II, 579.
Sa-ser, II, 545.
Sa-hor, I, 241.
Sāketa, I, 21.
Sags-kha, II, 1061.
Sadnagara, II, 797, 811.
San-yaṅ, II, 806.
Sābhar, I, 241.
Samantabhadra, II, 452.
Samantāloka, I, 5.
Si-ha-ci'u, I, 53.
Siṅha'i gliṅ, I, 315; II, 580 (see Seṅga'i gliṅ).

Sītā, II, 854.
Sil-ma, II, 743.
Sil-ma-la, II, 942.
Sil-ma-la-kha, II, 986.
Sum-mkhar, II, 550.
Sum-bcu, II, 948.
Sum-pa sKyil-mkhar, II, 420.
Sum-pa ne'u-mkhar, II, 440.
Sum-'phreṅ, II, 860.
Sum-yul, II, 670.
Se-mkhar-chuṅ, II, 778.
Se-gle, II, 615, 620, 637.
Se-ba-luṅ, II, 457, 616, 620.
Se-bo, II, 1088.
Se-sbrag, I, 138.
Se-mo-che, II, 769.
Se-mo-do, II, 461, 499, 522, 675.
Se-ra, I, 75; II, 729.
Se-gseb, II, 569.
Seṅga'i gliṅ, II, 797.
Seṅ-ge-gliṅ, II, 686.
Seṅ-ge-rgyab, I, 197.
Seṅ-ge sgo-mdun, II, 544.
Seṅ-ge-rdzoṅ, I, 197; II, 869.
Seṅ-ge-ri, II, 676.
Seṅ-ge-rin, II, 678.
Seṅ-ge-luṅ, II, 525.
Ser-skya'i-gži, I, 11.
Ser-chags, II, 699.
Ser-phreṅ, II, 519.
Ser-ba dgon-pa, I, 319.
Ser-bu dben-tsha, II, 421.
So-thaṅ, I, 96.
So-sa gliṅ, II, 730.
Sog, I, 238; II, 501, 542, 549, 555.
Sog-chu, II, 524, 637.
So-zam, II, 492.
Somapurī, II, 844, 845.
Sol-thaṅ, I, 273 (see next entry).
Sol-nag Thaṅ-po-che, I, 75, 76, 88, 93; II, 1062 (see Thaṅ-po-che).
Srad, I, 214; II, 419.
Sram-pa, I, 111, 115.
Sri, I, 258.
Srin-chu, II, 906.
Srin-po-ri, I, 140, 349; II, 450, 600, 601, 799, 1069, 1071.
Sru, II, 1013.
Sru-yul-sgaṅ, II, 1011.
Srug-gan-pa, II, 1011.
Sreg-pa-luṅ, II, 659.
Sro-gu-luṅ, I, 63.
Stham-vihara, I, 247.
Svayambhū-cāitya, II, 869, 971.

Svayambhūnātha-cāitya, I, 230; II, 799, 821, 853, 1033.
gSa'-'phur, II, 516.
gSag-mo'i steṅs, II, 507.
gSaṅ-sṅags-mkhar, II, 1078.
gSaṅ-phu, I, 141, 155, 201, 307, 308, 310, 322, 325, 332, 334, 335, 339, 340, 341; II, 464, 490, 524, 525, 529, 532, 570, 596, 630, 678, 751, 781, 802, 1043, 1080.
gSaṅ-phu brag-nag, II, 806.
gSam-khaṅ, II, 591.
gSar-mda' khra-luṅ, II, 1042.
gSar-len, II, 464.
gSal-rje-gaṅs, II, 696, 988.
gSer-khuṅ-sgaṅ, II, 849.
gSer-gyi-rgyal-mtshan, I, 241.
gSer-gyi Bya-skyibs-can, II, 540.
gSer-gyu, II, 987.
gSer-gcig-ma, II, 745.
gSer-ldiṅs, II, 421.
gSer-luṅ, I, 188, 189; II, 994.
gSer-lha, II, 937.
bSag-mo, II, 722.
bSam-gliṅ, II, 519.
bSam-gtan-gliṅ, I, 153; II, 814, 823, 827, 831, 836, 968.
bSam-sdiṅs, II, 750, 829.
bSam-yas (Samye), I, 42, 43, 44, 60, 93, 95, 102, 103, 106, 201, 254, 257, 258, 261, 309, 315, 326, 328, 329, 336, 366, 378; II, 443, 492, 498, 568, 570, 575, 577, 582, 606, 642, 663, 792, 806, 807, 844, 942, 957, 975, 1030, 1070.
bSam-yas Khrims-khaṅ-gliṅ, II, 822.
bSam-yas 'Chims-phu, I, 110, 173; II, 812.
bSi-chon (Szechwan), I, 48.
bSil-ba-tshal, II, 701, 869, 1028,
Ha'o-gaṅs, II, 664, 986.
Ha'o-rgol, I, 109.
Ham-mdo, I, 301.
Harimaṇḍa, II, 1058.
Hastināpura, I, 4, 14.
Hwaṅ-je'u (Hwang-chou), I, 56.
He-bo, II, 443.
He-ma-khaṅ, I, 230.
Hor, I, xvii; II, 471, 486, 492, 551, 702.
Hor-thaṅ, II, 686.

Lha, I, 256.
Lha-khaṅ, I, 138.
Lha-khaṅ chen-mo, I, 216.
Lha-khab, II, 686.
Lha-khyim, II, 513.
Lha-ṅu, I, 301.
Lha-rje, I, 71.
Lha-rje-rags, I, 256.
Lha-steṅs, II, 490, 514, 550.
Lha-thel Rin-chen-gliṅ, II, 602.
Lha-ldan, I, x, xi, 45, 46.
Lha-gdoṅ, I, 132; II, 690, 691, 695.
Lha-mdo, I, 75.
Lha-naṅ, I, 372.
Lha-phu, II, 444.
Lha-phu sPaṅ-rtsa, II, 733.
Lha-phyug, II, 715.
Lha-brag-kha, I, 280.
Lha-rtse, I, 205, 208; II, 778.
Lha-rtse'i brag, I, 207.
Lha-rtse bhig-tig, I, 64.
Lha-žiṅ khri-dgu, I, 79.
Lha-zur, I, 182, 184.
Lha-ri, I, 175.
Lha-ri-kha, II, 715.
Lha-ri-gyaṅ-mtho, II, 715.
Lha-ri sñiṅ-po, II, 908.
Lha-ri-mo, II, 678.
Lha-ri rtsa-brgyad, I, 78.
Lha-luṅ, I, 191; II, 479, 694.
Lha-sa, I, ii, x, xi, 42, 46, 52,

60, 71, 140, 148, 195, 223, 254, 256, 258, 260, 265, 273, 279, 288, 294, 323, 325, 326, 341, 354, 373, 384; II, 406, 407, 420, 450, 465, 473, 479, 490, 492, 494, 498, 499, 504, 508, 509, 530, 542, 549, 586, 590, 591, 631, 636, 639, 640, 641, 643, 648, 668, 672, 673, 680, 717, 729, 734, 738, 743, 776, 777, 780, 799, 802, 849, 854, 855, 878, 885, 895, 911, 912, 957, 973, 984, 1030, 1044, 1069, 1082, 1093.

Lha-sa rKyaṅ-thaṅ, II, 498.

Lha-sa gTsug-lag-khaṅ, II, 1006 (see Jo-khaṅ).

Lhag-ru, II, 723.

Lhaṅ-tsho, II, 865.

Lhan, II, 941.

Lhab, I, 156.

Lhar-che-sgra, I, 95.

Lhiṅ-pa, I, 75.

Lhun-grub-steṅs, II, 492, 543.

Lhun-grub Lha-rtse, I, ii; II, 827, 1090.

Lho, I, 292, 332; II, 399, 438, 581, 720.

Lho-kha, I, 256; II, 468, 477, 656, 984, 1082.

Lho-gra, I, vi.

Lho-rgyud, I, ii; II, 479, 988, 1090.

Lho-stod, I, 132; II, 430, 432.

Lho-nag lha-mo, II, 409.

Lho-brag, I, 132, 159, 302, 373; II, 403, 414, 416, 437, 606, 607, 656, 657, 676, 680, 682, 693, 695, 710, 829, 930, 941, 963, 970, 975, 1009, 1042, 1070.

Lho-brag mkhar-chu, II, 676, 814 (see mkhar-chu).

Lho-brag chag-pa, I, 322.

Lho-brag gtam-śul, II, 657.

Lho-brag sTeṅs-chen-po, II, 964.

Lho-brag Ba-śi, I, 76.

Lho-brag Bya-se, I, 126.

Lho-brag Ye-raṅ, I, 679.

Lho-brag-roṅ, II, 930.

Lho-brag Sribs-mo ser-phug, II, 988.

Lho-mon, II, 672.

Lho Ye-phug, II, 565.

Lhog-tshaṅ-steṅs, II, 587.

A-rmo-nig (*A-mo-li-ka*), I, 21.

A-'o-mdo, II, 986.

A-la, II, 493.

Ajita, I, 4.

Anavatapta, II, 540, 726, 1091.

Amdo, I, ii, xvii, 173, 213, 334, 386; II, 418, 480, 501, 595, 607, 696, 777, 1073, 1075, 1079.

Ayodhyā, I, 4, 14, 15:

Ar, I, 330.

Aśmaka, I, 13.

Aśvamukha, II, 1091.

Āṭavaka, I, 22.

Ābhīra, II, 869.

Ārya-Jamali, I, 392 (see *Ārya-wa-ti*).

Āryadeśa, II, 754, 755, 756, 761.

Ārya Wa-ti, II, 1008 (see *'Phags pa 'Ja-ma-li* and *'Phags-pa Wa-ti*).

Indasāla-guhā, I, 371.

U-skyu-'gul, II, 1002.

U-rgyan, I, 230; II, 517, 526, 669, 745, 962 (see Oḍḍiyāna).

Uttarapatha, I, 25.

Uraśā, I, 4, 14.

Uruvāsa, II, 798.

Uruvilvā, I, 20.

E, I, vi.
E-chuṅ, II, 597.
E-vaṃ, II, 535, 536.
E-la-myaṅ, II, 507.

O-dkar, I, 183.
Oṅ-po, II, 919.
Otantapurī, I, 243; II, 1031.
Oḍḍiyāna, I, 242, 359, 361, 362, 367, 368; II, 526, 527, 530, 539, 552, 562, 598, 669, 700, 701, 745, 753, 846, 853, 858, 893, 920, 949, 955, 962, 971, 1039, 1049 (see U-rgyan).

ERRATA

Part I

p. xii, note, read later.

p. 12, l. 6, read Droṇodana.

12, l. 24, read sPyi-bo-nas skyes.

13, l. 18, read kLu-dbyaṅs-kyi rgyal-po.

16, l. 5, read sTobs-po-čhe.

55, l. 31, read Tai-

n. 44, read 'Gos.

56, l. 13, read Tai-Liao.

l. 8,9, read Činggis.

l. 11, read Sečen.

l. 20, read Tai-Yüan.

note 48, read name of.

57, l. 1, read (Ch'in Shih Huang-ti).

l. 5, read Chin.

l. 28, read Tumbinai

l. 29, read Sečen.

58, l. 2, n. 50, read Činggis.

59, l. 19, read Tai-Ming.

60, l. 3, read Činggis.

72, l. 29, read lČe Dwal-sgaṅ-pa.

79, l. 25, read Ka-ba Dar-seṅ.

87, n. 2, read 'byor.

98, l. 15, read zur-pa.

108, l. 32, read bLon-.

131, l. 35, read sTon-pa.

162, l. 30, read dgc-sloṅ.

180, l. 11, read Śer-.

186, l. 14, read Phyā-pa.

187, l. 32, read Dags-čhuṅ-pa.

195, l. 27, read 'Khrul-žig Seṅ-ge-rgyab-pa.

200, l. 30, read Ṅag-gi.

201, l. 5, read Kun-dga'.

p. 214, l. 6, 2125 read Tai-Yüan.
l. 28, read bSod-nams.
l. 35, read sTag-tshaṅ.
216, l. 14, reap kung-ming.
l. 6, 13, 29, 30, read Sečen.
219, l. 25, read dGon-pa-pa.
225, l. 22, read an.
233, l. 12, read 'Jaṅ-pa.
234, l. 5, read Bya-ze-pa.
235, l. 5, read Phu-čhuṅ-ba.
236, l. 7, read Rin-čhen-gsal.
242, note, read Puṇyaśrī.
256, l. 13, read Gam-pa byaṅ-thaṅ.
263, l. 9, read 'Phraṅ-kha Ber-čhuṅ.
269, l. 20, read gÑos Bra-gor-pa.
l. 21, read Rog-dmar-zur-pa.
276, l. 36, read Luṅ-gi dbaṅ-phyug.
277, l. 29, read Luṅ-gi.
298, l. 10, read Phyā-pa.
302, l. 11, read secret preceptor dBaṅ.
308, l. 23, read rGya-ma-pa.
309, l. 8, read Rin-saṅ-ba.
l. 8, read -dbyaṅs.
310, l. 30, read Luṅ-gi.
314, l. 17, read gLan-čhu-mig-luṅ-ṅu-ba.
321, l. 15, read Yer-pa-ba.
329, l. 20, read Phyogs-las.
331, l. 17, read rGya-'čhiṅ-ru-ba.
336, l. 26, read Rig-pa'i ral-gri.
l. 28. read Rig-pa'i ral-gri.
338, l. 33, read Den-ldan-pa.
339, l, 9, read Rig-pa'i ral-gri.
343, l. 30, read Ña-dbon.
343, l. 4, read Sar-spos.
346, l. 31, read grub.
352, l. 21, read Śrī-Sarvarahasyanibandha...

p. 354, l. 7, read Je-ser.
355, l. 20, read sPyaṅ-tshaṅ-pa.
364, l. 16, read Tre-bo.
367, l. 21, 22, read Śer-phyin.
373, l. 34, read rKyaṅ-pa.
374, l, 3, read Čhos.
376, l. 13, read mṄon-pa-pa.
377, l. 32, read Śer-phyin.
379, l. 14, read mṄon-pa-pa.
l. 31, read gLo-bo.
380, l. 18, read Rus-sbal.
395, l. 15, rean Pham-mthiṅ-pa.

Part II

400, l. 11, read sPyi-ther-ba.
401, l. 22, read by many...
402, l. 1, read Pham-mthiṅ-pa.
405, l. 32, read bSod-nams.
419' l. 31, read Thaṅ-pa-pa.
421, l. 1, read Sa-rbo.
437, l. 24, read Ti-pu-pa.
439, l. 11, read Lo-byi-mgo-pa.
l. 12, read gLan-byi-mgo-pa.
440, l. 6, read Lo-byi-mgo-pa.
441, l. 12, read Phag-mo gru-pa.
l. 21, read bZaṅ-pa.
452. l. 19, read dPa'-bas-byin.
462, l. 21, read gSer-sgom.
474, l. 6, read mTsho—.
476, l. 1, read 428.
l. 14, read Btsan—.
493, l. 21, read Rol-pa'i.
504, l. 28, read Ri-bo-sgaṅ-pa.
507, l. 1, read Lha-mo-skyid.
517, l. 25, read Žwa-dmar-pa.
l. 30, read gNam-mtsho-ba.
518, l. 21, read many.

p. 519, l. 3, read Sar-spos.
519, l. 24, read Lho La-yag-pa.
533, l. 9, read brTag-gñis.
535, l. 8, read Dol-po-pa.
541, l. 36, read gŽon-nu-dpal-pa.
546, l. 24, read Ri-mi-'babs-pa.
554, l. 18, read Yan-thub-bu.
556, l. 27, read Phyā-pa.
568, l. 6, read gods.
l. 15, read Yel-pa.
l. 19, read Lo-ro ras-pa.
572, l. 30, read dBon.
579, l. 3, sead Lho-gdoṅ-pa.
l. 11, read Thog-kha-pa.
l. 24, read he went.
581, l. 36, read mGon-po-rgyal.
582, l. 1, read dPon.
583, l. 15, read dPon.
584, l. 17, read dPon.
585, l. 33, read Byaṅ-rtse.
588, n. 16, read rgyan.
597, l. 35. read gÑal-pa.
601, l. 29, read Bal-bu goṅ-pa.
608, l. 12, read gÑis-pa.
631, l. 22, read the.
l. 10, read Bya-bral-pa.
632, l. 29, read gYuṅ-'druṅ.
635, l. 14, read Kun-dga'-bo.
638, l. 17, read Rin-čhen-dpal-pa.
640, l. 3, read Don-dam bsñen-pa.
l. 6, read Śrī-Kālacakropadeśa—.
643, l. 14, read bZaṅ-dpal-pa.
648, l. 19, read bKra-śis dpal-pa.
l. 28, read gÑa'-khri.
654, l. 20, read sTeṅ-pa.
657, l. 27, read dGon-gsar-pa.

p. 678, l. 14, read by the upādhyāya.
680, l. 18, read Yu-pi-ba.
688, l. 24, read lČog-ro.
690, l. 26, read Drod-čhuṅ.
692, l. 9, read Zur-phug-pa.
694, l. 12, read dpal-pa.
l. 16, read of sKyes-mčhog-pa.
695, l. 3, read Śes-rab dpal-pa.
696, l. 4 & 5, read Drod-čhuṅ-pa.
698, l. 11, read ldan.
699, l. 4, read ordinations.
706, l. 22, read Phyar-čhuṅ.
711, l. 19, read Yaṅ-rtse-ba.
715, l. 28, read Ñi-ma-'od.
722, l. 30, read bSam-gtan dpal-pa.
l. 32, read Seṅ-ge dpal-pa.
727, l. 20, read So-ba.
l. 23, read Phu-ri-ba.
733, l. 15, read rMog-gčog-pa.
740, l. 2, read Mahākāla.
l. 12, read Tshad-ma-pa.
752, l. 8, read Drag-po-čhe-pa.
756, l. 23, read Tre-bo.
758, l. 7, read dGon-pa-pa.
764, l. 12, 21, and 22, read Ṣaḍaṅga.
768, l. 13, read 'Gar-ston.
l. 15, read Tre-bo.
769, l. 10, read 'J̌am-gsar.
772, l. 27, read baγsi.
773, l. 25, read Byaṅ-sems.
774, l. 19, read bLa-ma.
l. 25, read J̌arγuči.
776, l. 4, read Dol-po.
790, l. 2, read rgyal-ba.
794, l. 35, read dpal-pa.
803, l. 23, read rDo-rJe dril-bu-pa.

p. 811, l. 35, read dpal-pa.
814, l. 27, read uaaya.
819, l. 23, read attaining.
842, l. 8, read Śa-ba- ri.
l. 14, read Yid-la.
845, l. 23, read Tārākurukulle, and 436.
851, l. 3, read Pham-mthiṅ-pa.
857, l. 26, read Śer-dad.
860, l. 3, read Nam-mkha'.
l. 5, read Ri-mi-'babs-pa.
862, l. 16, read Pa-tshab.
l. 18, read Rog-pa dMar-pa.
863, l. 2, read dṅos—.
866, l. 3, read Śa-ba-ri.
869, l. 22, read Gaṅgābhadrī.
873, l. 29, read Se-čhuṅ-ba.
874, l. 27, read rMa-sgom.
875, l. 29, read rGya-loṅ.
881, l. 32, read Mal-Ka-ba-čan-pa, and mThiṅ-gaṅ-pa.
890, l. 13, read sÑe-mdo-ba.
896, l. 22, read at kLags-pa-lam.
900, l. 5, 12, read Čhag Brag-dmar-pa,
905, l. 19, read sGam-po-pa.
909, l. 1, read Ba-ri-ba.
919, l. 18, read rGya sGom-pa.
923, l. 26, read gYas-mo.
925, l. 9, read Phyar-čhen.
928, l. 22, read Riṅ-mo-ba.
931, l. 17, read Čhos-sgo-ba.
939, l. 27, read rGya-ma dbon-ston.
942, l. 27, read dKon-skyabs.
948, l. 12, read Ñams snaṅ-ma.
954, l. 19, read exists.
955, l. 14, 21, read Prajñāsiddha.
963, l. 18, read mkhan-po.

p. 966, l. 22, read Žig-po.
968, l. 30, read Kṛṣṇa.
970, l. 14, read Ye-śes dpal-pa.
982, l. 19, read Rog-pa sar-ma.
986, l. 34, read daughters.
987, l. 36, read bstan-bsruṅs.
988, l. 27, read dMu-yan.
991, l. 33, read mi-'babs-pa.
996, l. 19, read sMa-ra.
1002, l. 34, 36, read dGon-pa-pa.
1004, l. 23, read rgya-dman.
1006, l. 5, read Mi-bskyod-.
1007, l. 24, read Sumanaḥśrī.
1018, l. 5, read mThoṅ-ba don-ldan.
l. 9, read dBaṅ Grags-pa rgyal-mtshan.
1024, l. 9, read grags.
l. 16, read rGya-ma-pa.
l. 36, read Žaṅ.
1025, l. 35, read Zla-ba rgyal-mtshan.
1039, l. 32, read Žwa-dmar-pa.
1042, l. 13, read Grags-pa seṅ-ge.
1043, l. 12, read gYuṅ-ston.
1044, l. 27, read latter.
l. 33, read Kun-bsod-pa, mKhas-grub.
l. 34, read dmar-khrid.
1051, l. 32, read Rin-po-čhe-ba.
1052, l. 4, read Śes-rdor-ba.
1055, l. 4, read Mal-gro.
l. 8, read Žaṅ.
1061, l. 1, read Roṅ-gliṅ.
1067, l. 1, read "premonition that an invitation"....
1069, l. 30, read bśes-gñen.
1072, l. 36, read sÑag-phu-pa.
1075, l. 14, read Khyuṅ-po.
1078, l. 15, read Lha sPur-gru-bži-pa.
1083, l. 3, read Śākya rgyal-mtshan.

About the Author

GEORGE NICHOLAS DE ROERICH

(August 16,1902 — May 21, 1960)

GEORGE NICHOLAS DE ROERICH was a prominent 20th century Tibetologist. He is known for his contribution to Tibetan dialectology, his monumental translation of *The Blue Annals,* and his *11-volume Tibetan-Russian-English Dictionary* (published posthumously).

After finishing his studies at Karl May School, he entered the Indian and Iranian department of Oriental Language at London University in 1918. He studied Sanskrit, Pali and Chinese languages in the Indian Philology Department of Harvard University. Roerich began his independent research at the age of 21. By December 1923, he had arrived at the base of the Himalayas as a member of a scientific expedition to Sikkim.

The plethora of materials collected during the Central Asia Expedition became the foundation for the establishment of the Himalayan Research Institute named 'Urusvati' in Darjeeling in 1928. He collaborated with Prince Peter of Greece and Denmark and Rahul Sankrityayana to translate the Buddhist text *Pramāṇavārttikam* from Tibetan into Sanskrit. He translated the lengthy pioneering work on Tibetan history, *The Blue Annals,* which was published in two volumes by the Asiatic Society in 1949 and 1954(and reprinted by MLBD in 1976).

After spending almost 30 years in India Roerich returned in 1957 to Soviet Russia, where he made efforts to revive the Russian School of Oriental Studies.